ANNUAL REVIEW OF PSYCHOLOGY

ANNUAL REVIEW OF PSYCHOLOGY

CALVIN P. STONE, *Editor*
Stanford University

QUINN McNEMAR, *Associate Editor*
Stanford University

VOLUME 5

1954

ANNUAL REVIEWS, INC.

STANFORD, CALIFORNIA, U.S.A.

ANNUAL REVIEWS, INC.
STANFORD, CALIFORNIA, U.S.A.

FOREIGN AGENCIES

H. K. Lewis & Company, Limited
136 Gower Street,
London, W.C.1

Maruzen Company, Limited
6, Tori-Nichome Nihonbashi
Tokyo

PRINTED AND BOUND IN THE UNITED STATES OF AMERICA BY
GEORGE BANTA PUBLISHING COMPANY

PREFACE

In presenting the fifth volume of the *Annual Review of Psychology* we desire to express our appreciation of the thoroughgoing co-operation of professional colleagues here and abroad who have prepared the chapters for this and the previous volumes of the *Review*. Evidences of their generous good will in accepting invitations and of thoughtful planning and perseverance in the task of bringing to their readers a representative, coherent digest of interesting contributions have been most heartening. To the authors, chiefly, is due the major credit for our having met each essential deadline, culminating in on-schedule publication of the five volumes.

During the preceding year, important changes took effect in the personnel of the Editorial Committee. Keenly noted was the loss of Donald W. Taylor, Associate Editor, whose resignation was accepted with regret at the beginning of the year to facilitate his discharging inescapable obligations connected with his research and other professional commitments. Beginning in 1947, Dr. Taylor co-operated in an advisory capacity on plans for the first volume of the *Review*. In 1949 his official work as Associate Editor began. During a six-year period his interest has been unflagging and second to none have been his constructive ideas on delimitation of chapters, choice of subjects for occasional review, nominations for chapter authorships, editorial practices, and a host of other details requiring official consideration. With his loss, we are happy to announce that Dr. Quinn McNemar of Stanford University has accepted the invitation of the Board of Directors to succeed Dr. Taylor, beginning in January, 1954.

During the present year Dr. Taylor kindly consented to edit the chapters on Vision and Audition; Dr. McNemar, the chapters on Statistics, Individual Differences, and Theory and Techniques of Assessment. Each was available as consultant on other chapters. The Editor is also indebted to Miss Marian Ballin, Graduate Student, for her careful work with galley for twelve of the chapters. Her wide acquaintance with psychological literature and technical training in editorial conventions greatly expedited the Editors' work.

Still other changes in make-up of the Editorial Committee in 1953 include the retirement of Dr. J. G. Miller, who completed his term of service, and the resignation of Dr. C. H. Graham one year before his term had expired. Having committments outside the States, he suggested that he be replaced by one who could participate more actively in the work of the Committee. His successor for the unexpired term is Dr. Clifford T. Morgan who will continue after 1953 for a regular five year term.

With the presentation of Volume 5, it is a pleasure here to take note of the informed, painstaking approach that has characterized the work of our editorial assistants who, throughout each year, perform many nonacademic, recurring functions that are essential to the production of the *Review*. When manuscripts arrive they collaborate in numerous ways to unify the joint efforts of authors and Editors. The Editors would individualize their indebtedness to Ruth Swan and Carol F. Kupke for providing the "know-how" to make the initial *Review* in psychology conform in style and format with those of the other well-established *Annual Reviews*. Other editorial assistants no less conscientious in discharging essential duties, slightly narrower in scope but none the less important, were Barbara Darniel, Joyce Fairweather, Robbie Bass, and Lillian Rutherford. The constant interest of our editorial assistants in each volume's receiving a favorable reception contributes innumerable emendations from which the readers derive many tangible benefits.

J.E.A. C.T.M.
N.D.C. Q.M.
J.G.D. R.L.T.
C.P.S.

TOPICS AND AUTHORS
ANNUAL REVIEW OF PSYCHOLOGY
VOLUME 6 (1955)

ERRATA

Volume 4

page 168, line 4: *for* is not now available *read* is now available from The Macmillan Company

page 221, line 42: *for* Mardee *read* Maree

page 224, line 29: *for* 4 *read* 5

page 456, reference 4: *for* (1938) *read* (1948)

CONTENTS

CHILD PSYCHOLOGY[1,2]

By Helen L. Koch

Department of Psychology and Committee on Home Economics, The University of Chicago, Chicago, Illinois

General Characterization and Evaluation of the Field

Writings that might be said to fall under the classification of child psychology have been located in the output of many disciplines, pure and applied. This state of affairs is no doubt as it should be, for problems seldom fall neatly within discipline lines, and interest in the behavior and welfare of the child should be widespread. But a heavy price is paid for the interest child psychology enjoys, for much of the exploring is in inexperienced hands. Often clumsy conceptualizations and procedural blunderings could have been avoided had there been acquaintance with the best that psychology and contributing disciplines had to offer. But what is more serious, hypotheses and faiths are confused with facts. As is usual in popular thinking, practical considerations are the focus of interest, and the implications of even well-founded principles are elaborated without any attention to the complexity of phenomena. Too many studies, though not without some merit, have little foundation in systematic theory. Their goal seems to be rather to observe and to see what "turns up." In the main, psychoanalytic interpretations are accepted uncritically as are also those based on projective tests.

It may be significant that the writer could not find in the products of the year the presentation of any new principle of substantial scope, and there were only about a half-dozen investigations that contributed to the clarification of even the semidescriptive old ones. These latter studies, since they are rare, have been singled out for special comment.

Basic Concepts and Descriptions of Behavioral Development

Riesen & Kinder (93), through the intensive observation and controls which only the use of animal subjects permits, have subjected to checking such descriptions of development as Gesell has popularized or formulated. Riesen & Kinder's subjects were 13 infant chimpanzees. The two authors question the usefulness for understanding the detail of human behavioral development of the phylogenetic law, though their skepticism is not with respect to the validity of the law. They find themselves at least not in dis-

[1] The survey of the literature to which this review pertains was completed May 1, 1953.

[2] The following abbreviations have been used in this review: WISC (Wechsler Intelligence Scale for Children); EEG (electroencephalogram); MMPI (Minnesota Multiphasic Personality Inventory); M-F Test (Masculinity-Femininity Test); TAT (Thematic Apperception Test); PMA (Thurstone Primary Mental Abilities Test).

agreement with the principle of alternating flexor and extensor dominance, albeit wanting for the present to suspend judgment. They question the principle of a rigid maturational sequence unless the sequence is composed of behaviors which develop far apart in time. No one of their subjects, for instance, followed exactly the 40-item sequence taken from the Gesell-Ames Schedules. Riesen & Kinder wonder if the description that development proceeds in a cephalocaudad direction applies beyond the prenatal period. They suspect that the so-called postnatal cephalocaudad sequence may be reducible to a complexity sequence. Their observations are not entirely congruent with the Coghill principle that the "part individuates out of the whole." Rather, Windle (118) is given some support. The independent action of parts, they think, depends on many variables, among which are stimulus characteristics. Disappearing reflexes were observed but of the current interpretation of these in terms of cortical maturation and the overlaying of lower-center functions Riesen & Kinder are not sure. They feel that evidence to date has not eliminated learning as the mechanism causing the disappearance. When they observed their animals daily, they witnessed no developments they would describe as saltatory. It is worthy of note in relation to the nature-nurture issue that chimpanzees reared by humans and those cared for by their own mothers did not differ significantly in their performance on the developmental items of the Gesell-Ames Schedules.

The Windle-Coghill controversy mentioned above and thought important because of its relation to the law that development proceeds from the undifferentiated to the differentiated received some attention from Humphrey (55) who, in a carefully documented theoretical article, defends the thesis that there are two kinds of reflexes, the monosynaptic stretch reflexes and the plurisynaptic cutaneous reflexes. These two classes, she thinks, are affected differentially by oxygen lack. Humphrey believes that workers who saw only generalized responses among the earliest the human organism made missed the localized stretch reflexes because of observing when the oxygen reduction was sufficient to dissipate them but still insufficient to block the plurisynaptic reflexes.

One of the important questions in psychology is the nature of the aspects of things to which organisms respond. The Gestaltists contend that animals respond chiefly to relations, to Gestalts; they offer the results of transposition experiments in support of their contention. Spence (106) has questioned this evidence. Hunter (56) offers a critical investigation bearing on the Köhler-Lashley-Spence (68, 71, 106) controversy. He concludes that the "absolute" theory of Spence is inadequate to account for the findings of his study but expresses the opinion that response is to both relational and absolute aspects of stimuli. Which discrimination will serve as the basis of a particular transposition is a function of many variables.

The kinds of relations cognized and abstracted were questions also of interest to Werner & Kaplan (117). These authors investigated how children of different ages handle the problem of inferring from context cues the meaning of strange words. The detail in the monograph is rich but cannot be specified here. The general developmental trend in the thinking of the children was in accord with principles Werner had enunciated earlier: i.e., from concrete to abstract; from syncretic to differentiated, precise, and independent.

R. R. Sears and the group of workers gathered about him have long been concerned with making child psychology a more deductive and less inductive science. They have been interested in testing the extent, on the basis of chiefly neo-Hullian principles of learning, to which they can deduce personality characteristics and the behavior of children from knowledge of the behavior of their parents, especially the latter's reward and punishment practices. Nowlis (85), one of Sears' cohorts, has described in more detail than has been given before, the goals, procedures, trials, and tribulations of the "Iowa" study of the relation of maternal behavior and child aggression and dependency. For those who tend to interpret a complex situation glibly in terms of a single principle, it might be pointed out that the original prediction the Iowa group made, namely, that children most frequently punished for aggression at home would show the least aggression at school, was not borne out. Only by supplementing the principle of reinforcement with others, such as the drive heightening effect of conflict, could predictions be made that were congruent with the curvilinear relation observed between the amount of punishment the children received for aggression at home and the amount of aggressive behavior they displayed at school.

Freud believed that the individual in his libidinal development normally goes through a series of stages, oral, anal, phallic, which are characterized by certain interests, dominant satisfactions, attitudes, and patterns of adjustment. An individual, according to Freud, may remain fixated at any one of these levels, or having tried unsuccessfully to function at a more mature level, may fall back (regress) to a less mature mode of functioning.

Two major investigations aimed to determine whether the attribute complexes Freud imputed to persons fixated at, or regressed to, a certain level can be discovered in the population. Barnes (9) included in the qualities and attitudes he measured (crudely) in a group of male college students the principal conscious attitudes Freud ascribed to the various fixation and regression types. These measures Barnes subjected to a factor analysis. While there are three factors out of eleven in the data which might, if interpretations were elastic enough, be viewed as those of oral, anal, and phallic character, most of the traits Freud alleges to be characteristic of a type are not weighted with the appropriate factor, though some important ones are. Efforts to take into account reaction-formation did not improve the picture. It may be, as many have thought, that Freud was a better observer than theorist and that he did in a hazy way differentiate some common personality types but was in error as to the determinants of the types and so in relation to the nature of the total picture. Barnes' data, of course, shed no light on the origin of the factors uncovered.

Blum & Miller (13) concentrated their study on the so-called oral type. Like Barnes, they offer no developmental or biographical data on their subjects but rather merely asked the question do the traits Freud attributes to the oral character really tend to cluster in some school-age children. Blum & Miller observed that their measures of food intake and food interest, social isolation, concern over giving, need for being liked, and tolerance for boredom were correlated to some extent. However, measures of suggestibility, depression, need to be ingratiating, and inability to divide loyalties were not associated with the aforementioned cluster. This is the same pattern of partial agreement, partial disagreement with Freudian theory that Barnes has noted. Blum & Miller did not see fit to consider explanations for their findings that would be alternative to the Freudian.

Friedman (43) has been concerned with the castration and Oedipus complex concepts which psychoanalysts consider extremely important for the interpretation of development. He has subjected to checking two assertions said to follow from the two concepts: (*a*) that castration fears (and hence repression of them) are high at about five years and then again at early adolescence and (*b*) that girls, after experiencing the castration complex, turn increasingly toward their fathers and away from their mothers. Friedman used a story completion test, containing stories about objects which, according to Freudian lore, are penis symbols (e.g., tails). The stories were developed in such a way that one completion theme that might readily occur would be the removal of the organ. If the story completion in terms of mutilation was not given, then it was assumed likely that repression, motivated by castration fears, was responsible. Friedman reports that, consistent with Freudian theory, the mutilation theme occurred less frequently in the story completions of 5-year-olds, especially boys, and in 11 to 14-year-olds than in the stories of children 7 to 10 years of age or over 14. It should be noted, however, that in presenting significance data. Friedman chose the particular age comparison most likely to yield a significant p. The comparison chosen varied from story to story. It would have been interesting, too, to have determined whether stories suggesting the mutilation of living things that are not regarded as penis symbols (or are there any such?) were less frequently forthcoming from children of certain ages than others.

Likewise with a story completion and a picture story test, Friedman gauged the parent preference of his subjects. Evidence of a mother preference by the girls was yielded by one technique but several other, less direct, approaches suggested the opposite. Hence, Friedman thinks his results are congruent with Freudian theory. The possibility of a cultural interpretation of his findings is not considered.

Personality Organization and Developmental Trends

Trait persistence.—The extent to which personality traits tend to persist in an individual through the years is a question of much significance. If persistence is observed, it is usually interpreted in terms of genetic influences, constant environmental forces, powerful abiding effects of early happenings (such as brain damage, or mental trauma). Seldom, however, have we been able to disentangle these influences, and relevant studies this year succeed no better. Despite lack of success in interpretation, it is of some interest merely to know what traits tend to be rather stable. Studies bearing obliquely on the issue [Blum & Miller (13); Barnes (9)] have already been mentioned. Smith (103) approaches the problem more directly, though her study lacks in adequate controls. Using a detailed diary kept by a mother relative to the activities of her six children (three males and three females), Smith rates these six individuals (in some cases also has them rate themselves and each other) as young children and then as elderly adults. The rank on the basis of age at which learning to talk and to read took place agrees perfectly with adult rank in academic achievement, and the estimates of childhood IQ are correlated perfectly with occupational status in maturity. Thirty-seven per cent of the childhood character and personality ratings agree with those made of the adult, and 33 per cent differ by no more than one point on the five-point scale. How much better than chance this is, Smith does not determine. Nor can we be sure of the independence of the judgments of adult and childhood status or of their relative freedom from bias. At any rate, among the apparently more stable traits were found affectionateness, sympathy, conscientiousness, carelessness, ambition, intelligence, contrariness, irritability, jealousy, quarrelsomeness, spunkiness, strength of will, nervousness, and physical attractiveness. Consistent with Tuddenham's (112) observation, Smith noted that the boys in the family improved more in status than did the girls.

Physique and temperament are believed by many to be related. Hence, although the investigation is only tangential to the psychology of personality, it seems appropriate to call attention here to Reynold's (92) excellent one on the distribution of subcutaneous fat in childhood and adolescence. Reynolds analyzed roentgenographic measures of subcutaneous fat in eight body areas, the measures taken annually for 12 years on 176 children. As evidence bearing on the stability of adipose character, the inter-age correlations may be cited. The correlations between measures procured at 7.5 and 13.5 years range, depending on the area assessed, from +.38 to +.83 for girls and from +.41 to +.71 for boys; while the correlations between measures taken at 11.5 and 16.5 years scatter from +.40 to +.71 in the case of girls and from +.61 to +.82 in boys. These coefficients indicate some stability in body type. The inter-area *r*'s, while positive, are low enough to bespeak of striking differences in build. Suggestive of but by no means proof of genetic correlates of individual differences in adiposity and in adiposity patterns, are the facts (*a*) that Reynold's subjects tended to resemble their parents (*r*, father-son = +.48; *r*, mother-daughter = +.35 for measures of subcutaneous fat on calf and chest) and (*b*) the amount of resemblance in adipose character the members of pairs of children showed was directly related to the degree of closeness of the pair members in genetic relationship. It is probably significant that the children (both male and female) with the greater fat breadths tended to mature earlier, though it should again be emphasized that this cannot be taken as evidence of genetic effects.

Age trends.—Ames this year has added two studies to her significant series of normative studies of preschool children. She has provided a catalogue of chiefly verbal behaviors exhibited by children 18 to 48 months of age and thought to be revealing of the child's sense of self (3). Lists of typical behaviors are given for half-year intervals, though, unfortunately, no frequency or variability data are presented.

Ames *et al.* (4) give Rorschach Test norms for half-year intervals from 2 to 6, and thereafter, at yearly intervals until 10 years. The volume is a significant contribution to the testing literature as well as the literature on mental growth.

Still another chiefly normative study of personality change, though social class differences are also focussed, was directed by Frank and co-workers (38) and is based on the results obtained with five projective tests. Although no systematic population sampling was attempted, 100 each of prepuberal, puberal, and adolescent girls, representing various social classes and circumstances, were the subjects. Some of the chief conclusions of Frank *et al.* are: (*a*) the adolescent girl, as compared with the younger, is more poised, realistic, critical of her family, active and interested in men; (*b*) the American girl tends to be somewhat dependent and fears growing up; (*c*) she is motivated by a desire to please more than by an intrinsic well-integrated value system; (*d*) middle-class girls are inclined to be anxious, tense, and ambitious but not mature emotionally, even at late adolescence; (*e*) high intelligence and superior school performance tend to block the whole-hearted embracing of the feminine role; (*f*) many lower-class girls have been severely traumatized, but those who have not, verge toward a more mature femininity than the girls of corresponding age from the middle class.

Unfortunately, in the case of the reports on some of the tests no quantitative data are offered, the writer merely giving her impressions and some illustrative material. Hence the reader is in no position to assess the impressions and interpretations given. One may also question, on the basis of studies such as Samuels' (97), whether different interpreters would receive similar impressions from the data basic to the monograph. Value judgments are made freely, judgments which to the reviewer seem at times distinctly oldworldish. As is characteristic of diagnoses based on projective tests, the "difficulties" of the subject receive much attention. Even if one grants the diagnoses correct, one may well wonder how a stress sign would be assessed if it could be viewed in the context of the individual's total response system and the character of the culture in which he must function.

Social Class Differences

Attitude and adjustment.—Auld (6), after reviewing the relevant literature, asserts that practically all studies show the higher classes to be superior to the lower in attitude and adjustment. Social class differences tend to be greater than economic group differences, though the two classifications overlap greatly. Davis (23), of course, would insist that Auld's is a necessary finding, because assessments are made in terms of middle-class rather than lower-class values. Although it might be interesting to debate this issue, let us merely survey the class differences observed.

The fact that lower-class children in telling stories interpreted their characters as motivated by less remote goals than did middle-class children is taken by Leshan (74) to mean that middle-class folk, as compared with lower, are more inclined to delay pleasure for the sake of future gain.

Consistent with this view is Ort's (86) observation that in the case of his middle-class group there was less concordance between what youths said their parents expected of them and what they did, than was true of the lower-class group. The lesser concordance in those of higher social status stemmed from the fact that the expectations held for the children involved more unpleasantness, *i.e.*, less immediate satisfactions, than those held for children lower in the social scale.

To determine directly just what parents struggle for in their children, Aberle & Naegele (1) interviewed a group of middle-class fathers. The traits stressed by these men, in their hopes for their sons were initiative, responsibleness, obedience, masculinity, medium aggressiveness, good achievement in school, and a business career; for their daughters, lovingness and docility. Marriage was the chief goal for the girls.

Lest comments on this point be taken as suggestive that life for the lower-class child is rosy, attention should be paid to studies like that of Drucker & Remmers (28) and Pattie & Cornett (87). The lower-class group among the seventh-grade children who the former authors had check the SRA-Youth Inventory indicated they had more basic personal problems than did the middle- and upper-class children. This is in agreement with the trend in the Frank (38) monograph. The Inventory, it should be added, was validated against school counsellors' judgments of the children's adjustments and was found to discriminate between extreme groups reasonably well (29).

Pattie & Cornett asked children from both underprivileged and favored neighborhoods to recall as many as possible memories of their life before five years. The proportion of unpleasant memories recalled by the children from the unfavorable environments was about twice as great as that for the children from the favorable. On the basis of this fact, Pattie & Cornett warn against the common practice of diagnosing as pessimists individuals who recall relatively more unpleasant experiences than do others. Experience and background need to be taken into account. Of course, one might raise the question of what does make a pessimist if not his experiences!

Turkish children from poor homes were more generous in a sharing test than were the economically more favored, according to Uğurel-Semin (113).

Concepts.—Estvan (34) questioned upper- and lower-class children (ages 10 to 11) to discover their conception of the extent and implications of poverty. In conception of extent the groups did not differ, but they did differ in their notions of the way the problem could be dealt with. As far as implications were concerned, the lower-class children stressed quantity lacks; the upper-class, quality lacks.

Language.—Children from the upper classes have long been known to have language skills superior to those from the lower. Consistent with this, is Irwin's (58) observation that after 18 months even the children from the professional and business groups differ in speed of speech acquisition, the former making the more rapid progress. Relevant, too, is Estes' (33) finding that her subjects from the professional and administrative groups scored higher on the WISC[2] than the children of day laborers, differences being more marked in the case of achievement on the verbal section than on the performance.

Because of considerations such as the above, efforts are being made to develop so-called culture-free intelligence tests (24, 32).

Effects of Family Attitudes and Practices

Effects on social-emotional behavior and attitudes.—Though not always has the effect of family attitudes on child behavior been well abstracted from that of a correlated complex, it is generally agreed that when parent attitudes are bad, the children have difficulty making a good social adjustment. But what are the bad attitudes? Some clarification of this point may be achieved by the summaries which follow.

Among the several studies dealing with variables correlated with the child's identification with his parents (this is a fuzzy concept) is that of Sopchak (105). He asked students to check the MMPI,[2] first to describe themselves, and then successively, as they thought their father, their mother, and most people would check it for themselves. Degree of similarity between self and parent descriptions was taken as a measure of identification. (How satisfactory this method is, we do not know, but it is essentially the same, though different instruments were employed, as has been used in the other studies on identification we shall mention later.) At any rate, the correlations obtained by Sopchak between the identification scores, especially those for identification with the father, and various measures of psychotic trends which the MMPI yields, were significant and, of course, negative.

Cava & Raush (16), estimating child conflict in twelfth-grade boys from lower-status homes by means of the Blacky Test, found that the boys who showed the least identification with their fathers tended also to show the most conflict, especially in the castration fear area.

Cass (15) noted that parent-child conflict (gauged by a sentence completion test) was greatest among a group of adolescent girls when the mother was low in awareness of the child's thoughts and feelings and high in restrictiveness. The measures of child identification with the mother when correlated with the mother's "awareness" score yielded a value of +.59 in the case of the girls, and +.17 in the case of the boys.

Schoeppe *et al.* (98) discovered that success in achieving emotional independence at adolescence and also in sex-role performance is significantly associated, in the case of males, with strong identification with the father. Severe parental control was associated in the population studied with poor performance in all the major developmental tasks of adolescence. Schoeppe *et al.* have based their conclusions on a great volume of material obtained in an intensive inter-disciplinary study of the adolescents of a given age in a small midwestern community.

The reverse of the picture just presented is described in the conclusion by Montalto (83) that her six-year-old subjects whose mothers were warm in affection and low in restrictiveness were the most stable. Montalto based her estimates of child adjustment on the Rorschach Test and her judgments of mothers on the Fels Child Research Station parent ratings. Montalto believes the various combinations of high restrictiveness, low restrictiveness, warmth, and coolness in the mother result in quite different personalities in the children.

To reflect the young child's view of its mother's functioning and its reaction to this, wishful and otherwise, Isch (59) used the Sears doll-play procedure. Each of 33 pre-schoolers had been observed with its mother in an experimental session. The children whose mothers in the experimental session had been aggressive with them tended in the doll play to fantasy the child doll or the mother doll the recipient of much aggression. If the mother had tended to ignore the child, then the child doll was fantasied as receiving aggression from the mother, whereas if the mother had been highly directive, then neither the child doll nor the mother doll was fantasied as aggressive, but the child doll was portrayed as highly directive and negativistic. The correlations between measures of the child's actual behavior and his fantasy tend to be insignificant or very low.

Effects on intelligence and language.—As evidence of the interest-stimulating effects of a good home, Fischer (35) presents data on institution babies. Several groups tested first at six months each averaged about 76 in IQ. All of the babies gained on retest. A group tested after adoption scored normal. Unfortunately the babies remaining in the institution were not tested at the same time; so it is difficult to tell whether the institution continued to be depressing. Irwin (58), in the same key, reports institution babies slow in speech acquisition.

Presenting the reverse side of the picture, Klatskin (66) announces that a group of 184 babies who are participating in the Yale-Senn program, hence receiving good pediatric care and with parents being counselled to be permissive and flexible, scored above average on all but five of the items of the Cattell Infant Intelligence Scale when one year old. Sixty-one per cent of the group walked at 12 months, as compared with only 28 per cent of the babies used to establish the Gesell norms. The lack of acceleration on the verbal items leaves one wondering. Does this illustrate Shirley's (101) contention that an early enthusiasm for motor activities may delay the onset of speech?

Mowrer (84) takes the view that, as in the case of talking birds, devotion by the baby to the person who cares for it, is highly important for the development of good motivation for speech learning.

Probably illustrating the effect on speech development of parental neglect and abuse is the case of extreme speech retardation which Du Pont *et al.* (30) describe. The speech difficulty in this eight-year-old boy cleared up considerably under simple nondirective therapy with no special attention to speech correction.

Effects of feeding practices.—Since some of the psychoanalysts painted very distressing pictures of the effects of early feeding frustrations, there has been much debate on this topic. Already we have mentioned the indirect approaches to the question by Barnes (9) and by Blum & Miller (13). Sewell (99) has taken a more direct route. He found no relation, however, between the type of feeding and weaning experience of his 161 child subjects while infants and their present self attitudes as measured by the California Test of Personality, ratings their teachers gave them on independence, emotional control, acceptance of authority, etc., or their mothers' reports of nervous habits, speech difficulties, sensitiveness, or fears. Rosenthal (94), on the other hand, comparing the mothers of a group of babies suffering from eczema with the mothers of a parallel group free from the disorder, reports that the former comforted and handled their babies little. We should like to see the investigation repeated with better matching and control of examiner bias.

The Wolfenstein (119) historical account of the trends in child feeding and infant care in the United States from 1914 to 1951 (the various editions of the Children's Bureau pamphlet, *Infant Care*, was the source material) made one view with some misgivings his present faiths, since the fashions during the last 35 years have been many. The present fashion is favorable to a child-cued program and highly permissive treatment.

Family effect on social goals.—Ambition or mobility was the subject of an investigation by McGuire (78). The offspring in socially mobile families and from families in which the two parents had different social-class backgrounds tended to be mobile, the incidence of mobility being 62 and 72 per cent, respectively, in the above mentioned groups and only 15 per cent in the offspring of nonmobile families.

Family effects on ethnic attitudes.—Goodman (45), in a very convincing study, using testing, intensive interviewing, and long observations of both parents and children, demonstrated a considerable degree of race consciousness among both Negro and white preschool children in mixed schools. Some of the awareness and attitudes stemmed clearly from parent teaching. Forty per cent of the Negroes and 24 per cent of the white children showed high race awareness; 15 per cent of both groups, very low awareness. About three-fourths of the Negro children would have preferred to be white. About one-fourth of Goodman's 103 four-year-old subjects exhibited a strongly entrenched system of color-related values.

Frenkel-Brunswik & Havel (41), Bird *et al.* (12), and Helfant (53) sketch the prejudice picture of the school-age child. All report some, but only a small-to-medium relation between the ethnic attitudes of parents and their children. Prejudice was fairly systematized and generalized in both and, according to Bird *et al.*, not related to the social, educational, or occupational level of the family or its church affiliation or attendance. Generally the culturally less favored were less prejudiced against the culturally more favored group than the latter were to the former.

Brunswik and Havel raise, but do not answer, the question as to whether prejudice is learned chiefly through direct and indirect teaching by family and peers or results from mechanisms such as displacement of hostility.

Ordinal position and sibling influence.—Studies in this area are few. Commenting on the Fels Research Institute findings, Lasko (72) states that mothers tend to be less warm with their first child than with later ones, though at the same time more child-centered and protective, at least during the child's first two years.

In a sharing test the only child was more selfish, on the average, than the child with sibs, according to Uğurel-Semin (113). Refutation of the idea that sibs strongly stimulate development in speech comes from Irwin (58).

Evidence of the effects of sibling rivalry was obtained by Lees (73). Among the adult miners who were given the opportunity for some college training, first-borns made especially good use of these opportunities, i.e., did well in their studies and improved their occupational status, if they had sibs who had done better than they socially or economically; otherwise, accomplishments were moderate. The performance of the second-borns seems to have been unrelated to their sibs' life status. Markedly fewer of the first-borns in the group had married, and they were less sociable than the second-borns.

Peer Relations

McGuire (79) contends that within the first half year after entering school, children have established their peer allegiances, and these tend to persist through the rest of the year. The friendship groups are composed usually of children of one sex. While a certain degree of general social conformity seems important for peer acceptance at these ages, the child who is too conforming and adult-centered is not popular.

Second-graders, when citing their reasons for liking a classmate, listed external characteristics, such as good looks or a nice home, according to Dymond *et al.* (31); whereas sixth-graders most frequently mentioned personal qualities, such as friendliness and cheerfulness.

In the studies listed below we have illustrations of four different methods of gauging a child's acceptability to his peers. Tuddenham (112) thinks his version of the "guess who" test furnishes good clues as to social adjustment. It indicates who accepts and who rejects the child and for what reason, whether those the child admires also admire him, whether he is generally approving or disapproving of his classmates, and whether his view of himself is consistent with that of others.

Clark & McGuire (18) have devised two instruments to gauge peer status. The basic data in both cases are derived from a standard sociometric procedure. Each positive and negative mention a child receives is then weighted, in the case of one instrument (80), by the arbitrary weight given to the social class of the child making the mention; in the other instrument (18), by the popularity in the class of the child making the mention.

Believing that the degree to which a school-age child has pregenital attitudes would be inversely related to the degree of his acceptability to his classmates, Miller & Stine (82) devised a story completion test and scoring scheme to reveal pregenital attitudes. The test was validated against a sociometric test criterion. The scores of the two instruments correlated negatively, as expected, but "anal" attitudes seemed to be associated with popularity. This latter fact may remind the reader of Davis's (23) contention that many so-called "anal" characteristics, e.g., thrift, cleanliness, thoroughness, are traits highly valued by the middle class. This is the class to which most of Miller & Stine's subjects belonged.

The hypotheses of Dymond *et al.* (31) and Ausubel & Schiff (7) that empathy, the ability to know how others think and feel, is significantly correlated with popularity and with age were verified. Self knowledge, according to Ausubel, was slightly less accurate than knowledge about others.

The Sexes

In a nicely conceived study of peer judgments, Tuddenham (112) employed a "guess who" technique with subjects from grades one to five. He reports the following findings: girls had the reputation among their classmates of being quiet, docile, and friendly; boys, of being aggressive, bold, and active. Girls generally were more approved than boys, but the boys' stock went up with age; the girls', if anything, went down. The children, as a rule, favored their own sex. The boys cast proportionally more favorable votes for their peers; the girls giving both more positive and more negative votes, a finding somewhat in line with that of Sherriffs & Jarrett (100) that women tend to more extreme grading than men. The boys were inclined to agree better with each other in their estimates of a given classmate than were the girls. The individual pupil's judgment of himself in various traits was not, in the main, in good accord with his classmates' assessment of him, but the degree of agreement increased with age, a trend similar to that reported by Ausubel & Schiff (7). The teacher's judgment of a given child and that of his classmates agreed only moderately, the extent varying with the trait and, as Ausubel & Schiff also noted, inversely with the age of the child.

Items related to the success individuals have in the major developmental tasks of adolescence vary somewhat with sex, according to Schoeppe *et al.* (98). Positive feeling for boys, for instance, was important for the success of the girl in her sex role in the population studied, whereas the reverse seemed not to hold for boys. Close conformity to the social code appeared to have been more important for girls than boys. For boys, success in the achievement of emotional independence was related to the adoption of the morality system of the father; while for girls, no significant relation with this latter variable was noted.

The idea that masculinity or femininity may be a biosocial complex is suggested by the data of Schoeppe *et al.*, and is borne out further by the findings of Ford & Tyler (36) who factored separately the Terman-Miles M-F[2] scores obtained from 153 female and 157 male ninth-graders. Two factors were adequate to account for the communalities in the responses of the males; three factors, in the responses of the females. The patterns of item loadings suggested that the factors, in the case of the boys, may be tough-mindedness and interest; in the case of the girls, sensitivity, interest, and social role. The latter factor seems consistent with the observation of Schoeppe *et al.* that conformity to the behavior code approved by the culture for females is very important for the girls.

Perhaps the findings of Veroff *et al.* (114) reflect some of the detail of this behavior code. These investigators gave a picture-story test depicting individuals at work to a group of 16- to 18-year-olds. More achievement themes occurred in the girls' stories when the picture contained a male than when a female figure, whereas the boys showed no such difference in reaction. The girls, moreover, did not, as the boys did, increase achievement themes when put under pressure to do well. It is the opinion of the investigators that their results support Mead's (81) idea that, at adolescence and after, the female stops competing with the male but rather competes and achieves through him.

Sex differences in race awareness among preschool children were noted by Goodman (45), the girls being the more race conscious. This seems in line with an oftrepeated finding that girls have stronger social interests than boys.

Following are some of the sex differences found by Ames *et al.* (4) in the responses of young children (two to ten years) to the Rorschach Test. R, A%, and A were higher for boys than girls; F, FC, and H%, lower. No consistent sex differences were apparent in D, F%, M, FM, m, W%, C, or Clob. No attempt will be made here to suggest what these differences may mean.

The view that a person who draws first, in the Draw-a-Person Test, a human figure opposite in sex to his own is a sexual invert has been challenged by Granick & Smith (48). The third of their female subjects who drew the opposite sex figure first and the eighth of their male subjects, did not differ in M-F score on the MMPI from those who drew the like sex figure first. The M-F scores of the two sexes in each of the aforementioned two groups differed significantly and to the same degree. All investigators [Weider & Noller (116); Knopf & Richards (69); etc.] agree, however, that the two sexes tend to draw first the figure of their own sex. Knopf & Richards hold the opinion that deviation from the trend is associated with anxiety in the child.

(See also Lorr & Jenkins (76) below for other findings on sex differences.)

Deviant Behavior and Attitudes

Among the deviant groups on whom attention will be centered are the children with behavior problems, the delinquent, the school failure, the neurotic. Discussion of psychotic children will be omitted.

To determine whether any order underlies the various behavior difficulties children fall victim to, Lorr & Jenkins (76) made a factor analysis of the Ackerson data on the forms of deviant behavior reported for a large population of children brought to a behavior clinic for help. The analysis yielded five common factors which the investigators interpret as follows: encephalitis or brain damage, unsocialized aggression, socialized delinquency, overinhibition, and schizoid character. The second-order factors Lorr & Jenkins label rebellion and schizoid disorganization. The analyses for the two sexes revealed slightly different patterns of factor weights, but the same factors. Male socialized delinquents, for instance, are more likely to steal, females to be untruthful. The overinhibited girl is likely to cry frequently; the boy not. Among the unsocialized aggressives, the girls tend to have tantrums, the boys to be destructive.

For the purposes of organization we shall follow Lorr & Jenkins' classification as far as possible.

Brain conditions and problem behavior.—A number of investigators [Lorenzo & Sidwell (75); Gunnarson & Melin (50); Kennard (64)] agree in finding a greater incidence of abnormal brain wave patterns in behavior problem children, and all are in accord, too, that brain damage can be associated with an abnormal EEG[2] and with behavior disorders. There is not, however, consensus as to what an abnormal EEG means. Kennard, for instance, after reviewing the literature, comes to the conclusion that an abnormal EEG (especially the pattern of high voltage fast waves) may be merely the internal correlate of emotion. She thinks there is no evidence to justify the view that once an individual shows a deviant brain wave pattern then he can be expected to continue to show it or that the abnormal pattern is necessarily a sign of a defective brain or constitution. Lorenzo asserts that an abnormal EEG was characteristic of more of the behavior problem children he worked with than any other physical, neurological, psychological, or sociological condition he explored. He admits that an "abnormal" family history increased the probability of an abnormal EEG in a child, a fact which may, of course, be interpreted to support either side of the controversy Kennard specifies.

It is frequently assumed that the abnormal EEG stems from brain damage received at birth, as from anoxia, among other things. Significant in this connection is the demonstration by Hurder & Sanders (57) of very high resistance by newborn rats to impairment of learning ability from severe anoxia (adult rats had not shown this). This finding is in line with current pediatric faiths.

Apropos of the problem of the relation of brain damage and behavior, one might mention the report by Keeler & Bender (63) on a 3- to 15-year follow-up of 20 children originally admitted to Bellevue Hospital with Sydenham's chorea. In the years following their release from the Hospital, 11 made a very poor social adjustment and 6 more only a fair one. Among those who made the poorest adjustment were those with evidence of permanent brain damage, with a low IQ, or a home of poor quality.

Delinquent and aggressive behavior.—The year's most extensive treatment of the problem of the aggressive child is given in a volume by Redl & Wineman (91). Believing extreme aggressiveness results from ego disturbances, these authors present their theories relative to what occasions the breakdown of controls or what interferes with their development, picture in vivid detail the defense mechanisms typical of the delinquent, and sketch the methods found useful in helping the residents of a home for disturbed children to develop effective "controls from within."

The extrapunitiveness Redl sees to be common in the aggressive child shows clearly in Rosenzweigs' (95) study of a group of clinic children. On the Picture-Frustration Test the clinic children gave more extrapunitive and fewer impunitive responses than normals.

That the aggression frequently found in habitual delinquents tends to be widely generalized is suggested once again by Wattenberg & Faigenbaum's (115) observation that there is little consistency in the type of offense in which a given individual indulges except in the case of the sex delinquent and auto thief.

Although delinquency is a legal category and no uniform personality characteristics mark the group, Gough & Peterson (46) are of the opinion that delinquents rather generally lack the ability to look at themselves as social objects, in Mead's terms, to take roles. On the basis of the theory, though it must be admitted some items quite irrelevant to the theory were included, Gough & Peterson constructed a questionnaire which was successful in identifying 78 per cent of the adolescent delinquents in one population and 66 per cent of the adult offenders in another. Twenty-three per cent of a group of normals were misclassified by the instrument. The delinquents, when compared with nondelinquent controls, were rated on the average as more rebellious, headstrong, defensive, dissatisfied, tense, anxious, wary, sensitive, and affected.

Examples of what might be called socialized delinquency may be found in Clark's (19) investigation of experiences in vandalistic episodes on the part of students. The incidence of experiences of this sort among the students was higher in males than females. More of the episodes, too, in the case of the males occurred after the boys were 10 years old; more of those in the case of girls, before 10. The crowd situation, enjoyment of excitement, and hostility to the individual or agency whose property was damaged were cited frequently as motivations for the acts of vandalism. Clark thinks vandalism, within limits, is normal and with this Crane (21) essentially agrees. He found that 41 per cent of the male gangs and 27 per cent of the female gangs he studied were predatory. Crane found gangs were usually one-sex organizations, reached a peak in frequency in the years 9 to 13, and had an average size of six to seven members. They tended to have a secret language or code, a secret meeting place, and in the case of male gangs, initiation rites.

It has been presented as a basic law of behavior that whenever an organism is prevented from achieving its desires it reacts aggressively. There has been much debate in regard to whether aggression is a necessary consequence of frustration. Of course, although the issue can receive no final test, it is of interest to know with what other kinds of responses organisms do meet blocking. On this point Davitz (25) contributes. He systematically exposed one group of boys to experiences which stressed and rewarded constructive activities and a matched group, to experiences in which aggressive behavior was reinforced. Following an imposed frustration, the behavior of the two groups was carefully observed. The aggressively trained boys behaved more aggressively after frustration than did the constructively trained. The latter also behaved generally less aggressively after than before training.

Neurotic behavior.—Anna Freud (42) gives a revealing review of some of the kinds of insults, fears, and dependency stimulations children often have when hospitalized or merely when ill at home. With a view to determining some of the psychological effects, especially the persisting ones, of an operation, Jessner *et al.* (60) observed 142 tonsillectomy and adenoidectomy cases before, during, and after the operation. Twenty per cent of the children had a severe persisting reaction, those children most upset by the operation experience being usually the ones who were disturbed individuals before. Symptoms observed by Jessner *et al.* in their traumatized subjects were nightmares, refusal to talk, tics, fears of white coats and of death, wetting and soiling, screaming, and increased dependency. Since the information the child had about the operation beforehand was not related to the severity of his reaction to the event, Jessner and his co-workers think information needs to be supplemented by other experiences such as acting out, perhaps.

"Accident proneness," which has frequently been interpreted as a neurotic sign, was the subject of an investigation by Krall (70). She located, through hospital records, 32 five- to eight-year-old children who had had at least three major accidents in four years. These children were observed in two doll-play sessions and their behavior compared with that of 32 controls matched in age and school grade. (Would that the matching had included environment or social class!) The "accident prone," in relation to the controls, were in the doll-play sessions more active, intense, indulged in more verbal aggression, and made more bids for attention. It is significant that the social histories of the "accident prone" revealed that the child in many cases was a member of a large family, was late in the birth order, came from a broken home, and had transferred frequently from school to school. It was suggested that, instead of giving an interpretation of the high accident rate of these children in masochistic terms or even in terms of cognitive dedifferentiation, as is usual, one might do well to consider the possibility that the accidents resulted from inadequate supervision and greater exposure to danger.

If nail biting were taken as a sign of neuroticism, then 61.6 per cent of Chicago's public school children of eight years would be neurotic! Malone & Massler (77) found the incidence of nail biting in five-year-olds was 38 per cent. It increased until eight years when it reached 61.6 per cent and then declined. However, at 18 years, 28 per cent of the pupils were still biting their nails. After 10 years girls offended less than did boys.

Since some attribute most feeding difficulties in babies to anxiety generated by poor handling, the observations of Jorup (62) on the 30 per cent of his 589 infant patients who were dyspeptic will be of special interest. Nine per cent of the babies had severe difficulty. The disorder, characterized by loose stools, high intestinal pressure, and pain, begins, according to Jorup, at birth and is relatively independent of diet or environment. Since anticholinergic drugs give immediate relief, Jorup believes the disorder stems from parasympathetic dominance. In support of the theory that the difficulty is constitutional, he points to the fact that the parents and sibs of dyspeptic babies are frequently sufferers from gastrointestinal disorders. Jorup's thesis is in accord with the fact that rats can be bred for differences in frequency of defecation and micturition (when under stress). Since, however, the visceral behavior and overt fear behavior are not well correlated, Bindra & Thompson (11) are of the opinion that what is inherited is a tendency to gastrointestinal lability rather than, as has been asserted, a tendency to fear.

Learning difficulties.—A great volume of literature indicates that learning is influenced by motivation. But what are these motivations in detail and what is the pattern of their effects? Gaier (44) was interested in some of the characteristics of the rigid learner. He used a unique technique, "stimulated recall," to get a picture of what 11 university students were thinking about, in respect to the course subject matter, themselves, and others, during the regular sessions of a university class. A tape recording was made of each session, and this was used to stimulate the student's recall of his thoughts and feelings. Also each student was given a battery of tests to measure general academic competence, a Rorschach test to gauge his anxiety, rigidity, and negativism, and finally the course examination consisting of two sections, one composed of "rote" questions and one of "thought" questions. The estimates of anxiety and rigidity made by three independent judges correlated negatively with all the tests of academic timber and of course learning, except the rote part of the final examination, and correlated positively with the amount of derogatory thinking about the self which the stimulated-recall sessions exposed. The negativism rankings also correlated positively with the amount of critical thinking about self and others in which the students indulged during class. Gaier thinks anxiety makes the student rigid and this in turn prevents him from dealing in a creative way with new experiences. One may wonder, of course, whether the student is anxious and critical because he is having to deal in his courses with material beyond his depth or whether the situation is as Gaier outlines.

Pushing the question one step back, Pearson (88) gives a lengthy review of kinds and sources of motivation disturbances as well as organic conditions believed to contribute to learning difficulties. Staver (109) and Sperry *et al.* (107), in their study of 15 to 17 poor achievers, point chiefly to parent attitudes as a source of trouble. The parents of their subjects had tended to discourage efforts of the child to get answers to his questions and to learn. They had explained little and had tried to keep the child dependent.

Like Staver's, Kimball's (65) results point back to disturbed relations with parents as a probable determinant of poor scholarship. Her subjects were 20 bright, prep-school boys who were failing badly in their studies. A sentence completion test, given in an English class, suggests that the boys had a poor relationship with their fathers, and the TAT[2] indicated that they had much hostile feeling. What is cause and what is effect, may here again be difficult to determine.

Graham (47), working with retarded readers, believes that most of them suffer from some specific blocking which causes them to resist instruction. He calls attention to the fact that when his group was tested with the WISC and the Wechsler-Bellevue Test, they scored above average on the object-assembly, picture-completion, picture-arrangement, block-design, and comprehension sections; below average, on the arithmetic, digit-span, digit-symbol, information, and vocabulary sections. This is a profile Wechsler gives (we wonder with what wisdom) for psychopaths.

At any rate, support for the view that the motivation to do good work in school stems often from quite other than mere interest in the subject matter is given by a study by Frandsen & Sessions (37). The investigators correlated the grades a given child made in his various school subjects and self-ratings on degree of interest in the subjects. These correlations ranged from −.80 to +.90, depending on the child and, no doubt, still other variables. The median correlation for the class was +.51. The children whose grades were unrelated or negatively related to the level of their interest were said to be extrinsically motivated; the others, intrinsically. There was no difference in the general adjustment of these two groups of students, according to the investigators.

Physical handicap and adjustment.—Holding the opinion that no really dependable information is available relative to the extent of physical handicaps among children, Barker *et al.* (8) made a thorough survey of one county in Kansas. In this county, 7 per cent of the boys and 4.8 per cent of the girls were suffering from a disability of some sort. Ninety per cent of the handicapped attended regular school; 6.5 per cent, no school. Speech and vision defects were the most common. The data of the study have many implications for education.

To determine whether a cardiac condition tends to maladjust a child seriously, Freed & Cruickshank (39) compared the performance of 71 cardiac cases with 71 matched normals on a sentence completion test designed to reflect adjustment. The authors conclude that both groups of children showed a good relationship to their fathers but, whereas the normals exhibited a better adjustment to their mothers than to their fathers, the reverse obtained for the cardiacs. The hypothesis is presented that the cardiacs have a less good relation to the mother because it is she who must constantly enforce the inactivity their heart condition dictates.

That cerebral palsy may interfere with perceptual as well as motor processes is suggested by the finding of Dolphin & Cruickshank (27) that, in a tactual discrimination task, a group of cerebral palsy victims were not so adept as normals in distiuguishing figure from ground.

Since it has been asserted, perhaps with not too much foundation, that children identify better with the figures on a TAT card if the figures are like them in sex, in color, etc., Greenbaum *et al.* (49) have raised the question of whether handicapped children will reveal more of themselves in a picture-story test in which the figures pictured are handicapped persons. The investigators presented to one group of orthopedically handicapped children pictures depicting cripples, and to the other group cards from the regular TAT series. The latter the authors believe encouraged more productivity than did the revised pictures, although in this latter case 50 per cent of the stories touched upon the handicap.

Mental defect.—Porteus & Corbett (90) have reviewed the statutory definitions of feeblemindedness in the United States since 1912 and the provisions for the commitment of children to institutions for mental defectives. The authors feel that the provisions often do not insure competent diagnosis and tend to stress too much mere test score. Some states have left the diagnosis entirely to physicians.

Of course, many question the wisdom of institutionalizing any but the most seriously defective. In relation to this issue, Charles's (17) study is timely. To discover what the feebleminded make of themselves he located and investigated 151 of the 206 feebleminded individuals whom Ballers had studied in 1935 and who were then over 21. The dullest 20 per cent are still institutionalized. The rest differ from the general population in that fewer have married, and the married have fewer children; also, their death rate has been higher, especially death by violence. Forty per cent of the males have violated the law (chiefly because of drunkenness) and 50 per cent have had some sort of relief aid in the 17-year period which included the depression years. The type of dwelling in which they live and the incidence of home ownership is average. Their children are, in the main, proceeding through school with little difficulty. Altogether, the picture is a not-too-discouraging one.

Cognitive Processes and Mental Measurement

Mental measurement.—Table I summarizes some of the inter-test relations explored in the year's writing. There seems to be agreement that the Stan-

TABLE I

Comparative Studies of Various Intelligence Tests for Children

Investigator	Age of Subjects: Range (yrs.)	Age of Subjects: M or Md (yrs.)	N	WISC Full Scale M (IQ)	WISC Full Scale σ	WISC Verbal Section M (IQ)	WISC Verbal Section σ	WISC Performance Section M (IQ)	WISC Performance Section σ	Tests Other than WISC: Test	Tests Other than WISC: M (IQ)	Tests Other than WISC: σ	Inter-Test Correlations: Test Correlated	Inter-Test Correlations: r
Triggs & Cartee (110)	5 to 6	—	46	107.56	13.21	103.39	14.19	111.07	13.73	Stanford Binet	124.11	9.72	WISC (Full) and Stanford	+.62
													WISC (Verbal) and Stanford	.58
													WISC (Performance) and Stanford	.48
Holland (54)	5 to 13	—	26	—	—	—	—	—	—		—	—	WISC (Full) and Stanford	.87
													WISC (Verbal) and Stanford	.83
													WISC (Performance) and Stanford	.73
Hanvick (52)	5 to 12	—	25	107.84	—	107.12	—	107.56	—	Goodenough, Draw-a-Man	94.12	—	WISC (Full) and Goodenough	.18
De Lattre & Cole (26)	10½ to 15½	—	50	112.00	—	108.00	—	114.00	—	Wechsler Bellevue (Full)	106.00	—	WISC (Full) and W-B (Full)	.87
										Wechsler Bellevue (Verbal)	102.00		WISC (Verbal) and W-B (Verbal)	.86
										Wechsler Bellevue (Performance)	109.00		WISC (Performance) and W-B (Performance)	.82
Cohen & Collier (20)	6½ to 8¾	—	51	99.80	14.26	98.50	14.48	101.10	14.51	Stanford Binet	104.8	15.07	WISC (Full) and Stanford	.85
													WISC (Verbal) and Stanford	.82
													WISC (Performance) and Stanford	.80
										Arthur	94.7	16.35	WISC (Full) and Arthur	.80 (eta)
													WISC (Verbal) and Arthur	.77 (eta)
													WISC (Performance) and Arthur	.81 (eta)
													Arthur and Stanford	.71 (eta)
Altus (2)	—	13½	55	—	—	—	—	—	—		—	—	WISC (Full) and California Mental Maturity	.81
													WISC (Verbal) and Progressive Readng	.84
													California Mental Maturity and Progressive Reading	.73
Ansbacher (5)	—	10½	100	—	—	—	—	—	—	Goodenough	101.8	14.25	Goodenough and PMA	.41
										Primary Mental Abilities	97.95	12.52	Goodenough and PMA (S+R+P sections of PMA)	.48
													Goodenough and MacQuarrie	
													Tracing	.34
													Tapping	.23
													Dotting	.16

ford Binet yields a higher IQ than the WISC and that the verbal section of the latter correlates somewhat better with the Stanford Binet than the performance section, in fact almost as well as the full scale. The low sigma of the Stanford scale at age five is once again revealed (110).

Triggs & Cartee (110) and Holland (54) disagree on the magnitude of the difference between the Stanford Binet and WISC scores in relation to the variables of age and size of IQ, Holland contending that there is no relation between these latter variables and the magnitude of the difference between the two tests. Although he employed some refinements of technique, e.g., control of practice effects which was lacking in the others' study, it is doubtful whether these are adequate to compensate for the paucity of his subjects and their wide irregular scatter.

De Lattre & Cole (26) found that their 10- to 16-year-old subjects scored better on the WISC than on the Wechsler-Bellevue Scale. The correlations between parallel subtests ranged from +.19 for picture arrangements to +.71 for digits, a warning against assuming that tests with similar names measure the same processes. The verbal section of the WISC correlated better with the Progressive Reading Test than did the California Mental Maturity Test.

Hanvik's (52) emotionally disturbed subjects scored significantly better on the WISC than on the Goodenough Draw-a-Man Test, the correlation between the two instruments being insignificant. Hanvik thinks the drawing test is more anxiety activating. Possibly the children were indifferent to the whole test situation but found it more difficult to resist when the experimenter was stimulating them directly and constantly offering new tasks.

Ansbacher (5) reports that the Draw-a-Man Test correlated +.41 with the Thurstone PMA[2] Test but scarcely at all with the MacQuarrie Mechanical Ability Test. His subjects were a group of 100 fourth-graders. Since the subtests in the PMA battery of space, perception, and reasoning showed the most relation to the Drawing Test, and the MacQuarrie Test *r*'s were very low, Ansbacher thinks this is evidence that the Drawing Test is less one of motor skills than of cognitive processes.

There has long been the suspicion that the examiner's relation with the preschool children he is testing determines in a major way the children's performance. Sacks (96) in a neat study tested this assumption. She carefully matched three groups on the basis of an initial Stanford Binet test score. Then for 10 days she tried to ingratiate herself with the children of one group by serving them well when at nursery school and to establish poor relations with a second group by being sober, indifferent, and denying help; she had no contact with the children of group three. If she was really able to control the tester's bias, her results are significant. On retest the groups gained on the average 14.5, 5.0, and 1.6 IQ points, respectively. Apparently mere familiarity with the tester had some favorable effect on test performance; good relations, considerable.

Darcy (22), after reviewing the relevant literature, concludes that bilinguals usually do less well on verbal intelligence tests than monoglots, but do not differ in achievement on performance tests. This is confirmed by Johnson (61(who worked with bilinguals whose second language was Spanish. Johnson's ingenious device for gauging degree of bilingualism should be mentioned, as it is apparently a better index than the Hoffman Test. The index is the ratio of the number of words in the first language recalled in five minutes to the number of words in the second language recalled in the same interval of time.

For studies of other variables which influence mental test performance see Estes (33); Fischer (35); and Klatskin (66).

Speech and language.—See Darcy (22); Du Pont (30); Irwin, (58); Klatskin (66); Mowrer (84); and Werner & Kaplan (117).

Perception, conception, thinking, memory.—While the studies in the area named are motley and difficult to relate, they point often to the developmental trend in thinking from syncretic to differentiated, from concrete to abstract, and from egocentric to social.

Following a Piaget type (89) of analysis of the reasons children gave for their responses in a sharing test, Ugurel-Semin (113) confirms the sequence he suggests. Following is the developmental sequence Semin noted: egocentric response, knowledge of the moral rule but action still egocentric, adult-dictated rule governs conduct, child assesses rule, modifying it in terms of his own experiences.

The development in the understanding of time which occurs between the years four and six has been described by Springer (108).

A contribution which lends some support to the genetic theory of consonance comes from Bugg & Thompson (14). They noted (*a*) that students who had learned to be appreciative of dissonant music rated a number of presented intervals the same in consonance as did a group of students who disliked dissonant music and (*b*) that the rating of the first group did not shift as their liking for dissonant music increased.

The law of primary reinforcement was verified by Siegel & Fashee (102) using preschool children, a Skinner lever-pressing device, and candy pellets as rewards. The more reward the children received the more difficult was extinction of the lever-pressing response.

There has long been interest in the question of whether childhood really is the happy period it seems when viewed from the adult point of vantage. No definitive answer is supplied to this question and several related issues by the studies of Smith (103). Tuckman & Lorge (111), and Barschak (10). Rather they tend merely to confirm the view that adults look upon the period of childhood as the halcyon days and think with no relish on getting old.

Major studies already mentioned which deal with problems of perception, conception, and thinking, are as follows: Ames (3); Ames *et al.* (4); Goodman (45); Werner & Kaplan (117).

LITERATURE CITED

1. Aberle, D. F., and Naegele, K. D., *Am. J. Orthopsychiat.*, **22,** 366–78 (1952)
2. Altus, G. T., *J. Consulting Psychol.*, **16,** 230 (1952)
3. Ames, L. B., *J. Genet. Psychol.*, **81,** 193–232 (1952)
4. Ames, L. B., Learned, J., Metraux, R. W., and Walker, R. N., *Child Rorschach Responses* (Paul B. Hoeber, Inc., New York, N. Y., 310 pp., 1952)
5. Ansbacher, H. L., *J. Consulting Psychol.*, **16,** 176–80 (1952)
6. Auld, F., Jr., *Psychol. Bull.*, **49,** 318–30 (1952)
7. Ausubel, D. P., and Schiff, H. M., *Child Development*, **23,** 111–28 (1952)
8. Barker, L. S., Schoggen, M., Schoggen, P., and Barker, R. G., *Child Development*, **23,** 215–26 (1952)
9. Barnes, C. A., *Genet. Psychol. Monographs*, **45,** 105–74 (1952)
10. Barschak, E., *Brit. J. Psychol., Gen. Sect.*, **43,** 129–40 (1952)
11. Bindra, D., and Thompson, W. R., *J. Comp. Physiol. Psychol.*, **46,** 43–45 (1953)
12. Bird, C., Monachesi, E. D., and Burdick, H., *J. Abnormal Social Psychol.*, **47,** 688–99 (1952)
13. Blum, G. S., and Miller, D. R., *J. Personality*, **20,** 287–304 (1952)
14. Bugg, E. G., and Thompson, A. S., *J. Gen. Psychol.*, **47,** 71–90 (1952)
15. Cass, L. K., *Am. J. Orthopsychiat.*, **22,** 305–13 (1952)
16. Cava, E. L., and Raush, H. L., *J. Abnormal Social Psychol.*, **47,** 855–56 (1952)
17. Charles, D. C., *Genet. Psychol. Monographs*, **47,** 3–72 (1953)
18. Clark, R. A., and McGuire, C., *Child Development*, **23,** 129–40 (1952)
19. Clark, W., *J. Social Psychol.*, **36,** 167–77 (1952)
20. Cohen, B. D., and Collier, M. J., *J. Consulting Psychol.*, **16,** 226–27 (1952)
21. Crane, A. R., *J. Genet. Psychol.*, **81,** 113–23 (1952)
22. Darcy, N. T., *J. Genet. Psychol.*, **82,** 21–58 (1953)
23. Davis, W. A., *Social Class Influences upon Learning* (Harvard University Press, Cambridge, Mass., 100 pp., 1948)
24. Davis, A. and Eells, K., *Davis-Eells Test of General Intelligence or Problem-Solving Ability* (World Book Co., Yonkers-on-Hudson, N. Y., 1952)
25. Davitz, J. R., *J. Abnormal Social Psychol.*, **47,** 309–15 (1952)
26. Delattre, L., and Cole, D., *J. Consulting Psychol.*, **16,** 228–30 (1952)
27. Dolphin, J. E., and Cruickshank, W. M., *J. Personality*, **20,** 466–71 (1952)
28. Drucker, A. J., and Remmers, H. H., *J. Abnormal Social Psychol.*, **47,** 379–81 (1952)
29. Drucker, A. J., and Remmers, H. H., *J. Appl. Psychol.*, **36,** 186–87 (1952)
30. Du Pont, H. J., Landsman, T., and Valentine, M., *J. Consulting Psychol.*, **17,** 122–25 (1953)
31. Dymond, R. F., Hughes, A. S., and Raabe, V. L., *J. Consulting Psychol.*, **16,** 202–6 (1952)
32. Eells, K., Davis, A., Havighurst, R. J., Herrick, V. E., and Tyler, R. W., *Intelligence and Cultural Differences* (University of Chicago Press, Chicago, Ill., 388 pp., 1951)
33. Estes, B. W., *J. Consulting Psychol.*, **17,** 58–63 (1953)
34. Estvan, F. J., *Genet. Psychol. Monographs*, **46,** 3–60 (1952)
35. Fischer, L. K., *Am. J. Orthopsychiat.*, **22,** 522–33 (1952)
36. Ford, C. F., Jr., and Tyler, L. E., *J. Appl. Psychol.*, **36,** 251–53 (1952)

37. Frandsen, A. N., and Sessions, A. D., *Educ. Psychol. Measurement*, **13**, 94–101 (1953)
38. Frank, L. K., Harrison, R., Hellersberg, E., Machover, K., and Steiner, M., *Monographs Soc. Research Child Development*, **16**, No. 53 (1951)
39. Freed, E. X., and Cruickshank, W. N., *Quart. J. Child Behavior*, **4**, 299–310 (1952)
40. Freeman, H. E., and Showel, M., *J. Social Psychol.*, **37**, 97–102 (1953)
41. Frenkel-Brunswik, E., and Havel, J., *J. Genet. Psychol.*, **82**, 91–136 (1953)
42. Freud, A., *The Psychoanalytic Study of the Child*, **7**, 69–81 (International Universities Press, Inc., New York, N. Y., 448 pp., 1952)
43. Friedman, S. M., *Genet. Psychol. Monographs*, **46**, 61–130 (1952)
44. Gaier, E. L., *Psychol. Monographs*, **66**(17), 28 pp. (1952)
45. Goodman, M. E., *Race Awareness in Young Children* (Addison-Wesley Press, Inc., Cambridge, Mass., 280 pp., 1952)
46. Gough, H. G., and Peterson, D. R., *J. Consulting Psychol.*, **16**, 207–12 (1952)
47. Graham, E. E., *J. Consulting Psychol.*, **16**, 268–71 (1952)
48. Granick, S., and Smith, L. J., *J. Consulting Psychol.*, **17**, 71–73 (1953)
49. Greenbaum, M., Qualtere, T., Carruth, B., and Cruickshank, W., *J. Clin. Psychol.*, **9**, 40–44 (1953)
50. Gunnarson, E., and Melin, K. A., *Acta Paediat.*, **40**, 496–501 (1951)
51. Haeusserman, E., *J. Genet. Psychol.*, **80**, 3–23 (1952)
52. Hanvik, L. J., *J. Clin. Psychol.*, **9**, 71–72 (1953)
53. Helfant, K., *Psychol. Monographs*, **66**(13), 23 pp. (1952)
54. Holland, G. A., *J. Consulting Psychol.*, **17**, 147–52 (1953)
55. Humphrey, T., *J. Psychol.*, **35**, 3–44 (1953)
56. Hunter J. M. L., *Brit. J. Psychol., Gen. Sect.*, **43**, 113–28 (1952)
57. Hurder, W. P., and Sanders, A. F., *J. Comp. Physiol. Psychol.*, **46**, 61–63 (1953)
58. Irwin, O. C., *J. Speech Hearing Disorders*, **17**, 369–79 (1952)
59. Isch, M. J., *J. Genet. Psychol.*, **81**, 233–58 (1952)
60. Jessner, L., Blom, G. E., and Waldfogel, S., *Psychoanalytic Study of the Child*, **7**, 126–69 (International Universities Press, Inc., New York, N. Y., 448 p., 1952)
61. Johnson, G. B., Jr., *J. Genet. Psychol.*, **82**, 3–10 (1953)
62. Jorup, S., *Acta Paediat.*, **41**, Suppl. 85, 110 pp. (1952)
63. Keeler, W. R., and Bender, L., *Am. J. Psychiat.*, **109**, 421–28 (1952)
64. Kennard, M. A., *Psychosomat. Med.*, **15**, 95–115 (1953)
65. Kimball, B., *J. Consulting Psychol.*, **16**, 353–58 (1952)
66. Klatskin, E. H., *J. Clin. Psychol.*, **8**, 230–37 (1952)
67. Kline, M. V., *J. Genet. Psychol.*, **82**, 137–42 (1953)
68. Köhler, W., *Dynamics in Psychology* (Liveright Publishing Corporation, New York, N. Y., 158 pp., 1940)
69. Knopf, I. J., and Richards, T. W., *J. Genet. Psychol.*, **81**, 99–112 (1952)
70. Krall, V., *J. Abnormal Social Psychol.*, **48**, 99–108 (1953)
71. Lashley, K. S., and Wade, M., *Psychol. Rev.*, **53**, 72–87 (1946)
72. Lasko, J. K., *Am. J. Orthopsychiat.*, **22**, 300–4 (1952)
73. Lees, J. P., *Brit. J. Psychol., Gen. Sect.*, **43**, 210–21 (1952)
74. Leshan, L. L., *J. Abnormal Social Psychol.*, **47**, 589–92 (1952)
75. Lorenzo, J. M., and Sidwell, R. T., *Quart. J. Child Behavior*, **4**, 326–37 (1952)
76. Lorr, M., and Jenkins, R. L., *J. Clin. Psychol.*, **9**, 16–19 (1953)

77. Malone, A. J., and Massler, M., *J. Abnormal Social Psychol.*, **47,** 193–202 (1952)
78. McGuire, C., *Marriage and Family Living*, **14,** 109–15 (1952)
79. McGuire, C., *Marriage and Family Living*, **15,** 17–22 (1953)
80. McGuire, C., and Clark, R. A., *Child Development*, **23,** 141–54 (1952)
81. Mead, M., *Male and Female: a Study of the Sexes in a Changing World* (William Morrow & Co., New York, N. Y., 477 pp., 1949)
82. Miller, D. R., and Stine, M. E., *J. Personality*, **20,** 162–74 (1952)
83. Montalto, F. D., *J. Projective Techniques*, **16,** 151–78 (1952)
84. Mowrer, O. H., *J. Speech Hearing Disorders*, **17,** 263–68 (1952)
85. Nowlis, V., *Am. J. Orthopsychiat.*, **22,** 286–99 (1952)
86. Ort, R. S., *J. Abnormal Social Psychol.*, **47,** 425–32 (1952)
87. Pattie, F. A., and Cornett, S., *J. Personality*, **20,** 315–21 (1952)
88. Pearson, G. H. J., *The Psychoanalytic Study of the Child*, **7,** 322–386 (International Universities Press, Inc., New York, N. Y., 448 pp., 1952)
89. Piaget, J., *The Moral Judgment of the Child* (The Free Press, Glencoe, Ill., 418 pp., 1948)
90. Porteus, S. D., and Corbett, G. R., *J. Psychol.*, **35,** 81–105 (1953)
91. Redl, F., and Wineman, D., *Controls from Within* (The Free Press, Glencoe, Ill., 332 pp., 1952)
92. Reynolds, E. L., *Monographs Soc. Research Child Development*, **15,** No. 2 (1950)
93. Riesen, A. F., and Kinder, E., *Postural Development of Infant Chimpanzee* (Yale University Press, New Haven, Conn., 204 pp., 1952)
94. Rosenthal, M. J., *Pediatrics*, **10,** 581–92 (1952)
95. Rosenzweig, S., and Rosenzweig, L., *J. Abnormal Social Psychol.*, **47,** 683–87 (1952)
96. Sacks, E. L., *J. Abnormal Social Psychol.*, **47,** 354–58 (1952)
97. Samuels, H., *Psychol. Monographs*, **66**(5), 20 pp. (1952)
98. Schoeppe, A., Haggard, E. A., and Havighurst, R. J., *J. Abnormal Social Psychol.* **48,** 42–52 (1953)
99. Sewell, W. H., and Mussen, P. H., *Child Development*, **23,** 185–91 (1952)
100. Sherriffs, A. C., and Jarrett, R. F., *J. Psychol.*, **35,** 161–68 (1953)
101. Shirley, M., *The First Two Years: Postural and Locomotor Development* (University of Minnesota Press, Minneapolis, Minn. 227 pp., 1931)
102. Siegel, P. S., and Fashee, J. G., *J. Exptl. Psychol.*, **45,** 12–14 (1953)
103. Smith, M. E., *J. Genet. Psychol.*, **80,** 151–82 (1952)
104. Smith, M. E., *Child Development*, **23,** 159–80 (1952)
105. Sopchak, A. L., *J. Abnormal Social Psychol.*, **47,** 159–65 (1952)
106. Spence, K. W., *Am. J. Psychol.*, **54,** 223–29 (1941)
107. Sperry, B. M., Staver, N., and Mann, H. E., *Am. J. Orthopsychiat.*, **22,** 356–65 (1952)
108. Springer, D., *J. Genet. Psychol.*, **80,** 83–97 (1952)
109. Staver, N., *Am. J. Orthopsychiat.*, **23,** 131–41 (1953)
110. Triggs, F. O., and Cartee, J. K., *J. Clin. Psychol.*, **9,** 26–29 (1953)
111. Tuckman, J., and Lorge, I., *J. Psychol.*, **34,** 137–50 (1952)
112. Tuddenham, R. D., *Psychol. Monographs*, **66**(1), 57 pp. (1952)
113. Uğurel-Semin, R., *J. Abnormal Social Psychol.*, **47,** 463–74 (1952)
114. Veroff, J., Wilcox, S., and Atkinson, J. W., *J. Abnormal Social Psychol.*, **48,** 108–19 (1953)

115. Wattenberg, W. W., and Faigenbaum, D., *J. Clin. Psychol.*, **9,** 78–81 (1953)
116. Weider, A., and Noller, P. A., *J. Clin. Psychol.*, **9,** 20–23 (1953)
117. Werner, H., and Kaplan, E., *Monographs Soc. Research Child Development*, **15**(1), 120 pp. (1950)
118. Windle, W. F., *Physiology of the Fetus* (W. B. Saunders Co., Philadelphia, Penna. 249 pp., 1940)
119. Wolfenstein, M., *Am. J. Orthopsychiat.*, **23,** 120–30 (1953)

LEARNING[1,2]

By Edward C. Tolman and Leo Postman
University of California, Berkeley, California

THEORY

Books by Hull (74) and Guthrie (62) have brought their respective $S\text{-}R$[2] theories up to date. A brief article by Tolman (165) gives a précis of his most recent general formulation. MacCorquodale & Meehl (110) have presented an elaboration of an earlier paper (112) in which they formalized expectancy theory by a set of postulates. They include reinforcement in addition to frequency of presentations, $S_1 \rightarrow R_1 \rightarrow S_2$, as probably an important determiner of expectancies.[3] This is the only point in their discussion to which the present reviewers would definitely take exception.

Hull's last book (74) is of great significance and will long stand as a memorial to his creative genius. It presents in final form his basic postulates and corollaries. It also contains many ingenious, though often not very rigorous, applications of these postulates and corollaries, through the derivation of theorems, to most of the factual problems of animal learning. One feature of the system as now presented, in which we naturally concur, is his latest equation for Reaction Potential,

$$_SE_R = D \times V_1 \times K \times {}_SH_R$$

(where D stands for drive strength, V_1 for stimulus-intensity dynamism, K for incentive motivation, and $_SH_R$ for habit strength). This formula makes somewhat the same distinction between learning ($_SH_R$)[2] and performance ($_SE_R$)[2] that we would. Two basic differences between Hull's system and ours are, however, to be noted: (*a*) Hull conceives what is learned to be an $_SH_R$ whereas we conceive it to be an expectancy, a "readiness" for an S_1 to be followed by an S_2 provided a certain type of R_1 occurs; and (*b*) Hull still asserts the acquisition of an $_SH_R$ to be a function of frequency of reinforcement (though no longer of amount of reinforcement). We would assert the acquisi-

[1] This review is based on publications covering the period from about May 1, 1952 to May 1, 1953. The writers wish to express their gratitude to Mr. J. Trevor Peirce for bibliographical assistance, and to Miss Pauline Austin for help in reading the proofs.

[2] The following symbols appear in this chapter. When special meanings are needed additional symbols are added to the basic letters. The meanings intended are explained by the authors where these first appear. CR (conditioned response); CS (conditioned stimulus); D (drive, drive strength); $_SE_R$ (excitatory strength); $_SH_R$ (habit strength); I_R (reactive inhibition); $_SI_R$ (conditioned inhibition); M (means); pR (pointer-reading response); R (response); r_G (fractional anticipatory goal response); *rs* (central neural surrogate response); S (stimulus); s_G (fractional goal stimulus); US (unconditioned stimulus).

[3] We have gratefully borrowed some features of their notation.

tion of an expectancy to be primarily a function of frequency of past occurrences of $S_1 \rightarrow R_1 \rightarrow S_2$, whether or not S_2 has had positive, negative or zero incentive value. However, positive or negative incentive values acting as perceptual emphasizers undoubtedly speed up acquisition.

Gleitman *et al.* (53) have attacked Hull's doctrine of extinction. They point out, for example, that insofar as Hull now defines responses not as specific muscle contractions but as oriented adjustments to the environment, $I_R{}^2$ (conceived as attributable to the building up of specific fatigue-like products) loses much of its applicability. Further, insofar as extinction is also said to be due to the building up of ${}_SI_R{}^2$, progressive increase in the latter should eventually overtake the amount of ${}_SH_R$ and cause the response to disappear permanently. Gleitman *et al.* also point to the difficulties, as had Ritchie (134), of the concept of the "not-response."

Seward has continued his bridge between *S-R* theory and expectancy theory by his construct of rs^2 (cf. 143). The *rs* performs for Seward much the same function that $r_G{}^2$ and $s_G{}^2$ perform for Hull and Spence. The *rs* is an assumed neurological mechanism by which the significate and also its goal character, if it should have one, are brought back to the *S* at the choice point and made a determiner of *R* at that point. In two recent papers (144, 145), he has specifically applied this concept of *rs*'s to the acquisition of motives.

The new edition (62) of Guthrie's book presents again his doctrine of single-trial *S-R* contiguity learning. Guthrie also asserts once more his doctrine that the *R* which gets conditioned is the "movement" which removes the organism from the given S. So-called adjusted, purposive "acts" are for him purely fortuitous, happy (or perhaps unhappy) combinations of conditioned "movements." It would seem to the reviewers that nature must be even cleverer about providing the right environmental stimuli for combining movements into adjusted, directed acts than we would have supposed her capable of.

There have also appeared several discussions concerning the legitimate objectives of learning theory. Kendler (81) argues that a behavioral theory can as such merely seek for operationally specifiable intervening variables. Insofar as the theorist gives substantive meanings to these intervening variables (i.e., asserts hypothetical constructs) he is going in for reifications which are not legitimate since they have no truth value. These constructs may, however, be helpful to the particular theorist, given his private style of thinking. Ritchie (135) in an oblique and witty reply points out that, if geographers had held to this same "modern methodology," they would not have found it permissible to ask whether the earth were round or flat! But, if Kendler be right, they should have arrived at the same rules for navigation. Ritchie's moral appears to be that if one assumes, for example, the model properties of *S-R* connections one really will arrive at different predictions for behavior than if one assumes the model properties of expectancies. Davis (32), at odds with all theoretical constructs at the merely behavioral level, suggests that what we need is a "physical psychology" in which stimuli, responses, and intervening processes would all be defined by their physical and physico-chemical characteristics. Kessen & Kimble (83) in criticizing Krech's neurological "dynamic systems" (90, 91) argue valiantly for the legitimacy of any sorts of theoretical constructs be they drawn by analogy from neurology, physics, sociology, aesthetics, or whatever.

Our classification of the empirical studies reflects the fact that our systematic approach leads us to employ four types of constructs in the analysis of stimulus-response associations, viz: discrimination, expectancy, drives and incentives, and performance. In line with this conceptual analysis we shall distribute our summaries of the empirical studies under the headings: (*a*) discrimination learning; (*b*) acquisition of expectancies in classical and instrumental conditioning; (*c*) performance in classical and instrumental conditioning, especially as determined by drive conditions; and, cutting across these categories, (*d*) verbal learning, and (*e*) motor learning.

DISCRIMINATION LEARNING

The process of discrimination is central to an expectancy theory of learning. In such a theory, the organism is conceived to discriminate and categorize environmental stimuli as signs, means, and significates. Our analysis of discrimination learning will focus on two major problems: (*a*) conditions governing perceptual discrimination per se; (*b*) the ways in which the discriminated features of the environment come to function as signs.

Conditions of Discrimination

When differential responses are systematically related to an orderly series of stimuli (such as black, gray, and white), a dimension of discrimination has been established. In experiments on discrimination learning, stimuli located at different points along such dimensions come to serve as differential signs to positive and/or negative significates. The more firmly the relevant dimensions of discrimination have been established, the more readily can expectancies be learned. A number of studies help to throw light on the process of perceptual learning in general as well as on the acquisition of specific dimensions of discrimination.

Early learning.—Hebb's (69) theory of perception, with its emphasis on the importance of early perceptual learning, has stimulated a number of empirical studies. Forgays & Forgays (47) and Hymovitch (76) studied the effects of varied infant environments on problem-solving by the adult rat. Both found that early opportunity for perceptual experience may have lasting beneficial effects. Partial support for this conclusion also comes from a study of Bingham & Griffiths (15).

The influence of early training on discrimination learning was studied by Siegel (149) who showed that ring doves reared under conditions of visual deprivation were significantly retarded in the later solution of a discrimination problem. According to Griffiths & Stringer (59), variations in the intensity of early stimulation were not, however, found to produce significant effects on adult learning in rats.

Perceptual training experiments.—Hypotheses about perceptual learning have also been tested in experiments investigating the effects of training on the discrimination of specific classes of stimuli. Lawrence, who had previously presented important evidence for the acquired distinctiveness of cues (98, 99), used a transfer situation to study the conditions governing the establishment of a new dimension of discrimination in rats (100). A difficult discrimination is established more effectively if it is preceded by training on an easy discrimination along the same dimension than if all training is given directly on the difficult stimulus pairs. A gradual change from an easy to a difficult discrimination is optimal for the establishment of the dimension. We would certainly agree with Lawrence's conclusion that increase in $_SH_R$ is not the only factor in discrimination learning, and that the animal must learn "to isolate functionally the relevant stimulus dimension from other background and irrelevant cues" (100, p. 516).

Several experiments have demonstrated the effects of training on perceptual discrimination in human subjects. Smith (152) was able to produce increases in the apparent size of geometric forms by giving his subjects controlled experience with shapes of large physical size. The effects of the experience were specific to the forms used in the training. Bevan & Zener (12), investigating the effects of practice on the perceptual thresholds for geometric designs, obtained general practice effects in recognition as well as increased sensitivity to the specific figures practiced. Atkinson & Ammons (8) found that latency of recognition decreases with practice on a given stimulus but failed to find evidence for a perceptual "learning to learn." Closely related in its implications to the studies just reviewed is an investigation of Forgays (46) which showed that (*a*) tachistoscopic recognition thresholds for words decrease with educational experience and (*b*) superior sensitivity to words presented to the right of fixation, as compared with words presented to the left of fixation, is similarly a function of educational level. These results, in agreement with previous findings from Hebb's laboratory (116, 125), point to the learned nature of highly specific visual discriminations.

The learning of a discrimination may often depend on the performance of an orientating response or "receptor-exposure act." The beneficial effects of training on discrimination may be due partly to the establishment of such orienting responses. Wyckoff (183) presents an elaborate theoretical discussion of the conditions governing the acquisition of observing responses in terms of reinforcement theory. He proposes that the discriminative stimuli come to function as secondary reinforcers for the observing response once the subject has learned to respond differentially to the discriminative stimuli. The author recognizes the danger of circularity in this argument and attempts to escape from it by a series of quantitative assumptions concerning the effects of primary and secondary reinforcement. The reviewers could not help but feel that his highly elaborate analysis represents a tenuous *ad hoc* use of the principle of secondary reinforcement.

Differential effectiveness of discrimination stimuli.—In analyzing response to a given stimulus unit, we must take account of the organism's discrimination system. By discrimination system we refer to the organisms' propensities to categorize and order stimuli along dimensions of discrimination. The discrimination system is specified in terms of the psychophysical functions characteristic of the organism. Several studies have appeared during the year which contribute to the specification of the discrimination systems of several species of laboratory animals.

Amsel (5), using rats, studied the rate of acquisition of a brightness discrimination as a function of the duration of the discrimination stimuli which consisted of black and white runways preceding a choice point. He found speed of learning a direct function of stimulus duration. A previous study by Eninger (37), using auditory discrimination stimuli had, on the other hand, found the shorter durations more effective. Another study by Eninger (38) compared the effectiveness of compound discrimination stimuli involving both visual and auditory sense modalities with stimuli involving only the one or the other of these modalities. The compound stimuli were more effective and visual cues resulted in faster learning than did auditory ones. Greater effectiveness of visual stimulus components, as compared to auditory and tactual ones, was also reported by Fink & Patton (42). The relative effectiveness of color and form in the discrimination learning of monkeys was compared by Cole (30). In tests pitting color against form he found color to be the dominant cue; further tests showed, however, that form discriminations may be learned simultaneously with the dominant color discriminations. Further evidence for the simultaneous establishment of discrimination along two dimensions (size and brightness) is presented by Grice (57) in a study of visual discrimination learning in rats.

The Discrimination of Signs

What are the ways in which the discriminated features of the environment come to function as signs? From the point of view of the present analysis the two stimuli in a discrimination setup come to function as differential signs, one pointing to a positive, the other to a negative significate. Hence, in an expectancy theory, the problem of the nature and temporal development of the differentiation between the positive and negative signs is an important issue.

The problem of patterning.—A significant contribution to this problem has been made by Bitterman and his associates in a series of papers which began some three years ago and of which several appeared during the current year (16, 161, 167, 182). The general thesis of these papers is that a distinction must be made between two nonadditive processes of perceptual organization in discrimination learning: (*a*) configurational learning which involves a "primitive, diffuse" perception of the situation, and (*b*) relational learning in which the organism comes to respond selectively to the abstracted separate sign features in the situation. This latter process of relational learning corresponds to Lashley's (96, 97) analysis of the discrimination process whereas configurational learning conforms to the description of Gulliksen & Wolfle (61). Using this two-factor theory, Bitterman and associates have been able to account for their own experimental findings which conform to neither Lashley's nor Spence's (153, 154) theories. Notable among the empirical findings was the speedier acquisition of a successive as compared with a simultaneous discrimination (179). This finding was not, however, confirmed by Spence (155). It may be mentioned in this connection that Loess & Duncan (103), comparing successive and simultaneous discrimination learning in humans, found (*a*) no difference between the two methods in learning an easy discrimination, and (*b*) simultaneous presentation superior in the learning of a difficult discrimination.

Spence (155) has criticized Bitterman's analysis, at the same time extending his own theoretical views so as to encompass the case of successive discrimination. Compounds such as "white-left" and "black-right" may acquire excitatory potential for the response of approaching. Such "transverse patterning" will, however, occur only under conditions which do not allow learning on the basis of simpler cue-position patterns. Bitterman (16), in a reply to Spence, summarizes the evidence for a two-factor theory and objects to the "theoretical and experimental constriction" of Spence's position.

The implications of Spence's theory of discrimination learning for transposition behavior were tested by Hunter (75) in a series of experiments on size discrimination in children. His results uniformly favor interpretation in terms of relational learning rather than reinforcement of absolute cue properties. On the other hand, a study by French (48), showing the dependence of discrimination learning in humans on the number of common stimulus elements receiving consistent reinforcement, is in agreement with an interpretation in terms of stimulus generalization. In this connection, mention should be made of an extension of Spence's analysis to multiple-choice learning in a paper by Cook (31).

Discrimination reversal.—Studies of discrimination reversal have frequently been viewed as "crucial experiments" for testing divergent interpretations of discrimination learning (as, for example, in the continuity-discontinuity controversy). A modified continuity position is presented by Gatling (50) in his investigation of the effects of repeated stimulus reversals. His results show progressive decreases in negative transfer effects as reversals are continued. He ascribes the increased efficiency of learning to the simultaneous operation of two factors: (*a*) a continuing build-up of habit strength which is transferred from reversal to reversal; and (*b*) the mastery of the reversal problem per se, i.e., essentially the acquisition of a reversal-learning set. Several studies of discrimination reversal in human subjects appeared during this year. In a series of three papers, Buss (22, 23, 24) addresses himself to the problem of "rigidity" in discrimination-reversal learning, i.e., to the conditions determining readiness to shift from old to new discriminations. He found (*a*) differential and partial reinforcement during original training more favorable to reversal than continuous reinforcement; (*b*) the ability to shift depends on the absolute values of the cues reinforced during training rather than on the relation among the cues. An interpretation of "rigidity" as learned behavior is also proposed by Schroder & Rotter (141) who show that the propensity to shift from one solution to another in a card-sorting problem depends on learned expectancies of alternative solutions. Results favoring the continuity hypothesis in human discrimination learning are reported by Walk (176). In two experiments reversal of the cues used in the preliminary training slowed down learning of a visual discrimination although the effects were of limited duration. Walk states that the positive stimulus appeared to have greater weight in determining discrimination than did the negative stimulus. It should be noted in this connection, however, that in a study of visual discrimination in rats Fitzwater (43) found preliminary training, which included experience with the positive and negative stimuli presented separately, more favorable than reinforced practice on the positive stimulus alone.

Discrimination-learning sets.—The continued confirmation of a series of related expectancies may give rise to generalized expectancies ("beliefs") embodying the common features of the specific expectancies. It is in terms such as these that we would conceptualize the learning sets demonstrated by Harlow (64). At the same time, we would point out that the phenomenon of learning sets underscores the inadequacy, or at least the limitations, of an analysis of discrimination learning based on the reinforcement of absolute cue values. Several experimental analyses of discrimination-learning sets appeared during the year. Harlow & Warren (66) report the establishment of learning sets in a series of 450 discrimination problems using planometric stimulus objects (the previously reported studies had used stereometric objects). Although learning sets were again demonstrated, the inter-problem improvement tended to be less than in the earlier studies, a result which is attributed to the greater similarity among the stimuli used in the new experiments. Riopelle (133) presents an experimental analysis of the acquisition of learning sets in monkeys for the solution of new and reversed discrimination problems. Initial disparities between the learning rates for the two types of problems gradually disappeared as the animals gained experience. Riopelle suggests that the acquisition of a learning set involves "transfer suppression," i.e., performances on successive problems in general, and reversal problems in particular, become increasingly independent of each other as the training continues. The course of the acquisition of discrimination-learning sets in chimpanzees and in children was studied by Hayes and associates (67). Their results point to qualitatively different stages in the acquisition of discrimination-learning sets: an early stage in which abstract principles are learned and a later stage characterized by the improvement of performance skills and work habits. The data fail to yield evidence for inter-species differences in the ability to acquire sets. In a further paper, Hayes *et al.* (68) investigate chimpanzees' ability to learn various numbers of discrimination problems simultaneously. A high degree of accuracy can be obtained with as many as 20 simultaneous problems.

We cannot leave the problem of discrimination learning without noting Harlow's (65) eloquent insistence that the motivation of his primate subjects in discrimination experiments is not to reduce visceral needs but to satisfy their curiosity and to manipulate environmental objects. Working in Harlow's laboratory, Butler (25) has presented convincing evidence for the strength and persistence of a visual-exploratory motive which is not derived from other biological drives.

ACQUISITION OF EXPECTANCIES IN CLASSICAL AND INSTRUMENTAL CONDITIONING

Before turning to the actual studies a brief expansion of our theoretical analysis will be helpful. The basic independent variable governing the acquisition of an expectancy is, according to us, one or more occurrences of a "stimulus-response-stimulus" sequence. We shall symbolize such an event by $\{(S_1, M):R_1 \rightarrow S_2\}$. This is to be read: an initial stimulus S_1 is presented and with it an associated "behavioral support" (see Tolman, 164, p. 96f) or "means," M, and, given this S_1 and this M,[2] a response-act, R_1, occurs and results in the stimulus S_2. Moreover, since such a sequence usually occurs within some drive context and may take place more than once, and since S_2 may have either positive, negative, or zero incentive value, the complete symbol will be $D\Sigma\{(S_1, M):R_1 \rightarrow S_2^*\}$ where D stands for an active drive or drives; Σ for number of occurrences; and (*) for the positive, negative or zero incentive value of S_2. Further, the consequence of such $D\Sigma\{(S_1, M):R_1 \rightarrow S_2^*\}$ occurrences is conceived by us to be the acquisition of an expectancy, symbolized as $(\dot{S}_1:\dot{R}_1\dot{S}_2^*)$. Such an expectancy is to be read: if a "discriminated" stimulus of type $\dot{S}_1$ be present, and if the "discriminated" response-act of type $\dot{R}_1$ be made, a "discriminated" stimulus of type $\dot{S}_2$ with "discriminated" incentive value (*) will appear. Given such an expectancy, if there be a drive D relative to which S_2^* is either positive or negative, then upon the presentation of S_1, there will occur a disposition to "go to," "escape from," "avoid," or "merely wait for" S_2^*. And this disposition will betray itself by a specific performance or pointer reading response pR (e.g., salivating, sweating, running, jumping, etc.) which is what the experimenter observes and measures.

In Table I are listed eight independent variables the consideration of which is suggested by the above analysis. These provide us with the categories under which we shall order the empirical studies.

Type or intensity of drive, D.—(*a*) Noxious light as D: Flynn & Jerome (45) were able to teach rats multiple-choice-box problems where D was the drive to avoid strong light and S_2^* a dark goal compartment. Caldwell & Womack (27) found also that albino mice could learn a maze to get out of light. (*b*) Intensity of relevant D: Teel (160) found, using rats, that rates for

TABLE I

INDEPENDENT VARIABLES GOVERNING THE ACQUISITION OF EXPECTANCIES

1. Type or intensity of D.[2]
2. Type or intensity of S_1.
3. Features of M.
4. Quality and incentive value of S_2* (Type and amount of reinforcement).
5. Frequency and probability with which S_2* follows R_1 (Frequency and pattern of reinforcement).
6. Time delays between R_1 and S_2* (Delay of reinforcement).
7. Intertrial intervals.
8. Derived incentive value of S_2* (Secondary reinforcement).

both learning and extinction did not differ for deprivation periods of 1, 7, 15, and 22 hr. of hunger. Apparently strength of D over a normal range does not affect acquisition though it may affect performance. (*c*) The effect of an irrelevant D on conditioning: The effect of an irrelevant drive upon the establishment of an association is illustrated in an experiment by Bahrick (9). This investigator subjected rats to sensory preconditioning with light and buzzer under two degrees of food deprivation. He then conditioned the rats to buzzer as sign for shock. Subsequently, he trained them on the light as sign for shock. The previous pairing of light and buzzer under high deprivation led to more rapid learning to avoid the light. Spence & Taylor (158) and Spence & Farber (157), using eyelid conditioning, found that anxious subjects, as measured on items from the Minnesota Multiphasic Personality Inventory, condition more readily and extinguish more slowly than non-anxious subjects. In such a situation, anxiety may be considered an irrelevant drive. Bitterman & Holtzman (17), using the galvanic skin response (*GSR*) also found that anxious subjects selected by a number of clinical measures, conditioned more rapidly and extinguished more slowly than non-anxious subjects. (*d*) Effect of anxiety on trial and error: Farber & Spence (40) found with a stylus maze that anxious subjects did more poorly, especially on difficult choice points. Where difficult discriminations have to be made between S_1's leading to different S_2*'s (blind ends versus true-path segments) anxiety may interfere with the building up of the appropriate expectancies or, as the authors suggest, tends to enhance indiscriminately all the response tendencies present.

Type of intensity of initial stimulus, S_1.—The readiness with which an expectancy is acquired may depend on the quality or intensity of the initial stimulus. It is to be noted, however, that we have already discussed most of the experimental evidence illustrating this relationship in the section above on conditions of discrimination.

Features of behavior support, M.—We shall consider here a group of experiments in which the environmental arrangements supporting the animal's response appear to be an important variable. (*a*) Time intervals in conditioning (that is, environmental supports for waiting): White & Schlosberg (180) conditioned a *GSR* with light as S_1 and shock as S_2^* with different intervals (*M*'s) requiring different R_1's of waiting between S_1 and S_2^*. They found that an interval of 0.5 sec. resulted in the fastest conditioning. They also note that the optimal time intervals for autonomic and skeletal conditioning are about the same. Fitzwater & Reisman (44) compared forward, backward, and simultaneous presentations of S_1 and S_2^* in instrumental finger withdrawal. The forward setup where S_1 preceded S_2^* by 0.5 sec. here also produced the clearest evidence of conditioning. Kaplan (80), using intermittent reinforcements, taught rats to push a lever where the resultant S_2^* was the going off, for 1.1 min., of a noxious light. For different groups the intervals between reinforcements were 0.2, 0.5, 1.0, 2.0, 3.0, or 5 min. The longer the time intervals the slower the rate of responding. That is, the longer the average time between the R_1's in any interval and the S_2^* at the end of that interval the less readily was the expectancy formed. (*b*) Supports for space and response learning: Hill & Thune (70) ran two groups of rats on single-choice elevated mazes. Their findings, in contrast to the earlier one of Tolman, Ritchie & Kalish (166), was that a "turning" R_1 was acquired more readily than a "going towards a given place" R_1. However, their maze-path arrangements (i.e., *M*) were different from those of Tolman *et al.* and seem to us to have favored response learning since the response group always made a right-angle turn whereas the place group had to make both right angle and obtuse turns. Moreover, the goal place did not occupy as distinctive a position with respect to the source of light. (*c*) Introduction of new *M*: Page & Hall (126) extinguished a conditioned avoidance response by restraining the rats (introducing a new *M*) for a brief interval after the coming of the CS[2] in the former shock compartment for five trials, and then testing in a series of ordinary extinction trials. These rats extinguished more rapidly than a control group not given this first "restraint" experience.

Quality and incentive value of the terminal stimulus, S_2^* (*Type and amount of reinforcement*).—Furchtgott & Rubin (49) ran rats, all 22 hours hungry, in a two-unit maze to different amounts of food: 2500 mg., 250 mg., 75 mg., 20 mg., and 0 mg. No differences in the learning curves were obtained save for the 0 mg. group which showed little manifest learning. We would suspect, however, that, if food had then been introduced, the 0 mg. group would have shown that they had achieved "latently" the same amount of actual learning. Bitterman, Reed & Krauskopf (18) compared the conditioning of *GSR* to light with a US (shock) of 3 sec. duration (i.e., strong negative reinforcement) and a US[2] (shock) of only 0.5 sec. duration (i.e., weak negative reinforcement). No differences were found. On the other hand, Spence (156) conditioned eyelid responses under two different strengths of US (air puff). On the next day half of each group of subjects was tested under strong and half under weak air puff. The number of CR's[2] was significantly more for the strong than for the weak US both in training and in the test. Again the question remains open as to whether the strength of the negative unconditioned stimulus affected learning or performance.

A study by Seeman & Williams (142) is concerned with the "Hull-Leeper" problem of the conditions under which different expectancies can be attached to different drive states. The animal must learn to discriminate between two drives as signs to different S_2*'s. These experimenters taught rats, when hungry, to run around the left arm of a maze to the goal box and food and, when thirsty, to run around the right arm of the maze to the same goal box and water. For the experimental group the final common path and the goal box were black for food and white for water. For the control group, they were black for both food and water. The former group learned faster. The two more distinct S_2*'s correlated with the two different drives favored acquisition of the two expectancies.

In general it is our view that it is frequency of stimulus-response-stimulus occurrences and not amounts of reinforcement which primarily affect acquisition. We believe, in contrast to Hull, that learning may occur in the absence of reinforcement. This last hypothesis is of course tested in experiments on latent learning to which we turn next.

Latent learning.—Interest in this problem continues unabated. The question no longer is whether latent learning does or does not occur. Rather a number of specific experimental variables are being explored in the hope of specifying the conditions of latent learning more and more precisely. (*a*) Spatial position of irrelevant incentive: Thistlethwaite (163) and McAllister (108) both investigated the effect on latent learning of the spatial position of food (irrelevant incentive) relative to the water when preliminary training was under thirst, and water was on both sides. Both investigators found that, when the food was placed close to the water, the rats did not show latent learning, but when the food was at some distance prior to the water they did show it. (*b*) Degree of motivation for relevant incentive: Johnson (79), using a T-maze with food in one goal box but no water in either arm, ran rats with different degrees of thirst. He found that the greater this original thirst, the greater the number of trials to learn to run to the food side when the rats were made hungry. This finding suggests that the more thirsty animals were perceptually more set for water (even though it was not there) and hence less ready to perceive the food. (*c*) Drive discrimination: Thistlethwaite (163) also tested the effect of preceding practice in drive discrimination. Two thirds of his rats were given preliminary practice in going to the food end of a straightaway when hungry and to the water end when thirsty. It was only these animals which showed latent learning. These results confirm the earlier findings of Christie (29). All such findings suggest that when in latent learning experiments the animal is switched to a new drive he must discriminate this new drive as well as remember where the appropriate goal S_2* has been if he is to perform correctly. (*d*) General maze-wiseness versus learning of true path: Muenzinger & Conrad (119), after giving their rats one, two, or three days of nonrewarded training in a six-unit symmetrical maze, reversed the path and tested under reward. Prior to introduction of reward, errors had been dropping out progressively. However, when the true path was reversed there was negative transfer only for the three-day group. The authors therefore distinguished between a general maze-wiseness acquired in the first two days, and a specific latent learning of the true path acquired later. (*e*) Place of prefeeding: Meehl & MacCorquodale (113) ran hungry unrewarded rats in the Blodgett maze for five days. Then the animals were prefed in a maze-like section placed in front of the starting box. When put back in the maze they exhibited a further drop in errors. The authors ascribe the effects of this prefeeding to a conditioning of the hunger drive to the maze environment. This conditioned hunger drive adds to the total drive strength which multiplies with habit strength to produce $_SE_R$. It seems to the reviewers a surprising assumption that at 22½ hr. of deprivation one prefeeding experience would add a substantial increment to the effective drive. (*f*) Effectiveness of unrewarded preliminary exploration: Gilchrist (52) gave different amounts of preliminary exploration of a T-maze without food and then trained with food. The more the preliminary exploration the faster the subsequent learning. Control groups exposed to similar amounts of previous exploration but with food showed no faster subsequent learning. Again it appears that it is the frequency of presentation rather than presence of positive reinforcement as such which determines acquisition.

Frequency and probability with which terminal stimulus, S_2, follows the response R_1 (Frequency and pattern of reinforcement)*—(*a*) Frequency: The influence of frequency per se is by now so well established that there appears to have been only one study during the year dealing with this variable alone. Siegel & Foshee (150), training children to press a bar for a candy reward, found that greater frequency in the original training caused greater resistance to extinction. (*b*) Probability of reward (reinforcement): A number of studies have been concerned with speed of acquisition and with resistance to extinction as determined by various schedules of partial reinforcement. Grant & Schipper (55) used 25 per cent, 50 per cent, 75 per cent, and 100 per cent reinforcements in eyelid conditioning. In general the greater the percentage of reinforcement, the faster the conditioning. They also found that the 50 per cent and 75 per cent groups showed greater resistance to extinction. Lewis (101), using a gambling setup with boys, also found that 50 per cent and 60 per cent groups extinguished more slowly than a 100 per cent group. However, Rubin (140), using a panel-pushing response with rats with distributed practice (40 min. intertrial intervals), found greater resistance to extinction for the continuously reinforced group. Grant, Schipper & Ross (56), with eyelid conditioning, did not, however, find that intertrial spacing reduced resistance to extinction following partial reinforcement. They suggest that the presence of human verbalization may account for the difference between their results and those of Sheffield's (148). In two experiments Bitterman and associates compared 50 per cent reinforcement when presented randomly and when presented alternately. With both humans (106) and rats (168) the alternate group extinguished faster. It appears to the reviewers that the results of the partial reinforcement experiments continue to pose a serious problem for *S-R* reinforcement theory. It is equally true that expectancy theory has not yet been elaborated to a point where it can give a consistent interpretation of this total body of data. The results do point to the conclusion, however, that organisms can learn probabilities, i.e., that probability of reward is one of the environmental features about which expectancies are formed.

Time delays between response, R_1, and terminal stimulus, S_2 (Delay of reinforcement).*—(*a*) Unfilled versus filled delay: Ferster (41) trained pigeons in a Skinner box with aperiodic partial reinforcement (average every 1 min.). He then introduced a 60-sec. delay (the box went dark) between successful peck and reinforcement; rate of pecking decreased. However, if the length of delay was increased gradually from 0 to 60 sec., the original pecking rate could be maintained. Each bird then filled in the delay with its own "superstitious" response. In another experiment birds learned to keep up the rate of pecking to one color of the target key which did not give food but which did (average every 1 min.) produce a second color of the target key in an arrangement by which this second color was followed regularly and automatically (after 1 min.) by food. The birds continued to peck but more slowly during this delay period. The pigeon apparently cannot learn to expect a delayed goal unless during the delay it can develop some sort of a bridging response (R_1) (superstitious or otherwise). (*b*) Long versus short delays: Logan (104) used a double-bar Skinner box. One bar delivered a pellet after 1 sec., the other after 5 sec. The short-delay bar was responded to faster and was preferred. Lambert & Solomon (94), after teaching rats to run a straight alley (with a number of jumps in it) to food, tested extinction by putting a block near the start, near the goal, or merely by removing food. Block near the start caused most rapid extinction, block near the goal the next most rapid, and no food produced the slowest extinction.

Intertrial intervals.—Stanley (159) extinguished a learned turning response in a single T-maze under massed (every 15 sec.) and under distributed (every 15 min.) extinction trials. There was faster extinction for the distributed trials. He also tested for extinction under satiation. The rats arrived equally soon at a 50 per cent choice whether their trials were massed or spaced. Baron (10) found with delayed eyelid conditioning no differences in original learning between a mean intertrial interval of 270 sec. and one of 120 sec. Vandermeer & Amsel (175) also found with eyelid conditioning no difference between spaced and massed trials. Teichner (162), teaching rats to depress a food tray in response to a signal, did find distributed trials better. Holland (72), teaching rats to choose between two levers, also found distributed trials better. As in other areas of investigation (see below under verbal and motor learning) the effects of distribution on acquisition and extinction seem to defy any simple generalization and to depend upon specific experimental conditions.

Derived incentive value of terminal stimulus, S_2 (Secondary reinforcement).*—Although there is by now a considerable body of experimental evidence in support of so-called secondary reinforcement, the nature of the "secondary reinforcers" is still moot. Even from the point of view of a reinforcement theory the distinction between primary and secondary reinforcer has become difficult. The presence or absence of biological need reduction has failed as the criterion. From our point of view environmental features can acquire incentive value and thus serve as way stations (subgoals) to the attainment of already existing goals. To what extent such subgoals can become goals in their own right seems to us to be an unresolved experimental question.

McClelland & McGown (109) found that, if there was an irregular and unpredictable association between a circular goal alley and when and how the rats were fed in it, this goal alley acquired more "secondary reinforcement" (i.e., subgoal-incentive value) than it did for rats which had always been fed regularly at one point in it. Bugelski, Coyer & Rogers (21) found no evidence that pre-nonfeeding in a goal box (after learning) caused extinction of a simple runway response. This was a repeat, with additional controls, of the earlier Seward & Levy experiment (146) which had seemed to give evidence of secondary nonreinforcement.

PERFORMANCE IN CLASSICAL AND INSTRUMENTAL CONDITIONING

If there is an expectancy ($\dot{S}_1 : \dot{R}_1 \dot{S}_2^*$), and if S_2^* has either positive or negative incentive value, the organism will have a disposition to get to, or to get away from, S_2^*. The strength of the disposition is a joint function of the strength of the expectancy, the incentive value of S_2^* and the drive condition. Specific performances serve as pointer-reading responses, *pR*'s, for inferring these dispositions to get to, or get away from, S_2^*. In short, we are maintaining the distinction between learning and performance suggested by Tolman (164) and Lashley (95), and more recently, reflected in the distinction between $_SH_R$ and $_SE_R$.

The studies now to be reviewed are ones which we interpret as throwing light on the ways in which expectancy, drive, and incentive value interact. Once an expectancy can be assumed to have been established, i.e., learning to be complete, the strength of the organism's dispositions to respond can be related to (*a*) type or intensity of *D* at the time of testing or (*b*) difference between training and test conditions with respect to S_1, *M*, and S_2^* (generalization with respect to sign, means, and significate). In this section we shall attempt an interpretation of the experimental data as regards these determinants of performance.

Drive and Performance

Intensity of drive.—Hillman, Hunter & Kimble (71) trained rats under two degrees of thirst in a 14-unit maze. No differences in error curves appeared, but the stronger deprivation group ran faster. A third and a fourth group were started on weak and strong deprivation respectively and then each shifted to the other deprivation. The error curves were not different from those of the first two groups. But the shifts from weak to strong motivation and vice versa caused respectively faster running and slower running. Deprivation affected performance but not acquisition. Variation in the strength of an irrelevant drive at the time of testing may also affect performance. Brandauer (19) trained rats in a Skinner-type box under one degree of hunger. He then divided his subjects into three groups and extinguished under three degrees of thirst. The greater the thirst the more persistent the bar pressing performance. These results supported Webb's earlier findings (178). Kendler *et al.* (82) taught rats to make a given turn in a T-maze to obtain food pellets. The rats were then subdivided into two groups, one 22 hr. thirsty and the other 3 hr. thirsty. When tested under these thirst conditions, significantly more of the 22 hr. thirsty group turned away from the food side. The greater the thirst the greater the negative incentive value of the expected food and the less the performance of going to it. (Kendler's own interpretation is in terms of the incompatibility of anticipatory goal responses).

Kohn (89) and Berkun, Kessen & Miller (11) have reported two important related studies in which plastic fistulas were sewn into rats' stomachs. Using rate of drinking milk (11) or rate of panel pushing for milk (89), they found that, in general, prefeeding with milk through the mouth was the most effective, injection of the same amount of milk directly into the stomach next most effective, while injection of the same volume of isotonic saline solution was least effective in reducing further drinking or panel pushing. In our interpretation of these results these three types of prefeeding reduced the drive to different degrees, and these resultant differences in drive intensity correspondingly influenced performance. (In a further study in this series Miller & Kessen (115) showed that milk injected into the stomach served as adequate reward for the learning of a T-maze even though it was less effective than milk taken by mouth.) Kaplan (80), in the study already mentioned above in which the rats were trained to turn off a noxious light, also tested the effects of lights of different intensities, 0 mL. to 2400 mL. Rate of responding increased rapidly from 0 mL. to about 500 mL. but decreased somewhat with lights from 500 mL. to 2400 mL. A too intense light caused less performance. Apparently too strong a drive stimulus had a depressant effect. Campbell & Kraeling (28) ran rats on an electrified straightaway in which the voltage in the start and middle sections was high and in the goal section lower. They found that the greater the drop from the same initial voltage the greater the running speed. Secondly, if the goal-box voltage was zero, all groups performed with the same high speed, irrespective of the starting-section voltage. Thirdly, a constant decrease in voltage between starting section and goal section had less effect when both start and goal voltages were high than when both were low. That is, the effect on performance of one and the same drop was greater as between two low voltages than as between two high voltages. (A Weber phenomenon?)

Type of drive.—Amsel & Roussel (6) taught hungry rats to run a straightaway to food in two successive goal boxes. After the running speeds had stabilized the rats were then "frustrated" in the first goal box on half their trials by not finding food in it. They definitely ran faster and showed lower latencies in leaving this first box on the frustration trials. The authors conclude that frustration in the first box was a new added drive which enhanced the performance of going to the second goal box. Zeeman & Radner (184) taught rats to cross the center of a tilting box to turn off light but could not teach them to cross to turn on light. It would seem plausible to us to assume that both expectancies concerning the appearance or nonappearance of the light were equally well established. But only the drive to get away from light produced performance.

It should be noted that some of the "latent-learning" studies summarized above might also have been considered with this group of studies. For in many of them the final test runs consisted in introducing a new *D*, appropriate to the previously irrelevant goal object, and when the new *D* was introduced the incentive value of the irrelevant goal became positive and the performance of going to it appeared.

Generalization

We may turn now to studies of generalization. In terms of our analysis such studies investigate the effect of differences between training and test conditions as regards S_1, M, and S_2*.

Generalization with respect to S_1.—These are studies which have been treated conventionally under the heading of stimulus generalization. Brush *et al.* (20) trained pigeons in the Skinner box to peck at a lighted circle 1.4 cm. in diameter. The birds were then tested on circles ranging from 2.6 to 0.2 cm. in diameter. A bell-shaped generalization curve (with the peak at the training size) was obtained. There was somewhat more generalization to the larger sizes. Kling (88) ran rats in a Grice alley to white discs. Each group was trained on successive trials to two different areas (both positive). Subgroups were extinguished on a single large area or on a single small area. The to-be-expected generalizations were found. Rosenbaum (138) studied generalization along the dimension of height under different strengths of an irrelevant drive (namely, anxiety). Training human subjects to make a voluntary movement of a bar to a visual rectangle, he induced different degrees of "anxiety" by giving strong shock, weak shock, and buzzer to different groups, if the responses were not quick enough. He tested on rectangles of other heights and the to-be-expected generalizations for response frequencies and response amplitudes were obtained. Strong anxiety (strong shock) produced the most generalization. Different results were however, obtained for latencies. The more different the test rectangle, the shorter the latency. This last finding is puzzling. May it be that responses to the remote test stimuli were made only when the subjects did not take time to make the required discrimination? Kimble & Kendall (86) studied, with rats, the effects of changes in S_1 in an extinction setting. They extinguished a "wheel-turning" response which turned off shock and which had been conditioned to a strong light as the sign for coming shock. They found that, if they began the extinction with a weak light, increasing it by gradual steps, none of which, when introduced, produced much avoidance, extinction was more rapid than with the use of the original stimulus at full strength. This was conceived as a validation of Guthrie's (62) "toleration method" for extinction.

Generalization wlh respect to M.—There have been almost no experiments in this area. Studies falling here would be ones testing new maze routes (short cuts, *Umwege*), or new time-intervals, or the like, to discover whether and how the disposition to respond supported by the original *M* will generalize to a new *M* or new *M*'s. One recent study which might, however, very tentatively be classed here would be that of Notterman, Schoenfeld & Bersh (124). They extinguished a conditioned heart-rate response in human subjects by three methods: Group I had no instruction; Group II the instruction "now no shock will follow"; Group III the instruction "tap electric key and no shock will follow." Group III extinguished most readily, Group II next and Group I not at all during the 11 extinction trials. The provision, by means of the different instructions for the different groups, of different new *M*'s during the waiting period caused different degrees of generalization.

Generalization with respect to S_2^*.—There seem to have been no studies during the year which fall under this heading. Experiments concerning this problem would be ones which after acquisition varied the nature or amount of S_2^* and related the subsequent dispositions to respond (performance) to such variations. Such data could also be used to gauge the relative incentive values of different S_2^*'s. The extinction situation represents the extreme case in which the new S_2^* has no incentive value and in this case the generalized readiness to respond is always lost in time.

Performance in the Presence of Alternative Expectancies

Several expectancies can be established in the same situational setting. So far we have discussed the relation of performance to expectancy as governed by drive and conditions of generalization. Several experiments suggest, however, that where alternate expectancies are built up the correlated dispositions to respond are affected by additional determinants.

Fixation.—We conceive fixation as the situation in which performance according to an early acquired expectancy interferes with performance according to a subsequently acquired expectancy. Wilcoxon (181) used special reinforcement schedules in the Maier "frustration" setup (111) to induce a strong expectancy highly effective in performance. His findings suggest that fixation is to be explained not as "frustration-instigated" behavior but as due to the dominance of the response disposition correlated with the original expectancy. It would appear that such factors as the special reward schedules and primacy of acquisition lead to the development of strong and resistant response dispositions which later interfere with the appearance of the new more appropriate response disposition, even though there was evidence in terms of "lookings" and "hesitations" that the corresponding new espectancies had actually been acquired.

Regression.—Aebli (4) trained rats to go to their preferred turn or to their nonpreferred side. He then shocked them just prior to choice. Those trained on the preferred side continued to choose that side; those trained on the opposite side "regressed" to the preferred side. He concludes that regression is to an unlearned preference.

Alternation.—Where two different expectancies for which the S_2*'s have equal incentive value are built up, as, for example, in a T-maze where both arms lead to food, animals show a tendency to alternate between sides. The following investigations are concerned with discovery of the conditions which favor or reduce such alternations. Riley & Shapiro (132) tested in a T-maze the effect of light versus heavy weights on doors and also the effect of massed versus distributed trials. Massed trials clearly produced more alternation. Heavy weights gave only slight evidence of producing more alternation. Rothkoff & Zeaman (139) tested amount of alternation in a simple T, as affected by preceding forced trials to one side, by changes of intramaze cues and by changes of extramaze cues. They found a tendency to go to a new "place" as well as to make a new "turn." They say ". . . the data did not do violence to a composite 'tired stimuli and tired response' type of theory." Montgomery (118), continuing previous studies, used the T-maze with opposite starting stems, and found that the rats were alternating with respect to goal places but not with respect to turns. Goodman, Moyer & Bunch (54) measured alternations in a simple T-maze filled with water in a nonhungry group of rats, a group subjected to shock, and a group subjected to airblast. No differences in tendencies to alternate appeared. We conclude that alternation is an expression of the alternate "fatiguing," not of muscles (I_R) but of response dispositions for, say, going to light versus going to dark or for making right-hand turns versus making left-hand turns.

Pointer-Reading Responses

Percentage correct responses, running times, rates of lever pressing, amplitudes, latencies, trials to extinction, etc., have all been used as *pR*'s[2] and have been assumed to be highly correlated. But many experiments make this assumption of high intercorrelations doubtful, and this lack of consistency among measures continues to pose a serious problem for any system (ours included) which attempts to use them interchangeably as dependent variables. Two recent experiments illustrate this lack of consistency among measures. Hall & Kobrick (63) measured the strength of a runway response in terms of latency, running time, and resistance to extinction. Latency and running were significantly but not highly correlated, but neither of them was correlated with resistance to extinction. Logan (105) reanalyzed the data of his experiment mentioned above (104) in which he used a double-bar Skinner box. The two bars had different delays of reward (1 sec. and 5 sec.). He had three measures: preferential latency for the short-delay bar, per cent of choice of the short-delay bar, and the difference between the response speeds to the two bars presented singly. He found good correlation between differential response speeds and preferential latency but no significant relationship between either preferential latency or differential response speeds and per cent choice of short-delay bar.

VERBAL LEARNING

The theoretical framework for most studies of verbal learning has remained associationistic. The conditions governing the formation of associations among the members of a verbal series continue to claim experimental attention. From the general point of view represented in this review, such studies serve to specify the conditions under which exposure to conjunctions of verbal stimuli serves to establish expectancies concerning such conjunctions.

Meaning and familiarity.—The related variables of meaningfulness and familiarity are stressed in several publications. Noble (121) has presented a theoretical analysis of verbal meaning in *S-R* terms and devised an index of meaning based on the number of different associations elicited by a given word. Using this index, Noble (122) then investigated the role of stimulus meaning in serial verbal learning. A number of performance criteria (pointer-reading responses) showed a direct relationship between degree of stimulus meaning and learning proficiency. The finding of Kurtz & Hovland (92) that verbalization during observation of stimulus objects increases accuracy of recognition and recall may be mentioned in this connection. The verbalization may be assumed to increase the richness of the associative context aroused by the stimulus objects.

Variations in meaning and familiarity produce parallel effects. Hovland & Kurtz (73) report that familiarization with nonsense syllables prior to learning speeds up acquisition. Such familiarization reduces the number of trials to mastery by a more or less constant amount for lists of different lengths. The results are in conformity with Robinson's Law of Acquaintance. In terms of information theory, familiarization reduces the amount of information conveyed by each syllable in the list.

Information theory is also applied by Aborn & Rubenstein (2), who investigated the influence of previously learned rules of organization on the immediate recall of nonsense syllables. The rules were such as to produce systematic variation in the amount of information per syllable. The lower the rate of information the more syllables were recalled.

The effects of previously learned associations on recall were demonstrated by Jenkins & Russell (78). Stimulus and response terms from the Kent-Rosanoff list were scattered at random through a list of words. Recall tests showed a strong tendency for the Kent-Rosanoff pairs to be recalled together. In the recall, the *S-R* sequence of the Kent-Rosenoff test was also maintained.

Conditions of practice and testing.—Under this heading, we shall make brief reference to a somewhat heterogeneous group of experiments which have varied conventional conditions of practice or testing or both in investigations of serial association. Meyer & Miles (114) investigated changes in the process of rote learning which result from continued practice (20 successive lists). They were unable to find systematic changes in the mathematical properties of learning curves at different stages of practice, and there is scant evidence for qualitative changes in the learning process.

An interesting variation in conventional procedures of serial learning is introduced by Deese & Kresse (33) in their study of the types of errors which account for the classical bow-shaped serial position curve. To gauge fully the response dispositions at different points in the series, subjects were given unlimited amounts of time for anticipation of each syllable. Two types of errors summate to form the serial position curve: a distribution of intralist intrusions symmetrical around the middle of the list, and failure-of-response errors which rise to an asymptote in the second half of the list.

Turning to conditions of testing, we note the failure of Rockway & Duncan (136) to find any evidence for pre-recall warming up in retention tests for serially learned verbal materials. They made every effort to duplicate the procedures of earlier investigators but could not reproduce the results. Another "now-you-see-it-now-you-don't" phenomenon! Also on the negative side are the results of Grings (60) who attempted an experimental test of the "extinction" theory of verbal forgetting proposed earlier by Underwood (169). Varying amounts of distraction introduced during the retention test failed to produce "disinhibition," i.e., did not lead to recovery of presumably extinguished verbal responses.

Distribution of practice and reminiscence.—The phenomena of distribution and reminiscence appear in both motor and verbal learning. There are important differences between the two areas, however, as regards both experimental facts and theoretical interpretations: (*a*) the range of conditions over which distribution makes a significant difference appears to be much more circumscribed in verbal than in motor learning; (*b*) the theoretical construct of reactive inhibition which has carried the main burden of theoretical interpretation of distribution effects in motor learning can be applied to verbal learning phenomena only with considerable difficulty. Over the last two years or so, Underwood has been conducting a systematic investigation of the effects of distribution in verbal learning. Several of these studies (170 to 174) appeared during the current year. His results emphasize the dependence of distribution effects on very specific experimental conditions and the lack of a general theory under which the experimental findings can be subsumed.

Among Underwood's findings we may briefly mention the following: (*a*) the activity used to fill the rest intervals may significantly influence the effects of distribution; thus the conventional activity of color naming induces a responding set which raises the frequency of errors as well as the frequency of correct responses (170); (*b*) whereas distribution has a beneficial effect on the learning of serial nonsense lists, no such influence is found with paired nonsense syllables (171, 172); (*c*) similarly, with meaningful materials (adjectives) serial learning is improved by distribution whereas paired associate learning is not (173, 174). It is important to note that careful analysis of the wide variety of learning and retention data obtained by Underwood fails to lend consistent support to any one theory of distribution, such as the reactive-inhibition theory or the differential-forgetting theory. Gibson's generalization hypothesis (51) also fails to handle some of the major findings of these studies. The theoretical analysis of distribution of practice in verbal learning is still a wide open problem, as was also found to be true for classical and instrumental conditioning.

The picture presented by recent studies of reminiscence in verbal learning is equally inconclusive. Using serial lists of nonsense syllables Archer (7) failed to find any evidence for reminiscence; variations in the association value of the syllables, the length of the rest interval, and in the rest-interval activity did not yield any reminiscence effects. The results flatly contradict earlier studies. Riley (131), on the other hand, obtained evidence for reminiscence in paired-associate learning with nonsense syllables when competing responses are attached to the stimulus terms. The results are at variance with a differential-forgetting theory and are consistent with a work-decrement hypothesis, although the exact nature and conditions of such decrements in verbal learning remain uncertain. In accordance with earlier studies, no reminiscence effects were found by Noble (122) in the serial learning of meaningful words. The description of reminiscence as a "now-you-see-it-now-you-don't" phenomenon (26) appears to be as apt as ever.

The law of effect in verbal learning.—Much of Thorndike's experimental evidence for the law of effect was obtained in verbal learning situations. Implications of the reinforcement hypothesis continue to be tested in such situations. Thus the problem of "learning without awareness" has been reopened. Thorndike had argued that such learning would be evidence for the automatic effects of reinforcement. Evidence for discrimination learning without awareness of the principle of solution is reported by Walk (176). Postman & Jarrett (129) found only scant evidence for learning without awareness in the acquisition of an associative response tendency. Their results do not, however, support invocation of a principle of insight. Skill in the application of a verbalized principle showed a gradual increase.

The spread of effect, originally offered as critical evidence for the law of effect, continues to be reanalyzed. Sheffield & Jenkins (147) offer new evidence in support of their argument that the guessing-sequence hypothesis is adequate to account for the spread phenomenon. In the absence of reward, duplication of other features of Thorndike's situation (e.g., fixed order of stimuli, set for recall of word-number connections) yields levels of response repetition equal to, or exceeding those obtained by Thorndike.

The role of anxiety in serial rote learning is analyzed by Montague (117) from the point of view of reinforcement theory (cf. similar studies by Spence and associates (40, 157). Anxiety, as a drive, is assumed to multiply with habit strength to determine excitatory potential of correct as well as incorrect responses. Anxiety should aid performance if correct response tendencies predominate and should hinder performance in the presence of incorrect competing tendencies (which are enhanced by the drive along with the correct ones). This implication was verified in a design employing nonsense-syllable lists of varying difficulty. Anxious subjects performed better on the easy lists and were surpassed by the nonanxious subjects on the difficult lists involving many incorrect response tendencies.

Failure and related motivational factors.—Verbal materials have frequently been used in the investigation of motivational factors in learning and retention, particularly to test the concept of repression or hypotheses stemming from it. Experimentally induced failure is one of the techniques used to create motivational conditions appropriate to the testing of such hypotheses. Several studies of this type appeared during this year. Eriksen (39) compared memory for completed and incompleted tasks by ego-involved and control subjects. Ego-involved subjects (*a*) recall relatively more completed tasks and (*b*) show greater variability than do control subjects. Eriksen interprets his data as demonstrating the importance of ego-defense in memory. Aborn (1) compared the relative effects of experimentally induced failure on materials learned intentionally and incidentally. Ego-threat had significant effects on memory for the incidentally learned materials only. In the case of incidental memory, such factors as rehearsal and overlearning presumably do not counterbalance the motivational effects. Murdock (120) investigated the effects of both failure and retroactive inhibition on mediated generalization. Both types of treatment served to reduce the amount of mediated generalization: failure by leading to the "suppression," and retroactive inhibition by producing extinction, of the mediating verbal responses.

An implication of repression theory was tested by Laffal (93) who compared words which produce association disturbances and words which do not with respect to speed of learning and retention. He found (*a*) slower acquisition of the disturbing words, and (*b*) no differences in retention for the two types of words. These contradictory findings lend only indifferent support to a repression hypothesis.

We feel that the effects of failure, stress, and related conditions on learning and retention can for the present be adequately and parsimoniously handled by the more mundane concepts of current learning theories. The invocation of ego defense or repression seems to put too heavy a conceptual burden on rather slender empirical facts.

Social attitudes.—The danger of erecting precarious theoretical superstructures on limited and uncertain data seems to us illustrated in a study of Rokeach (137) concerned with attitude as a determinant of distortion in recall. Low- and high-prejudiced subjects were shown photographs of whites and Negroes with fictitious names attached to them. In a recall test, the high-prejudiced group recalled certain names (Gray, Greene, Lynch) more often than the low-prejudiced group to both Negro and white faces, whereas the low-prejudiced group was partial to the name Jones. To explain these rather puzzling results, the author invokes the following concepts: Freud's theory of slips, a continuum of cognitive reorganization ranging from assimilation to various degrees of compromise and contrast, tolerance af ambiguity, tolerance of incongruity, closure! The ratio of concepts to data appears somewhat high.

Doob (34) investigated the effects of attitude on incidental memory for controversial items and found quantity of recall to be associated with intensity of attitude. In the same investigation, the effects of serial position on items evoking different attitudes were studied. In the case of items evoking strong drives, primacy increases amount of recall; in the case of items evoking weak drives, recency is more effective, probably by reducing the amount of retroactive inhibition to which the items are subjected. The picture presented is highly complex but we note with interest the attempt to apply systematic learning principles to memory data obtained under naturalistic conditions.

Perlmutter & de Montmollin (128) compared the performance of groups and individuals in a rote-learning task. Groups were found to be superior to average individual learners in total scores, but the best individual performers surpassed the group. The learning performance of individuals was improved by prior participation in group work. In a further study, Perlmutter (127), using Bartlett's method of repeated reproduction, compared the products of individual and group memory. He concludes that some of the group products are not derivable from the individuals' products. The reviewers express their bewilderment at the implied resurrection of the unlamented late group mind!

MOTOR LEARNING

For an expectancy theory, specific motor acts serve as "pointer readings" for inferring the organism's cognitive dispositions. Variations in motor behavior would, therefore, be treated primarily under the general heading of performance. However, expectancy theory has not developed a systematic description of motor learning. For an *S-R* reinforcement theory, on the other hand, motor learning provides important opportunities for testing hypotheses about both learning and performance. Much of the current experimental work in motor learning centers around the implications of Hull's concepts of reactive inhibition (I_R) and conditioned inhibition ($_SI_R$). The specific experimental designs are concerned primarily with the effects of post-practice rest intervals on the acquisition and performance of motor responses. The inhibition built up during practice is assumed to dissipate during the rest. Much effort is now being devoted to obtaining as precise information as possible concerning the conditions under which inhibition grows and dissipates and the quantitative laws of these phenomena. Without reviewing these studies in detail, we shall consider some of the main experimental problems and conclusions.

Distribution of practice.—Several studies have compared acquisition and performance of motor skills under distributed and massed practice. In general, spacing has a beneficial effect on acquisition and performance. The effects appear, however, to be transient. Thus Adams (3) reports that both his distributed and massed group were approaching the same asymptote of performance on the pursuit rotor. Using three different psychomotor tests, Reynolds & Bilodeau (130) found that distributed practice during acquisition resulted in superior performance on all tests. On tests of retention 10 min. and 24 hr. later the two groups become increasingly alike. Bilodeau (14) observed the effects of massing and distribution over an extended period of practice and found that performance depended more on the number of days of prior practice than on conditions of distribution. Kimble & Shatel (87) present data supporting Kimble's previous analysis (84) of inhibitory processes in motor learning. According to this view, reactive inhibition decreases with continuing practice since with declining motivation the subject will allow less and less I_R to accumulate before he rests. Conditioned inhibition, on the other hand, is assumed to increase with practice in a negatively accelerated fashion. A review of the evidence supporting Kimble's theory is presented by Wasserman (177).

Reminiscence.—The reminiscence experiment is, of course, a special case of distribution of practice. The theoretical analysis of reminiscence effects in motor learning follows the same general line as the analysis of distribution effects: virtually all the investigators take their lead from the concept of reactive inhibition. A number of parametric studies has appeared, relating postrest gain to such variables as amount of prerest practice, duration of the rest period, and effortfulness of the task (e.g., 13, 36, 123). It would be difficult to summarize the experimental findings in terms of a few generalizations, beyond the fact that reminiscence does occur following massed practice. The reviewers are impressed with the dependence of the functional relationships on the specific experimental conditions.

Important questions concerning the interpretation of reactive inhibition are raised by a series of studies demonstrating reminiscence in bilateral transfer. Irion & Gustafson (77) found significant postrest gains in pursuit-rotor performance even though subjects shifted from right to left hand following the rest intervals. Similar results are reported by Kimble (85) whose subjects shifted from nonpreferred to preferred hand following the rest. Findings such as these throw doubt on a conception of reactive inhibition as localized in specific effector organs. Stimulated by this problem, Grice & Reynolds (58) compared the effects of varying amounts of rest on ipsilateral and bilateral transfer reminiscence. For both conditions, postrest gains were an increasing function of the amount of rest. Although the ipsilateral group showed larger gains than the bilateral group the data suggests that the general shape of the function is the same. Grice & Reynolds ascribe the postrest gains in bilateral transfer to "temporary inhibitory factors either associated with generalized postural adjustment or of a perceptual or central character." Such an interpretation seems to broaden the connotations of reactive inhibition very considerably. This general conclusion is in harmony with that reached above in connection with the experiments on alternation behavior in rats.

Rest intervals usually result in warm-up decrements which may be attributable to a loss of set or postural adjustment. Hence postrest performance may be improved by warming-up activities during the rest interval. Silver (151) has systematically explored the effects of varying amounts and distribution of warm-up activity during a rest interval. Warm-up activity clearly improved postrest performance provided the amount of such activity did not itself produce too high a degree of inhibition. Distributed warm-up activity is, therefore, more beneficial than massed warm-up activity.

Transfer.—Motor learning is convenient for the study of transfer processes because specific stimulus and response elements can often be identified precisely. Duncan (35) investigated transfer between two motor tasks as determined by two variables, degree of learning of first task, and intertask similarity. Degree of positive transfer was a direct function of both these variables. There was no evidence for interference between tasks. Both response generalization and "learning how to learn" may account for the uniformly positive transfer effects. Evidence for negative transfer effects appears, however, in studies of retroactive inhibition in motor learning. Lewis, Smith, & McAllister (102) studied retroactive inhibition in performance on a two-hand coordinator when original and interpolated tasks required a reversal of movements. They found amount of retroactive inhibition to vary with the degree of interpolated learning but, contrary to their expectations, differential amounts of retroactive facilitation were not developed. Using the same apparatus, McAllister (107) studied the effect of different degrees of original learning on retroactive interference. Interference increases as a function of original learning level, reaches a maximum and then appears to decline with overlearning of the original task (this finding is similar to results obtained with verbal materials). Relearning data showed the interference effects to be relatively enduring.

LITERATURE CITED

1. Aborn, M., *J. Exptl. Psychol.*, **45,** 225–31 (1953)
2. Aborn, M., and Rubenstein, H., *J. Exptl. Psychol.*, **44,** 260–66 (1952)
3. Adams, J. A., *Am. J. Psychol.*, **65,** 404–14 (1952)
4. Aebli, H., *J. Comp. Physiol. Psychol.*, **45,** 258–63 (1952)
5. Amsel, A., *J. Comp. Physiol. Psychol.*, **45,** 341–46 (1952)
6. Amsel, A., and Roussel, J., *J. Exptl. Psychol.*, **43,** 363–68 (1952)
7. Archer, E. J., *J. Exptl. Psychol.*, **45,** 245–52 (1953)
8. Atkinson, R. C., and Ammons, R. B., *J. Exptl. Psychol.*, **43,** 173–78 (1952)
9. Bahrick, H. P., *J. Comp. Physiol. Psychol.*, **46,** 39–42 (1953)
10. Baron, M. R., *J. Exptl. Psychol.*, **44,** 438–41 (1952)
11. Berkun, M. M., Kessen, M. L., and Miller, N. E., *J. Comp. Physiol. Psychol.*, **45,** 550–54 (1952)
12. Bevan, W., Jr., and Zener, K., *Am. J. Psychol.*, **65,** 434–42 (1952)
13. Bilodeau, E. A., *J. Exptl. Psychol.*, **43,** 381–90 (1952)
14. Bilodeau, E. A., *J. Exptl. Psychol.*, **44,** 108–13 (1952)
15. Bingham, W. E., and Griffiths, W. J., Jr., *J. Comp. Physiol. Psychol.*, **45,** 307–12 (1952)
16. Bitterman, M. E., *Psychol. Rev.*, **60,** 123–26 (1953)
17. Bitterman, M. E., and Holtzman, W. H., *J. Abnormal Social Psychol.*, **47,** 615–23 (1952)
18. Bitterman, M. E., Reed, P., and Krauskopf, J., *Am. J. Psychol.*, **65,** 256–62 (1952)
19. Brandauer, C. M., *J. Exptl. Psychol.*, **45,** 150–52 (1953)
20. Brush, F. R., Bush, R. R., Jenkins, W. O., John, W. F., and Whiting, J. W. M., *J. Abnormal Social Psychol.*, **47,** 633–40 (1952)
21. Bugelski, B. R., Coyer, R. A., and Rogers, W. A., *J. Exptl. Psychol.*, **44,** 27–30 (1952)
22. Buss, A. H., *J. Exptl. Psychol.*, **44,** 222–27 (1952)
23. Buss, A. H., *J. Exptl. Psychol.*, **45,** 75–81 (1953)
24. Buss, A. H., *J. Exptl. Psychol.*, **45,** 153–56 (1953)
25. Butler, R. A., *J. Comp. Physiol. Psychol.*, **46,** 95–98 (1953)
26. Buxton, C. E., *Psychol. Bull.*, **40,** 313–40 (1943)
27. Caldwell, W. E., and Womack, H. L., *J. Psychol.*, **35,** 353–60 (1953)
28. Campbell, B. A., and Kraeling, D., *J. Exptl. Psychol.*, **45,** 97–101 (1953)
29. Christie, R., *J. Exptl. Psychol.*, **43,** 281–88 (1952)
30. Cole, J., *J. Comp. Physiol. Psychol.*, **46,** 16–18 (1952)
31. Cook, J. O., *Psychol. Rev.*, **60,** 15–22 (1953)
32. Davis, R. C., *Psychol. Rev.*, **60,** 7–14 (1953)
33. Deese, J., and Kresse, F. H., *J. Exptl. Psychol.*, **44,** 199–202 (1952)
34. Doob, L. W., *J. Abnormal Social Psychol.*, **48,** 199–205 (1953)
35. Duncan, C. P., *J. Exptl. Psychol.*, **45,** 1–11 (1953)
36. Ellis, D. S., Montgomery, V., and Underwood, B. J., *J. Exptl. Psychol.*, **44,** 420–27 (1952)
37. Eninger, M. U., *J. Exptl. Psychol.*, **41,** 440–45 (1951)
38. Eninger, M. U., *J. Comp. Physiol. Psychol.*, **45,** 604–8 (1952)
39. Eriksen, C. W., *J. Abnormal Social Psychol.*, **47,** 230–35 (1952)
40. Farber, I. E., and Spence, K. W., *J. Exptl. Psychol.*, **45,** 120–25 (1953)
41. Ferster, C. B., *J. Exptl. Psychol.*, **45,** 218–24 (1953)

42. Fink, J. B., and Patton, R. M., *J. Comp. Physiol. Psychol.*, **46**, 23–27 (1953)
43. Fitzwater, M. E., *J. Comp. Physiol. Psychol.*, **45**, 476–81 (1952)
44. Fitzwater, M. E., and Reisman, M. N., *J. Exptl. Psychol.*, **44**, 211–14 (1952)
45. Flynn, J. P., and Jerome, E. A., *J. Comp. Physiol. Psychol.*, **45**, 336–40 (1952)
46. Forgays, D. G., *J. Exptl. Psychol.*, **45**, 165–68 (1953)
47. Forgays, D. G., and Forgays, J. W., *J. Comp. Physiol. Psychol.*, **45**, 322–28 (1952)
48. French, R. S., *J. Exptl. Psychol.*, **45**, 25–34 (1953)
49. Furchtgott, E., and Rubin, R. D., *J. Comp. Physiol. Psychol.*, **46**, 9–12 (1953)
50. Gatling, F., *J. Comp. Physiol. Psychol.*, **45**, 347–51 (1952)
51. Gibson, E. J., *Psychol. Rev.*, **47**, 196–229 (1940)
52. Gilchrist, J. C., *J. Comp. Physiol. Psychol.*, **45**, 198–203 (1952)
53. Gleitman, H., Nachmias, J., and Neisser, U., *Psychol. Rev.* (In press)
54. Goodman, R. W., Moyer, K. E., and Bunch, M. E., *J. Comp. Physiol. Psychol.*, **45**, 460–67 (1952)
55. Grant, D. A., and Schipper, L. M., *J. Exptl. Psychol.*, **43**, 313–20 (1952)
56. Grant, D. A., Schipper, L. M., and Ross, B. M., *J. Exptl. Psychol.*, **44**, 203–10 (1952)
57. Grice, G. R., *J. Gen. Psychol.*, **47**, 65–70 (1952)
58. Grice, G. R., and Reynolds, B., *J. Exptl. Psychol.*, **44**, 247–52 (1952)
59. Griffiths, W.J., Jr., and Stringer, W.F., *J. Comp. Physiol. Psychol.*, **45**, 301–6 (1952)
60. Grings, W. W., *Am. J. Psychol.*, **65**, 594–96 (1952)
61. Gulliksen, H., and Wolfle, D. H., *Psychometrika*, **3**, 127–49 (1938)
62. Guthrie, E. R., *The Psychology of Learning*, Revised ed. (Harper & Brothers, New York, N. Y., 310 pp., 1952)
63. Hall, J. F., and Kobrick, J. L., *J. Comp. Physiol. Psychol.*, **45**, 280–82 (1952)
64. Harlow, H. F., *Psychol. Rev.*, **56**, 51–65 (1949)
65. Harlow, H. F., *Psychol. Rev.*, **60**, 23–32 (1953)
66. Harlow, H. F., and Warren, J. M., *J. Comp. Physiol. Psychol.*, **45**, 482–89 (1952)
67. Hayes, K. J., Thompson, R., and Hayes, C., *J. Comp. Physiol. Psychol.*, **46**, 99–104 (1953)
68. Hayes, K. J., Thompson, R., and Hayes, C., *J. Comp. Physiol. Psychol.*, **46**, 105–7 (1953)
69. Hebb, D. O., *The Organization of Behavior* (John Wiley & Sons, Inc., New York, N. Y., 335 pp., 1949)
70. Hill, C. W., and Thune, L. E., *J. Exptl. Psychol.*, **43**, 289–97 (1952)
71. Hillman, B., Hunter, W. S., and Kimble, G. A., *J. Comp. Physiol. Psychol.*, **46**, 87–89 (1953)
72. Holland, G. A., *J. Comp. Physiol. Psychol.*, **46**, 90–94 (1953)
73. Hovland, C. I., and Kurtz, K. H., *J. Exptl. Psychol.*, **44**, 31–39 (1952)
74. Hull, C. L., *A Behavior System* (Yale University Press, New Haven, Conn., 372 pp., 1952)
75. Hunter, I. L. M., *Brit. J. Psychol., Gen. Sect.*, **43**, 113–28 (1952)
76. Hymovitch, B., *J. Comp. Physiol. Psychol.*, **45**, 313–21 (1952)
77. Irion, A. L., and Gustafson, L. M., *J. Exptl. Psychol.*, **43**, 321–23 (1952)
78. Jenkins, J. J., and Russell, W. A., *J. Abnormal Social Psychol.*, **47**, 818–21 (1952)
79. Johnson, E. E., *J. Comp. Physiol. Psychol.*, **45**, 526–30 (1952)
80. Kaplan, M. E., *J. Comp. Physiol. Psychol.*, **45**, 538–49 (1952)
81. Kendler, H. H., *Psychol. Rev.*, **59**, 269–77 (1952)

82. Kendler, H. H., Levine, S., Altchek, E., and Peters, H., *J. Exptl. Psychol.*, **44,** 1–3 (1952)
83. Kessen, W., and Kimble, G. A., *Psychol. Rev.*, **59,** 263–67 (1952)
84. Kimble, G. A., *J. Exptl. Psychol.*, **39,** 15–23 (1949)
85. Kimble, G. A., *J. Exptl. Psychol.*, **43,** 391–92 (1952)
86. Kimble, G. A., and Kendall, J. W., Jr., *J. Exptl. Psychol.*, **45,** 87–90 (1953)
87. Kimble, G. A., and Shatel, R. B., *J. Exptl. Psychol.*, **44,** 355–59 (1952)
88. Kling, J. W., *J. Exptl. Psychol.*, **44,** 339–46 (1952)
89. Kohn, M., *J. Comp. Physiol. Psychol.*, **44,** 412–22 (1951)
90. Krech, D., *Psychol. Rev.*, **57,** 283–90 (1950)
91. Krech, D., *Psychol. Rev.*, **57,** 345–61 (1950)
92. Kurtz, K. H., and Hovland, C. I., *J. Exptl. Psychol.*, **45,** 157–64 (1953)
93. Laffal, J., *J. Abnormal Social Psychol.*, **47,** 454–62 (1952)
94. Lambert, W. W., and Solomon, R. L., *J. Comp. Physiol. Psychol.*, **45,** 269–79 (1952)
95. Lashley, K. S., in *The Foundations of Experimental Psychology,* Chap. 14, 524–63 (Murchison, C., Ed., Clark University Press, Worcester, Mass., 907 pp., 1929)
96. Lashley, K. S., *J. Gen. Psychol.*, **26,** 241–65 (1942)
97. Lashley, K. S., and Wade, M., *Psychol. Rev.*, **53,** 72–87 (1946)
98. Lawrence, D. H., *J. Exptl. Psychol.*, **39,** 770–84 (1949)
99. Lawrence, D. H., *J. Exptl. Psychol.*, **40,** 175–88 (1950)
100. Lawrence, D. H., *J. Comp. Physiol. Psychol.*, **45,** 511–16 (1952)
101. Lewis, D. J., *J. Exptl. Psychol.*, **43,** 447–50 (1952)
102. Lewis, D., Smith, P. N., and McAllister, D. E., *J. Exptl. Psychol.*, **44,** 44–50 (1952)
103. Loess, H. G., and Duncan, C. P., *J. Exptl. Psychol.*, **44,** 215–21 (1952)
104. Logan, F. A., *J. Exptl. Psychol.*, **43,** 393–99 (1952)
105. Logan, F. A., *Psychol. Rev.*, **59,** 300–7 (1952)
106. Longnecker, E. D., Krauskopf, J., and Bitterman, M. E., *Am. J. Psychol.*, **65,** 580–87 (1952)
107. McAllister, D. E., *Am. J. Psychol.*, **65,** 218–32 (1952)
108. McAllister, W. R., *J. Comp. Physiol. Psychol.*, **45,** 531–37 (1952)
109. McClelland, D. C., and McGown, D. R., *J. Comp. Physiol. Psychol.*, **46,** 80–86 (1953)
110. MacCorquodale, K., and Meehl, P. E., *Psychol. Rev.*, **60,** 55–63 (1953)
111. Maier, N. R. F., *Frustration, the Study of Behavior without a Goal* (McGraw-Hill Book Co., Inc., New York, N. Y., 264 pp., 1949)
112. Meehl, P. E., and MacCorquodale, K., *Psychol. Rev.*, **58,** 230–33 (1951)
113. Meehl, P. E., and MacCorquodale, K., *J. Exptl. Psychol.*, **45,** 20–24 (1953)
114. Meyer, D. R., and Miles, R. C., *J. Exptl. Psychol.*, **45,** 109–15 (1953)
115. Miller, N. E., and Kessen, M. L., *J. Comp. Physiol. Psychol.*, **45,** 555–64 (1952)
116. Mishkin, M., and Forgays, D. G., *J. Exptl. Psychol.*, **43,** 43–48 (1952)
117. Montague, E. K., *J. Exptl. Psychol.*, **45,** 91–96 (1953)
118. Montgomery, K. C., *J. Comp. Physiol. Psychol.*, **45,** 287–93 (1952)
119. Muenzinger, K. F., and Conrad, D. G., *J. Comp. Physiol. Psychol.*, **46,** 1–8(1953)
120. Murdock, B. B., Jr., *J. Exptl. Psychol.*, **44,** 156–64 (1952)
121. Noble, C. E., *Psychol. Rev.*, **59,** 421–30 (1952)
122. Noble, C. E., *J. Exptl. Psychol.*, **43,** 437–46 (1952)

123. Norris, E. B., *J. Exptl. Psychol.*, **45**, 260–64 (1953)
124. Notterman, J. M., Schoenfeld, W. N., and Bersh, P. J., *J. Abnormal Social Psychol.*, **47**, 674–77 (1952)
125. Ohrbach, J., *Am. J. Psychol.*, **65**, 555–62 (1952)
126. Page, H. A., and Hall, J. F., *J. Comp. Physiol. Psychol.*, **46**, 33–34 (1953)
127. Perlmutter, H. V., *J. Psychol.*, **35**, 361–70 (1953)
128. Perlmutter, H. V., and de Montmollin, G., *J. Abnormal Social Psychol.*, **47**, 762–69 (1952)
129. Postman, L., and Jarrett, R. F., *Am. J. Psychol.*, **65**, 244–55 (1952)
130. Reynolds, B., and Bilodeau, I. McD., *J. Exptl. Psychol.*, **44**, 19–26 (1952)
131. Riley, D. A., *J. Exptl. Psychol.*, **45**, 232–38 (1953)
132. Riley, D. A., and Shapiro, A. M., *J. Comp. Physiol. Psychol.*, **45**, 468–75 (1952)
133. Riopelle, A. J., *J. Comp. Physiol. Psychol.*, **46**, 108–14 (1953)
134. Ritchie, B. F., *Psychol. Bull.*, **41**, 640–52 (1944)
135. Ritchie, B. F., *Psychol. Rev.*, **60**, 216–21 (1953)
136. Rockway, M. R., and Duncan, C. P., *J. Exptl. Psychol.*, **43**, 305–12 (1952)
137. Rokeach, M., *J. Abnormal Social Psychol.*, **47**, 482–88 (1952)
138. Rosenbaum, G., *J. Exptl. Psychol.*, **45**, 35–43 (1953)
139. Rothkoff, E. Z., and Zeaman, D., *J. Psychol.*, **34**, 235–55 (1952)
140. Rubin, L. S., *J. Comp. Physiol. Psychol.*, **46**, 28–32 (1953)
141. Schroder, H. M., and Rotter, J. B., *J. Exptl. Psychol.*, **44**, 141–50 (1952)
142. Seeman, W., and Williams, H., *J. Exptl. Psychol.*, **44**, 40–43 (1952)
143. Seward, J. P., *Psychol. Rev.*, **54**, 83–98 (1947)
144. Seward, J. P., *Psychol. Rev.*, **59**, 405–13 (1952)
145. Seward, J. P., *Psychol. Rev.*, **60**, 99–110 (1953)
146. Seward, J. P., and Levy, N., *J. Exptl. Psychol.*, **39**, 660–68 (1949)
147. Sheffield, F. D., and Jenkins, W. O., *J. Exptl. Psychol.*, **44**, 101–7 (1952)
148. Sheffield, V. F., *J. Exptl. Psychol.*, **39**, 511–26 (1949)
149. Siegel, A. I., *J. Comp. Physiol. Psychol.*, **46**, 115–19 (1953)
150. Siegel, P. S., and Foshee, G., *J. Exptl. Psychol.*, **45**, 12–14 (1953)
151. Silver, R. J., *J. Exptl. Psychol.*, **44**, 88–95 (1952)
152. Smith, W. M., *Am. J. Psychol.*, **65**, 389–403 (1952)
153. Spence, K. W., *Psychol. Rev.*, **43**, 427–49 (1936)
154. Spence, K. W., *Psychol. Rev.*, **44**, 430–44 (1937)
155. Spence, K. W., *Psychol. Rev.*, **59**, 89–93 (1952)
156. Spence, K. W., *J. Exptl. Psychol.*, **45**, 57–63 (1953)
157. Spence, K. W., and Farber, I. E., *J. Exptl. Psychol.*, **45**, 116–19 (1953)
158. Spence, K. W., and Taylor, J. A., *J. Exptl. Psychol.*, **45**, 265–72 (1953)
159. Stanley, W. C., *J. Exptl. Psychol.*, **43**, 249–60 (1952)
160. Teel, K. S., *J. Comp. Physiol. Psychol.*, **45**, 188–91 (1952)
161. Teas, D. C., and Bitterman, M. E., *Psychol. Rev.*, **59**, 130–40 (1952)
162. Teichner, W. H., *J. Exptl. Psychol.*, **44**, 170–78 (1952)
163. Thistlethwaite, D., *J. Comp. Physiol. Psychol.*, **45**, 517–25 (1952)
164. Tolman, E. C., *Purposive Behavior in Animals and Men* (The Century Co., New York, N. Y., 463 pp., 1932)
165. Tolman, E. C., *Psychol. Rev.*, **59**, 389–400 (1952)
166. Tolman, E. C., Ritchie, B. F., and Kalish, D., *J. Exptl. Psychol.*, **36**, 221–29 (1946)

167. Turbeville, J. R., Calvin, A. D., and Bitterman, M. E., *Am. J. Psychol.* **65,** 424–33 (1952)
168. Tyler, D. W., Wortz, E. C., and Bitterman, M. E., *Am. J. Psychol.*, **66,** 57–65 (1953)
169. Underwood, B. J., *J. Exptl. Psychol.*, **38,** 429–39 (1948)
170. Underwood, B. J., *J. Exptl. Psychol.*, **43,** 329–40 (1952)
171. Underwood, B. J., *J. Exptl. Psychol.*, **44,** 80–87 (1952)
172. Underwood, B. J., *J. Exptl. Psychol.*, **45,** 133–42 (1953)
173. Underwood, B. J., *J. Exptl. Psychol.*, **45,** 143–49 (1953)
174. Underwood, B. J., *J. Exptl. Psychol.*, **45,** 253–59 (1953)
175. Vandermeer, S., and Amsel, A., *J. Exptl. Psychol.*, **43,** 261–66 (1952)
176. Walk, R. D., *J. Exptl. Psychol.*, *Psydhol.*, **44,** 410–19 (1952)
177. Wasserman, H. N., *Psychol. Rev.*, **59,** 278–84 (1952)
178. Webb, W. B., *J. Exptl. Psychol.*, **39,** 1–14 (1949)
179. Weise, P., and Bitterman, M. E., *Psychol. Rev.*, **58,** 185–95 (1951)
180. White, C. T., and Schlosberg, H., *J. Exptl. Psychol.*, **43,** 357–62 (1952)
181. Wilcoxon, H. C., *J. Exptl. Psychol.*, **44,** 324–33 (1952)
182. Wodinsky, J., and Bitterman, M. E., *Am. J. Psychol.*, **65,** 563–72 (1952)
183. Wyckoff, L. B., Jr., *Psychol. Rev.*, **59,** 431–42 (1952)
184. Zeaman, D., and Radner, L., *J. Exptl. Psychol.*, **45,** 239–44 (1953)

VISION[1,2]

By Austin H. Riesen
Department of Psychology, The University of Chicago, Chicago, Illinois

The physiology of vision has just been reviewed by Chang (48). Vernon's book on visual perception (229) is almost up to date, yet not enough so as to include the newer titles from her contribution to Volume 4 of this series. Her approach to perception while in sympathy with phenomenology is different from that of Gibson, emphasizes individual differences, and is well balanced on the nativism-empiricism problems. The past year has brought publication of a number of specialized books on applied areas in vision, Volume 2 in the series by Linksz (143), Geldard's general text (91) on *The Human Senses*, and several important new translations. Foremost among the latter is that by Boeder of Tschermak-Seysenegg's *Introduction to Physiological Optics* (227). Now for the first time we can read in English a full discussion of the physiological psychology of visual action.

Middleton (153) represents the renewed enthusiasm for giving consideration to the human eye and its addenda for obtaining, storing, and evaluating information. Nonvisual aids such as radar have been oversold to the extent that we, the people, "are likely to under-rate the importance of actual seeing," Middleton says. His bibliography includes many hard-to-find technical publications on outdoor seeing. Studies reviewed in the later sections of the present chapter show that increasing attention is being given the problem of how and when man makes an adequate evaluation of his visual environment. But first, what is new in our understanding of visual capacities and their development?

Basic Psychophysical Functions

Methods.—Verplanck, Collier & Cotton (230) question the general assumption that each trial in a psychophysical experiment on the visual threshold is an independent event. Using procedures modeled in several respects after ones employed by Hartline or by Hecht, they find that if S[2] reports "yes" after one flash he is more likely to do the same on the next trial, or conversely. Statistically significant dependence was found with as many as 10 responses intervening between the correlated responses. Theories

[1] The survey of the literature reported here covered the 15 months ending May 1, 1953. The survey was done and the present chapter prepared during the author's appointment as Visiting Research Professor at the University of Rochester.

[2] The following abbreviations and symbols are used in this chapter: S (subject); cff (critical flicker frequency); ERG (electroretinogram); C.I.E. (Commission Internationale d'Eclairage), also known in the United States as I.C.I. (International Commission on Illumination); j.n.d. (just noticeable difference); RDP (receptor type distribution pattern).

of the threshold which have assumed independence may need to be re-examined. Equally important is the question of what produces the interdependence of contiguous groups of trials. Blackwell (22) is on the trail of this problem. He suggests a number of procedures for keeping the subject at the peak of performance. Among these are: fairly extensive experience for the subject, forced choice, training on the procedure with knowledge of results, and a minimum of variation in the luminances used within a block of trials.

Where verbal instruction and report cannot be used, as in work with young children or animals, the problem of obtaining peak performance is much increased. Fields (76) reports preliminary findings with a procedure that results in considerably better visual acuity scores for the white rat than have ever been obtained previously. Misumi (155) criticizes some earlier methods and offers data on the development of size constancy in human infants based on a preference-response for the larger of two objects.

Absolute thresholds.—Two independent studies deal with the distribution of scotopic sensitivity along various meridians of the visual field. Lange (137) measured along vertical, horizontal, and diagonal meridians to 30° from the fovea. He reports that sensitivity declines with age over the entire retina. His results agree with those of Riopelle & Bevan (191) in finding the fovea to have the highest threshold of any region (except the blind spot) out to 30°. However, the latter investigators mapped to 56° and along twice as many meridians and found for their eight Ss a region beyond 45° below the fovea that was even less sensitive than the fovea. Regions of maximum sensitivity were found on the horizontal meridian between 15° and 30° from the fovea, the temporal region being slightly more sensitive than the nasal.

Davy (65) describes experiments on the $I \times t$ relationship for multiple flashes of light in the peripheral retina and finds that threshold energy is the same for rapidly successive flashes as for single flashes within a critical interval. Beyond 0.4 to 0.5 sec. of temporal separation, threshold energy is the same for each of two flashes as it is for one flash. At this point S first reports seeing two flashes consistently. Bouman (27) measured thresholds for line-shaped targets, 2′ in width and 2′ to 256′ long. Results agree with predictions from quanta theory. It is again concluded that two quanta must be absorbed within about 0.1 sec. and within a given area (Ricco's region). For green flashes Ricco's region subtends visual angles up to 32′, which is somewhat larger than for circular flashes. For red flashes the limit is about 8′, as compared with 2 to 4′ in the case of circular test flashes. Intensity, size, and distance functions were measured by Kaneko & Obonai (126) in a study of areal interaction. With low intensities (up to eight times threshold value) the inducing stimulus facilitated perception of the test stimulus. Beyond this an inhibitory effect began. This was a negatively accelerated increasing function of the intensity and the area of the inducing stimulus. Walsh (237) could find no dependence of visual thresholds on the amplitude or the phase of the alpha rhythm at the moment of stimulation, thus failing to find support for the interesting hypothesis that the alpha rhythm "scans" the striate cortex. Reaction times also were not related to phase or amplitude of alpha at the moment of stimulation.

Conditions of preadaptation were varied systematically in studies of the subsequent course of dark-adaptation by Mote and co-workers. Varying intensity and duration of pre-exposure through the range for which $I \times t = C$, they (159) find this relationship holds up to a value of 3,320 mL.-sec. Beyond this, intensity becomes a more potent factor than duration. Their other studies (1, 157, 158) are concerned with the effects of intermittent pre-exposure. For low values of $I \times t$ neither rate of intermittence nor intensity variation disrupted the Bunsen-Roscoe relation. For larger values the hypothesis of Wald and Clark is found generally acceptable: Slower recovery is an expression of the regeneration of rhodopsin from the vitamin A stage, which becomes predominant over the regeneration from retinene. To obtain quantitative data for an analysis of various possible nervous and photochemical mechanisms in dark adaptation, Bouman (25) presented red or green test flashes of various sizes during 0.5 sec. interruptions of either red or green adapting fields. Ricco's region, where integration of energy occurs, is found to diminish with increases in preadaptation level, but only for green light. "For red flashes even for the dark adapted eye Ricco's region hardly exceeds the size of one receptor" (25, p. 950). This is a remarkable result for test patches 7° toward the periphery of the visual field.

Wald (232) fails to find that pre-exposure to ultraviolet light results in a prolongation of dark adaptation time. He does confirm the fact that ultraviolet is an adequate stimulus for the aphakic eye. Other work on spectral sensitivity is reviewed below under color discrimination.

Differential brightness thresholds.—Holding adaptation levels constant at various points in the luminance scale, Kern (128) explored brightness discrimination functions. Maximum sensitivity, $B/\Delta B$, for each function occurs at the respective light intensity to which the eye is adapted. An absolute maximum is found at one Apostilb (10^{-1} mL.). At low background brightnesses the contrast threshold data are considered to be well described by the two-quanta theory (26), and independence of the adapting processes in each eye is found to be complete when variation of pupil size is eliminated. Using rod vision 7° nasal from the fovea, Bouman & Blokhuis (28), studied the visibility of black against an illuminated background. They conclude that response is possible if two quanta are intercepted from the background stimulation at the retina. A 60 per cent chance of seeing criterion was again employed. Difference thresholds for two luminous points as a function of the separation between them were studied by Flamant (78). A separation of 10′ to 15′ was found to be optimum. With a constant separation of 10′, sensitivity was measured for various positions on the retina between the fovea and 2° nasally and temporally. Flamant found maximum sensitivity at the center of the fovea for red and green monochromatic light. A range between 10′ and 40′ from the center proved most sensitive for blue.

In accordance with his alternation of response theory, Bartley (14) finds brightness enhancement at certain rates of intermittency to be susceptible to the effects of fluctuating or steady stray light. Fry & Alpern (87) report data confirming the stray light hypothesis and denying interaction mediated by retinal mechanisms as the explanation for effects of peripheral glare sources upon apparent brightness. Reduced receptor sensitivity produced by whole-body x-irradiation (369 to 469 r's) is held responsible (88) for changes in the performance of rats on brightness discrimination problems.

Both Brindley (33) and Rouse (195) report studies of the Bunsen-Roscoe Law at supra-threshold levels. Brindley used white light and a large range of times and intensities. For flashes giving a sensation of equal brightness the product of time and intensity was found to remain equal for durations from 1.54×10^{-3} to 4.11×10^{-7} sec., and for intensities up to about 3×10^{8} photons (trolands). Within this range of duration flashes that appeared equal at the fovea also appeared equal in the light-adapted and the dark-adapted periphery. Rouse, using central fixation, studied the intensity-time relationship necessary for differential thresholds of red, green, and blue flashes on a surrounding white-lighted field. The critical duration was the same for all wave lengths. There is no evidence here for temporal or structural differences in the retinal processes associated with color vision.

Flicker-fusion thresholds were measured by Lloyd (142) for various foveal and peripheral areas. For areas with diameters of 1° or 2° thresholds were similar for fovea and periphery (20° below fovea). At low intensities the periphery was slightly more sensitive, and at medium intensities the fovea had higher cff[2]. The larger field (2°) produced higher cff in both locations. For 6° and 14° peripheral areas there were still further increases. Erlick & Landis (75) find lower cff with advance in age, which they attribute chiefly to a lengthened restoration period during the dark phase. Peckham & Arner (173) report that they could predict changes in acuity from changes in cff measured morning and evening on college students driving automobiles in the Arizona desert.

Binocular flicker has been studied again in a comprehensive research by Baker (11), and again Sherrington's conclusion that each eye acts independently is disproved. Baker also reports variation in cff with size of field within the fovea. There is a limited flexibility in the correspondence of position on the two retinas which must be stimulated for binocular interaction to occur.

Acuity.—Using a black Landolt C on an illuminated background, Pirenne & Denton (176) have extended Schlaer's acuity-intensity function down to −4 Trolands or Log −6 candles/M^2. Brief exposures were used. For a wide range of intensities the quantity of light striking the retinal image of the smallest detail detectable is of the order 140 to 900 quanta/sec. The minimum number of quanta absorbed by the receptors per unit action time (0.1 sec.) is between 2 and 10, whether absolute threshold or acuity is taken as the index of seeing. Barlow (13) reports that, although individual fixation pauses show very little movement (root mean square deviations of 0.25′ of arc during 0.4 sec.), successive fixation points scatter around a mean position with a root mean square deviation of 5′ of arc. Ditchburn & Ginsborg (69) find similar amplitudes of physiological nystagmus. Ratliff (185) shows that eye movements and physiological nystagmus hinder rather than aid monocular acuity.

Effects of pupil size on acuity are reported by Leibowitz (138), whose data indicate that the natural pupil is normally too dilated for maximum acuity in the range of .01 through 1 mL. of field luminance. Groot & Gebhard (102) have evaluated, weighted, and combined the available data on pupil size as a function of adapting luminance. They present a very useful table on retinal illumination for the average eye with known field luminance which incorporates corrections for the Stiles-Crawford effect. By pharmacological means (adrenalin and cocaine) in normal persons and in persons with Horner's syndrome, Monjé (156) studied the neural mechanisms that control accommodation. He concludes that control is exerted by oculomotor and sympathetic centers through labile tonus-maintaining mechanisms, that there is no relaxed position, and that age, heterophoria, and other factors related to individual differences all contribute to accommodation responses. Fry (83) discusses some psychological factors in visual acuity and believes that improvement in the identification of blurred retinal images can result from practice, and, furthermore, that "an effort to see" may improve acuity by producing changes in accommodation, pupil size, or intraocular pressure. Bahr (9) agrees that the problem of measuring the depth of focus of the eye is extremely difficult. Acuity criteria and type of illumination are highly significant parameters. Bahr reports data on one aphakic S with a constant correction of +13 diopters who showed the required acuity through a range of 2 diopters under daylight fluorescent and 5 diopters with a mercury lamp. Wulfeck's normal subjects showed a similar range of depths of field (242). Using an infrared double spot light source, Wulfeck photographed the third Purkinje image to find average accommodation times varying from 0.24 to 0.45 sec., depending upon target size and whether near-far or far-near shifts were required.

Scotopic or night visual acuity has received careful study in the experiments of Brown *et al.* (34). Their test fields were gratings subtending 7.3° of visual angle. Improving acuity as a function of dark adaptation is seen only as a single cone curve when measured with fine gratings, but for coarser gratings rod portions of the curves appear after 10 to 15 min. Fry & Alpern (86) report an investigation of the effects of flashes of light on scotopic acuity. Flashes were varied in brightness and duration, and acuity was measured in terms of the width of a black line necessary for visibility against a background luminance equated to that of moonlit sky. Pupil size was held constant (2 mm. artificial pupil). Several basic principles evolved, the most general being that the effects of flashes which did not directly strike the part of the retina used in viewing the acuity target can be accounted for in terms of stray light. There was no spread of adaptation processes from one part of the retina to another. To help determine the part played by pupillary responses to light flashes, Fry & Allen (85) report the first studies of many that will have to be done before accurate predictions can be made of the course of pupillary constriction and recovery. As a limiting case it is found that 3 sec., 8°, centrally fixated flashes of high brightness permit full recovery within the first minute following the flash. Koomen, Scolnik & Tousey (131) measured accommodation in dim light and in darkness by photographing the Purkinje images of two spots of light. Subjects remained focused for far vision or in one case accommodated about 1 diopter, which was taken as evidence that night myopia is a result of spherical aberration with increase in size of pupil, rather than a result of an accommodative response.

Color discrimination.—Outstanding among a number of new books on theoretical and applied aspects of color are those of Judd (124) and of The Optical Society of America Committee (170). In the latter, Newhall was primarily responsible for excellent chapters, with good bibliographies, on psychological processes in color vision. The Committee now abandons the position taken by the 1922 Committee on Colorimetry, which defined color as a sensation. It is clear from the Introduction that this abandonment in favor of a psychophysical point of view was not achieved without a struggle. In addition to chapters on methods in these new books, there are several papers which make important methodological points or describe new apparatus. The representativeness of the C.I.E.[2] Standard Observer is questioned (119, 123). Nickerson (166) and co-workers present a table of C.I.E. tristimulus values with Munsell renotations for all Munsell standard papers made to July, 1950. A recheck and extension of data on the spectral energy distribution of light sources A, B, and C are provided by Davis *et al.* (64). Burnham (42) describes a new colorimeter, and Schmidt (199, 200) discusses procedures for testing color blindness.

In a statistical study of color-matching Brown (35) finds normal distributions about a color center, and the magnitudes of one-standard-deviation ellipsoids are shown to be smaller than those misrepresented as such in earlier work. By contrast with the fineness of hue discriminability, the number of absolutely identifiable hues is astonishingly small. Halsey & Chapanis (106), in order to minimize somewhat the effects of habitual color names, taught subjects identifying numbers for spectral hues. Presenting the hues one at a time and using a high criterion of accuracy, they found that there were only 10 or 12 absolutely identifiable hues through the spectral range for which there are more than 150 hues that can be discriminated by direct comparison.

Several researchers have measured effects of chromatic surroundings, of adaptation, or of field size on color perception. Brown (36) finds that 2° fields give poorer discrimination and are more affected by surrounding colors than are 12° fields. Burnham (41) reports that larger areas of color appear brighter and more saturated than small ones of the same physical intensity. Hunt (116), using a binocular matching technique, shows that maximum saturation is obtained with low levels of adapting intensity and high test-color intensity. He reports that the dark-adapted eye sees a pale blue rather than colorless light. Burnham, Evans & Newhall (43) also had their observers match fields presented separately to the two eyes. A change from an adapting artificial daylight to tungsten light produced a shift in the perceived colors toward the blues on the order of 20 j. n. d.[2] The converse produced a shift toward the yellows. Jameson & Hurvich (123) measured the spectral sensitivity for a 1° foveal field as it depends on the state of adaptation: dark or light neutral, blue, green, yellow, or red. A slight Purkinje shift was found for the small central field, which the authors prefer to explain on other than a rod-participation basis. A prominent shoulder at 600 to 610 mμ almost disappears with red adaptation. The data do not fit the commonly cited trichromatic response curves, but other curves could presumably be made to agree with the results and still remain within the general framework of three-color theory.

Frank defect in color vision and variability in presumed normals are active topics of investigation. Wright (241) has given a fascinating account of his discovery of about 40 tritanopes through publication of a color chart in a picture weekly. One near monochromat was also found. On the basis of numbers responding Wright estimates an incidence of tritanopia somewhere between 1 person in 13,000 and 1 in 65,000. Genetic transmission seems to differ from that for protonopia or deuteranopia, but workup of family lines is still in progress. All tritanopes had "large field" defects of which they were quite aware. According to Halsey & Chapanis (107) protanopes give matches with blue-green standards that diverge markedly from Judd's predictions based on Pitt's data for spectral colors. Matches by deuteranopes and the neutral matches by protanopes agree well with Judd's predictions. Constants for isochromaticity lines are given. These authors (49) report that photopic thresholds for red light (640 mμ) in an unselected sample of color-deficient individuals vary in a fairly continuous distribution, there being only a slight indication of bimodality. Burnham (41) finds marked individual differences in components selected on a three-knob colorimeter to match Munsell colors, which he believes are attributable to differences in sensitivity. Ishak (119, 120) also reports variations from individual to individual for tristimulus values of the spectrum. He feels that the C.I.E. chromaticity coordinates are based on too few observers. Egyptian and British observers are found not to differ significantly in their means for the red coordinates, but for the green the mean is significantly higher and for the blue lower in the Egyptians (119). Differences in densities of ocular pigmentation are ruled out.

Walls & Mathews (236), from an extensive review of some color vision literature and their own data, come out with 61 summarizing conclusions. Their highly argumentative monograph is certain to provoke rejoinders. They urge adoption of their sensitive methods for the information of great theoretical interest that these are producing. They cling tenaciously to a three-color theory, reject the notion of macular pigmentation as an explanation of individual differences, and accept the evidence for nonuniform distribution of chromatic receptors in the fovea. Maxwell's spot is regarded as an entoptic indicator of the distribution of receptors. The primary objective of their research is to relate foveal receptor-type distribution patterns (RDP's) to various types of color-blindness. The blue RDP[2] in protanoids is considered evidence that where redness receptors are absent their places in the retina are occupied by supernumerary blueness receptors. Deuteranopes and achromates do not see an RDP. Based on the different patterns of the RDP that normal subjects report, they can be classified into six types. Tentative quantitative interpretations of the relative numbers of receptor-types in different zones of the RDP are offered by Walls & Mathews as a basis for discussion and further work. Weale (238) measured both spectral sensitivity and wave length discrimination out to 70° from the fovea. Three regions of maximum sensitivity do not have clear parallels in fineness of wave length discrimination. Weale believes that differences in hue discrimination with retinal location will be accounted for in terms of post-receptor mechanisms.

Three-receptor theory is being challenged. It is probably an oversimplification. Motokawa & Ebe (162) find maxima for spectral sensitivity at seven different wave lengths: six appearing at the fovea (415, 465, 515, 575, 610, and 650 mμ) and the seventh at 507 mμ 20° from the fovea. Motokawa & Ebe used alternating current to elicit phosphenes and found threshold-energy minima at specific frequencies. Sensitivity to these frequencies could be further enhanced by low intensity monochromatic light. The optimum spectral hue for a given AC frequency was identified. The range of AC frequencies employed corresponds nicely with that which Lindsley (141) reports he can pick up in the optic tract, although the visual cortex fails to follow frequencies beyond the middle of this range. The optimum sensitizing spectral wave lengths for the fovea correspond well, as Motokawa & Ebe point out, with the threshold sensitivity maxima found by Thomson (223). Thomson's three red-insensitive observers lacked the maximum at the longest wave length. Additional data on the interchangeability of wave length with frequency of stimulation at the retina are presented by Motokawa & Ebe (160, 161) and by Hess (113). Two flashes of white light can be used to produce the same supernormality effect as a colored light if the proper interval between flashes is used (160), or intermittent white light will produce "subjective" color when applied to one retina, as opposed to the two retinae in alternation (113). The methods and abundant research coming from Motokawa's laboratory have been reviewed by Gebhard (90), and a stimulator suitable for pursuing research with these techniques is described (12). Gebhard (89) failed to find more than one minimum in a strength-frequency curve, but he only sampled two frequencies above 25 c.p.s.

From a different approach Tschermak-Seysenegg (227) rejects three-component theory as inadequate. Although he thinks in terms of four primaries for chroma, he posits six visual substances. The complexity of retinal photochemistry is becoming increasingly apparent (48). There is evidence that absorption maxima vary considerably with pH. Dartnall (62, 63) reports two new visual pigments, which he identifies by their wave lengths of maximum absorption, a practice which he suggests should become general. Collins (59) describes a series of experiments which demonstrate the close relation of indicator yellow to rhodopsin. Far from accepting it as an artifact, he regards indicator yellow as a key substance in visual chemistry.

The retinal mechanism responding to red light has been found to have another index in the X wave of the electroretinogram (ERG). Armington (3) and Schubert & Bornschein (201) independently report that in protanopes the X wave, which according to Armington is most easily elicited by light in the region of 630 mμ, is not present. Armington reports further that this component of the ERG[2] dark adapts rapidly (within 2 or 3 min.). Armington, Johnson & Riggs (4) have analyzed the A wave of the ERG into two components, the second of which, in sequence of appearance, is dependent upon dark-adaptation and shows scotopic spectral sensitivity. Temporal factors relating the rod and cone systems are studied further by Bouman & Brink (29) and by Bartley & Wilkinson (15). At threshold levels the two systems show mutual dependence (29).

Developmental Processes in Vision

Genetics and early maturation.—The development of vision is an exceedingly intricate process which is beyond the scope of any single discipline. Experts in the area are showing an increasing ability to take a multiplicity of factors into account. This is clearly revealed, for example, by Sorsby (216, p. x) in the Preface to his *Genetics in Ophthalmology* where he states: "The fatalism with which genetic affections are generally regarded is as unfounded in reason as it is unjustified by achievement already reached." The implication here that not all the eggs are in one basket is born out in many of the new studies of hereditary and environmental factors in visual development.

Section I in Sorsby's book is theoretical, covering modes of inheritance, human pedigrees, varieties of genetic disease, and prospects of controlling genetic disease. Section II treats ocular anomalies per se, and Section III is a discussion of metabolic and systemic functions and their ocular effects. The genetics of color blindness, thoroughly reviewed in Sorsby's book, is also related to specific types of defect by Jaeger (121, 122), by Walls & Mathews (236), and by Wright (241). Jaeger questions whether red-green disturbances are always sex-linked recessives, reporting the case of a deuteranomalous woman who has two sons, one deuteranomolous and the other normal.

The problems of how and why vision begins to function are being attacked anew with some definitive methods. During the first two or three days after birth there is no ERG or it amounts to only a slight rise in base line [Zetterström (246)]. The B wave increases gradually with age and by three months a measurable potential of 0.10–0.20 mv. has developed. The A wave develops between the sixth and twelfth months. Does this imply that the color receptors follow a similar time course of development? Unfortunately, our knowledge of the structural changes in the retina during infancy is too meagre to enable any close correlation with the ERG changes at present. In premature infants of the lowest weight group the ERG appears after a considerably longer time.

> The fact that ERG appears in children born only a few weeks before term, within the same time as is required for children born at term, supports the theory that extrauterine factors are of great importance for the appearance of ERG (247, p. 408).

Brattgård (31) studied the effects of withholding light stimulation in newborn rabbits on the chemistry of retinal ganglion cells. The method, developed in Hydén's laboratory, permits the determination of lipids, nucleoproteins, and proteins in single nerve cells, and the finding is that ganglion cells in young eyes deprived of light lack the pentose nucleoprotein fraction. This is interpreted by Brattgård as indicating that early postnatal absence of stimulation leads to incomplete development of the nerve cells and to disturbances in their metabolism that are not immediately recovered. The work has not gone far enough to indicate whether the changes may be irreversible; however, if such proves to be the case, it would seem that we have here an explanation of some results of prolonged light deprivation reported for chimpanzees (186). The work strongly confirms the need for diffuse light stimulation when the development of pattern vision is studied by a deprivation technique, as in several recent studies (186, 188, 204). But is there no "spontaneous" neural activity in light deprived animals? Brattgård believes that the ganglion cells and those in the nuclear layers of the retina are the only nerve cells which can be effectively excluded from stimulation experimentally. Denton & Pirenne (68) agree in that they affirm "biological noise" or background excitation of the retina to be extremely low.

Development of acuity.—The satisfactory determination of acuity in very young children is still a difficult problem. Bouman *et al.* (30) have suggested an "objective" method, calibrated against Snellen opto-types, which may prove useful for this purpose. Keiner (127) claims to find an acuity of 5/5 in many children by the age of three years. Sabatini (196), by contrast, reports improving acuity through age nine, or the fourth grade level. Both investigators urge the importance of psychological factors, and their apparently divergent results are testimony to the fact that acuity is not a "pure" factor and that different procedures will emphasize different components or requirements. By retinoscopy Hirsch (114) determined that between the ages of five and fourteen years the mean refractive state moves in a minus direction about 0.5 diopter. The median shows this change to a lesser extent, indicating a disproportionate contribution of extreme cases. Fewer than 1 per cent of the five and six year olds had myopia in excess of 1.00 diopter. More than 5 per cent had this extent among the thirteen and fourteen year olds. A rather sudden increase in myopia occurs at puberty, a year or two earlier in girls than in boys. For changes in senescence Dufour & Cuendet (70) attempt to develop a single quantitative index for combined acuity, sensitivity, and visual field losses, and Kleemeier (129) shows that reported loss of hue discrimination in older persons is based on methods that have not ruled out the factor of acuity.

Amblyopia *ex anopsia* is considered to be secondary to poorly developed binocular coordination (127, 143, 216). Keiner cites his ERG results as further evidence that these monocular acuity deficiencies are central rather than retinal processes.

Binocular coordination and stereoscopic vision.—A developmental point of view on the origins of binocular fusion and stereoscopic vision is steadily making inroads on the position that innately determined reflexes (or field forces) constitute the sufficient basis for these functions. On occasion the newer viewpoint is carried to extremes, particularly when urgent needs for the clinical treatment of "squint" arise. Nevertheless, some sound research is being stimulated by these needs. Keiner (127) reports observations on newborn babies of dissociated wandering eye movements and spontaneous monocular reactions, which give way after one to three weeks to transitory conjugate fixation movements in response to a moderately strong light stimulus located a short distance from the eyes. A difference in the reactivity, at a slightly later stage, to stimulation of the nasal and temporal halves of the retina leads Keiner to conclude that the crossed pathways are more predominantly connected with the binocular gaze center than are the uncrossed. After further study of 984 cases of squint, this author concludes that there is almost total dissociation of the two eyes at birth; familial predispositions are strong, but there is no such entity as congenital squint. Rather, strabismus is a manifestation of a retarded developmental process which normally reaches its highest activity at the end of the first six months and is complete at about eighteen months. During this crucial period binocular "reflexes" are being conditioned, in the Pavlovian sense, to visual stimuli which originally elicited only monocular optomotor responses. Hormonal, refractive, early illnesses, and a variety of other factors which may contribute to the retardation of this process are suggested. A majority of Keiner's cases of strabismus was apparent before the age of one year, many cases spontaneously recovering later in childhood, but the longer a squint was allowed to persist, the more difficult retraining of the optomotor reflexes became. Baird (10), Lancaster (135), and Lange (136) come to similar conclusions concerning the prior importance of fixational, rotational, and fusional responses in the developmental sequence, and the need for exercising these functions as opposed to concern over visual acuity. Where binocular anomalies have developed, operation on the eye muscles is sometimes sufficient to permit the attainment of fusion or stereoscopic vision or both, according to Riise (189) and Portmann & Dufour (178), but the latter study indicates considerably improved prognosis where orthoptic re-education is added to the treatment. This is also the conclusion of a recent symposium by Rodman *et al.* (193).

Sabatini (196) reports that stereoscopic vision continues to improve in school children through the fourth grade. Walls (235) makes an impassioned plea for extending even a normal person's zone of single binocular vision (Panum's areas) by adding to the visual training armamentarium. Just what such training would do, if anything, to the still larger zones wherein depth is perceived in the presence of double images [Ogle (168)], no one has yet been able to say.

The psychological-physiological basis for the development of anomalous correspondence is obscure. Its stability and extent is in dispute, largely because the properties of the "false macula" differ considerably among different cases, but also because of the assumptions held by the clinician making the study. Colson (60) believes, with Verhoeff, that a squinting eye shows false correspondence to the fovea of the eye in central fixation anywhere along the line between and including the location of the "false macula" and the true fovea of the squinting eye. Halldén (105) used an afterimage method to measure the angle of anomaly. Five of nine young adults were found to have harmonious anomalous correspondence, i.e., the angle of objective squint and the angle of anomaly were equal. By introducing prisms before one eye while these subjects were fusing, Halldén recorded fusional movements which completely compensated for the prisms. Sensory fusion was also demonstrated where the movement could not quite overcome the full power of the prism. Halldén is willing to entertain a conditioned response theory of the development of anomalous correspondence. Kretzschmar (132) set out to determine whether there was a redistribution of corresponding points over the entire horizontal axis of visual space. Such a reallocation of local sign is reported, the amount of displacement closely approximating the objective angle of squint. Small angle squint with anomalous correspondence is notoriously difficult to re-educate (178). Apparently this condition is a fairly satisfactory biological state of affairs. Vukovich & Müller (231) have asked the question: what happens to fusion zones where there is merely a demonstrable heterophoria? They find that in exo- and esophoria there are opposite shifts in the boundaries of Panum's areas, in peripheral as well as in central vision. An average horopter, however, remains within both ranges of single vision and is asymmetrical with respect to each type of deviant fusional zone.

All these data raise the question: what happens to accommodation in conjunction with atypical eye rotations? Fry (84) reports that, although accommodation and convergence are closely linked physiologically, some increase in the flexibility of the relationship can be achieved by training. He believes that fusional convergence and accommodative convergence, while operating through different mechanisms, may, nevertheless, utilize a common center in the midbrain. Lord (144) measured eye rotations with changes of accommodation and reports failure to confirm Hering's law, although a change of accommodation was found to be associated with a saccadic excursion of the eye. In a subject who showed suppression in one eye, no movements accompanied change in accommodation, and "it thus seems likely that binocular visual experience is entirely responsible for eye movements associated with change of accommodation . . ." (144, p. 671). Piper (175) does not assume such independence. On the contrary, he hooks up accommodation with convergence or divergence of the eyes and then places this compound mechanism all at the mercy of the autonomic nervous system. The main experimental findings are that in esophoria accommodation for near is slow, and the converse holds for exophoria. Arguing from the effects of drugs on accommodation [Monjé (156)], Piper concludes that if the parasympathetic division is poorly controlled (released, as in youth) then adjustment for near is accompanied by an overshooting impulse and esophoria results. The adult tends toward sympathetic release and outward deviations. No data on the relative incidence of these phorias with age are given. It will come as something of a shock to old line physiologists to read that: "For most observers the conscious estimate of the position of an object plays a part at least as important as accommodation in determining convergence" [Asher (5, p. 675)]. Those who have accepted some form of conditioning theory may be able to look with favor upon this statement. The data presented by Asher are quantitative and worthy of consideration.

Binocular equivalence and binocular rivalry.—Binocular equivalence, insofar as it is measured by learned responses to stimuli presented initially to only one eye, is far from complete in adult birds [Levine (139)], and even less so in young birds deprived of form vision from the time of hatching [Siegel (204)]. Riesen, Kurke & Mellinger (188) report that, whereas young, visually experienced cats show transfer of monocularly learned habits immediately, cats whose prior visual experience through one eye was restricted to diffuse light could not perform habits when seeing through that eye, even when these habits had been overlearned during use of the other eye. They interpret these results as indicating that binocular equivalence in the adult mammal is dependent in part upon early conditioning processes involving sequences of activity in specific neural pathways. They assume that these coordinating pathways can be initially activated as discrete pathways only by patterned visual stimulation. It would be extremely helpful in this connection to know whether interocular transfer of afterimages of movement of the kind described by Walls (234) would occur in the case, say, of a person just operated upon for congenital cataract. Ohwaki & Kihara (169) report observations of the so-called "Bocci image" (a faint afterimage observed in one eye after stimulation of the other) and regard this as having some of the characteristics of eidetic images. These authors find variation with age.

The problem of the sensory integration of impulses from the two eyes has one of its counterparts in the process of rivalry. Phylogenetically, monocular vision is prior to binocular. Evidence cited above is in agreement with the view that this is true also in human ontogenesis. Optic pathways in the mammal are obviously better arranged for binocular coordination of sensory input than are those of the bird. Nevertheless, even in adult man vision seems to become monocular under certain conditions. Asher has just revived an old theory of du Tour, supported it with some new observations on rivalry in stereoscopically presented patterns, and proposed that (6, p. 49), "of a pair of corresponding points, one always suppresses the other." Binocular depth is related to the rivalry in the suppression process. Asher overcomes the problem of binocular color mixture by postulating a mosaic effect in which a fine grain mental picture results from the close intermingling of dominant and suppressed points. Alexander & Bricker (2) report only partial success in their effort to influence rate of rivalry by raising or lowering contrast. Steinitz (220) questions the doctrine of precise correspondence of points and urges adoption of a more plastic conception. His argument becomes circular when he says that images fuse when and because they occupy the same position in psycho-optical space.

Development of pattern recognition and space perception.—Gibson & Waddell (99) have demonstrated that depth perception is dependent upon differentiated retinal images. Gibson & Dibble (98) eliminate the perception of a surface as a possible "elementary" impression. Teas & Bitterman regard their experiments as evidence that aggregations of afferent visual processes function initially as "loosely organized wholes out of which the perception of objects and relations is subsequently differentiated" (222, p. 140). These observations place a high premium on the study of area processes in vision. Boring (23, 24) and Gibson (94) have argued about the best approach. Developmental studies are contributing to the knowledge of this subject, and other work will be covered below.

Hebb's theoretical position has been the inspiration for a number of developmental studies in man and animal. Experimental variation of the early visual environments of rats has produced consistent evidence for the contribution of the opportunity for visual exploration to later behavior (20, 80, 117). A late "free" environment is not a substitute for an early one. "Playthings" also help. Siegel's experiments with the ring dove (205) provide further evidence that visual learning is a cumulative process.

Pattern discrimination, as measured by word recognition, is somewhat specific to the area stimulated on the retina if there has been differential practice for such areas [Mishkin & Forgays (154), Orbach (171)]. Better recognition for words in the right side of the visual field is found only in the later grades of elementary school (79). These data are taken as evidence against an innate equipotentiality of different parts of the visual field.

Thresholds for the perception of patterns are shown to vary with recent past experience in studies by Atkinson & Ammons (7) and Bevan & Zener (19). The apparent size and distance of a triangle was altered by recent experience with objects of this shape [Smith (210)]. The apparent size and distance of a control figure was not altered. Kume (133) concludes that past experience is one of the main factors determining size constancy. In a distorted-room setting marriage partners were found to be less susceptible to size distortion than were strangers [Wittriech (240)]. Harper (108) reports that figures which are characteristically red (like a lobster) require more red in the background before they become indistinguishable from it than do figures which ordinarily have no characteristic color (like an oval) but which are equally red for this particular experiment.

Several comparative studies on primates deal with phylogenetic aspects of pattern vision. Gorillas at a fairly early age perform complex patterned string problems at levels superior to those of monkeys [Riesen *et al.* (187)]. Complex visual pattern discrimination in the chimpanzee is demonstrated in the work of Hayes & Hayes (111, 112) on picture identification and imitation behavior. According to Cole's experiments (58), form is subordinate to color when monkeys can learn visual discrimination habits on the basis of either cue. Nevertheless, by eliminating the color cue on critical trials, Cole found that form was effective in determining response in favor of this previously rewarded subordinate stimulus. Butler (45) interprets his new observations to mean that there is a primary motivation toward visual exploration in the monkey.

These recent studies contribute to the understanding of how learning supplements in a highly significant way the innate visual adaptive responses of the organism. We cannot say that all innately determined responses are seen prior to those dependent upon associative processes. Fear of strange stimuli, shown to be present in human infancy by Gesell and co-workers and by other earlier studies, and now demonstrated for primates (186) and dogs (151), certainly requires learning but apparently has a strong innate determinant. The protective blinking reflex to menace (127, 186) and the visual placing response (188) are further examples of behaviors that become highly automatic, yet depend on prior environmental conditions suitable for the establishment of conditioned responses. Keiner (127, p. 131) conceives of vision as resulting from the cooperation of optomotor, associative, and perceptual components. The interaction of these factors during early development is clearly indicated in an increasing number of experimental studies.

Agnosia.—Once established, visual recognition behavior may be lost again through brain damage, accidentally or experimentally produced. Interpretations of such losses are entering a new theoretical phase [Bay (16); Bender (17); Semmes (202)]. It is proposed that "associative" cortex may return impulses to the primary sensory areas and there stabilize or modulate the sensory process. Instability of sensory thresholds is found even in "pure" agnosias (16), and sometimes the most sensitive test employs simultaneous bilateral stimulation where central interaction accounts for the loss of response to the damaged side [Bender (17); Denny-Brown *et al.* (67)].

Parietal and temporal association areas are implicated in form recognition [Chow (51, 52); Denny-Brown *et al.* (67); and Riopelle *et al.* (190)]. Chow finds that the conditions of postoperative visual experience are a factor in the "spontaneous" recovery of lost habits following removal of temporal cortex, and Riopelle and co-workers report that the "learning set" task was seriously affected by bilateral (two stage) invasion of the temporal lobes, whereas solutions of patterned string problems were not.

Vision with spatial inversion.—Snyder & Pronko (213) have repeated the

Stratton experiment, essentially, with Snyder wearing the inverting lenses for a 30-day period. There actually appears to have been more nausea, eye fatigue, and headache after removal of the lenses than when they were first donned. The authors take the extreme empiricistic position in their interpretation.

Spatial Discriminations

Form perception.—Sleight & Duvoisin (209) have compiled an annotated bibliography of form perception in which emphasis is placed on the relative discriminability of geometric shapes. With sorting time as the criterion, Sleight (207) finds that discriminability for some geometric forms is better than for others by a factor of ten. The "easy" and "hard" figures do not bear any clear relation to "simple" figures in the Gestalt sense. Threshold studies give different and apparently contradictory results, depending upon the method. Naruse (165) used brightness thresholds and found triangles and rectangles were more easily seen than circles. Cheatham (50) used Pieron's method for measuring perceptual latency and reports that angles were seen later than smooth contours. Bruner *et al.* (37) find, in line with the well-known Carmichael, Hogan and Walter experiment, that ambiguous figures given verbal labels in advance of exposure are reproduced more in accordance with such a label than when they are not labeled or are given another label. The horizontal-vertical illusion in lines [Pollock & Chapanis (177)] or in geometric figures [Sleight & Austin (208)] does not hold for all subjects. In general, lines tilted 20° to 30° to the left look longer than lines in any other orientation. Lichte (140) measured shape constancy for a square rotated on its vertical axis until it appeared equal in shape to one of four standard rectangles. The Brunswik ratio (index of constancy) decreased as angle of rotation increased. Wide individual differences were found.

Apparent size is determined by retinal angle if distance cues are effectively eliminated [Hastorf & Way (110)]. Under the conditions of Smith's (212) experiments perceived size may lie outside the range between the limits that would be predicted from the "law of size-constancy" and the "law of the visual angle." Young (244) reports that Emmert's law does not accurately predict the size of afterimages over large distances. With high stimulus luminances, afterimages were smaller than would be expected.

The principle of closure in form perception continues to resist precise definition. For specific sets of experimental conditions some limiting factors are being measured. Depending on the size of gap, and on the time of exposure, an incomplete circle is changed in tachistoscopic perception toward "closure" or its opposite, enlargement of the gap [Tresselt & Simberg (226)]. As either supplementary or as alternative to orthodox Gestalt theory, which relates closure, proximity, and the like to dynamic processes of the brain field, current studies propose and find evidence for ecological or "expectancy" factors [Brunswik & Kamiya (39); Postman & Bruner (182)]. Apparently failing to confirm this experiential interpretation is Michael's study

(152), in which Navajo and white subjects did not show significant differences in the numbers of "closure" responses. Turner (228) proposes an aesthetic factor as a supplement to the principle of *Prägnanz*. George (92) confirms the Hebb-Foord findings and rejects this principle for delayed reproductions. The derived principle, flexibility of closure, is found stable enough as a measure of individual differences to give good correlations with analytical ability or deductive thinking [Pemberton (174)]. Ogasawara (167) describes a quantitative study of displacement effects: the change in apparent size of a circle when a concentric circle is added to the figure.

Figural aftereffects.—Christman (54), Deatherage & Bitterman (66), and Kakizaki (125) report phenomena which can be fitted into the theory of satiation, but Azuna (8) and Luchins & Luchins (145) find the need for supplementary principles to explain certain aftereffects and changes in illusions. Köhler, Held & O'Connell (130) discuss some facts of visual perception not explained by the neural conduction doctrine. In support of their field theory they report extensive records taken chiefly over the striate cortex when objects were moved through the visual field. The same electrical polarity relations occurred whether the moving objects were bright or dark. Are these figure currents related to the phenomenon recently reported by Burns & Grafstein (44)? They describe a surface-positive response obtained from stimulating an isolated slab of cortex with intact blood supply. The response "spreads without attenuation in all directions from the stimulated point." Knife cuts are said to show that the spread depends on dendrites and synapses lying below 1 mm. in the grey matter.

An alternative theory which attempts to account for the better known effects on perception of previous form stimulation in terms of principles of conduction along discrete pathways is offered by Osgood & Heyer (172). They point out, after Marshall and Talbot, that by the time retinal events produce effects at the cortex, some dispersion in space and time will have occurred. The spatial distribution of excitation along contours will have a shift in its maximum as the result of previous excitation. Thus, "inspection" contours leave individual neurones in unequal states of recovery according to symmetrical distributions, which will then shift the zone of maximum excitation when a new contour appears in an adjacent region. This theory would demand an increase in threshold for luminous points near zones of previous stimulation by an inspection figure. Two recent studies [Bevan (18); Yokose & Uchiyama (243)] report just such changes, although it is odd that both should have been motivated by the conception that they would support Köhler's theory. Both the satiation theory and this neuron recovery theory still leave much to be desired in the way of precision before they can be put to critical tests. At present, it is difficult to see at just what points they may be incompatible, if they really are. There is still the big question of what happens beyond the striate cortex. Field theory has nothing to say on this problem, and two recent studies demand a central explanation for perceptual changes that cannot be referred to past or present retinal events or their isomorphic counterparts [Mull, Arp & Carlin (164); Solomon & Werner (215)]. Three dimensional phenemona of apparent movement, such as those described and correlated with objective conditions by Burke (40), Ekman (72), Hall *et al.* (104), and Smith (211), are also difficult to translate into theoretical terms.

Size and depth perception.—The extensive and highly competent discussions of space perception in Linksz (143) and Tschermak-Seysenegg (227) should be recommended reading for every psychologist. Linksz describes many teachable demonstrations and both authors discuss European findings that are being "rediscovered" in America, often without benefit of familiarity with the previous work. Linksz (143, p. 426) describes a convincing self-demonstration of convergence as a cue to distance (and size) for relatively near objects. Chalmers (47), using a dark tunnel to control secondary cues, compares monocular and binocular viewing conditions for size and distance judgments. Monocular vision fails beyond 25 feet and binocular vision begins to fail at 30 to 80 feet. Gumbel (103) reports an advantage for binocular viewing in depth judgments even at scotopic levels of illumination. Physiological mechanisms which mediate the accommodation, convergence, and binocular disparity factors in space perception are further discussed by Asher (5, 6) and by Ludvigh (146).

The apparent slant of a plane surface normally depends on a variety of cues. Cibis *et al.* (57), introducing cues, one at a time, find that perspective attributable to horizontal boundaries (for a small, rectangular surface rotated about the vertical axis) proves more effective than vertical stripes or irregular markings. Stereoptic cues were almost as effective as the strongest perspective cue under their conditions. Gibson and co-workers find that a gradient of density of visual detail is one sufficient and highly effective condition for producing the perception of slant (97), but motion perspective is not (96).

When do two-dimensional forms appear three-dimensional? Wallach & O'Connell (233) point out that no rules of "spontaneous organization" are adequate to predict this. Of course, the empiricists have their answer. In the case of moving forms, produced by turning a three-dimensional wire-edged or solid form behind a translucent screen so that only a two-dimensional shadow is seen by the observer, one essential condition for the perception of a third dimension is that the shadow must display contours or lines which change their length and their direction simultaneously. This is Wallach's "kinetic depth effect." For any other form to appear three-dimensional there must have been previous perception of that form in three dimensions, these authors conclude. Fry (82) presents a general mathematical formulation of relations governing stereopsis and geometrical perspective for plane figures.

Size and distance judgments are intimately related, and Gibson (94) makes a plea against trying to separate the two factors except for very limited experimental purposes. Boring (23, 24) says that such analysis is the essence of scientific method in psychology. Through an ingenious use of reversible figures Hochberg & Hochberg (115) attempt to separate familiar size from relative size as determinants of perceived distance. That their experiment does so is open to question. Where they try to eliminate familiarity, they use the identical boy in two sizes for comparison figures. He is familiar by the time he is perceived on both surfaces. Kume's method (133) seems to eliminate familiarity more adequately for he used disks which lack identity. Both experiments are said to show that larger objects are seen as nearer than smaller ones, where distance is ambiguous.

Visibility, Detection, Orientation

Problems of outdoor visibility are treated at length by Middleton (153). Many specialized topics in this area are currently under investigation. Examples are the Tousey & Koomen study (225) of the increasing visibility of stars during twilight and the research by Sexton, Malone & Farnsworth (203) of the visibility of different colors against a simulated sea background. The poor visibility of yellow came out in both studies, interestingly enough, since this has been thought the color of choice for life rafts. Orange Aldebaran appeared early in the night sky, relative to its magnitude. Red was more visible than other hues against the blue-grey of the ocean. Visual problems to be expected in very high altitude flying are discussed by Cibis (56).

Problems of lighting, legibility, and spatial arrangement in visual displays are central in human engineering research. The new *IES Lighting Handbook* (118) is invaluable for psychologists concerned with this area. The problem of specifying luminance at mesopic and scotopic levels is reviewed, and a luminance scale is offered for converting from cone to rod levels by a series of multiplying factors [Bridgman (32)]. Spragg & Rock (217, 218) find a critical brightness level of 0.02 ft. L. for dial reading, above which there is little or no improvement in speed or accuracy, and color is a minor factor. Illumination (not luminance) was the factor studied by Tinker (224) in an investigation concerned with reading six-point italic type. The critical level he reports was between 10 and 25 ft. candles. Fluorescent flicker is found to reduce cff but not significantly affect reading performance (245). The legibility of letters and digits was studied by Crook, *et al.* (61) and Schapiro (198). Widths and spacing of markers and pointers in dial design for precision of reading were investigated by Carr & Garner (46). Christensen (53) finds interactions between type of dial, exposure time, and practice. Eriksen (73, 74) studied the general problem of locating specified objects within a multitudinous display. Hue proved more effective than any other single dimension in facilitating speed of the locating and designating response. Objects unique in several dimensions were still more quickly located.

Solomon & Postman (214) report that frequency of experimental usage is a determinant of thresholds for tachistoscopic recognition for nonsense words. McGinnies, Comer & Lacey (150) found that word length and word frequency (familiarity) were, both separately and in interaction, significant determiners of variation in recognition thresholds. Lacy, Lewinger & Adamson (134) used instructions to manipulate thresholds for "taboo" words. The highly familiar sequences, the alphabet, and numbers from 1 to 20, were used by Mowbray (163) to compare the efficiency of vision and audition, singly or in competition, for the detection of missing elements. For the single modality audition was less efficient. Errors increased about equally in both modalities when two tasks were presented simultaneously, except that a significantly larger increase in errors of commission occurred with visually presented sequences.

Orienting with respect to the gravitational vertical is dependent upon cooperation or conflict between visual and proprioceptive mechanisms. Where there is conflict the response may be a compromise one (95, 97, 148) or one modality may dominate (148). Instructions and the sophistication of S are variables which can influence the relative dominance of conflicting cues [Mann & Boring (149)]. Prior tilt of the test rod effects the perceived vertical [Werner & Wapner (239)]. Mann (147) studied the duration of the oculogyral illusion by using a flickering vertical line presented above critical fusion frequency to produce a "picket fence" phase. The relation between revolutions per minute and duration fits Mayne's formula. Visual cues utilized in orientation during flight in aircraft are discussed by Cibis (55) and Rose (194), who agree that size of image is an important cue, that binocular cues are relatively unimportant, and who are not in full agreement as to whether motion parallax or linear perspective should be considered the other cue of major importance. Gerathewohl (93) discusses the problem of predicting the disorienting effects that will be encountered under subgravity or zero-gravity states. Accidents on superhighways involving vehicles moving in the same direction at different rates of speed prompted the experiment by Stalder & Lauer (219). They investigated the effect of visual patterns on the perception of relative motion, and found that a sharply delineated area was superior to small light spots or checkerboard in producing accurate estimates of the rates of approach.

Emphasis on perceptual variables in eye-hand coordination is seen in a number of recent studies (77, 101, 184, 192, 197). Space does not permit discussion of this very important applied area of research.

Motivation in Visual Perception

Motivation was seen to be a minor but somewhat troublesome variable in simple threshold studies (22). It is undoubtedly more significant in highly ambiguous conditions of stimulation and response. The literature in this area is still full of contradictions. Motivating conditions are too often inferred rather than controlled, although an increasing number of studies are dealing more effectively with this variable. Whether to regard a given change in response as a measure of a perceptual process or an alteration in response tendency as a result of a shift in "set" is a difficult theoretical issue. Some progress is being made in the effort to disentangle this issue experimentally [Postman & Crutchfield (183)]. Whether motivation operates directly at the moment of perception and response, or whether it has operated exclusively in prior situations to produce selective learning is not always clear in a given experiment. The reader interested in following current theoretical issues in this area should consult Postman's recent discussion (179).

The concept of "perceptual defense" is under dispute. An experiment by Taylor (221), who conditioned the galvanic skin response to geometrical figures, supports the position that discrimination is possible before a visual stimulus can be identified verbally. Postman, Bronson & Gropper (180) find no support for the concept of "perceptual defense" as a variable influencing thresholds for emotionally toned words, nor do Bitterman & Kniffin (21). Postman & Brown (181) were able to alter word recognition thresholds by manipulating the preceding success or failure experiences of the subjects. Their results are closely related to those cited earlier on the effects of frequency and expectancy (134, 150, 214).

Fraser (81) used a new visual vigilance task in which the presence or absence of the experimenter produced a reliable difference in the number of signals seen, a difference contributed entirely by seven of the 18 Ss. The nature of motivational differences is merely implied. Gilchrist & Nesberg (100) varied hunger or thirst by imposing up to 20-hr. of food or 8-hr. of fluid deprivation. Positive time error in the illuminance matches of objects related to need increased with increases in the periods of deprivation. This is a variation of the experiments on changes in the magnitude of a psychophysical dimension as related to symbols of need-reducing objects. Effects on the apparent size of objects are reported in experiments by Bruner & Rodrigues (38), Dukes & Bevan (71), and Singer (206). Hastings (109) used a modified "thereness-thatness" demonstration of Ames and reports that Ss rating high on insecurity tended to see objects nearer than did more secure subjects.

LITERATURE CITED

1. Adair, E. R., "Duration and Light-Dark Ratio of Intermittent Preadaptation as Factors Influencing Human Dark Adaptation," *J. Opt. Soc. Amer.*, **43,** 22–27 (1953)
2. Alexander, L. T., and Bricker, P. D., "Figure-Ground Contrast and Binocular Rivalry," *J. Exptl. Psychol.*, **44,** 452–54 (1952)
3. Armington, J. C., "Component of the Human Electroretinogram Associated with Red Color Vision," *J. Opt. Soc. Amer.*, **42,** 393–401 (952)
4. Armington, J. C., Johnson, E. P., and Riggs, L. A., "The Scotopic A-Wave in the Electrical Response of the Human Retina," *J. Physiol. (London)*, **118,** 289–98 (1952)
5. Asher, H., "Stimulus to Convergence in Normal and Asthenopic Subjects," *Brit. J. Ophthalmol.*, **36,** 666–75 (1952)
6. Asher, H., "Suppression Theory of Binocular Vision," *Brit. J. Ophthalmol.*, **37,** 37–49 (1953)
7. Atkinson, R. C., and Ammons, R. B., "Experiential Factors in Visual Form

Perception: II. Latency as a Function of Repetition," *J. Exptl. Psychol.*, **43,** 173–78 (1952)

8. Azuna, H., "The Effect of Experience on the Amount of the Müller-Lyer Illusion," *Japan. J. Psychol.*, **22,** 111–23 (1952)
9. Bahr, G. von, "Studies on the Depth of Focus of the Eye," *Acta Ophthalmol.*, **30,** 39–44, (1952)
10. Baird, J. M., "Individual Correction of Strabismus," *Am. Orthoptic J.*, **2,** 25–34 (1952) (Suppl. *Trans. Am. Acad. Opththalmol. Otolaryngol.*)
11. Baker, C. H., "The Dependence of Binocular Fusion on Timing of Peripheral Stimuli and on Central Process: 1. Symmetrical Flicker, 2. Asymmetrical Flicker, 3. Cortical Flicker," *Can. J. Psychol.*, **6,** 1–10, 84–91, 123–30, 151–63 (1952)
12. Barger, D. M., and Gebhard, J. W., "An Electronic Stimulator for Use on the Human Eye," *Am. J. Psychol.*, **65,** 450–57 (1952)
13. Barlow, H. B., "Eye Movements during Fixation," *J. Physiol. (London)*, **116,** 290–306 (1952)
14. Bartley, S. H., "Brightness Comparisons When One Eye is Stimulated Intermittently and the Other Eye Steadily," *J. Psychol.*, **34,** 165–67 (1952)
15. Bartley, S. H., and Wilkinson, F. R., "Certain Factors in Producing Complexity of Response to a Single Pulse of Light," *J. Psychol.*, **35,** 299–306 (1953)
16. Bay, E., "Analyse eines Valles von Seelenblindheit," *Deut. Z. Nervenheilk.*, **168,** 1–23 (1952)
17. Bender, M. B., *Disorders in Perception* (Charles C Thomas, Publisher, Springfield, Ill., 109 pp., 1952)
18. Bevan, W., Jr., "The Influence of Figural After-Effects upon Visual Intensity Thresholds," *J. Gen. Psychol.*, **45,** 189–207 (1951)
19. Bevan, W., Jr., and Zener, K., "Some Influences of Past Experience Upon the Perceptual Thresholds of Visual Form." *Am. J. Psychol.*, **65,** 434–42 (1952)
20. Bingham, W. E., and Griffiths, W. J., Jr., "The Effect of Different Environments during Infancy on Adult Behavior in the Rat," *J. Comp. and Physiol. Psychol.*, **45,** 307–12 (1952)
21. Bitterman, M. E., and Kniffin, C. W., "Manifest Anxiety and 'Perceptual Defense'," *J. Abnormal Social Psychol.*, **48,** 248–52 (1953)
22. Blackwell, H. R., "Studies on Psychophysical Methods for Measuring Visual Thresholds," *J. Opt. Soc. Amer.*, **42,** 606–16 (1952)
23. Boring, E. G., "Visual Perception as Invariance," *Psychol. Rev.*, **59,** 141–48 (1952)
24. Boring, E. G., "The Gibsonian Visual Field," *Psychol. Rev.*, **59,** 246–47 (1952)
25. Bouman, M. A., "Mechanisms in Peripheral Dark Adaptation," *J. Opt. Soc. Amer.*, **42,** 941–50 (1952)
26. Bouman, M. A., "Peripheral Contrast Threshold for Various and Different Wavelengths for Adapting Field and Test Stimulus," *J. Opt. Soc. Amer.*, **42,** 820–31 (1952)
27. Bouman, M. A., "Visual Thresholds for Line-Shaped Targets," *J. Opt. Soc. Amer.*, **43,** 209–11 (1953)
28. Bouman, M. A., and Blokhuis, E. W. M., "The Visibility of Black Objects Against an Illuminated Background," *J. Opt. Soc. Amer.*, **42,** 525–28 (1952)
29. Bouman, M. A., and Brink, G. van den, "On the Integrate Capacity in Time and Space of the Human Peripheral Retina," *J. Opt. Soc. Amer.*, **42,** 617–20 (1952)

30. Bouman, M. A., Ten Doesschate, J., and Du Marchie Sarvaas, G. J., "A Modification of Goldmann's Apparatus for the Objective Determination of the Visual Acuity," *Ophthalmologica*, **122**, 368–74 (1951)
31. Brattgård, S.-O., "The Importance of Adequate Stimulation for the Chemical Composition of Retinal Ganglion Cells during Early Post-Natal Development," *Acta Radiologica, Suppl.* **96**, 80 pp. (1952)
32. Bridgman, C. S., "Correction of Low Intensity Luminance Functions for the Purkinje Effect," *J. Opt. Soc. Amer.*, **42**, 832–36 (1952)
33. Brindley, G. S., "The Bunsen-Roscoe Law for the Human Eye at Very Short Durations," *J. Physiol. (London)*, **118**, 135–39 (1952)
34. Brown, J. L., Graham, C. H., Leibowitz, H., and Ranken, H. B., "Luminance Thresholds for the Resolution of Visual Detail during Dark Adaptation," *J. Opt. Soc. Amer.*, **43**, 197–202 (1953)
35. Brown, W. R. J., "Statistics of Color-Matching Data," *J. Opt. Soc. Amer.*, **42**, 252–56 (1952)
36. Brown, W. R. J., "The Effect of Field Size and Chromatic Surroundings on Color Discrimination," *J. Opt. Soc. Amer.*, **42**, 837–44 (1952)
37. Bruner, J. S., Busiek, R. D., and Minturn, A. L., "Assimilation in the Immediate Reproduction of Visually Perceived Figures," *J. Exptl. Psychol.*, **44**, 151–55 (1952)
38. Bruner, J. S., and Rodrigues, J. S., "Some Determinants of Apparent Size," *J. Abnormal Social Psychol.*, **48**, 17–24 (1953)
39. Brunswik, E., and Kamiya, J., "Ecological Cue-Validity of 'Proximity' and of other Gestalt Factors," *Am. J. Psychol.*, **66**, 20–32 (1953)
40. Burke, L., "On the Tunnel Effect," *Quart. J. Exptl. Psychol.*, **4**, 121–38 (1952)
41. Burnham, R. W., "Comparative Effects of Area and Luminance on Color," *Am. J. Psychol.*, **65**, 27–38 (1952)
42. Burnham, R. W. "A Colorimeter for Research in Color Perception," *Am. J. Psychol.*, **65**, 603–8 (1952)
43. Burnham, R. W., Evans, R. M., and Newhall, S. M., "Influence on Color Perception of Adaptation to Illumination," *J. Opt. Soc. Amer.*, **42**, 597–605 (1952)
44. Burns, B. D., and Grafstein, B., "The Function and Structure of Some Neurones in the Cat's Cerebral Cortex," *J. Physiol. (London)*, **118**, 412–33 (1952)
45. Butler, R. A., "Discrimination Learning by Rhesus Monkeys to Visual-Exploration Motivation," *J. Comp. and Physiol. Psychol.*, **46**, 95–98 (1953)
46. Carr, W. J., and Garner, W. R., "The Maximum Precision of Reading Fine Scales," *J. Psychol.*, **34**, 85–94 (1952)
47. Chalmers, E. L., "Monocular and Binocular Cues in the Perception of Size and Distance," *Am. J. Psychol.*, **65**, 415–23 (1952)
48. Chang, H.-T., "Physiology of Vision," *Ann. Rev. Physiol.*, **15**, 373–96 (1953)
49. Chapanis, A., and Halsey, R. M., "Photopic Thresholds for Red Light in an Unselected Sample of Color-Deficient Individuals," *J. Opt. Soc. Amer.*, **43**, 62–63 (1953)
50. Cheatham, P. G., "Visual Perceptual Latency as a Function of Stimulus Brightness and Contour Shape," *J. Exptl. Psychol.*, **43**, 369–80 (1952)
51. Chow, K. L., "Conditions Influencing the Recovery of Visual Discriminative Habits in Monkeys Following Temporal Neocortical Ablations," *J. Comp. and Physiol. Psychol.*, **45**, 430–37 (1952)
52. Chow, K. L., "Further Studies on Selective Ablation of Associative Cortex in

Relation to Visually Mediated Behavior," *J. Comp. and Physiol. Psychol.*, **45,** 109–18 (1952)

53. Christensen. J. M., "Quantitative Instrument Reading as a Function of Dial Design Exposure Time, Preparatory Fixation, and Practice," *Tech. Rept.* 52–116 (Wright Air Development Center, Wright-Patterson Air Force Base, Ohio, 51 pp., 1952)
54. Christman, R. J., "Figural After-Effects Utilizing Apparent Movement as Inspection-Figure," *Am. J. Psychol.*, **66,** 66–72 (1953)
55. Cibis, P. A., "Problems of Depth Perception in Monocular and Binocular Flying, *J. Aviation Med.*, **23,** 612–31 (1952)
56. Cibis, P. A., "Retinal Adaptation Applicable to Visual Problems in Flight at Increasing Altitudes," in *Physics and Medicine of the Upper Atmosphere,* 562–66 (White, C. S., and Benson, O. O., Jr., Eds., University of New Mexico Press, Albuquerque, N. M., 611 pp., 1952)
57. Cibis, P. A., Gerathewohl, S. J., and Rubinstein, D., "Depth Perception in Monocular and Binocular Vision," *Special Report, Distrib. No. 1858* (USAF School of Aviation Medicine, Randolph Field, Texas, 12 pp., 1953)
58. Cole, J., "The Relative Importance of Color and Form in Discrimination Learning in Monkeys," *J. Comp. and Physiol. Psychol.*, **46,** 16–18 (1953)
59. Collins, F. D., "Rhodopsin and Indicator Yellow," *Nature,* **171,** 469–71 (1953)
60. Colson, Z. W., "Verhoeff's Theory of Anomalous Projection," *Am. J. Ophthalmol.*, **35,** 807–11 (1952)
61. Crook, M. N., Hanson, J. A., and Wulfeck, J. W., "The Legibility of Type as a Function of Reflectance of Background under Low Illumination," *Tech. Rept.* **52–85** (Wright Air Development Center, ARDC, USAF, Wright-Patterson Air Force Base, Ohio, 15 pp. 1952)
62. Dartnall, H. J. A., "Visual Pigment 467, a Photosensitive Pigment Present in Tench Retinae," *J. Physiol.* (*London*), **116,** 257–89 (1952)
63. Dartnall, H. J. A., "A New Visual Pigment Absorbing Maximally at 510 mμ," *J. Physiol.* (*London*), **117,** 57 (1952)
64. Davis, R., Gibson, K. S., and Haupt, G. W., "Spectral Energy Distribution of the International Commission on Illumination Light Sources A, B, and C," *J. Opt. Soc. Amer.*, **43,** 172–76 (1953)
65. Davy, E., "The Intensity-Time Relation for Multiple Flashes of Light in the Peripheral Retina," *J. Opt. Soc. Amer.*, **42,** 937–41 (1952)
66. Deatherage, B. H., and Bitterman, M. E., "The Effect of Satiation on Stroboscopic Movement," *Am. J. Psychol.*, **65,** 108–9 (1952)
67. Denny-Brown, D., Meyer, J. S., and Horenstein, S., "The Significance of Perceptual Rivalry Resulting from Parietal Lesion," *Brain,* **75,** 433–71 (1952)
68. Denton, E. J., and Pirenne, M. H., "On the Functional Stability of the Retina," *J. Physiol.* (*London*), **117,** 55 (1952)
69. Ditchburn, R. W., and Ginsborg, B. L., "Involuntary Eye Movements during Fixation," *J. Physiol.* (*London*), **119,** 1–17 (1953)
70. Dufour, R., and Cuendet, J. F., "Appreciation Quantitative des Perturbations des Fonctions Visuelles," *Ophthalmologica*, **123,** 249–55 (1952)
71. Dukes, W. F., and Bevan, W., Jr., "Size Estimation and Monetary Value: A Correlation," *J. Psychol.*, **34,** 43–53 (1952)
72. Ekman, G., "The Laws of the Wandering Phenomenon. Contribution to the Theory of Perception," *Acta Psychologica*, **8,** 154–68 (1952)

73. Eriksen, C. W., "The Location of Objects in a Visual Display as a Function of the Number of Dimensions on Which the Objects Differ," *J. Exptl. Psychol.*, **44,** 56–60 (1952)

74. Eriksen, C. W., "Object Location in a Complex Perceptual Field," *J. Exptl. Psychol.*, **45,** 126–32 (1953)

75. Erlick, D., and Landis, C., "The Effect of Intensity, Light-Dark Ratio, and Age on the Flicker-Fusion Threshold," *Am. J. Psychol.*, **65,** 375–88 (1952)

76. Fields, P. E., "The Efficiency of the Serial Multiple Visual Discrimination Apparatus and Method with White Rats," *J. Comp. and Physiol. Psychol.*, **46,** 69–76 (1953)

77. Fitts, P. M., and Simon, C. W., "Some Relations between Stimulus Patterns and Performance in a Continuous Dual-Pursuit Task," *J. Exptl. Psychol.*, **43,** 428–36 (1952)

78. Flamant, F., "Seuils Differentiels D'intensite de Deux Points Lumineux," *Rev. opt.*, **31,** 113–20 (1952)

79. Forgays, D. G., "The Development of Differential Work Recognition," *J. Exptl. Psychol.*, **45,** 165–68 (1953)

80. Forgays, D. G., and Forgays, J. W., "The Nature of the Effect of Free-Environmental Experience in the Rat," *J. Comp. and Physiol. Psychol.*, **45,** 322–28 (1952)

81. Fraser, D. C., "The Relation of an Environmental Variable to Performance in a Prolonged Visual Task," *Quart. J. Exptl. Psychol.*, **5,** 37–38 (1953)

82. Fry, G. A., "The Relationship Between Geometrical Perspective and Stereo Cues," *Am. J. Optometry*, **29,** 353–68 (1952)

83. Fry, G. A., "Psychological Factors in Visual Acuity," *Am. J. Optometry*, **29,** 624–30 (1952)

84. Fry, G. A., "Research in Accommodation and Convergence," *Am. J. Optometry*, **29,** 169–76 (1953)

85. Fry, G. A., and Allen, M. J., *Effect of Flashes of Light on Night Visual Acuity*, Part II, (Armed Forces—National Research Council Vision Committee Secretariat, University of Michigan, Ann Arbor, Michigan, 17 pp., 1953)

86. Fry, G. A., and Alpern, M., *Effect of Flashes of Light on Night Visual Acuity*, Part I, (Armed Forces—National Research Council Vision Committee Secretariat, University of Michigan, Ann Arbor, Michigan, 28 pp., 1953)

87. Fry, G. A., and Alpern, M., "The Effect of a Peripheral Glare Source upon the Apparent Brightness of an Object," *J. Opt. Soc. Amer.*, **43,** 189–95 (1953)

88. Furchtgott, E., "The Effects of X-Irradiation on Brightness Discrimination," *J. Psychol.*, **34,** 37–41 (1952)

89. Gebhard, J. W., "Thresholds of the Human Eye for Electric Stimulation by Different Wave Forms," *J. Exptl. Psychol.*, **44,** 132–40 (1952)

90. Gebhard, J. W., "Motokawa's Studies on Electric Excitation of the Human Eye," *Psychol. Bull.*, **50,** 73–111 (1953)

91. Geldard, F. A., *The Human Senses* (John Wiley & Sons, Inc., New York, N. Y., 365 pp., 1953)

92. George, F. H., "Errors of Visual Recognition," *J. Exptl. Psychol.*, **43,** 202–6 (1952)

93. Gerathewohl, S. J., "Physics and Psychophysics of Weightlessness—Visual Perception," *J. Aviation Med.*, **23,** 373–95 (1952)

94. Gibson, J. J., "The Visual Field and the Visual World: A Reply to Professor Boring," *Psychol. Rev.*, **59,** 149–51 (1952)

95. Gibson, J. J., "The Relation between Visual and Postural Determinants of the Phenomenal Vertical," *Psychol. Rev.*, **59,** 370–75 (1952)

96. Gibson, J. J., and Carel, W., "Does Motion Perspective Independently Produce the Impression of a Receding Surface?" *J. Exptl. Psychol.*, **44,** 16–18 (1952)

97. Gibson, J. J., and Cornsweet, J., "The Perceived Slant of Visual Surfaces—Optical and Geographical," *J. Exptl. Psychol.*, **44,** 11–15 (1952)

98. Gibson, J. J., and Dibble, F. N., "Exploratory Experiments on the Stimulus Conditions for the Perception of a Visual Surface," *J. Exptl. Psychol.*, **43,** 414–19 (1952)

99. Gibson, J. J., and Waddell, D., "Homogeneous Retinal Stimulation and Visual Perception." *Am. J. Psychol.*, **65,** 263–70 (1952)

100. Gilchrist, J. C., and Nesberg, L. S., "Need and Perceptual Change in Need-Related Objects." *J. Exptl. Psychol.*, **44,** 369–76 (1952)

101. Gilinsky, A. S., and Brown, J. L., "Eye Dominance and Tracking Performance," *Tech. Rept. 52–15* (Wright Air Development Center, Wright-Patterson Air Force Base, Ohio, 1952)

102. Groot, S. G. de, and Gebhard, J. W., "Pupil Size as Determined by Adapting Luminance," *J. Opt. Soc. Amer.*, **42,** 492–95 (1952)

103. Gumbel, E. J., "A Study of Depth Perception in the Light and Dark Adapted Eye," *Am. J. Optometry*, **29,** 613–23 (1952)

104. Hall, K. R. L., Earle, A. E., and Crookes, T. G., "A Pendulum Phenomenon in the Visual Perception of Apparent Movement," *Quart. J. Exptl. Psychol.*, **4,** 109–20 (1952)

105. Halldén, U., "Fusional Phenomena in Anomalous Correspondence," *Acta Ophthalmol.*, Suppl. 37, 93 pp. (1952)

106. Halsey, R. M., and Chapanis, A., "On the Number of Absolutely Identifiable Spectral Hues," *J. Opt. Soc. Amer.*, **41,** 1057–58 (1951)

107. Halsey, R. M., and Chapanis, A., "Experimental Determination of Some Iso-Chromaticity Lines in Color-Deficient Vision," *J. Opt. Soc. Amer.*, **42,** 722–39 (1952)

108. Harper, R. S., "The Perceptual Modification of Colored Figures," *Am. J. Psychol.*, **66,** 86–89 (1953)

109. Hastings, P. K., "A Relationship between Visual Perception and Level of Personal Security," *J. Abnormal Social Psychol.*, **47,** 552–60 (1952)

110. Hastorf, A. H., and Way, K. S., "Apparent Size With and Without Distance Cues," *J. Gen. Psychol.*, **47,** 181–88 (1952)

111. Hayes, K. J., and Hayes, C., "Imitation in a Home-Raised Chimpanzee," *J. Comp. and Physiol. Psychol.*, **45,** 450–59 (1952)

112. Hayes, K. J., and Hayes, C., "Picture Perception in a Home-Raised Chimpanzee" (Unpublished data)

113. Hess, E. H., "'Subjective' Colors: Retinal vs. Central Origin," *Am. J. Psychol.*, **65,** 278–80 (1952)

114. Hirsch, M. J., "The Changes in Refraction between the Ages of 5 and 14—Theoretical and Practical Considerations," *Am. J. Optometry*, **29,** 445–59 (1952)

115. Hochberg, C. B., and Hochberg, J. E., "Familiar Size and the Perception of Depth," *J. Psychol.*, **34,** 107–14 (1952)

116. Hunt, R. W. G., "Light and Dark Adaptation and the Perception of Color," *J. Opt. Soc. Amer.*, **42,** 190–99 (1952)

117. Hymovitch, B., "The Effects of Experimental Variations on Problem Solving in the Rat." *J. Comp. and Physiol. Psychol.*, **45**, 313–21 (1952)
118. *IES Lighting Handbook* (2nd ed. Illuminating Engineering Society, New York, N. Y., 974 pp., 1952)
119. Ishak, I. G. H., "The Spectral Chromaticity Coordinates for One British and Eight Egyptian Trichromats," *J. Opt. Soc. Amer.*, **42**, 534–39 (1952)
120. Ishak, I. G. H., "Determination of the Tristimulus Values of the Spectrum for Eight Egyptian Observers and One British Observer," *J. Opt. Soc. Amer.*, **42**, 844–49 (1952)
121. Jaeger, W., "Werden die angeborenen Störungen des Rotgrünsinns ausnahmslos recessiv-geschlechtsgebunden vererbt?" *Albrecht von Graefe's Arch. Ophthalmol.*, **152**, 379–84 (1952),
122. Jaeger, W., "Beitrag zur Frage der Genlokalization der Farbensinnstörungen," *Albrecht von Graefe's Arch. Ophthalmol.*, **152**, 385–88 (1952)
123. Jameson, D., and Hurvich, L. M., "The Spectral Sensitivity of the Fovea and its Dependence on Adaptation" (Color Control Division Report No. A-131, Eastman Kodak Co., Rochester, New York, 65 pp., 1953)
124. Judd, D. B., *Color in Business, Science and Industry* (John Wiley & Sons, Inc., New York, N. Y., 401 pp., 1952)
125. Kakizaki, S., "The Effects of Preceding Conditions upon Binocular Rivalry (II)," *Japan. J. Psychol.*, **20**, 11–17 (1950)
126. Kaneko, T., and Obonai, T., "Factors of Intensity, Quantity and Distance in Psychophysiological Induction," *Japan. J. Psychol.*, **23**, 73–79 (1952)
127. Keiner, G. B. J., *New Viewpoints on the Origin of Squint* (Martinus Nijhoff, The Hague, Netherlands, 222 pp., 1951)
128. Kern, E., "Der Bereich der Unterschiedsempfindlichkeit des Auges bei festgehaltenem Adaptations-zustand," *Z. Biol.*, **105**, 237–45 (1952)
129. Kleemeier, R. W., "The Relationship between Ortho-Rater Tests of Acuity and Color Vision in a Senescent Group," *J. Appl. Psychol.*, **36**, 114–16 (1952)
130. Köhler, W., Held, R., and O'Connell, D. N., "An Investigation of Cortical Currents," *Proc. Am. Phil. Soc.*, **96**, 290–330 (1952)
131. Koomen, M.J., Scolnik, R., and Tousey, R., "Measurement of Accommodation in Dim Light and in Darkness by Means of the Purkinje Images," *J. Opt. Soc. Amer.*, **43**, 27–31 (1953)
132. Kretzschmar, S., Jr., "A Propos de la Fousse Correspondence Retinienne," *Ophthalmologica*, **123**, 343–48 (1952)
133. Kume, K., "On the Relation between the Perceived Size and the Viewing Distance with Some Consideration of the Factors Determining Size Constancy," *Japan. J. Psychol.*, **22**, 235–44; **23**, 32–43 (1952)
134. Lacy, O. W., Lewinger, N., and Adamson, J. F., "Foreknowledge as a Factor Affecting Perceptual Defense and Alertness," *J. Exptl. Psychol.*, **45**, 169–74 (1953)
135. Lancaster, W. B., *Refraction and Motility* (Charles C Thomas, Publisher, Springfield, Ill., 310 pp., 1952)
136. Lange, C. W., "Visual Efficiency Development," *Optometric Weekly*, **43**, 83–85, 279–82, 493–96 (1952)
137. Lange, F., "Untersuchungen zur normalen Verteilung des Lichtsinns in der Netzhaut und iher Altersabhängigkeit," *Albrecht von Graefes Arch. Ophthalmol.*, **153**, 93–104 (1952)

138. Leibowitz, H., "Effect of Pupil Size on Visual Acuity for Photometrically Equated Test Fields at Various Levels of Luminance," *J. Opt. Soc. Amer.*, **42**, 416–22 (1952)

139. Levine, J., "Studies in the Interrelations of Central Nervous Structures in Vision: III. Localization of the Memory Trace as Evidenced by the Lack of Inter- and Intraocular Habit Transfer in the Pigeon," *J. Genetic Psychol.*, **81**, 19–27 (1952)

140. Lichte, W. H., "Shape Constancy: Dependence upon Angle of Rotation; Individual Differences," *J. Exptl. Psychol.*, **43**, 49–57 (1952)

141. Lindsley, D. B., "Effect of Photic Stimulation in Visual Pathways from Retina to Cortex," *Science*, **117**, 469 (1953)

142. Lloyd, V. V., "A Comparison of Critical Fusion Frequencies for Different Areas in the Fovea and Periphery," *Am. J. Psychol.*, **65**, 346–57 (1952)

143. Linksz, A., *Physiology of the Eye*, **2**, *Vision* (Grune & Stratton, Inc., New York, N. Y., 869 pp., 1952)

144. Lord, M. P., "Eye Rotations with Change of Accommodation," *Nature*, **170**, 670–72 (1952)

145. Luchins, A. S., and Luchins, E. H., "On the Relationship between Figural After-Effects and the Principle of Prägnanz," *Am. J. Psychol.*, **65**, 16–26 (1952)

146. Ludvigh, E., "Possible Role of Proprioception in the Extraocular Muscles," *Arch. Ophthalmol.*, **48**, 436–41 (1952)

147. Mann, C. W., "An Analysis of the Oculogyral Effect," *J. Aviation Med.*, **23**, 246–53 (1952)

148. Mann, C. W., "Visual Factors in the Perception of Verticality," *J. Exptl. Psychol.*, **44**, 460–64 (1952)

149. Mann, C. W., and Boring, R. O., "The Role of Instruction in Experimental Space Perception," *J. Exptl. Psychol.*, **45**, 44–48 (1953)

150. McGinnies, E., Comer, P. B., and Lacey, O. L., "Visual Recognition Thresholds as a Function of Word Length and Word Frequency," *J. Exptl. Psychol.*, **44**, 65–69 (1952)

151. Melzack, R., "Irrational Fears in the Dog," *Can. J. Psychol.*, **6**, 141–47 (1952)

152. Michael, D. M., "A Cross-Cultural Investigation of Closure," *J. Abnormal Social Psychol.*, **48**, 225–30 (1953)

153. Middleton, W. E. K., *Vision Through the Atmosphere* (University of Toronto Press, Toronto, Canada, 250 pp., 1952)

154. Mishkin, M., and Forgays, D. G., "Word Recognition as a Function of Retinal Locus," *J. Exptl. Psychol.*, **43**, 43–48 (1952)

155. Misumi, J., "Experimental Studies of the Development of Visual Size Constancy in Early Infancy," *Japan. J. Psychol.*, **20**, 16–24 (1950)

156. Monjé, M., Über Pharmakodynamische und Klinische Untersuchungen der Akkommodation," *Albrecht von Graefe's Arch. Ophthlamol.*, **152**, 357–78 (1952)

157. Mote, F. A., and Reed, E. C., "The Effect of Extending the Duration of Various Light-Dark Ratios of Intermittent Pre-exposure upon Dark Adaptation in the Human Eye," *J. Opt. Soc. Amer.*, **42**, 333–38 (1952)

158. Mote, F. A., and Reed, E. C., "The Effect of High Intensity and Short Duration versus Low Intensity and Long Duration of Intermittent Pre-exposure upon Human Dark Adaptation," *J. Opt. Soc. Amer.*, **42**, 521–25 (1952)

159. Mote, F. A., and Riopelle, A. J., "The Effect of Varying the Intensity and the Duration of Pre-exposure upon Subsequent Dark Adaptation in the Human Eye," *J. Comp. and Physiol. Psychol.*, **46**, 49–55 (1953)

160. Motokawa, K., and Ebe, M., "Retinal Colour Processes Caused by Intermittent White Light," *Nature*, **170**, 79–80 (1952)

161. Motokawa, K., and Ebe, M., "Selective Stimulation of Color Receptors with Alternating Current," *Science*, **116**, 92–94 (1952)

162. Motokawa, K., and Ebe, M., "Retinal Receptors Isolated with AC Method and Polychromatic Theory," *J. Opt. Soc. Amer.*, **43**, 203–9 (1953)

163. Mowbray, G. H., "Simultaneous Vision and Audition: The Detection of Elements Missing from Overlearned Sequences," *J. Exptl. Psychol.*, **44**, 292–300 (1952)

164. Mull, H. K., Arp, K., and Carlin, P., "Indications of a Central Factor in Uncontrolled and Controlled Shifts in Cube Perspective," *Am. J. Psychol.*, **65**, 89–90 (1952)

165. Naruse, G., "The Influence of Form upon the Visual-Perception-Threshold," *Japanese J. Psychol.*, **21**, 26–35 (1951)

166. Nickerson, D., Tomaszewski, J. J., and Boyd, T. F., "Colorimetric Specifications of Munsell Repaints," *J. Opt. Soc. Amer.*, **43**, 163–71 (1953)

167. Ogasawara, J., "Displacement-Effect of Concentric Circles," *Japan. J. Psychol.*, **22**, 224–34 (1952)

168. Ogle, K. N., "On the Limits of Stereoscopic Vision," *J. Exptl. Psychol.*, **44**, 253–59 (1952),

169. Ohwaki, Y., and Kihara, T., "A New Research on the So-Called 'Bocci Image'," *Tôhoku Psychologica Folia*, **13**, 157–80 (1953)

170. Optical Society of America, Committee on Colorimetry, *The Science of Color* (Thomas Y. Crowell Co., New York, N. Y., 400 pp., 1953)

171. Orbach, J., "Retinal Locus as a Factor in the Recognition of Visually Perceived Words," *Am. J. Psychol.*, **65**, 555–62 (1952)

172. Osgood, C. E., and Heyer, A. W., Jr., "A New Interpretation of Figural After-Effects," *Psychol. Rev.*, **59**, 98–118 (1952)

173. Peckham, R. H., and Arner, W. J., "Visual Acuity, Contrast, and Flicker, as Measures of Retinal Sensitivity," *J. Opt. Soc. Amer.*, **42**, 621–25 (1952)

174. Pemberton, C. L., "The Closure Factors Related to Other Cognitive Processes," *Psychometrika*, **17**, 267–88 (1952)

175. Piper, H. F., "Augenhaltung und Akkommodationsimpuls," *Albrecht von Graefes Arch Ophthalmol.*, **152**, 719–30 (1952)

176. Pirenne, M. H., and Denton, E. J., "Accuracy and Sensitivity of the Human Eye," *Nature*, **170**, 1039–42 (1952)

177. Pollock, W. T., and Chapanis, A., "The Apparent Length of a Line as a Function of its Inclination," *Quart. J. Exptl. Psychol.*, **4**, 170–84 (1952)

178. Portmann, V. P., and Dufour, M., "The Place of Orthoptics in the Treatment of Convergent Concomitant Strabismus," *Ophthalmologica*, **123**, 294–303 (1952)

179. Postman, L., *The Experimental Analysis of Motivational Factors in Perception*, (Presented at the symposium on Current Research and Theory in Motivation, In press, University of Nebraska, Lincoln, Nebraska, 1953)

180. Postman, L., Bronson, W. C., and Gropper, G. L., "Is There a Mechanism of Perceptual Defense?" *J. Abnormal Social Psychol.*, **48**, 215–24 (1953)

181. Postman, L., and Brown, D. R., "The Perceptual Consequences of Success and Failure," *J. Abnormal Social Psychol.*, **47**, 213–21 (1952)

182. Postman, L., and Bruner, J. S., "Hypothesis and the Principle of Closure: The Effect of Frequency and Recency," *J. Psychol.*, **33**, 113–25 (1952)

183. Postman, L., and Crutchfield, R. S., "The Interaction of Need, Set, and Stimulus-Structure in a Cognitive Task," *Am. J. Psychol.*, **65**, 196–217 (1952)

184. Poulton, E. C., "The Basis of Perceptual Anticipation in Tracking," *Brit. J. Psychol. (Genet Sect.)*, **43**, 295–302 (1952)

185. Ratliff, F., "The Role of Physiological Nystagmus in Monocular Acuity," *J. Exptl. Psychol.*, **43**, 163–72 (1952)

186. Riesen, A. H., "Post-Partum Development of Behavior," *Chicago Med. School Quart.*, **13**, 17–24 (1951); (Unpublished data)

187. Riesen, A. H., Greenberg, B., Granston, A. S., and Fantz, R. L., "Solutions of Patterned String Problems by Young Gorillas," *J. Comp. and Physiol. Psychol.*, **46**, 19–22 (1953)

188. Riesen, A. H., Kurke, M. I., and Mellinger, J. C., "Interocular Transfer of Habits Learned Monocularly in Visually Naive and Visually Experienced Cats," *J. Comp. and Physiol. Psychol.*, **46**, 166–72 (1953)

189. Riise, P., "Results in Binocular Vision by Early Operation in Esotropia," *Acta Ophthalmol.*, **31**, 117–25 (1953)

190. Riopelle, A. J., Alper, R. G., Strong, P. N., and Ades, H. W., "Multiple Discrimination and Patterned String Performance of Normal and Temporal-Lobectomized Monkeys," *J. Comp. and Physiol. Psychol.*, **46**, 145–49 (1953)

191. Riopelle, A. J., and Bevan, W., Jr., "The Distribution of Scotopic Sensitivity in Human Vision," *Am. J. Psychol.*, **66**, 73–80 (1953)

192. Riopelle, A. J., and Stritch, T. M., "Placing Precision and Angle of Regard," *J. Exptl. Psychol.*, **44**, 407–9 (1952)

193. Rodman, S. I., Bair, D. R., Sugar, H. S., and McPhail, A., Symposium: "Intermittent Exotropia," *Am. Orthoptic J.*, **2**, 5–24 (1952) (Suppl. *Trans. Am. Acad. Ophthalmol. Otolaryngol.*)

194. Rose, H. W., "Monocular Depth Perception in Flying," *J. Aviation Med.*, **23**, 242–45 (1952)

195. Rouse, R. O., "Color and the Intensity-Time Relation," *J. Opt. Soc. Amer.*, **42**, 626–30 (1952)

196. Sabatini, R. W., "Vision—its Maturational and Perceptual Behavior," *Optometric Weekly*, **43**, 969–73 (1952)

197. Sandström, C. I., "Sex Differences in Localization and Orientation," *Acta Psychologica*, **9**, 82–96 (1953)

198. Schapiro, H. B., "Factors Affecting Legibility of Digits," *Tech. Rept. 52–127* (Wright Air Development Center, ARDC, USAF, Wright-Patterson Air Force Base, Ohio, 17 pp., 1952)

199. Schmidt, I., "Effect of Illumination in Testing Color Vision with Pseudo-Isochromatic Plates," *J. Opt. Soc. Amer.*, **42**, 951–55 (1952)

200. Schmidt, I., *Comparative Evaluation of the Hardy-Rand-Rittler Polychromatic Plates for Testing Color Vision, Project No. 21-31-013* (Air University, USAF School of Aviation Medicine, Randolph Field, Texas, 10 pp., 1952)

201. Schubert, G., and Bornschein, H., "Beitrag zur Analyze des menschlicken Elektroretinogramms," *Ophthalmologica*, **123**, 396–413 (1952)

202. Semmes, J., "Agnosia in Animal and Man," *Psychol. Rev.*, **60**, 140–47 (1953)

203. Sexton, M. S., Malone, F. L., and Farnsworth, D., *The Relative Detectability of Red-Purples, Reds, and Yellow-Reds, in Air-Sea Rescue* (Medical Research Laboratory Report No. 195, U. S. Naval Submarine Base, New London, Conn. 15 pp., March, 1952)

204. Siegel, A. I., "Interocular Transfer of a Visual Motor Task in Normally Reared and 'Hood-Reared' Ring Doves," *Am. Psychol.*, **7**, 242 (1952)
205. Siegel, A. I., "Deprivation of Visual Form Definition in the Ring Dove. I. Discriminatory Learning," *J. Comp. and Physiol. Psychol.*, **46**, 115–19 (1953)
206. Singer, J. L., "Personal and Environmental Determinants of Perception in a Size Constancy Experiment," *J. Exptl. Psychol.*, **43**, 420–27 (1952)
207. Sleight, R. B., "The Relative Discriminability of Several Geometric Forms," *J. Exptl. Psychol.*, **43**, 324–28 (1952)
208. Sleight, R. B., and Austin, T. R., "The Horizontal-Vertical Illusion in Plane Geometric Figures," *J. Psychol.*, **33**, 279–87 (1952)
209. Sleight, R. B., and Duvoisin, G., *An Annotated Bibliography of Form Perception* (JHU Report 166-1-153, Office of Naval Research, Washington, D. C., 28 pp., 1952)
210. Smith, W. M., "Past Experience and the Perception of Visual Size," *Am. J. Psychol.*, **65**, 389–403 (1952)
211. Smith, W. M., "Sensitivity to Apparent Movement in Depth as a Function of Stimulus Dimensionality," *J. Exptl. Psychol.*, **43**, 149–55 (1952)
212. Smith, W. M., "A Methodological Study of Size-Distance Perception," *J. Psychol.*, **35**, 143–53 (1953)
213. Snyder, F. W., and Pronko, N. H., *Vision with Spatial Inversion* (University of Wichita Press, Wichita, Kansas, 144 pp., 1952)
214. Solomon, R. L., and Postman, L., "Frequency of Usage as a Determinant of Recognition Thresholds for Words," *J. Exptl. Psychol.*, **43**, 195–201 (1952)
215. Solomon, P., and Werner, H., "Studies on Contour: III Negative After-Images," *Am. J. Psychol.*, **65**, 67–74 (1952)
216. Sorsby, A., *Genetics in Ophthalmology* (Butterworth & Co. Ltd., London, England and C. V. Mosby Co., St. Louis Mo., 251 pp., 1951)
217. Spragg, S. D. S., and Rock, M. L., "Dial Reading Performance as a Function of Brightness," *J. Appl. Psychol.*, **36**, 128–37 (1952)
218. Spragg, S. D. S., and Rock, M. L., "Dial Reading Performance as a Function of Color of Illumination," *J. Appl. Psychol.*, **36**, 196–200 (1952)
219. Stalder, H. I., and Lauer, A. R., *Effect of Pattern Distribution on Perception of Relative Motion in Low Levels of Illumination*, 25–35 (Highway Research Board Bull., 56, pp., Washington, D. C., 1952),
220. Steinitz, W., "Allgemeine Theorie der binocularen Raumwahrnehmung," *Psychol. Forsch.*, **24**, 93–132 (1952)
221. Taylor, F. W. R., "The Discrimination of Subliminal Visual Stimuli," *Can. J. Psychol.*, **7**, 12–20 (1953)
222. Teas, D. C., and Bitterman, M. E., "Perceptual Organization in the Rat," *Psychol. Rev.*, **59**, 130–40 (1952)
223. Thomson, L. C., "The Spectral Sensitivity of the Central Fovea," *J. Physiol.*, **112**, 114–32 (1951)
224. Tinker, M. A., "The Effect of Intensity of Illumination upon Speed of Reading Six-Point Italic Print," *Am. J. Psychol.*, **65**, 600–2 (1952)
225. Tousey, R., and Koomen, M. J., "The Visibility of Stars and Planets During Twilight," *J. Opt. Soc. Amer.*, **43**, 177–83 (1953)
226. Tresselt, M. E., and Simberg, A. L., "A Quantitative Experimental Investigation of the Phenomenon of Closure," *J. Gen. Psychol.*, **48**, 21–27 (1953)

227. Tschermak-Seysenegg, A. von, *Introduction to Physiological Optics*, (Boeder, P., Transl., Charles C Thomas, Springfield, Ill., 299 pp., 1952)

228. Turner, M. B., "The Relation of Preferences to Figural Reproductions," *Am. J. Psychol.*, **65**, 161–76 (1952)

229. Vernon, M. D., *A Further Study of Visual Perception* (Cambridge University Press, New York, N. Y., 289 pp., 1952)

230. Verplanck, W. S., Collier, G. H., and Cotton, J. W., "Nonindependence of Successive Responses in Measurements of the Visual Threshold," *J. Exptl. Psychol.*, **44**, 273–82 (1952)

231. Vukovich, V., and Müller, J., "Heterophorie und Binocularsehen," *Albrecht von Graefe's Arch. Ophthalmol.*, **153**, 83–92 (1952)

232. Wald, G., "Alleged Effects of the Near Ultraviolet on Human Vision," *J. Opt. Soc. Amer.*, **42**, 171–77 (1952)

233. Wallach, H., and O'Connell, D. N., "The Kinetic Depth Effect," *J. Exptl. Psychol.*, **45**, 205–17 (1953)

234. Walls, G. L., "Interocular Transfer of After-Images," *Am. J. Optometry*, **30**, 57–64 (1953)

235. Walls, G. L., "The Common-Sense Horopter," *Am. J. Optometry*, **29**, 460–77 (1952) ,

236. Walls, G. L., and Mathews, R. W., *New Means of Studying Color Blindness and Normal Foveal Color Vision* (University of California Press, Berkeley, Calif., 172 pp., 1952)

237. Walsh, E. G., "Visual Reaction Time and the α-Rhythm, an Investigation of a Scanning Hypothesis," *J. Physiol. (London)*, **118**, 500–8 (1952)

238. Weale, R. A., "Spectral Sensitivity and Wave-Length Discrimination of the Peripheral Retina," *J. Physiol. (London)*, **119**, 170–90 (1953)

239. Werner, H. and Wapner, S., "Experiments on Sensory-Tonic Field Theory of Perception: IV. Effect of Initial Position of a Rod on Apparent Verticality," *J. Exptl. Psychol.*, **43**, 68–74 (1952)

240. Wittreich, W. J., "The Honi Phenomenon: A Case of Selective Perceptual Distortion," *J. Abnormal Social Psychol.*, **47**, 705–12 (1952)

241. Wright, W. D., "The Characteristics of Tritanopia," *J. Opt. Soc. Amer.*, **42**, 509–21 (1952)

242. Wulfeck, J. W., *New Techniques for an Experimental Analysis of Accommodation Time* (Doctoral thesis, Univ. of Rochester, Rochester, N. Y., 129 pp., 1952)

243. Yokose, Z., and Uchiyama, M., "The Measurement of the Field-Forces in Visual Perception," *Japan. J. Psychol.*, **22**, 41–56 (1951)

244. Young, F. A., "Studies of the Projected After-Image: II The Projected Ground and the Projected Image. III. Projection over Large Distances," *J. Gen. Psychol.*, **47**, 195–205, 207–12 (1952)

245. Zaccaria, A., Jr., and Bitterman, M. E., "The Effect of Fluorescent Flicker on Visual Efficiency," *J. Appl. Psychol.*, **36**, 413–16 (1952)

246. Zetterström, B., "The Clinical Electroretinogram. IV. The Electroretinogram in Children during the First Year of Life," *Acta Ophthalmol.*, **29**, 295–304 (1951)

247. Zetterström, B., "The Electroretinogram in Prematurely Born Children," *Acta Ophthalmol.*, **30**, 405–8 (1952)

HEARING[1,2]

By James P. Egan[3]

The Hearing and Communication Laboratory, The Department of Psychology, Indiana University, Bloomington, Indiana

Auditory science continues its steady development in both its pure and applied aspects, and the past year has seen the publication of several important summaries that will help psychologists keep abreast with the advances in the knowledge about hearing. The recent *Handbook of Experimental Psychology* (96) continues to be the best single source for a detailed presentation of the facts and concepts of audition. Geldard (38) has provided us with a new general treatment of the senses, and the wealth of information organized by him shows how mature the study of sensation has become. Hirsh's book (49) presents the basic data and the fundamental concepts of selected areas of psychoacoustics and then shows how this material is related to the measurement of deafness. His discussions of auditory fatigue and recruitment are particularly welcomed, since these important topics have a widely scattered literature. For those psychologists interested in deafness and related problems, the quadrennial review of *Progress in Ophthalmology and Otolaryngology* (56) will be helpful. A collection of the papers read at the First International Course in Audiology held at Stockholm in September, 1950, constitutes two separate volumes of *Acta Oto-Laryngologica* (1). Taken as a group these paper provide an excellent source book for studies in audiology.

Fletcher's comprehensive monograph (29) in some 450 pages reports primarily the extensive researches conducted by investigators at the Bell Telephone Laboratories over the past 35 years. The concept of the critical band and its relation to hearing functions, the computation of the articulation index from a few physical and psychophysical parameters, Fletcher's space-time pattern theory of hearing, and many other facts and principles established since the first edition of 1929 are included. It is indeed fortunate that Dr. Fletcher has brought together in a single volume the monumental contributions made at the Bell Telephone Laboratories while he was Director of Acoustical Research.

Anatomy and Physiology

The fundamental advances toward our understanding of the mechanical and electrical dynamics of the cochlea have been crystallized in the splendid

[1] The survey of the literature to which this review pertains was completed in June, 1953.

[2] The following abbreviations were used in this review: DL (difference limen); SPL (sound pressure level); j.n.d. (just noticeable difference); MCL (most comfortable listening level).

[3] The writer acknowledges the aid of Mr. Edward C. Carterette in the preparation of this review.

review by Licklider (65). Thus, without slighting this important area of work, we shall examine only a few articles dealing with the anatomy and physiology of hearing.

Anatomy of the cochlea.—New techniques are being applied in a concerted effort to establish information on the detailed structure of the cochlear partition and the innervation of the organ of Corti. It is more evident than ever that a clear and final understanding of the events that transpire between the motion of the tympanic membrane and the discharge of the auditory nerve must rest upon the facts of the function and morphology of the observed physical elements themselves.

Wolff (113) provides us with a more complete evaluation of the superb work of Alfonso Corti (1851) and includes some of her own beautiful photographs on the microscopic anatomy of the cochlea. From her observations she believes that the tectorial membrane is attached at the so-called Hensen's node to the inner hair cells, and she expresses no doubt that the outer hair cells are imbedded in the tectorial membrane.

Katsuki & Covell (59) studied the organ of Corti under phase contrast microscopy. They throw doubt upon the function of Hensen's cells as supporting elements for the organ of Corti, provide further evidence that the hair cells are the most fragile components of the organ of Corti, and agree with Hilding's description of the tectorial membrane.

Engström & Wersäll (25) are studying by modern electron microscopical methods the structure of the outer hair cells of the inner ear.

For a very long time there has been controversy over the question as to whether the tectorial membrane is attached to the organ of Corti. The alterations produced by dissection and fixation have made it difficult to determine the precise microanatomy of the ear. Hilding (48) dissected some 130 temporal bones, mostly fresh, about 100 of which were from man. Whenever feasible, dissection was made immediately without fixation, and staining was done *in situ* with simple stains. According to his observations the tectorial membrane is inserted upon the organ of Corti and is in contact with the hairs of the hair cells. In certain preparations, the basilar membrane and the organ of Corti were made to rise and fall and the tectorial membrane rode upon the organ of Corti without apparent shearing motion at right angles to the long axis of the cochlear partition. Certain important properties of the tectorial membrane were determined. The following theory was then proposed. Because the fibrils of the tectorial membrane are almost parallel and are directed toward the apex and outwardly, and because the tectorial membrane is nonelastic in the longitudinal direction but is elastic in the transverse direction, an extended movement of the tectorial and the basilar membranes will nevertheless result in a shearing force between these two membranes at only a small locus of flexure as the travelling wave proceeds down the cochlea. If Hilding's model is correct, it provides a mechanical sharpening mechanism for frequency resolution by the cochlea. [See (65, pp. 89–92).]

Certain dimensions of the cochlea are important for understanding its mechanical and electrical action. Fernández (26) provides data for the guinea pig similar to those published by Wever (108) for man. Some of the dimensions plotted as a function of the distance along the basilar membrane for the cochlea of the guinea pig are: the distance across Rosenthal's canal and the osseous spiral lamina, the width and thickness of the basilar membrane, the cross sectional area of the three channels of the cochlea, and the angles formed by the axes of the outer and inner hair cells with one another and with the basilar membrane.

Spatial origin of the cochlear microphonic.—Tasaki & Fernândez (99) developed techniques by which they could (*a*) record simultaneously electrical responses from different turns of the guinea pig cochlea, (*b*) perfuse the cochlea with chemicals (potassium chloride), and (*c*) polarize the sensory endings in the cochlea by D.C. Very fine electrodes were introduced into a given turn of the cochlea, one into the scala vestibuli and the other into the scala tympani (differential recording); great care was taken to avoid injury to the scala media. Reversible changes in the magnitude of the cochlear microphonic and nerve potentials were induced with a perfusion of the canals with a potassium chloride solution, or by a polarizing D.C. across the cochlear partition. The potentials recorded were shown to arise from activity in the neighborhood of the electrodes and to be independent of the cochlear microphonic originating in other turns of the cochlea. It was shown that the cochlear microphonic is generated in the basal turn in response to both low and high frequencies, whereas the third and apical turns respond only to low frequencies. Previous investigators who have recorded the aural microphonics as a function of the stimulating frequency with one electrode on the round window and the other on the neck evidently were not obtaining information about the activity of the cochlea in the upper turns. Obviously, this is not to say that the electrical activity recorded at the round window is uninformative, for example, see Heise & Rosenblith (46).

Neural activity of the medial geniculate body.—Galambos *et al.* (33, 35, 87) present in detail the results of their meticulous exploration with microelectrodes of the potentials whose origin was shown to be in the neural structures of the pars principalis of the medial geniculate body in cats. Of their major findings we mention only those concerned with the latency, the intensity, suppression (masking), and the tonotopic organization of the neural activity of the medial geniculate body. (*a*) Latency: the first sign of electrical activity after an acoustic click occurs at about 6 msec. with a small range of latencies, and spike potentials arise at about 10 msec. It is estimated that the major afferent volley to the medial geniculate in response to a sharp click is temporally dispersed about 10 times by the acoustic pathway. (*b*) Intensity of acoustic click: As stimulus intensity increases, the latency decreases and the percentage of clicks that evoke spikes rises from zero to a maximum (80 to 100 per cent) in about 20 db. (*c*) Suppression: At the medial geniculate, one of the most striking effects of pure tone stimuli is their suppression of the electrical response due to a click. (*d*): Tonotopic organization: Pure tone audiograms on medial geniculate units indicate that the typical element responds to a relatively wide range of frequencies at its threshold intensity.

The range of effective frequencies becomes even wider as the stimulus intensity is increased. These latter results are not in accord with data from other lines of investigation which have indicated tonotopic organization.

Hearing and cochlear lesions.—Schuknecht & Neff (91) provide new information as to the effect upon hearing in cats of surgical insult to the receptor and neural elements in the apical region of the cochlea. The absolute thresholds for pure tones were determined by avoidance conditioning both before and after the cochlea was entered with a very small needle. The cochleas were examined histologically. When damage to the hair cells was confined to the apical region, audiograms showed that the principal hearing loss was below 1000 c.p.s. As the damage became more extensive, sensitivity at the higher frequencies was also diminished.

Hearing and cortical lesions.—Further evidence on the complex organization of the different areas of the auditory cortex involved in frequency and intensity discrimination was published by Meyer & Woolsey (76). The original article must be consulted to appreciate the high caliber of this research, and only the principal results can be given here. Cats were trained to respond to a small change in the frequency (in some cases, intensity) of a pure tone of 1000 c.p.s. Then, bilaterally symmetrical cortical ablations of various combinations of auditory area I, auditory area II, somatic area II, and the posterior ectosylvian gyrus were made. Retraining was then undertaken. The results show that it is possible, through surgical intervention, to dissociate frequency from intensity discrimination. Removal of all the combined areas listed above abolished frequency discrimination but left intensity discrimination relatively unimpaired. Ablations of less than all these areas did not result in quantitative deterioration of frequency discrimination.

Toxic effects of streptomycin.—Large doses of streptomycin in its present form result in damage to the sensory epithelium of the vestibular and auditory apparatus. Space permits only references (10, 43, 44, 90, 102).

Psychophysics of Thresholds and Attributes

Absolute sensitivity and Brownian motion.—Under ideal conditions for the detection of a signal, certain of our sense organs respond to an incredibly small amount of energy. In fact, the random fluctuations of pressure on a membrane as a result of Brownian noise in the air is not far below the pressure required at the absolute threshold of hearing at 2000 c.p.s. De Vries (22) points out that in the consideration of the energetics of the threshold, the important quantity is the Brownian motion of the eardrum, because this membrane is not only acted upon by Brownian noise of the air, but it is coupled to a system (the middle and inner ear) that generates Brownian noise. His calculations show that Brownian motion at the eardrum is above the measured threshold. He then reasons that since the threshold is determined in the presence of Brownian noise, the actual threshold energy is the sum of the measured stimulus energy and the Brownian motion. De Vries then goes on to consider the Brownian motion in the inner ear, and his calculations show that at threshold the power from the stimulus available to a single hair cell (if not amplified) is far below that attributable to the Brownian motion in the cells. The observations by Davis *et al.* (18) and by Békésy (5, 6) establish the existence of D.C. potentials across and within the cochlear partition which are maintained continuously by the metabolism of the sensory cells. Amplification of the stimulus energy is thus possible, and the energy available for excitation of the nerves may greatly exceed the energy from the acoustic stimulus. De Vries holds that electrically the cells are rigidly coupled in parallel so that the electrical effects of Brownian motion of an individual cell are distributed and therefore suppressed. On the other hand, a stimulus moves a number of cells in phase and the potentials generated act together.

The audibility curve.—The accurate calibration of audiometers requires that the procedure for measuring the threshold of hearing in terms of minimum audible pressure be standardized, and that a large group of normal listeners be tested by this procedure over the entire audible range. Dadson & King (17) report on their progress in the standardization of audiometers and procedures for determining the absolute threshold. It is hoped that such data will establish a standard reference zero based on the normal ear. Their results are in excellent agreement with those reported below by Wheeler & Dickson, and in substantial agreement over the range 250 to 8000 c.p.s. with the results of Sivian & White for minimum audible pressure (94). Dadson & King's data show greater sensitivity outside this range. Histograms at each frequency tested show how the absolute thresholds are distributed. Wheeler & Dickson (109) considered carefully the factors that are important in the standardization of audiometry. Their subjects were males with normal ears between the ages of 18 and 23. The precision measurements were made from 256 to 8192 c.p.s., and frequency distributions of absolute thresholds based on 1028 ears are shown graphically.

Heise (45) determined for the pigeon the absolute thresholds for pure tones and for white noise by an operant conditioning technique. Sensitivity to pure tones was similar to that of human subjects at low frequencies, but the thresholds for the pigeons increased abruptly above 4000 c.p.s.

Free-field versus ear canal pressures: the missing 6 db.—In a series of experiments, Munson & Wiener (79) have tried to resolve the mystery of the missing 6 db (9, 89, 94). The problem is simply this: at low frequencies, below about 300 c.p.s., an earphone must generate a greater sound pressure in the ear canal than a free-field sound pressure that has the same sensory effect. The explanation of this difference is difficult because the human head is very small compared to the wave lengths of these low frequencies, and therefore diffraction effects are negligible (110, 111). Furthermore, even when the sound pressure is measured in the ear canal for the two conditions of listening, there is the discrepancy of at least 6 db in order to produce the same response. From Thévenin's theorem one would expect that the single ear would not care whether the sound pressure was generated by an earphone or by a loudspeaker. But somehow the listener takes the difference in the source of the sound into account and thereby requires a difference in intensity of about

6 db in judging the two sounds equivalent. Now, at the quiet absolute threshold this difference in the energy required between listening to an earphone and to a loudspeaker might be the result of the masking effect of physiological noises, such as the rush of blood and the pounding of the heart, or of the seashell effect created by the presence of the earphone and muscle tremor (13). But at higher intensities of the stimulus these masking noises are negligible, and equal loudness matches between a tone from an earphone and a tone of the same frequency from a loudspeaker end up with 6 db missing.

In addition to (*a*) the hypothesis of masking by self-noise, Munson & Wiener consider the following factors that might be responsible for the discrepancy at higher stimulus intensities. (*b*) The hypothesis of poor receiver fit—that the low frequency leak was less during the measurements of the sound pressure by the use of a probe tube than during the loudness balance. But in their new experiments the sound pressure was measured during the progress of the loudness balance, and the hypothesis discarded because the pressure difference was still about 6 db. (*c*) That the static pressure attributable to the application of the earphone to the ear might be responsible was abandoned because they found that this static pressure diminishes rapidly to less than 1 mm. of mercury during a loudness test. (*d*) The middle ear muscles might contract when an earphone is applied to the pinna. Their experiments on this point make it an unlikely factor.

Munson & Wiener also report the following experiment. Earphones are worn throughout a series of loudness balances. The listener matches in loudness a tone generated by the earphones to a tone of the same frequency that is generated by a loudspeaker but which reaches the receptors by leaking under the receiver caps or by any other available path. Probe tubes (78), inserted into the ear canals with the earphones on the ears, measure the sound pressures during the loudness balance. In one experiment, no significant differences were found between the sound pressures from the two sources. But in a later experiment the sound pressure under the earphone was again about 6 db greater when the sound was coming from the earphone than when the tone was leaking into the ear canal from the loudspeaker. It is probably important that the experimenters could not conceal from the listener the source of the sound. This last experiment and its replication with their disconcerting results still leave us with a baffling problem.

Related to the problem just discussed are Benson's (8) cautions regarding the calibration and use of probe-tube microphones.

Masking.—Webster *et al.* (107) secured the masked absolute thresholds for pure tones in the presence of a thermal noise that had the energy rejected over part of the frequency scale. For a noise with a gap that is one octave in width, a sinusoidal signal at the center of the gap is just audible when its intensity is about 25 db less than that required in the presence of unfiltered noise. These results are of practical interest, because a steady noise with a gap in it might be used to make transient, extraneous noises less distracting without reducing the audibility of the signal. They also measured the change in pitch of pure tones near the abrupt slopes in the noise spectrum, and their results agreed substantially with earlier findings.

Frequency discrimination.—The arduous task of measuring the smallest change in frequency or intensity that can be detected by the human listener needs to be undertaken from time to time. Our techniques improve, and our understanding of auditory discrimination enables us to define more precisely just how the data should be secured. For over 20 years the data of Shower & Biddulph (93) have been used to define the resolving power of the ear with respect to frequency. These investigators employed a form of frequency modulation, and it has never been clear that their results were obtained under stimulus conditions that exhaust the listener's capacity for frequency discrimination. Harris (41) has given the questions of stimulus control, psychophysical method, and training of subjects careful consideration and has provided us with new data on pitch discrimination at various frequencies from 60 to 4000 c.p.s. Below 1000 c.p.s., his results differ substantially from Shower & Biddulph's, and it seems clear that different auditory functions are measured by the two studies being discussed. The present writer would maintain that Harris' stimulus conditions are preferred over Shower & Biddulph's for the purpose of defining pitch discrimination.

Auditory flutter.—Pollack (83) furthered our understanding of auditory flutter (*a*) by measuring thresholds of detection of changes in the rate of interruption of a white noise, (*b*) by constructing a psychological scale of auditory flutter, and (*c*) by determining the accuracy of estimation of the rate of interruption. With this information at hand, Pollack considered the question of whether the neural mechanism underlying the perception of auditory flutter is substitutive or additive. Since the subjective size of the j.n.d.[2] of auditory flutter is roughly proportional to the number of j.n.d.'s above threshold, he concludes that the neural mechanism for the perception of a periodically interrupted white noise is more like that of loudness (additive) than like that of pitch (substitutive).

Loudness of noise.—Pollack (84) determined equal loudness contours for bands of noise and found that these contours are closely similar to those for pure tones. He measured also the contribution to the loudness of noise made by various frequency bands over a wide range of noise levels. Near the quiet absolute threshold, the stimulus is slightly more effective if the noise energy is concentrated in a narrow frequency band than if it is spread over a wider band. However, above threshold, a noise of constant band pressure level (constant overall S.P.L.[2]) is louder if the energy is scattered along the frequency scale than if it is concentrated. Pollack interprets his findings by employing the assumption that the displacement of the basilar membrane is a nonlinear function of the mechanical excitation. He assumes that a narrow band of noise quickly overloads the system, whereas, with a wider band of noise, frequency analysis of the cochlea results in less displacement and less overload at any given point.

Another explanation might be, however, that the overload or nonlinearity comes about from the distribution of thresholds of elements in the various neural channels. The all-or-none pulses in the nerve fibers that represent the energy concentrated in a given frequency region of the acoustic stimulus soon reach a maximal rate (34), and it might be that the spreading of the excitation along the basilar membrane brings in more responding fibers than does an increase in intensity at a given locus. This latter interpretation does not assume mechanical overload until more intense levels of excitation are reached. It is here offered as an alternative interpretation to that of Pollack's because he found that the weakest intensity at which it is more effective to spread the noise frequencies than to concentrate them is far below the intensity at which the cochlear microphonic begins to show overload.

Volume of noise.—Thomas (101) extended his earlier investigation of the volume of pure tones (100) to the volume of bands of noise. Bands of noise of various widths were compared with a narrow, standard band with respect to both loudness and volume. The equal-loudness equations differed systematically from those of equal volume. As a band of noise is increased in width, its band pressure level must be decreased in order to maintain equal loudness, and then it must be further decreased in intensity in order to maintain equal volume with the narrow, standard band. The results based on the loudness matches agree substantially with those obtained by Pollack (84).

Three articles (37, 57, 106) on the effect of interaural phase differences on the masked thresholds and the perception of pure tones must be left for a later reviewer.

Auditory Fatigue

Auditory fatigue does not refer to a specific state or condition of the end-organ and nerves. The defining operation merely consists in a measured increase in the quiet absolute threshold following stimulation. Auditory fatigue, defined in this way, can be obtained under a wide range of stimulus conditions, but it now appears unlikely that the mechanisms responsible for the threshold changes are the same for the various conditions. Zwislocki & Pirodda (114) provide a convincing argument for distinguishing between adaptation (short-duration auditory fatigue or residual masking) and transient acoustic trauma (temporary hearing loss or stimulation deafness). If the threshold shift is measured at a number of frequencies following exposure to a pure tone, a curve showing the spread of adaptation or fatigue is obtained. Their experimental analysis indicates that adaptation has the following characteristics: The maximum amount of adaptation occurs at the frequency of the fatiguing pure tone and is even found after stimulation with very weak intensities. Furthermore, immediately (within 50 msec.) after cessation of intense stimulation with a pure tone, the greatest threshold shift occurs at the frequency of the fatiguing stimulus. Transient acoustic trauma, as the authors term it, is greatest about one half octave above the fatiguing stimulus. It is evident only after relatively intense stimulation and after a rest period. The acoustic trauma persists much longer than the threshold shift resulting from adaptation. Zwislocki & Pirodda conclude that adaptation depends upon a decrease in the sensitivity of the sensory cells and of the peripheral nerve fibers, whereas transient acoustic trauma has its locus in the sensory cells.

Since complete recovery is obtained even with severe temporary hearing losses, it is not yet clear whether permanent acoustic trauma is an extension of the same process as transient acoustic trauma, or is a different type of injury, such as an anatomical dislocation of the hair cells.

Rawnsley & Harris (85) have continued their studies of short-duration auditory fatigue. In the present study they investigated the effect of the intensity of the fatiguing stimulus on the degree of fatigue with the recovery interval as a parameter. With short intervals of time between the cessation of the fatiguing stimulus and the onset of the test tone, fatigue is demonstrable after stimulation for only 400 msec. at a sensation level of only 10 db. From such data it is possible to plot the course of recovery from auditory fatigue. Their data show that at low fatiguing intensities the amount of fatigue (threshold shift) is independent of the duration of the fatiguing stimulus, and this result is in support of the contention of Zwislocki & Pirodda that short-duration auditory fatigue is a different process from transient acoustic trauma.

Rawnsley & Harris (86) attempted to determine the "tuning" of the cochlea by measuring in considerable detail the spread of fatigue (or residual masking) to frequencies closely adjacent to the fatiguing tone. The fatiguing tone was sounded for 435 msec. After a silent interval of 35 msec., the test tone (50 msec. in duration) was presented. They found nearly uniform fatigue from 990 through 1010 c.p.s. following exposure to a fatiguing stimulus of 1000 c.p.s. However, since the tone used to test for a threshold shift was of very short duration, it consisted of a narrow band of energy. If the cochlea had infinite resolving power, the curves relating fatigue to the center frequency of such a test stimulus would have a broad maximum about as wide as that of the test stimulus. Hence, the authors should not be disturbed by the lack of sharp "tuning" as measured by their technique.

Hirsh & Ward (51) studied the recovery of the absolute threshold after strong acoustical stimulation. The most important aspect of their results is that the recovery from fatigue is not always a simple monotonic function, but is in many cases diphasic. A typical diphasic recovery curve shows an initial rapid recovery occupying about 1 min., with a subsequent rise in the threshold followed by its slow return to normal. Such recovery curves are most apparent when the fatiguing stimulus is of low frequency, especially 500 c.p.s. In the first experiments a click was used to trace the course of recovery from fatigue. Since this click had a broad spectrum, the recovery from fatigue was also investigated by measuring the absolute threshold for bands of noise each 250 mels wide, and for pure tones. With a fatiguing stimulus of 500 c.p.s., 120 db S.P.L., and 3 min. of stimulation, it was found that the bounce or diphasic character of the recovery curve shows up most clearly for bands of noise, and for pure tones, between 1000 and 5000 c.p.s. Many of their diphasic recovery curves show that the absolute threshold at the maximum of the bounce is greater than the threshold measured immediately after cessation of the fatiguing stimulus. Wide individual differences are reported as to the degree of the bounce in the recovery curve, but its consistent appearance for certain subjects upon repetition of the same conditions establishes that the process of recovery from fatigue is in these cases complex. Although there were important differences between the procedures used by Hood (52) and those used in this study, nevertheless it is surprising that Hood did not record diphasic recovery curves. Only further research can resolve this discrepancy.

Sensori-Neural Deafness

Until recently, it was accepted doctrine that peripheral deafness, as opposed to central deafness, could be classified into two distinct types. Pure conductive deafness, or transmission-deafness, results from disturbances in the mechanical transmission system. In the treatment of transmission-deafness, the hearing loss can be successfully considered as identical with the insertion of an equivalent attenuation in a communication circuit terminated by the normal ear. Nerve or "perceptive" deafness results from sensori-neural dysfunction. In many cases of nerve deafness, the resulting hearing loss cannot be compensated for by an increase in the gain of a linear communication circuit, because the rate of change of loudness with respect to intensity is greater in these cases than for the normal listener. For over 15 years, the accepted explanation of this phenomenon of loudness recruitment has been in terms of the loss of sensori-neural units that become an increasingly smaller percentage of the total number of activated fibers as stimulus intensity increases. Injury to the hair cells has been considered physiologically equivalent to injury to the VIIIth cranial nerve (97, p. 288).

The recent studies, principally from the clinic, may force us to abandon this simple theory of recruitment and to recognize three types of peripheral deafness: transmission-deafness, cochlear or scalar deafness, and VIIIth nerve or neural deafness. At the same time these investigations may provide psychophysical tests that will help the clinician to differentiate a lesion or malfunction in the hair cells from damage to the VIIIth nerve.

The distinction between these three possible type of peripheral deafness revolves about the phenomenon of loudness recruitment. Transmission-deafness may be distinguished from sensori-neural deafness by a comparison of the absolute thresholds obtained by bone and by air conduction. Theoretically, measures of recruitment are unnecessary to establish whether or not the increased threshold of hearing is a result of transmission loss or to hair cell and nerve injury. However, the phenomenon of recruitment appears at the moment to provide a means of distinguishing scalar from VIIIth nerve disturbances.

It now seems that loudness recruitment is correlated with cochlear or scalar disturbances, especially with damage to the hair cells, whereas in VIIIth nerve injury recruitment is partial or absent. Most of the cases to be reported of cochlear disturbances with probable hair cell involvement are those with Ménière's disease, in which the cardinal symptoms are vertigo, tinnitus, and deafness. In their fundamental research, Dix, Hallpike & Hood (23) state that the structural changes in the inner ear found in Ménière's disease are limited to Corti's organ, and that the nerve fibers and cells of the spiral ganglion are normal. In their 30 cases with Ménière's disease, loudness recruitment was present and complete.

In order to study the effect on hearing of lesions in the VIIIth nerve, patients with tumors of the cerebellopontine angle have been given various tests, both direct and indirect, of recruitment. Dix *et al.* (23) reported that recruitment was absent in 14 of their 20 cases of VIIIth nerve degeneration.

Because of the great importance of these phenomena, both in their theoretical and clinical aspects, several papers dealing with this topic will be reviewed in detail and at least brief comment devoted to several others. Important papers not reviewed here are Flett (30), Fowler & Zeckel (31), Furstenberg (32), Lempert *et al.* (64), Lindsay (66), Lindsay *et al.* (67), McKenzie (74), and Williams (112). These studies have appeared over the past two years.

Measures of recruitment.—The direct measure of recruitment in terms of loudness balances is tedious, time-consuming, and not always possible. Many other measures which might indicate recruitment have been explored and several found valuable. The ensuing discussion will be clarified by a summary of the principal measures of recruitment which show characteristic differences in the two types of deafness (see Table I). For a more complete list and discussion of these measures, see Garner (36), Hirsh (49), and Harris (42).

The new clinical evidence.—Eby & Williams (24) employed Fowler's "alternate binaural loudness balance test," in the study of (*a*) 32 patients with unilateral deafness in which the diagnosis was Ménière's disease (end-organ lesion), (*b*) one case with unilateral deafness considered to be the result of a vascular accident involving the organ of Corti, and (*c*) 16 patients with unilateral auditory nerve deafness attributable to a variety of causes.

Consider first the 33 cases whose deafness was presumably a result of lesions of the end-organ. Loudness recruitment was present in all cases and was incomplete in only two of the 33; diplacusis binauralis dysharmonica was present in 23 of the 27 cases tested. In 15 of the 17 tested for speech intelligibility with phonetically balanced lists, the per cent correctly received reached a maximum and then declined. The range between the threshold for speech reception and the most comfortable listening level (MCL)[2] was narrowed to 18 db. The threshold of discomfort for speech was within the limits of their audiometric scale in all cases tested.

In eight of the 16 cases with auditory nerve deafness, the diagnosis of nerve fiber involvement was substantiated by the operative findings. For these eight cases, VIIIth nerve tumors and lesions in the cerebellopontine angle were found. Loudness recruitment was not present for these eight cases, and only partial recruitment occurred in three of the remaining eight patients. Diplacusis binauralis was not found in 15 of the 16 tested. In five of the six cases given speech tests, the articulation scores continued to improve up to the limit of the intensity of the audiometric scale. The MCL

TABLE I[4]

The Typical Results of Measures of Recruitment that Seem to Distinguish Scalar from VIIIth Nerve Deafness

Measure	Scalar Deafness	VIIIth Nerve Deafness
Binaural loudness balance	Rapid growth of loudness: recruitment	Normal growth of loudness: no recruitment
Equal-loudness contour	Near normal at high intensities	Same aberrant contour as shown at threshold
Variability of absolute threshold (Békésy audiogram)	Small variability at frequencies which show recruitment	Normal variability
Difference limen for intensity near threshold	Same size as at high sensation levels	Same as normal ear at low sensation levels
Short-duration auditory fatigue	Greater fatigue corresponding to greater loudness	Amount of fatigue same as normal ear with same sensation levels
Diplacusis binauralis	Marked pitch distortion	Little pitch distortion
Hearing loss for speech	Not discriminative	Not discriminative
Discrimination loss for speech	Marked loss, which increases with increasing intensity	Loss relatively constant as intensity increases

was wider for this group with nerve fiber deafness than for the 33 with end-organ damage. It averaged 29 db. The threshold of discomfort was beyond the limit of the audiometric scale.

This study with its excellent case material gives clear support to the thesis that scalar deafness has different effects on hearing from neural deafness.

Lüscher (71) in a paper based on extensive experience in the detection of recruitment by measurement of the DL[2] for intensity further documented the thesis that the presence of recruitment generally indicates a cochlear lesion. Considerable evidence is added to previous data that show the identical behavior of recruitment and the DL for intensity. In another paper

[4] It must be stressed that this Table is presented primarily to contrast the (probable) differences between two types of sensorineural deafness. Cases showing inconsistent results have been reported which are, perhaps, attributable to mixed deafness, but the data do not permit any final conclusions. Of those measures listed, short-duration auditory fatigue is the least documented for the differential diagnosis of scalar and VIIIth nerve deafness.

Lüscher & Zwislocki (72) compared the results of their technique, which employs amplitude modulation for measuring the DL for intensity, with that used by Denes & Naunton (21), and prefer the use of amplitude modulation in the detection of recruitment.

Jerger (58) simplified Lüscher's technique for the determination of the DL for intensity, standardized his procedure on 39 normal ears and then administered this test to 89 cases showing hearing losses. Of these 89, 15 were pure conductive cases who showed DLs of the same magnitude as the normal ear. The remaining 74 cases comprised the group showing a sensori-neural loss of which 53 had abnormally small DLs, thus indicating recruitment. The otological diagnosis, made independently of Jerger's tests, support the contention that the DL is small in acoustic trauma, Ménière's disease, and endogenous deafness. Normal DLs were found in cases diagnosed as cerebellopontine angle tumor, streptomycin damage, and disorders of the central nervous system.

Lund-Iversen (70) determined the DL for 10 normal and 71 deaf individuals. These measurements apparently were made with the stimulus 40 db above the patient's threshold, and no differences in the size of the DLs were found. It would seem that the DL for intensity will indicate recruitment best if the measurement is carried out at low sensation levels. At high intensities the DL for the recruiting ear will be nearly the same as for the normal ear.

In three of the above studies (58, 70, 71), abnormally large DLs were reported in a few cases. There seems to be agreement that these large DLs have no peripheral organic basis for the indicated hearing loss.

Hood (53), and Hallpike & Hood (40), have continued their studies of auditory fatigue and its relationship to clinical tests of deafness. It will be recalled (52) that in Hood's study of perstimulatory auditory fatigue, a loudness balance was made with the two ears simultaneously stimulated, but with the fatiguing tone having been on for a period of time. The considerable degree of fatigue measured in this way contrasts with the absence of fatigue measured by matching two tones alternately presented, one to each ear. Hood explains the difference in the results obtained by these two methods in terms of the on-effect. In their more recent reports (40, 53), the auditory fatigue of normal and deaf individuals was determined by continuous and simultaneous stimulation of both ears. Of course, in the normal listener, no fatigue is demonstrable by this technique, since one ear fatigues as rapidly as the other. In unilateral transmission-deafness, as fatigue proceeds, no change in stimulus intensity in the normal ear is required to balance the loudness of the tone in the deaf ear. The initial loudness balance introduces a difference in intensity between the two ears such that the mechanical excitation in the two cochleas is the same. From then on, fatigue proceeds in the ear with transmission-deafness at the same rate as in the normal ear. A very different result is obtained when this procedure in employed in cases of unilateral Ménière's disease. Here, the difference is absolute thresholds between the normal and impaired ear still shows up in loudness balances made at low stimulus intensities. But, as the two tones continue to sound, one in each ear, fatigue proceeds more rapidly in the impaired ear than in the normal, and the intensity in the normal ear must be decreased for a loudness balance. When high stimulus levels are employed, only a small difference in intensity is initially required for a loudness balance, and this fact is recruitment in the impaired ear. However, as stimulation continues the final balancing intensity in the normal ear must be reduced so much that little or no recruitment is manifest. They conclude that over a period of continuous stimulation the phenomenon of loudness recruitment in Ménière's disease is transient, and that in the adapted ear the impairment is still measureable at high stimulus intensities.

Pirodda & Zwislocki (82) continued the study of short-duration auditory fatigue as a measure of the recruitment phenomenon. They conclude that the measurement of fatigue over a considerable range of frequencies is necessary for adequate demonstration of the presence of recruitment. They believe that this testing technique is probably too protracted for practical purposes of routine testing.

In a detailed and thorough monograph, Lundborg (69) evaluated the variability of the absolute threshold (Békésy audiograms) obtained on 72 cases with different types of sensori-neural deafness. In scalar lesions or end-organ deafness (acoustic trauma or Ménière's disease), the Békésy audiogram indicated complete recruitment, while in retrocochlear lesions of the auditory pathways (intracranial tumor) the majority of the audiograms indicated absence of recruitment.

Kristensen & Jepsen (61) also stress the importance of determining the presence or absence of recruitment in the differential diagnosis between Ménière's disease and acoustic neurinoma.

The numerous investigations concerned with loudness recruitment make it clear how interrelated are the various functions of hearing; for example, Bocca (11) has described a new test for the diagnosis of various types of peripheral deafness. The intensity of a temporally continuous noise is increased until it just masks a tone of 15 db (sensation level). The noise is then interrupted at a rate of one per second and the subject can usually again hear the tone. The rate of interruption is increased without altering the burst intensity until the tone is again just masked (see also, 77). This critical rate of interruption turns out to be the same in cases of conduction and VIIIth nerve deafness as in the normal. In the cases of cochlear deafness, but with the exception of those with Ménière's disease, the critical rate was much lower than the normal.

In several of the investigations on loudness recruitment the phenomenon of hyper- or over-recruitment is reported. For an equal loudness match, less stimulus intensity is required for the recruiting ear than for the normal, contralateral ear. Such over-recruitment is never more than a few decibels. Harris (42) says that there is no good explanation of this phenomenon of over-recruitment. However, Hirsh (49, p. 219) points out that if the "normal" ear has a slight transmission loss, say 5 db, and if at high intensities equal mechanical excitation in the two cochleas is required for equal loudness, then the "normal" ear with a slight transmission-deafness will require a greater intensity of the stimulus, by 5 db in this example, than that required for the deafened, completely recruiting ear.

The relation between the intelligibility of speech and the intensity at which it is received (articulation-gain function) provides important diagnostic information. In pure transmission-deafness, the articulation-gain function is simply translated with unaltered form with respect to the axis that represents the intensity of received speech. In sensori-neural deafness, however, the function is not only translated with respect to intensity, but the maximum articulation score is considerably less than for the normal ear. The loss in discrimination for speech cannot be compensated for by increasing the intensity of the speech.

Huizing & Reyntjes (54) provide further evidence that the articulation-gain function for the ear showing marked recruitment reaches a maximum and then declines as the intensity of speech is increased. The recruitment phenomenon results in a rapid growth of loudness as speech is increased in intensity. However, the severe distortion correlated with recruitment apparently causes a decline in the intelligibility of speech.

Azzi (3), in a lengthy discussion of speech audiometry, also reports this third type of articulation-gain function.

Cawthorne & Harvey (15) found that the articulation gain-function for 37 out of 40 cases with Ménière's disease reached a maximum and immediately declined. The decrease in the percentage of words recognized as the speech intensity was increased was so great that they describe the function as "hump-backed." In these cases, the pure tone audiogram often showed only a moderate loss, and this loss was usually uniform with frequency. Cases with severe traumatic deafness also showed the "hump-backed" articulation curve. Day (20) states that the pure tone audiogram does not nearly describe the great difficulty in understanding of speech that certain patients show with Ménière's disease. Day points out that roaring tinnitus and distortion attributable (probably) to severe recruitment conspire to reduce markedly the ability to understand conversational speech. Barber & Ireland (4) concur with Day that the final assessment of retained hearing should not be based on the patient's ability merely to detect the presence of a stimulus, and Knight & Littler (60) believe that it is generally more satisfactory to evaluate the speech audiogram itself than to predict it from the pure tone audiogram. Some of the procedures and advantages of speech audiometry are pointed out by Walsh (105). He also reported that recruitment or over-recruitment was present in almost every case of Ménière's disease. The discrimination loss was universally high. In many cases these high discrimination losses were in contrast to the relatively moderate hearing loss. Furthermore, an end-organ lesion seems to be indicated by a high discrimination loss with a relatively small hearing loss for speech.

Bocca & Pellegrini (12) obtained articulation-gain functions with normals in which various types of deafness were simulated by using frequency selective circuits both with and without expansion. They matched the frequency selective circuits to the audiograms and in many cases the resulting articulation curves for the normal ears obtained with frequency distortion and expansion resembled those of patients with frequency distortion and recruitment (expansion?) arising from disorders of the ear. They believe that the marked frequency distortion present in patients showing high-tone deafness is compensated for by recruitment, especially in the reception of meaningful words. Studies of this type are far too rare and this writer believes that a more complete understanding of deafness would be achieved by simulating deafness in its various forms by means of communication circuits and masking noises.

The methods developed by Fletcher for calculating articulation scores for communication systems both with and without noise, but for normal listeners, are applied (28) after simplification to the perception of speech by persons with abnormal hearing. There is little question that the hearing loss for speech (threshold shift in decibels) can be predicted from the pure tone audiogram with considerable accuracy from well-known formulae. To predict, as Fletcher wishes to do, the entire course of the articulation curve using difficult test items for cases with either nerve or mixed deafness is quite another matter. The articulation index is obtained as a product of four factors: the frequency distortion (relative response at different frequencies), the sensation level of the speech sounds, the ear (amplitude) distortion which depends on how near the sounds are to the threshold of feeling, and the proficiency factor which depends on how well the listener knows the speech sounds. Both bone and air conduction audiograms for pure tones are needed so that the degree of transmission-deafness and nerve-deafness may be evaluated separately. The effect of transmission-deafness is taken as identical with a loss in gain, and the effect of nerve-deafness is considered to be identical with the effect of masking in the normal ear. The computations are made by applying appropriate weighting functions to each of six frequencies. The details are too involved to present here. The agreement between the calculated and obtained scores is fairly good, but a final evaluation of the generality of Fletcher's methods must wait until data are obtained from patients known to have either scalar or VIIIth nerve lesions. From the reports already reviewed, it would seem that an additional factor that handles marked recruitment will be required in certain instances of scalar deafness.

Very little work has been reported on animal research on labyrinthine hydrops. One interesting study is that of Fernández, Ludwig & McAuliffe (27) who were interested in standardizing the procedure of electrocoagulation of the vestibule in the treatment of hydrops of the labyrinth. They recorded the cochlear microphonic and action potentials both before and after various forms of surgical insult to the membranous labyrinth of guinea pigs, and then examined the structures histologically. The increases in the electrical "thresholds," both cochlear microphonic and action potential, correlated well with the degree of injury to the hair cells.

This topic of recruitment and types of deafness has been discussed at length because of its great importance, not only to the clinic, but to the sensory psychologist. If it turns out that two distinct types of sensori-neural deafness must be recognized, then new evidence may be forthcoming to help us solve such problems as the mechanism of stimulation of the auditory nerve cells, the physiological basis of loudness, diplacusis binauralis, tinnitus, the discrimination of speech sounds, and other phenomena.

Theory.—The two types of sensori-neural deafness might arise from the following mode of action of the hair cells and the VIIIth nerve. With hair cell damage, the associated nerve elements are not activated at low stimulus intensities and the absolute threshold is increased. At higher levels of the stimulus, the activity of the hair cells responsible for firing the nerve spreads in locus and brings into action those nerve elements which normally would be fired by their own sensory cells. At still higher levels, the VIIIth nerve is discharging as if all hair cells were intact. Loudness is then fully recruited. In VIIIth nerve damage, certain nerve elements are permanently lost, and even at high intensities they remain nonfunctional. If at each stimulus intensity the number of inactive elements is a constant fraction of the active fibers [Dix *et al.* (23)], little or no loudness recruitment would occur.

The present writer suggests that discrimination loss for speech is severe for the ear showing end-organ damage because (*a*) dL/dI is abnormally large, and (*b*) with speech as a stimulus dI/dt is also large, therefore dL/dt is very great. For the ear showing VIIIth nerve damage, dL/dt for speech is probably reduced over that for the normal ear, and the discrimination loss resembles the effect of a passive filter.

Audiometric Changes Following Fenestration

A few of the studies regarding the effect of the fenestration operation upon hearing loss and methods for predicting this loss will be discussed. Other reports not reviewed here are those of Lempert (63), Skoog (95), McKenzie (75), and Asherson (2).

Shambaugh (92) presents the results of the measurement of hearing loss both before and after the fenestration operation in 164 consecutive cases. Of importance is the simple formula developed for predicting the probable outcome of the operation. This formula is based on two assumptions: (*a*) it is assumed on good evidence (14) that the bone conduction audiogram suitably corrected for the Carhart or otosclerotic notch is a reliable and valid measure of cochlear reserve, and (*b*) with factual support (19) it is also assumed that the successfully fenestrated ear has a definite residue of unrestored conductive loss attributable to the altered mechanics of sound conduction. The formula predicts surprisingly well the actual hearing by air conduction six months following fenestration.

McConnell & Carhart (73) confirmed the observation that the bone conduction audiogram obtained from patients with stapes fixation gives an under estimate of the true cochlear reserve. Their results also agree with those of Davis & Walsh (19) in showing that the minimum hearing loss to be expected after this operation is 20 db, and that the maximum preoperative conductive loss produced by stapes fixation is 60 db.

Thurlow *et al.* (103) give us a further description of the long-term study of the results of both speech and pure tone tests of hearing administered routinely both before and after the fenestration operation. This statistical study based on about 100 additional patients confirms the conclusions of their previous studies. This series of papers might well serve as a model for this type of evaluation of clinical procedures in audiology.

Cawthorne & Harvey (15) add more evidence that a close correlation exists between the hearing loss for pure tones and for speech in pure transmission-deafness. In mixed deafness, the correlation is somewhat reduced.

Nilsson (80) measured with a free-field audiometer the change in hearing for pure tones at various stages during fenestration operations performed under local anesthesia. In most cases when the labyrinth is opened, there is an immediate improvement in hearing for both air and bone conduction.

Link & Zwislocki (68) go into considerable detail regarding the difficulties in the measurement of the cochlear reserve by means of bone conduction audiometry. Such audiometry is necessary since Fowler's recruitment test cannot be relied upon alone to distinguish transmission-deafness from retrocochlear lesions. As a result of the complex way in which the ear is stimulated by a bone conduction receiver, nearly the least favorable point of application of the stimulus for diagnosis is the mastoid process. They compared bone conduction thresholds measured at the mastoid and the temple in normal ears and in patients with middle ear infections. They masked the contralateral ear by means of a narrow band of noise, centered about the frequency of the test stimulus, and the intensity of this noise was automatically adjusted to maintain the appropriate degree of masking as the intensity of the test stimulus was varied. The principal measurements were made with the ear canal not occluded. Their results confirm Békésy's earlier findings that the threshold measured at the temple is about 10 db more than if measured at the mastoid process, and that this difference is essentially independent of frequency. They conclude that tests made at the temple circumvent the effects of the middle ear upon the bone conduction thresholds better than when measured at the mastoid process, and they recommend application of the receiver to the temple in spite of the loss in efficiency at this locus.

Benedict's study (7) is concerned with the correlation between anatomical structure as altered by fenestration and hearing as measured by instrumental avoidance conditioning. Clinical otosclerosis was simulated in the monkey's ear by removing the incus (mastoidectomy), and thus interrupting the chain of ossicles. Removal of the incus resulted in a hearing loss of about 45 db that was fairly uniform from 150 to 4000 c.p.s. Then, following Lempert's surgical technique, K. Lowry fenestrated the ear in various ways, the animals' hearing was tested, and histological examination was undertaken. Since the oval window was not occluded, the fenestration operation added a third functional window to the inner ear. No obvious correlation was found between the thresholds and the condition of the fistula. However, this finding should not be too disturbing, since there were (apparently) always at least two mobile windows in the inner ear.

Van Eyck (104) discovered a pigeon with a congenital ankylosis of the oval window that was similar to the stapes ankylosis in human otosclerosis. After electrophysiological study of the ear of this pigeon both before and after fenestration, he concluded that sound is transmitted to the cochlea by way of the round window, and that the function of the new window is to permit liquid motion.

Huizinga (55) discussed the reaction of Tullio and the fenestration operation, and made it clear why the patient is not troubled with this reaction.

Tinnitus and Paracusis

Subjective tinnitus aurium is a fascinating phenomenon in the normal ear, but one which can be annoying or even intolerable to the patient suffering from certain otologic diseases. Such tinnitus is usually localized at one or both ears, and it can be described with some specificity. Although tinnitus is extremely common in many otologic disorders little research has been directed toward more precise description or measurement of it. Tinnitus may change the sound of an acoustic stimulus and thus it resembles an illusion; but it can be heard in the quiet. Sometimes it is hallucinatory and is given objective reference; but under observation the same tinnitus may be localized in the ear and the hallucination disappears. Tinnitus may seem loud; but its equivalent acoustic intensity is never very great. Because of the difficulties in obtaining accurate descriptions of the auditory quality and intensity of tinnitus, Goodhill (39) has made a recording of a variety of sounds so that the individual can make a more accurate description of his tinnitus.

After a study of tinnitus aurium in both normal and deaf individuals, Heller & Bergman (47) conclude that the qualitative characteristics of the tinnitus experienced by the normals were similar to those reported by the patients. The relative frequencies of occurrence of different auditory qualities were nearly the same in the two groups.

Sullivan & Hodges (98) studied the phenomenon of Paracusis Willisii by determining the quiet and masked absolute thresholds for pure tones. With the noise level used for masking, the masked thresholds above 1500 c.p.s. obtained from patients with bilateral conductive deafness are on the average nearly the same as the masked thresholds for the normal ear.

In the quiet, when speech is intended for the normal listener, the paracusic is at a severe disadvantage. In noisy surroundings, however, when the speech intensity has been adequately increased for the normal listener, the paracusic may also hear. In this connection, see Kryter (62).

Other Developments

This review does not include a considerable number of very fine articles on hearing and related topics which have appeared during the past year. Practically the entire field concerned with the physical analysis and the perception of speech has not been treated. At least we must mention the diversified group of papers presented at the *Conference on Speech Analysis*, and published as a unit (16). There have been papers and monographs on audiometry, such as Palva's *Finnish Speech Audiometry* (81), and the description of new recorded speech tests for the measurement of hearing and discrimination loss (50). An adequate survey could not be accorded in this review to the problems that arise when man is exposed to the intense noises of industrial and military situations (88). Because these developments are too important and involved to treat briefly, their summary and evaluation must remain for a later review.

LITERATURE CITED

1. *Acta Oto-Laryngol.*, **40** (1951); **41** (1952)
2. Asherson, N., *J. Laryngol. and Otol.*, **66,** 552–69 (1952)
3. Azzi, A., *Rivista audiologia practica*, **3–4**, 45–72 (1951)
4. Barber, H. O., and Ireland, P. E., *Laryngoscope*, **62,** 566–76 (1952)
5. Békésy, G. von, *J. Acoust. Soc. Amer.*, **23,** 576–82 (1951)
6. Békésy, G. von, *J. Acoust. Soc. Amer.*, **24,** 72–76 (1952)
7. Benedict, M. R., *Laryngoscope*, **62,** 1293–1315 (1952)
8. Benson, R. W., *J. Acoust. Soc. Amer.*, **25,** 128–34 (1953)
9. Beranek, L. L., *Acoustic Measurements*, 730–39 (John Wiley & Sons, Inc., New York, N. Y., 914 pp., 1949)
10. Berg, K., *Acta Oto-Laryngol.*, Suppl. 97, 77 pp. (1951)
11. Bocca, E., *Acta Oto-Laryngol.*, **39,** 452–63 (1951)
12. Bocca, E., and Pellegrini, A., *Acta Oto-Laryngol.*, **39,** 473–84 (1951)
13. Brogden, W. A., and Miller, G. A., *J. Acoust. Soc. Amer.*, **19,** 620–23 (1947)
14. Carhart, R., and Hayes, C., *Laryngoscope*, **59,** 1084–1101 (1949)
15. Cawthorne, T., and Harvey, R. M., *J. Laryngol. and Otol.*, **67,** 233–47 (1953)
16. Conference on Speech Analysis, *J. Acoust. Soc. Amer.*, **24,** 581–642 (1952)
17. Dadson, R. S., and King, J. H., *J. Laryngol. and Otol.*, **66,** 366–78 (1952)
18. Davis, H., Fernández, C., and McAuliffe, D. R., *Proc. Natl. Acad. Sci. U. S.*, **36,** 580–87 (1950)
19. Davis, H., and Walsh, T. E., *Laryngoscope*, **60,** 273–95 (1950)
20. Day, K. M., *Laryngoscope*, **62,** 547–55 (1952)
21. Denes, P., and Naunton, R. F., *J. Laryngol.*, **64,** 375–98 (1950)
22. De Vries, H. L., *J. Acoust. Soc. Am.*, **24,** 527–33 (1952)
23. Dix, M. R., Hallpike, C. S., and Hood, J. D., *J. Laryngol. and Otol.*, **62,** 671–86 (1948)
24. Eby, L. G., and Williams, H. L., *Laryngoscope*, **61,** 400–14 (1951)
25. Engström, H., and Wersäll, J., *Acta Oto-Laryngol.*, **43,** 1–10 (1953)
26. Fernández, C., *J. Acoust. Soc. Amer.*, **24,** 519–23 (1952)
27. Fernández, C., Ludwig, H., and McAuliffe, D. R., *Laryngoscope*. **62,** 1159–74 (1952)
28. Fletcher, H., *J. Acoust. Soc. Amer.*, **24,** 490–97 (1952)
29. Fletcher, H., *Speech and Hearing in Communication* (D. Van Nostrand Co., Inc., New York, N. Y., 461 pp., 1953)
30. Flett, R. L., *Laryngoscope*, **62,** 556–61 (1952)
31. Fowler, E. P., Jr., and Zeckel, A., *Psychosomatic Medicine*, **15,** 127–39 (1953)
32. Furstenberg, A. C., *Ann. Otol. Rhinol. Laryngol.*, **61,** 692–96 (1952)
33. Galambos, R., *J. Neurophysiol.*, **15,** 381–400 (1952)
34. Galambos, R., and Davis, H., *J. Neurophysiol.*, **6,** 39–58 (1943)
35. Galambos, R., Rose, J. E., Bromiley, R. B., and Hughes, J. R., *J. Neurophysiol.*, **15,** 359–80 (1952)

36. Garner, W. R., *Ann. Rev. Psychol.*, **3**, 85–104 (1952)
37. Garner, W. R., and Wertheimer, M., *J. Acoust. Soc. Amer.*, **23**, 664–67 (1951)
38. Geldard, F. A., *The Human Senses* (John Wiley & Sons, Inc., New York, N. Y., 365 pp., 1953)
39. Goodhill, V., *Ann. Otol. Rhinol. Laryngol.*, **61**, 778–88 (1952)
40. Hallpike, C. S., and Hood, J. D., *J. Acoust. Soc. Amer.*, **23**, 270–74 (1951)
41. Harris, J. D., *J. Acoust. Soc. Amer.*, **24**, 750–55 (1952)
42. Harris, J. D., *Psych. Bull.*, **50**, 190–99 (1953)
43. Hawkins, J. E., Jr., and Lurie, M. H., *Ann. Otol. Rhinol. Laryngol.*, **61**, 789–806 (1952)
44. Heck, W. E., Lynch, W. J., and Graves, H. L., *Ann. Otol. Rhin. Laryngol.*, **62**, 101–6 (1953)
45. Heise, G. A., *Am. J. Psychol.*, **66**, 1–19 (1953)
46. Heise, G. A., and Rosenblith, W. A., *J. Comp. Physiol. Psychol.*, **45**, 401–12 (1952)
47. Heller, M. F., and Bergman, M., *Ann. Otol. Rhin. Laryngol.*, **62**, 73–83 (1953)
48. Hilding, A. C., *Trans. Am. Acad. Ophthalmol. Otolaryngol.*, **57**, 35–45 (1953)
49. Hirsh, I. J., *The Measurement of Hearing* (McGraw-Hill Book Co., Inc., New York, N. Y., 364 pp., 1952)
50. Hirsh, I. J., Davis, H., Silverman, S. R., Reynolds, E. G., Eldert, E., and Benson, R. W., *J. Speech Hearing Disorders*, **17**, 321–37 (1952)
51. Hirsh, I. J., and Ward, W. D., *J. Acoust. Soc. Amer.*, **24**, 131–41 (1952)
52. Hood, J. D., *Acta Oto-Laryngol.*, Suppl. 92, 57 pp. (1950)
53. Hood, J. D., *J. Laryngol. and Otol.*, **65**, 530–44 (1951)
54. Huizing, H. C., and Reyntjes, J. A., *Laryngoscope*, **62**, 521–27 (1952)
55. Huizinga, E., *Laryngoscope*, **62**, 741–51 (1952)
56. Ireland, P. E., and Sullivan, J. A., Eds., Part II, *Progress in Ophthalmology and Otolaryngology* (Grune & Stratton, New York, N. Y., 665 pp., 1952)
57. Jeffress, L. A., Blodgett, H. C., and Deatherage, B. H., *J. Acoust. Soc. Amer.*, **24**, 523–27 (1952)
58. Jerger, J. F., *Laryngoscope*, **62**, 1316–32 (1952)
59. Katsuki, Y., and Covell, W. P., *Laryngoscope*, **63**, 1–17 (1953)
60. Knight, J. J., and Littler, T. S., *J. Laryngol. and Otol.*, **67**, 248–65 (1953)
61. Kristensen, H. K., and Jepsen, O., *Acta Oto-Laryngol.*, **42**, 552–60 (1952)
62. Kryter, K. D., *J. Acoust. Soc. Amer.*, **18**, 413–17 (1946)
63. Lempert, J., *Am. Med. Assoc. Arch. Otolaryngol.*, **56**, 101–13 (1952)
64. Lempert, J., Wolff, D., Rambo, J. H. T., Wever, E. G., and Lawrence, M., *Ann. Otol. Rhinol. Laryngol.*, **61**, 717–46 (1952)
65. Licklider, J. C. R., *Ann. Rev. Psychol.*, **4**, 89–110 (1953)
66. Lindsay, J. R., *Trans. Am. Acad. Ophthal. Otolaryngol.*, **57**, 27–34 (1953)
67. Lindsay, J. R., Schuknecht, H. F., Neff, W. D., and Kimura, R. S., *Ann. Otol. Rhinol. Laryngol.*, **61**, 697–716 (1952)
68. Link. R., and Zwislocki, J., *Arch. Ohren-, Nasen- u. Kehlkopfheilk. ver. Z. Hals-, Nasen- u. Ohrenheilk.*, **160**, 347–57 (1951–1952)
69. Lundborg, T., *Acta Oto-Laryngol.*, Suppl. 99, 111 pp. (1952)
70. Lund-Iversen, L., *Acta Oto-Laryngol.*, **42**, 219–24 (1952)
71. Lüscher, E., *J. Laryngol. and Otol.*, **65**, 486–510 (1951)
72. Lüscher, E., and Zwislocki, J., *J. Laryngol. and Otol.*, **65**, 187–95 (1951)
73. McConnell, F., and Carhart, R., *Laryngoscope*, **62**, 1267–92 (1952)
74. McKenzie, K. G., *Laryngoscope*, **62**, 562–65 (1952)
75. McKenzie, W., *J. Laryngol. and Otol.*, **66**, 211–25 (1952).

76. Meyer, D. R., and Woolsey, C. N., *J. Neurophysiol.*, **15**, 149–62 (1952)
77. Miller, G. A., and Garner, W. R., *J. Acoust. Soc. Amer.*, **20**, 691–96 (1948)
78. Munson, W. A., and Wiener, F. M., *J. Acoust. Soc. Amer.*, **22**, 382–86 (1950)
79. Munson, W. A., and Wiener, F. M., *J. Acoust. Soc. Amer.*, **24**, 498–501 (1952)
80. Nilsson, G., *Acta Oto-Laryngol.*, **39**, 329–37 (1951)
81. Palva, T., *Acta Oto-Laryngol.*, *Suppl.* **101**, 128 pp. (1952)
82. Pirodda, E., and Zwislocki, J., *Acta Oto-Laryngol..*, **42**, 152–60 (1952)
83. Pollack, I., *Am. J. Psychol.*, **65**, 544–54 (1952)
84. Pollack, I., *J. Acoust. Soc. Amer.*, **24**, 533–38 (1952)
85. Rawnsley, A. I., and Harris, J. D., *J. Exptl. Psychol.*, **43**, 138–42 (1952)
86. Rawnsley, A. I., and Harris, J. D., *Rept. No. 199*, **11** (16), 1–14 (Med. Research Lab., U. S. Navy Bur. Med. Surgery, New London, Conn., 1952)
87. Rose, J. E., and Galambos, R., *J. Neurophysiol.*, **15**, 343–57 (1952)
88. Rosenblith, W. A., Wheeler, D. C., and Smedal, H., *Rept. No. PNR-133* (Psycho-Acoustic Lab., Harvard Univ., Cambridge, Mass., 25 pp., 1952)
89. Rudmose, W., *J. Acoust. Soc. Amer.*, **22**, 674 (1950)
90. Ruedi, L., Furrer, W., Luthy, F., Nager, G., and Tschirren, B., *Laryngoscope.* **62**, 333–51 (1952)
91. Schuknecht, H. F., and Neff, W. D., *Acta Oto-Laryngol.*, **42**, 263–74 (1952)
92. Shambaugh, G. E., Jr., *Laryngoscope*, **62**, 461–74 (1952)
93. Shower, E. G., and Biddulph, R., *J. Acoust. Soc. Amer.*, **8**, 275–87 (1931)
94. Sivian, L. J., and White, S. D., *J. Acoust. Soc. Amer.*, **4**, 288–321 (1933)
95. Skoog, T., *Acta Oto-Laryngol.*, *Suppl.*, 100, 134–43 (1952)
96. Stevens, S. S., Ed., *Handbook of Experimental Psychology*, Chap. 21, 25–28 (John Wiley & Sons, Inc., New York, N. Y., 1436 pp., 1951)
97. Stevens, S. S., and Davis, H., *Hearing, Its Psychology and Physiology* (John Wiley & Sons, Inc., New York, N. Y., 489 pp., 1938)
98. Sullivan, J. A., and Hodges, W. E., *Laryngoscope*, **62**, 687–703 (1952)
99. Tasaki, I., and Fernández, C., *J. Neurophysiol.*, **15**, 497–512 (1952)
100. Thomas, G. J., *Am. J. Psychol.*, **62**, 182–201 (1949)
101. Thomas, G. J., *Am. J. Psychol.*, **65**, 588–93 (1952)
102. Thomas, J. A. B., *J. Laryngol. and Otol.*, **65**, 472–76 (1951)
103. Thurlow, W. R., Davis, H., Walsh, T. E., and Eldert, E., *Laryngoscope*, **61**, 124–37 (1951)
104. Van Eyck, M., *J. Laryngol. and Otol.*, **65**, 183–86 (1951)
105. Walsh, T. E., *J. Laryngol. and Otol.*, **67**, 119–27 (1953)
106. Webster, F. A., *J. Acoust. Soc. Amer.*, **23**, 452–62 (1951)
107. Webster, J. C., Miller, P. H., Thompson, P. O., and Davenport, E. W., *J. Acoust. Soc. Amer.*, **24**, 147–52 (1952)
108. Wever, E. G., *Theory of Hearing*, (John Wiley & Sons, Inc., New York, N. Y., 484 pp., 1949)
109. Wheeler, L. J., and Dickson, E. D. D., *J. Laryngol. and Otol.*, **66**, 379–95 (1952)
110. Wiener, F. M., *J. Acoust. Soc. Amer.*, **19**, 143–46 (1947)
111. Wiener, F. M., and Ross, D. A., *J. Acoust. Soc. Amer.*, **18**, 401–8 (1946)
112. Williams, H. L., *Am. Med. Assoc. Arch. Otolaryngol.*, **56**, 24–44 (1952)
113. Wolff, D., *Am. Med. Assoc. Arch. Otolaryngol.*, **56**, 588–609 (1952)
114. Zwislocki, J., and Pirodda, E., *Experientia*, **8**, 279–84 (1952)

THE CHEMICAL SENSES[1]

By Bernice M. Wenzel

Department of Psychology, Barnard College, Columbia University, New York, New York

In reviewing the chemical senses for Volume 1 of the *Annual Review of Psychology*, 1950, Geldard remarked that it was still too early to determine whether the interest then being shown would turn out to be more than a flurry. Since the number of articles reviewed here annually has tended to increase, it seems fair to say, after five years, that interest in the field is definitely strengthening, as evidenced not only by the number of publications but also by the appearance of at least some continuity. An encouraging symptom of vigor in an experimental area can be detected when one man's conclusion becomes the source of the next man's hypothesis. Such a symptom is now just noticeable, especially in studies of taste. Still another type of evidence is afforded by the ambitious and very well-attended two-day conference, sponsored jointly by science and industry, to discuss basic research problems in odor (4). The next five years can be expected to provide some real progress in experimental findings.

Before we take up the research articles, a few reviews will be mentioned. The chemical senses have been plagued with too many reviews of too few facts but some which have appeared this year are contributions, nonetheless. Beidler (1) has written a summary of current information concerning taste receptors for a general semiscientific audience. It is both a comprehensive and comprehensible account and is highly recommended. Another review, this one on smell, is by Geldard (3). It, too, is an excellent summary of the principal facts and speculations in the field. This reviewer wishes, as the only change, that somewhat less attention had been given to systems of classification and a little more paid to the possibility of using olfactometers with more suitable controls than those of Zwaardemaker and of Elsberg. As an example of the type of review that is fairly common in scientific literature of industrial origin, that of Crocker (2) may be cited. The following quotation generally typifies the underlying theme of such articles. "Sensation is subjective. Nobody can touch or measure anything that is subjective. Sensation is unique for any particular person. It is dealt with by the psychologist" (2, p. 169A).

Gustation

Neurophysiology.—This is one of the most active areas, having several studies involving cortical or glandular extirpation. Bonvallet *et al.* (9) give the results of recording potentials from central gray matter evoked by stimulation of the afferent nerves of the cat's tongue. Potentials with variable latencies and amplitudes were recorded from the entire head of the

[1] The period covered by this review is approximately from June, 1952 to June 1953.

caudate nucleus, the lateral and central nuclei of the amygdaloid complex, the claustrum, and the septal region. Stable responses appeared in the putamen. Such data can be of assistance in charting the exact course of the entire gustatory pathway. It is not clear from the abstract, however, whether taste mediating nerves alone were stimulated.

Benjamin & Pfaffman (8) investigated the role of a specific cortical area, as located by evoked potentials from the chorda tympani and the glossopharyngeal nerves, in the rat's taste discrimination. The region excised was the inferior portion of Area 1 on the postorbital surface just above the rhinal fissure. The behavioral measure was the threshold for quinine aversion. It is hard to appreciate the full significance of the experiment from an abstract and a brief paper read at a meeeting, but the suggestion is that the cortical region concerned is of some importance for taste discrimination and that subcortical damage may be critical. These results seem to be in agreement with the taste localization by Patton & Amassian (24) based on a study of evoked potentials.

It has been reported previously that temporal lobectomy in monkeys may produce dietary changes. Bagshaw & Pribram (7) have tried to shed some light on this phenomenon by studying changes in the acceptance threshold for quinine hydrochloride as a function of the region of temporal cortex removed. Acceptance was markedly increased following removal of the insula, operculum, and anterior supratemporal plane from three monkeys, and there was a slight increase with excision of only the insula and operculum in one monkey. Removal of the insula alone in one monkey or in combination with the supratemporal plane in another monkey had no effect. The authors suggest an analogy with vision, consisting of a primary system and a crucial center spot. This experiment could profitably be followed by a series designed to measure the effect of various combinations of damage on discriminations among taste stimuli, once the present findings are confirmed on more animals.

In the same area of food habits, Anand & Brobeck (6) have shown that bilateral lesions in the lateral or medial group of amygdaloid nuclei of rats had no effect on amount of food eaten as compared with controls of the same age, although previous studies on dogs and monkeys had shown this effect.

A worthwhile attempt was made by Jones & Jones (16) to repeat the Allen & Weinberg study (5) on fusion frequency of taste sensations from direct electrical stimulation of receptors. The earlier data had been offered as evidence for four distinct taste systems on the basis of different fusion frequencies. Jones & Jones were unable to obtain reports of anything but continuous sensations from six subjects, some being experienced and some inexperienced observers. Their reasonable suggestion is that the previous results should not be used as evidence until the cause of the discrepancies is made clear.

The role of the chorda tympani and glossopharyngeal nerves in the rat's sensitivity for sodium chloride and for quinine sulfate has been evaluated by Pfaffman (26). Four experimental animals, with section of the chorda tympani alone and tested before regeneration was possible, were compared with four control animals. He found essentially no difference in the preference-aversion function for sodium chloride, and only a slight lessening of aversion to quinine (one animal was added to each group for the quinine tests). Cutting both nerves in six animals resulted in significant reduction of both preference and aversion for salt and aversion for quinine. In other words, the ability to discriminate among the different concentrations was greatly reduced but not entirely gone. It appears, then, that taste stimulation, as mediated by these nerves, functions to a large extent in the preference-aversion responses to sodium chloride. After histological study, Pfaffman attributed what little sensitivity remained to taste buds of the pharynx and the roof of the mouth, those of the latter being on the papillae of the naso-incisor ducts. The discovery of taste buds in these ducts is reported here for the first time.

Carr (11) has tested Richter's hypothesis that receptor sensitivity is lowered with need by comparing the preference threshold, Richter's measure of sensitivity, with the sensory threshold. The sensory threshold for sodium chloride was measured in 11 rats, before adrenalectomy, by a conditioning technique. The mean daily intake of 3 per cent sodium chloride and of tap water was also measured for 10 days. The postoperative measures for seven rats consisted of 10 days of comparative intake of salt solution and water, then measurement of the sensory threshold, followed by 10 more days of comparative intake. A significant increase occurred in amount of salt solution drunk in both postoperative periods, but the postoperative sensory threshold did not change. The sensory thresholds found were comparable to those obtained by Pfaffman & Bare (25) in direct electrical recording of receptor sensitivity. Carr's results are certainly of great interest but probably should not be considered completely conclusive until alternative ways of measuring the sensory threshold have been tried (see Cubbage & MacPhee below). His procedure involved giving a shock if water was drunk. Use of shock in this way for threshold determinations is dubious in that it introduces an unassessed variable.

Individual differences.—This section is something of a catchall for experiments dealing with individual differences per se as well as those concerned with factors which might increase variability among subjects.

The following experiment was designed to test the same hypothesis as that of the last experiment in the preceding section. Starting from Richter's premise, Meyer (21) tested the interesting hypothesis that the threshold for glucose in human subjects would change as a function of food deprivation. Nine subjects went without food for 34 hr. while the threshold for glucose was measured along with control thresholds for two less vital substances (sodium chloride and quinine bisulfate), at nine different times. At the end of the deprivation period they ate freely, and the thresholds were again measured. The curve of threshold against deprivation time for each substance had essentially a zero slope. Analysis of variance showed the effect of deprivation to be insignificant but intersubject thresholds were significantly different. These data are the third set which fail to support Richter's hypothesis. It could be argued in this case that the need was not severe enough or prolonged sufficiently to affect the receptors. However, even at the end of the 34 hr. period, there was no sign of a downward trend. It seems to be time to start looking elsewhere for the explanation of increased intake of appropriate substances with need.

Meyer's experiment is also relevant to the reports of Goetzl's group appearing in recent years on the effects of diurnal variations associated with ingestion of food on gustatory and olfactory sensitivity. This year Irvin & Goetzl (15) reported experiments that show a significant decrease in threshold for sodium chloride as time since last meal increases, and a significant rise immediately after eating. The time involved is merely that between breakfast and lunch on one day. It is puzzling, to say the least, that the results of Meyer and of Goetzl *et al.* are so sharply at variance. Meyer himself does not even refer to the work of Goetzl *et al.* so there are no suggestions from him, and the published accounts of procedure are not detailed enough to reveal grounds for any critical differences. Since the problem under investigation is an important one, not only from the point of view of receptor action but also methodologically for experiments where such a variable is not wanted, it deserves further consideration. Previous reviewers have commented critically on Goetzl's failure to mention, if not include, some needed controls. One further recommendation might be to set up the procedure in such a way that the experimenter has no knowledge of the degree of food deprivation represented by each subject.

Four recent papers deal directly with some aspect of individual differences. Thieme (28) has contributed one on tasting of phenylthiocarbamide. It provides merely the frequencies of nontasters in a total of 3,229 Puerto Ricans, divided into 15 geographic regions and 10 ethnic groups. The total frequency was 12 per cent, with no significant differences between regions or groups. A study of individual reactions to the primary tastes was made by Kahn (17), but unfortunately the data suffer from an end effect. His concentrations of most of the substances were not weak enough to measure thresholds accurately. The author concluded that variability was present, although no formal statistical estimate was made. The problem is a worthy one, however, for information on individual reactions is greatly needed. Pfaffman (27) has approached this same problem by way of species differences. Using the rat, rabbit, and cat, he took recordings from the chorda tympani after stimulation of the tongue by substances for the primary tastes. The response to hydrochloric acid was similar in all animals but responses to the other stimuli differed to such an extent that Pfaffman warns that ". . . any general theory of taste must take species differences into account." In line with this idea, Murray *et al.* (23) described a series of four ingenious experiments which show a definite difference between rats and human beings in their reactions to sodium sucaryl. Solutions which human subjects judged equally sweet and preferable to saccharin were avoided by rats when paired with water, although the rats preferred saccharin to water. The authors suggest that the differences could be a matter of differential sensitivity to the "sweet" and "bitter" components of sucaryl. This phenomenon may be related to an earlier speculation that saccharin tastes bitter to dogs (see 30, p. 120).

Changes in identification thresholds for the primary tastes after stimulation by monosodium glutamate were studied by Mosel & Kantrowitz (22). They tested four subjects just before, and 5 min. after, a 7-sec. exposure to a strong solution of monosodium glutamate. The thresholds for salt and sweet remained unchanged but those for sour and especially for bitter decreased. This whole matter is somewhat confused, both in terms of previous research results and of everyday experience. Therefore, the authors could have made a greater contribution if they had included a control group and more subjects so that more sensitive statistical techniques could have been applied and confidence increased.

Studies on insects.—In the hands of competent workers, certain insects have proved to be very convenient subjects for investigating chemical sensitivity. The accessibility of their receptors is an especially valuable characteristic. There are two experiments to report here, both excellent examples of good design.

The relative acceptance by the honeybee of sugars present in nectar was studied by Wykes (31) under both field and laboratory conditions. In the field, sucrose, glucose, and fructose were used, and the measure of preference was the number of bees on each dish at 10 min. intervals for 3 or 4 hr. Sucrose and glucose were preferred significantly over fructose but a mixture of the three sugars in equal parts was always preferred over any one, a mixture of any two, or an unequal mixture of the three. Maltose, not present in nectar, was added in the laboratory tests where the measure was uptake during 1 or 2 hr. Here the order from most to least preferred was sucrose, glucose, maltose, and fructose. Again, the sucrose-glucose-fructose mixture in equal parts stood out; it was consumed to a significantly greater degree than was predicted from the mean uptake of the constituents. The implication is clear that the sugar composition of nectar may be an important factor in influencing visits of bees to flowers.

The basic problem of adaptation has been attacked systematically by Dethier (13), using the tarsal receptors of the blowfly and solutions of sucrose. The insect was held in a paraffin block so that only his front parts were free. The indication of adaptation was retraction of, or failure to extend, the proboscis when the legs were put in sucrose. It was found that the time for complete adaptation increased as the logarithm of the adapting sucrose concentration. Continued stimulation from supraliminal concentrations had no further effect on the threshold; time may be a factor in changing the threshold when subliminal concentrations are used, however. With continuous stimulation at one intensity, intermittent bursts of activity occurred. In looking for the site of adaptation, two techniques were utilized with opposing results. If one leg was tied while the other was adapted, no response was made when the resting leg was then stimulated; this indicated central control. When the two legs were stimulated differentially by sucrose and by water in a divided dish and then the leg that at first had been in water, and hence unadapted, was put into sucrose a response occurred 66.6 per cent of the time. Dethier speculates that there may be two centers involved. Simultaneous stimulation by mixtures of acceptable and unacceptable substances resulted in adaptation to both at the same rate. Further studies of this type would provide useful data to aid in understanding the action of the receptors.

Taste and flavor testing.—An extensive literature exists on these problems, but only a few of the more basic references, concerned chiefly with methodology, are included here. A good summary of techniques in panel testing is presented by Konigsbacher *et al.* (18). They include the use of rating scales and flavor profiles, the use of binary test systems, and some general discussion of statistical treatments and applications. Binary test systems may be exemplified by the triangle test wherein each judge is asked to select from three samples the one which is different. Tests of this sort could be convenient in the psychophysical laboratory for sorting subjects quickly into broad categories of sensitivity. Further attention to the importance of the experimental design and the availability of powerful statistical tools is given in articles by Mason & Koch (20) and by Bradley (10). The latter is particularly recommended for the discussion of statistical methods and its extensive classified bibliography. A methodological experiment testing the effect of certain features of the design on judgment of flavor characteristics was reported by Hopkins (14).

An interval scale for sweetness was constructed by MacLeod (19) from half-judgments for sucrose and glucose separately and from judgments of equivalent sweetness between the two sugars. MacLeod's attempt to evaluate validity by cross predictions within the obtained data can be implemented by testing predictions to other situations. Such a scale, if its validity can be established and if it can be used reliably, would be a great aid both in applied and theoretical problems.

Learning.—A study of Pavlovian conditioning by Travina (29) showed that "alimentary" conditioned responses could be established with equal ease when the unconditioned stimulus was provided by the normal act of eating or by stimulating surgically exposed portions of the tongue. This result would be expected on the basis of various experiments using inadequate stimulation for the unconditioned stimulus.

Cubbage & MacPhee (12) have given an interesting demonstration of maze learning in rats as a function of gustatory cues. They used a linear maze with four choice points. There was a nozzle holding eight drops of liquid in front of each door, and there were two doors at each choice point. Sixteen rats were divided into two equated groups. Group I learned the maze first with cues present, then ran without cues; Group II followed the reverse procedure. When cues were present, the nozzle in front of the correct door contained salt solution while the other had water. In the control condition, both nozzles held water. Running under 24 hr. water deprivation and with one trial per day, Group I met the criterion (group mean of 0.75 errors on four successive days) with cues in 32 trials; when cues were removed, the error curve rose. Group II, running first without cues, performed at chance for 20 trials after which cues were added and the criterion was met in 20 trials. The results were highly significant, with p less than .001 for the effect of cues. This technique could be readily adapted to threshold studies and studies of sensory equivalence using rats and other animals.

Olfaction

As in previous years, articles on olfaction dealing with the results of actual research are less plentiful than on gustation. The area cannot be said to be suffering from neglect, however, for it is being discussed a great deal and an increasing amount of work can be hopefully anticipated.

Neurophysiology.—Bonvallet *et al.* (9, 42a), in the study discussed earlier, evoked potentials in several central areas following stimulation by means of bipolar electrodes in the two olfactory bulbs. The largest, fastest, and most stable responses to rapid stimulation (50/sec.) were recorded in the prepiriform and piriform cortex, the anterior commissure and its branches, the ventral part of the head of the caudate nucleus, the olfactory tubercle, and the anterior limbs of the internal capsule. Their conclusion is that these regions constitute the direct olfactory system. Potentials with longer latency were detected in the claustrum, putamen, globus pallidus, and the lateral, central, and basal amygdaloid nuclei (the medial was not explored). The slowest responses, with latencies longer than 10 msec., occurred in the septum and the dorsal part of the head of the caudate nucleus. It is considered that the septum and hippocampus receive no direct fibers. All of the rapid responses were completely homolateral except for a few rare bilateral ones in the anterior commissure. These results from stimulation confirm some earlier pathways mapped by means of degeneration. They point once more to the intricacy of the olfactory central connections as well as to the neuroanatomical interactions with other sensory systems. Some potentials were recorded even in the cerebellum.

Adrian (32 to 36), in the last year and a half, has continued to summarize in very brief articles his results obtained by direct electrical recordings from the olfactory bulb of the rabbit. He has been aided in this work by a special high-pass filter, designed in his laboratory, which rejects frequencies below 400 c.p.s., making the continuous background potentials much less troublesome in interpreting the spikes associated with stimuli. He no longer holds his earlier notion that the mechanical effect of the passage of air through the nostrils in normal breathing produced potentials in the olfactory nerves. When there was an odorant in the air which was drawn through the nose by means of a syringe, the rate of flow had to be 4 cc. before it was effective. At rates from 6 to 30 cc., threshold was inversely related to concentration while latency was constant at all rates. Thresholds and latencies varied with the substance and the region tested. By recording in different parts of the bulb, he found that an abrupt discharge occurred near the anterior pole to stimulation by esters. Hydrocarbons resulted in a more gradual discharge deep in the posterior half. He speaks of evidence for the same relationship in the cat, plus a third posterior dorsal region where a discharge could be recorded from stimulation by amines. It is certainly possible, as he hints, that spatial distribution of this sort may underlie olfactory discrimination. In addition, he shows that various groups of receptors are differentially sensitive. One electrode can be placed to record large spikes from a single neuron as well as smaller spikes from neighboring multiple units. Such a preparation in the anterior and posterior areas showed little difference in sensitivity, but it was not so in the middle. There, a unit which responded to a water soluble substance rarely responded to a lipoid soluble substance. In addition, the former response was characterized by abrupt onset and high frequency while the latter was often of low frequency. At the time of writing, he was unable to say how many receptor types there may be. It is hoped that he will soon present a more complete account of these researches, comparable to his review in 1950 (36a), for their importance seems very great indeed.

Two further papers attest the growth of interest in the recording of electrical activity. Additional data have been obtained from the rabbit by Walsh (53) who confirms the general finding of a high level of resting activity, but with intermittent discharges when odorous room air is drawn through the nose. Upon application of specific odorous materials, a massive discharge was recorded. The principal contribution of Walsh's report is concerned with adaptation. With prolonged stimulation, there was first a spurt of activity, but adaptation occurred from three to five respiratory cycles later in the pause between exhalation and inhalation. He notes that there were individual differences in responsiveness to different substances. Walsh was able to record spikes from single units in the opossum by means of micropipette electrodes under very light anesthesia. The picture was essentially the same as that from larger regions, viz., spontaneous resting discharge and increased frequency in the presence of odorous material. No information was included in the printed abstract which would allow comparison with any of Adrian's specific findings.

The work of Sem-Jacobsen *et al.* (50) is a fitting climax for this discussion of centrally recorded activity inasmuch as this group has described responses measured in a human subject. Opportunity was taken of examination procedures preliminary to leukotomy on a 53-year-old psychotic woman to implant depth electrodes in the vicinity of the olfactory nerves and bulb. The left frontal electrode actually rested on the cribriform plate for some distance and gave less background discharge, as would be expected, than leads in the bulb. Inhalation of an odorous substance served to initiate, in less than 1 sec., a rhythmic series of 28 to 32 c.p.s. and intensity of 60 μv. They feel that the bulb is the origin of the discharges recorded since axon spikes are absent and the discharge is a rhythmic one, actually the first example of a rhythmic response occurring to a constant stimulus rather than to an intermittent one. No direct data are presented for pure air as stimulus. A number of odorous substances of unspecified strength and purity were used as stimuli, and the intensity of response was graded. Little response was noted to room air, hyocyamus, acetone, and alcohol; moderate response occurred to oil of wintergreen, bitter almonds, onions, turpentine, camphor, raspberry, and cinnamon; the "best" responses appeared to lilac perfume, oil of cloves, oil of lemon, benzine, coffee, oil of peppermint, oil of lavender, and valerian. Some of these rankings are quite surprising but should not be considered too seriously because of the poor co-operation received from the subject. Lack of co-operation was a real hindrance, too, in any attempts to relate the neural responses to discriminative ability. Responses were completely abolished at all stages of thiopental (barbiturate) anesthesia, which is not true of animal preparations. Some extracranial recording was done successfully through the nasal fossa, but it was not as clear as that from the depth electrodes. If it is at all feasible to record in this way, however, the technique should certainly be exploited, for even reduced data might be better than no data. Two hypotheses are advanced regarding the nature of the olfactory system in the human. First, we should consider the possibility of a population of neurons with a characteristic frequency of discharge remaining inactive until a stimulus disturbance, even a steady, continuing stimulus, sets the oscillation going. Second, based on the finding of an almost linear relationship between intensity of response and intensity of stimulation, is the suggestion that amplitude, rather than frequency-modulation underlies the olfactory system in contrast with most afferent systems. The experiments reported above may have opened a most fundamental research area in which real progress could occur.

Psychotic subjects are involved in two further papers included in this section. Alliez & Pujol (37) have studied the coincidence of olfactory hallucinations and paranoia, a relationship often noted by others. On the basis of an analysis of several cases, with disorders both prolonged and recent and involving both pleasant and unpleasant odors, they suggest that the temporal lobe should be investigated in this connection. The electroencephalograms on these patients showed irregularities in the temporal lobe. The authors compare the often complex hallucinations to Penfield's reports (49) of "forced thinking" occurring upon stimulation of cortical epileptogenic foci. Finally, Wenzel (54) has reported on measurements of olfactory thresholds pre- and postoperatively on 22 experimental patients and 4 controls in the second Greystone project. The experimental subjects underwent a variety of brain operations for the alleviation of psychosis. The only ablation considered to have a possible influence on olfactory acuity was transorbital lobotomy. The tests employed the Elsberg apparatus, with coffee, phenyl ethyl alcohol, and peppermint oil as stimuli. The subjects' inability to follow instructions reliably made it impossible to use the thresholds in any but a relative way, but it was clear that none of the operations had any effect either to raise or to lower acuity.

Apparatus.—The ever-puzzling question of how to stimulate the human olfactory receptors has received some attention in the form of a blow by Jones (43) aimed at the Elsberg olfactometer. Many blows have been directed at this instrument, but Jones' paper is probably the first to criticize it on the basis of direct empirical evidence. What might be called "Elsberg thresholds" were obtained on 10 subjects for three different concentrations of *n*-octane and amyl acetate. On the assumption that the number of odorous molecules entering the nostril is a significant variable for sensation, it would be predicted that greater pressures (i.e., larger volumes) would be needed for detection of the weaker concentrations. This expectation was not realized; the thresholds for the different concentrations could not be shown to differ statistically. The conclusion is that blast-injection thresholds are not directly comparable to thresholds obtained by presenting a series of concentrations of the odorant. So much work needs to be done in this area that it is discouraging to find only the above article. Inadequate methods must certainly be eliminated but so also must adequate ones be provided. A next step would seem to be to develop techniques for controlling the natural sniff.

In the spirit of the quotation from Crocker in the introduction to this review, Langley & Polin (46) avoid the whole question of the human observer by replacing the osmoscope with a chemical measure of deodorant capacity. They developed a system in which odorous air is circulated in contact with a deodorant and the resultant is drawn off for chemical analysis to determine how much of the odorous components has been removed or modified. Such a test is appropriate only when suitable analytic procedures are possible. Even then, the chemical reduction would have to be made meaningful in terms of a human being's impression of odor reduction.

Individual differences.—In a search for an easily obtained and valid indicator of systemic fatigue, a group of investigators (52) carried out two preliminary experiments using healthy young men as subjects to test the use of the olfactory threshold for this purpose. In one experiment, thresholds for phenyl ethyl alcohol were measured by a modified stream injection technique at four different times. Tests were made $2\frac{1}{2}$ hr. after breakfast and lunch on two successive days, with the afternoon test on the first day immediately preceded by controlled exercise (walking up and down stairs). In the other experiment, thresholds were obtained for dry coffee by means of blast injection $1\frac{1}{2}$ hr. after breakfast and $4\frac{1}{2}$ to $5\frac{1}{4}$ hr. after dinner on the same day. The evening session was calculated to take advantage of the normal accumulation of fatigue throughout the day. In neither experiment was there any indication whatsoever that thresholds were varying with fatigue. The hypothesis was considered not worth pursuing. Given more sensitive measuring devices and perhaps greater amounts of fatigue, some relationship might be detectable.

Kirk & Stenhouse (44) have given figures on a sample of the white population of Australia for incidence of inability to smell potassium, or possibly hydrogen cyanide. (The title speaks of potassium cyanide but the two names are used about equally often in the article with no clarification. Hydrogen cyanide seems more likely to be odorous.) The difference between adult males and females, 18 per cent and 4 per cent, respectively, suggests sex linkage which is somewhat supported by the data for 148 children of 122 parents included in the above figures. In addition, the intensity of the sensation for smellers seems to be affected by other genetic factors.

Odor and chemical constitution.—Stoll (51) reports briefly on variations in odor associated with an homologous series of bicyclic farnesyl synthetic compounds. As usual, intensity of odor is said to decrease with molecular weight and character of odor changes as well. He believes that both intensity and character of odor are determined by the form and size of the molecule while the functional groups are only partially influential. For example, in the macrocyclic series the epoxydes are less odorous whereas in this series they are more odorous. On the basis of his finding of adaptation in 10 to 20 sec. for molecules in the middle of the series, he suggests that there are fewer receptive centers for relatively larger molecules. Otherwise, adaptation would be slow since these molecules would take longer to reach all the centers.

The promising beginning of a systematic exploration of adaptation has been made by Cheesman & Mayne (40). They hope to work out a hierarchy of materials in terms of the degree of community between pairs of substances as indicated by the slope of the adaptation function relating them. Such a hierarchy could then presumably be related to the chemical and physical characteristics of the substances. Their general procedure is of interest in that the masking thresholds were group measures. In summary, all subjects were tested at once, each one taking a sniff of the adapting substance and then sniffing various concentrations of the test material and recording a positive or negative response for presence or absence of odor. The 50 per cent threshold was calculated by probit analysis and log-log plots made of threshold as a function of adapting concentration. The substances used in this experiment were isopropanol, cyclopentanone, and dioxan. When both stimuli were the same the slope of the best-fitting line was -0.7; when they were different the slopes varied from -0.2 to -1.0.

Studies on insects. A paper related to the preceding topic of chemical constitution, using blowflies as subjects, describes the function between rejection thresholds and concentration of homologous aliphatic alcohols as measured by Dethier & Yost (41). The same series of alcohols had previously been used in tests on tarsal receptors. Rejection, measured by per cent of flies at a porthole that admitted odorous air as compared with a porthole for pure air, increased with log of concentration and varied directly with vapor pressure. As the chain length increased, rejection occurred at logarithmically decreasing concentrations with no further stimulation beyond decanol. When thresholds are expressed as thermodynamic activity, all of the alcohols are equally stimulating although this relationship is somewhat obscured at the extremes. It leads to the hypothesis that the critical process for olfaction in this case is one of equilibrium. Stimulation of tarsal receptors had not shown such a relationship. The reports from Dethier's laboratory should be followed closely by those interested in olfaction for their implications go beyond insect physiology.

Two further studies will be reported briefly. In one, Barnhart & Chadwick (38) showed that flies apparently contribute something to spots which they visit (dishes of mush bait, in this study) which increases their attractiveness for other flies. What the substance might be or by what mechanism it acts, is not discussed. Glynne Jones (42), in testing repellents for honey bees, found that repellency of phenol increased, decreased, and then increased again as concentration was increased. He concluded that olfaction was effective for the weaker stimuli but that the common chemical sense, which the psychologist would prefer to subsume under cutaneous sensitivity, supplanted it when stronger stimuli were used.

Industrial problems.—Minimal representation is included in this section for two industrial problems which are intimately concerned with odors, viz., ventilating and air conditioning, and use of chlorophyll as a deodorant. In the first, Kuehner (45) has summarized his experiments concerned with determining the strength of odor which is intolerable in an occupied space. Naturally, he first faced the problem of how to measure odor level and finally resorted to a dilution method, similar to the familiar Fair and Wells technique. The entire procedure and the report's generality have been criticized by various persons, among them a psychologist whose main objection is to the insistence on judges who are in extremely high agreement, thus eliminating individual differences which the industry must take into account. He mentions other dubious points in the procedure as reported, such as omission of any statement as to precautions against adaptation, the use of only two observers, and the discarding of "divergent readings."

If this review is to typify its period, it can hardly ignore chlorophyll. An uncritical account of the range of its effectiveness as a deodorant has been prepared by Lesser (47) who takes at face value results obtained by some inadequate experimental procedures. A series of experiments with uniformly negative results has been reported by Brocklehurst (39). He made use of either chemical tests (see Langley & Polin above) or the human nasal instrument to evaluate odor reduction. With the former, he found no difference in amount of methyl mercaptan remaining in a circulating system after contact with one of his chlorophylls as compared with the amount left after contact with water. Of more interest to the psychologist are those tests wherein the sensation of odor was the criterion. In a variety of ways, several odorants were put in contact with one or another chlorophyll preparation for varying times. In each case, the test was mere presence or absence of odor and, with a couple of minor exceptions, odor was present in each test case. Brocklehurst has been criticized for making no effort to measure degree of odor and for using many odorants (such as perfumes) which were never claimed to be susceptible to chlorophyll. A very few clinical trials were also run, again with completely negative results. The author is roundly criticized in several letters to the editor for chemical and other errors, including some already stated here, and especially for failing to specify his chlorophylls exactly after criticizing previous workers for the same thing. One final article on chlorophyll is included since it gives a clue to the chemical action when deodorization actually occurs, as it does with many compounds containing sulfur. Mitchell (48) reports that benzyl mercaptan in an aqueous solution of sodium chlorophyllin or sodium copper chlorophyllin becomes odorless in 24 hr., forming a suspension of odorless dibenzyl disulfide. The same thing happens in air but requires at least 10 days. Nothing happens, with or without chlorophyll, if no oxygen is present. The effect of the chlorophyll is greatly to speed the action of oxygen, but it is not a true catalysis since a given quantity of chlorophyllin is limited in the amount of odorant it can affect, in spite of the fact that its chemical behavior, color, and spectrophotometric properties are unchanged.

In conclusion, the present reviewer wishes to underline a point of view implicitly represented in several places above. The time has come in the study of chemoreception when it is not enough to present data from two or three subjects, obtained in a poorly designed experiment. If researchers are to build on each other's work, each has an obligation to conduct his experiment in such a way as to make possible a proper statistical estimate of the significance of his findings. Failure to utilize modern techniques of design and analysis in experimenting merely adds confusion where an abundance of the same already exists.

The following four articles arrived too late for original inclusion in the chapter but will be briefly reviewed here because of their importance. All are concerned with the interaction of the olfactory system with other aspects of physiology. David *et al.* (40a) have shown that the female cat's sexual cycle can be altered by electrical stimulation of the olfactory bulbs. The data are rather skimpy and irregular, but the relationship is an interesting one. The indication is that both the hypophysis and ovary are affected.

LeMagnen has continued his physiological investigations. In an experiment with Rapaport (46a) he has found that rats with severe deficiency of vitamin A are unable to make odor discriminations which are normally possible. The yellow color of the olfactory area has suggested the importance of this vitamin in its functioning. LeMagnen has also investigated some of the relationships between olfaction and sex in the white rat (46b). He has established the fact that rats in different sexual conditions present different odors to other rats since the latter respond differentially in a choice situation where olfactory cues are the only ones present. The sexual condition of the observing rat also affects its performance. Somewhat inconsistent results were obtained in experiments designed to study the effect of different sexual conditions on ability to discriminate between presence or absence of certain odors in varying concentrations. The last article in this series (46c) is a general review of the effects of olfaction on psychophysiological functions and is recommended for its inclusiveness.

LITERATURE CITED

General

1. Beidler, L. M., "Our Taste Receptors," *Sci. Monthly*, **75,** 343–49 (1952)
2. Crocker, E. C., "The Nature of Odor," *Tappi*, **35,** 169–75A (1952)
3. Geldard, F. A., *The Human Senses*, 270–94 (John Wiley & Sons, Inc., New York, N. Y., 365 pp., 1953)
4. N.Y. Acad. Sci. and Am. Soc. Heating and Ventilating Engrs. Conf., "Basic Odor Research Correlation" (April 23–24, 1953); *Ann. N. Y. Acad. Sci.* (In press)

Gustation

5. Allen, F., and Weinberg, M., "The Gustatory Sensory Reflex," *Quart. J. Exptl. Physiol.*, **15,** 385–420 (1925)
6. Anand, B.K., and Brobeck, J.R., "Food Intake and Spontaneous Activity of Rats with Lesions in the Amygdaloid Nuclei," *J. Neurophysiol.*, **15,** 421–30 (1952)
7. Bagshaw, M. G., and Pribram, K. H., "Cortical Organization in Gustation (*Macaca mulatta*)," (Paper delivered at meeting Eastern Psychol. Assoc., Boston, Mass., April 24, 1953); *J. Neurophysiol.* (In press)
8. Benjamin, R. M., and Pfaffman, C., "Cerebral Mechanisms in Taste Discrimination," *Am. Psychologist*, **7,** 251 (1952)
9. Bonvallet, M., Dell, P., and Hugelin, A., "Projections olfactives, gustatives, viscérales, vagales, visuelles et auditives au niveau des formations grises du cerveau antérieur du chat," *J. physiol.* (*Paris*), **44,** 222–24 (1952)
10. Bradley, R. A., "Some Statistical Methods in Taste Testing and Quality Evaluation," *Biometrics*, **9,** 22–38 (1953)
11. Carr, W. J., "The Effect of Adrenalectomy upon the NaCl Taste Threshold in Rat," *J. Comp. Physiol. Psychol.*, **45,** 377–80 (1952)
12. Cubbage, I. H., and MacPhee, H. M., "Gustatory Cues as Sensory Control in Maze Learning" (Paper delivered at meeting Eastern Psychol. Assoc., Boston, Mass., April 25, 1953)
13. Dethier, V. G., "Adaptation to Chemical Stimulation of the Tarsal Receptors of the Blowfly," *Biol. Bull.*, **103,** 178–89 (1952)
14. Hopkins, J. W., "Laboratory Flavor Scoring: Two Experiments in Incomplete Blocks," *Biometrics*, **9,** 1–21 (1953)
15. Irvin, D. L., and Goetzl, F. R., "Diurnal Variations in Acuity of Sense of Taste for Sodium Chloride," *Proc. Soc. Exptl. Biol. Med.*, **79,** 115–18 (1952)
16. Jones, M. H., and Jones, F. N., "The Critical Frequency of Taste," *Science*, **115,** 355–56 (1952)
17. Kahn, S. G., "Taste Perception—Individual Reactions to Different Substances," *Illinois Acad. Sci. Trans.*, **44,** 263–69 (1951)
18. Konigsbacher, K. S., Danker, W. H., and Evans, R. L., "The Evaluation of Odors and Flavors," *Drug & Cosmetic Ind.*, **70,** 332–33, 406–11 (1952)
19. MacLeod, S., "A Construction and Attempted Validation of Sensory Sweetness Scales," *J. Exptl. Psychol.*, **44,** 316–23 (1952)
20. Mason, D. D., and Koch, E. J., "Some Problems in the Design and Statistical Analysis of Taste Tests," *Biometrics*, **9,** 39–46 (1953)

21. Meyer, D. R., "The Stability of Human Gustatory Sensitivity during Changes in Time of Food Deprivation," *J. Comp. Physiol. Psychol.*, **45**, 373–76 (1952)
22. Mosel, J. N., and Kantrowitz, G., "The Effect of Monosodium Glutamate on Acuity to the Primary Tastes," *Am. J. Psychol.*, **65**, 573–79 (1952)
23. Murray, E. J., Wells, H., Kohn, M., and Miller, N. E., "Sodium Sucaryl: A Substance which Tastes Sweet to Human Subjects but is Avoided by Rats," *J. Comp. Physiol. Psychol.*, **46**, 134–37 (1953)
24. Patton, H. D., and Amassian, V. E., "Cortical Projection Zone of Chorda Tympani Nerve in Cat," *J. Neurophysiol.*, **15**, 245–50 (1952)
25. Pfaffman, C., and Bare, J. K., "Gustatory Nerve Discharges in Normal and Adrenalectomized Rats," *J. Comp. Physiol. Psychol.*, **43**, 320–24 (1950)
26. Pfaffman, C., "Taste Preference and Aversion Following Lingual Denervation," *J. Comp. Physiol. Psychol.*, **45**, 393–400 (1952)
27. Pfaffman, C., "Species Differences in Taste Sensitivity," *Science*, **117**, 470 (1953)
28. Thieme, F. P., "The Geographical and Racial Distribution of ABO and Rh Blood Types and Tasters of PTC in Puerto Rico," *Am. J. Human Genet.*, **4**, 94–112 (1952)
29. Travina, A. A., "Conditioned Reflexes (in Response to) Stimulation of (Surgically) Exposed Portions of the Tongue with Alimentary Substances," *Zhur. Vyssheĭ Nervnoĭ Deyatel' im. I. P. Pavlova*, **2**, 126–32 (1952); *Psychol. Abstr.*, **27**, 1649 (1953)
30. Wendt, G. R., *Ann. Rev. Psychol.*, **3**, 105–30 (1952)
31. Wykes, G. R., "The Preferences of Honeybees for Solutions of Various Sugars which Occur in Nectar," *J. Exptl. Biol.*, **29**, 511–19 (1952)

Olfaction

32. Adrian, E. D., "Differential Sensitivity of Olfactory Receptors," *J. Physiol. (London)*, **115**, 42P (1951)
33. Adrian, E. D., "High-Pass Filter for Recording Axon Potentials," *J. Physiol. (London)*, **115**, 41–42P (1951)
34. Adrian, E. D., "Olfactory Discrimination," *Année psychol.*, **50**, 107–13 (1951)
35. Adrian, E. D., "The Role of Air Movement in Olfactory Stimulation," *J. Physiol. (London)*, **114**, 4–5P (1951)
36. Adrian, E. D., "The Discrimination of Odours by the Nose," *Schweiz. med. Wochschr.*, **82**, 36–39 (1952)
36a. Adrian, E. D., "The Electrical Activity of the Mammalian Olfactory Bulb," *EEG Clin. Neurophysiol.*, **2**, 377–88 (1950)
37. Alliez, J., and Pujol, R., "Hallucinations olfactives et délires d'influence," *Ann. méd. psychol.*, **110**, 156–61 (1952)
38. Barnhart, C. S., and Chadwick, L. E., "A 'Fly Factor' in Attractant Studies," *Science*, **117**, 104–5 (1953)
39. Brocklehurst, J. C., "An Assessment of Chlorophyll as a Deodorant," *Brit. Med. J.*, 541–44, 621–22, 674 (1953)
40. Cheesman, G. H., and Mayne, S., "The Influence of Adaptation on Absolute Threshold Measurements for Olfactory Stimuli," *Quart. J. Exptl. Psychol.*, **5**, 22–30 (1953)
40a. David, R., Thierry, G., Bonvallet, M., and Dell, P., "Effects de la stimulation des bulbes olfactifs sur le cycle sexuel de la chatte," *Compt. rend. soc. biol.*, **146**, 670–72 (1952)

41. Dethier, V. G., and Yost, M. T., "Olfactory Stimulation of Blowflies by Homologous Alcohols," *J. Gen. Physiol.*, **35**, 823–39 (1952)
42. Glynne Jones, G. D., "The Responses of the Honey-bee to Repellent Chemicals," *J. Exptl. Biol.*, **29**, 372–86 (1952)
42a. Hugelin, A., Bonvallet, M., David, R., and Dell, P., "Topographie des projections centrales du système olfactif," *Rev. neurologique*, **87**, 459–63 (1952)
43. Jones, F. N., "A Test of the Validity of the Elsberg Method of Olfactometry," *Am. J. Psychol.*, **66**, 81–5 (1953)
44. Kirk, R. L., and Stenhouse, N. S., "Ability to Smell Solutions of Potassium Cyanide," *Nature*, **171**, 698–99 (1953)
45. Kuehner, R. L., "The Bacteria and Odor Problem in Occupied Spaces," *Heating, Piping, Air Conditioning*, **24**, 113–18 (1952); **25**, 143–46 (1953)
46. Langley, L. L., and Polin, H. S., "Objective Method of Determining Deodorant Capacity," *Federation Proc.*, **12**, 83 (1953)
46a. LaMagnen, J., and Rapaport, A., "Essai de détermination du rôle de la vitamine A dans le mécanisme de l'olfaction chez le rat blanc," *Compt. rend. soc. biol.*, **145**, 800–4 (1951)
46b. LeMagnen, J., "Les phénomènes olfacto-sexuels chez le rat blanc," *Arch. sci. physiologiques*, **6**, 295–332 (1952)
46c. LeMagnen, J., "L'olfaction. Le fonctionnement olfactif et son intervention dans les régulations psycho-physiologiques," *J. physiol. (Paris)*, **45**, 285–326 (1953)
47. Lesser, M. A., "Pros and Cons of Chlorophyll as a Deodorant," *Drug & Cosmetic Ind.*, **71**, 30–31, 128–33 (1952)
48. Mitchell, W., "Chlorophyll: A Reply to the Critics," *Perfumery Essent. Oil Record*, **44**, 124–27 (1953)
49. Penfield, W., and Rasmussen, T., *The Cerebral Cortex of Man* (The Macmillan Co., New York, N. Y., 248 pp., 1950)
50. Sem-Jacobsen, C. W., Bickford, R. G., Dodge, H. W., and Petersen, M. C., "Human Olfactory Responses Recorded by Depth Electrography," *Proc. Staff Meetings Mayo Clinic*, **28**, 166–70 (1953)
51. Stoll, M., "Odor and Constitution (VII)," *Drug & Cosmetic Ind.*, **71**, 608–9, 682–83 (1952)
52. *U. S. Army Med. Research Dev. Bd., Proj. DA*-49-007-*MD*-222 (*O. I.* 19–52), "The Effects of General Activity and Extended Diurnal Variation on Olfactory Sensitivity (Office of Surgeon General, Tech. Report No. 11, 1952)
53. Walsh, R. R., "Electrical Activity in the Mammalian Olfactory Bulb," *Federation Proc.*, **12**, 150–51 (1953)
54. Wenzel, B. M., in *Psychosurgical Problems*, 107–9 (Mettler, F. A., Ed., The Blakiston Co., New York, N. Y., 357 pp., 1952)

INDIVIDUAL DIFFERENCES[1]

By John B. Carroll

Graduate School of Education, Harvard University, Cambridge, Massachusetts

As any reasonably sophisticated reader of this volume will recognize, some overlap between this chapter and others is inevitable. This review of recent research, however, is oriented around what may be regarded as the central problems of the "field" of individual differences: (*a*) whether it may be said, in any sense, that dimensions of individual differences exist, and if so, what these dimensions are; (*b*) whether these dimensions can be accounted for in terms of lower order concepts of psychology, such as learning; and (*c*) how dimensions of individual differences may be most effectively measured.

The theory and results of factor analysis will be used as a point of departure, partly because the reviewer finds it interesting to do so, but also because it is his conviction that the study of correlation matrices by factor analysis is the method of choice in the identification of basic variables. Our premises are as follows: tests, ratings, and other measurement procedures may overlap considerably with regard to the traits they measure; we can determine the extent of overlap by noting their intercorrelations; and finally, it is the function of factor analysis to summarize the overlaps found in a set of measures and to indicate, to the extent possible, mutually nonoverlapping clusters of measurements. Any such cluster may then be regarded as measuring an underlying trait of individual differences. Of course, factor analysis usually attempts to do more than this; it describes each test variable as a linear function of a certain number of "common factors." The controversies about methods of factor analysis stem largely from the fact that mathematically an infinite number of ways of doing this are possible, but if it is remembered that the basic objective of factor analysis is to identify nonoverlapping (or at least, linearly independent) clusters of variables, and that the achievement of this objective may necessitate series of factor-analytic experiments, many of the controversial points can be resolved (22, 43). The usually justifiable requirement that the coefficients of the factors in the linear description of tests be generally zero or positive enables a reasonable choice among the infinitely numerous alternative solutions.

These considerations seem to have been overlooked by Loevinger (73) in her examination of the position of factor analysis in psychological theory. Despite her able exposition of various factorial procedures, she fails to point out adequately the positive contributions that factor analysis can make, and gives false impressions regarding some aspects of theory and practice in the field. For example, her statement that blind rotation of axes (that is,

[1] The period covered by this review is approximately May, 1952 to May, 1953. References to work falling outside this period are in general not listed in the bibliography, but can easily be found in the articles under discussion.

rotation performed without a knowledge of the identities of the test variables) is "neither widely practiced nor widely advocated" is simply not true, in the reviewer's experience. Again, in criticizing the hypothesis that "tests can be regarded as precise mathematical functions of factors," she writes:

> . . . tests cannot be considered precise mathematical functions of anything, for as psychological tests are now constructed, two people with the same score will in general have done different items correctly. Thus the items must measure different abilities, and a given total score will represent different sets of abilities for different people.

In the first place, this statement ignores the well-known theorem that a test score can be regarded as composed of a true score and an error score. In Lord's (75) model for items measuring a single underlying ability, it is evident that two people getting the same score could have passed different items, and this would happen solely by virtue of the fact that a true probability of passing an item (which may lie between zero and unity) can only be manifested as an a posteriori probability of either precisely zero or precisely unity (that is, after the item has actually been passed or failed). The difference between the two probabilities is error, and such errors are inevitable, even in the most carefully conducted psychophysical experiments. In all psychophysical dimensions known thus far, it is found that in the region of the limen the true probability of detecting a stimulus or a stimulus difference is less than one and greater than zero. In the second place, Loevinger's argument doubles back on itself. As soon as she mentions "different sets of abilities" she postulates the very things which factor analysis seeks to discover. In the case of a test with a complex factorial composition, it is perfectly easy to show that a given score might represent different sets of abilities, and this is nothing that would alarm a student of factor analysis. Loevinger invites factor analysts to demonstrate the status of factors by methods completely independent of factor analysis; in reply, one may say that if she will accept Mill's method of concomitant variation as this "independent method," this can be done very easily.

There remain, of course, fundamental questions as to the psychological meaning of a "factor," but these questions are the same ones that can be raised about the concept of a psychological "trait." This is not the place to take up this problem; we shall only cite Coombs' discussion of it (28). Sakoda (99) wonders whether factors (or traits) may not more appropriately be identified with situations rather than with individuals, but his discussion misses the point that nobody has ever expected individuals' traits to manifest themselves except in various "situations" or stimulus constellations.

Dimensions of Individual Differences

In some ways, the reviewer regrets that in this section it is impossible to list and describe all the factorial dimensions discovered or confirmed in the literature under discussion, for these dimensions constitute the chief substantive results of these studies. Nevertheless, the interested reader will be well advised to resort to the original articles, in view of the fact that no brief phrases that might be used here could suffice to give an adequate idea of the nature of these dimensions.

Dimensions of ability.—Zimmerman's (119) orthogonal reanalysis of Thurstone's original primary mental abilities data (110) is a welcome contribution, bringing that early study more into line with the results of current studies and also with other reanalyses of the Thurstone data. The verbal and numerical factors are better defined, and the factorial content of the fluency, memory, perception, and reasoning domains has now become considerably clearer. Perhaps an oblique solution would make the factors even more psychologically meaningful. Guilford, Fruchter & Zimmerman (57) report a factor analysis of 39 experimental tests and 7 reference tests. Seven of the 13 factors were clearly identifiable with previous known factors, and several relatively new factors were identified. It is of interest that two independent orthogonal solutions were made and reported; despite one or two substantial differences between the solutions, one gets the impression that they were nearly equivalent with respect to providing a basis for the interpretation of the factors.

Some students of factor analysis in Great Britain, led by Burt (20) and Vernon (112), have supported a theory of a "hierarchical organization of cognitive ability." The evidence brought forth by Moursy (83) demands serious consideration. Nearly all the currently available analytic procedures are applied to the correlations between 20 tests designed to measure four types of ability: sensorimotor, perceptual, associative, and relational. By the method which Moursy prefers, a "general cognitive ability" is found in all tests of the battery; the tests are then subdivided into those measuring "practical ability" and "intellectual ability"; finally, these groups are still further subdivided. The results appear to confirm the initial hypothesis of hierarchical organization, and the solution seems to have been unique and not subject to arbitrary manipulation. The "simple structure" analysis offered by Moursy was orthogonal, and not a very good one at that. Moursy might have confirmed the hierarchical hypothesis alternatively by an oblique simple structure solution containing two correlated second-order factors.

Guilford *et al.* (58), Corter (30), and Myers (84) report factor analyses in the domain of reasoning abilities. The first of these confirms the existence of several factors found in other studies. Corter's study was especially designed to test certain hypotheses as to stages in the process of reasoning, but was not particularly successful in this respect. The results of Myers' study again support the proposition that there are both speed and level-of-mastery components in timed tests, as had been shown previously (35), but much more research on this problem is needed.

At least four studies of factors in the perceptual domain appeared during the last year. Thurstone's "speed of closure" and "flexibility of closure" factors are investigated by Pemberton; in the first of her studies (88) evidence is found that flexibility of closure generalizes to tasks requiring higher cognitive functions, specifically those requiring "analytical reasoning"; in the second study (89), scores on these closure factors are found to be related to temperament variables as measured by certain objective personality inventories. Persons high on flexibility of closure tend to be socially retiring, independent of other's opinions, and averse to routine, according to this report. Persons high on speed of closure tend to be sociable, artistic, systematic, neat, and possibly "intolerant of ambiguity," in Frenkel-Brunswik's sense. A major contribution to the description of the perceptual domain is made by Roff (94), who identifies several factors similar to those in previous studies as well as several new factors. Some of the new factors appear only in motion picture tests, which were also analyzed by Fruchter & Mahan (50) with results somewhat parallel to those of Roff.

One of the most interesting reports to appear recently concerns tests of "creative thinking," by Guilford *et al.* (60). A number of hypotheses about factors in creative thinking are confirmed, and several extremely intriguing factors are disclosed. It would seem that the farther one moves away from the academically flavored types of tasks included in the usual intelligence tests, the more one finds identifiable factors which may have considerable relevance to the study of higher-level mental processes. One awaits the results of a similar exploration of "evaluative abilities," now under way by Guilford *et al.* (59).

Dimensions of individual differences measured by psychomotor tests have also received considerable attention. Roff (95) isolates six psychomotor factors, most of them new, and Fleishman (46) finds that the same factors in the respective trials of two rudder-control tests exist regardless of the order in which they are administered.

Dimensions of personality.—New evidence on the factorial structure of objective personality inventories is furnished in the extremely instructive research of Baehr (9), who made a second-order factor analysis of nine first-order factors previously identified by Thurstone in three personality schedules by Guilford. Two of the four factors which emerged were found to correspond to variables postulated in the Heymans-Wiersma conceptual scheme of temperament traits. Next, by a direct first-order factor analysis of 22 behavior items selected from the original inventories in such a way as to exclude first-order contrasts, three of the second-order factors previously identified were obtained as first-order factors. By showing that a factor can appear either in the first-order or the second-order domain, depending upon the selection of variables, the study suggests a hierarchical organization of personality traits much like that which, as Moursy suggests, exists for cognitive abilities. Cattell & Horowitz (25) published another in a series of factor studies of personality, this one being concerned with personality traits in the domain of "altruism."

A study by Carroll (23) shows that to some extent, the five traits presumably measured by Guilford's Inventory of Factors STDCR can be differentiated not only in the scores of the personality inventory itself but also, and even better, in terms of self-ratings and peer-ratings on scales especially constructed to correspond to the traits.

Several studies (not all using factor analysis, however) are concerned with the so-called trait of masculinity-femininity. Ford & Tyler (47) find that Terman and Miles' masculinity-femininity test contains at least two dimensions, for both sexes; one dimension has to do with interests, and the other with emotional characteristics. Lee (72) believes that since Bennett's Mechanical Comprehension Test (MCT) predicts masculinity-femininity scores better than it does any criterion of mechanical ability, it can be regarded as a nonfakable masculinity-femininity test. One wonders which dimension of masculinity-femininity identified by Ford & Tyler is the one correlated with the MCT, and what implications Lee's results have for the factorial interpretation of the MCT. Gough (55) has constructed a new "psychological femininity" scale, but does not concern himself with the possible lack of unidimensionality in his scale.

It is apparent, also, that problems of multiple dimensionality are latent in the measure of "authoritarianism" proposed by Adorno *et al.* (1). Hofstaetter (62) showed that this scale actually measures five factors which are largely independent: anti-Negroism, anti-Semitism, national pride, puritanism, and state socialism. We may agree wholeheartedly with Hofstaetter's conclusion that, as he puts it, "there is no justification for combining these independent dimensions of variability into one type, 'the authoritarian personality'."

The utility of factor-analytic procedures in the identification of entities in abnormal behavior was demonstrated in two studies. Degan (37) reanalyzed T. V. Moore's data on symptoms of manics, depressives, and schizophrenics. The nine first-order factors which were isolated were regarded as syndromes; when these were subjected to a second-order analysis, four factors emerged, identified as corresponding to the well-known diagnostic classifications of mania, hebephrenic schizophrenia, depression, and catatonic schizophrenia. Eysenck (42) studied intercorrelations between 20 scores on a variety of tests administered to 100 normals, 50 schizophrenics, and 50 manic depressives. In centroid analyses of the conventional type he found that the factor patterns for normals resembled those of psychotics to a considerable extent. By using the method of "criterion analysis" which he had developed earlier, he claimed to show that schizothymia-cyclothymia does not exist as a separate dimension of personality found only in psychotics. Thus, the study showed what has been hypothesized for many years: that the difference between normality and psychosis is a matter of degree rather than kind. Such a conclusion, of course, does not preclude a concern with the dynamic processes which take some individuals into mania and others into schizophrenia. It would now be interesting, incidentally, to attempt a study of normals using the variables which Degan investigated. One wonders, also, whether the battery of tests used by Eysenck was sufficiently diversified to enable a univocal test of his hypothesis as to the continuity between normality and psychosis.

Attention should be called to two books on personality study (41, 45), both concerned to a considerable extent with problems of identifying individual difference dimensions.

Dimensions of interests and attitudes.—The original Allport-Vernon Study of Values test was subjected to a factor analysis by Brogden (17) in a study which was more thoroughgoing than an earlier one by Lurie (79). The results paralleled Lurie's quite well and at the same time shed light on the proper interpretation of the six evaluative scores originally set forth by Allport and Vernon. It is shown that these scores are not factorially pure, but are in most cases averages of at least two of the more refined factors isolated by Brogden. In all, Brogden was able to identify 10 first-order evaluative factors; one interpretable factor in the second-order domain was thought to represent the difference between "idealism" and "practicality." Even though not analyzed factorially (possibly because overlaps in the scoring keys and the forced-choice feature of the preference test cause a degree of experimental dependence not desirable in factor studies), the data presented by Stanley & Waldrop (107) concerning intercorrelations of scores on the Study of Values and the Kuder Preference Record are of some interest in showing that the scales from the two instruments that might logically be expected to correspond do not actually intercorrelate very highly. In the light of Brogden's analysis of the Study of Values and various studies of the Kuder Preference Record, it would seem that the discrepancies are due to differing factorial compositions of the scales.

Strong & Tucker (108) were able to construct a number of relatively independent scales for the measurement of interests in various medical specialties. A factor analysis of the scales is presented. One continues to wonder at the proliferation of scales on the Strong Interest Inventory in view of the fact that it has previously been shown practicable to compute occupational scores as linear combinations of a small number of interest factors. Barnett *et al.* (11) found that the occupational level scale of the Strong test is not a measure of achievement drive but of the socioeconomic level where the individual will be most comfortable. Garry (52) discovered that the ability to fake scores on the Strong Interest Blank seems to be an ability which is independent of intelligence, sex, or information regarding the occupations involved. Perhaps this ability would be found to have some sort of diagnostic significance if further investigated. Long (74) developed a Job Preference Survey which is designed to be appropriate for placement of unskilled and semiskilled workers. To judge from their intercorrelations, the six components of work interest seem to be relatively independent: (*a*) routine—varied, (*b*) indoor—outdoor, (*c*) hazardous—nonhazardous, (*d*) sedentary—bodily active, (*e*) isolated—gregarious, and (*f*) precise—approximate. It would be desirable to attempt to tie these interests to a broader framework of personality structure. Some of them may be associated with cognitive abilities.

Dimensions of criterion measures.—In the search for dimensions of individual differences, it is useful to investigate what are commonly called "criterion measures," that is, measures of performance in various occupational pursuits and in various complex tasks. An occupation itself constitutes a situation in which the behavior of the individual can be measured, and is thus analogous to a psychological test, though of much greater complexity and duration. It is likely that occupations, considered as tasks, will tap dimensions of individual differences which are well-nigh inaccessible to the usual psychological testing procedures; this, at least, is suggested by the findings of Brown & Ghiselli (18) that in general there is a very low relation between the validity of a test in predicting trainability and its validity in predicting job performance. To quote these writers, "The abilities important for learning a job may differ markedly from those important in the maintenance of proficiency on the job." At the same time, it must be remembered that each occupation or complex task presents a distinct situation. A factorial dimension emerging in studies of occupational criteria may be specific to the occupation involved, and since it would be rare to find individuals who could be measured in more than one occupation, the cross-identification of factors among occupations is somewhat difficult. Nevertheless, the results of factorial studies of occupational criteria are often useful, even though they may leave the investigator unable to devise suitable predictors of these criteria. Indeed, even the criterion factors will often seem extremely inconstant and elusive. This is illustrated particularly well in a study by Bach (8); despite the finding that somewhat the same factors were identified in ratings of practice teaching and in ratings of in-service teaching, the relations between preservice and in-service ratings were negligible.

Newman, French & Bobbitt (85) find three factors observable in performance at the United States Coast Guard Academy: adaptability to academy life and activities, athletic proficiency and attitude, and academic grades. Studies by Ryans (96) and Ryans & Wandt (97) show that the factors emerging from ratings of observed teacher behaviors in the elementary school are much the same as those in the secondary school. In a factorial investigation of measurements applied to industrial trainees Bajard (10) found one factor common to his tests and his criterion measurements; two other factors were specific to the tests.

Several mathematical techniques and experimental designs to aid in the interpretation of relations between predictors and criteria can be mentioned here only briefly. Wrigley (118) has proposed and illustrated a technique whereby criterion variables are factor-analyzed and predictor regression weights for estimating the criterion factor scores are computed. The procedure has certain resemblances to canonical correlation. Fruchter (49) has considered the problem of describing criterion measures in terms of a set of predictor variables. This problem arose in the United States Air Force, where groups of recruits are assigned to different technical courses after their basic training. Fruchter's technique involves locating the criterion measurements obtained in each of the technical schools in the space of the predictor matrix. In his empirical data, the proportions of criterion variance accounted for by predictor variables range from .14 to .93; predictor factors identified as verbal comprehension, numerical facility, mechanical experience, and visualization contribute to the various specialty criteria in a manner which coincides fairly well with what one might expect in view of the nature of these factors and the content of the specialties. For example, the mechanical experience factor appeared most strongly in mechanical courses and not at all in such specialties as medical corpsman.

Experimental studies of individual difference dimensions.—The time does not seem to have arrived when, as hoped by Thurstone and other pioneers of factor analysis, the dimensions of individual differences isolated by this technique could be subjected to experimental study of the type which would manipulate learning, motivation, and similar independent variables. The few investigations which have been of this type seem never to have been consciously designed with such an end in view; they have stemmed from other approaches. Nevertheless, some of these studies can be turned to use in the field of individual differences. One example from recent literature may be cited. Maltzman & Morrisett (81) traced the effects of different kinds of training on the solution of anagrams. Now, anagram tests have frequently been used in factor studies of verbal fluency. It is therefore interesting to learn that subjects trained with a diversified list of anagrams make significantly better progress in solving anagrams in a particular semantic category than subjects trained in solving anagrams both of that category and equally of another category. The experiment was conducted in order to test certain propositions about habit strength. To students of individual differences, however, it prompts the hypothesis that verbal fluency as measured by anagrams tests is partly a function of the restricted versus diversified character of the incidental environmental training which the subject has received.

Several other studies of problem solving performances suggest that the factor of individual differences which is most often known as the "reasoning factor" does not need to be regarded merely as a statistical artifact arising from the intercorrelations of tests. O'Connor (86), in a correlational study, found that "intolerance of ambiguity" is related to poor abstract reasoning ability only when it is associated with ethnocentrism. Schroder & Rotter (102) discovered that they could experimentally create different degrees of rigidity which would differentially affect performance in a problem solving task. Thus, they regard rigidity "not as a trait or entity but as a kind of behavior predictable from specific learning experiences." Cowen, Wiener & Hess (31) obtained a correlation of .42 between rigidity scores on Luchins' water-jar task and a specially constructed "alphabet-maze" designed to measure a different aspect of rigidity in behavior. Thus, rigidity now seems to be a fairly general source of individual differences in performing certain kinds of tasks, particularly those involving reasoning. It is of some interest, incidentally, that Cowen *et al.* report U-shaped distributions for their measures. Such distributions are usually hard to come by.

Factorial interpretations of certain well-known tests.—One may applaud the trend toward investigations of the factorial composition of certain widely used clinical tests. Ansbacher (6) correlated scores on the Goodenough Draw-a-Man test with scores on Primary Mental Abilities tests and certain of the MacQuarrie tests. Higher correlations were found for Reasoning (.40), Space (.38), and Perception (.37) than for Verbal Meaning (.26) and Number (.24). Since the test correlated to the extent of .34 with the MacQuarrie tracing subtest, Ansbacher suggested that the Draw-a-Man test also measures "youthful willingness to follow directions." Unfortunately, one cannot tell from this investigation whether the connections between the Draw-a-Man test and Primary Mental Abilities tests are due to group factors or to a general factor of intelligence.

The Wechsler-Bellevue test also came under scrutiny from the standpoint of a factor-analytic rationale. In the first of two papers, Cohen (26) found that the test can be resolved into three common factors (connected by a second-order general factor) which he called "verbal," "non-verbal organization," and "freedom from distractability" respectively, and that the factorial composition of the subtests is in general highly consistent whether one tests psychoneurotics, schizophrenics, or brain-damaged cases. In the subsequent paper (27), Cohen proposed a "factor-analytically based rationale for the Wechsler-Bellevue." Disagreeing with the test rationales offered by Wechsler and by Rapaport, he finds that test performance in patient populations can be interpreted readily in terms of his common factors. Little evidence is found for test specificity, as would be required by the Wechsler and Rapaport rationales. On the other hand, some of the Wechsler-Bellevue subtests seem to operate differently in different neuropsychiatric groups; thus, interpretation of the tests is partly dependent on the diagnosis. Cohen's work has a strong appeal but suffers somewhat from the fact that only the subtests of the Wechsler-Bellevue were studied. No "reference" tests of previously established factors were included in the analysis.

Variables Associated with Individual Differences

In the studies to be discussed below, we shall consider some constitutional and environmental variables which may account for individual differences. As has been true of similar research in the past, most of these investigations are limited by the fact that they are not sufficiently discriminating with respect to the variables of individual differences which are studied. When the dependent variable is a complex hodgepodge like "general intelligence," we cannot draw any conclusions as to which aspects of individual differences are associated with a given genetic or environmental vraiable.

The stability of individual differences.—Before investigating variables associated with individual differences we may well look to the stability of these differences. Very little has been contributed to the literature on this problem recently. The study by Husén (65) merely confirms existing evidence that intelligence test scores are stable for adults over periods of a year, and that the correlations obtained will depend upon the extent to which the tests are equivalent. Though based on only six cases, a study by Smith (106) is interesting because it is perhaps the first longitudinal study covering a 50-year period. A notebook kept by a mother on her six children for eight years furnished the data for this study; the life histories of these individuals 50 years later were also available. Considerable consistency was found in such areas as health, learning ability, personality, and interests.

Genetic and physiological variables.—In an elaborate statistical treatment of certain data from the so-called Scottish Survey, Roberts (92) claimed to find further evidence for Pearson's hypothesis of two types of mental deficiency: the type which is found in the lower tail of the normal curve and which may be described in terms of multi-factorial genetics, and the abnormal, qualitatively different type ascribed to the operation of a single gene. Nevertheless, it is probable that both these types would be regarded as endogenous by Feldman (44), who found that exogenous mental defectives do better on the Bender Gestalt tests. Biesheuvel (13) summarizes the arguments against the use of IQ tests in studies of heredity and environment or in studies concerned with a putative decline in the intelligence of the population. He sees no evidence that the national intelligence in South Africa is declining, and confirms certain indications of the Scottish Survey on family size and intelligence. Short (104) finds reason to believe that imagery types (visual versus verbal) may be of an inherited character, since they are associated with alpha rhythm, also known to be hereditary.

In view of the tremendous difficulties entailed in establishing any association between ethnicity and individual differences, current research on this problem seems limited to small scale descriptive studies. Anastasi & D'Angelo (4) examined Negro-white differences in language development and Goodenough Draw-a-Man IQ. In a sample of 100 preschool children, no differences in IQ were significant; in language development, the only significant result was a race×sex interaction wherein Negro boys developed faster than girls, while the opposite tendency (consistent with the results of previous research) was noticed among the white children. Perhaps this result could be traced to environmental and cultural factors.

There is, however, increased interest in the effect of aging on individual differences. Vincent (113) finds that the decline of mean score on various intelligence tests with age can be regarded as practically constant, that this decline operates for both timed and untimed tests (provided they are influenced only to a minor extent by knowledge), and that the mean annual decline from age 21 to 60 is approximately $.03\sigma$. Welford (115) presents experiments on the effect of aging on various types of skilled performances. He ascribes the resulting decline to failures of central receptor mechanisms. A factor analysis of the Wechsler-Bellevue test by Birren (15) is interesting because its results compare very favorably with those of Cohen (26), previously cited, for three neuropsychiatric groups. Birren finds four oblique factors, three of which were identified as Verbal Comprehension, Closure, and Rote Memory. Comparison of the patterns of factor loadings suggests that these are the same, respectively, as Cohen's Verbal, Nonverbal Organization, and Freedom from Distractability factors. Thus, Cohen and Birren differ only in the subjective interpretations which they give the factors, which are in any case highly similar. Since the two studies appear to have been performed quite independently, and even on different types of populations, the results constitute fresh and interesting evidence for the invariance of factor analytic results. Birren notes, incidentally, that his elderly sample shows loss on all three factors, but greatest relative loss on the closure factor.

If the various types of ability decline differentially, it has been reasoned, comparisons of losses on different factors should result in a measure of mental impairment. It seems that investigators in this field have not adequately taken into account a factor-analytic rationale. Two recent research papers on this topic seem to do little more than illustrate the complexity of the problem. Garfield & Blek (51) emphasize that there is an interaction between age and mental impairment that must be taken account of. Corsini & Fassett (29) offer a substitute for Wechsler's mental deterioration index which works better even when applied to Wechsler's own data.

If the data had been analyzed more thoroughly and rigorously, the results presented by Kurland & Gilgash (71) might have thrown further light on the operation of glutamic acid dosage with mental defectives. Administration of this drug for a month apparently produced a significant rise on the Wechsler-Bellevue test, but the effect seems to have been more marked on the performance scales than on the verbal scales.

Environmental variables.—While it is too early to expect follow-ups of the work of Eells *et al.* (39), several exploratory studies on socioeconomic status variables associated with intelligence tests have appeared. Estes (40) found status differences at age 7½. A more careful look at some of Estes' results, however, shows that significant socioeconomic differences on certain scales (particularly the "verbal" scales) seem to be present even at age 10½. These scales are of course arbitrary combinations of scores on separate test performances, and not factor-analytically established scales. The differences associated with such a variable as socioeconomic status can be made meaningful only if they are in terms of linearly independent variables. Tate (109) compared groups of five-year-olds, contrasted in socioeconomic status, on the Leiter International Performance Scale and certain other tests of intelligence. The conclusion of the author that the Leiter International Performance Scale is no more culture-free than the Stanford-Binet or the Arthur Performance Scale seems fairly well supported by her data. In the area of personality testing, Auld (7) reviewed the by now substantial amount of evidence that social class is associated with responses on various personality tests, both objective and projective. Auld concludes that the psychologist must take these social class differences into account; otherwise, says Auld, the psychologist is "likely to assume a bias in favor of his own social class, the middle class."

Socioeconomic status is a gross variable which masks the specific influences of various kinds of experience. Fortunately, at least a few studies of the effects of specific training appeared in the last year. A study by Klatskin (69) suggests that the currently popular "lenient" child-care procedures make for a slight rise in scores on infant intelligence tests. This sort of thing happens with laboratory rats, too, to judge from researches reported by Bingham & Griffiths (14) and Forgays & Forgays (48), who found that rats raised in infancy in "rich" environments learn mazes better as adults; nevertheless, these workers have not yet been able to pin down exactly what makes an environment "rich" for a newborn rat. Boger (16) conducted an experimental study of the effect of special exercises with blocks, geometric problems, and puzzles on the intelligence test scores of elementary pupils in rural schools. Experimental groups were significantly better than control groups after $3\frac{1}{2}$ months' training, particularly on the spatial relationship part of the California Test of Mental Maturity. This finding suggests tentatively that the space factor, as it is usually identified, may be attributable partly to differences in experience with the tasks used in measuring this factor. There are, in fact, disappointingly few studies to date concerning the effects of specific kinds of training upon the factorial compositions of tasks. One recent investigation from France, by Goguelin (54), is of interest despite the fact that the results cannot be neatly integrated with those obtained from samples in the United States. Goguelin made factor analyses of the same seven subtests of a mechanical comprehension battery for four groups with different amounts and kinds of technical training. The differences in the factor loadings are explained on the hypothesis that some tests were performed by technically trained people primarily on the basis of their technical knowledge, but by nontechnical people primarily on the basis of what Goguelin calls "a more or less intuitive reasoning ability."

Perhaps because of recent world events and movements of peoples, there is a continuing interest in the effect of bilingualism on measured intelligence. Nothing in the extensive review by Darcy (34) of 110 references in the literature would tend to set aside the hypothesis that bilingualism depresses scores on certain intelligence tests simply because the bilingual child (bilingual in the sense of using two languages, but not necessarily with equal competence) is not likely to have as good a mastery of the language of testing as a comparable unilingual child. Darcy herself concludes that bilinguals suffer from a language handicap in taking verbal tests, but that there is no indication of inferiority of bilinguals on nonlanguage tests, provided adequate controls have been exercised. Recent papers by Darcy (33), Anastasi & Cordova (3), and Johnson (66) show results consistent with these conclusions. Jones (67) found that in the case of Welsh-English bilingual children, the difference between nonverbal and verbal IQ tends to diminish as reading age in English increases.

There are several studies which deal with certain effects of the measurement procedure upon intelligence test scores. Peel (87) examined practice effects on Moray House intelligence tests; Sacks (98) found that the examiner's establishment of pleasant social relations with three-year-old nursery school children makes for significantly higher tested IQ's; and Sarason & Mandler (101) showed that individuals with a high anxiety drive in the testing situation tend to perform more poorly than otherwise on group intelligence, aptitude, and achievement tests. If the Sarason-Mandler effect is a highly general one, it may mean that test scores ought to be adjusted for anxiety drive, both in research and practice. This is a problem which will doubtless receive more study in the near future.

Psychometric Methodology

Under the heading of psychometric methodology, the predominantly important topics are (*a*) techniques of identifying dimensions of individual differences, (*b*) problems involved in constructing measurements, and (*c*) the appropriate scaling of these measurements. These topics will be discussed in inverse order, however, because recent thought has emphasized the problems inherent in measuring a unidimensional trait.

Scaling theory.—An important contribution to the theory of all psychological scaling (including both psychophysical and psychometric) is the monograph by Coombs (28), who desires to construct a mathematical model to fit behavior rather than to attempt to fit behavior to a preconceived model. Implied in this effort is the rejection of the numerical assumptions latent in many previous theories of scaling, with the result that in Coombs' opinion scaling must be distinguished from measurement, which implies number. Coombs' model concerns various procedures for seeking relations between individuals and stimuli. Values for individuals and for stimuli are found on scales which yield orders of magnitude rather than numerical quantities. Of particular interest in the present connection is Coombs' mathematical definition of a perfect trait (perfect in the sense that it orders both individuals and stimuli in a corresponding way). Thus far, Coombs has not published any material explicitly applying his approach to mental test data, but such an application seems clearly possible.

Mathematical theory of ability tests.—The theory of mental tests has taken substantial forward strides in the hands of Lord (75), who shows that when the items of a test are measures of a single common factor of ability, the characteristics of the test score distribution can be predicted with high accuracy from the parameters relating to the difficulty and the validity of the items. He has confirmed with admirable mathematical rigor the hypothesis of several previous workers that the regression of test scores on true ability is curvilinear in the general case. His formulations also enable the prediction of bivariate frequency distributions between tests measuring a single ability but composed of items with any specified difficulty values and validities.

Further, it is found that the relations between item parameters and the reliability and discriminating power of a test can be precisely specified. These results are all for free response tests, that is, where the examinee has no opportunity to pass an item by guessing. Later, however, Lord published two papers relating to multiple choice tests (76, 77), the second of which also presents formulae for maximum likelihood estimates of true scores. Cronbach & Warrington (32) have come to several conclusions identical to Lord's but chiefly by empirical rather than by mathematical investigation. Plumlee (91) developed formulae to show the effect of item difficulty and chance success on product moment item correlations and on test reliability. Finally, a mathematical investigation by Angoff (5) and an empirical study by Wesman & Kernan (116) concern the problem of estimating the unspeeded reliability for time-limit tests. Many of these studies are of fundamental significance; unfortunately, their results are of too great complexity for further description here. It would appear, at any rate, that a theory of mental tests which employs orthodox quantitative concepts is of great practical value. Perhaps this is another way of saying that some of the quantitative assumptions to which Coombs would take exception actually fit the data quite well.

Other problems in test construction.—Anastasi (2) showed sequential sampling of cases to be an efficient and accurate method of determining item parameters such as difficulty and validity. Kuang (70) compared three methods of item analysis: F. B. Davis's procedure, biserial r, and probit analysis. It was found that they produce tests about equal in reliability, but that they differ in the computational labor involved, the Davis technique being the fastest and probit analysis the slowest. Lorge & Kruglov (78) concerned themselves with the problem which arises when one wishes subject matter experts to estimate item difficulties in advance of any tryout of items. They found that estimates could be made more accurately when the judges are given anchoring information consisting of the difficulty values of representative items tried out previously.

Factor analysis methodology.—Guttman (61) clarifies certain relations between Thurstone's, Holzinger's, and his own approaches to the computation of multiple group factors. In a critical review of statistical significance tests in factor analysis, Burt (21) summarizes several methods which may not be familiar to American investigators. He is in a generous frame of mind on the question of "when to stop factoring," but more severe when it comes to "demonstrating" factors. He is properly critical of the practice of testing the significance of residuals against the sampling distributions of zero correlations. His idea of testing the significance of the difference between observed and reproduced correlations further suggests a possible means of testing the significance of a factor loading even in an oblique reference frame, for possibly one could compare the observed reproduced correlation with the reproduced correlation under the hypothesis of a zero factor loading.

Several solutions have been offered for finding the orthogonal structure which best fits a given oblique structure (53, 56). Sandler (100) suggests that the rotation of factor axes can be facilitated by selecting certain persons as extreme deviates in the factors represented and, by Burt's reciprocity principle, inserting these persons into the test space. Sandler does not, however, give any convincing demonstration that his method would be useful when one does not know what the factors are in advance of the analysis. Carroll (24) has recently offered a method for obtaining an approximation to simple structure by completely objective techniques rather than by the usual graphical procedures; unfortunately, the method presently requires almost prohibitive computations.

Other techniques and problems.—Much interest has been evinced lately in the multiple discriminant function, designed to give a best-fitting set of weights for *n* tests in descriminating between *k* groups. Tiedeman & Sternberg (111) have provided an illustration of the possibilities of this technique in curriculum guidance in secondary schools, but Webster's (114) paper suggests that the technique may also be useful in the investigation of individual differences as such. For example, in his study the technique disclosed a result that otherwise might not have been apparent, namely, that certain Thematic Apperception Test variables significantly discriminated "dominant" from "submissive" men only among those who were "secure."

Sidman (105) cautioned against the rather common practice of educing functional relations from group data when these are actually averages from individual curves. Averaging, he pointed out, may mask the possibly differing forms and parameters of individual curves.

Psychometric Instruments

Attention should be called to the publication of Buros's *Fourth Mental Measurements Yearbook* (19). Buros has performed a distinct service for all persons concerned with tests in continuing to provide a comprehensive listing and review of currently available instruments.

New tests.—Davis & Eells (36) brought out a series of tests for primary and elementary school children which they presume to be culture-fair for children of different socioeconomic levels. Two attempts have been made to simplify the Vigotsky test for clinical use (90, 103). These researches fail, however, to clarify what the Vigotsky test measures. Apparently, it does not measure "intelligence" in the usual sense.

Work has continued on the development of abbreviated scales of intelligence. Hunt & French (64) offer extended norms for their so-called CVS Abbreviated Intelligence Scale and provide evidence of its validity for rough screening on intelligence and for certain kinds of psychiatric classification.

Standardization and evaluation of tests.—Numerous investigations concerning the standardization of intelligence tests continue to appear. Representative of these are: Roberts & Mellone's (93) study of the comparability of Terman-Merrill IQ's at different ages; Justman & Wrightstone's (68) study of the Pintner and the Henmon-Nelson tests; Holland's (63) comparison, for normal children, of the Wechsler Intelligence Scale for Children (WISC) and the Stanford-Binet; Delattre & Cole's (38) comparison of the WISC and the Wechsler-Bellevue, again for normal children; and Beverly & Bensburg's (12) comparison of the Leiter, Cornell-Coxe, and Stanford-Binet tests as applied to mental defectives. Typically, these studies report differences in mean level of IQ or mental age obtained with different tests; in view of the high correlations usually reported (which are not at all surprising in view of the generally common factorial content of the tests), it would perhaps be more useful if these writers were to report, in addition, detailed tables of score equivalences.

Millard (82) and Wickert (117) agree in finding that despite its title, the test known as *How Supervise?*, designed for measuring knowledge of foremanship and industrial supervision, functions essentially as an intelligence test, at least for nonhigh school graduates. If it measures knowledge of principles of supervision at all, it does so only for highly educated groups. These results may be partly accounted for by Maloney's (80) finding that the test is at the "difficult" level of readability. It may be commented that the readability of a test, or of the test instructions, is probably often a good indication of the extent to which it measures the verbal comprehension factor of ability.

LITERATURE CITED

1. Adorno, T. W., Frenkel-Brunswik, E., Levinson, D. J., and Sanford, R. N., *The Authoritarian Personality* (Harper & Brothers., New York, N. Y., 990 pp., 1950)
2. Anastasi, A., "An Empirical Study of the Applicability of Sequential Analysis to Item Selection," *Educ. Psychol. Measurement*, **13**, 3–13 (1953)
3. Anastasi, A., and Cordova, F. A., "Some Effects of Bilingualism upon the Intelligence Test Performance of Puerto Rican Children in New York City," *J. Educ. Psychol.*, **44**, 1–19 (1952)
4. Anastasi, A., and D'Angelo, R. Y., "A Comparison of Negro and White Preschool Children in Language Development and Goodenough Draw-a-Man IQ," *J. Genetic Psychol.*, **81**, 147–65 (1952)
5. Angoff, W. H., "Test Reliability and Effective Test Length," *Psychometrika*, **18**, 1–14 (1953)
6. Ansbacher, H. L., "The Goodenough Draw-a-Man Test and Primary Mental Abilities," *J. Consulting Psychol.*, **16**, 176–80 (1952)
7. Auld, F., Jr., "Influence of Social Class on Personality Test Responses," *Psychol. Bull.*, **49**, 318–32 (1952)
8. Bach, J. O., "Practice Teaching Success in Relation to Other Measures of Teaching Ability," *J. Exptl. Educ.*, **21**, 57–80 (1952)
9. Baehr, M. E., "A Factorial Study of Temperament," *Psychometrika*, **17**, 107–26 (1952)
10. Bajard, G., "Analyse Factorielle de Critères Professionnels," *Bull. Institute Natl. Étude Travail et Orientation Profession.*, **8**, 122–27 (1952)
11. Barnett, G. J., Handelsman, I., Stewart, L. H., and Super, D. E., "The Occupational Level Scale as a Measure of Drive," *Psychol. Monographs*, **66** (10), 37 pp. (1952)
12. Beverly, L., and Bensberg, G., "A Comparison of the Leiter, the Cornell-Coxe, and Stanford-Binet with Mental Defectives," *Am. J. Mental Deficiency*, **57**, 89–91 (1952–53)
13. Biesheuvel, S., "The Nation's Intelligence and its Measurement," *S. African J. Sci.*, **49**, 120–38 (1952)
14. Bingham, W. E., and Griffiths, W. J., Jr., "The Effect of Different Environments during Infancy on Adult Behavior in the Rat," *J. Comp. Physiol. Psychol.*, **45**, 307–12 (1952)
15. Birren, J. E., "A Factorial Analysis of the Wechsler-Bellevue Scale Given to an Elderly Population," *J. Consulting Psychol.*, **16**, 399–405 (1952)
16. Boger, J. H., "An Experimental Study of the Effects of Perceptual Training on Group IQ Test Scores of Elementary Pupils in Rural Ungraded Schools," *J. Educ. Research*, **46**, 43–52 (1952–53)
17. Brogden, H. E., "The Primary Personal Values Measured by the Allport-Vernon Test, 'A Study of Values,' " *Psychol. Monographs*, **66**(16), 31 pp. (1952)
18. Brown, C. W., and Ghiselli, E. E., "The Relationship between the Predictive Power of Aptitude Tests for Trainability and for Job Proficiency," *J. Appl. Psychol.*, **36**, 370–72 (1952)
19. Buros, O. K., Ed., *Fourth Mental Measurements Yearbook* (Gryphon Press, New Brunswick, N. J., 1163 pp., 1953)
20. Burt, C., "Subdivided Factors," *Brit. J. Psychol.* (*Stat. Sect.*), **2**, 41–63 (1949)

21. Burt, C., "Tests of Significance in Factor Analysis," *Brit. J. Psychol.* (*Stat. Sect.*), **5,** 109–33 (1952)
22. Carroll, J. B., "Factor Analysis in Educational Research," *Rev. Educ. Research,* **21,** 368–88 (1951)
23. Carroll, J. B., "Ratings on Traits Measured by a Factored Personality Inventory," *J. Abnormal Social Psychol.*, **47,** 626–32 (1952)
24. Carroll, J. B., "An Analytical Solution for Approximating Simple Structure in Factor Analysis," *Psychometrika,* **18,** 23–38 (1953)
25. Cattell, R. B., and Horowitz, J. Z., "Objective Personality Tests Investigating the Structure of Altruism in Relation to Source Traits A, H, and L," *J. Personality,* **21,** 103–17 (1952)
26. Cohen, J., "Factors Underlying Wechsler-Bellevue Performance of Three Neuropsychiatric Groups," *J. Abnormal Social Psychol.*, **47,** 359–65 (1952)
27. Cohen, J., "A Factor-Analytically Based Rationale for the Wechsler-Bellevue," *J. Consulting Psychol.*, **16,** 272–77 (1952)
28. Coombs, C. H., *A Theory of Psychological Scaling* (Engineering Research Institute, University of Michigan, Ann Arbor, Mich., Bulletin 34, 94 pp., 1952)
29. Corsini, R. J., and Fassett, K. K., "The Validity of Wechsler's Mental Deterioration Index," *J. Consulting Psychol.*, **16,** 462–68 (1952)
30. Corter, H. M., "Factor Analysis of Some Reasoning Tests," *Psychol. Monographs,* **66**(8), 31 pp. (1952)
31. Cowen, E. L., Wiener, M., and Hess, J., "Generalization of Problem-Solving Rigidity," *J. Consulting Psychol.*, **17,** 100–3 (1953)
32. Cronbach, L. J., and Warrington, W. G., "Efficiency of Multiple-Choice Tests as a Function of Spread of Item Difficulties," *Psychometrika,* **17,** 127–47 (1952)
33. Darcy, N. T., "The Performance of Bilingual Puerto Rican Children on Verbal and on Non-Language Tests of Intelligence," *J. Educ. Research,* **45,** 499–506 (1951–52)
34. Darcy, N. T., "A Review of the Literature on the Effects of Bilingualism upon the Measurement of Intelligence," *J. Genetic Psychol.*, **82,** 21–58 (1953)
35. Davidson, W. M., and Carroll, J. B., "Speed and Level Components in Time-Limit Scores: A Factor Analysis," *Educ. Psychol. Measurement,* **5,** 411–27 (1945)
36. Davis, A., and Eells, K., *Davis-Eells Tests of General Intelligence or Problem-Solving Ability* (World Book Co., Yonkers, N. Y., 1952)
37. Degan, J. W., "Dimensions of Functional Psychosis," *Psychometric Monographs,* No. 6, 41 pp. (1952)
38. Delattre, L., and Cole, D., "A Comparison of the WISC and the Wechsler-Bellevue," *J. Consulting Psychol.*, **16,** 228–30 (1952)
39. Eells, K., Davis, A., Havighurst, R.J., Herrick, V.E., and Tyler, R.W., *Intelligence and Cultural Differences* (University of Chicago Press, Chicago, Ill., 388 pp., 1951)
40 Estes, B. W., "Influence of Socioeconomic Status on Wechsler Intelligence Scale for Children: An Exploratory Study," *J. Consulting Psychol.*, **17,** 58–62 (1953)
41. Eysenck, H. J., *The Scientific Study of Personality* (George Routledge & Kegan Paul, Ltd., London, England, 320 pp., 1952)
42. Eysenck, H. J., "Schizothymia-Cyclothymia as a Dimension of Personality: II. Experimental," *J. Personality,* **20,** 345–84 (1952)

43. Eysenck, H. J., "The Logical Basis of Factor Analysis," *Am. Psychologist*, **8**, 105–14 (1953)

44. Feldman, I. S., "Psychological Differences among Moron and Borderline Mental Defectives as a Function of Etiology," *Am. J. Mental Deficiency*, **57**, 484–94 (1952–53)

45. Ferguson, L. W., *Personality Measurement* (McGraw-Hill Book Co., Inc., New York, N. Y., 457 pp., 1952)

46. Fleishman, E. A., "A Factor Analysis of Intra-Task Performance on Two Psychomotor Tests," *Psychometrika*, **18**, 45–55 (1953)

47. Ford, C. F., Jr., and Tyler, L. E., "A Factor Analysis of Terman and Miles' M-F Test," *J. Appl. Psychol.*, **36**, 251–53 (1952)

48. Forgays, D. G., and Forgays, J. W., "The Nature of the Effect of Free-Environmental Experience in the Rat," *J. Comp. Physiol. Psychol.*, **45**, 322–28 (1952)

49. Fruchter, B., "Ability Patterns in Technical Training Criteria," *J. Appl. Psychol.*, **36**, 381–84 (1952)

50. Fruchter, B., and Mahan, W. W., "Some Perceptual Factors Measured by Motion Picture Tests," *J. Educ. Psychol.*, **43**, 430–35 (1952)

51. Garfield, S. L., and Blek, L., "Age, Vocabulary Level, and Mental Impairment," *J. Consulting Psychol.*, **16**, 395–98 (1952)

52. Garry, R., "Individual Differences in Ability to Fake Vocational Interests," *J. Appl. Psychol.*, **37**, 33–37 (1953)

53. Gibson, W. A., "Orthogonal and Oblique Simple Structures," *Psychometrika*, **17**, 317–23 (1952)

54. Goguelin, P., "Études sur Deux Tests. I. Un Nouveau Test Technique. II. Test des Phrases en Désordre," *Rev. Psychol. Appl., Paris*, **2**, 229–38 (1952)

55. Gough, H. G., "Identifying Psychological Femininity," *Educ. Psychol. Measurement*, **12**, 427–39 (1952)

56. Green, B. F., "The Orthogonal Approximation of an Oblique Structure in Factor Analysis," *Psychometrika*, **17**, 429–40 (1952)

57. Guilford, J. P., Fruchter, B., and Zimmerman, W. S., "Factor Analysis of the Army Air Forces Sheppard Field Battery of Experimental Aptitude Tests," *Psychometrika*, **17**, 45–68 (1952)

58. Guilford, J. P., Green, R. F., Christensen, P. R., Hertzka, A. F., and Kettner, N. W., "A Factor-Analytic Study of Navy Reasoning Tests with the Air Force Aircrew Classification Battery," *Reports from Psychol. Laboratory, Univ. So. Calif.*, No. 6, 23 pp. (1952)

59. Guilford, J. P., Hertzka, A. F., Berger, R. M., and Christensen, P. R., "A Factor-Analytic Study of Evaluative Abilities. I. Hypotheses and Description of Tests," *Reports from Psychol. Laboratory, Univ. So. Calif.*, No. 7, 19 pp. (1952)

60. Guilford, J. P., Wilson, R. C., and Christensen, P. R., "A Factor-Analytic Study of Creative Thinking. II. Administration of Tests and Analysis of Results," *Reports from Psychol. Laboratory, Univ. So. Calif.*, No. 8, 24 pp. (1952)

61. Guttman, L., "Multiple-Group Methods for Common-Factor Analysis: Their Basis, Computation, and Interpretation," *Psychometrika*, **17**, 209–22 (1952)

62. Hofstaetter, P. R., "A Factorial Study of Prejudice," *J. Personality*, **21**, 228–39 (1952)

63. Holland, G. A., "A Comparison of the WISC and Stanford-Binet IQ's of Normal Children," *J. Consulting Psychol.*, **17**, 147–52 (1953)

64. Hunt, W. A., and French, E. G., "The CVS Abbreviated Intelligence Scale," *J. Consulting Psychol.*, **16,** 181–86 (1952)
65. Husén, T., "The Stability of Intelligence Test Scores," *Acta Psychol.*, **9,** 53–81 (1953)
66. Johnson, G. B., Jr., "Bilingualism as Measured by a Reaction-Time Technique and the Relationship between a Language and a Non-Language Intelligence Quotient," *J. Genetic Psychol.*, **82,** 3–10 (1953)
67. Jones, W. R., "The Language Handicap of Welsh-Speaking Children," *Brit. J. Educ. Psychol.*, **22,** 114–23 (1952)
68. Justman, J., and Wrightstone, J. W., "A Comparison of Pupil Functioning on the Pintner Intermediate Test and the Henmon-Nelson Test of Mental Ability," *Educ. Psychol. Measurement*, **13,** 102–9 (1953)
69. Klatskin, E. H., "Intelligence Test Performance at One Year among Infants Raised with Flexible Methodology," *J. Clin. Psychol.*, **8,** 230–37 (1952)
70. Kuang, H. P., "A Critical Evaluation of the Relative Efficiency of Three Techniques in Item Analysis," *Educ. Psychol. Measurement*, **12,** 248–66 (1952)
71. Kurland, A. A., and Gilgash, C. A., "A Study of the Effect of Glutamic Acid on Delinquent Adult Male Mental Defectives," *Am. J. Mental Deficiency*, **57,** 669–80 (1952–53)
72. Lee, M. L., "Relationship of Masculinity-Femininity to Tests of Mechanical and Clerical Abilities," *J. Appl. Psychol.*, **36,** 377–80 (1952)
73. Loevinger, J., "Intelligence," in *Theoretical Foundations of Psychology*, 557–601 (Helson, H., Ed., D. Van Nostrand Co., Inc., New York, N. Y., 787 pp. 1951)
74. Long, W. F., "A Job Preference Survey for Industrial Applicants," *J. Appl. Psychol.*, **36,** 333–37 (1952)
75. Lord, F. M., "A Theory of Test Scores," *Psychometric Monographs*, No. 7, 84 pp. (1952)
76. Lord, F. M., "An Investigation of the Relation of the Reliability of Multiple-Choice Tests to the Distribution of Item Difficulties," *Psychometrika*, **17,** 181–94 (1952)
77. Lord, F. M., "An Application of Confidence Intervals and of Maximum Likelihood to the Estimation of an Examinee's Ability," *Psychometrika*, **18,** 57–76 (1953)
78. Lorge, I., and Kruglov, L., "The Improvement of Estimates of Test Difficulty," *Educ. Psychol. Measurement*, **13,** 31–46 (1953)
79. Lurie, W. A., "A Study of Spranger's Value Types by the Method of Factor Analysis," *J. Social Psychol.*, **8,** 17–37 (1937)
80. Maloney, P. W., "Reading Ease Scores for File's *How Supervise?*" *J. Appl. Psychol.*, **36,** 225–27 (1952)
81. Maltzman, I., and Morrisett, L., Jr., "Different Strengths of Set in the Solution of Anagrams," *J. Exptl. Psychol.*, **44,** 242–46 (1952)
82. Millard, K. W., "Is *How Supervise?* an Intelligence Test?" *J. Appl. Psychol.*, **36,** 221–24 (1952)
83. Moursy, E. M., "The Hierarchical Organization of Cognitive Levels," *Brit. J. Psychol.* (*Stat. Sect.*), **5,** 151–80 (1952)
84. Myers, C. T., "The Factorial Composition and Validity of Differently Speeded Tests," *Psychometrika*, **17,** 347–52 (1952)
85. Newman, S. H., French, J. W., and Bobbitt, J. M., "An Analysis of Criteria for Validation of Selection Measures at the U. S. Coast Guard Academy," *Educ. Psychol. Measurement*, **12,** 394–407 (1952)

86. O'Connor, P., "Ethnocentrism, 'Intolerance of Ambiguity,' and Abstract Reasoning Ability," *J. Abnormal Social Psychol.*, **47,** 526–30 (1952)
87. Peel, E. A., "Practice Effects between Three Consecutive Tests of Intelligence," *Brit. J. Educ. Psychol.*, **22,** 196–99 (1952)
88. Pemberton, C. L., "The Closure Factors Related to Other Cognitive Processes," *Psychometrika*, **17,** 267–88 (1952)
89. Pemberton, C. L., "The Closure Factors Related to Temperament," *J. Personality*, **21,** 159–75 (1952)
90. Penny, R., "The Vigotsky Block Test: A Form of Administration," *Australian J. Psychol.*, **3,** 65–83 (1951)
91. Plumlee, L. B., "The Effect of Difficulty and Chance-Success on Item-Test Correlations and Test Reliability," *Psychometrika*, **17,** 69–86 (1952)
92. Fraser Roberts, J. A., "The Genetics of Mental Deficiency," *Eugen. Rev.*, **44,** 71–83 (1952)
93. Fraser Roberts, J. A., and Mellone, M. A., "On the Adjustment of Terman-Merrill I.Q.'s to Secure Comparability at Different Ages," *Brit. J. Psychol.* (*Stat. Sect.*), **5,** 65–79 (1952)
94. Roff, M., "A Factorial Study of Tests in the Perceptual Area," *Psychometric Monographs*, No. 8, 41 pp. (1952)
95. Roff, M., "The Pilot Candidate Selection Research Program. V. A Factorial Study of the Motor Aptitudes Area," (USAF School of Aviation Medicine, Randolph Field, Texas, Project No. 21-29-008, Report No. 5, 25 pp., 1953)
96. Ryans, D. G., "A Study of Criterion Data (A Factor Analysis of Teacher Behavior in the Elementary School)," *Educ. Psychol. Measurement*, **12,** 333–44 (1952)
97. Ryans, D. G., and Wandt, E., "A Factor Analysis of Observed Teacher Behavior in the Secondary School: A Study of Criterion Data," *Educ. Psychol. Measurement*, **12,** 574–86 (1952)
98. Sacks, E. L., "Intelligence Scores as a Function of Experimentally Established Social Relationships between Child and Examiner," *J. Abnormal Social Psychol.*, **47,** 354–58 (1952)
99. Sakoda, J. M., "Factor Analysis of OSS Situational Tests," *J. Abnormal Social Psychol.*, **47,** 843–52 (1952)
100. Sandler, J., "A Technique for Facilitating the Rotation of Factor Axes, Based on an Equivalence between Persons and Tests," *Psychometrika*, **17,** 223–29 (1952)
101. Sarason, S. B., and Mandler, G., "Some Correlates of Test Anxiety," *J. Abnormal Social Psychol.*, **47,** 810–17 (1952)
102. Schroder, H. M., and Rotter, J. B., "Rigidity as Learned Behavior," *J. Exptl. Psychol.*, **44,** 141–50 (1952)
103. Semeonoff, B., and Laird, A. J., "The Vigotsky Test as a Measure of Intelligence," *Brit. J. Psychol.* (*Gen. Sect.*), **43,** 94–102 (1952)
104. Short, P. L., "The Objective Study of Mental Imagery," *Brit. J. Psychol.* (*Gen. Sect.*), **44,** 38–51 (1953)
105. Sidman, M., "A Note on Functional Relations Obtained from Group Data," *Psychol. Bull.*, **49,** 263–69 (1952)
106. Smith, M. E., "A Comparison of Certain Personality Traits as Rated in the Same Individuals in Childhood and Fifty Years Later," *Child Development*, **23,** 159–80 (1952)
107. Stanley, J. C., and Waldrop, R. S., "Intercorrelations of *Study of Values* and

Kuder Preference Record Scores," *Educ. Psychol. Measurement*, **12,** 707–19 (1952)

108. Strong, E. K., Jr., and Tucker, A. C., "The Use of Vocational Interest Scales in Planning a Medical Career," *Psychol. Monographs*, **66**(9), 61 pp. (1952)
109. Tate, M. E., "The Influence of Cultural Factors on the Leiter International Performance Scale," *J. Abnormal Social Psychol.*, **47,** 497–501 (1952)
110. Thurstone, L. L., "Primary Mental Abilities," *Psychometric Monographs*, No. 1 121 pp. (1938)
111. Tiedeman, D. V., and Sternberg, J. J., "Information Appropriate for Curriculum Guidance," *Harvard Educ. Rev.*, **22,** 257–74 (1952)
112. Vernon, P. E., *The Structure of Human Abilities* (Methuen & Co., Ltd., London, England, 160 pp., 1950)
113. Vincent, D. F., "The Linear Relationship between Age and Score of Adults in Intelligence Tests," *Occupational Psychol.*, **26,** 243–49 (1952)
114. Webster, H., "Rao's Multiple Discriminant Technique Applied to Three TAT Variables," *J. Abnormal Social Psychol.*, **47,** 641–48 (1952)
115. Welford, A. T., *Skill and Age* (Oxford University Press, London, England, 161 pp., 1951)
116. Wesman, A. G., and Kernan, J. P., "An Experimental Comparison of Test-Retest and Internal Consistency Estimates of Reliability with Speeded Tests," *J. Educ. Psychol.*, **43,** 292–98 (1952)
117. Wickert, F. R., "Relation between *How Supervise?*, Intelligence, and Education for a Group of Supervisory Candidates in Industry," *J. Appl. Psychol.*, **36,** 301–3 (1952)
118. Wrigley, C., "The Prediction of a Complex Aptitude," *Brit. J. Psychol.* (*Stat. Sect.*), **5,** 93–104 (1952)
119. Zimmerman, W. S., "A Revised Orthogonal Rotational Solution for Thurstone's Original Primary Mental Abilities Test Battery," *Psychometrika*, **18,** 77–93 (1953)

PERSONALITY[1,2]

By Irvin L. Child

Department of Psychology, Yale University, New Haven, Connecticut

In agreement with Sears (37), the writer feels that the subject matter of personality study may usefully be classified into three general categories: personality structure, psychodynamics, and personality development. These categories are not rigidly separated, but are useful labels for certain clusterings either of theoretical interest, of research methods, or of type of evidence sought for. Within each of these categories, of course, there is no sharp boundary between general study of personality and such specific interests, covered elsewhere in this volume, as the investigation of child behavior, abnormal behavior, and techniques of assessment and diagnosis. The writer has no interest in helping to preserve the integrity of personality study as an isolated entity, welcoming instead the fact that as general psychology becomes more adequate to deal with the whole range of human behavior there is ever less occasion to recognize personality study in the traditional sense as a discipline in any way distinct. The general approach adopted in planning this chapter has been that of concentrating on those topics in personality study that seem least likely to receive extended attention in other chapters. Within the rather restricted yet heterogeneous field that is delimited in this way, the writer has none the less been highly selective.

One topic, psychodynamics and performance, will receive extended attention just because it happens to be especially conspicuous in the research studies published during the past year. Several other topics in psychodynamics will then be treated more briefly. Illustrative of the lack of rigid separation among the three categories of personality study mentioned above is the fact that much of the research reviewed under these topics might, with a slight shift in theoretical interest, be classified under personality development or, if attention were focussed on the kind of evidence appealed to, be classified under personality structure.

Within the delimited field reviewed here, there has been so little research during the past year on personality development that this category will be omitted from separate consideration. There remains the study of personality structure. Here the reviewer has been highly selective in a way that is not easily communicated; he has simply picked out for special attention certain research which seemed to him, for diverse reasons, especially likely to be of great general interest.

[1] The survey of the literature pertaining to this review was completed in May, 1953.

[2] The following abbreviations were used in this review: MMPI (Minnesota Multiphasic Personality Inventory); US (unconditioned stimulus).

Psychodynamics and Performance

The past year has seen a remarkable burst of research publication on psychodynamic influences on intellectual performance; it is remarkable, in part, for the extent to which various scholars working independently of each other but under the common influence of the general state of the science, have formulated similar hypotheses and tested them in similar fashion. Earlier work has been reviewed, and theoretical integration has been offered, by Lazarus, Deese & Osler (29) and by Child & Waterhouse (13, 14) and these efforts are being brought more up to date by Deese & Lazarus (16). In view of this fact, what seems most appropriate here is a review of the developments that seem most distinctive during the past year. As it happens, these developments are particularly appropriate in a review on personality, for they are concerned with personality variables in relation to the psychodynamics of performance. In particular, three separate measures of personality variables, apparently developed quite independently, have been used in these studies.

General scale of manifest anxiety.—The first of these variables is the measure developed and most fully reported by Taylor (43). It is based on a questionnaire which consists of anxiety items taken from the Minnesota Multiphasic Personality Inventory, together with buffer items. Those items were first selected which four out of five clinicians agreed to be indicative of manifest anxiety, but about a quarter of the items were later eliminated for lack of high correlation with total score. On the basis of the way the scale was constructed, it has been widely taken as a measure of manifest anxiety. Recently evidence has become available which may have a direct bearing on its validity, though the evidence certainly does not lead to any unambiguous conclusion. Taylor (43) reports a very large difference in average score on this scale between normal subjects and psychiatric patients, and suggests that this may constitute some positive evidence for the validity of the scale. Holtzman, Calvin & Bitterman (27) report very high correlations between the Taylor scale and a scale developed by Winne (49) from the MMPI[2] by the criterion of high discrimination between normals and neurotics, and they too suggest that this is positive evidence for the validity of the Taylor scale. Deese, Lazarus & Keenan (17), on the other hand, confirm the latter finding and also report a high correlation between the Taylor scale and a scale of psychasthenia (largely a result of overlapping items) but feel that these relationships cast some doubt on the simple view of what the Taylor scale measures which is represented in most of the publications making use of it. Actually the most pertinent evidence on validity, in relation to the purposes for which the scale has been used, may be that provided by an incidental finding of a study by Bitterman & Holtzman (4). Thirty-seven subjects were divided into high and low anxiety categories by a conference of four raters, who made use of various MMPI scores, the Rorschach, and information about response to experimental stress. The relation of this dichotomy to one based on the Taylor scale alone was not significant. These various facts suggest the difficulties that may generally be encountered when a complex personality scale comes to be used not for some practical aim for which discrimination may be useful even if the basis of discrimination is not understood, but instead for theoretical purposes which require relating scores to a single theoretically defined intervening variable. For the other personality measures which will be reviewed later, there is no parallel evidence to complicate the picture of their possible meaning, but this is doubtless just because inquiry into their validity has not been pushed as far.

This scale of general manifest anxiety was first used by Taylor (42) in a study in which extreme groups, very high or very low on the scale, were compared with respect to eyeblink conditioning. She found significantly more conditioned responses in the high anxiety group and interpreted this as an outcome of higher drive level in this group. (She pointed out that the effect of drive might be either directly on performance or by way of an influence on the habit-strength increment resulting from each rewarded response, or both together.) This finding was confirmed by Spence & Taylor (40), separately for two intensities of the air puff which served as US,[2] and by Spence & Farber (39); the latter authors also showed that the higher performance level of the high anxiety subjects was maintained during extinction. A study by Hilgard, Jones & Kaplan (26), using unselected subjects from the whole normal range, instead of preselected extreme groups, confirmed the relation between conditioning and anxiety score only as to direction, with results which are far short of being significant. However, one study by Spence & Taylor (41), which used an unselected group, did significantly confirm the finding which had otherwise been based on extreme groups alone. The evidence adds up to a perfectly clear conclusion at the empirical level. In eyeblink conditioning, performance level is positively correlated with score on the Taylor scale. It seems likely, moreover, that this is a more or less continuous relationship throughout the normal range (41), though Spence & Taylor (41) mention unpublished studies which indicate that the relationship may be curvilinear rather than rectilinear. The finding of faster conditioning with high anxiety is, it should be added, consistent with earlier studies of conditioning rate as a function of pathological anxiety [see Welch (46)]. That the finding has some generality, at least for conditioned responses based on anxiety-arousing unconditioned responses, is suggested by the fact that these earlier studies have used stimuli and responses different from those used by the Iowa group, as has a recent study on normal subjects by Bitterman & Holtzman (4).

From these findings about simple conditioning, the Iowa studies go on to consider the possible effects of anxiety as a variable in more complex learning situations. The principal lines of theoretical reasoning used here are those presented by Taylor & Spence (44) and repeated by Farber & Spence (24). The theoretical distinction they make among various learning tasks has to do with the number of competing response tendencies aroused. In simple conditioning, the situation is so controlled that a single stimulus-response tendency is aroused, with no appreciable competition; here the effect of increased anxiety is simply to improve performance through increasing the drive which, by Hullian theory, enters as a multiplier in determining the strength of this single S-R tendency. But in a more complicated learning task, such as serial rote learning, there are likely to be several competing tendencies present at any one point, and heightened drive will, according to Hullian postulates, have a multiplicative effect upon the strength of all these tendencies. If the correct response is not the one with greatest habit strength, the result will be to increase the advantage in response strength of those incorrect responses which are above it in the response hierarchy. Thus the probability of evocation of the correct response will be lowered, and the persistence of the dominant incorrect responses will be more protracted, so that during this period performance of subjects with high anxiety will be inferior to that of subjects with low anxiety. This much seems to be a thoroughly sound and direct derivation from Hullian theory. But at this point the theoretical reasoning of Taylor & Spence (44) becomes, in the opinion of the reviewer, rather careless. For they also suggest that if the correct response is the one of greatest strength, then the responses lower in the hierarchy will have a greater probability of being evoked in the presence of high anxiety than in the presence of low anxiety! Since they mention, in this connection, response threshold and behavioral oscillation, which they happen not to mention in connection with the preceding argument, the two arguments appear, at first glance, not to be contradictory. In the opinion of the reviewer, however, the two arguments as presented are contradictory, and only the first one seems to represent a correct derivation from the postulates employed. The same view is perhaps implied in a paper by Montague (33), for in a similar theoretical discussion he employs only the first of these two arguments.

By whatever mode of reasoning, then, Taylor & Spence predict that in situations where numerous incorrect response tendencies are aroused high anxiety should make for poorer performance than low anxiety; this effect is just the opposite of that found in simple conditioning. The available evidence will be reviewed in relation to this prediction before returning to the problem of theoretical interpretation. Several studies in the Iowa series report the relative performance of high anxiety and low anxiety subjects on learning tasks where incorrect response tendencies are likely to be conspicuous. Taylor & Spence (44), using a sort of verbal multiple-T maze, found high anxiety subjects to be significantly inferior to low anxiety subjects. Lucas (30) found high anxiety subjects to be inferior in immediate memory for consonant lists which contained confusing duplications. Farber & Spence (24) obtained the same result with a stylus maze. These latter authors, moreover, had employed some of the same subjects on the stylus maze and in a conditioning study. Normalizing the scores on each task to render them comparable, they were able to make a direct comparison of performance by the same high and low anxiety subjects in the two kinds of learning situations.

There is a clear interaction, with high anxiety subjects being inferior to low anxiety subjects in maze learning and superior to them in simple conditioning.

The theoretical considerations from which this gross variation of the effect of anxiety according to type of task was predicted would, of course, also lead to a prediction of quantitative variation of the effect according to the extent to which strong competing response tendencies are aroused. Two approaches have been used in an attempt to verify this prediction. One is to investigate the magnitude of the anxiety effect as a function of the difficulty of particular choice points in the maze, on the obvious assumption that greater difficulty implies more successful competition from incorrect response tendencies. Taylor & Spence (44) and Farber & Spence (24) both report a high correlation between difficulty of choice point and amount of difference between the two groups of subjects in performance on that choice point, and regard this as some confirmation of the theoretical prediction. To the reviewer this evidence carries no conviction, for it seems too likely to be a mere artifact of the system of measurement employed. The range of difficulty, at least in the data of Farber & Spence's study, is from a low percentage of errors up to something in the vicinity of 50 per cent of errors, and it seems likely that an effect essentially constant in nature would vary in magnitude through this range in just about the observed manner; this would be true, for example, of the effects of sampling error. (At the same time, both these pairs of authors note that anxiety has a detrimental effect even on easy choice points to an extent that is perhaps incompatible with their assumptions alone; in the opinion of the reviewer, this finding suggests the influence of other competing responses made specifically to the anxiety, such as will be mentioned again later.) More convincing evidence is actually provided by a finding reported by Farber & Spence in a slightly different connection. When high anxiety and low anxiety subjects are matched for total score on the stylus maze, significant evidence (at the 5 per cent level) is found that the high anxiety subjects perform better than the low anxiety subjects on the easiest choice points, while performing worse on the most difficult choice points.

The second approach to this problem of quantitative variation of the effect with amount of response competition consists of experimental introduction of variables which should directly influence amount of response competition. In an experiment by Lucas (30) the experimental variable introduced for this purpose was the extent to which, in a list of consonants presented in an immediate memory task, some of the consonants were repeated in differing locations within the list. Significant evidence was found that with either two or five such duplications, the inferiority in performance of a high anxiety group was greater than with no duplications. Montague (33), in a study of serial rote learning, introduced two experimental variables for this purpose, intra-list similarity and association value of the nonsense syllables used. Some evidence was obtained that both high intra-list similarity and low association value, presumably both making for relatively strong competing responses, tend to produce a decrement in performance in high anxiety subjects in comparison with low anxiety subjects.

These various lines of evidence do add up to a convincing demonstration that as the task becomes more complex (in the sense of involving conflict among various response tendencies) there is a tendency for high anxiety subjects to show increasingly poor performance in comparison with low anxiety subjects. If one shares the view of Taylor & Spence (44) that this relationship would be expected from a simple application of Hullian theory regardless of whether the correct response is highest in the response hierarchy, then this conclusion tends to confirm this simple application of Hullian theory. If, with the reviewer, one feels that their prediction here is faulty, then the theoretical implication of these findings is not so clear, for the simple application of Hullian theory would lead to this prediction only in those cases where the correct response is not at any given point dominant in the hierarchy. In this event, there is no clear theoretical basis for predicting the overall direction of effect of anxiety on performance in a complex task. To verify this interpretation one would need a trial-by-trial analysis to determine whether high anxiety subjects show greater stability of both their correct and their incorrect responses than do low anxiety subjects. One can certainly agree with Taylor & Spence (44, p. 64) that "further experimentation needs to be carried out in learning situations in which the number and relative strengths of the responses competing with the correct one can be controlled and manipulated." But at the present stage of knowledge, the reviewer is of the opinion that the most plausible general interpretation of these findings about task complexity is that the disruptive effects of various responses to anxiety vary with the nature of the task: that in simple conditioning, where a stable relationship is established between a single stimulus and a single response, what internal responses the subject is making at the time do not have any great effect, whereas the presence of high drive level does make for heightened performance; but that in complex situations, where the subject is already in conflict between various response tendencies relevant to the task, the presence of irrelevant responses made to anxiety heightens the conflict and interferes with performance to a greater extent than the increased drive improves it. In those specific instances where the correct response tendency is not the strongest of the task-relevant response tendencies, of course, the simpler sequence of events outlined by Taylor & Spence should be operating also to further strengthen this effect.

This line of interpretation is recognized both by Montague (33) and by Lucas (30), though it is made use of only by Lucas. In the reviewer's opinion, it is an essential line of interpretation (for reasons which will be indicated in dealing with personality variables other than the Taylor scale). The Iowa studies seem to have missed its importance thus far for two reasons. The first reason has to do with the nonexperimental nature of the Iowa studies. In view of the origin of these studies in a strongly experimental tradition, it is a curious fact that with the single exception of the Lucas study they have made no attempt to vary anxiety experimentally but have been content to deal with anxiety exclusively as a preexisting personality variable. The Lucas study illustrates what is also shown in other studies to be reviewed below, that when anxiety is simultaneously varied experimentally and personality-wise, complications appear. For example, Lucas found that when anxiety was varied experimentally by varying the number of failure experiences, one class of subjects showed a decrement in performance with increasing anxiety while another class of subjects showed an increment. The interpretation which seems to be called for, and which Lucas was not able to supply within the simplified conceptual framework he was using, is that different classes of subjects (such as those high and low on the Taylor anxiety scale) have different response tendencies evoked by situationally produced anxiety. This is the second reason that the Iowa studies have missed this essential line of interpretation—that despite their origin in a framework of learning theory they have paid no attention to possible differences among subjects in their previously learned response-tendencies to the cues provided by anxiety. It is in connection with these two points that the Iowa studies are valuably supplemented by the studies now to be reviewed which have used other personality variables.

Scale of anxiety in the testing situation.—Mandler & Sarason (31) have developed a questionnaire which, like the Taylor questionnaire, is intended to measure anxiety as a personality variable. A more specific measure is attempted here, however; it is a measure not of general anxiety but of anxiety in the situation of being tested. The hypotheses that have been tested with the Taylor questionnaire all have to do, of course, with effects of anxiety as aroused in the situation in which performance is measured. To the extent, then, that individuals differ with respect to anxiety arousal by different kinds of situations, and that questionnaires can really discriminate between anxiety in general and anxiety in one class of situation, the Mandler-Sarason questionnaire should be an even more appropriate and precise instrument for verifying hypotheses about the effects of anxiety when the hypotheses predict performance in a situation in which the subject is being tested. This questionnaire asks the subject not about anxiety in general or in a variety of situations, but only about anxiety in connection with being tested (in course examinations, in individual intelligence testing, and in group intelligence testing).

Mandler & Sarason (31) offer one item of direct evidence for the validity of their questionnaire. The examiner, testing subjects without any knowledge of their questionnaire responses, made ratings of overt manifestations of anxiety in the testing situation. These ratings yielded a point correlation of .59 with anxiety tendency as measured by the questionnaire. Even though the subjects were from the extremes of the distribution of questionnaire scores, this seems to the reviewer to be impressive direct evidence of validity.

This measure of test anxiety has been studied in relation to performance on several kinds of tasks. All of these tasks are ones of high complexity, and attention was not focussed on task differences. In comparison with the Iowa studies, these studies have the special value of presenting evidence on the interaction of personality differences not with task variables but with a set of experimental variables which might all be regarded as falling in the general class of experimental manipulation of anxiety arousal. Review of these studies here will be concentrated on this problem; as there was no such similar concentration of attention on this one problem in the original studies, however, it will be noted that some of the statistical tests relevant to this problem were not made in the published articles and have to be roughly estimated for present purposes.

In a series of three experiments Mandler & Sarason (partly in collaboration with Craighill) have explored the ways in which the dependence of test performance upon experimentally aroused anxiety varies according to status of the subject on the personality variable of test anxiety. Throughout these studies the general procedure has been to use subjects who are preselected for having either extremely high or extremely low scores on the test anxiety questionnaire, and then to subject each of the two extreme groups to identical variations of experimental procedure.

In the first of these studies (31), performance was measured on the Kohs block-design test, and the experimental variable consisted of failure, success, and neutral stimulation. This variable was introduced through statements of the examiner, informing the subject either that he had done very poorly on the preceding tests, or that he had done extremely well (accompanied by a challenge to continue doing as well), or else making no reference to standards or to previous performance. The effect of failure versus neutral stimulation is the finding most closely parallel to that of other studies. The tendency was for failure stimulation (in comparison with neutral) to produce a decrement in performance in the high anxiety group, but to produce an increment in performance in the low anxiety group. Only the second of these two effects reaches ordinary standards of statistical significance; no test is made of the difference between the two groups in the effect, but it seems probable that it would be significant. The interpretation offered has to do, of course, with personality differences between the two groups. The high anxiety group, it is suggested, have a strong previously acquired tendency to react to anxiety, in a test situation, with responses not relevant to the task, and the reference by the examiner to the test situation and to failure in it serves to elicit such responses more strongly than before and thus to interfere with adequate performance. The low anxiety group, on the other hand, have little tendency to make task-irrelevant responses; when some degree of anxiety is evoked by the mention of failure, it is then supposed, anxiety contributes to the total drive strength motivating task-relevant responses and thus leads to improved performance.

A subsidiary finding of great importance because of its novelty, even though it is not statistically significant, has to do with the effects of success stimulation. A tendency appears for success stimulation to operate in essentially the same way as failure stimulation; that is, for success stimulation (in comparison with neutral stimulation) to depress performance in the high anxiety group and to improve performance in the low anxiety group. The interpretation offered is that reference to performance in the test situation in connection with success tends to elicit internal responses in about the same way as in connection with failure, differentially for the high and low anxiety groups. If this finding is further confirmed, of course, it has important methodological implications, for it suggests that attempts to control failure stimulation by success stimulation do not provide an appropriate control, that in certain respects these two types of stimulation have identical effects which can be demonstrated only by having some clearly neutral kind of stimulation as a control. In addition, of course, this finding would contribute to clarifying just what it is about frustration or stress which influences performance, by indicating that it is something which is shared by frustration and by certain kinds of clear success, the presence of stimulation which elicits anxiety about evaluation of future performance in relation to goals and standards of performance.

In a second experiment (36), the experimental variable of anxiety arousal consisted of another kind of variation in statement to the subject. A digit symbol test was used, of sufficient length that no one could finish any trial in the time allowed. In one condition, subjects were told that they should be able to finish in the time allowed; in the other condition, they were told that they were not expected to finish. In the low anxiety group, the expect-to-finish instructions produced very markedly better performance than the other instructions. The interpretation made is similar to that offered in the first experiment; the expect-to-finish instructions led to increased drive which, in these subjects, served to motivate task-relevant responses. The instructions might be thought of as frustrating in character (and similar instructions have been used by other experimenters with the intention of producing frustration), and it is of interest, in this connection, to note that the effect was apparently just about as large on the first trial, when the subjects had had no opportunity to discover that they would in fact not be able to finish, as on subsequent trials which had been preceded by this frustrating discovery. Again, then, there is a suggestion here that some of the effects of frustration on performance are indirect results of direct effects which may also be produced in other ways than by frustration.

In the high anxiety group, an opposite effect of this instruction variable was predicted, on the grounds that such subjects would predominantly react to the statement that they should finish with task-irrelevant responses. Such a reversal of effect was found on two of five trials, but not on the other three. There certainly does, however, appear to be a clear difference in effect between the two anxiety groups which is probably statistically significant, though it was not tested.

In a third experiment (36), the experimental variable was ego-involvement as manipulated through instructions. As in many previous experiments on ego-involvement, half the subjects were told that the purpose of the testing was individual evaluation while the other half were told that the experimenter's interest was in studying the task. The task used was a stylus maze. Rather consistently, ego-involvement favored better performance in the low anxiety group, and poorer performance in the high-anxiety group, though most of the differences which the authors tested were not statistically significant.

In the theoretical argument presented in their first paper (31), Mandler & Sarason also arrived at certain predictions about absolute differences in performance between high anxiety and low anxiety subjects, which derived from essentially the same theoretical notions which have been referred to above in describing the experimental aspects of their work. Of necessity, these predictions cannot be as definitively tested because of the possible role of ability differences as sources of, rather than results of, anxiety level. In all three articles (31, 35, 36) published by this group, however, there are results which on the whole are consistent with predictions of this sort which they make. Their theoretical statement also includes a prediction that high anxiety subjects should under favorable conditions of repeated and rewarded practice learn to respond to their anxiety with appropriate task-relevant responses, and thus have a motivational resource for improvement through practice which exceeds the parallel resources of the low anxiety subjects. The item of evidence which to the reviewer seems most striking as a confirmation of this suggestion is a nonexperimental finding reported in their third article (35). It was found that scores on aptitude tests taken upon college entrance have a definitely lower average in high anxiety subjects than in low anxiety subjects, whereas the relation between the two groups in college grade average is slightly reversed. No test was made of the significance of this difference in relationship, but it appears probable that it would be significant. The interpretation made by the authors is that in progress through a college course the high anxiety person has the opportunity to learn to respond to his anxiety with task-relevant responses, so that the disadvantage he has in novel anxiety-arousing situations (such as taking intelligence tests) disappears or may even in time be turned into a motivational advantage.

These various studies done with the Mandler-Sarason scale of test anxiety seem to justify a definite conclusion. It is that the subjects with high test anxiety differ from the subjects with low test anxiety in the habits of responding to anxiety which have been built up through the course of their life. High anxiety subjects evidently have habits of responding to anxiety with various responses, internal and external, which are incompatible with efficient pursuit of a complex task; hence these subjects do worse in a situation which evokes much anxiety (through ego-involving instructions, announcement of failure, etc.) than in a situation which does not evoke much anxiety. Low anxiety subjects, on the other hand, evidently lack strong habits of responding to anxiety with task-irrelevant responses, so that anxiety-arousing instructions have as their main effect on these subjects an improvement of performance through increase in drive. (The increase in drive in an anxiety-arousing situation must of course be supposed to occur in the high anxiety subjects also, but its direct effect in improving performance to be obscured through interference by the task-irrelevant responses made to it.) It seems to the reviewer that these facts about the interaction of anxiety as a personality variable and as an experimental variable rather conclusively eliminate the simple application by Taylor & Spence (44) of the response-hierarchy concept as the main explanation of performance decrement with high anxiety, though their explanation may indeed be essential and adequate for certain simple instances. For the more general problem, it would appear that the preexperimental acquisition of response tendencies to anxiety as a cue must be taken into account. Here perhaps are the "new theoretical assumptions regarding the properties of anxiety and failure" which Lucas (30, p. 65) suggests are called for in order to explain those findings of his which parallel those of the Mandler-Sarason studies, though he suggests instead a different set of assumptions. He suggests, in effect, that as the level of anxiety increases (either as a function of personality or as a function of experimental manipulation), favorable effect on task-relevant responses increases first more rapidly, and then less rapidly, than the effect on interfering responses. The reviewer would agree that such an assumption may be necessary, particularly to explain why high anxiety subjects sometimes perform better than low anxiety subjects, even on complex tasks, in situations that are relatively nonanxiety-arousing. But if one searches for a theoretical background for this otherwise *ad hoc* assumption, it seems likely to be found in knowledge of the circumstances under which irrelevant response-tendencies have been learned by various persons, and hence of the cuing off of those responses by different levels of anxiety in different persons. In that case, one comes back to the necessity for attention to individual differences in the outcome of previous learning as an essential part of an adequate explanation.

Scale of tendency to make interfering responses to frustration.—The third personality variable which is relevant to this topic is one which has been used only in two experiments reported in a single paper by Waterhouse & Child (45). It is a measure derived from a questionnaire intended to sample the individual's characteristic responses to frustration, with respect to strength and pervasiveness of tendency to react to frustration with responses which would tend to interfere with adequate performance of a task. In the principal experiment, a variety of intellectual and motor tasks were employed, and frustration was introduced experimentally by informing half the subjects that they were doing very poorly. Subjects above the median on the interfering response questionnaire performed worse under frustration than under neutral conditions, whereas an opposite effect was found in subjects low on the interfering response questionnaire, and this interaction was statistically significant. In a subsidiary experiment this finding was confirmed, though not quite at the 5 per cent confidence level, with different tasks, subjects, and mode of inducing frustration. This finding is now so familiar from the Lucas and the Mandler-Sarason studies that there is no need to elaborate it or its interpretation here. The novelty in this study is that an attempt was made to measure directly a tendency to make interfering responses, whereas this tendency was in the other studies only introduced hypothetically as an explanatory device. In the other studies it was assumed that strength of anxety proneness as a personality variable could be taken as an index of tendency to make interfering responses to the cues provided by anxiety. The fact that the Waterhouse-Child scale of interference tendency shows a correlation only in the neighborhood of .50 with the Mandler-Sarason scale of test anxiety (35) may possibly justify an assumption that the two variables have a degree of independence sufficient to warrant their joint use. Particularly if measures of anxiety proneness and interference tendency could be made purer and more independent of each other, joint use of the two measures might be useful in seeking further disentanglement of the two opposing effects of anxiety on performance.

Miscellaneous studies of psychodynamics and performance.—In addition to the studies already reviewed, which have used personality measures especially devised for theoretical relevance to this problem, several other recent studies have been concerned with the relation of personality characteristics to psychodynamic influences on performance, measuring personality characteristics with standard tests. One test used in this connection is the Rorschach. Several years ago Williams (48) reported a very high relationship between certain Rorschach variables and performance changes under experimentally induced stress. Eriksen, Lazarus & Strange (21), in a somewhat comparable experiment, have failed to find any significant evidence of relationships between Rorschach variables and performance changes under stress. This outcome, and the similar outcome of several other comparable studies as reported or summarized by Carlson & Lazarus (8), lead the reviewer to suppose that Williams' findings may have been a product of sampling error. For lack of repetition of experiments, there are probably many statistically significant conclusions which are widely accepted despite being a product of only sampling error, and this recent work provides an instructive example of the value of repetition or near-repetition of psychological studies.

Another test used for a similar purpose is the Rosenzweig Picture-Frustration Test. Hybl & Stagner (28) studied reaction to stress on three fairly complex tasks, and administered the P-F Test to their subjects. Two groups of subjects selected as showing maximum or minimum disruption under stress showed several significant differences on the P-F Test. For example, those most affected by stress show significantly higher scores on intropunitive and lower scores on impunitive, tendency than do those least affected by stress. Perhaps the results may be viewed as tending to confirm the idea that disruption of performance under stress is associated with a general tendency to react to frustration with disrupting response tendencies, but the reviewer is not well enough acquainted with the P-F Test to judge with any confidence.

Interpretation is complicated by the fact that the high and low groups here differ with respect to psychiatric diagnosis as well as stress reaction. To the thesis that response to stress is a function of general personality characteristics, the Hybl & Stagner study also contributes by finding very high correlations among the various complex tasks used, with respect to the effect of stress upon performance.

Certain other studies published during the past year, while not concerned with personality variables, fit in well with some of the findings of the research already reviewed. Thus the point that the effects of anxiety vary with different kinds of tasks is reinforced by a finding by Moldawsky & Moldawsky (32), that in a group of college students performance on a digit span test was disrupted by an anxiety-inducing procedure, where performance on a vocabulary test was not. The important role of interfering responses evoked by a frustrating situation is stressed by Child & Waterhouse in two theoretical articles (13, 14). Particularly pertinent to the present discussion is their critique (13) of the Barker, Dembo & Lewin (2) experiment on regression. The broad generalization often drawn from the Barker, Dembo & Lewin study, that frustration tends to produce regression (in the sense of primitivation or disorganization of behavior), can hardly go unchallenged today. Child & Waterhouse attempt to show, partly through reanalysis of the data published by Barker, Dembo & Lewin, that that experiment demonstrates primarily that the extent to which regression (in this sense) results from frustration is a function of the extent to which the specific occurrence of frustration gives rise to response tendencies incompatible with high level performance in the behavior which is being observed.

Aggression

Scientific evidence on the determinants of aggression as a reaction to frustration has received a notable addition in the demonstration by Pastore (34) of the importance of arbitrariness of the frustrating situation as an influential variable. The evidence was derived from a study based on essentially the technique used by Doob & Sears (18), in which subjects are asked to indicate their probable reactions to a number of frustrating situations. Pastore prepared descriptions of situations in pairs (to be presented to different subjects), distinguished by whether the social origin of the frustration lay in an arbitrary act of another person or in a more justified act. Aggressive responses were much more numerous for the more arbitrary set of situations. The theoretical significance of this finding is certainly not clear, as Pastore recognizes in discussing various interpretations that might be made. But the clear demonstration of the importance of this variable should be a useful stimulant for further research on this problem which has been so oddly neglected in psychological research.

One way in which the relationship between arbitrariness and aggressive reaction might arise, of course, is through characteristic sequences of learning in the life history of individuals in our society, or perhaps in any society.

While there has been a frequent general assumption that learning is responsible for the frustration-aggression sequence, or at least greatly modifies it, and Whiting (47) has argued for this view from ethnographic evidence, psychologists seem not to have begun a direct test of this hypothesis until the recent work of Davitz (15). Davitz gave groups of children in a summer camp repeated training, either in aggressive games or in constructive activities, in a specific playroom. He subsequently subjected them to a frustrating experience and immediately introduced them into the same playroom again. Their behavior during this postfrustration period was then studied in relation to which of the two kinds of training they had undergone. It was found that the aggressively trained subjects behaved more aggressively and less constructively than did the constructively trained subjects. The highly specific and similar nature of the two situations in this experiment (that of training, and that of subsequent observation of behavior) of course limits the breadth of generalization that one can feel to be immediately justified, as the author recognizes. But for the situation used, there is very clear evidence of the important role of previous learning in influencing the overt response to frustration.

While Davitz's experiment has been introduced here in connection with the topic of aggression, it also has a very suggestive bearing upon the previous topic of psychodynamics and performance. A slightly different experiment might well demonstrate that previous training in aggression (or in some other task-irrelevant responses), in comparison with no such training, tends to lower quality of performance in a task because of producing interfering responses. In the studies cited in the preceding section, where explanatory use was made of the previous learning by subjects of responses to frustration, no evidence was actually available about that learning; it was merely inferred from present characteristics of subjects, and constitutional differences could perfectly well have been the major source of those characteristics so far as present evidence could show.

Identification

Several studies have attempted to verify hypotheses associated with the concept of identification. All of these have employed a cross-sectional method obtaining from subjects some index of identification and at the same time a measure of other characteristics which might be associated with degree of identification. Sopchak (38) measured identification by the degree of similarity between a subject's own responses on the MMPI[2] and the responses which he believed his father (or, separately, his mother) would be likely to give. For male subjects, Sopchak reports a negative relationship between degree of identification and all nine maladjustment measures on the MMPI, with some slight evidence of a closer relationship for identification with father rather than mother. One might wonder whether this finding results merely from a uniform tendency for children to think of their parents as giving "normal" responses; some of the other possible criticisms, inevitable in the light of the methods used, are discussed by Sopchak. For a much smaller group of female subjects, the results were more complicated; for identification with father, the results with males were confirmed, but for identification with mother consistent though not significant results suggest a relation in the opposite direction. For both sexes, the relation to general identification score appears to be greater for the "psychotic" variables than for the "neurotic" variables.

Cass (9, 10) employed a more varied questionnaire in attempting to measure identification, a questionnaire concerned with a variety of personal preferences. Her index of identification was the degree of agreement between the child's own responses and the mother's own responses. She tests several relationships between this index and other variables. The one most pertinent for comparison with Sopchak's results is delinquency; she finds no evidence of a relationship between delinquency and identification scores (10). Possibly this is because, as Sopchak argues, the child can only identify with the image he has of his parent, not with the parent as he actually is; on the other hand, Sopchak's technique has the difficulty that it may only be measuring projection. In this field where measurement offers such problems, it may be useful in further studies of identification to include both indices. Results confirmed through both indices will have greater plausibility than those confirmed through only one of the two fallible indices.

Meanwhile, there might well be wonder whether any such techniques as those used by Cass and Sopchak penetrate at all to the largely unconscious processes to which the term identification has been applied by clinicians. Evidence supplied by Cava & Raush (12) is very encouraging on this point. They obtained from boys in the twelfth grade a measure parallel in nature to that of Sopchak, but based on the Strong Vocational Interest Blank. The subjects responded to the Blank for themselves, and as they guessed their fathers would respond. The measure of identification consisted of the number of items on which these two responses were the same. The same subjects were also given the Blacky Test [see Blum (5)], in which stories are told in response to pictures of dogs in situations relevant to important sources of human conflict.

> The following dimensions of the test were chosen for investigation because of their theoretical relationship to the identification process: (*a*) Oedipal Intensity, (*b*) Castration Anxiety, (*c*) Identification, and (*d*) Ego Ideal. A fifth index representing an over-all estimate of conflict in these four areas was also used (12, p. 855).

Scores for disturbance in each of these areas were found, as predicted, to be negatively related to the measure of identification (or of perceived similarity, as the authors call it); for one of the areas, and for the over-all disturbance score, the relationship was statistically significant.

Personality Structure

Trait concepts associated with psychoanalytic theory of psychosexual development.—Psychoanalytic theory of psychosexual development suggests, though without necessarily implying, a number of predictions about intercorrelations among behavior tendencies. For example, if the theory interprets several personal characteristics as an outcome of anal fixation, it is possible to suppose that these characteristics should be correlated with each other because of their common origin. Various empirical correlations have received special attention in the past because they tend to confirm or to nullify such predictions. Surprisingly, however, it is only recently that comprehensive studies directed at testing a variety of such predictions have begun to appear.

In a way, the most comprehensive of these studies is that by Barnes (3), which is concerned with a variety of interrelationships predicted from the notions of oral, anal, and phallic levels of development. From the psychoanalytic literature, Barnes derived a number of trait adjectives associated with each of these developmental levels. The status of subjects on each of these traits was then measured by their responses to five or ten questionnaire items, involving either self-rating or expression of attitudes. Such trait scores were obtained for a large sample of male college students and intercorrelated, and a factor analysis was performed. There did not emerge any set of three factors corresponding to the three psychosexual levels. This is a valuable fact to have established, however skeptical one might be in advance about the suitability of the kind of data employed. The value of Barnes' study does not stop with this general negative finding, however. He reports some partial groupings of traits which are in accord with certain of the predictions based on psychoanalytic concepts, and these positive findings too will need to be taken into account in reaching, in the future, some satisfactory evaluation of the psychoanalytic trait concepts.

Another more specific study of similar nature has been published by Blum & Miller (7). It is concerned only with correlations predicted from the concept of oral character. While the authors say they are using "conventional psychological methods," their specific choice of methods is highly ingenious and well adapted to the problem. Studying third-grade children, they used as a basic measure of orality the frequency of nonpurposive mouth movements. They then tested the relation of this measure to a variety of behavioral observations, sociometric measures, and teachers' ratings which they felt might be symptomatic of oral character traits. There was sufficient confirmation of predictions to encourage further research which Blum (6) indicates is in progress. A major difficulty with the Blum & Miller study as so far reported is that the results seem to lend themselves to explanation in terms of a more general variable of nervousness or maladjustment, instead of requiring interpretation by reference to a specifically oral variable.

These two studies represent important additions to a growing body of data available for empirical evaluation of these trait concepts which have been derived from psychoanalytic theory. The earlier studies have been most recently reviewed by Blum (6). Inconclusive but suggestive, must be the verdict on all this work to date. Each study is subject to one or more criticisms which prevent it from leading to strong conviction either way about the value of these trait concepts. While the defects are various, one deficiency of all these studies [with the single exception of that by Goldman-Eisler (25)] is that they do not combine the structural study with a study of antecedent variables which might eventually permit the nailing down of appropriate labels for those clusterings which are consistently confirmed in the structural analysis.

Trait concepts associated with psychodiagnostic categories.—No attempt will be made here to provide a general review of research relating to abnormal behavior. An exception will be made, however, in the case of certain work by Eysenck which seems to have special methodological significance for other problems of personality study.

The contribution of special significance here is to be found in Eysenck's (23) use of what he terms "criterion analysis." The data for such an analysis consist of scores on a number of variables for individuals in two groups which differ in some way believed to be relevant to those scores, e.g., scores of normal and neurotic subjects on tests believed to be sensitive to neuroticism. Independently for each group, a factor analysis is performed. Rotation for the first factor is then done in such a way as to maximize the correlation between the factor loading of the variables and the accuracy with which the variables discriminate between the two groups; again, this is done independently for each group, except of course that the criterion of discrimination is the same for both rotations. The use of such a criterion as a basis for rotation seems to justify a high degree of confidence that the underlying variable within each group identified by the factor is the same variable on which the two groups are distinguished. Inspection of the factor loadings, then, may give more accurate information than was available before about the precise nature of the variable. In just this way, Eysenck offers a contribution to the measurement and to the understanding of two dimensions, a neurotic dimension and a psychotic dimension.

This method seems capable of fruitful application in a number of ways. True, criterion groups are not available for many of the dimensions which the student of personality wishes to explore. But important criterion groups may be found for many dimensions when they are looked for. In particular, it would seem that this method might add to the value of studies exploring the relation of a variety of supposedly consequent variables to a single antecedent variable, where roughly identifiable position on the antecedent variable provides the basis for segregation of subjects into two groups.

That the technique of criterion analysis is no cure-all for the problems of identifying and interpreting basic dimensions of variation in personality, and that just as much care as ever is needed in planning a study which will use it, is well illustrated by one point made by Eysenck in a rather different connection. In a study which was exploring both the psychotic dimension and a possible schizothymic-cyclothymic dimension (for which the criterion groups were patients diagnosed as schizophrenic or manic depressive), Eysenck (22) reports that he found no evidence for the latter dimension. He shows quite clearly, however, that this is because the psychotic dimension had already been isolated in the same study. Criterion analysis applied to the schizophrenics and manic depressives alone yielded a factor which was nicely correlated with the group difference. It was only because a group of normals was simultaneously being studied, that this factor was seen to be identical with that distinguishing normals from the psychotic group as a whole, and not a distinctive schizothymic-cyclothymic factor.

Search for basic traits through factor analysis.—Several articles during the past year have reported results of factor analyses of personality measures. In the opinion of the reviewer, the significance of such results is so completely dependent upon systematic comparison of findings of diverse studies that there is little point in reviewing separately all the specific contributions in any one year. One of the recent studies, however, is of such distinctive interest as to warrant separate attention here. This is the study by Cattell & Cross (11), which reports the results of a factor analysis of intraindividual variation on motivational variables, and compares them with the results of earlier analyses of interindividual variation on the same or similar variables.

Cattell & Cross dealt with 20 statements expressing specific motivational interests, statements which for the most part had shown high loadings on nine factors identified in two interindividual studies. Responses of a subject to these statements were obtained by three different techniques (scores obtained by the three techniques then being pooled), twice a day for 40 days. Intercorrelations among the 20 variables, with respect to session-to-session variation, were then calculated and factor-analyzed.

Perhaps of greatest interest is Cattell & Cross's finding that most of the factors emerging from this analysis could reasonably be identified with factors previously emerging from interindividual correlations. Obviously it would be premature to attempt to draw any conclusions, from this one analysis, about which motivational factors will be found dependably to show this consistency for interindividual and intraindividual variation, and which factors will not. But further study of this sort may have important implications, or at least pose important problems, for theoretical interpretation. Among the various hypotheses that may be used in explaining interindividual variation in personality, some should lead to a prediction of a corresponding temporal variation within the individual and some should not. At one extreme, the hypothesis that a particular trait is primarily a function of some definite physicochemical condition in which an individual varies from time to time, but for which each individual's variation is around a mean level characteristic for him, would suggest that manifestations of the trait might well vary in much the same way as between individuals and within an individual from time to time. At another extreme, the hypothesis that certain items of behavior vary together among individuals because they covary in subcultures and each individual has learned the pattern of his particular subculture, would not necessarily suggest any corresponding covariation within the individual from time to time. The careful comparison of inter- and intraindividual variation might be an important tool in distinguishing among various traits with respect to the nature of their origin.

A second point of interest in Cattell & Cross's paper is that it provides a new and instructive illustration of how controlled techniques and statistical manipulations ordinarily used for the verification of general hypotheses can be applied to the understanding of specific cases. The reviewer is somewhat skeptical about the efficiency of P-technique as an ordinary clinical instrument, but it can obviously yield results of great interest where there is justification for the necessary expenditure of time.

Mode of ego defense.—In discussing selective recall of failures and successes, several psychologists have suggested that individual differences in this measure reflect a general tendency to react to ego threat in some specific manner. Direct evidence that this is so, however, has been mostly confined thus far to Alper's very suggestive findings (1) which, because they are based on so few cases, cannot be very conclusive. Now Eriksen (19, 20) has provided some more substantial evidence. His evidence is limited to the specific point that there is some generality of mode of ego-defense. In one study (19), he shows that selective recall of successes rather than failures is associated with manifestations of perceptual defense in another experimental situation. In another study (20) he shows that selective recall of successes rather than failures is associated with difficulties in the rote learning of materials which seem to be emotionally disturbing to the subject. While Eriksen does not in these papers attempt to push back to the more general personality differences which may lie behind these consistencies, he establishes the existence of a consistency much more securely than before.

LITERATURE CITED

1. Alper, T. G., "Memory for Completed and Incompleted Tasks as a Function of Personality: Correlation between Experimental and Personality Data," *J. Personality*, **17,** 104–37 (1948)
2. Barker, R. G., Dembo, T., and Lewin, K., "Frustration and Regression," *University of Iowa, Studies in Child Welfare*, **18,** 1–314 (1941)
3. Barnes, C. A., "A Statistical Study of the Freudian Theory of Levels of Psychosexual Development," *Genetic Psychol. Monographs*, **45,** 105–75 (1952)
4. Bitterman, M. E., and Holtzman, W. H., "Conditioning and Extinction of the Galvanic Skin Response as a Function of Anxiety," *J. Abnormal Social Psychol.*, **47,** 615–23 (1952)
5. Blum, G. S., "A Study of the Psychoanalytic Theory of Psychosexual Development," *Genetic Psychol. Monographs*, **39,** 3–99 (1949)
6. Blum, G. S., *Psychoanalytic Theory of Personality* (McGraw-Hill Book Co., Inc., New York, N. Y., 219 pp., 1953)
7. Blum, G. S., and Miller, D. R., "Exploring the Psychoanalytic Theory of the 'Oral Character'," *J. Personality*, **20,** 287–304 (1952)
8. Carlson, V. R., and Lazarus, R. S., "A Repetition of Meyer Williams' Study of Intellectual Control under Stress and Associated Rorschach Factors" (In press)
9. Cass, L. K., "An Investigation of Parent-Child Relationships in Terms of Awareness, Identification, Projection and Control," *Am. J. Orthopsychiat.*, **22,** 305–13 (1952)
10. Cass, L. K., "Parent-Child Relationships and Delinquency," *J. Abnormal Social Psychol.*, **47,** 101–4 (1952)
11. Cattell, R. B., and Cross, K. P., "Comparison of the Ergic and Self-Sentiment Structures found in Dynamic Traits by R- and P-Techniques," *J. Personality*, **21,** 250–71 (1952)
12. Cava, E. L., and Raush, H. L., "Identification and the Adolescent Boy's Perception of his Father," *J. Abnormal Social Psychol.*, **47,** 855–56 (1952)
13. Child, I. L., and Waterhouse, I. K., "Frustration and the Quality of Performance: I. A Critique of the Barker, Dembo, and Lewin Experiment," *Psychol. Rev.*, **59,** 351–62 (1952)
14. Child, I. L., and Waterhouse, I. K., "Frustration and the Quality of Performance: II. A Theoretical Statement," *Psychol. Rev.*, **60,** 127–39 (1953)
15. Davitz, J. R., "The Effects of Previous Training on Postfrustration Behavior," *J. Abnormal Social Psychol.*, **47,** 309–15 (1952)
16. Deese, J., and Lazarus, R. S., "The Effects of Psychological Stress upon Performance: A Theoretical Analysis and Review of Recent Developments" (Mimeographed by the authors, 1953)
17. Deese, J., Lazarus, R. S., and Keenan, J., "Anxiety, Anxiety-Reduction and Stress in Learning," *J. Exptl. Psychol.* (In press)
18. Doob, L. W., and Sears, R. R., "Factors Determining Substitute Behavior and the Overt Expression of Aggression," *J. Abnormal Social Psychol.*, **34,** 293–313 (1939)
19. Eriksen, C. W., "Defense against Ego-Threat in Memory and Perception," *J. Abnormal Social Psychol.*, **47,** 230–35 (1952)
20. Eriksen, C. W., "Individual Differences in Defensive Forgetting," *J. Exptl. Psychol.*, **44,** 442–46 (1952)

21. Eriksen, C. W., Lazarus, R. S., and Strange, J. R., "Psychological Stress and Its Personality Correlates: Part II. The Rorschach Test and other Personality Measures," *J. Personality*, **20**, 277–86 (1952)

22. Eysenck, H. J., "Schizothymia-Cyclothymia as a Dimension of Personality," *J. Personality*, **20**, 345–84 (1952)

23. Eysenck, H. J., *The Scientific Study of Personality* (The Macmillan Co., New York, N. Y., 320 pp., 1952)

24. Farber, I. E., and Spence, K. W., "Complex Learning and Conditioning as a Function of Anxiety," *J. Exptl. Psychol.*, **45**, 120–25 (1953)

25. Goldman-Eisler, F., "Breastfeeding and Character Formation," in *Personality in Nature, Society, and Culture, Second Edition*, 146–84 (Kluckhohn, C., Murray, H. A., and Schneider, D. M., Eds., Alfred A. Knopf, Inc., New York, N. Y., 701 pp., 1953)

26. Hilgard, E. R., Jones, L. V., and Kaplan, S. J., "Conditioned Discrimination as Related to Anxiety," *J. Exptl. Psychol.*, **42**, 94–99 (1951)

27. Holtzman, W. H., Calvin, A. D., and Bitterman, M. E., "New Evidence for the Validity of Taylor's Manifest Anxiety Scale," *J. Abnormal Social Psychol.*, **47**, 853–54 (1952)

28. Hybl, A. R., and Stagner, R., "Frustration Tolerance in Relation to Diagnosis and Therapy," *J. Consulting Psychol.*, **16**, 163–70 (1952)

29 Lazarus, R. S., Deese, J., and Osler, F., "The Effects of Psychological Stress upon Performance," *Psychol. Bull.*, **49**, 293–317 (1952)

30. Lucas, J. D., "The Interactive Effects of Anxiety, Failure, and Intra-Serial Duplication," *Am. J. Psychol.*, **65**, 59–66 (1952)

31. Mandler, G. and Sarason, S. B., "A Study of Anxiety and Learning," *J. Abnormal Social Psychol.*, **47**, 166–73 (1952)

32. Moldawsky, S., and Moldawsky, P. C., "Digit Span as an Anxiety Indicator," *J. Consulting Psychol.*, **16**, 115–18 (1952)

33. Montague, E. K., "The Role of Anxiety in Serial Rote Learning," *J. Exptl. Psychol.*, **45**, 91–96 (1953)

34. Pastore, N., "The Role of Arbitrariness in the Frustration-Aggression Hypothesis," *J. Abnormal Social Psychol.*, **47**, 728–31 (1952)

35. Sarason, S. B., and Mandler, G., "Some Correlates of Test Anxiety," *J. Abnormal Social Psychol.*, **47**, 810–17 (1952)

36. Sarason, S. B., Mandler, G., and Craighill, P. G., "The Effect of Differential Instructions on Anxiety and Learning," *J. Abnormal Social Psychol.*, **47**, 561–65 (1952)

37. Sears, R. R., "Personality," *Ann. Rev. Psychol.*, **1**, 105–18 (1950)

38. Sopchak, A. L., "Parental 'Identification' and Tendency toward Disorders as Measured by the Minnesota Multiphasic Personality Inventory," *J. Abnormal Social Psychol.*, **47**, 159–65 (1952)

39. Spence, K. W., and Farber, I. E., "Conditioning and Extinction as a Function of Anxiety," *J. Exptl. Psychol.*, **45**, 116–19 (1953)

40. Spence, K.W., and Taylor, J.A., "Anxiety and Strength of the UCS as Determiners of the Amount of Eyelid Conditioning," *J. Exptl. Psychol.*, **42**, 183–88 (1951)

41. Spence, K. W., and Taylor, J. A., "The Relation of Conditioned Response Strength to Anxiety in Normal, Neurotic, and Psychotic Subjects," *J. Exptl. Psychol.*, **45**, 265–72 (1953)

42. Taylor, J. A., "The Relationship of Anxiety to the Conditioned Eyelid Response," *J. Exptl. Psychol.*, **41**, 81–92 (1951)

43. Taylor, J. A., "A Personality Scale of Manifest Anxiety," *J. Abnormal Social Psychol.*, **48**, 285–90 (1953)
44. Taylor, J. A., and Spence, K. W., "The Relationship of Anxiety Level to Performance in Serial Learning," *J. Exptl. Psychol.*, **44**, 61–64 (1952)
45. Waterhouse, I. K., and Child, I. L., "Frustration and the Quality of Performance: III. An Experimental Study," *J. Personality*, **22**, 298–311 (1953)
46. Welch, L., "Human Conditioning and Anxiety," *Ann. N. Y. Acad. Sci.*, **56**, 266–72 (1953)
47. Whiting, J. W. M., "The Frustration Complex in Kwoma Society," *Man*, **44**, 1–4 (1944)
48. Williams, M., "An Experimental Study of Intellectual Control under Stress and Associated Rorschach Factors," *J. Consult. Psychol.*, **11**, 21–29 (1947)
49. Winne, J. F., "A Scale of Neuroticism," *J. Clin. Psychol.*, **7**, 117–22 (1951)

SOCIAL PSYCHOLOGY AND GROUP PROCESSES[1,2]

By Richard S. Crutchfield

Department of Psychology and Institute of Personality Assessment and Research, University of California, Berkeley, California

The field of social psychology continues in healthy ferment. Over-all the impression is one of vigor and freshness of ideas, balanced by a growing sophistication and maturity of theory, problems, and methods.

Significant trends in social psychology over recent years persist in current work and become even more firmly established. Interdisciplinary relations with sociology, anthropology, and other social sciences, are broadened. The inherent unity of social psychology with the area of personality becomes more pronounced. Field research takes its proper place alongside laboratory research, and the latter shakes off some of its earlier narrowness and artificiality. Rigorous conceptualization and model-construction abound. The frontier field of group dynamics shows perhaps the greatest upsurge of all, with its convincing demonstrations of how crucial psychological variables can be dealt with experimentally in genuine group settings. Appropriate to its central psychological significance, the study of social perception makes progress, though all too haltingly. Attitude change research has been rescued from the doldrums by its present emphasis upon explicit conceptualization, careful design, and attachment to larger theory. And subsidiary to all these areas, methodological and technical advances more than keep pace.

In contrast to these trends it is easy to detect a favorable decline in the kind of unconnected, socially irrelevant, and atheoretical studies that have traditionally abounded in the field of social psychology.

One trend not manifested as emphatically as might be desired is that toward insightful social psychological theorizing which, distinct from the more formal and systematic hypothetico-deductive type of which there is a considerable amount, is theorizing in its most fundamental sense, namely, the creative conception of psychological relationships which must occur before the more formal research and theory construction can proceed.

All in all, the year's work has been largely in the nature of a consolidation of the above trends and of laying of groundwork for things to come. It can not properly be called a vintage year, in view of the relative scarcity of products having genuine brilliance, flavor, and richness. But that there are noteworthy exceptions to this becomes abundantly clear in the review which follows.

[1] The survey of literature to which this review pertains was completed in June, 1953. Mrs. Britomar Handlon and Mr. William T. Richardson have been invaluable in collecting material for the review.

[2] The following abbreviation is used in this review: MMPI (Minnesota Multiphasic Personality Inventory).

Systematic Treatment of the Field of Social Psychology

A penetrating treatise on fundamental problems of social psychology has been written by Asch (6). Though cast superficially in the form of a textbook, it is directed at a more profound level than is true of the typical text. Its intent is to bring into sharper focus and to seek theoretical and empirical clarification of the underlying psychological assumptions of social psychology. It is not offered as a comprehensive "system" of social psychological theory, but rather as a connected series of discussions of the basic nature of social phenomena.

The orientation is that of Gestalt theory, the fruitfulness of which Asch wishes to demonstrate for social psychology. But a reader unsympathetic to the Gestalt view need not take alarm; the discussion is valuable for its sensitive isolation and analysis of critical theoretical issues confronting the social psychologist, no matter what his systematic persuasion may be.

As might be expected of the Gestalt orientation, heavy stress is laid on the necessity for phenomenological description of the structural properties of experience and action. The keynote is the role of insight and understanding in the processes of human interaction. The superiority of concepts stressing sensible and insightful cognitive relations over arbitrary ("blind") connections is argued at every opportunity, especially in reference to social perception, social suggestion, and attitude change. These topics are richly illustrated from Asch's own pioneering experimental research on how people perceive others, how individual judgment is distorted by group pressure, etc.

Considerable attention is given to analysis of aspects of social phenomena that many social psychologists have been reluctant to explore, such as the psychological basis of group interaction, the "group mind" concept, social value, and cultural relativism. The flavor of Asch's thinking is well exemplified by his treatment of "doctrines of man." He disagrees sharply with the psychological assumptions and implications of several prevailing "doctrines," especially, the ego-centered character of man, the supremacy of irrational emotions, the primacy of rationalization in human thinking, the basis of human experience in arbitrary association and conditioning, and the roots of adult attitudes in childhood experiences. That he exaggerates the case against these doctrines, doing less than justice to their positive contributions, is undeniable, but in this fashion he makes explicit the tacit assumptions in these doctrines and illuminates difficulties inherent in them.

Along more conventional lines are textbooks by Sprott (118), on a fairly nontechnical level; by Britt (19), a revision of an earlier book; and by Bonner (17), characterized by a heavy emphasis upon ethnological data and cross-cultural comparisons of human behavior.

Relationships of social psychology to other disciplines.—Several writers address themselves to the question of the systematic status of social psychology in relation to other fields. Tolman (126) presents an analysis of the relations between sociology and psychology by comparing the nature of independent, intervening, and dependent variables in the two disciplines. Sociology, as well as anthropology, is concerned with such independent variables as the "surrounds" (climate, geography, history, other groups, etc.), and special personality characteristics and psychological processes of members of the given group; with such intervening variables as social structures, ideologies, and roles; with such dependent variables as role performances and group productions. Psychology, on the other hand, is concerned with such independent variables as constitutional factors and physiological drive states in the individual, and physical and social stimulus factors affecting him; with such intervening variables as values, cognitions, and behavior-field forces; with such dependent variables as behavioral achievements or attempted achievements. With this schema of relevant variables for the two disciplines, Tolman seeks to clarify the types of theoretical and research problems that properly fall under such headings as sociological theory, psychological theory, social psychology, and psychological sociology.

Lindesmith & Strauss (81) criticize attempts to extend the concepts and theories of the experimental psychology of learning (drawn heavily from animal psychology) to the problems of social psychology, which they regard as properly treated only at the human level. On the other hand, Smith & Ross (115) provide an informative review of the literature on social behavior of vertebrates, 1939 to 1950, with an argument for the importance of work in comparative social psychology. They stress the needs for extending social study of animals to more species and to wider settings, and for the guiding of such research by a more systematic conceptual framework.

Bendix (11) points out shortcomings in the usual psychiatric conceptions of collective behavior which, in his opinion, give insufficient weight to the mores and folkways of a society as the critical determinants of behavior.

How interdisciplinary planning for team research on social behavior in communities (the Springdale Project) may be made effective is discussed by Bronfenbrenner & Devereux (20).

Group Processes

Models and methods in group study.—Research and theorizing on group processes are increasingly sophisticated in emphasis upon formal conceptualization, mathematical model-construction, and rigorous experimental design. This is paralleled by rapid growth of techniques for the study of groups.

One of the more impressive attempts in conceptual formalization is Simon's (113) demonstration of "how the mathematization of a body of theory can help in the clarification of concepts, in the examination of the independence or non-dependence of postulates, and in the derivation of new propositions that suggest additional ways of subjecting a theory to empirical testing." Taking an example from Homans' *The Human Group* (60), he sets up equations involving four group variables: intensity of interaction among members, level of friendliness among members, amount of activity carried on by members of the group, and amount of activity imposed on the group by the external environment. From these equations he derives the verbalizations of Homans, plus certain others. The special importance of Simon's study lies not so much in the particular deductions produced as in the demonstration of the effectiveness of a mathematical model in arriving at them by formal procedures. The weakness lies in the point, acknowledged by the author himself, that the equations must necessarily leave out many variables and that numerous simplifying assumptions must be made. As is true of most models in present-day social science, even the best, this one consists more in over-simplification than in idealization, which is the proper ultimate aim of a model.[3]

Stephan & Mishler (119) concern themselves with another aspect of the application of mathematical functions to study of groups. They work out a simple mathematical function that appears to express quite well the distribution of participation within a particular type of small discussion-group. Thirty-six groups, varying in size from 4 to 12 members, were observed in a total of 81 meetings. An exponential function that accommodates the observed data on distribution of participation is:

$$P_i = ar^{i-1}$$

where P is the estimated percentage for subject ranked i, r is the ratio of percentages for adjacent ranks, and a is the estimate for subject ranked 1. (The ranking refers to the number of units of participation.)

When three conditions are fulfilled—(*a*) that there is a range of verbal participation potential among the members, (*b*) that there is no systematic interference with free competitive expression of these potentials, and (*c*) that there is an absence of well differentiated roles among the members—then the size of the group is found to be an important parameter affecting the magnitude of the ratio in the basic equation.

A three-dimensional model for visual analysis of group structure is described by Chapin (23). The three dimensions are (*a*) position (official), (*b*) distance (differences between individuals in scores of status scales, etc.), and (*c*) direction (toward upper status or lower status as expressed by incoming versus outgoing sociometric choices). Two main assumptions are involved in the model, first, that equality in incoming and outgoing sociometric choices is a rough measure of intragroup reciprocity, and second, that the relative size of this intragroup reciprocity is one measure of the cohesion or solidarity of the whole group.

A particularly promising mathematical model for the study of groups, as well as for wider problems in psychology and sociology, is the theory of graphs discussed by Harary & Norman (51). These two mathematicians provide an engagingly clear and concise outline showing the relevance of

[3] This distinction between "over-simplification" and "idealization" in mathematical models in the social sciences has been discussed by Kaplan (67).

this discipline of mathematics for such problems of conceptualization as those to be found in group patterns and networks. Typical problems are those having to do with group structure, communication, stability and change, efficiency, etc. Comparison of graph theory with Lewin's topological representation is made, and the authors introduce some new concepts into the theory of graphs with discussion of their psychological implications.

In response to recent criticisms of the J-curve as an effective model for analysis of conformity behavior, Solomon (116) comments on the need for restricting use of the J-curve to the kinds of appropriate conformity situations for which it was intended, on the soundness of the scaling methods used in developing the method, and on the impropriety of skewness and kurtosis as alternative measures of conformity, inasmuch as the J-curve assumes not an infinite number, but only four, principal variables: conformity producing agencies, simple chance as a leveling out factor, physiological or biological factors, and personality deviations. Argyle (5) discusses problems of experimental design in the study of small social groups.

Theory of groups.—Horowitz & Perlmutter (61) give an extended discussion of the concept of the social group. They argue for the propriety and necessity of development of laws of group behavior pertaining to group learning, group memory, group perception, and the like, as distinct from, and not merely reifications of, laws of individual behavior of perception, memory, and learning. They point to ambiguities and inconsistencies in the position of Krech & Crutchfield (71) on this matter, although acknowledging that those authors have argued for the essential independence of several "levels" of study of behavioral processes.

A thoroughgoing treatment of the theory of group learning is provided by Cattell (22). Groups, he asserts, have three aspects: (*a*) population characteristics, which are the averages of characteristics of individual members; (*b*) structural characteristics; and (*c*) syntality characteristics, where syntality is to the group what personality is to the individual. Group learning is defined as "a change in syntality when the group is exposed to a certain environmental situation." Of the three general types of individual learning, conditioning, insightful, and trial-and-error, only the latter is important in group learning. The investigation of group learning may begin by exploration of the variables from classical learning, such as frequency, motivation, etc., but more interesting are the "internal dependent variables," e.g., size of group, length of association of its members, type of leadership, etc. Illustrative hypotheses relating to such group variables are, that large groups learn more slowly than small groups and that groups with a formally appointed leader learn more rapidly than leaderless groups. Cattell's treatment is refreshing and enlightening, though on the side of conceptual development it may reflect too much reliance on principles of individual learning as it addresses itself to what is asserted to be a distinctly separate problem, that of group learning.

An outline of group relationships designed to clarify and organize problems of research is presented by Landecker (74). He discusses four types of group integration: (*a*) cultural, the degree to which cultural standards are mutually consistent within the group; (*b*) normative, the degree to which conduct in the group conforms to its standards; (*c*) communicative, the degree to which members of the group are linked to one another by exchanges of meanings; and (*d*) functional, the degree to which they are linked to one another by exchanges of services.

Determinants of group formation and structure.—One of the critical problems in understanding group structure and behavior concerns what is contributed by the specific characteristics of individual members who constitute the group. Relatively little experimental work has yet been done on this problem. A significant study by Haythorn (55) seeks to evaluate the influence of individual members on small groups by systematically rotating the membership of the groups in such a way as to isolate the influence of a given individual without regard for the makeup of any particular group. Sixteen male students of the Navy Reserve Officers' Training Corps met in groups of four, working on a syllogistic reasoning task, a mechanical assembly task, and a discussion task. Each subject worked with each other subject only once, taking part in five different groups. Ratings were made of various characteristics of group behavior and of individual behavior in the group, such as aggressiveness, cooperativeness, efficiency, etc. Personality questionnaire data were also obtained. In general, it is found that the behavior of individual members significantly affects the characteristics of small groups; for example, effective group functioning is facilitated by cooperativeness, efficiency, and insight, while behavior termed "striving for individual prominence" reduces group cohesiveness and friendliness. As to personality relationships, it appears that mature, accepting persons facilitate the group activity, while suspicious, nonaccepting persons depress the smooth functioning of the group. The importance of this study is less in its verification of somewhat obvious relationships between group behavior and characteristics of members than in its demonstration that these two sets of variables can be effectively separated in an experimental setting.

Gilchrist (45) has studied the formation of social groups under conditions of success and failure. After working individually at tasks in which failure and success were arbitrarily manipulated by the experimenter, and then announced, subjects were required to choose their preferred work partner in a further group task involving a pair. One experimental variable was granting or not granting the choice. Another was the arbitrarily controlled success or failure of the formed group. Choices after the group experience were also determined. It appears that when such an unorganized collection of individuals is required to form groups, the individuals tend to form them around those others who have been successful. Failures do not tend to form groups, that is, by reciprocating one another's choices on the basis of mutual failure. The emergence of such failure groups is to be understood as determined by events occurring after the initial grouping choice has been made. The evidence also points to the conclusion that knowledge of an individual's level of aspiration about a task and of his expectations of success or failure with other individuals may lead to a reliable prediction of his choices of group partners, and hence, in a larger framework, to predictions about the emergence of specific groupings. The study also throws light on the comparative strength of expectations of success and failure with others before and after actual work experience with them.

A highly significant study of group behavior by Festinger, Pepitone & Newcomb (41) deserves detailed review. Their concern is with consequences of what may be called deindividuation in a group, characterized in their own words as follows:

> There occurs sometimes in groups a state of affairs in which the individuals act as if they were "submerged in the group." Such a state of affairs may be described as one of de-individuation; that is, individuals are not seen or paid attention to as individuals. The members do not feel that they stand out as individuals. Others are not singling a person out for attention nor is the person singling out others.

The experimental design was directed toward study of two propositions: (*a*) that deindividuation in a group is accompanied by a reduction in inner restraints for the members; (*b*) that groups characterized by such deindiv,duation and reduction of inner restraints are more attractive to their memibers To accomplish deindividuation in 23 groups of four to seven members each. conditions were set so as to encourage a reduction of inner restraints in discussing feelings of hostility toward their parents. The degree of such reduction in each group was measured by the relative predominance of negative over positive statements concerning parents. The degree of deindividuation was measured by the extent to which the group members were unable after the group discussion to identify which members had made certain statements.

The first proposition is confirmed by a statistically significant correlation for the 23 groups between the above two measures, degree of reduction of inner restraints and degree of deindividuation. Four alternative theories to account for this obtained relationship are discussed and refuted: namely, repression, laws of memory, division of attention, and individual reactions other than the group phenomenon. The second proposition, saying that deindividuation is related to attractiveness of the group to its members, the latter being determined by the subject's expression of desire to carry on further discussions with his group, is also confirmed.

This study is noteworthy for its effective demonstration of how a long alleged but unverified group phenomenon of central theoretical importance can be brought under precise measurement and conceptual exploration.

Intragroup tensions.—An effective combination of conceptualization, methodology, and social relevance is found in Herbst's study of the family (58). Using a Lewinian approach, he distinguishes three concepts, the "family field," the "family structure," and the "tension balance." The total family field can be constructed from an analysis of the "path field" of each member, which in turn derives from a study of his participation pattern in various family activities. Herbst finds that within the population of Australian families he studies, the family field is virtually a cultural constant. Evidence for this is seen in the finding that given the number of regions in which a family member participates, it is possible to predict accurately which ones they are. On the other hand, family structure shows wide variations among families in his sample, characterized by four quite different patterns of husband-wife power-interaction: (*a*) husband dominant, (*b*) wife dominant, (*c*) autonomic, with separation of spheres of influence, (*d*) syncratic, with joint, co-operative determination. Each type of pattern has associated with it a different level of tension in the family. Herbst's analysis permits him to draw a number of inferences concerning tension levels, balance, and change. For instance, although in specific areas of syncratic co-operative relationships tension may be high, the total family tension is low, thus typifying a generally efficient and harmonious family structure. Conversely, autocratic and autonomous relationships may achieve reduction of tension in connection with specific family areas at the serious cost of increased general family tension.

In connection with other aspects of the problem of tensions in groups, Thibaut & Coules (125) make an experimental evaluation of the role of communication in the reduction of interpersonal hostility. Their study is directed at both the "catharsis" hypothesis [Dollard *et al.* (31)] and the "autistic hostility" hypothesis [Newcomb (95)]. The experiment involved groups consisting of two persons, one of whom was a confederate of the experimenter, the other being the real experimental subject. The two persons looking at one another through a window, wrote and exchanged messages revealing information about themselves in order that they could later write a personality sketch of the other. The confederate's messages were standardized and designed to show him as opinionated and arrogant. The final one from him consisted of an outright attack on the other subject. Half of the experimental subjects were permitted to reply to this note and half were not. All then wrote new personality sketches of the other. Those allowed to reply to the final note showed fewer unfriendly elements in the personality sketch than did those not permitted to respond, thus supporting the hypothesis that "the communication of hostility to an instigator will tend to reduce the residual hostility toward that instigator." The effects are found to interact with those pertaining to the "autistic hostility" hypothesis, in that the higher the level of postexperimental hostility revealed in the sketch the stronger the desire to discontinue the message sending in the no-communication group, and that initially hostile subjects, when compared with initially friendly subjects, initiate a smaller volume of communication during the preinstigation period. In this study one is struck once again by the ingenuity with which previously unverified hypotheses about complex aspects of group functioning are being put to precise test in contemporary experimental research in group dynamics.

Further light on the nature of interpersonal tensions in groups is given by Zajonc's study (137) of aggressive attitudes of the "stranger" as a function of conformity pressures. Twenty Indian students of shorter residence in the United States were compared with 20 of longer residence for their attitudinal aggression against, and difficulty in conformity with, a number of American behavior patterns, such as scholastic competition, treatment of women, dating, kissing in public, etc. Results confirm hypotheses based on the sociological concept of the "stranger" and on the Dollard (31) frustration-aggression sequence. Zajonc holds that the "stranger" needs to conform, is frustrated in this need by his super-ego bound in another culture, is thereupon instigated to aggressive response, is free to express his aggression because of the permissiveness of his role as "stranger," and hence finds the instigation to aggression reduced. The frustration-aggression hypothesis, long prominent in social psychological theorizing, is extended in a needed direction by Pastore (99), who supplies evidence that the perceived "arbitrariness" of the frustration is significantly related to the amount of aggression elicited.

Group productivity.—On the continuing problem of the productivity of small groups, McCurdy & Lambert (83) describe a situation in which, on a problem requiring genuine co-operation, small groups do not work more successfully than do individuals. The authors explain the apparent discrepancy of these findings with earlier findings, such as those by Watson (129) and Shaw (111), where group performance exceeded that of individuals, by pointing out that in the present experiment the problem (levers to be pushed to turn on lights in a kind of "group maze") is such that the less alert and less adequate individual member will necessarily interfere to some extent with the group progress, inasmuch as his contribution is as required as that of better members. In previous studies, on the other hand, the group tasks were such as to involve a cumulative product, or such as to reflect mainly the performance of certain group members who were superior in insight, reasoning, etc., upon whom the burden of group responsibility tended to fall. A subsidiary finding of McCurdy & Lambert is that in their group situation neither a "democratic" nor an "authoritarian" atmosphere proves the more favorable in terms of group productivity.

The relative superiority of groups over individuals in the learning of nonsense syllables is by no means clear-cut according to the work of Perlmutter & Montmollin (100), who find that although groups of three who learn and recall syllables by a "method of agreement" are superior to the average individual working alone, in many cases individuals surpass the group score. There appears to be evidence that individuals who have first participated in the group learning task do better when subsequently shifted to working alone than do individuals who have not had the benefit of the prior group experience.

A methodologically and conceptually sophisticated study by Darley, Gross & Martin (27) throws light on some of the factors associated with group productivity. They arranged a contest among 13 university living groups, the goal being to prepare a "plan for better co-operative living" in the co-operative housing project. The criterion of group productivity for each house was the over-all quality rating given by a committee of judges to the house's report after a month long period of preparation. The predictor variables in the study were derived from five hypotheses regarding factors associated with group productivity. All other things being equal, the productivity of a group will depend upon the extent to which (*a*) the group goal is accepted, (*b*) the previous group experience has been successful and satisfying, (*c*) appropriate use is made of differential skills within the group membership, (*d*) leadership is both accepted and persistent, and (*e*) there are available within the group individuals of requisite ability or special skill. Rather than being content with a single datum relating to each of these hypotheses (a shortcoming common to many studies), these experimenters worked out 18 predictor variables pertaining to the five hypotheses, the data being gathered from a variety of sources, including participant-observation, attendance records, autobiographical reports, sociometric measures, etc. Rank-order correlations ($N=13$) of the predictor variables with the criterion of group productivity are such as to lend support to all five of these hypotheses; for example, efficiency of house organization for the contest correlates .86, support of formal leader correlates .51, and enthusiasm for the task correlates .59 with the criterion. It is equally significant for more general implications of the conceptualization problem in group research that the several predictor variables which clustered under the heading of a given hypothesis did not necessarily show very high communality and did not all yield significant correlations with the criterion. As the authors remark, this "emphasizes the importance of careful derivations of behavioral coordinates in testing the relationships involved in group processes."

Related to the problem of group productivity is a validation of a sociometric regrouping procedure reported by Van Zelst (127). Carpenters, formed into work teams according to their sociometric choices, show significant differences from a control group in job satisfaction, labor turnover, and labor and material costs.

Israeli (64) describes a provocative study of group interaction in creative and critical activity; it is a topic that has attracted virtually no systematic attention in past research and that has tended to concentrate on group productivity having to do with logical problem-solving, quantity of output, and the like, rather than with the higher forms of creativity. Experimental use is made of a technique termed "method of serial production," in which a creative work, such as a poem, an essay, or a drawing, is spontaneously and quickly constructed and criticized by one person after another in a chain-like order in a small group. The interest centers on the character of the social interaction between an artist and other artists, between a critic and other critics, and between artists and critics, and on the influence of such interactions on the nature of the final creative product. Experimental details are scantily reported and the results presented must be considered as merely indicative of the research potentialities of this area. Representative of the reported findings of the study are: (*a*) that the initial step in a construction dominates later development, "a weak, ambiguous, or unstructured beginning hampers writers who follow" whereas "a strong and coherent opening challenges and directs their work"; and (*b*) that "creative performance seems to be blocked towards the end of a sequence" resembling "satiation in productive thinking as considered by Duncker."

The influence process in groups.—In a study involving a complex manipulation of conditions and variables, Festinger *et al.* (40) explore the influence process in groups containing extreme deviates in opinion. Subjects (of whom there were 443, in groups of six to nine) were required to take a position on the probable outcome of a labor dispute. All communications among group members were written and were actually constructed arbitrarily by the experimenters to simulate the opinions of the other group members. The independent variables manipulated were: (*a*) high versus low cohesiveness, (*b*) degree of deviation (manipulated by giving the subject false information about the positions of other subjects in the group), (*c*) presence or absence of alleged "experts," and (*d*) the alleged availability or unavailability of the actual outcome of the labor dispute. The dependent variables measured were: (*a*) readiness to change one's opinion, (*b*) attempts to influence others in the group, and (*c*) redefinition of the boundaries of the group, as measured by lowered communication to deviate persons.

In general, deviates are found to be more ready to change their opinions and show less confidence in their opinions. Those who change communicate less than others, that is, make less attempt to influence others; those deviates who do not change, tend to redefine the group boundaries by communicating only with those close to their own position and not with the majority farthest removed from their own position. The effect of high cohesion introduced into the groups is generally to accentuate the influence on the deviates. They attempt more to influence others in the cohesive group; the nonchanging deviates redefine the group boundaries to a greater degree. Where the correct answer is supposed to "exist," the amount of change is increased, and the attempts to influence others decreased. The major finding of the study in the words of the authors is, "The relative strength of the tendency to redefine the boundaries of the group in response to pressures toward uniformity increases for a member as the discrepancy between his opinion and the modal opinion in the group increases."

Striking effects of group pressure on the modification of individual judgments are reported by Asch (6), who employs a novel technique whereby all but one member of a group of subjects are confederates of the experimenter, instructed to report falsely on a simple visual judgment of comparative length of lines, the one remaining, naïve subject being the only person actually tested in the situation. By this means, experimental manipulation can readily be made of such variables as degree of discrepancy of the false group report from the correct judgment, size of the group, size of the majority which agrees on the false judgment, etc. Asch finds that even under these conditions of highly structured stimulus material, many subjects are markedly influenced to go along with the group judgment. Apparently only a minor part of the effect is related to genuine perceptual distortion, most being ascribable to judgmental distortion or distortion of report. The size of the group can be reduced sharply to about three members without appreciable loss in effectiveness of pressure, but the introduction of a single other person who gives the correct answer, thus breaking the unanimity of the opposition, largely eliminates the subject's tendency to distort.

Asch finds marked individual differences in responsiveness to the group pressure. Light on the nature of the personality correlates of such "independence" and "yielding" is given by a study of Barron (7), using some of Asch's subjects. "Independents" and "Yielders" are found to be equally stable in personality (as inferred from MMPI[2] responses), but to differ in values and self-descriptions. "Independents" more than "Yielders" tend to value the individual as opposed to the group, to prefer complexity to simplicity, and to see themselves as original, emotional, and artistic, rather than obliging, optimistic, efficient, kind, and determined.

Kelley & Volkart (69) explore the resistance to change of group-anchored attitudes by measuring Boy Scouts' attitudes about Boy Scout activities before and after hearing an adult read a paper criticizing these activities. Half were told that their answers were strictly private; half, the opposite. Three hypotheses were tested: (*a*) the amount of change in expressed attitudes produced by a standard communication contrary to the norm will be less under public than under private conditions (not confirmed); (*b*) when the influence to change is of standard strength, there will be an inverse relationship between change and value of membership to the individual (confirmed); (*c*) the foregoing relationship will be greater under private than under public conditions (confirmed).

A quite different approach to the study of group influence on individual behavior is the experiment of Schachter & Hall (108) in which a speaker attempts to recruit subjects for a psychological experiment under four conditions of group-derived restraints. In order, from lowest to highest degree of restraint, these were: (*a*) half the group being secretly instructed to raise their hands; (*b*) the whole group being required to fill out a form indicating their interest in volunteering; (*c*) forms made available to anyone who wanted to take one and to be filled out then and there; (*d*) request of show of hands of those wishing to volunteer, forms being passed out to those with hands up. Follow-up contacts were made by a combination of letter and phone call. The results are that the proportion of persons volunteering is higher for the low-restraint conditions, but that these persons are less likely actually to show up. Thus, the two extremes of restraint condition are less economical than the moderate restraint condition. With low restraint, more volunteer but fewer show up; with high restraint, too few volunteer.

A study of group influence more in the tradition of the older work on social facilitation and inhibition is that of Wapner & Alper (128), who find that the presence of an audience increases the time for subjects to make choices among alternative words to follow phrases, an unseen audience having a greater delaying effect than a visible audience. The effect is accentuated for items having personal reference for the subject.

Leadership and group influence.—Maier & Solem (84) treat of another aspect of the influence process in showing how under proper leadership conditions, minority opinions may be more effectively utilized in shaping the group's thinking. Thirty-four groups of five or six persons each were supplied with a discussion leader while working on a logical reasoning problem. As controls, 33 groups were supplied with an observer. The leaders' function was to facilitate the discussion; the observers simply observed. Neither leaders nor observers expressed their own views. Group members were asked to render individual answers to the problem before and after an 8-min. discussion. Beforehand, 45 per cent of the members of both experimental and control groups gave correct answers. After the discussion, correct answers in the groups with leaders rose to 84 per cent, as compared with 72 per cent in the leaderless groups. Further analysis revealed that the major part of the obtained difference was attributable to the relatively greater influence that individuals with minority opinions exerted in the leader groups. These results are interpreted to mean that a discussion leader can function to upgrade a group's thinking by permitting an individual with a minority opinion time for discussion. In a leaderless discussion, the majority is more likely to dominate and the potential contribution of the minority to be lost.

In reviewing this study it is important to note that the problem was one calling for a logical solution. It would be of great interest to compare these findings with those on a problem where the solution was less clear-cut, or where the subject-matter of the group task consisted of attitudes and opinions rather than of matters of fact.

The comparative effect of supervisory and participatory leadership on opinion change in small discussion groups is studied by Hare (53) in a repetition of the Preston & Heintz experiment (102). The results confirm the earlier findings that participatory leadership is more productive of opinion change than is supervisory leadership, in which the leader does not join the discussion. It is interesting that the Preston & Heintz results were obtained with college students and the Hare results with groups of boys averaging 13 years of age, the leaders averaging 14 years. An incidental finding of some interest is that the supervisory leaders themselves showed the least change in opinion.

Berkowitz (13) contributes an analysis of the phenomenon of leadership-sharing in small, decision-making groups, based upon a study of 72 conference groups in business, industry, and government. Westerlund (131) reports an experimental study of different leadership methods in a Stockholm telephone exchange, a study fertile of hypotheses but inconclusive as to results.

Leadership measurement and training.—Maier & Zerfoss (85) describe "multiple role playing" (MRP) techniques as a training and research method in leadership. Maier (86) demonstrates that supervisors in industry, after eight hours training in group-decision methods, are markedly more efficient in bringing about desired decisions by groups in an MRP test situation than are untrained supervisors.

The leaderless group discussion situation has been shown to have some value in the assessment of leadership potential. On the basis of a statistical analysis of data from 67 such leaderless discussion situations, Bass, Klubeck & Wurster (9) examine the validity of the technique and arrive at certain implications concerning ways of increasing the validity.

Considerable interest in dealing with the leaderless group discussion technique has attached to the question of whether or not seating arrangement affects the emergence of leaders. Bass & Klubeck (8) report experimental results in the negative.

With relevance to an interesting aspect of leadership attitude and behavior, Eager & Smith (34) administered the Sanford Authoritarian-Equalitarian Scale to 11 college women counselors in a health camp for underprivileged children. Later the children took a "Guess Who" questionnaire, which provided data on their perceptions of the leadership style of the counselors. There is clear evidence that their impressions of the counselors scoring high on the Sanford A-E scale differed coherently from their impressions of those scoring low, thus providing one minor piece of validation of the A-E scale as a measure of leader behavior.

Fleishman (43) offers a questionnaire developed for the objective description of leadership behavior of supervisors in industry, providing measurement of two relatively independent leadership dimensions: "consideration for others" and "initiating structure."

Personal factors in leadership.—Few new studies are available concerning the relation of personal factors to leadership. Martin, Gross & Darley (88) conducted an empirical study of 13 groups of girls living in a university cooperative village, among whom formal, informal, and mixed-type leaders were distinguished. Of approximately 100 personal variables available, only two differentiate these leader types: (*a*) higher level paternal occupation mark the formal leaders, and (*b*) better self-estimates of emotional development mark the mixed type leaders. All three leader types identify to a significantly greater degree with middle class standards than do the followers or group isolates, and all indicate greater experience in precollege family activities. Gordon (47) presents results generally consistent with the implications of Stogdill's earlier review (120), showing that women dormitory students nominated as corridor leaders tend to be rated high on responsibility, ascendency, and absence of hypersensitivity, while there is no similar relation with ratings of sociability and refinement.

Opinion and Attitude Change

The year's work in the social psychology of attitudes is distinguished by a swelling stream of excellent experimental studies of attitude change, especially those concerned with the specification of conditions governing change.

As part of a program of research on the dynamics of attitude change, Jarrett & Sherriffs (66) compare the degree of influence on an attitude by arguments presented in three contexts: (*a*) an exposition frankly favorable to a particular attitudinal position, (*b*) a debate between apologists of opposing positions, and (*c*) an impartial presentation of the two incompatible arguments. It is hypothesized that in the first context, expressed attitudes should change in the direction of the argument. In the second context, expressed attitudes should move in the direction of the pre-existing bias, the amount of change depending upon the degree of emotional involvement in the issue. (The latter part of this hypothesis was not properly subject to test as a result of the lack of a satisfactory measure of emotional involvement.) In the third context, expressed attitudes should become more moderate in position. The results are on the whole consistent with these three hypotheses.

Hovland & Mandell (62) report an experimental comparison of conclusion-drawing by the communicator and by the audience. A talk on currency devaluation was presented on tape. Two variables were manipulated: (*a*) conclusions drawn by the speaker, versus conclusions left unstated; (*b*) the speaker presented as a member of a class which would have a stake in the conclusions drawn, versus a speaker presented as impartial. Tests of opinion before and after the speech were given. The salient findings are that having conclusions drawn by the speaker is most effective in changing the audience's attitude, that there tends to be greater attitude change for the impartial speaker situation, and that there is "no support for the hypothesis that drawing one's own conclusions is particularly effective when one suspects the motives of the communicator." Interesting incidental results are that the biased communicator is rated by the audience as having given a more one-sided presentation, though in fact his talk was identical with that of the impartial speaker, and that there is no difference in the factual information retained by the listeners for the "suspicion-arousing" and the impartial talks.

The effects of different intensities of fear arousal in communications were explored by Janis & Feshbach (65) in a study of propaganda on dental hygiene among high school students. Illustrated talks inducing strong, mild, or minimal fear were given, with attitude testing one week before, immediately after, and one week after. The minimal fear appeal proved most effective in eliciting resistance to subsequent counter-propaganda, and in eliciting a higher degree of verbal adherence to a set of recommended practices. These findings are interpreted as supportive of the following hypothesis: "When fear is strongly aroused but is not fully relieved by the reassurances contained in a mass communication, the audience will become motivated to ignore or to minimize the importance of the threat." Or, more generally: "Other things being equal, the more persistent the fear reaction, the greater will be the (acquired) motivation to avoid subsequent exposures to internal and external cues which were present at the time the fear reaction was aroused."

An interesting "sleeper" effect in opinion change is demonstrated by Weiss (130). In a standard learning situation, 228 subjects learned to associate labels of "true" or "false" with each of eight statements concerning effects of smoking. Some subjects were then exposed to a brief counter-communication discounting the truth value of the learned associations; others had no such counter-communication. Pre- and posttests on an opinion questionnaire about the effects of smoking reveal a smaller loss in effectiveness of the original communication after six weeks for the group having had the immediate counter-communication, thus demonstrating a "sleeper" effect.

Questions concerning the effect of repeating the same oral propaganda on the attitude of listeners are raised experimentally by Cromwell & Kunkel (26). Although their results do not clearly indicate a cumulative effect of such repetition after 30 days, the inadequacy of the experimental design renders the findings inconclusive.

One more demonstration of the by now thoroughly verified fact that one critical source of constraint on the effectiveness of prestige suggestion is the degree of structuredness of the judged material is given by Moos & Koslin (92) who measure the influence effect of rankings of importance of statements taken from the *Congressional Record* allegedly made by Republican or Democratic leaders. Suggestion was exhibited on the vaguer statements, i.e., those appealing to broad norms, but not on the less vague. An excellent theoretical and empirical discussion of this whole matter of degree of structure and ease of suggestion effect is found in Asch's book (6), previously mentioned.

Parrish & Campbell (98) find that radio transcriptions in monologue form do not differ in their opinion-change effectiveness from those in dialogue form, though the former are more frequently judged to be "propagandistic." A methodological finding is that an indirect measure of propaganda effect, in the form of an information test, is a more sensitive indicator than the more usual direct attitude test.

How the expression of an opinion varies with the person's "definition of the situation" under which it is elicited is shown by Gorden (46). Private responses to an ostensibly anonymous questionnaire on opinions about Russia were compared with the same person's public responses during an interview in the presence of other persons, all of whom were residents of a co-operative living project. Each person also gave his estimates of the group's opinion on the issues. It is found that a person's publicly expressed opinion tends to compromise the difference between his own private opinion and his estimate of group opinion. Case studies of extreme conformists and nonconformists in this respect suggest that four factors may distinguish them: (*a*) degree of identification with the group, (*b*) conception of group attitude toward nonconformity, (*c*) own role in group, and (*d*) negativism.

A fairly rare opportunity for measurement of effect of a dramatic news event on shifts of opinion is described by Taves (124). Before and after a multiple killing in a small town, intensive interviews of a cross section of the community were taken on a number of community issues. The killing apparently produced several shifts in opinion, generalized considerably beyond the immediate character of the crime. More people questioned the "goodness" of the police department, the integrity of the elected city officials, the adequacy of welfare services, and the power of "influence" groups.

Opinion-Attitude Methodology

Attitude scales and scaling.—The literature on the Guttman and related methods of scale-analysis continues to grow. Stouffer *et al.* (121) contribute what they call the H-technique for building scales with increased precision. In their words,

> The method simply consists of determining a given cutting point in a Guttman or Lazarsfeld latent distance scale not by means of a single response, but rather by means of several responses, which are formed into a new "contrived item." The object is to maximize the information available from the basic data, and hence to strengthen confidence in the scalability of the area under consideration and the generality of the dimension which the scale is defining, and to improve the ranking of individuals through reduction of scale error.

On the problem of classifying nonscale response patterns in a Guttman scale, Henry (57) describes a simple method of placement, and Borgatta & Hays (18) point out some limitations on the arbitrary classification by the method of "perfect types," stating what they believe to be a better solution.

Schuessler (109) explores some problems of item selection in scale-analysis, concluding on the basis of an empirical study that an objective method of listing the content of the attitude area is needed. Two suggested procedures for this are: (*a*) to construct the universe operationally in terms of a content analysis of some body of material that lends itself to this method; and (*b*) to obtain from a random sample of people a complete verbal expression of the attitude being studied. The author also points out that categories contrived in the method of successive approximations are not necessarily homogeneous. A simplified and improved version of the Guttman scalogram board is recommended by Marder (87).

Hovland & Sherif (63, 112) provide new light on certain judgmental phenomena in connection with the derivation of Thurstone-type attitude scales. They present evidence that those persons whose judgments are skewed tend to hold extreme views and that arbitrarily throwing out their judgments restricts the range of the scale. Also, there is evidence that the more emotionally involved judges (e.g., Negroes on a scale of attitude toward Negroes) use a more constricted scale, and that neutral items are displaced away from the subject's own position.

Riley & Toby (105) make an interesting proposal concerning the scaling of social objects ("object scales"), as differentiated from the usual scaling of persons ("subject scales"), which would provide a systematic empirical approach to the concept of group definition of objects, and their ordering along various dimensions. They say, "Subject scales measure the extent to which individuals share a common component. Object scales on the other hand may result from group definitions which are contributed to in different ways by different group segments."

Survey methodology.—Methodological developments in survey research continue along numerous fronts, such as methods of data collection, problems of coding, sampling, interviewer bias, validity of interviews, etc.

Metzner & Mann (90) address themselves to a study of the persistent problem of comparison of the fixed-alternative questionnaire and the open-ended interview. They discover marked discrepancies in personal background data as obtained by the two instruments. The interview yields a significantly higher percentage of electrical utility employees expressing satisfaction with their work than does the anonymous questionnaire. White collar employees show greater consistency on the two forms than do other employees.

The comparative merits of field coding and office coding are examined by Woodworth & DeLott (136) with somewhat inconclusive indications that the two methods do yield differences in frequency of use of precoded categories and in frequency of "don't know" responses, fewer of these being obtained from field coders.

On questions of sampling methodology, Alpert (4) points out qualifications in the use of quota, cluster, and probability sampling deriving from certain sociological factors bearing on grouping of people. Maslow & Sakoda (89) examine volunteer-error in the Kinsey study with the finding that volunteers are higher than nonvolunteers on a measure of "self-esteem" and that "self-esteem" correlates significantly with unconventional sex behavior. The specific implication is that sex studies using volunteers as a sample require correction for volunteer-error, and this has more general implications, of course, for all kinds of studies using the volunteer sample method.

Procedures for detection and control of interviewer bias are suggested by Ferber & Wales (39). The sending of letters forewarning respondents of the specific topics to be covered in a coming opinion poll does not produce appreciable differences in answers obtained in the poll [Nuckols (96)]. Ervin & Bower (36) give some practical advice on the increasingly important technical problem of language translation in international surveys.

In the sadly underdeveloped area of validation of survey methods, Larsen (76) contributes an interesting experimental study of the comparative validity of telephone and face-to-face interviews on the measurement of message diffusion from leaflets. The Washington Public Opinion Laboratory had leaflets dropped which requested, among other things, that the recipients mail them in. The relevant areas were then interviewed by telephone and by face-to-face interviews. The telephone sample was found to show more exaggeration in their report of what they had done, pointing to the necessity for especial caution in interpretation of data obtained from telephone interviews.

Another aspect of validity of interviews is treated by Miller (91), who describes the construction and validation of several question batteries designed to predict voter turnout in a Congressional election in Waukegan, Illinois. Before and after election interviews were conducted with a carefully drawn probability sample, whose reports on voting behavior were objectively checked against official voting records. Seventy-two items were analyzed as to their predictive power and several batteries constructed on an empirical basis. The best battery still resulted in inclusion of at least 15 per cent nonvoters, and even this represents some overstatement of validity of the battery, inasmuch as no cross-validation is available.

Reviews are available of polls and survey research programs in France [Dorsey (32)], Western Germany and West Berlin [Kellerer (68)], Holland [DeJong (28)], and in agencies of the United States government [Alpert (3)].

Communication and Rumor

Communication theory and research.[4]—Deutsch (29) discusses communication models in the social sciences, pointing out that the functions of such models are "the organizing, the heuristic, the predictive, and the measuring," and that the adequacy of a model can be evaluated in respect to criteria of originality, simplicity, and realism. On a more concrete level, Eisenstadt (35) draws a number of theoretical implications about the communication process from a study of 250 new immigrant families being absorbed in Israel. One of the main functions of communication within the social system is to maintain effective performance of social roles inherent in it, thus insuring full social participation and identification with its values. The individual is most receptive to those communications which help him to satisfy various needs and specifically to perform different status-conferring roles. In general, "the communications concerning the technical aspects of new social roles are more effectively transmitted than are those relating to institutional values and symbols."

In another field study of communication as observed within a real life setting, in a rural Greek village, Stycos (122) finds that in accordance with the "opinion leader" hypothesis, the importance of the opinion leader is enhanced in an area of low literacy and meager access to mass media, and his role as opinion leader somewhat formalized. Moreover, "information controllers" who have access to radios may emerge in positions to control the flow of news.

In laboratory experimentation on the communication process, Grace (49) reports on the effects of different degrees of knowledge about an audience on the content of communication. The task was for the subject to study a set of objects on a table for two minutes, then report on them to an audience consisting of another person. This was done under three conditions: (*a*) without knowledge of the sex of the audience, (*b*) with knowledge of the sex of the audience, and (*c*) with careful briefing about the sex of the audience. Both male and female undergraduates served as subjects, and in each of the three conditions half reported to a male audience and half to a female audience. It

[4] Communication theory, in its more specialized sense of information theory, psycholinguistics, etc., is treated by Dr. Miller elsewhere in this volume.

appears that the selectivity of content of a person's communications under these conditions is influenced both by his own values and by a clear understanding by him of the nature of the audience to which he will communicate.

A special issue of the *Public Opinion Quarterly* devoted to problems of international communications research is edited by Lowenthal (82), with contributions by Lazarsfeld (79), Lasswell (77), and others. Of particular interest are White's (132) discussion of the problem of resistance to international propaganda among both friends and foes, and a symposium on content analysis for the Voice of America.

Spiegelman, Terwilliger & Fearing (117) study the content of comic strips as an important mass medium of communication. Their most interesting finding is that there is an inverse relationship between reality of depicted situation and of characterization; if the situation is "real," the actors are caricatured; if it is "irreal," the actors will be treated more realistically.

A semipopular account of propaganda analysis, public opinion, and mass communication, which utilizes surprisingly little of the more recent psychological insights and findings on these topics, has been written by Lee (80).

Berelson's *Content Analysis in Communication Research* (12), an extensive revision of an earlier account, is an exceptionally useful discussion of the definition, rationale, uses, and methods of content analysis.

Rumor.—Dodd (30) reports progress on a large-scale experimental program to study rumor, with emphasis upon social factors regulating rate and other characteristics of message diffusion. An attempt is made to give a formal analysis of message diffusion, though question remains whether much is to be gained from such a formalization. A suggested refinement of the Allport & Postman "law of rumor" (2) is offered by Chorus (24) who points out the relevance of a factor of insightfulness by the person in modifying the tendency to transmit the rumor.

A case report of rumor transmission in a catastrophic situation (the Darjeeling landslides of June, 1950, in India) is presented by Sinha (114). The data provide support for the view that transformations tend to be in the direction of exaggeration. Rather pronounced distortions in immediate perception by participants are also reported.

Socio-Political Attitudes and Participation

The most interesting of the year's studies of socio-political attitudes have to do with their personal determinants, especially in relation to the variable of liberalism-conservatism. That liberalism-conservatism can properly be considered a unitary dimension is challenged by the study of Kerr (70) who intercorrelated measures of political, economic, social, religious, and aesthetic liberalism on 246 university men; he found these five dimensions to be relatively independent of one another. Using the separate liberalism measures, data are presented to show that Republican Party membership is associated with political liberalism and economic conservatism, and that Roman Catholics, Protestants, Jews, and those without church affiliation fall in that order along the scale from religious conservatism to liberalism. Within the political liberalism test itself, a cluster analysis of items indicates the presence of three relatively separate factors: empathy with elected personnel, devotion to civil liberties, and participation tendency. As is true of many similar correlational studies in the field of attitudes, serious questions must be asked about the representativeness of the sampling of subjects as well as of the items included in the questionnaires. University students may well manifest such differentiations of sentiment about issues of liberalism-conservatism but the same may not be true of other, less highly selected populations, for whom a more generalized liberal or conservative point of view may exist.

In a sample of British students, Sanai (107) reports significant positive correlations of "alterationism" (radicalism) with emotionality and introversion, and with Theoretical and Aesthetic values on the Allport-Vernon test; with Religious value the correlation is negative.

Helfant (56) finds that adolescents' international attitudes (e.g., attitude toward Russia) are more closely correlated with the attitudes of their parents than with their own feelings of outwardly direct hostility, as measured by the extrapunitive scores on the Rosenzweig Picture-Frustration Test and on related techniques. The obtained correlations between adolescent and parental attitudes are smaller than previously reported, due perhaps to the fact that in this study a more valid appraisal of parental attitudes was achieved than is often the case in such studies.

In a study handicapped by inadequate design and sampling, Dreger (33) attempts to compare extremes of religious liberalism and conservatism, measured by a Salvation Opinionnaire, in respect to several measures of personality, such as emotional maturity, rigidity, emotional control, dependence need, etc. By and large the results are negative, 30 church going "liberals" not differing in any of the generally hypothesized ways from 30 church-going "conservatives." However, it must be noted that these comparisons are within church-goers; religious "liberals" who are not church-goers might show differences not tapped in the present comparison.

A preliminary presentation of some of the data being gathered by the Appeals of Communism Project at Princeton University is made by Krugman (72). Intensive interviews with 50 former members of the American Communist Party, divided into two groups, middle-class intellectuals (journalists, writers, artists, professionals, etc.) and trade union officials, reveal that the intellectuals are more likely than the union officials to have had emotional adjustment problems prior to joining, to have been attracted by the opportunities to defy authority, to have been status-anxious, and in general to have satisfied their unconscious needs through the Party. Such a study suffers, of course, from the inherent weakness of its necessary method, that of retrospective reporting by the ex-Communist on the motivational factors involved in joining. A shortcoming that could be remedied is the lack of comparative personality data on matched control groups of middle class intellectuals, and trade union officials, who had not joined the Communist

Party. Such data would help clarify essential differences which appear to exist between the two groups compared in this study.

Political participation.—Personality correlates of political interest and political apathy are examined by Mussen & Wyszynski (93) in a study of 156 undergraduates, divided into two extreme groups on the basis of questioning concerning their present and anticipated political participation. The apathetic and interested groups do not differ ideologically, as measured by the A-S, E, F, and PeC Scales of *The Authoritarian Personality* study (1). But differences are found on a number of projective questions designed to elicit personality attributes previously hypothesized to relate to extent of political participation, for instance by Riesman & Glazer (104). Those at the active extreme tend to be self-accepting of their own emotions, conflicts, and feelings, concerned with emotional and intellectual expression rather than with conventional values and standards, and outwardly oriented toward others and their welfare. Those at the politically apathetic extreme, on the other hand, tend to be fundamentally hostile yet unable to accept their hostile impulses, and as a result appear submissive to authority, over stressing of conformity, incapable of enjoying deep emotional experience, and in effect unable to become genuinely concerned with others or with the general welfare. In general, these differences lead the authors to conclude that

> political apathy and activity are specific manifestations of more deep-lying, and pervasive passive and active orientations. . . . Political activity or apathy are not functions *only* of the general social structure and current historical events. The personality of the individual operating within the socio-historical context must also be considered.

While the foregoing formulation is provocative, one is struck by technical limitations of the study, especially the choice of subjects, the lack of means of getting at actual political participation behavior rather then mere expression of intention, and the quite modest size of the personality differences found.

Added light is thrown on determinants of participation by the study of Gough (48) in connection with the development of a scale to predict "social participation" among high school seniors. The criterion of participation was the number of extracurricular activities in which the student was involved. Extreme highs and lows in participation were compared in responses to a large battery of specially devised items, and a final scale of discriminating items was refined and validated. Study of the diagnostic items reveals that the more participative students tend to be characterized by greater candor and frankness, self-discipline, tolerance of others, and a sense of identification with and acceptance by the group. Although it is social participation of a particular sort which is here involved, it is presumed that these results have some significance for the problem of participation in general, including political participation. In this light, it is of interest that the kinds of personality differences isolated do provide some support for earlier views about the psychological determinants of participative action.

Robinson's (106) further analysis of data from *The People's Choice* [Lazarsfeld *et al.* (78)], involving a factorial analysis of different components of participative political activity, uncovers three independent factors: (*a*) spectator interest, indicated by tendency to read about the campaign, etc., but not necessarily related to basic involvement or voting behavior; (*b*) citizen interest, indicated by above average voting tendency, but with no particular attention toward influencing others; and (*c*) partisan interest, indicated by primary concern with influencing others regarding the issues and candidates.

Wiebe (133) evaluates the actual influence of watching the televised Kefauver crime hearings on people's political participation. A study of a sample of 260 New Yorkers showed that, although the problem was broadly perceived, the hearings did not stimulate the individuals to engage in constructive problem solving behavior. Wiebe relates the findings to a concept of "social impotence" which has bearing on reference group theory.

A formulation of hypotheses concerning socio-psychological factors determining the difference between intention to vote and actual voting is offered by Suchman (123), with attention both to factors relating to the campaign situation itself and to personality factors in the individual voter.

Ethnocentrism and Prejudice

A steady stream of studies of ethnic prejudice continues to flow, focussed primarily on the determinants and correlates of prejudice, the effect of personal contact on prejudice, the relation of expression of prejudice to overt behavior, and the comparison of prejudice among various groups. To this reviewer there seem to be few truly outstanding developments in the field during the year's work. The studies are mainly extensions of lines of inquiry previously set in motion, rather than significant departures or innovations in theory and method.

Determinants and correlates of prejudice.—In an investigation of personal values as factors in anti-Semitism, Evans (37) gave the Allport-Vernon Study of Values and the Levinson-Sanford Anti-Semitism Scale to college students. In general accord with his hypothesis, it is found that the value-patterns of those high in anti-Semitism stress political and economic values, whereas for those low in anti-Semitism stress is on aesthetic and social values. Another evidence of relation of personality factors to ethnic attitudes is presented by O'Connor (97), who finds among a sample of 77 Harvard undergraduates that scores on the Ethnocentrism Scale are positively associated with "intolerance of ambiguity" and with poor ability to solve abstract reasoning problems. In a similar vein, Block & Block (16) find that ethnocentrism (measured on the Berkeley Ethnocentrism Scale), submission to authority suggestion in continuing a spool-packing task after the subject is "satiated," and rapid establishment of a norm in autokinetic judgment, all cluster together and may be inferred to reflect a compulsive "structuring" approach to a somewhat unpredictable environment.

Frenkel-Brunswik & Havel (44) report a study of 81 white American

Gentile children, 10 to 15 years of age, interviewed about their attitudes toward five minority groups: Negroes, Mexicans, Chinese, Japanese, and Jews. The children varied from extreme highs to extreme lows on the Ethnocentrism Scale. Prejudice, as measured by this scale, correlates .67 with an over-all interview rating on general prejudice, and intercorrelations ranging from .69 to .97 are found among ratings on prejudice toward the various minority groups. These findings give some (though far from conclusive) support to the notion of a generalized prejudice factor in the children. A tendency is found for the high ethnocentric subjects to dichotomize, to exaggerate adherence to conventional values, to avoid insight into the characteristics of the in-group, and to feel fear of threats and danger from the out-group. The authors see some distressing social implications in their results:

> The children's attitudes are usually a mixture of prejudice and tolerant ideologies. Our high-scoring subjects, on the whole, were freer in expressing prejudice than the low-scoring children were in expressing tolerance. Furthermore, the middle scorers who are more representative of the bulk of the population show great similarity in their responses to the high scorers. Thus the attitudes of the children as a group are predominantly prejudiced ones.

Hofstaetter (59) criticizes studies such as the above and others which reflect the influence of *The Authoritarian Personality*, as overemphasizing personality factors in prejudice at the expense of important sociological factors. On the basis of what appears to be a technically faulty factorial study of responses to a short attitude questionnaire, he concludes that there is no justification for including such independent dimensions as anti-Negroism, anti-Semitism, national pride, Puritanism, etc., in a single type, the so-called "authoritarian personality."

Contact and prejudice.—Observations of the relationship of intergroup contact and racial attitudes in such diverse settings as a Utah mining town, the Pocahontas coal field, department stores, and public housing projects, can be found in Harding (52). One of the studies included is especially notable both for its methodological care and its real life setting. Wilner, Walkley & Cook (134) analyze residential proximity and intergroup relations in public housing projects. Intensive interviews with large numbers of white housewives provided data for assessing the amount and kind of contact with Negroes and the relation of degree of proximity to attitudes toward Negroes. Marked proximity influences are found, thus providing

> strong support for a hypothesis that has gained increasing acceptance in recent years: that contact among racial groups of equal or nearly equal socio-economic class and status-roles is a favorable condition for the modification of ethnic attitudes. The data from these studies indicate that this is particularly likely to be the case in situations where the social climate supports such contact.

Bird, Monachesi & Burdick (15) find that in a neighborhood undergoing infiltration by Negroes, white residents express markedly varied racial attitudes. The majority are ambivalent in attitude, feeling both inability to overcome what they recognize as "unfounded prejudice" and resentment that the proximity of the Negroes causes them to become aware of hitherto suppressed feelings of prejudice. It appears that one consequence of the lack of clarity and uniformity of the adult attitudes is that the white children are not afforded a consistent, clear set of evaluations of Negroes, the result being that their attitudes do not closely resemble their parents' attitudes.

Expressed attitudes and overt behavior.—Along the lines of the classic study of LaPiere (75) on relation of attitude expression to overt behavior, Kutner, Wilkins & Yarrow (73) find that restaurants when queried by mail or by phone about reservations for a party including both whites and Negroes attempt to avoid making such reservations, yet when parties of white and Negro women together actually appear at the restaurant, they are regularly seated and served.

To evaluate the actual place of attitudes toward minority groups in the larger life-space of the residents of a small midwestern community, Brookover & Holland (21) used three techniques of assessing attitudes: an attitude scale, a formal interview, participant observation. They find that the adults of the community, when directly asked, express consistent and highly unfavorable attitudes toward minority groups; yet at the same time in normal everyday conversation, relations with minority groups are not at all a common topic, nor are minority groups frequently mentioned in response to nondirective questions. The inference is that minority group attitudes are not salient in this community and that answers to a direct questionnaire may not reflect the true attitudinal situation.

Comparative prejudice among whites and Negroes.—Three studies throw limited light on the matter of comparative prejudice among whites and Negroes. Prothro & Jensen (103) supply data on attitudes of Negro and white college students in the deep South with respect to the Church, Jews, whites, and Negroes. Contrary to previous findings, their results do not support the view that the attitudes of whites and Negroes are highly similar. In the same vein, Gray & Thompson (50) find that Negro students in Georgia consistently show more ethnic prejudice than white students as measured by the Bogardus Social Distance Scale. On the other hand, a subsidiary finding of the Bird, Monachesi & Burdick study (15) mentioned previously is that in a neighborhood where whites and Negroes both live, the white and Negro children are remarkably alike in their expression of attitudes toward Jewish children.

Social Perception

Bieri (14) reports experimental confirmation of the hypothesis that in a constructive interaction situation, one's perception of another will change in the direction of increased similarity to oneself. Pairs of students who were strangers interacted in a discussion of the course and discussion of a hypothetical vacation together. Before and after the interaction situation, each subject predicted the other's responses on a modified Rosenzweig Picture-Frustration Test.

The influence of the individual's value-system on his perception of people is investigated by Fensterheim & Tresselt (38). The objects of judgment were 24 pictures of men and women. The subjects rated each picture on a like-dislike dimension and also assigned to each that one of six statements drawn from the six Allport-Vernon values which best described the picture and that one which least-well described it. The hypothesis that the perceiver's own major values will be projected in his perception of liked pictures is confirmed. The liked stimuli are judged to have the subject's own high values. A further hypothesis that the subject will use his own major values as "anchoring points" for judging the pictures is not confirmed; rather, his own low values tend to serve as anchors. The interpretation offered is in terms of the "strangeness" of the stimuli.

On the other hand, evidence that perception of other people's values is by no means entirely a matter of projection is shown by Precker (101). All 242 student members of a college community ranked 39 value-criteria as pertaining to themselves. In addition, sociometric choices were made of peer-associates and of near-authority figures (advisors). The subjects tend to choose persons in both categories whose value-patterns objectively resemble their own. This tendency is most marked in the case of reciprocal sociometric choices.

Hastorf & Bender (54) emphasize the need for theoretical and operational differentiation of empathy and projection in the judgments of other people. Each of 50 students took the Allport-Vernon test of values and also predicted the value scores for another student he knew well. Two deviation scores were obtained: one, the difference between predicted and true value score (empathy); the other, the difference between predicted and self-score (projection). For 20 of the subjects predictions were closer to the true scores of the others; for 28 the predictions were closer to own scores. The authors characterize the above two types of subjects as "empathizers" and "projectors," a distinction the value of which will remain unclear until some sharper way to differentiate the types can be found, and validity tested.

Fiedler, Warrington & Blaisdell (42) find that fraternity men perceive fellow group members they like best to be more like themselves than fellow group members they like least, although there is no such objective relationship found between the self-descriptions, obtained through a Q-sort procedure.

Following along lines of thought emerging from the Berkeley studies of the "authoritarian personality," Scodel & Mussen (110) test the hypothesis

> that authoritarians, because of their lack of insight into others and their need to consider themselves members of the in-group, would perceive non-authoritarian peers to have attitudes and personality characteristics similar to their own. Non-authoritarians, on the other hand, being more insightful and more individualized in their approaches to others, would judge authoritarians accurately with respect to attitudes and personality characteristics.

Twenty-seven pairs of subjects, each consisting of a person scoring high on the F-scale (authoritarian) and a person scoring low (nonauthoritarian) interacted in a brief neutral discussion session. Afterwards each member tried to predict how his partner would answer the F-scale items and 30 selected MMPI items. The results are taken to confirm the hypothesis, inasmuch as the highs do not perceive lows as having F scores significantly different from their own, whereas lows do ascribe to the highs F scores that are significantly higher than their own. Some reservations may be entered, however. For one thing, the lows do only slightly better than the highs in accuracy of prediction of the partner's MMPI responses, and this indicates a limitation upon the hypothesized differences in perceptual functioning in the two groups. For another thing, the lows may not be more accurate in their F score prediction, but may merely express a stereotype of their own that others are more "authoritarian" than themselves. Needed controls could be introduced by also having the lows judge lows and the highs judge highs.

Far off the beaten track of most of the foregoing studies of social perception, which primarily concern themselves with the mechanism of projection in perceiving others, is a study by Wittreich (135) on the so-called "Honi phenomenon." Married persons looked at their spouses and at strangers in the two windows of the Ames' distorting room and noticed that the distortion in size of the spouse was less than in the case of the stranger. In a check experiment in which the person being judged walked from one corner of a large distorting room to the opposite corner, changing perceptually from small through normal to large in size, the above finding is verified, namely, that the marital partner is perceptually more stable in normal size than a stranger. The finding is a remarkable one and because of its theoretical importance should be further investigated with a variety of needed controls, especially those concerned with determining whether the phenomenon is essentially judgmental rather than perceptual and the conditions which favor or disfavor the effect.

In a curious experiment by Cofer & Dunn (25) evidence is found that previous reinforcement of the words "hot" or "cold" for two groups of subjects significantly influence the way they rate related personality traits of photographed persons. The finding may have implication for the kind of earlier studies of social perception carried out by Asch (6), Kelley, and others.

Social Psychology and the Atomic Age

In accepting the fifth Kurt Lewin Memorial Award, Myrdal (94) discusses some of the psychological impediments to effective international cooperation. Bauer (10) writes an enlightening account of basic changes in the Soviet conception of human nature, brought about as a function of ideological, practical, and political pressures, a book which is both an essay in psychological history and a study in political control.

But aside from such rather general exceptions, it can not escape attention that this review of the year's work in social psychology includes little that is aimed directly at the deepest social issue of our atomic age—international conflict.

Perhaps this is as it should be. It may indeed be true that in our longer perspective (assuming that such shall continue to exist), the greatest contribution that scientific social psychology can make to the problem of international conflict is in increasing our understanding of the concrete processes of group dynamics, attitude change, prejudice, and social perception, to which most of the year's research has been devoted.

LITERATURE CITED

1. Adorno, T. W., Frenkel-Brunswik, E., Levinson, D. J., and Sanford, R. N., *The Authoritarian Personality* (Harper & Brothers, New York, N. Y., 990 pp., 1950)
2. Allport, G. W. and Postman, L., *The Psychology of Rumor* (Henry Holt & Co., Inc., New York, N. Y., 247 pp., 1947)
3. Alpert, H., *Public Opinion Quart.*, **16**, 33–41 (1952)
4. Alpert, H., *Social Forces*, **31**, 30–33 (1952)
5. Argyle, M., *Brit. J. Psychol.*, (*Gen. Sect.*), **43**, 269–79 (1952)
6. Asch, S. E., *Social Psychology* (Prentice-Hall, Inc., New York, N. Y., 646 pp., 1952)
7. Barron, F., *J. Personality*, **21**, 278–97 (1953)
8. Bass, B. M., and Klubeck, S., *J. Abnormal Social Psychol.*, **47**, 724–27 (1952)
9. Bass, B. M., Klubeck, S., and Wurster, C. R., *J. Appl. Psychol.*, **37**, 26–30 (1953)
10. Bauer, R. A., *The New Man in Soviet Psychology* (Harvard University Press, Cambridge, Mass., 229 pp., 1952)
11. Bendix, R., *Am. J. Sociol.*, **18**, 292–303 (1952)
12. Berelson, B., *Content Analysis in Communication Research* (The Free Press, Glencoe, Ill., 220 pp., 1952)
13. Berkowitz, L., *J. Abnormal Social Psychol.*, **48**, 231–38 (1953)
14. Bieri, J., *J. Abnormal Social Psychol.*, **48**, 61–66 (1953)
15. Bird, C., Monachesi, E. D., and Burdick H., *J. Abnormal Social Psychol.*, **47**, 688–99 (1952)
16. Block, J., and Block, J., *Human Relations*, **5**, 91–98 (1952)
17. Bonner, H., *Social Psychology: an Interdisciplinary Approach* (American Book Co., New York, N. Y., 439 pp., 1953)
18. Borgatta, E. F., and Hays, D. G., *Public Opinion Quart.*, **16**, 410–16 (1952)
19. Britt, S. H., *Social Psychology of Modern Life* (Rinehart & Co., Inc., New York, N. Y., 703 pp., 1952)
20. Bronfenbrenner, U., and Devereux, E. C., *Human Relations*, **5**, 187–204 (1952)
21. Brookover, W. B., and Holland, J. B., *Am. Sociol. Rev.*, **17**, 196–202 (1952)
22. Cattell, R. B., *J. Social Psychol.*, **37**, 27–52 (1953)
23. Chapin, F. S., *Social Forces*, **31**, 20–25 (1952)
24. Chorus, A., *J. Abnormal Social Psychol.*, **48**, 313–14 (1953)
25. Cofer, C. N., and Dunn, J. T., *J. Personality*, **21**, 223–27 (1952)
26. Cromwell, H., and Kunkel, R., *J. Social Psychol.*, **35**, 175–84 (1952)
27. Darley, J. G., Gross, N., and Martin, W. C., *J. Appl. Psychol.*, **36**, 396–403 (1952)
28. DeJong, W., *Public Opinion Quart.*, **16**, 71–76 (1952)
29. Deutsch, K. W., *Public Opinion Quart.*, **16**, 356–80 (1952)
30. Dodd, S. C., *Public Opinion Quart.*, **16**, 247–62 (1952)
31. Dollard, J., Doob, L. W., Miller, N. E., Mowrer, O. H., and Sears, R. R., *Frustration and Aggression* (Yale University Press, New Haven, Conn., 209 pp., 1939)
32. Dorsey, J., *Public Opinion Quart.*, **16**, 225–35 (1952)
33. Dreger, R. M., *Psychol. Monographs*, **66**(335), 1–18 (1952)
34. Eager, J., and Smith, M. B., *J. Abnormal Social Psychol.*, **47**, 265–67 (1952)
35. Eisenstadt, S. N., *Public Opinion Quart.*, **16**, 42–58 (1952)

36. Ervin, S., and Bower, R. T., *Public Opinion Quart.*, **16,** 595–604 (1952)
37. Evans, R. I., *J. Abnormal Social Psychol.*, **47,** 749–56 (1952)
38. Fensterheim, H., and Tresselt, H., *J. Abnormal Social Psychol.*, **48,** 93–98 (1953)
39. Ferber, R., and Wales, H. G., *Public Opinion Quart.*, **16,** 107–27 (1952)
40. Festinger, L., Gerard, H. B., Hymovitch, B., Kelley, H. H., and Raven, B., *Human Relations*, **5,** 327–46 (1952)
41. Festinger, L., Pepitone, A., and Newcomb, T., *J. Abnormal Social Psychol.*, **47,** 382–89 (1952)
42. Fiedler, F. E., Warrington, W. G., and Blaisdell, F. J., *J. Abnormal Social Psychol.*, **47,** 790–96 (1952)
43. Fleishman, E. A., *J. Appl. Psychol.*, **37,** 1–6 (1953)
44. Frenkel-Brunswik, E., and Havel, J., *J. Genetic Psychol.*, **82,** 91–136 (1953)
45. Gilchrist, J. C., *J. Abnormal Social Psychol.*, **47,** 174–87 (1952)
46. Gorden, R. L., *Am. Sociol. Rev.*, **17,** 50–58 (1952)
47. Gordon, L. V., *J. Social Psychol.*, **36,** 245–48 (1952)
48. Gough, H. G., *J. Social Psychol.*, **35,** 227–33 (1952)
49. Grace, H. A., *J. Social Psychol.*, **36,** 89–96 (1952)
50. Gray, J. S., and Thompson, A. H., *J. Abnormal Social Psychol.*, **48,** 311–13 (1953)
51. Harary, F., and Norman, R. Z., *Graph Theory, As a Mathematical Model in Social Science* (Institute for Social Research, University of Michigan, Ann Arbor, Mich., 45 pp., 1953)
52. Harding, J., *J. Social Issues*, **8**(1) (1952)
53. Hare, A. P., *J. Abnormal Social Psychol.*, **48,** 273–75 (1953)
54. Hastorf, A. H., and Bender, I. E., *J. Abnormal Social Psychol.*, **47,** 574–76 (1952)
55. Haythorn, W., *J. Abnormal Social Psychol.*, **48,** 276–84 (1953)
56. Helfant, K., *Psychol. Monographs*, **66**(13) 1–23 (1952)
57. Henry, A. F., *Public Opinion Quart,.* **16,** 94–106 (1952)
58. Herbst, P. G., *Human Relations*, **5,** 3–36 (1952)
59. Hofstaetter, P. R., *J. Personality*, **21,** 228–39 (1952)
60. Homans, G. C., *The Human Group* (Harcourt, Brace and Co., Inc., New York, N. Y., 484 pp., 1950)
61. Horowitz, M. W., and Perlmutter, H. V., *J. Social Psychol.*, **37,** 69–95 (1953)
62. Hovland, C. I., and Mandell, W., *J. Abnormal Social Psychol.*, **47,** 581–88 (1952)
63. Hovland, C. I., and Sherif, M., *J. Abnormal Social Psychol.*, **47,** 822–32 (1952)
64. Israeli, N., *J. Social Psychol.*, **35,** 73–89 (1952)
65. Janis, I. L., and Feshbach, S., *J. Abnormal Social Psychol.*, **48,** 78–92 (1953)
66. Jarrett, R. F., and Sherriffs, A. C., *J. Abnormal Social Psychol.*, **48,** 33–41 (1953)
67. Kaplan, A. (Paper presented at the Berkeley Conference for the Unity of Science, Berkeley, California, July 3, 1953)
68. Kellerer, H., *Intern. J. Opinion Attitude Research*, **5,** 511–18 (1951)
69. Kelley, H. H., and Volkart, E. H., *Am. Sociol. Rev.*, **17,** 453–65 (1952)
70. Kerr, W. A., *J. Social Psychol.*, **35,** 111–25 (1952)
71. Krech, D., and Crutchfield, R. S., *Theory and Problems of Social Psychology* (McGraw-Hill Book Co., Inc., New York, N. Y., 639 pp., 1948)
72. Krugman, H. E., *Public Opinion Quart.*, **16,** 331–55 (1952)
73. Kutner, B., Wilkins, C., and Yarrow, P. R., *J. Abnormal Social Psychol.*, **47,** 649–52 (1952)
74. Landecker, W. S., *Social Forces*, **30,** 394–400 (1952)

75. LaPiere, R. T., *Social Forces*, **13**, 230–37 (1934)
76. Larsen, O. N., *Am. Sociol. Rev.*, **17**, 471–76 (1952)
77. Lasswell, H. D., *Public Opinion Quart.*, **16**, 491–500 (1952)
78. Lazarsfeld, P. F., Berelson, B., and Gaudet, H., *The People's Choice* (Columbia University Press, New York, N. Y., 178 pp., 1948)
79. Lazarsfeld, P. F., *Public Opinion Quart.*, **16**, 481–490 (1952)
80. Lee, A. M., *How To Understand Propaganda* (Rinehart & Co., Inc., New York, N. Y., 281 pp., 1952)
81. Lindesmith, A. R., and Strauss, A., *Am. J. Sociol.*, **18**, 272–79 (1952)
82. Lowenthal, L., *Public Opinion Quart.*, **16**(4) (1952)
83. McCurdy, H., and Lambert, W. E., *J. Personality*, **20**, 478–94 (1952)
84. Maier, N. R. F., and Solem, A. R., *Human Relations*, **5**, 277–88 (1952)
85. Maier, N. R. F., and Zerfoss, L. F., *Human Relations*, **5**, 177–86 (1952)
86. Maier, N. R. F., *Human Relations*, **6**, 161–73 (1953)
87. Marder, E., *Public Opinion Quart.*, **16**, 417–31 (1952)
88. Martin, W. E., Gross, N., and Darley, J. G., *J. Abnormal Social Psychol.*, **47**, 838–42 (1952)
89. Maslow, A. H., and Sakoda, J. M., *J. Abnormal Social Psychol.*, **47**, 259–62 (1952)
90. Metzner, H., and Mann, F., *Am. Sociol. Rev.*, **17**, 486–97 (1952)
91. Miller, M., *Public Opinion Quart.*, **16**, 381–99 (1952)
92. Moos, M., and Koslin, B., *Public Opinion Quart.*, **16**, 77–93 (1952)
93. Mussen, P. H., and Wyszynski, A. B., *Human Relations*, **5**, 65–82 (1952)
94. Myrdal, G., *J. Social Issues*, Suppl. Series, No. 6, 1–31 (1952)
95. Newcomb, T., *Human Relations*, **1**, 3–20 (1947)
96. Nuckols, R. C., *J. Appl. Psychol.*, **37**, 121–25 (1953)
97. O'Connor, P., *J. Abnormal Social Psychol.*, **47**, 526–30 (1952)
98. Parrish, J. A., and Campbell, D. T., *J. Abnormal Social Psychol.*, **48**, 3–9 (1953)
99. Pastore, N., *J. Abnormal Social Psychol.*, **47**, 728–31 (1952)
100. Perlmutter, H. V., and Montmollin, G. de, *J. Abnormal Social Psychol.*, **47**, 762–69 (1952)
101. Precker, J. A., *J. Abnormal Social Psychol.*, **47**, 406–14 (1952)
102. Preston, M. G., and Heintz, R. K., *J. Abnormal Social Psychol.*, **44**, 345–55 (1949)
103. Prothro, E. T., and Jensen, J. A., *Social Forces*, **30**, 426–28 (1952)
104. Riesman, D., and Glazer, N., in *Studies in Leadership* (Gouldner, A. W., Ed., Harper & Brothers, New York, N. Y., 1950)
105. Riley, M. W., and Toby, J., *Am. Sociol. Rev.*, **17**, 287–96 (1952)
106. Robinson, W. S., *Am. Sociol. Rev.*, **17**, 151–56 (1952)
107. Sanai, M., *J. Social Psychol.*, **36**, 3–13 (1952)
108. Schachter, H., and Hall, R., *Human Relations*, **5**, 397–406 (1952)
109. Schuessler, K. F., *Am. Sociol. Rev.*, **17**, 183–92 (1952)
110. Scodel, A., and Mussen, P., *J. Abnormal Social Psychol.*, **48**, 181–84 (1953)
111. Shaw, M. E., *Am. J. Psychol.*, **44**, 491–504 (1932)
112. Sherif, M., and Hovland, C. I., *J. Abnormal Social Psychol.*, **48**, 135–41 (1953)
113. Simon, H. A., *Am. Sociol. Rev.*, **17**, 202–11 (1952)
114. Sinha, D., *Brit. J. Psychol.*, (*Gen. Sect.*), **43**, 200–9 (1952)
115. Smith, W. I., and Ross, S., *Psychol. Bull.*, **49**, 598–627 (1952)
116. Solomon, R. S., *J. Abnormal Social Psychol.*, **48**, 153–54 (1953)

117. Spiegelman, M., Terwilliger, C., and Fearing, F., *J. Social Psychol.*, **35**, 37–57 (1952)
118. Sprott, W. J. H., *Social Psychology* (Methuen & Co., London, England, 268 pp., 1952)
119. Stephan, F. F., and Mishler, E., *Am. Sociol. Rev.*, **17**, 598–608 (1952)
120. Stogdill, R. M., *J. Psychol.*, **25**, 35–71 (1948)
121. Stouffer, S. A., Borgatta, E. F., Hays, D. G., and Henry, A. F., *Public Opinion Quart.*, **16**, 273–91 (1952)
122. Stycos, J. M., *Public Opinion Quart.*, **16**, 59–70 (1952)
123. Suchman, E. A., *Public Opinion Quart.*, **16**, 436–37 (1952)
124. Taves, M. J., *J. Social Psychol.*, **35**, 161–73 (1952)
125. Thibaut, J. W., and Coules, J., *J. Abnormal Social Psychol.*, **47**, 770–77 (1952)
126. Tolman, E. C., *J. Abnormal Social Psychol.*, **47**, 291–98 (1952)
127. Van Zelst, R. H., *J. Abnormal Social Psychol.*, **47**, 299–301 (1952)
128. Wapner, S., and Alper, T. G., *J. Abnormal Social Psychol.*, **47**, 222–29 (1952)
129. Watson, G. B., *J. Abnormal Social Psychol.*, **23**, 328–36 (1928)
130. Weiss, W., *J. Abnormal Social Psychol.*, **48**, 172–80 (1953)
131. Westerlund, G., *Group Leadership: A Field Experiment* (Nordisk Rotogravyr, Stockholm, Sweden, 1952)
132. White, R. K., *Public Opinion Quart.*, **16**, 539–51 (1952)
133. Wiebe, G. D., *Public Opinion Quart.*, **16**, 179–200 (1952)
134. Wilner, D. M., Walkley, R. P., and Cook, S. W., *J. Social Issues*, **8**, 45–69 (1952)
135. Wittreich, W. J., *J. Abnormal Social Psychol.*, **47**, 705–12 (1952)
136. Woodward, J. L., and DeLott, J., *Public Opinion Quart.*, **16**, 432–35 (1952)
137. Zajonc, R. B., *Human Relations*, **5**, 205–16 (1952)

INDUSTRIAL PSYCHOLOGY[1]

By Alastair Heron[2]

Unit for Research in Occupational Adaptation, Medical Research Council, London, England

It may well be that in the last five years we have experienced the end of an era in the history of industrial psychology. No startling development took place, no text appeared to establish a landmark, no new theory provoked widespread discussion and opened fresh vistas; but perhaps something less sensational may be detected. Discontent can sometimes be divine, provided it results in thinking which ultimately issues in more appropriate activity. Such a kind of discontent has appeared among psychologists concerned with the application of their scientific insights and skills to the problems of an industrial society. Some of the necessary thinking seems to have been done, and a little of it has been evidenced by changing activities.

Editorial policy and critical comment are agreed that the task of those called on to write these annual chapters is mainly "to derive some kind of order, even if only provisional, from the chaotic mass of current publications; to provide context, note trends, and as far as possible assess significance" (54). Consequently, though the literature has been exhaustively examined, no attempt is made to report more than a few of the books and articles appearing during the year. Those referred to have been selected mainly on the criteria of quality, interest, or novelty, but a few are added more as warnings than as models. Quality is not always measured in terms of experimental or statistical elegance, but it must be said that many reports have been passed by for gross defect in these respects. Interest has been interpreted in as catholic a manner as the limitations of the reviewer permitted, and novelty may often mean little more than a promising variation upon an old and familiar theme.

In order to set in perspective the published output of a single year it first seems desirable to stand back and take a quick look at our subject. The resulting selection appears so striking when kept in strict chronological order that no attempt has been made to organize it in other ways. More than 25 years ago it was already agreed that one of the functions of the British Industrial Health Research Board was "to advise the Medical Research Council upon the best means of securing the fullest application of the results of (its research) work to the needs of industry." By 1928 it was recognized that the objectives of industrial psychology were to acquire understanding and con-

[1] The period fully covered by this review ends at March 31, 1953, but a few additional books and journals were seen in April, 1953.

[2] The reviewer is very grateful to Professors Aubrey Lewis and L. S. Hearnshaw, and to Drs. H. J. Eysenck, C. B. Frisby, and Stephen Wiseman, for their critical comments upon a first draft of this chapter.

trol of the relations between the worker on the one hand, and his work, his work-mates, his supervisor, and his employer on the other. At that time the emphasis was explicitly stated as "being placed on the individual rather than on the group." Weber, Viteles, and others were already drawing attention to the criterion problem and the issue about the "one best way" had been stated by C. S. Myers and others. In 1930 Myers reminded psychologists in a characteristically balanced way of their twofold responsibility to statistical procedures:

Nothing is more important than that the experimental psychologist (sic!) should be well-grounded in the theory and practice of statistical measurement. But at the same time nothing is more important than that he should know when and how to use this statistical knowledge and skill, employing them not merely mechanically and mathematically but with due regard to psychological considerations.

In 1932 Viteles felt obliged to draw attention to the tendency of industrial investigators to duplicate testing devices "at a time when the more complete evaluation and standardisation of existing apparatus and techniques are most needed." He was able to quote Kornhauser's 1930 challenge, "Among the few greatest questions of our age is that which asks what modern industry means to the individual worker with reference to his satisfactions and fullness of life," and to conclude his still classic text (112) by placing an unerring finger upon the crucial role of the business executive.

Fifteen years of economic depression and war with their consequences bring us, in 1947, to Maier's recognition that "the most undeveloped aspect of industrial progress is management of labour power, an aspect which must be considered seriously in the scientific age" (79). A year later, Ghiselli & Brown stated the new emphases of industrial psychology to be implicit in an aim of "maximum production consistent with the abilities, energies, interests and motives of the worker" (43). By 1950 Shartle (99) could point out that the Armed Services work of psychologists had been "well done and well sold" but "short in criteria" and with "insufficient emphasis on leadership." Quoting Wagner, Shartle redirected attention to the interview and the problem of integrating the data obtained. A year later Bellows (12) could see an increase in leadership studies and the use of the leaderless group discussion technique. In 1952 Brown & Ghiselli (18) were expressing anxiety about a large number of articles on tests (echoing Viteles just 20 years before) and stressing the current need for more work on placement and training and for psychologists to know industry and report their work accurately and adequately. They noted the continuation of "the relatively recent interest . . . in group problems" and a trend towards "the development and use of personality tests" in selection work. Last year Harrell (51) noticed the increased popularity of studies concerned with "the effectiveness of training supervisors in human relations" and with "the relations of supervisors and employees."

As we pass on now to glance briefly at a highly selected sample of recent endeavour, much will seem familiar: sometimes because it has been going on for 30 years; sometimes because 20 years ago our elders had seen it to be important, but we have only just got round to it; and sometimes because it is in line with current fashion. In such a panorama of familiarity, it may be relatively easy to note anything strange and new.

European Work

A useful glimpse of a cross section of the work of European psychologists is available in *Applied Psychology*, the Proceedings of the 1951 International Congress of Psychotechnics (33). It contains summaries, varying in length, of 40 papers delivered by psychologists from Italy, France, Sweden, Germany, Yugoslavia, Belgium, Portugal, Austria, Norway, Switzerland, Great Britain, Denmark, and Holland. Heterogeneity of methodological sophistication characterises the general picture. Many papers reflect the continued disregard of statistical evaluation and sound experimental design which is by no means confined to the Continent. Scandinavian papers evidence an increasing interest in both the "testing" and the "human relations" approaches.

The titles of four French journals (21, 22, 88, 107) are listed for convenience in the bibliography at the end of this chapter. Their contents reflect a trend toward the more refined statistical methods such as factor analysis, discriminant function, and sequential analysis. Psychomotor tests, many of them ingenious, still dominate the selection field, but the close attention paid to work done in the United States and Great Britain is likely to lead to the use of objective personality tests as these become available. Attention is also drawn to *La Revue Suisse de Psychologie*, which publishes some papers in German or in French that are of interest to industrial psychologists, and to *Mensch und Arbeit*, which is published in Vienna. Articles in these journals are almost without exception qualitative in nature, but if the attention of British and American industrial psychologists were redirected towards a search for fresh hypotheses, it would be both smug and foolish not to acquaint themselves with the careful thinking of their Continental colleagues. A note by Froehlich & Davis (38), based on "visits to Germany in 1948, 1951, and 1952, an incomplete review of current German literature, and personal consultation with German nationals visiting America" accords with the information reaching this reviewer through similar means. These authors are mainly concerned with vocational guidance and in this connection stress the continued lack of standardised tests and the use of subjective evaluations prepared by the psychologist for the vocational advisor.

There are without doubt marked differences in training, outlook, and practice between the majority of Continental psychologists and those active elsewhere. Much has been done to further the common cause, but a great need remains for adequate provision of opportunities for personal encounter over periods measurable in weeks or months rather than the hectic few days of an infrequent congress. The same is also true, though to a lesser extent, of those active in research in Britain and in North America.

General Textbooks

Among the new and revised textbooks appearing during the year, two appear worthy of special mention. A half-length version of his *Applied Psychology* has been published by Burtt (23), who in spite of readable and frequently "popular" writing, still manages to underpin most of his material with the necessary facts. His statistical appendix for beginners serves, however, to remind this reviewer that it really is about time that more psychologists were introduced to Kendall's *Rank Correlation Methods* (68) and the virtues of "tau"; "rho" has had a very long inning without competition. *Readings in Experimental Industrial Psychology*, Blum's (15) valuable collection of papers already well known to the active research worker, but not known nearly well enough to the students, the novices, and many others whom it is harder to excuse, may do something to raise the standards of research design and reporting to a new and higher level.

The writer may perhaps be forgiven for expressing his view that we could well do without any further textbooks of "Industrial Psychology" until a really new one becomes possible.

Job Evaluation and Work Measurement

Ninth in the series of Purdue "Studies of Job Evaluation" (the eighth appeared in 1949) is one by Miles (82) on the development of a check list for office jobs, originally designed by Culbertson and Dudek and described in unpublished theses. For some reason or other this had to be read with intense concentration several times before it became clear just what was being compared with what. If others experience similar difficulties it will be a pity, because the design appears sound and the outcome encouraging. Perhaps the difficulty lies in the old phenomenon of overfamiliarity with the data on the part of the article-writer, which reviewers and abstracters encounter all too frequently in spite of the ceaseless work of editors. Howard & Schutz (61) use factor analysis to continue the pastime of exposing the essential unidimensionality of job evaluation schemes, accounting for 99 per cent of the variance among 11 "attributes" by means of a single factor which they identify as "skill demands." One may express the hope that the time has now come to call a halt; there are other more important exercises for Ph.D. candidates to do. Davis (29) draws fresh attention to the psychological consequences of leaving the design of "payment systems" entirely in the hands of production engineers and work-study experts. Her investigation, carried out in five modern factories, covered 386 men and 402 women by means of individual interviews. Two-thirds were dissatisfied in varying degrees with the group bonus systems in force, and in no group were more than half the workers prepared to describe themselves as satisfied. She concludes that the resulting conflicts are basically emotional rather than intellectual and recommends that general policy should be framed jointly by management, personnel officers, and medical officers, regarding the work-study engineers as technical experts who would be asked to "implement the policy."

While on the subject of work measurement, three papers may be mentioned from Smith and various collaborators (93, 108, 115) describing further work with the "Universal Motion Analyser," an electronic device for measuring travelling time and manipulative time separately. They report (*a*) that "pull" movements are significantly slower than "turn" movements; (*b*) that contrary to motion-study statements, extending distance of travel does also increase manipulative time; (*c*) learning affects the manipulative component three times as much as the travel one; (*d*) that in the type of motions analysed by them it is not true that increased pattern complexity reduces movement efficiency; and (*e*) that some positive transfer effect can be observed on the manipulative component, but not on travel. Summarised, these data strongly suggest need for research into the manipulative components of work behaviour with less attention than heretofore on the travel aspect except to keep it short. It will be interesting to observe the printed reaction of the motion-study pundits to what will undoubtedly be described as an artificial laboratory set-up from which no generalisations into real life can validly be made. Psychologists interested in this field will do well to consider how such blanket criticisms can be met by careful evaluation of the motivational elements in such studies. We do not know as yet, for example, whether differences in such elements would operate equally on both travel and manipulative components of motion. If it could be shown that they do, the work now reported would rest on firmer foundations.

Industrial psychologists will probably hail with relief the important book by Abruzzi, *Work Measurement* (1), in which he describes the application of statistics of quality control to both time and motion study. His research goal was "to develop estimating procedures that could be verified in terms of the modern theory of experimental inference." His results provide the long-awaited demonstration that standard data procedures are largely unvalidated, and that as psychologists have long suggested, there is no "one best way"; he also places on the shoulders of the scientific work-study experts a heavy responsibility to abolish ratings of worker performance, and to substitute objective procedures such as those he describes. Abruzzi's data showing that "independent standard elements" in time study and "independent motions" in motion analysis are frequently correlated, are strongly reminiscent of equally untenable claims for the independence of trait ratings which can also be shown as intercorrelated. In all these fields the independence has too long rested on intuitive judgments.

Vocational Guidance

Those who naively imagine that vocational guidance is either a highly developed precision instrument or a rather hit-and-miss affair will do well to read Stott's honest presentation of the problem of validation in this field (103). Like the interview itself, the case is not proven; unlike the interview, validation problems are intrinsically resistant to solution. Paradoxically, it is from vocational advisors that most help should be forthcoming if we are to see the improvement of the interview by alternate modification and re-evaluation through rigorous statistical treatment. Jahoda (64), in a valuable interview study of school leavers, their job attitudes and choice of first job, found that present youth employment services come into action too late because the informal influence of parents, relatives, and friends has already been effective in the majority of cases. This study is distinguished by the way in which it combines thorough field work with awareness of the need for statistical checks on the data obtained. In amplifying a "theory of occupational choice—a largely irreversible process involving compromise as an essential aspect," Ginzberg (46) draws attention to a pressing need for more and better research into the relation of emotional factors to work, especially in distinguishing the "work-oriented from the pleasure-oriented person." It may be commented here that although we are familiar with both these kinds of people (though usually by other names), we are still largely in a state of ignorance concerning the way in which such personalities are formed or the extent to which they are modifiable. Although it may prove even more difficult to carry out suitable research than to formulate it, this nevertheless appears to be one of the points at which psychologists in various fields could, and should, get together.

Strong (104) continues publication of long term follow-up data on his Vocational Interest Blank with material about engineer interests. The noteworthy point in this 19 years' follow-up is his statement that assumed equivalence of "A-ratings" can be dangerous and that it is the occupation with the highest score which is most likely to count. It may be hoped that this will not have the effect of stimulating unfounded claims to precise score values, especially as it is clear that Strong supports nothing of the kind. The assessment of vocational interests by questionnaire methods has been extended by the monograph of Strong & Tucker (105). Working under contract for the United States Army Medical Corps, and assisted by a team of five graduate students, they developed blanks for the medical specialties of internal medicine, surgery, pathology, and psychiatry, as well as taking the opportunity to revise the "physicians-in-general" scale. This monograph is especially recommended to the attention of those who are dubious about this sort of approach, because the facts necessary for evaluation are all there, either in the text or in the six technical appendices. This reviewer's impression is that Strong has strengthened his case.

Garry (40) showed that Strong Vocational Interest scores can be consistently faked on request, and that in the student population this ability was uncorrelated with intelligence, sex, or information about the occupation. As this is in line with Strong's own statement and that of others, and with findings on several personality inventories, we now need a different kind of investigation showing in a variety of motive situations how much faking is actually done. A possible model for such research is Green's 1951 study of patrolmen (49), in which he used the same personality schedules and inventories in circumstances (*a*) when the situation was likely to motivate responses in the direction of faking and (*b*) in another real-life situation in which similar respondents knew that nothing depended on their answers.

Zuckerman (126) seems justified in claiming the results to be clear-cut in an article reporting his comparison of like/indifferent/dislike response arrangement with "forced-choice" layout in vocational interests blanks. No significant difference was found between the two arrangements, as assessed by discriminatory power and split-half reliabilities, but he is right to point out that the results obtained may be peculiar to the group of professional persons studied.

Gustad (50) contributes to current work on the Occupational Interests Level Scale with a paper in which by clearly presented statistical data he shows that sampling problems are as crucial in this connection as in others and that college populations have their limitations even if only through restriction of range. The pity is that such discoveries are so frequently made after the completion of research projects. The same scale was investigated also by Barnett *et al.* (7) in separate studies synthesised into a monograph under the direction of Super. Of these the most interesting is perhaps Barnett's pioneer study of vagrants in which he suggests that the scale might be used as an "index of the occupational and/or social level which the individual is likely to find congenial." Worthy of comment is the way in which Super has here made real the concept of a team approach in doctoral research administration; may we see more of it. Not to be overlooked is a suggestion by Steinberg (102) that the Kuder Preference Record may be useful in vocational guidance as a means of detecting neurotic tendencies. His nonneurotic group was as impure as usual in such studies, but he still found differences significant at the 1 per cent level, justifying a suggestion that further work along these lines might be profitable.

Selection and Placement

Application forms.—In a chapter on the applications of psychology in the Defence departments, appearing in *Current Trends in British Psychology*, Wilson (121) quotes an interesting illustration of the validity of the Royal Navy's biographical data form which it takes 15 min. to administer. An experienced personnel selection officer used the form alone to grade the suitability of 500 men for a training course, and obtained a validity of .554 with "success in the course" (criterion not described). The standard test battery, with which her grading correlated .312, had a validity of only .393. In concluding the summary in which this example is given, Wilson makes the important point that although the actual work of the Armed Forces psychologists appears to be mainly technological research, the solutions they find depend always upon quite general developments in psychological or statistical work. This reference to the need for unity in psychology is strongly reminiscent of one of the last papers of Bingham (14), who died during the year. Further reference to this topic will be found in the concluding section of this chapter. A useful contribution to the problem of accuracy with application blanks comes from Mosel & Cozan (84) who commendably used evaluative procedures identical with those of Keating, Paterson & Stone (67) in order to permit comparison of findings. The principal result draws attention to the direction of distortion rather than to its amount, which is small.

Interviewing.—The shortcomings of psychometric prediction are so thoroughly publicized by those who use such methods, that it is hardly surprising to find repeated claims for the so-called "clinical approach" as an alternative. Harrison & Jackson (52) consider that "the effect of applying these (clinical) methods can be objectively and empirically validated." Readers are invited to consider the resulting paper, without bias if possible, and to draw their own conclusions. This reviewer's concept of validation differs from that of Harrison & Jackson but more broadminded critics may be satisfied. Kephart's *The Employment Interview in Industry* (69), a useful book for personnel managers, is inaccurately titled. "Personnel Selection in Industry" for the title might have implied too much but on the whole would have been nearer the mark. Very much more than interviewing is described in order to put the actual interview as such into perspective, and in fact the treatment of the interview itself is on the slight side. Industrial psychologists interested in the interview and who have not yet studied the relevant chapters in Vernon & Parry's book (111) are, in the light of Kephart's treatment of the subject, strongly urged to do so. Rodger (90) makes a spirited defence of the interview on the principal grounds that because people will in any case go on using interviews the task of the psychologist is to remove the defects. While supporting the use of objective tests and the search for better ones, he considers the case against the interview as not proven. With this balanced judgment the present reviewer concurs; but what a job it is getting interview users to advance the cause of scientific rigour!

Tests.—We may open this section with a reference to Brown & Ghiselli (19), who continue in their role of avuncular advisors by offering a reminder of the dangers implicit in using valid predictors of training success as predictors of job proficiency or vice versa. In another paper (20) they provide fresh data obtained from taxicab drivers concerning the relation between job tenure or labour turnover and various tests used as predictors. In general these data support previous findings of U-shaped relationships between tests and turnover, but the exceptions seem enough to preclude any firm pronouncement. In this reviewer's experience the only safe procedure is actually to examine the shape of the regression in every instance. An insignificant correlation does not always mean no predictive value, and critical cutoff points may exist in any particular instance.

Ralph & Taylor (87) used the General Aptitude Test Battery twice on a class of 49 medical students, using grade-point averages after five quarters' training as first criterion, and those after the full four years' course as second criterion. In spite of preselection and consequent restriction of range the verbal-numerical-spatial combination gave multiple R's of .56 and .60 on the two occasions. This finding is unusual in medical student selection, suggesting deficiencies both in the original selection procedures and in the make-up of the criteria, neither of which is the fault of these investigators. They are undoubtedly justified in asking for further research and especially for "thorough evaluation by means of well-designed studies" before any new procedures are widely installed. In this connection considerable interest will be focussed on the 10 years' study under way in England under the auspices of the Nuffield Trust.

In a brief report Wesman (118) gives some five years' follow-up data about the Differential Aptitude Tests. Among the points stressed by him it is as well to mention (*a*) the specificity of validity, (*b*) the evidence obtained for the depression of validities as a result of imperfect criteria such as course grades, and (*c*) the consistently greater predictability of grades for girls than for boys. Levine & Tupes (76) confirm the continuing validity of the United States Air Force pilot stanine, quoting biserial coefficients all around .55 to .60, and provide data to suggest that it would not be difficult to raise it still higher by substituting certain tests now available and by rekeying the scoring of existing tests.

Chriswell's report (26) of a structural dexterity test is less valuable than it might have been simply because he apparently rushed into print before completing the evaluation. It is not good enough to say "more significant results might be obtained with age held constant"; that is the reporter's job, not the reader's. Similarly it is not satisfactory to report two selected multiple R's out of a possible number of at least five without stating either the basis of selection or any of the usual information required by the reader in order to evaluate the quoted figures. In spite of these defects of reporting, the test itself looks promising enough to justify further trial under research conditions. Wyndham (123), describing selection of machine shop operators using drills, taps, and hand presses, reports a multiple R of .50, using the Minnesota Rate of Manipulation Test (both parts) plus an *ad hoc* "deburring test," with bonus earnings as criterion. Reliability of the *ad hoc* test is estimated as averaging about .8 using the intercorrelations of half-tests over four trials. The sample was 40 experienced operators and no cross validation is yet available. Goguelin (47) gives further details of his work on the selection of Paris streetcar drivers using Lahy's battery of tests. This paper provides a Thurstone factor analysis by the complete centroid method leading to four interpreted factors, based on the intercorrelations of 33 tests with age held constant. The four factors are described as "mental adaptation," "concrete intelligence," "physiological adaptation," and "duration of reaction." The sample consisted of 284 drivers. A second sample of 450 was tested with nine of the tests in the first battery and two rotated factors corresponded in part with two of the factors from the first analysis. He also supplies a table of test/retest coefficients over periods between six months and one year in respect of portions of his original sample of subjects; N's are either 40 or 26. The coefficients range from $-.31$ to $+.83$, which would seem to raise some problems for the users of the tests in selection work. Nevertheless it is good to see such data analysed exhaustively in this way instead of being accepted uncritically on an impressionistic basis as is so commonly done. Germaine, Browne & Bellows (42) ask some awkward questions about physical profiling systems at the end of their useful summary of those developed by the Armed Forces of Great Britain, Canada, and the United States. In particular they state themselves as "unable to find any reports of studies regarding reliability and validity of these systems."

The literature on that aspect of prediction work misnamed "personality" continues to be scanty. Krathwohl (73), in an attempt to assess the specificity of "industriousness" by means of the differences between achievement and aptitude scores, concludes that he has extended the findings of Hartshorne, May & Shuttleworth (53) by showing that an individual should not be considered industrious as such but rather as industrious in particular activities. Those wishing to continue trials of personality inventories in employee selection had better read Ghiselli & Barthol's cautionary two-page note (44). It might be added that the predictive value of some of the low but significant validities quoted should always be sized-up against costs in time and personnel for administration and scoring. Objectively scored tests of emotional stability of the type described by Eysenck (34) have been used by Heron in two studies reported during the year. In one of these (59), forming part of an intensive medical study of the incidence of rheumatism among British colliery workers, it was shown that as one proceeds from colliery office, through surface maintenance men, and those spending part-time above ground and part-time below, to the full-time face-workers, instability as measured by the test battery increases. In the other (57), where the object was to ascertain the extent to which psychological handicap is reflected in occupational maladjustment of unskilled workers, significant correlations were obtained with highly reliable supervisory ratings. These studies need further confirmation with other groups of unskilled workers before the predictive value of the tests employed can be established but may be said to represent a breakaway from interviews and multidimensional inventories. Heller (55), in a study of female hosiery workers, used a simplified form of the actual linking operation to predict success among new trainees by means of level-of-aspiration scoring. Pending replication, the value of the report lies at present in the attempt to extend level of aspiration studies to standardised tests of a work sample type.

Group selection methods.—Four further papers by Bass and his collaborators (8, 9, 10, 122) continue his examination of the leaderless group discussion technique. Data obtained from university students and Army and Air Force cadets include validities (using criterion ratings by peers or superiors) ranging from .17 to .42 and reliabilities from .80 to .88. Pooled discussions which are quoted in one of the papers show that, using the same data, validities are somewhat higher. It is suggested that low validities may be in part a result of restriction in range of criterion ratings dependent upon combination of candidates available in a given study, and narrow range of discriminations by discussion observers. Scores for leadership group discussion were found to correlate .37 with ascendancy and .22 with sociability on the Guilford-Zimmerman Temperament Survey, using a population of college women. Using a group of strangers instead of people acquainted with one another they obtained an average reliability of .92 and a weighted average correlation with future leadership status eight months later of .47. Semeonoff (97) draws attention to the possibility that L.G.D. reliability measurement could be tackled somewhat differently by means of separate measures of the number of times each particular participator was "active" (defined as speaking) and "passive" (was spoken to) respectively. He hypothesises that if two active (A) counts and two passive (P) counts intercorrelate highly within each category, reliability is demonstrated. He contrasts this with his own (unpublished) observations that A/P correlations were often greater than A/A or P/P ones, suggesting lack of consistent leadership behaviour. Evaluation of the group selection procedure is somewhat furthered by Higham (60) in respect of 50 sales representatives chosen for the chocolate and cocoa firm involved. Using as criterion a five-point grading on general efficiency by the sales manager, 74 per cent were regarded as successful, 18 per cent left voluntarily although satisfactory, and 8 per cent were asked to leave. It is noteworthy that the chosen 50 were apparently selected largely on the group procedure as no differences could be shown between them and 200 rejects, on test scores, schooling, interests, or careers in the Armed Services.

When these data are added to the summaries already provided in recent reviews, it seems that this technique has possibilities in certain circumstances and it is greatly to be hoped that in spite of the difficulties of validation those using it in varying situations will feel a high sense of responsibility in order to ensure a continuing flow of reliable information. We are as yet without important data concerning the limitations upon the use of the technique which may arise in connection with the variables of intelligence, education, or social class.

Criteria

In a thoughtful, provocative, and realistic address to his French colleagues, Bonnardel says, "The examination of criteria of success is something which psychologists must carry out systematically before all else" (16). He would therefore share the reviewer's pleasure at finding a considerable increase in the number of useful studies in this field. Severin (98) exposes some of the gaps in our knowledge concerning the ability of tests and ratings to predict job performance, stressing in the process the danger of substituting one criterion for another without prior determination of their equivalence, and adds his support to the current *caveats* about substituting training records for job performance criteria. Fruchter (39) provides an interesting suggestive illustration of the Guilford-Gulliksen thesis that criteria as well as predictors should be factor-analysed. If someone with adequate research facilities will now do what Fruchter would like to have done, they will have rendered a considerable service. A plea may be entered here that such work should be carried out somewhere else than in the Armed Services or a university. Hemphill & Sechrest (56) provide a depressingly interesting example of the possible lack of meaning in highly self-consistent criteria based on ratings. This is a study of criteria of air crew effectiveness where both superiors' ratings and sociometric indexes correlated significantly with bombing accuracy (a criterion of near zero reliability) because both the former had presumably used knowledge of bombing activity reports as part-bases for their judgments. In a study of Army noncommissioned officers Klieger & Mosel (72) provide data which suggest that the reliability of ratings is affected not only by the degree of ratee acquaintance, but also by the manner in which experience with the ratee is perceptually organised through status and role relationships.

The considerable literature on sales success through the years is not particularly encouraging reading, but a paper by Rush (94) may suggest why this is so. He used factor analysis to demonstrate that criteria of sales success were complex, and multiple correlation to suggest that differential prediction of various subcriteria was both feasible and desirable. The construction and use of a report form suitable for clerical officers in a large bank is reported by O'Neil (86). The special feature of this attempt is the apparently successful outcome of a determination to revise descriptive phrases in each of the eight five-item ratings until an approximately normal distribution was achieved instead of the initial (and usual) bunching and negative skewing. Factor analysis, however, indicated that the final outcome is probably a highly reliable rating of a single overall trait of efficiency. A complete absence of reference to the work of others mars this businesslike article. Weschler, Massarik & Tannenbaum (117) found clearly significant differences in the United States Civil Service Commission efficiency ratings when experimental conditions were introduced, by far the greater number of shifts being in the downward, i.e., less favourable, direction. Does this do more than confirm yet again the fact that the error of leniency is nearly always with us? If it does no more, then perhaps at least one or two additional people will be stimulated into a re-examination of their merit-rating procedures.

Acquaintance or buddy ratings were used by Husén (62) in a study for the Swedish Army as an additional criterion for validating psychological test batteries designed to select officer cadets. The method of paired comparisons was used within units of 20 students, involving for three variables 11,400 comparisons per unit. High or fairly high correlations were found, that between total rank order (TRO) by fellow students on all three variables (military fitness, intelligence, and capacity for leadership) and commanding officer's rank order (CORO) being .81; that between TRO and self rank order (SRO), .64; and between CORO and SRO, .59. Husén raised the problem of criterion selection and decided in this case that the acquaintance ratings can be used for establishing the relevance of a test to military achievement but not as a criterion of cadet school achievement. For research purposes Heron (58) established two criteria of occupational adjustment among unskilled workers. One in effect validated a factory work-study index by comparing equated production over various types of work with actual counts of units produced of a single specified type. The other, a criterion of job adjustment defined as the extent to which a man was a source of concern to his supervisor, was found to have a retest reliability over a five weeks' interval of .78, and also shown by factor analysis and analysis of variance to be unidimensional for six raters. The technique, which involved a double sorting procedure leading to a forced normal distribution on a five-point descriptive scale, has proved serviceable in other situations.

Stagner, Flebbe & Wood (101) introduced a paper with the statement that "the number of studies dealing with job satisfaction has become so large that the newcomer to the field may well be appalled." One can only hope that the newcomer will be more appalled by the low correlation between quality and quantity than by the absolute number of studies. Stagner *et al.* find union-management relations, grievance handling, supervision, and working conditions ranking 1 to 4 in importance to their sample of 100 railroad workers, using as criterion the magnitude of the difference between percentage of positive answers returned by the 50 high and 50 low satisfaction groups respectively. The authors call for more study of satisfaction at the on-the-job level: that is, personal relationships, rewards and punishments directly connected with the day's work. Weitz (116) puts forward the thesis that a worker's stated sources of job satisfaction are more meaningful if we can get some idea of how generally dissatisfied he is with everyday life, and illustrates it with some preliminary results. It occurs to the reviewer that the common element here may prove to be the extent of instability or maladjustment in the personality of the individual worker. In a brief summary of validation data on his Tear Ballot, Kerr (70) provides a small but useful bibliography of job satisfaction studies including some as yet unpublished. One of these, by Hoover, is quoted as showing the correlation between mean job satisfaction of each of 26 work groups at the beginning and end of a three years' period to be statistically insignificant. Without the full data this is difficult to evaluate, but it is to be hoped that the study will eventually be published since it may raise issues of importance both to research workers and to practitioners.

Robinson & Hoppock (89) continue the useful series of summaries of job satisfaction researches, providing a 23-item bibliography. They note a trend "in the direction of a probing for individual adjustment and group adjustment causes," commenting that "many researchers . . . appear now to accept the thesis that such factors as job security, wages, physical working conditions, etc., are symptoms . . . not causes in themselves." Probably the most striking result of an as yet unpublished study by Kristy (74) is "the clear determination that there is almost no relationship between proficiency and satisfaction among (British) post office counter clerks." By means of a group factor analysis of the combined matrix of proficiency and satisfaction variables, he finds that proficiency divides into (*a*) general ability, and (*b*) reliability defined as "getting along effectively without having to bother the supervisor"; and that satisfaction divides into (*a*) pleasant feeling towards the job and (*b*) satisfaction with the physical demands in relation to the rewards. Support for the latter dichotomy appears in some recently completed and as yet unpublished results obtained by the reviewer in a study of autobus conductors. Bernberg (13) found no significant relationship between assessments of morale obtained by questionnaires from 890 workers in an aircraft factory, and indicators of their efficiency. A supervisors' merit rating accounted for 42 per cent of the variance of the efficiency indicators, and the four measures of morale intercorrelated highly. It is therefore difficult to see why Bernberg used a combined score for efficiency but the four separate scores for morale. The former is described as the sum of the scores of the specific indicators. Apart from the fact that this does not indicate whether standard or other transformed scores were summed, it raises the basic question whether all the distributions involved were suitable for combining. Merit ratings, for example, may be well distributed and subject only to mild skewness in favourable circumstances with well-constructed scales, while frequencies of absence and lateness are notoriously J-shaped, especially in a short period such as 20 weeks. Papers of this kind lose a great deal of their potential interest and value to those reading them unless authors are forthcoming on points such as those raised.

Miscellaneous Topics

Rehabilitation.—Maule (81) used some of the governmental and private-enterprise industrial rehabilitation services of Great Britain as a medium for trying out the project method of teaching among a mixed postgraduate group of psychologists and medicals. Apart from comments on the usefulness of the project, Maule makes three points about the current trends in rehabilitation which are of interest. First, possession of the same specific disability is an unsound basis for classification; second, physical handicap is often overemphasised at the expense of occupational abilities; third, rehabilitators are apparently rather antiscientific so far as validating their work is concerned.

Ageing.—Problems of ageing received attention from Tuckman & Lorge (109) and from Kirchner, Lindbom & Paterson (71), who tackled the question of attitudes towards employment of older people, the former authors among graduate students and the latter among laundry rank-and-file workers and supervisors. Graduate students are reported as accepting erroneous ideas about older people more than would be expected of such a selected population, while in the laundry (and in a factory used for cross-validation) the neutrality of the under-30's among rank and file contrasted with the increasing favourableness in older age. This is not as platitudinous as might appear at first glance, the attitude of the under-30's being the critical element and the one to which further attention should be given.

Work environment.—Attention may be directed to three papers on perceptual aspects of the work environment. Spragg & Rock (100) contribute two careful studies of brightness levels in dial readings, showing that such levels should be kept above the critical range 0.02 to 0.05 foot-lamberts but that further increase adds nothing to error reduction and little to time reduction. Use of red lighting requires these limits to be exceeded, but not beyond 0.1 foot-lamberts. The first paper recognises limiting conditions not provided for in this experimental design and requiring further research. Zaccaria & Bitterman (124) used critical fusion frequency as a measure of fatigue when investigating the effects of fluorescent lighting on both A.C. and D.C. supplies. They concluded, apparently with justification, that single-lamp or in-phase multiple-lamp fluorescent installations are undesirable from the point of view of objective fatigue. No effects on speed of reading were observed. In an interesting paper describing the development of a new indicator of machine tool travel, Gibbs (45) stresses the way in which existing methods of display often dominate industrial tasks, and in the reviewer's judgment rightly emphasises that producing a practical working model is likely to achieve change much more quickly than verbal recommendation.

Accidents and absence.—Maguire, Pearson & Wynn (78) give examples of the use of various statistical tests in studying the homogeneity or heterogeneity of the time intervals in industrial accident data. They draw the analogy between quality control and accident control statistics but rightly stress the important differences between the two fields of study. That old veteran "accident-proneness" continues to receive attention, Webb & Jones (114) reporting that the index of reliability (demonstrating proneness) can be obtained equally well by the Poisson-fit and by the correlational approaches (incidentally still of the order of .2 on fresh data!), while Adelstein (2) continues the 1951 South African onslaught of Arbous & Kerrich (5) in a long paper followed by contributions from such well-known figures as Irwin and Chambers. The last two papers (Adelstein; Arbous & Kerrich) are now obligatory reading for all future investigators. Frank (37) gives details of the use of a new but unpublished technique developed by Arbous and Sichel for the analysis of absence data. Briefly the method is to establish "absence-proneness" in a given group of workers by correlating absences in a given year with those in the next; if this correlation is significant, to use the bivariate distribution for predicting future absence by means of a mathematical model based on the negative binomial distribution. Frank's data are encouraging for the use of this approach, and the paper is likely to be of considerable interest to those concerned with studies of absence.

Supervision

Evaluating procedures.—A promising dimensional approach to the objective assessment of supervisory behaviour comes from Fleishman (36), and it is to be hoped that others will give his Supervisory Behavior Description Form further trial, especially in situations where external criteria are available as validation.

File's "How Supervise?" has attracted attention from several sources. Millard (83) follows up the lead given by Slocum, Mosier, Harrell, and Sartain concerning the relationship between "How Supervise?" and general mental ability. It seems a pity that he used the Adaptability Test as a measure of intelligence following Sartain and more so that Carter (24), who quotes no references, fails to publish his obtained correlations between "How Supervise?" and the Otis test. Wickert (120) gives a correlation with the language-factor score of the California Mental Maturity Test, calling it "verbal intelligence." When a matter is a live issue it gives cause for regret that authors are not especially conscientious in making available every scrap of relevant data for the use of others. As it is, all we now know from these studies is that "How Supervise?" is almost certainly correlated significantly with word knowledge and educational level, especially if a wide range of these is involved, but we do not know whether it is affected by general mental ability. Whether it is an intelligence test or not, Part III of it correlated .65 with a rating of supervisory ability by fellow supervisors for two of three small groups of supervisors studied by Carter in a metal plant. This is one of several studies noticed this year where authors have apparently been unable to resist the temptation of proceeding to the use of multiple R on samples ranging from 12 to 20 cases. Incidentally Carter would be hard put to it to explain why, for the group of supervisors whose ability was not predicted at all by "How Supervise?" an r of .66 was found with the "Artistic" section of the Kuder Preference Record!

Training of supervisors.—The scanty research literature on training referred to by previous reviewers receives a welcome addition from Castle (25) in a paper reporting the development of two attitude scales and a role playing test for use in evaluating supervisor training procedures. Although the results of their preliminary use are inconclusive, as a contribution to methodology the article merits close attention by those better equipped with facilities for development and further research. *Principles of Human Relations* is the title of Maier's textbook (80) contribution in this field. Although it contains some material previously published in journal articles the bulk of the content is fresh. For those to whom the expression "human relations" has become anathema, this text is recommended reading if only because this author has his feet firmly planted on scientific ground. He gives reasons why the training techniques he describes justify serious attention and does not fail to relate his case material to his general psychology. Maier also provides evidence that he at least has not been blinded by success to the need for further well-planned research, suggesting ways in which training situations using role playing can be valuable opportunities for a variety of research purposes from the influencing of opinion to the effect on decision making of various kinds of participants. This book is a welcome contrast to the vague and verbose affirmations about human relations which have been the cause of much understandable resistance to this development in the field of scientific industrial psychology.

Psychology of Industrial Relations by Lawshe *et al.* (75) is "directed specifically at industrial people in supervisory and managerial ranks." Its competent and up-to-date nontechnical coverage of employee-centred industrial psychology would make it a useful handbook for supervisors and managers already convinced by Maier's programme, but it may be doubted whether its succinct summaries of good practice would cut much ice with the unconverted autocrats. Even if they responded to the businesslike appeal to use psychologically right methods in order to make employees happier in order to raise productivity in order that we shall "all have more," it is doubtful whether they could wear their sheepskins convincingly enough to achieve the objective. A not unreasonable analogy is the attempt to promote happier family living by buying Dad the right sort of book at Christmas. His problem is to get into the state of mind where he can do what the book says!

Attitudes and Morale

Vigorous criticism of that Hawthorne experiment known as the "Relay Assembly Test Room" comes from Argyle (6). Those concerned with the planning of fresh studies of working groups would be well advised to consult this paper whether on doing so they agree with Argyle or not. It is at least refreshing to see someone at last calling a halt to the procession of perfunctory references to the Hawthorne studies and their principal generalisations. A good looking paper on group productivity, complete with all the statistical data one now feels able to expect, laid out in a neat businesslike fashion, and dealing with a topic of current interest, is provided by Darley, Gross & Martin (28). The work reported is described as the first in a series of studies of group behaviour. There is a criterion of productivity, the dependent variable; there are 18 independent variables to predict it, a table of rank order (rho) correlations; and a choice of five multiple R's using different (selected) combinations of two, three, or four variables. The discussion is sophisticated both theoretically and statistically, including a half-column on the assumption of linear and additive relations between the predictors and the criterion. This reviewer became deeply interested in considering how the authors might have avoided the element of subjectivity involved in selecting the variables for their reported multiple R's, and as a result he at first completely overlooked the crucial fact, clearly stated by the authors, that this monumental structure rested on a frail foundation of 13 cases. Gekoski (41) in a related paper also used multiple R, on an N of 21, but largely prevents overenthusiasm by twice repeating that the results cannot be more than suggestive. These papers draw attention to the methodological problems presented to the well-trained psychologist by the implicit difficulties of obtaining large samples of groups. It is the opinion of others beside this reviewer that the right way to face these problems is to exercise restraint in the use of statistical procedures which demand for their valid use resources which we often cannot obtain.

The Man on the Assembly Line by Walker & Guest (113) is a cleanly written report of a well-planned attitude survey carried out in a new automobile plant. It will undoubtedly be read by those who get a copy into their hands, and if some research workers and teachers in the field of industrial psychology feel a bit lost without all the tables they are used to, the novelty may do no harm. This investigation is similar in some respects to several carried out in Great Britain during the last 10 years by teams of the Medical Research Council, but the principal differences are of some interest. Walker & Guest's interviewers reached all their sample at home on the telephone and saw their subjects at home by appointment. In Britain, assembly line workers seldom have or aspire to telephones and tend to resent home visits anyway. Over 90 per cent of the American sample had received more than elementary schooling, half of them having graduated from high school. Even allowing for their being atypical of American assembly workers, they would still contrast with their British opposite numbers, almost all of whom would have finished school at 14 or 15. Such divergencies underline the problem of generalisation where all such studies are concerned; but where findings are the same in spite of such social and educational differences we shall all the more confidently add to our general fund of firm knowledge.

In a survey of worker attitudes in seven factories of a company operating a scheme of establishment for wage earning employees which accorded quasi staff status and accompanying security, Denerley (31) repeated the frequent finding in attitude surveys that the aims of the scheme were not understood. Psychologists seem nearly as bad in communicating to employers the research findings about poor communications as are the employers themselves at communicating. Turning for the moment to the more mechanical aspects of the problem of communication, mention should be made of a paper by Twedt (110) who lifts evaluation of readership to a more sophisticated but still convincing level in his competent study of 34 advertising variables including Flesch readability and abstraction scores. He found that pictorial colour and size factors could account for more than half the variance in readership scores, that size plus number of colours plus square inches of illustration gave an R of .77 with readership, and that the regression equation stood up well when applied to six other business magazines. This approach seems promising but Twedt realises that it needs to be applied to other types of advertising location before any generalisation can be made. If it be established that the variables he names are the important ones, the social psychologists can get busy on the implications.

In the second of two studies, Comrey, Pfiffner & Beem (27) provide independent confirmation for the findings by Katz *et al.* (65, 66) that employees in more productive work groups tend to have greater pride in their work group. These now well-established facts should be considered in close relation to other data concerning the small relationship existing between efficiency and job satisfaction. We are evidently still a long way from understanding the composition of morale.

Leadership and Management

Van Zelst (125) and Tobolski & Kerr (106) provide a little more data about the Empathy Test, the former reporting correlations about .7 with leadership ability among 64 trade union business agents; the latter an r of .7 with new car sales success. One wonders what the average correlation would be between the two qualities if they could have been tested within the two populations studied! A well-planned study by Jackson (63) extends the Bell & French (11) laboratory study of leadership in small groups to a real life setting among telephone installation and repair sections. Like them he found that leadership skills satisfactory to one group proved consistently so in another, redirecting our attention once again to the personality of the group leader and away from the personality needs of those led. Jackson is probably right, however, to underline the contrasting fact that his data show attitudes about other aspects of the job to be more related to the personal frame of reference of the respondent.

Westerlund (119) gives rather profuse details of a well-designed study carried out in the Stockholm long-distance telephone exchange. Co-operation of management, unions, and operators was obtained for an experiment in which a system of group leadership was substituted for the traditional pattern of functional supervision. The first-named characterises current British and American practice; the latter, still in use in Sweden, involved the operator in responsibilities spread over a large number of superiors. Apart from the successful practical outcome (management agreed on the basis of the results to start a change-over to group leadership) the report may represent an important landmark in Scandinavian industrial psychology. The bibliography is comprehensive and remarkably up-to-date, and the statistical methods employed in testing a series of hypotheses are appropriate for the data involved. It is unfortunate that rather too much tabular material has been included, most of which could with profit to the text have been omitted or relegated to the appendix. Browne & Neitzel (17) have experimented with the Stogdill & Shartle scales for investigating responsibility, authority, and delegation of authority, relating results to the Harris "Morale Scale." Some ingenious comparison scores were devised and this article may be said to represent a necessary but tentative stage in the process of quantifying relationships which have hitherto been largely verbalized. This gives rise to a point which it is hoped editors may feel able to note, that until new and exploratory techniques are well-known, authors using them should be asked to do more than quote four-year-old references in lieu of giving summarised descriptions illuminated by examples.

During the year, the National Institute of Industrial Psychology published the results of a government-sponsored survey of *Joint Consultation in British Industry* (85). While it is undesirable to attempt a summary of this work here it should be said that many of its findings will be of interest to others outside the United Kingdom. The difficulties of the industrial psychologist in Great Britain may perhaps be estimated from the fact that of the 4719 manufacturing establishments approached by questionnaire only 751 replied. It was found that the foremen were the least favorable to joint consultation as it is generally constituted; only 39 per cent actively supported it while 47 per cent accepted it and 14 per cent resented it. In a sociological study of joint consultation in three British factories, Scott (96) comes by different methods to somewhat similar general conclusions as does the National Institute of Industrial Psychology survey. His suggestions for further work include "determining whether there is a particular type of social structure within which both high morale and high productivity co-exist . . . (and) why the behaviour of different leaders differs." On the methodological side, Scott supports the group discussion as a research technique but realises the need for further experimentation in methods of quantifying the data it provides. Rose (92) lists 23 hypotheses which he suggests might be used as a starting point for rigorous investigation of mediation techniques. These hypotheses arose from his first-hand studies of mediation procedures.

Mace (77) describes the widespread provision in the United States of education for management at the university or college level using the Harvard Business School as a leading example. After indicating in a shrewd and interesting way the sources of difficulty inherent in the philosophies of British university and industrial leaders, he expresses his belief that institutions such as he describes are a desirable development. In the reviewer's opinion Mace is right to emphasize that even in the United States there seems need for closer collaboration between the business schools and other departments in which psychologists are engaged in research.

In the report by Scott just referred to he says:

> the operational role of management rather than the mere presence of higher management at meetings . . .is an important point which appears to have been neglected in the literature. The paternalistic tradition . . . underlies the behaviour of top management and is responsible for the fact that consultation is not really "joint" . . . and why they (employee representatives) are preoccupied so exclusively with "welfare."

Davis (30) reports an unusual study by independent investigators of the merit rating scheme used by a small factory employing 500 workers. The supreme importance of the personal values and behaviour of the senior executives is described in connection both with the inception and installation of the scheme and in attempting to account for the health of the working community. Davis suggests in conclusion that "there are perhaps more gaps in our knowledge of why men work hard and contentedly than of why they do not."

Those concerned with the problem of administrative communication should read at least the final chapter in Ronken & Lawrence, *Administering Changes* (91). The authors, after presenting a case study of the introduction of a new manufacturing process, list five tentative generalisations about the way in which communication is dependent both upon skill and circumstance. They relate those to a central concept, "the need for self-awareness in the administrator" and make it clear that they regard this as an attitude which can be learned. As this process of learning involves alteration of social perceiving to a degree which requires a great deal of the individual in the way of motivation and security, there is obviously an important task for the psychologist here, provided he is the whole man rather than the preoccupied specialist in some narrow field.

Another example of the case-study approach is Scott & Lynton's *Three Studies in Management* (95). The special value of this book may lie in the fact that the three studies present such variations on the theme of change that the reader is at once impressed by the unlikelihood of a generally applicable formula for success. Those especially concerned with the psychological problems of selection and of training which may arise when a factory is built for an industry new to an old community will find one of these studies especially interesting, while another study shows in a striking manner what can be done when management is really permissive and reassuring in its attitude toward the training programme. In an appendix the authors are downright in their views about the methodological problems of social science. They are fully justified in asking whether the attitude questionnaire responses of "Yes" are necessarily equivalent in significance from Smith to Jones, especially when they give clear indications of their awareness that "the degree to which detail can be usefully abstracted varies with the purpose for which the data are to be evaluated." But their hesitations about what might be called a behavioural view of questionnaire responses extend further: to observations by a trained investigator and to the recollections of a local participant source of second-hand information. In the two latter there is the real problem of significance by selection which they imply is also true of "abstraction by statistics." Such an implication is by no means necessarily correct. Whether it is or not will depend in the event upon the appropriateness of the statistical methods to the purpose in hand and on the skill and integrity of the users of such methods. This said, let it be added immediately that much of this appendix on research method can be read with considerable profit by most industrial psychologists.

The basic problem, that of changing the attitudes of top management, referred to explicitly by Maier (80) and largely ignored by Lawshe (75), may prove pretty intractable in the present generation. However, it has been tackled in advance by the Harvard Business School, which for some years has been turning out young executives familiar with these needs and experienced in facing them in their own persons. The case-method of teaching, of which we have read in articles and reports of addresses, is now set out fully in the *Case Method of Teaching Human Relations and Administration* edited by Andrews (4). A careful reading of this book will probably convince even the most sceptical that something of profound importance is being done, and that those who are doing it are prepared to admit the difficulties frankly. There are three sections to this symposium. The first, "Teaching and Learning," makes clear the theory, spirit, use, and consequences of the case method at Harvard Business School. The second indicates and illustrates its extension into industry. The last, "Research Problems in Human Relations," stakes a claim for the "clinical method" which is sufficiently well-argued to merit serious consideration even from the toughest of tough-minded critics. The principal representative of the clinical method in the book is Lombard (pp. 225 to 240) who says baldly ". . . the techniques of the controlled experiment are not what I wish students of human behavior would learn from the natural sciences." Before dismissing him and his colleagues as unscientific, one would do well to examine the reasoning with which he supports this statement.

Indications

When commencing this review, the writer made no apology for providing a reminder of what has gone before, believing as he does that during a forced march someone from time to time must accept responsibility for glancing over his shoulder and reporting what he sees. An inspection of the contemporary scene and our adaptation to it is at once depressing and encouraging. We still spend too much time producing new tests instead of improving, adapting or re-analysing old ones. Many of us are still lopsided in our attitude to and use of statistical procedures. We still often fail to use our psychological insight in the use of our techniques, the teaching of our students, the writing of our books and articles, or the conversion of our employers in university, government, or industry. We write too much, talk too much, and think too little. On whichever side of the Atlantic we live, we are too prone to ignore or to belittle the products of the other.

It is encouraging to see in the results of the year under review that at long last the criterion is receiving the attention it merits; that training, both of supervisors and of executives, is now a major interest; and that studies of leadership and group behaviour are beginning to be the objects of more scientific enquiry. Catch-phrases such as "accident-proneness," "the one best way," and "the intuitive approach" have been vigorously attacked with possibly mortal consequences, while human relations has been rescued from the bog into which it had been dragged.

In a paradoxical age of passing fashions and repetitive movements it is difficult to note significant trends with any confidence. Perhaps it will be more profitable to consider our professional status and aims and to make explicit some of the immediate needs. Bingham (14) reminded us that we were in serious danger of being torn apart. Psychology is a branch of scientific enquiry, a means to selected ends, and a personal skill. There is current evidence that industrial psychology lacks integration. Workers in this field can too easily be either scientific or practical, rigorous or realistic, academic or practising. This suggests that present and pressing needs are of two distinct kinds, each more appropriate to some of us than to others but both relevant to the work of all.

One need may be met if those who as yet do not know industry well were to face up to some questions posed during the year by Gorsuch (48): (*a*) Why do psychologists have such difficulty in gaining acceptance in industry? (*b*) How do psychologists spend their time in industry? (*c*) What can we do to provide better psychologists for industry? (*d*) How well are psychologists equipped to solve business problems? Are we getting too smug? Do we have the necessary tools? If not, what are we doing about it?

The other need has been outlined by Flanagan (35) who, when wishing to advance some suggestions for research on what he calls "important social problems," significantly felt it necessary to begin with a summary restatement of the basic ingredients of scientific study. Going on to develop his main theme he said:

This does not mean that I prefer applied research to basic research. There seems adequate evidence at the present time that work on applied problems can lead to the discovery of basic scientific knowledge. The terms in which the problem is formulated and the general research methods used are the determining factors in whether a research study yields a specific result or one which may be generalised.

In view of the current emphasis on research into the social aspects of industrial adaptation, we may perhaps fittingly end by considering a view expressed by Drucker (32). He calls for research to be directed at the relationship between men, the group, and the actual job they are doing, and suggests that overemphasis on the human relations approach has distracted attention from the demands made by the job itself on the individual. This corrective is timely; we may need to be reminded that, important though they are now, at last, seen to be, social pressures are not the only ones. We need a balanced approach, the recollection that "psychology developed its applied areas because of public demand that the psychologist contribute his knowledge and skill to efforts to solve some of the urgent problems of man in a complex society" (3). We can agree with Drucker when he insists that in addition to more adequate methodology, the most urgent need is for better basic concepts; it may well be that as with psychology generally, so with industrial psychology in particular, the time has now come when most of us must ask those who support our work to permit a pause while we think.

LITERATURE CITED

1. Abruzzi, A., *Work Measurement* (Columbia University Press, New York, N. Y., 290 pp., 1952)
2. Adelstein, A. M., *J. Roy. Statist. Soc.*, [A]**115**, 354–410 (1952)
3. American Psychological Association, *Ethical Standards of Psychologists* (American Psychological Association, Washington, D. C., 171 pp., 1953)
4. Andrews, K. R., Ed., *Case Method of Teaching Human Relations and Administration* (Harvard University Press, Cambridge, Mass., 271 pp., 1953)
5. Arbous, A. G., and Kerrich, J. E., *Biometrics*, **7**, 340–432 (1951)
6. Argyle, M., *Occupational Psychol.* (*London*), **27**, 98–103 (1953)
7. Barnett, G. J., Handelsman, I., Stewart, L. H., and Super, D. E., *Psychol. Monographs*, **66**(10), 37 pp. (1952)
8. Bass, B. M., and Coates, C. H., *J. Abnormal Social Psychol.*, **47**, Suppl., 321–25 (1952)
9. Bass, B. M., Klubeck, S., and Wurster, C. R., *J. Appl. Psychol.*, **37**, 26–30 (1953)
10. Bass, B. M., McGehee, C. R., Hawkins, W. C., Young, P. C., and Gebel, A. S., *J. Abnormal Social Psychol.*, **48**, 120–28 (1953)
11. Bell, G. B., and French, R. L., *J. Abnormal Social Psychol.*, **45**, 764–67 (1950)
12. Bellows, R. M., *Ann. Rev. Psychol.*, **2**, 173–92 (1951)
13. Bernberg, R. E., *J. Social Psychol.*, **36**, 73–82 (1952)
14. Bingham, W. V., *Am. Psychologist*, **8**, 115–18 (1953)
15. Blum, M. L., Ed., *Readings in Experimental Industrial Psychology* (Prentice-Hall, Inc., New York, N. Y., 455 pp., 1952)
16. Bonnardel, R., *Trav. Humain*, **15**, 1–16 (1952)
17. Browne, C. G., and Neitzel, B. J., *J. Appl. Psychol.*, **36**, 86–91 (1952)

18. Brown, C. W., and Ghiselli, E. E., *Ann. Rev. Psychol.*, **3**, 205–32 (1952)
19. Brown, C. W., and Ghiselli, E. E., *J. Appl. Psychol.*, **36**, 370–72 (1952)
20. Brown, C. W., and Ghiselli, E. E., *J. Appl. Psychol.*, **37**, 9–12 (1953)
21. *Bull. centre études et récherches psychotechniques*, **1** (1952)
22. *Bull. inst Natl. étude travail et orientation professionnelle*, **8** (1952)
23. Burtt, H. E., *Applied Psychology* (Prentice-Hall Inc., New York, N. Y., Abridged Edition, 465 pp., 1952)
24. Carter, G. C., *J. Appl. Psychol.*, **36**, 393–95 (1952)
25. Castle, P. F. C., *Occupational Psychol.* (*London*), **26**, 191–205 (1952)
26. Chriswell, M. I., *J. Appl. Psychol.*, **37**, 13–15 (1953)
27. Comrey, A. L., Pfiffner, J. M., and Beem, H. P., *Personnel Psychol.*, **6**, 65–79 (1953)
28. Darley, J. G., Gross, N., and Martin, W. C., *J. Appl. Psychol.*, **36**, 396–403 (1952)
29. Davis, N. M., *Brit. J. Ind. Med.*, **10**, 18–26 (1953)
30. Davis, N. M., *Occupational Psychol.* (*London*), **27**, 57–68 (1953)
31. Denerley, R. A., *Occupational Psychol.* (*London*), **27**, 1–10 (1953)
32. Drucker, P. F., *Am. J. Sociol.*, **58**, 358–63 (1953)
33. Elmgren, J., and Rubenowitz, S., Eds., *Applied Psychology* (Orstadius Boktryckeri AB, Goteborg, Sweden, 214 pp., 1952)
34. Eysenck, H. J., *The Scientific Study of Personality* (George Routledge & Sons, Ltd., and Kegan Paul, Trench, Trubner & Co., Ltd., London, England, 320 pp., 1952)
35. Flanagan, J. C., *Psychometrika*, **17**, 359–68 (1952)
36. Fleishman, E. A., *J. Appl. Psychol.*, **37**, 1–6 (1953)
37. Frank, A., *Bull. Natl. Inst. Personnel Research* (*Johannesburg*), **4**, 110–22 (1952)
38. Froehlich, C. P., and Davis, F. G., *Personnel Guid. J.*, **31**, 462–64 (1952)
39. Fruchter, B., *J. Appl. Psychol.*, **36**, 381–84 (1952)
40. Garry, R., *J. Appl. Psychol.*, **37**, 33–37 (1953)
41. Gekoski, N., *Personnel Psychol.*, **5**, 281–92 (1952)
42. Germaine, G. L., Browne, C. G., and Bellows, R. M., *Occupations*, **30**, 579–83 (1952)
43. Ghiselli, E. E., and Brown, C. W., *Personnel and Industrial Psychology* (McGraw-Hill Book Co., Inc., New York, N. Y., 475 pp., 1948)
44. Ghiselli, E. E., and Barthol, R. P., *J. Appl. Psychol.*, **37**, 18–20 (1953)
45. Gibbs, C. B., *Occupational Psychol.* (*London*), **26**, 234–42 (1952)
46. Ginzberg, E., *Occupations*, **30**, 491–95 (1952)
47. Goguelin, P., *Trav. Humain*, **15**, 185–218 (1952)
48. Gorsuch, J. H., *Personnel*, **29**, 153–57 (1952)
49. Green, R., *Educ. Psychol. Measurement*, **11**, 503–15 (1951)
50. Gustad, J. W., *J. Appl. Psychol.*, **36**, 75–78 (1952)
51. Harrell, T. W., *Ann. Rev. Psychol.*, **4**, 215–38 (1953)
52. Harrison, R., and Jackson, T. A., *J. Appl. Psychol.*, **36**, 373–76 (1952)
53. Hartshorne, H., May, M. A., and Shuttleworth, F. K., *Studies in the Organization of Character* (The Macmillan Co., New York, N. Y., 503 pp., 1930)
54. Hearnshaw, L. S., *Occupational Psychol.* (*London*), **27**, 110–11 (1953)
55. Heller, F. A., *Occupational Psychol.* (*London*), **26**, 86–95 (1952)
56. Hemphill, J. K., and Sechrest, L. B., *J. Appl. Psychol.*, **36**, 323–27 (1952)
57. Heron, A., *J. Appl. Psychol.*, **36**, 385–87 (1952)

58. Heron, A., *Occupational Psychol. (London)*, **26**, 78–85 (1952)
59. Heron, A., and Braithwaite, D., *Brit. J. Ind. Med.*, **10**, 27–31 (1953)
60. Higham, M. H., *Occupational Psychol. (London)*, **26**, 169–75 (1952)
61. Howard, A. H., and Schutz, H. G., *J. Appl. Psychol*, **36**, 243–46 (1952)
62. Husén, T., *Occupational Psychol. (London)*, **26**, 176–82 (1952)
63. Jackson, J. M., *Human Relations*, **6**, 25–44 (1953)
64. Jahoda, G., *Occupational Psychol. (London)*, **26**, 125–40, 206–24 (1952)
65. Katz, D., Maccoby, N., and Morse, N. C., *Productivity, Supervision and Morale in an Office Situation* (Institute for Social Research, University of Michigan, Ann Arbor, Mich., 84 pp., 1950)
66. Katz, D., Maccoby, N., Gurin, G., and Floor, L. G., *Productivity, Supervision and Morale among Railroad Workers* (Institute for Social Research, University of Michigan, Ann Arbor, Mich., 61 pp., 1951)
67. Keating, E., Paterson, D. G., and Stone, C. H., *J. Appl. Psychol.*, **34**, 1–5 (1950)
68. Kendall, M. G., *Rank Correlation Methods* (Griffin Books, London, England, 160 pp., 1948)
69. Kephart, N. C., *The Employment Interview in Industry* (McGraw-Hill Book Co., Inc., New York, N. Y., 277 pp., 1952)
70. Kerr, W. A., *Personnel Psychol.*, **5**, 105–13 (1952)
71. Kirchner, W., Lindbom, T., and Paterson, D. G., *J. Appl. Psychol.*, **36**, 154–56 (1952)
72. Klieger, W. A., and Mosel, J. N., *Personnel Psychol.*, **6**, 57–63 (1953)
73. Krathwohl, W. C., *J. Appl. Psychol.*, **36**, 103–6 (1952)
74. Kristy, N. F., *Criteria of Occupational Success among Post Office Counter Clerks* (Doctoral thesis, Univ. of London, London, England, 1952)
75. Lawshe, C. H., *The Psychology of Industrial Relations* (McGraw-Hill Book Co., New York, N. Y., 350 pp., 1953)
76. Levine, A. S., and Tupes, E. C., *J. Appl. Psychol.*, **36**, 157–60 (1952)
77. Mace, C. A., *Occupational Psychol. (London)*, **26**, 61–69 (1952)
78. Maguire, B. A., Pearson, E. S., and Wynn, A. H. A., *Biometrika*, **39**, 168–80 (1952)
79. Maier, N. R. F., *Psychology in Industry* (George G. Harrap & Co., Ltd., London, England, 463 pp., 1947)
80. Maier, N. R. F., *Principles of Human Relations* (John Wiley & Sons, Inc., New York, N. Y., 474 pp., 1952)
81. Maule, H. G., *Occupational Psychol. (London)*, **26**, 225–33 (1952)
82. Miles, M. C., *J. Appl. Psychol.*, **36**, 97–102 (1952)
83. Millard, K. A., *J. Appl. Psychol.*, **36**, 221–24 (1952)
84. Mosel, J. N., and Cozan, L. W., *J. Appl. Psychol.*, **36**, 365–69 (1952)
85. National Institute of Industrial Psychology, *Joint Consultation in British Industry* (Staples Press, Ltd., London, England, 276 pp., 1952)
86. O'Neil, W. M., *Occupational Psychol. (London)*, **26**, 141–57 (1952)
87. Ralph, R. B., and Taylor, C. W., *J. Appl. Psychol.*, **36**, 107–11 (1952)
88. *Rev. Psychol. appl.*, **2**, (1952)
89. Robinson, H. A., and Hoppock, R., *Occupations*, **30**, 594–98 (1952)
90. Rodger, A., *Occupational Psychol. (London)*, **26**, 101–6 (1952)
91. Ronken, H. O., and Lawrence, P. R., *Administering Changes* (Harvard University Graduate School of Business Administration, Boston, Mass., 324 pp., 1952)

92. Rose, A. M., *Personnel Psychol.*, **5,** 187–200 (1952)
93. Rubin, G., von Treba, P., and Smith, K. U., *J. Appl. Psychol.*, **36,** 272–76 (1952)
94. Rush, C. H., Jr., *Personnel Psychol.*, **6,** 9–24 (1953)
95. Scott, J. F., and Lynton, R. P., *Three Studies in Management* (George Routledge & Sons, Ltd., Kegan Paul, Trench, Trubner & Co., Ltd., London, England, 220 pp., 1952)
96. Scott, W. H., *Industrial Leadership and Joint Consultation* (University Press, Liverpool, England, 207 pp., 1952)
97. Semeonoff, B., *Psychol. Bull.*, **49,** 540–41 (1952)
98. Severin, D., *Personnel Psychol.*, **5,** 93–104 (1952)
99. Shartle, C. L., *Ann. Rev. Psychol.* **1,** 151–72 (1950)
100. Spragg, S. D. S., and Rock, M. L., *J. Appl. Psychol.*, **36,** 196–200 (1952)
101. Stagner, R., Flebbe, D. R., and Wood, E. V., *Personnel Psychol.*, **5,** 293–306 (1952)
102. Steinberg, A., *Educ. Psychol. Measurement*, **12,** 96–104 (1952)
103. Stott, M. B., *Occupational Psychol.* (*London*), **26,** 158–68 (1952)
104. Strong, E. K., Jr., *J. Appl. Psychol.*, **36,** 65–74 (1952)
105. Strong, E. K., Jr., and Tucker, A. C., *Psychol. Monographs*, **66,** (9), 61 pp. (1952)
106. Tobolski, F. P., and Kerr, W. A., *J. Appl. Psychol.*, **36,** 310–11 (1952)
107. *Trav. Humain*, **15,** (1952)
108. von Treba, P., and Smith, K. U., *J. Appl. Psychol.*, **36,** 348–53 (1952)
109. Tuckman, J., and Lorge, I., *J. Appl. Psychol.*, **36,** 149–53 (1952)
110. Twedt, D. W., *J. Appl. Psychol.*, **36,** 207–15 (1952)
111. Vernon, P. E., and Parry, J. B., *Personnel Selection in the British Forces* (University of London Press, London, England, 324 pp., 1949)
112. Viteles, M. S., *Industrial Psychology* (W. W. Norton & Co., Inc., New York, N.Y., 652 pp., 1932)
113. Walker, C. R., and Guest, R. H., *The Man on the Assembly Line* (Harvard University Press, Cambridge, Mass., 180 pp., 1952)
114. Webb, W. B., and Jones, E. R., *Psychol. Bull.*, **50,** 133–36 (1953)
115. Wehrkamp, R., and Smith, K. U., *J. Appl. Psychol.*, **36,** 201–6 (1952)
116. Weitz, J., *Personnel Psychol.*, **5,** 201–5 (1952)
117. Weschler, I. R., Massarik, F., and Tannenbaum, R., *J. Social Psychol.*, **36,** 205–22 (1952)
118. Wesman, A. G., *Personnel Guid. J.*, **31,** 167–70 (1952)
119. Westerlund, G., *Group Leadership* (Nordisk Rotogravyr, Stockholm, Sweden, 257 pp., 1952)
120. Wickert, F. R., *J. Appl. Psychol.*, **36,** 301–3 (1952)
121. Wilson, N. A. B., in *Current Trends in British Psychology*, 22–33 (Mace, C. A., and Vernon, P. E., Eds., Methuen & Co., Ltd., London, England, 262 pp. 1952)
122. Wurster, C. R., and Bass, B. M., *Educ. Psychol. Measurement*, **13,** 122–31 (1953)
123. Wyndham, A. J., *Bull. Ind. Psychol. Personnel Practice* (*Melbourne*), **8**[3], 12–21 (1952)
124. Zaccaria, A., Jr., and Bitterman, M. E., *J. Appl. Psychol.*, **36,** 413–16 (1952)
125. Van Zelst, R. H., *J. Appl. Psychol.*, **36,** 293–95 (1952)
126. Zuckerman, J. V., *J. Appl. Psychol.*, **36,** 79–85 (1952)

COMPARATIVE PSYCHOLOGY[1,2]

By Roger W. Russell

Department of Psychology, University College, London, England

A chapter on Comparative Psychology differs in certain very significant ways from other chapters included in the *Annual Review of Psychology*. Basically it is unique in the sense that the term "comparative psychology" refers to a method of approach rather than an area of problems. It may be concerned with problems pertinent to most of the other chapters in the *Review;* its coherence lies in the application of the logic underlying the comparative methods of science. Schneirla (1) in considering some conceptual trends in comparative psychology has made this point a major issue by commenting that: "the practical consideration of paramount importance here is not how many types of animals we use in our investigations, but whether or not we use the comparative methods of science in working with them."

The logic of the comparative methods is based upon critical comparisons of phenomena that are truly homologous rather than merely analogous. The term "homology" implies that the phenomena are alike in origin and in fundamental structure. Russell (2) in considering the development and use of this logic has indicated how widely it has been applied in the study of language and communication; of social behavior, culture patterns and social institutions; as well as in attacks on problems of interest to the biological sciences. Because of its nature this comparative approach of the study of behavior is in no way limited to comparisons among individuals or groups differing phyletically, although in certain professional groups it has come to have such a meaning. Psychologists in some countries still understand it as covering many of the problems in child, abnormal, and social, as well as animal, psychology. Regardless of the basis upon which the groups compared have been classified comparative studies have in common a search for similarities and differences in the homologous behavior phenomena of a variety of living organisms.

Because comparative psychology is defined by method rather than problems peculiar to its investigations it does, to some extent at least, cut across the classification scheme upon which other chapters of the *Review* are based. Its findings can, and should, be considered in other chapters. Authors of this chapter in previous *Reviews* have recognized this and have set a precedent of limiting their writing mainly to information on problems for which the study of infrahuman animal behavior is particularly adapted. The present chapter will conform to this precedent.

[1] The material in this review covers approximately the period from April 1, 1952 to April 1, 1953.

[2] The following abbreviations are used: ACTH for adrencorticotrophic hormone; ESC for electroshock convulsion.

Experimental Psychogenetics

In 1951 Hall (3) brought to the attention of psychologists the potential values of research into the influences of genetic factors on behavior. His review of the present status of psychogenetics revealed how little systematic experimental work has been done in which the orientation of the research design has been that of the student of behavior.

Experimental psychogenetics is a field of research which must depend upon the use of infrahuman subjects (4). It is limited by the fact that man, with his particular culture patterns and long life span, cannot be employed as a subject for research. Experimental attacks on problems in this field are, therefore, the real responsibility of the animal psychologist.

Stob & Andrews (5) have shown how certain constitutional features such as body weight, thyroid weight, and histology, and gonad weight and histology respond differently in different inbred lines of mice to thiouracil and thyroprotein. The effects of ingesting the latter at the level of 0.22 per cent of the diet was to increase body weight in some lines, but to decrease it significantly in others. The seven lines studied could be divided into three size groups and the effects of thiouracil in small amounts (0.05 per cent of diet) were to depress growth in the large lines and not in the medium or small lines. Significant interactions between body size and treatment, sex and treatment, and line and treatment were found with respect to thyroid weight. No consistent effects of the drugs on gonad weight or histology were noted. There are a number of studies in the literature of psychogenetics to show that complex behavior patterns may be influenced genetically, either in whole or in part, but none of these studies is more striking than Hauschka's (6) report on mutilation patterns and cannibalism in mice. The incidence of parental cannibalism in animals from eight different strains kept on the same adequate diet, ranged from 0 to 45 per cent. In the subline where this behavior was most frequent it showed little fluctuation during 13 sibmated generations. Mothers of this subline restricted themselves to anatomically defined mutilation and amputation patterns and often reared their uniformly injured infants. Estes (7) has reported significant correlations between the racing class of high-spirited thoroughbred broodmares and offspring and of phlegmatic broodmares and their offspring. Although concerned with quite different characteristics of living organisms these three studies illustrate the first of four major steps experimental psychogenetics is taking: the determination of whether or not specific behavior patterns are influenced by genetic factors.

The second step begins when such influences have been established and undertakes to study the number and nature of the genetic factors involved. Hauschka (8), who appears to enjoy discovering genetic oddities, has reported observations of "whisker-eating" mice, whose performance followed a precise working pattern. Animals with this behavior anomaly were found in several heterozygous genotypes and in two inbred strains, but not in five other pure lines. All animals had been maintained on the same diet. From his observations Hauschka has concluded that multiple factors may be involved in influencing this behavior, single factors being definitely ruled out.

The third step in experimental psychogenetics is concerned with the location of the gene or genes on the chromosome. Falconer (9) has shown how linkage between characteristics can aid in such mapping. In the house mouse, "reeler" is a recessive gene which impairs locomotion through a disturbance of balance. By proper breeding procedures Falconer has shown this gene to be linked with two other genes, whose loci, in linkage group iii, were already known.

The old problem of interaction between genetic and environmental factors often has given rise to queries which, in the opinions of many, have turned out to be pseudoquestions. Recently Falconer (10) has stated the case for a real problem of environment and selection. In his opinion most geneticists would argue that performance in a favorable environment has a different genetic basis than performance in an unfavorable environment. A superior genotype in one environment could not be expected to be superior in a different environment. It seems probable that the student of psychogenetics will eventually have to face up to interactions of this kind.

Effects of Early Environmental Conditions on Later Behavior

Several systems in psychology have emphasized the important effects early environmental conditions may have on later behavior, particularly the appearance of behavior disorders. Recent experiments have studied effects produced by three general classes of conditions: those affecting body structure or function, intense stimulation, and "differential environments."

An experiment by Levinson (11), to be described more fully later, examined the effects of different amounts of x-irradiation at one of five stages of gestation on the maze learning performance of 50-day old rats. In terms of the usual measures of maze learning, performance was found to decrease as a function of the amount of fetal irradiation given. It was also noted that variability in performance increased with treatment. Armitage (12) gave varying dosages of the barbiturates, sodium barbital, and sodium pentobarbital, to pregnant female rats 19.5 days after breeding and studied the performance of the offspring in two mazes and one reasoning situation. Comparisons between the performances of drug and control groups indicated significant reductions of performance in the former. Two studies have been concerned with the effects of early anoxia on later learning performance. Becker & Donnell (13) asphyxiated guinea pigs in utero by occluding the maternal uterine vessels after one animal in each litter had been delivered as a control. One group of animals was released in time sufficient for spontaneous recovery; a second group was asphyxiated until comatose, totally apneic, and atonic, and then artificially revived with gas mixtures. Learning performance was tested 8 to 10 weeks later in problem boxes of two levels of difficulty. Analysis of the learning data for both levels of difficulty revealed significantly greater error and perseveration scores for the experimental as compared with control animals. Retest two weeks after learning showed retention to be affected in a similar manner. Hurder & Sanders (14) divided their rats into control and experimental groups at approximately one hour after birth. Two experimental groups were then placed in a decompression chamber, where one remained for 3 hr. at a simulated altitude of 30,000 feet and the other, for 38 min. at 34,000 feet. At 100 days of age, control and experimental groups were trained on a Stone multiple-T alley maze. The learning scores of the three groups were not significantly different.

Griffiths & Stringer (15) reported an experiment on rats designed to determine the effects of intense stimulation during infancy on adult behavior. One group of animals served as controls, and four experimental groups were exposed, each for a 3 min. period, daily during the first nine days of life and twice daily until the fifty-seventh day, to one of the following forms of stimulation: intense auditory stimulation, rapid rotation, extremes of environmental temperature, and electric shock. Beginning at 60 days of age, all groups were tested in four different situations: the Warner-Warden maze, a modified Lashley discrimination apparatus, the Hall open-field test for emotionality, and a test chamber for audiogenic seizures. No significant differences appeared between the performances of the experimental and control groups.

Three reports examine the effects on the later behavior of early experience in differential, or varied, environments as compared with restricted environments. Although the specific nature of the environments varied in the three studies, in all cases they were arranged on the one hand to allow wide access to a variety of different features and conditions, and, on the other, to restrict movement to a very limited field such as a laboratory cage. Bingham & Griffiths (16) reared groups of rats in such contrasting environments for 30 days, beginning at 21 days of age. Two weeks later tests began in five different situations: the Warner-Warden maze, an inclined-plane maze, a modified Lashley jumping apparatus, the Hall open-field temperament test, and a test chamber for audiogenic seizures. Measures of the behavior elicited in each of these situations showed that animals reared in the free environments were superior to those reared in the restricted environments in maze-learning performance only, no significant differences appearing in the other measures taken. Hymovitch (17) blinded his rats, some in early life and others at maturity, and reared them either in a "free-environment box" or in environments allowing various amounts of restricted activity. At maturity the animals were tested on the Hebb-Williams closed-field apparatus and on an enclosed, 10-unit T maze. Differences between early and late blinded animals were not significant nor were the performances of the free and restricted groups on the T maze. However, the free groups were superior to the restricted in their performance in the closed-field test. Two additional groups were studied. In one, free-environment experience was received during early life and restricted-environment experience later on; in the other, this order of experiences was reversed. In the adult tests the former group was clearly superior to the latter. Forgays & Forgays (18) in an experiment of similar design to those just described have obtained similar results. Attempts to explain the results of these experiments have been in terms of differential opportunities during rearing for perceptual experience and learning.

Sensory Processes

During the year covered by this review research continued on traditional problems in sensory processes, with an occasional suggestion of a new problem or a modification of technique. Fingerman (19) and Fingerman & Brown (20, 21) reported the results of three experiments designed to study color sensitivity in *Drosophila melanogaster*. These investigators interpreted their evidence as indicating that *Drosophila* possesses a true color vision. The evidence comes in part from observations of the strength of phototaxis in response to white and monochromatic lights following differential adaptation of the eyes to various light stimuli. Response to colored light was lost with reduction of the intensity of the stimulus, suggesting the existence of photopic and scotopic mechanisms as in the vertebrate eye. Because the genetics of *Drosophila* are so well established it was possible to select six groups of animals differing presumably in eye coloration only. Using phototactic orientation in response to 17 selected wave lengths between 366 and 700 mμ, spectral response curves were plotted for each of the groups. These curves were found to differ not only in over-all strength, but also in form, and appeared to be dependent upon the differential absorption of light by the various eye-pigments. The suggestion that the duplicity theory may apply to the compound eye is further supported on the anatomical basis that both long- and short-axoned retinula cells have been found in several Arthropoda. A final study in this series was designed to search for a Purkinje shift in *Drosophila* vision. The investigators observed the way in which the spectral response curve altered as the intensity of light was decreased. Maximal response to monochromatic light of relative intensities of 1 and 1/10 was in the region of 520 to 540 mμ and for relative intensities of 1/100 and 1/1000, in the region of 480 to 500 mμ, a shift of approximately 40 mμ. These studies furnish interesting comparative data relating certain processes in the compound eye with those in the differently structured vertebrate eye.

Montgomery & Heinemann (22) have argued that if von Frisch's findings on polarized sky light, as a basis of navigation in bees, is applicable to homing birds then the latter should be able to discriminate readily between patterns of light polarized in one plane and patterns polarized in a plane orthogonal to the first. Using homing pigeons as subjects, they presented the required stimulus patterns on a ground glass stimulus key. Responses to polarized light in one plane only were rewarded. The birds were maintained at 80 to 85 per cent of their normal body weights during acquisition and extinction trials. The results gave no evidence of discrimination between the planes of polarized light. On the other hand, brightness discrimination was learned very rapidly.

Dice & Barto (23) have reported on the ability of mice (*Peromyscus*) to hear ultrasonic sounds. Two sources were employed, one ranging from 500 to 16,000 c.p.s. and the other from 10 to 100 kc.p.s.; sound pressures of 1, 5, 10, or 20 dynes per cm.[2] at the animal's ear were used as desired. Activation of conditioned responses indicated supraliminal stimulation effective over a range from 500 to 95,000 c.p.s. in animals 25 to 70 days old, this range tending to decrease with age.

Another sign that research on animal behavior is keeping up with the times has come from an experiment by Alexander & Githler (24) regarding the chronic effects of jet engine noise on the structure and function of the cochlea. This study was not only of practical value in suggesting that jet engine noise presents an occupational hazard, but it contributed to our understanding of the function of the cochlear apparatus and of histological and electrical methods of examining it. Guinea pigs with normal hearing were exposed for a 15 min. period to the noise generated by a jet engine having an ambient sound level at cage distance in excess of 140 db. over a measurable frequency range of 25 to 7,500 c.p.s. Six to eight weeks later the sensitivity of each ear was determined by measuring cochlear potentials for 10 frequencies between 200 and 10,000 c.p.s. after which they were examined histologically. The group loss in sensitivity was found to be 34 db. Damage in the cochlea extended between 6 and 12 mm. from the basal end, with more destruction in the base than in the apex, which was interpreted as supporting the contention that the total cochlea is involved in response to sound. Electrical and histological techniques provided comparable information, the former showing depressed activity in accordance with the distribution of damage as determined by the latter.

Effects of Brain Damage and X-Irradiation

A number of investigators have reported the effects of experimentally induced brain damage or of x-irradiation on various aspects of animal behavior. The latter studies, especially, illustrate the way in which a matter of wide concern to society can exert its influence on trends of scientific research, and very probably they are destined to become rapidly developing areas of investigation. Because of space limitations these topics will be left to the chapter on Physiological Psychology.

Audiogenic Seizures

The early experiments of Maier and his collaborators on abnormal behavior in the rat, recently summarized in his book on frustration (25), had the effect of introducing a controversy which has stimulated a large amount of research, has ramified far beyond its original frame of reference, and has not yet reached generally satisfactory conclusions. The search for conditions critical to the production of the several forms of audiogenic seizures reported in the early studies still goes on.

Michels & Bevan (26), using rats, and Rabe (27), using mice, have examined the effects of the size of the test chamber on production of audiogenic seizures. In the first of these studies three sizes of test chamber, in the ratios of 1:2:4, were used. Groups of animals were given, individually, two minute stimulations in these chambers, one on each of 18 alternate days. The results revealed no significant differences in the frequencies of seizures among the groups, although significant differences did appear in the mean latencies of first running attacks in the largest and smallest chambers. Rabe's experiment was based on the hypothesis that the characteristic reactions of animals in the test chamber serve an "... abreactive function, and the cumulative frustration effect was produced by motor restraint." The design of Rabe's study was similar to the one just described, although the precision in varying test-chamber size was lacking. Significant differences were found between the duration of seizures in the two chambers. The strain of mouse studied is characterized by a high fatality rate from convulsions; in this regard large differences were observed between animals tested in the two chambers, 85 per cent of those confined dying as compared with 25 per cent deaths of those not confined. Since these two studies were not designed for purposes of comparison it is impossible to know whether the differences in results represent species differences or are functions of other conditions imposed by the experimental situation.

The search for genetic influences on susceptibility to audiogenic seizures has almost run the gamut of possibilities from single Mendelian characteristics to multiple factors. Now Frings & Frings (28) have reported "few" differences in seizural behavior among three strains of mice, except for the distributions with respect to age of maximal effect, and even here their figures showed great overlap. This may suggest that genetic factors may have little influence and is contrary to the more carefully planned genetic study by Hall (29).

A number of studies deal with the effects of experimental alteration of internal conditions of the organism on susceptibility to audiogenic seizures. Hurder & Sanders (30) have reported an experiment designed to test the hypothesis that ACTH[2] injections, sufficient to increase adrenal cortical size, modify the susceptibility of rats to audiogenic seizures. All animals were tested for seizure susceptibility and later injected with ACTH. Two hours after injections they were again tested. This second test failed to reveal significant changes in the susceptibility of animals susceptible or nonsusceptible on the initial test. Later assay of the adrenal glands showed the glands of susceptible animals to be heavier than those of nonsusceptible animals. These differences between effects of injected ACTH and gland size are puzzling and suggest that further research along these lines should be encouraged. Previous research (31) has suggested that susceptibility to audiogenic seizures is related to certain forms of middle ear infection, although this relation has been questioned (32). Recently, two studies have been reported in which vestibular dysfunction and middle ear disorder have been experimentally induced and their effects upon seizures observed. Finger, Brice & Day (33), using three groups of rats, injected one group with streptomycin, another with dihydrostreptomycin, and the third with isotonic sodium chloride solution. The large doses of streptomycin used impaired vestibular function markedly and auditory function to a much lesser extent. The susceptibility to audiogenic seizures of animals so affected showed no significant change from that of the two control groups, and the conclusion was drawn that vestibular excitation can be eliminated as a critical condition for convulsions induced by sound stimulation.

Marx & Chambers (34) used plastic-acetone injections into the nasopharyngeal openings of the right eustachian tubes of rats to produce middle ear disorders. On the basis of pretests these had been classified nonsensitive to audiogenic seizures. Controls were given only acetone solution, which had negligible effects. Repeated tests failed to produce convulsions under either condition, although later autopsy showed heavy fluid or pus in the middle ears of all but two of the experimental animals. The results strongly suggest that middle ear disorder per se is not a critical condition for susceptibility to audiogenic seizure.

Body temperature, another internal condition of the organism which might possibly influence susceptibility, has been subjected to experimental examination by Fuller & Rappaport (35). The effects on seizure frequency of 3 min. immersion in water at different temperatures were observed with most striking results. When wet the convulsion-susceptible mice were immune to convulsions, an immunity which disappeared when the animals were dried off rapidly and tested after 2 hr. or allowed to dry in their home cages and tested 24 hr. after immersion. The evidence upon which the researchers based their view that lowered body temperature was the important factor in the immunity comes from a comparison of the frequencies of seizure among animals immersed at 5°C., 23°C., and 38°C. Although immersion at all these temperatures reduced the frequency of convulsions, immersion at 5°C. was more effective than at 23°C., and both provided greater immunity than immersion at 38°C. Whether or not body temperature is the critical condition in these effects will need further analysis.

An experiment by Marx & Van Spanckeren (36) illustrates the way in which the behavior of an organism may interact with its susceptibility to audiogenic seizures. It was designed to test the hypothesis that reduction in seizural behavior will occur if the susceptible animal has learned to control the inducing stimulus. Experimental subjects were first trained to turn off the stimulus by tilting or touching a wooden pole extending into the test chamber, control animals being tested in a chamber containing a pole which did not allow control of the stimulus. After a training criterion had been reached the experimental animals were advanced to the next stage of the research design in which the pole was introduced at various intervals of time following the onset of the whistle. Several of the experimental animals were able to make the instrumental responses to the pole at delay intervals of 16 sec. or longer, and they showed significantly fewer signs of audiogenic seizure than did their matched controls. These results generally confirmed the hypothesis under test, but their real significance lies in the evidence they have provided that audiogenic seizures may be influenced to some extent by learned control.

Effects of Electroshock Convulsions on Behavior

In 1937 Bini (37) reported on the use of electric current to induce grand mal type convulsions in dogs, a technique which soon became the most frequently employed therapeutic method in the somatic treatment of man's behavior disorders. Since this initial experiment a large amount of research has been and continues to be reported in which the effects of ESC[2] on the behavior of several species of animals have been studied.

Research has centered around the general question of what parameters, organismic and environmental, of the ESC situation influence its effects. Pierce & Patton (38) designed an experiment to study electroconvulsive thresholds as a function of the age and weight of the rats used. They found age-weight, threshold-weight, and age-threshold correlations to be high, and similar, in magnitude. Further analysis suggested that body weight is more effective in influencing convulsive threshold than is age, although when body weight is held constant an increase in age is associated with a decrease in threshold. Electric shock produces convulsions with three distinct phases; they are shock, tonic, and clonic. Townsend, Russell & Patton (39) found that the duration of each of these phases is independent of the intensity and duration of the current inducing the convulsion, provided the current is of sufficient magnitude to reach the convulsive threshold. On the other hand, durations of the shock and clonic phases showed a small, but significant, curvilinear relationship with the cumulative effects of a series of treatments. Kurahashi (40), using cats as subjects, designed his research to compare the effects on learning of convulsive and subconvulsive stimulation and of two different intervals between treatment, 24 and 48 hr. Decrements in learning were clearly observable following convulsions, but stimulation leading to "misfits" produced no measurable effects. Recovery was faster following subconvulsive than following convulsive stimulation. The results were interpreted as indicating greater effects on learning and slower recovery with the shorter than with the longer intervals between treatments. Brown & de la Garza (41) observed that rats given ESC both during and before the learning period begins are unable to inhibit anticipatory responses when performing in a maze. The preshock group also were more erratic in their performance.

The points of greatest departure from previous research on the effects of ESC on learning and retention have been either the use of new species as subjects or of new problems to be learned and retained. Hamilton & Patton

(42) studied the difference in rates of spontaneous recovery between (*a*) rats receiving ESC immediately after establishment and extinction of a conditioned escape response and (*b*) control animals undergoing no experimental treatment during a period of time equivalent to that required for the ESC treatment. The results indicate that ESC favors spontaneous recovery, but that this effect is only transitory. Brown & de la Garza (41) have investigated the effect of ESC on the anticipatory responses of rats during the learning of a multiple-T maze under conditions of dim illumination and homogeneous surroundings. Controls learned the maze during a period in which they received one trial per day for 15 days, while the convulsed animals did not reach the criterion of learning. The main difference between the groups appeared to lie in the failure of the convulsed animals to inhibit anticipatory responses. Braun and his colleagues (43, 44) reported experiments on rhesus monkeys, designed to study the effects of ESC on the learning and retention of problems varying in difficulty. Twenty convulsions, induced at a rate of three per week, resulted in an impairment in the retention of an object-quality discrimination learning set, established prior to the shock series, but an impairment which was small in magnitude and very temporary in duration (43). The differences between the convulsed and control animals were most apparent on the differential cue trials when there appeared a tendency of the convulsed animals to adopt a response pattern of perseverating on the side which previously had been correct. This latter observation is of particular interest when compared with studies of reactions to stress generally in which rigidity in adhering to previously learned responses despite their inadequacies is most marked. A second experiment (44) dealt with the effects of a series of 20 ESC treatments on the performance of the monkey in a task of greater complexity, the oddity problem as used by Harlow and his collaborators (45). No significant differences in learning performance were found between the convulsed and control animals, both groups showing the progressive interproblem improvement characteristic of the formation of a learning set. Braun has interpreted these results as showing that, with the monkey, effects of ESC are not related to problem difficulty as they appear to be with the rat. Thus, the comparison of different species with regard to these particular aspects of behavior has led to the discovery of significant phylogenetic differences, the type of observation for which the comparative method is admirably suited. However, since training on the problems began 94 days after the last ESC and extended over four additional months, the possibility exists that temporary effects related to difficulty of problem may have dissipated prior to the learning.

Bendig & Patton (46) obtained positive results in a study of the effects of ESC on latent learning. Rats fed *ad libitum* with food and water in their home cages were given a series of trials in a one choice T maze with escape from water as the form of motivation. Food pellets were present on the same one of the two landing platforms during these trials. Following ESC treatment of the experimental animals, both controls and experimentals were given a series of test trials while operating under 23 hr. food deprivation. The results support the conclusion that ESC significantly decreased the effects of "latent learning."

Two studies at the University of Chicago laboratory have added to our knowledge concerning the effects of ESC on a "conditioned emotional response." By reinforcing a light stimulus with electric shocks to the feet, Brady & Hunt (47) rapidly produced in their rats a response of crouching and defecating to the presentation of the light alone. After the response was established experimental animals were given a series of ESC and the controls an equal number of pseudo-ESC. The convulsions had the immediate effect of almost eliminating the condition response. Hunt, Jernberg and Brady (48) showed that similar effects also appear in terms of a marked reduction of lever pressing in the Skinner box. In both experiments the effects were only temporary, the conditioned responses reappearing during the first 30-odd days following the treatment. That a "vestigial form" of the conditioned response survived even these temporary effects was suggested by the fact that experimental extinction following treatment interfered with the reappearance of the response.

In his studies on the effects of ESC upon learning in monkeys Braun (49) has included a study of delayed responses. Such responses, presumably involving symbolic behavior and memory function, showed no long-term impairment following ESC. The design of the experiment did not allow examination of the possibility that temporary losses might appear.

During the past few years several studies have been reported in which the effects of ESC on the behavior of animals treated while under the influence of various drugs have been examined. Recently Thomas & Stone (50) have convulsed albino rats after treatment with dilantin sodium, an anticonvulsant. No significant differences were observed in the subsequent maze performance of these animals and that of a shock-control group, although the ESC was associated with performance significantly worse than that of a drug-control group. Hunt, Jernberg & Lawlor (51) have studied the effect of ESC, administered under ether anaesthesia, on a conditioned emotional response. Three groups of rats were used, the first receiving ESC only, the second being convulsed while under the anaesthesia, and the third receiving ESC followed by anaesthesia. The results confirmed previous reports by other investigators that ESC does not have its usual effects on behavior of the rat if the convulsions are prevented from occurring by anaesthesia at the time of treatment.

Studies of Conflict and Behavior Disorders

Pavlov (52) once wrote: " . . . the decision, or the conditions favorable to a decision, of many important questions of etiology, the natural systematization, the mechanism and finally the treatment of neuroses in the human being lies in the hands of the animal experimenter." Contemporary investigators have taken this charge very seriously as evidenced by the relatively large number of recent studies of conflict and abnormal behavior patterns employing animals as subjects. The current trend is to view these studies in the framework of learning rather than frustration theory.

Some time ago Miller (53) described three basic varieties of response competition or conflict. Recently he and his collaborators, using rats as subjects, have reported a series of three experiments designed to test the extension of his original analysis to certain details of the phenomena of "displacement." Miller & Kraeling (54) studied the generalization of conflict to new stimulus situations. An approach-avoidance conflict was established by training hungry animals to run from one end to the other of a short alley in order to reach foot and then giving them electric shocks until they failed to touch the food on three successive trials. Miller's analysis would predict that such conflict would be revealed in vacillations between approach and avoidance responses at some point in the alley. The generalization of this conflict was studied by testing some of the animals in the same alley in which they were trained, others in a somewhat different alley, and still others in a very different alley. Appropriate control groups were included in the research design. Animals tested in all the alleys showed the vacillation predicted, indicating generalization of the conflict. By observing the proportion of animals touching the food in the different alleys during test trials it was concluded that approach generalized more strongly than avoidance. In a second experiment Murray & Miller (55) compared generalization gradients of approach and avoidance when the age of the habits and the number and distribution of training trials were controlled. Four groups of animals were used, two reinforced by food and two by electric shock. One of each of these latter groups was given continuous and the other partial reinforcement. The strength of pull on release after being restrained halfway to the goal served as the measure of the strength of approach and avoidance responses. Four test trials were run, two in the same alley in which the animal had been trained and two in a different alley. The steepness of the gradients of generalization was represented in each case by the difference between the strength of the pull in the two alleys and proved to be greater for avoidance than for approach. This difference in slope was highly significant when the measures of the test trials were averaged, although it did not appear in the first test trial of the group receiving continuous reinforcement. Another experiment by Miller & Murray (56) was designed to test the prediction that the gradient of stimulus generalization should be steeper for responses motivated by a learned, response-produced drive dependent upon external cues than for a primary drive independent of external cues. Avoidance responses were established to electric shock in an alley containing distinctive cues. Half the animals were then tested with the shock turned off so that they were motivated only by the secondary drive of "fear," which was assumed to vary with the cues in the alley. The other half were tested with the shock on and hence motivated by a primary drive, which could not be assumed to vary with alley cues. Half of each of these two groups were tested in the same alley in which they had been trained and the other half in a different alley. Strength of response was measured in terms of the force exerted by the animals against a temporary restraint. The gradient of stimulus generalization of the secondary-drive animals was steeper than that of the primary-drive animals and confirmed the prediction under test. The authors suggested that alternative explanations of the results are improbable, but cannot be entirely eliminated.

Other studies have been concerned with different manifestations of behavior under stress. Ullman (57) has followed up some of his earlier research on the production of a "compulsive eating symptom" in rats. He had suggested that four drives were operating in the situation to which his animals were exposed: hunger, hunger-fear, pain, and pain-fear. An observed increase in eating during electric shock was presumed to occur because eating had become a generalized tension-reducing response in the situation, a point of view supported by the fact that the animals ate when shock was applied despite having been previously satiated. In his follow-up study Ullman has set out to discover the relative importance of each of three variables intimately concerned in producing the symptom: level of hunger, amount of food-taking training, and intensity of electric shock. In a factorial research design each of these variables was present at two different levels, and the results indicated that the combination of conditions most favorable to the development of "compulsive eating" was: the lesser training in eating and the higher levels of hunger and shock.

In another experiment Datel & Seward (58) reported on observations of the persistence of an ear-scratching response in the rat. Collodion was applied to the ears of the experimental animals on five successive days, producing intense ear-scratching behavior. Control animals received no such application and showed no such heightened level of scratching activity. The groups had been equated on frequency of scratching during a four-day observation period. Ear-scratching was sampled during 10 min. observation periods once each day. Analysis of the results showed that for at least 16 days after cessation of treatment mean scratching scores for the experimental animals were significantly higher than those for the controls. The possibility that these results might be explained by residual after-effects of the collodion on the tissues was ruled out on two grounds: first, five or six days after applications of collodion ceased evidence of skin irritation and sensitization had disappeared; and, second, the difference between the groups did not diminish with time. Several possible explanations of the results were discussed, the favored approach being via Hull's concepts of secondary motivation and secondary reinforcement.

Bailey & Miller (59) have studied simple approach-avoidance conflict by observing the differential effects of a depressant drug, sodium amytal, on the relative strengths of the competing response tendencies. Hungry cats were subjected to conflict involving approach to food and avoidance of electric shock. When the animals remained away from the food on three successive test trials they were divided into two groups, the experimentals being given an intraperitoneal injection of sodium amytal and the controls an injection of normal saline. During test trials run at 5, 10, 15, and 20 min. after injection the two groups showed significantly different reactions to the conflict situation, all the experimental animals but only one control approaching the food within four trials. These are the results predicted on the grounds that sodium amytal should have a greater effect in reducing the fear motivating avoidance than the hunger motivating approach. Of interest are the authors' remarks that completely negative results were obtained in exploratory studies using rats as subjects. This is another suggestion that important differences may await research designed with phyletic comparisons in view.

The extensive series of studies by Maier and his colleagues (25) on the characteristics of behavior induced by "frustration" in the insoluble problem situation have been concerned almost entirely with responses made at single choice points. At the 1953 Annual Meeting of the British Psychological Society, Watson (60) reported a study of stereotyped behavior in a multiple-choice insoluble problem situation. Rats were presented with an insoluble problem involving four choices, thus providing a large number of possible seriation response patterns. Stereotypes, many extremely persistent, developed, involving sequences of responses. The animals received 200 trials under these conditions. After this phase of the research was completed, a soluble problem was introduced, which all the animals learned. Analysis of the results suggested that behavior on both the insoluble and soluble problems was consistent with that which would be predicted from conventional learning theory.

During the period of the present review the question as to whether reactions to stress fit into the general framework of learning theory or if another type of schema is required has received considerable attention. The controversial center of a number of contributions has been Maier's theory based upon qualitative distinctions between "goal-motivated" and "frustration-instigated" behavior. The majority of contributors have been rather unhappy with Maier's formulations, although at least one, Austin (61), has concluded that Maier's research program in the case of frustration has achieved some success. Maier's present position was stated in a 1951 paper (62) in which he argued that certain features of the experimental results obtained by other workers are not satisfactorily covered by current anxiety-reduction theory and that certain of the findings in his own laboratory could not be explained in terms of learning theory. The rebuttal of these arguments has come in the form of reinterpretations of the controversial results and of experiments designed to test various aspects of Maier's theory.

Wolpe (63, 64) in critiques of the literature on "experimental neuroses," has rejected Maier's theory on the grounds that it is based upon a misinterpretation of the "abnormal behavior fixations" appearing under conditions of the insoluble problem. Wolpe has pointed out that Maier found it necessary to compel his animals to jump by use of air blast or electric shock. Each time an animal was compelled to jump the response ended the blast or shock and, consequently, led to a reduction of the drive that forced the response. The response was not unrewarded as Maier has assumed. Wolpe has also suggested that the punishment, e.g., nose-bumping, associated with the stereotyped response is ineffective as a response-eliminating agent in relation to the strength of reinforcement associated with escape from the air blast or shock. It is not possible here to examine the details of Wolpe's analysis of "abnormal fixation" experiments, but the example given above illustrates the general approach which has led him to favor explanations based upon learning rather than frustration theory.

Although the manner in which Maier's theory has been formulated makes critical tests of it difficult to design, two studies have been reported which were planned to examine certain deductions from it. The results of both of these studies support interpretations based on learning theory. Knöpfelmacher (65) has taken as his point of departure Maier's assumption that the rigidity of stereotyped responses is a function of frustration. Continued punishment during the trials of Maier's customary research procedure should not only fail to decrease rigidity but actually to increase it. If this continued frustration were eliminated, for instance, by rewarding the stereotyped responses once they were established, the stereotype should become more amenable to extinction or, at least, not less amenable. On the other hand, if principles of learning theory are operating, reinforcement of the stereotyped response should tend to strengthen it. Rats were used as subjects and exposed to an insoluble problem in a discrimination unit employing escape from water as motivation. Each animal forming a stereotype was assigned to one of four groups. The first group served as a control and the other three were given 60, 120, and 180 rewarded trials, respectively. Finally, all groups were tested on a soluble problem in the same apparatus. Analysis of the results showed that none of the stereotypes was sufficiently rigid to meet Maier's criterion of "fixated" responses. The strengths of the stereotypes were directly proportional to the number of rewarded trials, which was interpreted as evidence that they were not qualitatively different from learned responses.

Wilcoxon (66) has presented additional evidence that conventional S—R learning theory can account for the phenomena reported by Maier. Two experiments were carried out. The first was designed to isolate the effects of partial and nondifferential reinforcement in the general situation employed by Maier. Three groups of rats were trained in an initial habit under different experimental training conditions: continuous reinforcement involving invariable reward for correct and punishment for incorrect responses; partial reinforcement where the correct response was rewarded half the time and punished the other half, while incorrect responses were always punished; and the conditions of the insoluble problem situation. Finally, all animals were tested on a new and soluble problem requiring abandonment of the initial habit. Analysis of the results showed that animals of the insoluble problem group took longer to establish a consistent response than did animals of the other groups. This was interpreted as indicating that nondifferential reinforcement per se increases variability, an interpretation "contrary to Maier's point of view." The results also supported the conclusion that partial reinforcement of the first habit is of primary importance in the development of fixations. It was observed that responses established under conditions of partial reinforcement were more rigid in the final tests than those established under conditions of the insoluble problem. Wilcoxon's second experiment was designed to examine techniques other than manual guidance for altering fixations once they were established. It provided results which indicated that such alteration was possible by applying relatively simple techniques based on learning principles.

Although most of the studies of reactions to stress have been oriented around problems of psychological theory, their potential value in supplementing clinical research in psychiatry and "psychosomatic" medicine has been recognized. Beach (67) has suggested that " . . . if 'psychosomatic' relationships in the human being are defined objectively and scientifically it becomes apparent that comparable phenomena occur in infrahuman animals." Russell (68) has pointed to certain problems in psychiatry which can only be attacked experimentally by the use of infrahuman subjects.

Concluding Remarks

Areas within comparative psychology have been selected for inclusion in the present review primarily in terms of the relative frequency with which they received attention from investigators during the period covered. In one case, experimental psychogenetics, research reports have been few, but promise great.

No radically new principles or techniques have been suggested in the publications of the comparative ethologists, whose general approach received so much attention in the past two *Reviews*. It would seem that we are now in a stage where this approach is undergoing careful and detailed scrutiny, as evidenced, for instance, by Ginsberg's (69) lengthy "reconstructive analysis" of the concept of instinct. During the past year research on animal learning has remained a "current trend" as it has for so many years in the past, but the new results are more suitably reviewed in the chapter on learning. Several investigations (70 to 73) have examined specific instances of the reciprocal relations between chemical balance within the organism and the behavior of the organism. There have been very few aspects of behavior which have not been examined as they occur in infrahuman animal species, but very few of these examinations have followed the design which the comparative sciences as a whole might have expected of a truly comparative psychology.

LITERATURE CITED

1. Schneirla, T. C., *Psychol. Bull.*, **49,** 559–97 (1952)
2. Russell, R. W., *The Comparative Study of Behaviour* (H. K. Lewis & Co., Ltd., London, England, 19 pp., 1952)
3. Hall, C. S., in *Handbook of Experimental Psychology,* 304–29 (Stevens, S. S., Ed., John Wiley & Sons, Inc., New York, N. Y., 1436 pp., 1951)
4. Russell, R. W., *Eugen. Rev.*, **45,** 19–30 (1953)
5. Stob, M., and Andrews, F. N., *Endocrinology,* **51,** 165–72 (1952)
6. Hauschka, T. S., *J. Heredity,* **43,** 117–23 (1952)
7. Estes, B. W., *J. Genet. Psychol.*, **81,** 273–88 (1952)
8. Hauschka, T. S., *J. Heredity,* **43,** 77–80 (1952)
9. Falconer, D. S., *Heredity,* **6,** 255–57 (1952)
10. Falconer, D. S., *Am. Naturalist,* **86,** 293–98 (1952)
11. Levinson, B., *J. Comp. and Physiol. Psychol.*, **45,** 140–45 (1952)
12. Armitage, S. G., *J. Comp. and Physiol. Psychol.*, **45,** 146–52 (1952)
13. Becker, R. F., and Donnell, W., *J. Comp. and Physiol. Psychol.*, **45,** 153–62 (1952)
14. Hurder, W. P., and Sanders, A. F., *J. Comp. and Physiol. Psychol.*, **46,** 61–63 (1953)
15. Griffiths, W. J., Jr., and Stringer, W. F., *J. Comp. and Physiol. Psychol.*, **45,** 301–6 (1952)
16. Bingham, W. E., and Griffiths, W. J., Jr., *J. Comp. and Physiol. Psychol.*, **45,** 307–12 (1952)
17. Hymovitch, B., *J. Comp. and Physiol. Psychol.*, **45,** 313–21 (1952)
18. Forgays, D. G., and Forgays, J. W., *J. Comp. and Physiol. Psychol.*, **45,** 322–28 (1952)
19. Fingerman, M., *J. Exptl. Zool.*, **120,** 131–64 (1952)
20. Fingerman, M., and Brown, F. A., *Physiol. Zool.*, **26,** 59–67 (1953)
21. Fingerman, M., and Brown, F. A., *Science,* **116,** 171–72 (1952)
22. Montgomery, K. C., and Heinemann, E. G., *Science,* **116,** 454–56 (1952)
23. Dice, L. R., and Barto, E., *Science,* **116,** 110–11 (1952)
24. Alexander, I. E., and Githler, F. J., *J. Comp. and Physiol. Psychol.*, **45,** 381–91 (1952)
25. Maier, N. R. F., *Frustration: the Study of Behavior Without a Goal* (McGraw-Hill Book Co., Inc., New York, N. Y., 264 pp., 1949)
26. Michels, K. M., and Bevan, W., Jr., *J. Genet. Psychol.*, **81,** 185–91 (1952)
27. Rabe, P. L., *J. Genet. Psychol.*, **81,** 3–17 (1952)
28. Frings, H., and Frings, M., *J. Mammalogy,* **33,** 80–87 (1952)
29. Hall, C. S., *J. Heredity,* **38,** 2–6 (1947)
30. Hurder, W. P., and Sanders, A. F., *Science,* **117,** 324–26 (1953)
31. Patton, R. A., *J. Psychol.*, **24,** 313–17 (1947)
32. Kenshalo, D. P., and Kryter, K. D., *J. Comp. and Physiol. Psychol.*, **42,** 328–31 (1949)
33. Finger, F. W., Brice, R. C., and Day, W. F., *J. Comp. and Physiol. Psychol.*, **45,** 163–69 (1952)
34. Marx, M. H., and Chambers, R. M., *J. Comp. and Physiol. Psychol.*, **45,** 239–45 (1952)
35. Fuller, J. L., and Rappaport, A., *J. Comp. and Physiol. Psychol.*, **45,** 246–49 (1952)

36. Marx, M. H., and Van Spanckeren, W. J., *J. Comp. and Physiol. Psychol.*, **45,** 170–79 (1952)
37. Bini, L., *Am. J. Psychiatry*, **94,** 172–74 (1931)
38. Pierce, J. F., and Patton, R. A., *J. Psychol.*, **33,** 79–86 (1952)
39. Townsend, J. C., Russell, R. W., and Patton, R. A., *J. Nervous Mental Disease*, **115,** 49–56 (1952)
40. Kurahashi, M., *Japan. J. Psychol.*, **22,** 7–11 (1951)
41. Brown, W. L., and de la Garza, C. O., *J. Genet. Psychol.*, **82,** 11–20 (1953)
42. Hamilton, C. L., and Patton, R. A., *J. Comp. and Physiol. Psychol.*, **45,** 600–3 (1952)
43. Braun, H. W., Patton, R. A., and Barnes, H. W., *J. Comp. and Physiol. Psychol.*, **45,** 231–38 (1952)
44. Braun, H. W., *J. Comp. and Physiol. Psychol.*, **45,** 585–88 (1952)
45. Harlow, H. F., in *Comparative Psychology*, 183–238 (Stone, C. P., Ed., Prentice-Hall, Inc., New York, N. Y., 525 pp., 1951)
46. Bendig, A. W., and Patton, R. A., *J. Exptl. Psychol.*, **44,** 352–54 (1952)
47. Brady, J. V., and Hunt, H. F., *J. Comp. and Physiol. Psychol.*, **45,** 180–87 (1952)
48. Hunt, H. F., Jernberg, P., and Brady, J. V., *J. Comp. and Physiol. Psychol.*, **45,** 589–99 (1952)
49. Braun, H. W., *J. Comp. and Physiol. Psychol.*, **45,** 352–57 (1952)
50. Thomas, H. F , and Stone, C. P., *J. Psychol.*, **33,** 127–32 (1952)
51. Hunt, H. F., Jernberg, P., and Lawlor, W. G., *J. Comp. and Physiol. Psychol.*, **46,** 64–68 (1953)
52. Pavlov, I. P., *Lectures on Conditioned Reflexes: Conditioned Reflexes and Psychiatry* (International University Press, Inc., New York, N. Y., 199 pp., 1941)
53. Miller, N. E., in *Personality and the Behavior Disorders*, 1 (Hunt, J. McV., Ed., The Ronald Press Co., New York, N. Y., 618 pp., 1944)
54. Miller, N. E., and Kraeling, D., *J. Exptl. Psychol.*, **43,** 217–21 (1952)
55. Murray, E. J., and Miller, N. E., *J. Exptl. Psychol.*, **43,** 222–26 (1952)
56. Miller, N. E., and Murray, E. J., *J. Exptl. Psychol.*, **43,** 227–31 (1952)
57. Ullman, A. D., *J. Comp. and Physiol. Psychol.*, **45,** 490–96 (1952)
58. Datel, W. E., and Seward, J. P., *J. Abnormal Social Psychol.*, **47,** 58–61 (1952)
59. Bailey, C. J., and Miller, N. E., *J. Comp. and Physiol. Psychol.*, **45,** 205–8 (1952)
60. Watson, R. H. J., *Stereotype Behaviour in a Multiple Choice "insoluble problem"* (Address delivered to the Animal Meeting of the British Psychological Society, Nottingham, England, April, 1953)
61. Austin, G. A., *Psychol. Rev.*, **59,** 202–8 (1952)
62. Maier, N. R. F., and Ellen, P., *Psychol. Rev.*, **58,** 435–45 (1951)
63. Wolpe, J., *Psychol. Rev.*, **60,** 111–16 (1953)
64. Wolpe, J., *Brit. J. Psychol.*, **43,** 243–68 (1952)
65. Knöpfelmacher, F., *Quart. J. Exptl. Psychol.*, **4,** 78–86 (1952)
66. Wilcoxon, H. C., *J. Exptl. Psychol.*, **44,** 324–33 (1952)
67. Beach, F. A., *Psychosomat. Med.*, **14,** 261–76 (1952)
68. Russell, R. W., in *Prospects in Psychiatric Research*, 86–108 (Tanner, J. M., Ed., Basil Blackwell & Mott, Ltd., Oxford, England, 197 pp., 1953)
69. Ginsberg, A., *J. Psychol.*, **33,** 235–77 (1952)
70. Gantt, W. H., *Psychosomat. Med.*, **14,** 174–81 (1952)
71. Mahl, G. F., *Psychosomat. Med.*, **14,** 182–210 (1952)
72. Clarke, J. R., *Endocrinology*, **9,** 114–26 (1953)
73. Siegel, P. S., and Taub, D. V., *J. Comp. and Physiol. Psychol.*, **45,** 250–53 (1952)

PHYSIOLOGICAL PSYCHOLOGY[1,2]

By R. A. Patton

Department of Psychology, University of Pittsburgh, Pittsburgh, Pennsylvania

The physiological psychologist does not deal with unique problems but seeks a common ground for a science of behavior with related disciplines such as biochemistry, neurophysiology, and other biological sciences. During the period covered by this review progress has been evident in the continued development of precise methods for evaluating behavioral changes as a function of specific central nervous system damage. The psychologist and the biochemist have worked more closely together on common problems. A number of new approaches to clinical behavioral problems have continued their development. No final answers to these problems have been presented. The studies reviewed below, however, give evidence of a satisfactory progress toward the formulation of the important questions.

Early Environmental Effects on Behavior

During recent years there has been an increasing interest in the important problem of the influence which early environmental conditions may exert on later behavior. One experimental approach has been the study of effects of early experiences upon later behavior where the early experience was extremely varied, as compared with a restricted environment. Hymovitch (1) blinded rats either in early life or at maturity and then reared them in a relatively free environment or in an environment which allowed only a restricted amount of activity. At maturity the animals were tested in a closed field apparatus designed by Hebb and Williams and on an enclosed 10-unit T-maze. It was found that the differences between early- and late-blinded animals were not significant. The differences in the performances of the free and restricted groups on the T-maze were likewise not significant. The free groups were found to be superior to the restricted groups when their performance was measured in a closed field test. In two additional groups free environmental experience was received during early life and restricted experience later on, while in another group this order of experience was reversed. In the tests conducted at maturity, the former group was found to be superior to the group receiving early restricted environment. In a comparable experiment, Forgays & Forgays (2) secured similar results which they interpreted in terms of the differences in opportunity for perceptual experience and learning in the various environmental situations. Bingham & Griffiths (3) maintained rats in similarly divergent environments for a 30-day period which began when the animals were 21 days of age. Tests were conducted two

[1] This review covers the period from June, 1952 to June, 1953.

[2] The following abbreviations are used in this chapter: ACTH (adrenocorticotropin); EEG (electroencephalogram).

weeks later in five different situations: an inclined plane maze, a jumping apparatus, an open field temperament test, a test for sound-induced seizures, and the Warner-Warden maze. Animals reared in the free environment were clearly superior to those reared in the restricted environment in maze learning performance while no significant differences appeared in the other tests.

A second approach to this problem consisted in the study of the effects of early experience of adverse environmental conditions such as x-irradiation or anoxia. In a study referred to later, Levinson (4) observed the relationship between different amounts of x-irradiation given at five stages of fetal life and the postnatal learning ability of rats. At 50 days of age the performance of the rats was found to decrease as a function of the amount of fetal irradiation applied. Greater variability in the performance of the irradiated animals was also reported.

Becker & Donnell (5) studied the effect of asphyxiation on guinea pigs by occluding the maternal uterine vessels after one animal in each litter had been delivered to serve as a control. One group of animals was released in time to recover spontaneously. A second group was asphyxiated until comatose and then artificially revived. Problem boxes were utilized 8 to 10 weeks later to evaluate learning performance. Problems of two levels of difficulty were utilized and greater error and perseveration scores were found for the experimental animals. Two weeks later retests showed that retention was affected by asphyxiation in a similar manner. Hurder & Sanders (6) used one-year-old rats exposed to different conditions in a decompression chamber. Two experimental groups were exposed to a simulated altitude of 30,000 ft. for 3 hr., and 34,000 ft. for 38 min. When 100 days of age the groups were trained on Stone's multiple-T alley-maze. Learning scores for the experimental animals were not significantly different from those of the controls.

Griffiths & Stringer (7) studied the effects of intense stimulation during infancy on adult behavior of the rat. The following four types of stimuli were used: rapid rotation, extremes of environmental temperature, auditory stimulation, and electric shock. Each rat in the experimental groups received a 3 min. period of stimulation daily during the first nine days of life and twice daily until the fifty-seventh day. At 60 days of age subjects were tested in four different situations: the Lashley-discrimination apparatus, the open field test for emotionality, a test for sound induced seizures, and the Warner-Warden maze. No significant differences appeared to distinguish the performances of the experimental groups from those of untreated control animals.

Sensory Processes

Although research on sensory processes is reviewed in the chapters on Vision and Audition, several studies will be covered here since they are relevant to the orientation of the present chapter.

Montgomery & Heinemann (8) have attempted to apply some of von Frisch's findings on the function of polarized light as a basis for navigation in bees, to homing behavior in birds. These authors reasoned that birds should be able to discriminate patterns of light polarized in one plane from polarized light patterns presented in another plane. Homing pigeons were used as subjects and the stimuli were presented on ground glass stimulus keys. The animals were rewarded only for responses to polarized light in one plane and maintained at 80 per cent of normal body weight during acquisition and extinction trials. This study gave no evidence that pigeons could discriminate between planes of polarized light, although they did discriminate brightnesses with ease.

Three well-designed studies were reported which dealt with color sensitivity in *Drosophila melanogaster*. Fingerman (9) and Fingerman & Brown (10, 11) have presented evidence indicating that this organism may possess true color vision. Observations were made on the strength of phototaxis in response to white and monochromatic light. Responses to colored light were lost with a reduction in the intensity of the stimulus, and the authors suggested the existence of photopic and scotopic mechanisms similar to those which have been described in the vertebrate eye. With different groups of organisms, spectral response curves were plotted when 17 wave lengths were presented and phototactic orientation responses noted. The well-established genetics of *Drosophila* permitted the careful selection of six groups of animals differing only in eye color. There was the suggestion that the spectral response curves differed not only in strength but also in form and might have been dependent upon a differential absorption of light by differing eye pigments. That the duplicity theory may possibly apply to the compound eye is supported by anatomical findings of both long and short axon retinal cells in different Arthropoda. The last study in this series investigated a possible Purkinje shift in the vision of *Drosophila*. Spectral response curves were observed to change as the intensity of light was decreased. The above mentioned investigations outlined both physiological and comparative data which relate the compound eye to the visual structures found in higher animal species.

Alexander & Githler (12) in a study related to military problems, studied the effects of jet engine noise on the function of the cochlea. Guinea pigs were exposed for a 15 min. period to jet engine noise which had an ambient sound level in excess of 140 db. over a measured frequency range from 25 to 7500 c.p.s. Six to eight weeks later auditory sensitivity was measured by observing cochlear potentials for 10 frequencies between 200 and 10,000 c.p.s. The group loss in sensitivity was found to be 34 db. Histologic examination of the ear structures revealed the existence of cochlear damage between 6 and 12 mm. from the basal end, supporting the contention that the entire cochlea is involved in responses to sound. Electrical techniques showed depressed cochlear activity which correlated with the evidence of histological damage. This investigation has a practical value in its applications to military problems and also presents additional information about cochlear function and methods for investigating it. Dice & Barto (13) studied the sensitivity of mice (*Peromyscus*) to ultrasonic stimulation. One sound source employed varied from 500 to 16,000 c.p.s. and the other from 10 to 100 kc.p.s. Sound pressures of 1, 5, 10, or 20 dynes per centimeter at the animal's ear were used. The appearance of conditioned responses was interpreted to indicate sensitivity over a range from 500 to 95,000 c.p.s. in animals from 25 to 70 days of age. Auditory sensitivity for these animals was found to decrease with age.

Bevan & Hunt (14) investigated the effects of sensory (proprioceptive) inflow on convulsive seizures produced in rats by maintaining them on a synthetic diet deficient in magnesium. Proprioceptive damage was induced by sectioning the dorsal funiculus of the cord at the cervical level. No differences were observed in either the frequency or the severity of the convulsive reactions which appeared in all deficient groups. As noted by a number of previous investigators, auditory stimulation was proved to be an effective method of inducing seizures in magnesium deficient animals.

The Effects of X-Irradiation

Furchtgott (15) has studied the influence of x-irradiation on the acquisition of a brightness discrimination habit under conditions of low illumination. Rats were irradiated over the whole body and their performance was later compared with that of controls. Irradiated animals were inferior to the controls, this difference being most apparent immediately after treatment. It was suggested that this evidence indicated that damage to peripheral receptors rather than central nervous damage was responsible for the observed effects. Levinson (4) observed the effects of irradiation during the fetal period upon postnatal learning in rats. Pregnant rats were exposed at five different stages of gestation to different specific dosages. Learning tests were subsequently carried out in the Lashley III maze when the young were 50 days old. With increasing amounts of irradiation significant impairment and variability of performance were found. It is of interest that the greatest effects on learning seemed to be apparent when treatment was given on the 13th day of gestation. In accordance with the findings of previous investigations, the suggestion was made that during the development of neural structures basic to maze learning a critical time might exist when they are particularly susceptible to damage. Another study in this research area was carried out by Arnold (16) who exposed the heads of rats to amounts of x-irradiation which were usually lethal when administered over the entire body. These animals had learned a Tolman-Honzik T-maze before treatment and were tested 1, 12, and 25 days after irradiation for retention. No significant impairment of performance resulted under the conditions described.

Two other studies have appeared in which the authors attempted to study behavior other than maze performance in relation to x-irradiation. Kimeldorf & Newsom (17) investigated external environmental factors influencing the survival of rats following irradiation. Such animals died when subjected to prolonged exposure to cold temperatures (6° C.). This temperature was well tolerated by normal animals. It was found that a similar dose of irradiation was not lethal for control animals at a normal room temperature of 23° C. Nims & Sutton (18) exposed rats to whole body x-irradiation and measured weight changes and water consumption. The over-all metabolism of fasted rats was not changed appreciably and the degree of hydration of tissues and weight loss seemed independent of the animal's initial weight. In nonfasted, irradiated rats, the weight loss persisted for a period of time which seemed proportional to the dosage received. Animals given sublethal dosages grew at a rate which was parallel to that shown by the control animals.

Experimental Brain Damage and Behavior

The study of relationships between functional areas of the brain and behavior has been of recurrent interest in the field of physiological psychology. The following studies are representative of the direction in which this type of research has been proceeding during the past year.

Rosner (19) trained groups of rats on two different tasks, a retracing, Lashley III maze and a nonretracing multiple-T maze. With lesions of less than 15 per cent of the neocortex the postoperative performance of the animals was not impaired. When lesions of over 20 per cent were made there was the tendency toward refusal to run the maze and aversion to operating the retracing doors. Mesocortex and allocortex lesions, involving phylogenetically older parts of the pallium, were associated with significantly poorer postoperative performance than was removal of neocortex only. Similar amounts of neocortex were destroyed in both groups. This study suggested the great importance of exploring the differential effects on behavior of cautery as against aspiration methods. There is some evidence that the effects of cautery may extend beyond the bounds of the lesion as defined by standard anatomical techniques (20). Forgays (21) showed that delayed aphasic, motor, sensory, and intellectual defects followed cerebral operations performed on human patients for the relief of epileptic seizures. Such delayed symptoms usually appeared about two days after operation and were followed by complete recovery in about a month without special training. All major subdivisions of the cortex were represented in operations with a group of 50 patients. Forgays (22) also reported that delayed behavioral disturbances followed frontal plus parietal lesions, and also bilateral parietal lesions. After the latter type of lesion the behavioral effects were less pronounced. If the lesions were made bilaterally in the frontal and occipital areas or in the anterior part of the cerebellum no significant behavioral impairment was found. In these studies the "closed field" test of rat "intelligence" devised by Hebb and Williams was used. It seems significant that the brain lesions described above produced behavioral disturbances which appeared at some time after cerebral injury. Recovery from these disturbances occurred after a few weeks without the necessity of retraining.

Pickett (23) trained blinded rats to run elevated mazes with narrow and wide pathways and also an alley maze, the animals being forced to rely mainly on tactual and kinesthetic cues. The mazes were rotated randomly in order to eliminate extramaze cues. Three groups of animals were used: the first had lesions of the motor and somatic cortical areas; the second, lesions of the posterior cortex excluding somatic areas; and the third, sham-operations. The results indicated that while the loss of motor areas handicapped performances on elevated areas, the cortical loss in the posterior areas did not do so. The results with the alley maze indicated that anterior lesions were not significantly more damaging than posterior lesions although a high correlation existed between loss of tissue and running ability. Two studies were reported by Chow (24, 25) on visual discrimination and conditioned reactions in the monkey. The experimental animals were trained and tested before and after the operations. In one group the prestriate areas, including lateral, medial, and frontal areas, were removed. Temporal neocortex was removed in another animal and the frontal eye fields were ablated in two other monkeys. The animals with bilateral temporal neocortical lesions were tested 12 days after operation but failed to score at better-than-chance levels. However, when the animals were trained on new discrimination problems after this test they showed quick recovery of the lost habits when tested again at the end of three months. The animals with extensive prestriate lesions failed to distinguish between food and inedible objects, and in addition were hyperactive and gave evidence of disorientation. In addition to showing the above symptoms an additional animal with the loss of temporal neocortex was retarded in relearning conditioned responses. No significant symptoms were associated with lesions in the frontal eye fields.

Zubek (26) reported the effects of extirpating somatic sensory areas I and II on roughness discrimination and tactual form discrimination in the cat and the rat. Cats showed amnesia for the testing situation when area II was removed either in combination with area I or alone. There was a loss of ability to learn or relearn fine discriminations. In the case of rats, it was found that ablation of either or both of these areas had no effect on tactual discrimination. While these studies with two animal species are not in agreement it is possible that the successful discriminations reported in the rat study were based on sensitivity other than tactual.

Evarts (27) studied the ability of the monkey to perform auditory discriminations after massive lesions involving up to 90 per cent of the auditory cortex. The author observed neither loss of ability to learn frequency discriminations nor loss of previously learned discriminations. The experiments required discrimination between tones of 350 and 3500 c.p.s. Meyer & Woolsey (28) investigated the effects of extirpations in various combination of auditory areas I and II, somatic area I, and the posterior ectosylvian gyrus on frequency and intensity discriminations. These lesions resulted in complete and lasting deficits for frequency discrimination but not for intensity discrimination. The extirpations of either auditory areas I and II alone, however, seemed to have little effect on either type of discrimination. In two other studies with monkeys, Evarts (29, 30) removed large amounts of auditory cortex and tested the animals on auditory-visual association problems. While these animals performed significantly better than chance they performed significantly less well than they did before operation. In other groups of animals the cortico-cortical connections (prestriate) were disrupted and auditory-visual associations were observed. Extensive lesions of the prestriate areas resulted in no loss in the complex problems utilized. Behavioral impairment in learning new tasks was not observed. Along with other evidence these results suggested that there are pathways other than the prestriate which mediate associations between visual and auditory inputs. It is possible that thalamic pathways are involved.

During the period covered by this review several investigators tested the capacity of experimental animals to solve problems involving anticipatory behavior or temporal discrimination. Utilizing a Hull-Hill (31) type maze, Carpenter observed the effects of removing parietal and frontal cortical areas on anticipatory behavior in the rat. Damage to the parietal region resulted in an increase in errors, whereas damage in the frontal area was associated with more anticipatory errors than were observed in control animals. The results of this study support the suggestion of previous authors that the increase in anticipatory errors may be understood in terms of a release from frontal inhibition. On the other hand, the impaired behavior of animals with parietal lesions might have resulted from an increase in perseveration associated with a release from parietal inhibition.

Warren & Harlow (32, 33) reported two studies of learning of pattern and object discriminations by monkeys after prolonged postoperative recovery from extensive bilateral lesions. The results showed that on pattern discrimination tests the frontal injury group did not differ significantly from the normal controls. Both groups of animals were definitely superior to the posterior group. Operated animals did not differ significantly from the normal controls on object discrimination tests. In the second investigation these authors observed the effects of additional contralateral lesions on discrimination behavior. Monkeys with extensive unilateral lesions and destruction of posterior association areas made significantly more errors than normal monkeys or animals with extensive unilateral damage and destruction of the contralateral frontal association areas. Harlow (34) also reported that although extensive unilateral cortical lesions left the operated group inferior on discrimination problems, they reached a high level of response after long training.

Leary *et al.* (35) continued the study of monkeys with anterior and posterior cortical lesions on double-alternation problems at the Wisconsin laboratory. Animals with frontal lesions demonstrated a strong tendency toward stereotypy while large numbers of single alternations were performed by animals with the posterior lesions. The Wisconsin group (36) presented additional evidence of a similar nature in monkeys tested on temporal pattern and discrimination problems. Brain lesions similar to those of the previous investigation were studied. It was found that the posterior lesion and the normal groups did equally well on delayed response problems. Both excelled the performance of animals with frontal injuries. With discrimination problems, however, the frontal lesion and normal animals excelled the performance of those with posterior damage. These results were interpreted as refuting the hypothesis of an equipotential associative cortex. There was evidence of "differential and complementary frontal and posterior syndromes," revealed by an inefficient performance on all discrimination learning tasks used and relatively efficient performance on tests of delayed response. Opposite results were found for animals with the anterior syndrome. The combined data in these and related studies from the Wisconsin laboratory has indicated that (*a*) differential localization of large bilateral cortical lesions produces differential syndromes of intellectual loss; (*b*) no function (such as discrimination learning) is totally destroyed even by large bilateral lesions; and (*c*) quantitative losses in learned performances associated with large cortical lesions are greatly reduced after prolonged testing. It would seem that many studies overlooked a possible source of important information about brain function if postoperative tests are conducted immediately without additional long-term observations being made.

Wade (37) compared the effects of prefrontal lobectomy and lobotomy on the behavior of the monkey. "Intellectual function" was found not to be impaired in several tests, but there was a decrement in the performance scores on the tests of delayed response. Section of the associative fibers seemed to produce instability in some conditioned reactions, but did not impair behavior on delayed response tests.

In a significant study Pribram *et al.* (38) made ablations in the dorsolateral frontal cortex in one group and the ventrolateral cortex in another group of guinea baboons. These operations were bilaterally symmetrical. Preoperative training on visual discrimination and delayed response was given. Postoperative tests yielded greater decrements on these tasks in the case of the dorsolateral animals than the ventrolateral group. These results suggested that pronounced behavioral effects associated with the ablation of frontal cortex in previous research must relate importantly to the loss of the dorsolateral region.

Brody & Rosvold (39) have contributed to methodology in their study of the relationships of prefrontal lobotomy to the social behavior of monkeys. A rigid dominance hierarchy was established in a group of animals which was characterized by aggressive attacks directed toward members lower down in the order. The stability of the established hierarchy was lost after prefrontal lobotomy. The observed changes in a small social group apparently resulted from a decrement in learned avoidance responses in the operated, low status monkeys. The observed changes in avoidance and aggressive behavior were apparent in the upwardly directed aggression and upward mobility in the hierarchy.

French, Amerongen & Magoun (40) presented evidence that there exists in the monkey, as in the cat, a centrally located region comprising the midbrain tegmentum, the subthalamus and hypothalamus, and the medial portion of the thalamus in which evoked potentials can be recorded from peripheral stimuli applied to the somatic, visual, auditory, and visceral systems. Evidence is discussed which indicates that this region functions as a unit and is subject to excitation by peripheral sensory stimulation. This excitation affects electrical activation of the cortex and behavioral reactions, such as awareness of stimulation, arousal to wakefulness, or attention in the animal. Lindsley *et al.* (41) had previously presented a report dealing with behavioral and EEG[2] changes resulting from chronic lesions in this region.

In a second investigation, French & Magoun (42) extended the study of chronic lesions in this important area. Electrolytic lesions were made in the central cephalic portion of the brain stem of nine monkeys. Information on the behavioral effects of destruction of this area was desired. Although complete destruction resulted in death, smaller lesions produced akinesis and hypersomnolence. Electroencephalograms were characterized by hypersynchrony not responsive to sensory arousal stimuli.

Anand & Brobeck (43) showed that bilateral electrolytic lesions in the amygdaloid nuclei of rats produced the following: (*a*) no change in food intake; (*b*) a decrease in spontaneous activity; (*c*) a transient fall in body temperature; (*d*) no development of savageness. Similar effects were observed in cats. In the latter animals food intake remained normal in those whose lesions did not invade the lateral hypothalamus. Beattie (44) has described a new instrument for the accurate placement of small brain lesions in the rat. The lesions are produced electrically with good control over various parameters of stimulation. The electrode is mounted on a pantograph-type carrier, readily removable to allow access to the field of operation.

Biochemical Correlates of Behavior

Several studies designed to investigate biochemical factors that may aid in differentiating between the behavior disorders have appeared recently. In a well designed experiment by Easterday and co-workers (45), groups of 10 subjects were given a controlled amount of exercise on a bicycle ergometer. In addition to a normal group, manic depressive, psychoneurotic, and schizophrenic patients were utilized. Blood glutathione, lactic acid, and pyruvic acid concentrations were determined from blood samples taken at 2, 5, 10, 20, 40, and 60 minutes after a standardized period of exercise. It was found that: (*a*) lactic and pyruvic acid values were significantly greater in females than in males; (*b*) no significant relationships appeared with respect to glutathione; (*c*) pyruvic acid values were significantly lower for normals than for the groups of patients; and (*d*) lactic acid values were significantly lower for normals than for the schizophrenic group. No inverse relationship between reduced glutathione and lactic acid was found for schizophrenics. These interactions were tested by analysis of variance and covariance, with appropriate control checks for variations in work done as related to the weight and height of subjects. The authors reported that significant increases in lactic acid production under exercise in schizophrenic patients, as compared with normals, suggested that glycolysis per se or the reduction of glucose to lactic acid is an efficient mechanism in schizophrenic patients. The apparent need for greater lactic acid production, however, suggested a disturbance in the mechanism for the biochemical transformation of chemical into mechanical energy rather than in the production of lactic acid itself. Further studies might well be oriented toward problems of phosphorus metabolism in schizophrenic patients.

The presence of a hyperglycemic factor in the urine of so-called schizophrenic patients has been reported by Meduna & Vaichulis (46). Meduna & McCulloch (47, 48) have reclassified these schizophrenics as "oneirophrenics" and have suggested a correlation between a hyperglycemic factor in the urine and an abnormal carbohydrate metabolism. A recent study was recently reported by Morgan & Pilgrim (49) which made a significant contribution to knowledge about this problem. These investigators confirmed the presence of a hyperglycemic factor in the urine of some schizophrenics. Methods for concentrating the factor were described and data presented for the yield and potency of the various fractions isolated. The factor has been tentatively identified as a protein or a substance closely bound to a protein. By a comparable fractionation of normal male urine, a measurable quantity of the hyperglycemic factor was not found. This study represents a step forward in the clarification of complex biochemical states underlying one of the most prevalent types of mental disorder.

Jacobs & Tempereau (50) published on the relationship of a proteolytic enzyme in schizophrenic patients. The subjects were 96 male schizophrenics who had not received previous psychiatric treatment. Thirty-six of these patients showed a high concentration of the enzyme (rennin-inhibitor). These patients also exhibited the following behavioral response patterns: (*a*) a low tolerance to frustration in the clinical situation and (*b*) the appearance of confusion, amnesia, or stupor in response to stress ordinarily ineffective in patients of this type. These authors felt that the clinical group having a high concentration of the enzyme most closely fits the traditional classification of catatonia.

Adreno-Cortical Mechanisms

During the past year a great many studies have appeared in the general scientific literature concerning adreno-cortical hormones. For the most part, however, these studies dealt with chemical and strictly physiological variables which are not the primary concern of this review. A few, however, are pertinent and will be covered.

Rosvold *et al.* (51), in a well controlled study, showed that when daily electroshock convulsions were administered to a group of 40 rats for a period of 10 days there was an accompanying increase in the size of the adrenals. The same type of experiment was repeated, using rats anesthetized by ether and pentobarbital sodium [nembutal; sodium 5-ethyl-5-(1-methylbutyl) barbiturate]. Electroshock was given to this and to a control group which was not anesthetized. No convulsive seizures occurred in the anesthetized group. Upon examination 10 days later the convulsed, control group showed enlarged adrenals while the anesthetized group did not show an increase.

Del Pozo (52) analyzed the possible effects of cortisone on the contraction of normal skeletal muscles. The experiment made use of cats with Achilles tendons cut and tied to a myograph. Biphasic electric shocks with a Grass stimulator were applied to the centrally cut sciatic nerve through shielded electrodes. Maximal shocks were used and several frequencies tested. Intra-arterial injections were made through the inferior mesenteric artery peripherally ligated and with retrograde cannulation. Intravenous injections were made through the jugular vein. It was found that doses of soluble cortisone of 6 mg./kg. produced an increase in amplitude of muscular response to the corresponding nerve. The enhancement of muscular contraction was also shown in the improvement of tension maintenance. Del Pozo pointed out that it was previously thought necessary to have an adrenal-cortex insufficiency to detect the effect of cortical hormones on muscular contractions. The results of this experiment show that this is not always the case.

Torda & Wolf reported three studies on the effects of ACTH[2] (53, 54, 55). It was shown that prolonged administration of ACTH increased the ability of the brain to synthesize acetylcholine (53). This increase amounted to 60 per cent in both hypophysectomized and nonoperated dogs. Using adrenalectomized rats a 20 per cent increase in synthesis of acetylcholine was observed. In another study (54) it was shown that in hypophysectomized dogs there was a decrease in the capacity to maintain action-potential amplitude in muscle fibers. ACTH restored the loss of this capacity, which remained unaltered during repeated stimulation. Torda & Wolf (55) also reported that ACTH increased the electrical activity of the brain; the EEG's showed increased voltage, occasional spiking, paroxysmal runs of low frequency, high voltage waves, and lowering of the convulsive threshold to pentomythelene tetrazol. The ACTH showed similar effects in hypophysectomized, adrenalectomized, nonoperated, and sodium injected animals. It was also shown that when the ACTH was administered in large quantities over long periods of time a decrease in cortical activity resulted.

Berkeley (56) tested the hypothesis that subjects who showed the widest divergence between goal and performance in a level-of-aspiration setting would also show the greatest increase in adrenocortical activity. Thirty-one males were used as subjects (only three of them being college students). These performed a manual level-of-aspiration task using an apparatus that could be manipulated by the experimenter to produce either success or failure by a desired amount. The score used was the difference between score obtained and score expected. Stressfulness was evaluated by the production rate of urinary 17-ketosteroids during the test period as against pretest controls. Discrepancy between aspiration and achievement with respect to both success and failure conditions was related to increase in output of 17-ketosteroid hormone. A multiple R of $+.70$ was obtained which is significant beyond the 1 per cent level of confidence.

Carr (57) tested the hypothesis that adrenalectomizing a rat lowers the taste threshold for sodium chloride when threshold is measured in behavioral terms and is uninfluenced by the rat's natural preference for salt. The rats were conditioned to drink salt water in preference to distilled water by shocking them if they chose distilled water and by varying the position of the vials in a random manner. After the conditioned response had been established the concentration of salt was decreased until frequency of its choice was not significantly greater than that of plain water. The preoperative rate of intake of a 3 per cent salt water solution was determined. Adrenalectomy was then performed and the postrecovery intake of 3 per cent salt water was again measured for the surviving animals. Postrecovery rate was significantly different from preoperative rate. The avoidance conditioning paradigm was again instituted, and it was shown that rather than a decrease of salt being necessary for discrimination the amount actually increased, although the increase was not significant. Carr concluded that the "need" for sodium chloride did not influence the ability of rats to detect it.

Siegel (58) injected rats intraperitoneally with blood serum drawn from hungry donors. These injected animals ate no more food over the subsequent two-hour interval than similar rats injected with blood serum from satiated donors. The findings were interpreted as having negative implications for a "hormone" theory of hunger. The volume of blood injected was inversely related to subsequent food intake of the animals.

Physiological Approaches to Clinical Problems

Wishner (59) undertook a study of the possible relationships between physiological and Rorschach measures of behavior characteristics. The data sought were in the area of the relationship between overt and physiological activity. Eleven psychoneurotic patients with anxiety as a major component, and 10 normals took the Rorschach test. On the same day, measurements of the physiological activity of the subjects were made under various stimulus conditions. These measures included electromyograms from the frontal and masseter muscles, electroencephalograms, heart rate, respiration rate, and the galvanic skin response. None of the Rorschach scoring categories, considered singly, differentiated between the two groups. Heart rate was significantly higher for the neurotic group, and respiration rate also tended in this direction. The normals had higher galvanic skin responses and muscle action potentials from the frontal muscles.

This past year was noted for additional research (see 60, 61, 62) on the relations between drive (anxiety) and learning, and these studies are considered by other reviewers. Although at present some of this research is not specifically oriented toward either clinical or physiological psychology, it is probable that in the near future both of these fields will feel the influence of this approach.

Malmo, Davis & Barza (63) reported an experimental study of a 19-year-old girl with apparently complete hysterical deafness. Electromyographic reactions to novel and intense auditory stimulation, and auditory conditioning were recorded. Initial auditory stimulation produced a startle reaction and emotional disturbance. Repetition of the stimulus one minute later produced no reaction and no change in an electromyogram. Auditory conditioning was obtained, the conditioned responses being confined to muscle potentials. The therapeutic usefulness of conditioning procedures in cases of hysterical deafness was suggested.

Klein & Krech (64) reasoned that if prolonged exposure to stimulation results in decreased conductivity of cortical tissue, this effect will be accentuated in cases of severe brain lesions. They compared brain-injured patients and controls on the degree and rate of satiation after exposure to a kinesthetic stimulus. The subjects, while blindfolded, rubbed the sides of a wooden standard and after varying periods of time judged the width of a control object by adjusting a tapering scale. Persistence of the effect was measured at stated intervals. It was found that the frequency and intensity of satiation effects were greater in the brain-injured. Also, in such patients satiation effects were reached more quickly and persisted longer than in normal controls. These findings suggested that a generalized effect of severe brain-injury is lowered conductivity.

Lazarus, Yousem & Arenberg (65) carefully studied the relationships between hunger and perception. Two experiments were described in which hunger was varied and thresholds of recognition determined tachistoscopically for food and nonfood objects in 110 subjects. Differential thresholds of recognition for the food versus nonfood items varied significantly with the degree of food deprivation and subjective hunger. Fifty-one additional subjects made guesses from a list of 16 names of objects, 10 of which were used in the tachistoscopic presentation. Half the list contained food items and half nonfood items. In this multiple-choice form of the experiment no relationship was found between hunger and perceptual recognition. The authors concluded that with precisely defined stimuli under unlimited exposure, tachistoscopic recognition thresholds are a function of the hunger need. This relationship, however, did not occur when the response variation of the subjects was limited by a multiple choice situation.

Semmes (66), in a stimulating review on experimental approaches to agnosia, suggested that in man, because of his capacities, injury, disease, or both, often produce disorders such as agnosia, apraxia, and aphasia which offer an extraordinary and largely unexploited field for research. The nature of behavioral impairment in primates following lesions of the parieto-temporo-preoccipital neocortex and of the "associative" cortex were discussed. She suggested two possibilities as to the nature of these deficits as they may relate to similar disorders in man: (*a*) there may be a loss of the capacity to utilize normal sense-data, as a basis for learned discriminations; or (*b*) the sense-data themselves are altered in an as yet unexplained way. A program of research was described in which these and other questions related to aphasia can be tested more feasibly with a series of brain-injured, human subjects. Suggestions were given for research on how somatic sensation and related abilities are altered by central and peripheral nervous lesions.

The New York group of investigators has maintained a continued interest in the systematic study of individuals who have suffered brain injuries (67 to 70). An earlier review by Bender & Teuber (71) critically summarized current ideas on the relationship of brain damage in humans to symptoms such as agnosia and alexia. A recent study by Battersby, Teuber & Bender

(72) presents data on problem solving behavior in men with frontal or occipital brain injuries.

Eighty World War II veterans were tested on a modification of the Maier String Problem. These subjects had sustained three types of injury: penetrating frontal, parieto-occipital, and peripheral nerve wounds (controls). Results with this test showed that brain-injury in frontal or parieto-occipital areas is less disruptive of problem solving than was indicated in previous reports. Some subjects took longer and were dependent on hints in achieving solution, but the group differences were too small to reach significance.

In normal subjects ability on the reasoning problems employed correlates more highly with ability to perceive hidden contours (Gottschaldt figures) than with ability to sort to a criterion (Weigl test). Neither of these correlations was significant in the brain-injured groups. Patients with anterior lesions did no worse than those with posterior injuries. These findings are not easily compatible with many current assumptions that the integrity of the frontal lobes is of singular importance for the solution of problems similar to those employed in these studies.

Marshall, Walker & Livingston (73) investigated the parameters of stimulation in a case of photogenic epilepsy. By use of intensity attenuation of a stroboscopic light with Polaroid filters, and also by noting the light required to give a positive EEG reaction of increased voltage with slowing, it was demonstrated that red light was at least 10 times as effective in triggering convulsive attacks as other types of colored light. Glasses eliminating this light component were of considerable aid to the patient.

Several reports have described new approaches or methods useful in physiological approaches to behavior, among them being Flanders (74) who has described a circuit for the continuous measurement of palmar resistance. The requirements that should be met if "resistance level" is to be useful as a measure of palmar skin resistance are outlined. Also, suggestions for meeting these requirements, based on equipment developed and used over a period of several years, were proposed.

In a related study on methodology, Grings (75) compared three different manifestations of electrical skin activity in human subjects. Data were presented on skin impedance as a function of the frequency of measurement current, resistance versus reactance components of skin impedance, and the relation between skin resistance and the magnitude of the measuring current. Relationships between AC and DC resistance components were shown to be linear, and the relation between skin potential and impedance quantities was nonlinear.

Other apparatus papers of interest are Baker & Taylor's (76) description of methods for recording changes in skin temperature. Barger & Gebhard (77) have developed an electronic stimulator for use on the human eye. This apparatus is of interest because of recent investigations in which the threshold of electrically induced sensations of light is used as an indicator of the effect of photic stimulation on the activity of visual mechanisms.

LITERATURE CITED

1. Hymovitch, B., *J. Comp. Physiol. Psychol.*, **45,** 313–21 (1952)
2. Forgays, D. G., and Forgays, J. W., *J. Comp. Physiol. Psychol.*, **45,** 322–28 (1952)
3. Bingham, W. E., and Griffiths, W. J., Jr., *J. Comp. Physiol. Psychol.*, **45,** 307–12 (1952)
4. Levinson, B., *J. Comp. Physiol. Psychol.*, **45,** 140–45 (1952)
5. Becker, R. F., and Donnell, W., *J. Comp. Physiol. Psychol.*, **45,** 153–62 (1952)
6. Hurder, W. P., and Sanders, A. F., *J. Comp. Physiol. Psychol.*, **46,** 61–63 (1953)
7. Griffiths, W. J., Jr., and Stringer, W. F., *J. Comp. Physiol. Psychol.*, **45,** 301–6 (1952)
8. Montgomery, K. C., and Heinemann, E. G., *Science*, **116,** 454–56 (1952)
9. Fingerman, M., *J. Exptl. Zool.*, **120,** 131–64 (1952)
10. Fingerman, M., and Brown, F. A., *Physiol. Zoöl.*, **26,** 59–67 (1953)
11. Fingerman, M., and Brown, F. A., *Science*, **116,** 171–72 (1952)
12. Alexander, I. E., and Githler, F. J., *J. Comp. Physiol. Psychol.*, **45,** 381–91 (1952)
13. Dice, L. R., and Barto, E., *Science*, **116,** 110–11 (1952)
14. Bevan, W., Jr., and Hunt, E. L., *J. Comp. Physiol. Psychol.*, **46,** 218–23 (1953)
15. Furchtgott, E., *J. Psychol.*, **34,** 37–41 (1952)
16. Arnold, W. J., *J. Comp. Physiol. Psychol.*, **45,** 358–61 (1952)
17. Kimeldorf, D. J., and Newsom, B. D., *Am. J. Physiol.*, **171,** 349–53 (1952)
18. Nims, L. F., and Sutton, E., *Am. J. Physiol.*, **171,** 17–21 (1952)
19. Rosner, B. S., *J. Comp. Physiol. Psychol.*, **46,** 56–60 (1953)
20. Caudill, C. M., Smith, G. A., French, L. A., Peyton, W. D., and Moore, G. E., *J. Neurosurg.*, **8,** 423–34 (1951)
21. Forgays, D. G., *J. Comp. Physiol. Psychol.*, **45,** 209–15 (1952)
22. Forgays, D. G., *J. Comp. Physiol. Psychol.*, **45,** 216–25 (1952)
23. Pickett, J. M., *Am. J. Psychol.*, **65,** 177–95 (1952)
24. Chow, K. L., *J. Comp. Physiol. Psychol.*, **45,** 109–18 (1952)
25. Chow, K. L., *J. Comp. Physiol. Psychol.*, **45,** 430–37 (1952)
26. Zubek, J. P., *J. Comp. Physiol. Psychol.*, **45,** 438–42 (1952)
27. Evarts, E. V., *J. Neurophysiol.*, **15,** 443–48 (1952)
28. Meyer, D. R., and Woolsey, C. N., *J. Neurophysiol.*, **15,** 149–62 (1952)
29. Evarts, E. V., *J. Neurophysiol.*, **15,** 191–209 (1952)
30. Evarts, E. V., *J. Neurophysiol.*, **15,** 435–41 (1952)
31. Carpenter, J. A., *J. Comp. Physiol. Psychol.*, **45,** 413–18 (1952)
32. Warren, J. M., and Harlow, H. F., *J. Genetic Psychol.*, **81,** 45–52 (1952)
33. Warren, J. M., and Harlow, H. F., *J. Comp. Physiol. Psychol.*, **45,** 119–26 (1952)
34. Harlow, H. F., *Biology of Mental Health and Disease* (Paul B. Hoeber, Inc., New York, N. Y., 496 pp., 1952)
35. Leary, R. W., Harlow, H. F., Settlage, P. H., and Greenwood, D. D., *J. Comp. Physiol. Psychol.*, **45,** 576–84 (1952)
36. Harlow, H. F., Davis, R. T., Settlage, P. H., and Meyer, D. R., *J. Comp. Physiol. Psychol.*, **45,** 419–29 (1952)
37. Wade, M., *J. Clin. Neurol.*, **96,** 179–207 (1952)
38. Pribram, K. H., Mishkin, M., Rosvold, H. E., and Kaplan, S. J., *J. Comp. Physiol. Psychol.*, **45,** 565–75 (1952)
39. Brody, E. B., and Rosvold, H. E., *Psychosomat. Med.*, **14,** 406–15 (1952)
40. French, J. D., Amerongen, F. K., and Magoun, H. W., *Arch. Neurol. Psychiat.*, **68,** 577–90 (1952)

41. Lindsley, D. B., Schreiner, L. H., Knowles, W. B., and Magoun, H. W., *EEG Clin. Neurophysiol.*, **2**, 483–98 (1950)
42. French, J. D., and Magoun, H. W., *Arch. Neurol. Psychiat.*, **68**, 591–604 (1952)
43. Anand, B. K., and Brobeck, J. R., *J. Neurophysiol.*, **15**, 421–30 (1952)
44. Beattie, J., *Quart. J. Exptl. Physiol.*, **37**, 225–32 (1952)
45. Easterday, O. D., Featherstone, R. N., Gottlieb, J. S., Nusser, M. L., and Hogg, R. V., *Arch. Neurol. Psychiat.*, **68**, 48–60 (1952)
46. Meduna, L. J., and Vaichulis, J. A., *Diseases Nervous System*, **9**, 248–60 (1948)
47. Meduna, L. J., and McCulloch, W. S., *Med. Clin. N. Amer.*, **29**, 147–51 (1945)
48. Meduna, L. J., *Oneirophrenia* (University of Illinois Press, Urbana, Ill., 390 pp., 1950)
49. Morgan, M. S., and Pilgrim, F. J., *Proc. Soc. Exptl. Biol. Med.*, **79**, 106–11(1952)
50. Jacobs, J. S. L., and Tempereau, C. E., *Arch. Neurol. Psychiat.*, **68**, 388–405 (1952)
51. Rosvold, H. E., Kaplan, S. J., and Stevenson, J. A. F., *Proc. Soc. Exptl. Biol. Med.*, **80**, 60–62 (1952)
52. Del Pozo, É. C., *Am. J. Physiol.*, **171**, 354–51 (1952)
53. Torda, C., and Wolf, H. G., *Am. J. Physiol.*, **168**, 406–13 (1952)
54. Torda, C., and Wolf, H. G., *Am. J. Physiol.*, **169**, 140–50 (1952)
55. Torda, C., and Wolf, H. G., *Am. J. Physiol.*, **169**, 150–58 (1952)
56. Berkeley, A. W., *J. Comp. Physiol. Psychol.*, **45**, 443–49 (1952)
57. Carr, W. J., *J. Comp. Physiol. Psychol.*, **45**, 377–80 (1952)
58. Siegel, P. S., and Taub, D. V., *J. Comp. Physiol. Psychol.*, **45**, 250–53 (1952)
59. Wishner, J., *J. Abnormal Social Psychol.*, **48**, 253–60 (1953)
60. Spence, K. W., and Farber, I. E., *J. Exptl. Psychol.*, **45**, 116–19 (1953)
61. Farber, I. E., and Spence, K. W., *J. Exptl. Psychol.*, 120–25 (1953)
62. Bitterman, M. E., and Holtzman, W. H., *J. Abnormal Social Psychol.*, **47**, 615–23 (1952)
63. Malmo, R. B., Davis, J. F., and Barza, S., *J. Personality*, **21**, 188–204 (1952)
64. Klein, G. S., and Krech, D., *J. Personality*, **21**, 118–48 (1952)
65. Lazarus, R. S., Yousem, H., and Arenberg, D., *J. Personality*, **21**, 312–28 (1953)
66. Semmes, J., *Psychol. Rev.*, **60**, 140–47 (1953)
67. Teuber, H., and Bender, M. B., *J. Gen. Psychol.*, **40**, 37–57 (1949)
68. Bender, M. B., and Teuber, H., *J. Psychol.*, **28**, 223–33 (1949)
69. Teuber, H., Bender, M. B., and Battersby, W. S., *Federation Proc.*, **9**, 125–26 (1950)
70. Wortis, S. B., Bender, M. B., and Teuber, H. L., *J. Nervous Mental Diseases*, **107**, 382–87 (1948)
71. Bender, M. B., and Teuber, H. L., *Progr. Neurol.*, **4**, 163–92 (1949)
72. Battersby, W. S., Teuber, H. L., and Bender, M. B., *J. Psychol.*, **35**, 329–51 (1953)
73. Marshall, C., Walker, E. A., and Livingston, S., *Arch. Neurol. Psychiat.*, **69**, 760–65 (1953)
74. Flanders, N. A., *Am. J. Psychol.*, **66**, 295–99 (1953)
75. Grings, W. A., *J. Psychol.*, **35**, 271–82 (1953)
76. Baker, L. M., and Taylor, W. M., *Am. J. Psychol.*, **66**, 124–25 (1953)
77. Barger, D. M., and Gebhard, J. W., *Am. J. Psychol.*, **65**, 450–57 (1952)

ABNORMALITIES OF BEHAVIOR[1]

By Jules H. Masserman, Zoltan Gross, and Curtis Pechtel
Department of Nervous and Mental Diseases, Northwestern University, Chicago, Illinois and the Downey Veterans Administration Hospital, Downey, Illinois

As in previous years, surveys of specialized literature in this field will be found in the *Annual Survey of Psychoanalysis* (42), the *American Journal of Psychiatry*, (3), *Progress in Neurology and Psychiatry* (135), and the *Year Book of Neurology and Psychiatry* (79). In the present chapter we shall attempt to integrate those experimental and clinical studies possessing general psychologic interest.

Experimental Investigations

Fixation and avoidance responses in animals.—Wilcoxon (150) found in a study of rats trained on the Lashley jumping apparatus under various conditions that partial reinforcement played a primary role in the development of stereotyped reactions, that such responses need not be considered abnormal, that they could easily be eliminated by training and that the data accorded so well with Hullian stimulus response theory as to render unnecessary Maier's concepts of "fixation habits." Bailey & Miller (7) taught 5 kittens and 12 cats to lift covers from food rewards and then shocked the animals to superimpose avoidance reactions. The latter were not affected by control injections of saline, but were mitigated by the administration of sodium amytal. The authors believe that amytal has a specific depressant effect on fear responses rather than acting like other hypnotics in disorganizing recently learned, complex and therefore relatively vulnerable patterns of behavior.

Physiologic correlates.—Beach (8) demonstrated in a comprehensive review of the field that psychosomatic responses can be elicited and studied advantageously in all species of animals. Mahl (82) in a special study of the physiologic concomitants of acute and chronic fear, measured gastric acidity and blood sugar levels in two monkeys at rest, in acute fear, and in chronic fear. Mahl's results were not in accord with Cannon's emergency theory, because in his data HCl secretion did not increase in response to acute stress but remained abnormally high during chronic fear, whereas the blood sugar level varied independently from the HCl.

Experimental neuroses.—Masserman & Pechtel (87) produced severe and persistent aberrations of behavior in monkeys by subjecting them to repeated conflicts between learned feeding patterns and apparently innate aversions to the appearance of a toy rubber snake. The experimental neuroses thus induced were characterized by inhibitions of feeding, generalized

[1] The survey of the literature to which this review pertains was completed in April, 1953.

phobias, gastrointestinal and cardiorespiratory dysfunctions, motor stereotypies or catalepsies, markedly increased homo- and autoeroticism, "hallucinatory" behavior (i.e., the animals would appear to seek and eat only imaginary pellets while avoiding real food), and marked changes of social conduct in relation to other animals or to the experimenter. The specific configurations of these patterns and the methods effective in individual and group therapy tended to vary with the species of monkey rather than with the nature or intensity of the trauma.

Wolpe (161) reported his observations on 12 cats subjected to grid shocks with or without learned feeding responses, and in general confirmed the results of similar experiments by previous workers. Nevertheless, he objects to Masserman's concepts of motivational conflict and Maier's thesis of "abnormal behavior fixations," and proposes instead that experimental neuroses are induced (*a*) by "ambivalent stimulation" arising from difficult discriminations, delay before reinforcement, or rapid reversals, and (b) "noxious stimuli" which interrupt learned responses. Wolpe postulates further that the specific patterns of the neurosis are learned and persist because the drives producing them are reduced by some degree of temporal and spatial escape from the anxiety-engendering stimulus. It may be noted, however, that these formulations eventuate in about the same procedures both for inducing and treating the neurotic deviations.

Masserman (86), in a review of the experimental data and basic concepts of biodynamics in relation to current tendencies to reintegrate biology, psychology, and medicine, concludes as follows:

This, then, is a summary . . . of a long series of experiments designed to analyze the biodynamics of behavior and to discern principles that would apply alike to "normal" and "abnormal" conduct, to animal and human subjects, and to experimental and clinical therapy. The gap between the responses of cats, dogs or monkeys in cages and the conduct of man in society is undeniably wide; certainly man, of all creatures, has developed the greatest facility in experiential association and integration, the highest capacity for symbolic, verbal and other imagery, and the most elaborate repertoire of "normal," "neurotic" and "psychotic" behavior patterns in a constantly changing social and cultural milieu. And yet, as elsewhere in medicine, the best way to unravel an especially complex problem is to take it into the laboratory as well as the clinic, investigate it by specially designed experiments, check their results with a rigid self-discipline that eliminates subtle errors and cherished preconceptions, and so advance bit by bit toward clearer formulations of general principles and more pertinent applications of them. In psychiatry, such experimental and operational approaches, when correlated with clinical practice, may not only dissolve the verbal barriers among the various schools and methods but may also foster a needed rapprochement between psychiatry on one hand and scientific medicine and the humanities on the other.

THE NEUROSES

Nosology.—During 1952 the fourth revision of the *Diagnostic and Statistical Manual of Mental Disorders* (109) was prepared by the Committee on Nomenclature and Statistics, American Psychiatric Association, and published in official form. A number of important changes in the etiologic and diagnostic concepts of various behavior disorders embodied in this manual may be reviewed as follows.

The new classification of mental disorders is proposed because (*a*) "only about 10 per cent of the total cases seen in the Armed Services fell into any of the categories ordinarily seen in public mental hospitals" (p. vi), and (*b*) two interim revisions (of the last official edition) by the Army and by the Veterans Administration had not proved completely satisfactory. The current manual explicitly (p. 9)

> recognizes the present day descriptive nature of all psychiatric diagnoses, and attempts to make possible the gathering of data for future clarification of ideas concerning etiology, pathology, prognosis and treatment in mental disorders . . . (and) for inclusion of new ideas and advances . . . without radical revision of the system of nomenclature.

In general, the manual fulfills these purposes, although there is little apparent logic of organization or codification in some of the proposed revisions. For example, on p. 92 the heading "††328 Chronic brain syndrome NOS" is inexplicably followed by a coequal heading "*321.1 Passive dependency* (†† includes passive-aggressive personality)," but nowhere is there any explanation of the system of coding, nor could a cryptographer of only ordinary skill divine the principles employed. Again, many specific sounding diagnostic distinctions without operational differences are retained: thus, "Psychoneurotic disorders (*310–318*, ††*328*) with or without somatizations, are listed separately from disorders of "Character, behavior and intelligence (*320–326*, ††*327*, ††*328*)" with no explanation as to how one could be neurotic without "a disorder of behavior" as the only index of disturbances either in "intelligence" or "character." Moreover, some of the proposed definitions lean too heavily on psychoanalytic or psychosomatic tenets that are as yet far from being sufficiently clear or valid. Thus, on p. 29, it is asserted that "psychophysiologic autonomic and visceral disorders . . . represent the visceral expression of affect which may be thereby largely prevented from being conscious," whereas the criteria used to differentiate organ neuroses from conversion, (itself a dubious dynamic concept) are that organ neuroses (*a*) involve the autonomic rather than the voluntary nervous system, (*b*) do not relieve anxiety, (*c*) are "physiologically rather than symbolically" determined, and (*d*) result in the "frequent production of structural changes which may threaten life." Somewhat less dogmatic but still controversial is the new taxonomy of the psychoneuroses, which are subclassified according to the manner in which "anxiety is . . . expressed . . . or controlled by various psychological defense mechanisms": e.g., dissociation, conversion, phobias, or depression. Under the "Personality Trait Disturbance" (another original category) various time-worn ambiguities (e.g., "Emotionally unstable personality") are also preserved; in this rubric, too, the new term "sociopath" (which replaces the epithetic psychopath) now includes the subtypes of antisocial, dyssocial, sex deviate, and drug addict. Supposedly cyclic disorders of behavior formerly termed manic depressive psychoses are more appropriately termed affective reactions with manic, depressed, and other manifestations. Even more boldly, the categorical diagnosis of schizophrenia has been discarded in favor of schizophrenic reactions, with acute undifferentiated, chronic undifferentiated, schizo-affective, childhood, and residual forms in addition to the usual hebephrenic, catatonic, and paranoid subtypes. Neurasthenia and hypochondriasis have, at long last, been eliminated altogether as disease entities, a loss to patients and physicians who long used them as convenient euphemisms, but a boon to more conscientious nosologists. The two most novel proposals in the new nomenclature, however, are these: first, to make the diagnosis of "mental deficiency" subsidiary to "chronic brain syndromes" with a primarily organic causation, and second, the addition of one of four phrases: "x1 with psychotic reaction," "x2 with neurotic reaction," "x3 with behavioral reaction," and "x4 with mental deficiency" to any diagnoses which need to be so modified. Finally, the manual incorporates the Army and Veterans Administration practice of adding specific notations as to the following: (*a*) external precipitating stress, (*b*) premorbid personality and predisposition, and (*c*) the degree of psychiatric impairment, i.e., minimal, mild, moderate, or severe.

Each of these changes will, no doubt, be approved and decried for different reasons by almost equal numbers of specialists in the field. Those trained in traditional nosology may be horrified by the progressive departures from the Kraepelinian system; others more dynamically inclined may point out that the manual still retains terms like psychoneurotic, cyclothymic, or for that matter neurotic and psychotic, the meanings of which, obscure enough originally, have become even more confused by decades of deviant interpretations. Nevertheless, many sections of the manual evince clear thinking, hard work, and reasonable compromise among conflicting tenets in the field; for this, Dr. George N. Raines, Chairman of the Committee, and his colleagues have earned the gratitude of all who for research and clinical purposes must attempt to classify the protean aberrations of human behavior.

Unfortunately, the nosologic confusion that the manual attempts to correct is still evident in much of the literature. Thus, Liber (74) attacks the term "neurosis" on the grounds that it encourages "loose thinking" in psychiatry and is too often used to cover errors in medical diagnosis. Similarly, Bowman & Rose (13) deplore the use of the phrase "sexual psychopath," whereas objections are also raised by Ascher (5) against the diagnosis of "neurotic depression" and by Weiss (147) against "neurocirculatory asthenia." Conversely, Cohen *et al.* (23) accept "neurocirculatory asthenia" and attempt to ascertain its "familial prevalence" whereas Wilson (153) describes still another "neurosis of everyday living" characterized by an "unconscious exaggeration of normal social patterns" such as race prejudice. Friedman (41) believes that neurotic patients may be distinguished from psychotic in that the actual or the screen memories of childhood in the neurotic group show neither a loss of personal identity nor a marked fear of such loss.

Interviewing.—In a comprehensive manual Menninger (90) gives detailed directions for various techniques of examining patients and their families, for recording case histories, and for planning therapy. Masserman (85) offers a briefer set of suggestions to aid the general practitioner in the essential psychosomatic supplementation of his methods of history taking, physical examination, and differential diagnosis, and Whitehorn (149) discusses anew the diagnostic and therapeutic psychodynamics of various interviewing techniques. In this connection Cameron (18) and Karnosh & Quinn (65) point out that of all the neuroses encountered in private practice anxiety states are the most frequent, the most easily diagnosed, and the most amenable to skillfully directed therapy.

Research Studies in Diagnosis

Physiologic.—Persky *et al.* (101) studied the excretions of hippuric acid after the administration of sodium benzoate to three groups of adults: normal, those exhibiting free anxiety, and those diagnosed as catatonic schizophrenics. When the normals were exposed to transient stresses of moderate severity, their hippuric output did not vary markedly; in contrast, the subjects with anxiety showed an increased average excretion correlated directly with the intensity of the affect, whereas the catatonics showed the lowest excretory rate with a tendency toward normal levels as the patients' behavioral status improved. Hemphill *et al.* (52) report that adult female patients in anxiety states feel fatigue more easily and have a lower perceptual sensitivity to pain than do patients with endogenous depressions. Seitz & Shipley (127) believe that there are demonstrable relationships between thoughts expressed by a patient and specific changes in his psychogalvanic skin responses as recorded continuously during a clinical interview; however, to one acquainted with the technical pitfalls of PGR determinations the correlations may appear to be questionable.

Psychologic.—A number of investigators have been interested in determining the effects of anxiety on various physiological and psychological processes. In some studies anxiety was presumably induced by the threat of mild shock or the necessity of scoring adequately on a test; in other instances persons who have in some way been diagnosed as anxious were compared with a normal population. Thus, Taylor & Spence (141) after choosing populations differentiated as extremes on the scale of Taylor's special test of anxiety and comparing the two groups in serial learning performance, found that anxious subjects were significantly inferior to the controls in learning competing responses (see also the chapter on Personality).

Psychosomatic Dysfunctions

Owen (139), in a recent symposium points out that localized somatic lesions often have broad "holosomatic" effects, and that physicians who treat only the local lesion will fail if they neglect its total setting. Dewan (139) states that mild depressions may simulate peripheral disease and that symptoms arising from anxiety about a particular organ must be differentiated from symptoms attributable to structural alterations in that organ. Williamson (139) notes in this connection that most complaints about heart-trouble in general practice are a result of cardiac neuroses, whereas Mac-

Donald (139) contends that illness and dependency would diminish among older people if our society did not encourage their early retirement. Prick & Calon (106) derive psychsomatic illness from an underlying neurosis, and add that infantile effects and impulses determine the organic area to be involved. Pearlman (99) adds that such illnesses may be used to maintain a comfortable equilibrium in which the patient gratifies covert dependent and narcissistic needs which would otherwise not be consciously acceptable. As to specific psychosomatic reactions, Abramson (1) acknowledges the allergic basis of bronchial asthma but insists that its intensity and persistence is maintained in an appreciable number of patients by unconscious conflicts. Fowler & Zeckel (37) report that common neurotic patterns and precipitating factors were found in a group of 23 patients with Ménière's disease; conversely Tissenbaum *et al.* (144) warn that Parkinson's syndrome, multiple sclerosis, and expanding brain lesions have often been initially misdiagnosed as psychiatric disorders.

Etiology of the Neuroses

Childhood experiences.—Spitz (136) reiterates the thesis that when congenital disease and other known physical factors are eliminated, the mother-child relationship is a major factor in the etiology of psychogenic diseases in infancy. Wolff & Bayer (160) believe that parents overly concerned with the infant's bodily functions may encourage later somatizations of neurotic symptoms. Johnson & Szurek (61) state that parents may unwittingly and also for vicarious gratification seduce the child to act out their own poorly integrated or forbidden impulses, thus establishing in the child superego defects which duplicate those of the parents. Wulff (162) and Sandford (123) likewise comment on the similarity of childhood neurotic symptoms and adult neuroses and attempt to explain the resemblance in conformity with standard psychoanalytic theory. Jackson *et al.* (59) note that children well adjusted to a favorable family environment show less emotional trauma when hospitalized. Johnson & Szurek (61) differentiate between neurotically hostile aggression in children and biologic "aggressiveness," a term which these and other writers seem to confuse with initiative. Sager (121), on the other hand, contends that aggressive behavior is always a reaction to injury or frustration and is not itself an instinct.

Prevention of Neuroses

Scheidlinger (124), Joseph *et al.* (64), and Luton (77) again point out the need for early recognition and control of neurotic processes through the practice of mental hygiene in schools, special clinics, and community programs. Bettelheim (12) and Sontag *et al.* (134) repeat the familiar theme that preventive psychiatry must deal with the factors that impair every child's ability to master his inner conflicts and the tasks imposed by society. In more general reviews, Coleman *et al.* (24) describe the advantages of the team-work approach in treating the child and its parents simultaneously, and Bender (9) outlines the various techniques, ranging from investigations of form perception to the development of group relationships which she has utilized with thousands of problem children at Bellevue Hospital. Arthur (4) asserts that only psychoanalysis can make conscious the repressed determinants of behavior disorders in children; however, without defining his concept of psychoanalysis, Arthur admits that nonanalytic therapy of both the parents and the child can be effective in alleviating undesirable patterns of conduct.

Hulse (56) reverts to the notion, long ago modified even in Freudian theory, that sexual frustration may be the primary cause of tension and anxiety, and therefore believes that the general practitioner should advise his neurotic patients to permit themselves greater freedom in conjugal relationships, apparently as a measure of mental hygiene.

Psychopathy and social deviation.—Sturup (138) points out that criminality is only an expression of society's rejection of the patient's form of conduct, as determined by his unique constitutional, psychophysical, cultural, and social background. The solution of the problem of deviations of behavior must therefore lie in a rapprochement of the two norms, though this is admittedly a difficult and often impossible condition. Nevertheless, Weber (146) believes that if the psychopath could be reached by intensive psychotherapy before late adolescence, sufficient advantage could be taken of his capacity for genuine affection and his tendency to identify with strong leaders to make the prognosis for social readjustment relatively favorable.

Therapy of the Neuroses

Jackman & Schorr (58), basing their conclusions on 25 cases, report that carbon dioxide inhalations are effective in decreasing anxiety, introspection, and conflict, and compare the method to a "chemical frontal lobotomy." However, Freeman (39) points out that in both ether and carbon dioxide therapy, unconscious dynamic forces are involved and must be assessed in the results.

Drug therapy.—Miller (92) employed 120 to 220 mg. of amobarbital sodium (amytal sodium; sodium 5-ethyl-5-isoamylbarbituric acid) in 20 to 25 cc. of 10 to 15 per cent ethyl alcohol intravenously for ambulatory narcoanalysis and reports that alcohol appears to counteract the unwanted side effects of the barbiturate and to facilitate verbal and affective release. Masserman & Pechtel (88) could demonstrate no beneficial effects of mephenesin (3-otoloxy-1, 2 propanediol) on neurotic animals; nevertheless Paul (98) reports relief of anxiety and tension in 26 of 30 neurotic patients given this drug and postulates that it produces muscle relaxation without hypnotic effects by acting on spinal internuncial neurons. Hill *et al.* (53) conclude that morphine reduces the disruptive effects on performance produced by the anticipation of pain.

Hormonal.—Brody (17) reports that cortisone and ACTH therapy may exacerbate adverse emotional responses ordinarily repressed in the absence of adrenal overstimulation. Lidz *et al.* (75) believe that the euphoria sometimes observed during ACTH therapy is in large part attributable to the relief of physical distress and may, as Hollender (54) warns, lead to addiction. Conversely Braceland (14) notes that anxiety and depression may supervene if the patient had unconsciously regarded his previous invalidism as a neurotic advantage.

Psychotherapy.—The literature in this field for 1952 fell mainly under the rubric of technical discussions of psychoanalytic technique, as reviewed by Saslow in this volume. Alexander & Ross (2) once again question the spurious dichotomies between so-called (*a*) psychoanalytic or deep as opposed to (*b*) superficial or brief techniques, and advocate instead more valid distinctions among (i) stereotyped and inefficient as contrasted with (ii) more skillful and effective methods of therapy.

Rennecker & Cutler (113), extending psychosomatic postulates to one extreme, recommend that in the therapy of cancer of the breast in women the patient's libido be mobilized to combat the illness. In practice, this is facilitated by complete candor leavened with emphasis on prognostically favorable factors and sympathetic aid in resolving her sexual, familial, and social anxieties. Relevant to such utilization of transference is Brewster's (15) reminder that dependent patients under intensive psychotherapy may suffer disruptive "separation reactions" during interruptions of their analysis.

Hypnotherapy.—Schenck (125) treated a patient with zoophobia by controlling anxiety through posthypnotic amnesias, and Paley (96) reports five cases of chronic alcoholism in which short term hypnosis encouraged "psychic surrender" and facilitated insight. Rosen (120) advocates hypnotherapy as a means of inducing emotional abreactions in patients who would otherwise be repressed and resistant; however, Rosen, apparently in accord with Bernheim's dictum "it is a wise hypnotist who knows who is hypnotizing whom," warns against the danger of participating too freely in the patient's fantasies. Finally, Reid & Finesinger (112) discuss insight in psychotherapy and discard the usual dichotomy of intellectual versus emotional understanding. Instead, they distinguish the following forms: (*a*) generic, i.e., "any cognitive act by which we grasp the significance of some pattern of relations," (*b*) neutral, which denotes intellectual understanding without affective discharge, and (*c*) dynamic, which alone is capable of inducing lasting therapeutic effects by objective and operational standards. It is not at all necessary that an interpretation be true to be effective; it need only be believed. However, in the authors' words, in some patients even this would only be adding "insight to injury."

Abnormal Behavior in Military Settings

Selection and performance.—According to Peterson & Chambers (102) only the helplessly dependent or aggressively immature need be excluded from service, since other neurotic characteristics are often compatible with military efficiency. Potter (104) studied 174 men separated from the Navy for unsuitability and concluded that although a large number of them had enlisted to escape an intolerable situation or were looking for excitement and adventure, there were no constant patterns in such individuals that would preclude their induction. Brill & Beebe (16) likewise point out that many men who seemed well adjusted in civilian life break down in combat, whereas others known to be neurotic functioned well; therefore, only those who clearly demonstrate an inability to adjust after a trial in service need be discharged.

Combat neuroses.—Wilkinson *et al.* (151) attribute the prolonged latent period of combat neuroses to the tendency of the soldier, for reasons of pride or group morale, to deny his anxiety and fatigue until he has reached the breaking point. Futterman & Pumpian-Mindlin (44) hold that the high frequency of traumatic war neuroses among rear echelon military personnel and immobilized combatants occurs because of their inability to discharge through motor activity the emotional reactions elicited by warfare. In other cases, war neuroses often involve guilt about assaulting or killing defenseless enemy personnel.

Reactions of prisoners of war.—Nardini, (94) on the basis of his personal observations during three and one-half years as a prisoner-of-war in the Philippines and Japan, states that survival depended upon the following factors: strong motivation for life with courageous exertion of will, good general intelligence, a hardy constitution, the cultivation of emotional indifference or a well-managed and balanced sensitivity, a sense of humor, the maintenance of obligations to others, a controlled fantasy life, successful active or passive resistance to the captors, pragmatic opportunism, the self-discipline retained from preceding years in the armed services, and plenty of luck.

Military psychoses.—Ripley & Wolf (116), who studied schizophrenic reactions in combat areas, conclude that some schizophrenic individuals functioned well in the Army despite psychopathologic symptoms for long periods prior to their acute episodes.

Military therapy.—Peterson & Chambers (102) state that the aims of military psychotherapy in the armed services are not different from those in civilian life, but that methods and approaches must be realistically adapted to the military situation. Chapman (20) outlines some of the special problems of psychiatric practice in a Naval Recruit Training Center, among which are the short period available for diagnosis and therapy, the difficulty of establishing rapport because of differences in rank between physician and patient, the absence of ancillary supporting figures such as the patient's family or friends, and the undeniable secondary gain of the neurosis. Grant (48) describes the methods employed in retraining individuals who would otherwise be discharged because of unsuitability: the patient's maladaptations to military regulations and relationships are sympathetically explored, but every effort is made to foster growth and maturity in an atmosphere of understanding; the inductee is taught to conform with certain basic rules of conduct by the use of moderate discipline when necessary, but individual privileges and group status are concurrently employed as incentives. By such means 59 per cent of 4,800 Navy, Marine, and Coast Guard personnel confined at a retraining command were returned to active duty, whereas without such treatment all would have been separated on grounds of unsuitability. Wolfe (159), for similar reasons, urges greater use of group psychotherapy in the treatment of Naval personnel. However, Peterson & Chambers (102) and Brill & Beebe (16) point out that the burden of guilt that a soldier feels when evacuated from combat for neurotic reasons may be additionally disruptive, whereas a discharge for psychoneurosis may seriously impair the individual's ability to readjust in civil life.

Postcombat.—Noble *et al.* (95) found a high incidence of psychiatric disability on the orthopedic and plastic surgical wards of a military hospital and suggest that the recognition and early handling of the emotional problems of wounded men can facilitate surgical management and reduce the possibility of later psychiatric illness. Schwartz & Inwood (126) found that 65 per cent of the psychiatric casualties evacuated from Korea to the United States were returned to duty in this country and therefore express optimism regarding the results of psychiatric treatment based on principles learned in World War II.

Civil defense.—Drayer (28) states that the principles of military psychiatry are equally applicable to civilian defense, but believes that it is premature to talk of psychiatric methods in this field when the civil defense program is as yet so inadequately conceived and its chance of being effective so pitifully small.

THE PSYCHOSES

For theoretical and speculative discussions of the psychoses the reader is again referred to the reviews listed in the introductory paragraph of this chapter. In the remaining sections we shall confine our discussion to literature dealing with (*a*) "process" research on the etiology, nature, and clinical expression of the protean abnormalities of behavior usually termed psychotic, and (*b*) clinical investigations of the techniques and results of various methods of therapy.

Process Oriented Research

This year's experimental work in psychopathology ranges from traditional univariate investigations (145) to those which attempt to incorporate personal values into perceptual and reactive functions. Five studies in the latter area deserve special mention because they represent newer orientations to research in abnormal psychology.

Rausch (110) and Sanders & Pacht (122), investigating the effects of the psychotic process on the perception of size, report that patients tended to overestimate the size of the stimulus objects, a phenomenon attributed in both instances to the effects of compensation. However, Rausch (110) speaks of "compensating for threats to the stability of the individual's ego structure" and Sanders & Pacht (122) speak of compensation "for the decrease in the visual angle," a postulate not as yet integrated with the concept of "ego structure." These studies, however, point to the possibility of developing correlations between perception of size and the more complex patterns ordinarily subsumed under "ego structure." Also in the area of perceptual functions, Roseman (119) and McGinnies & Adornetto (78) interpret their results in terms of the dynamics of other personality variables.

If the recent work by Postman, Bronson & Gropper (103) on the manipulation of recognition thresholds of taboo words can be generalized to other perceptual phenomena, it would appear that the problem of personality organization resolves itself into problems of set or attention. This is in accord with the suggested orientations of Shakow (129) and Hebb (51) and with the expectancy theories of Postman *et al.* (103). In this context one should also note Huston & Senf's (57) study of attention disturbances in schizophrenia and depression.

Pascal & Swensen's (97) work on the learning process in mentally ill patients supports Shakow's (129) position that schizophrenia may produce impairment in performance, but not in ability or capacity. Other investigators (25, 27, 31, 78) this year have also reported that the performance of psychotic patients is more variable than the performance of the normal controls and that this variability reflects the operation of selective perceptual mechanisms consistent with the organization of the patient but not necessarily with the stimulus situation. If this is true it would seem reasonable to postulate a specific form of schizophrenic organization rather than disorganization. Studies such as those of Eriksen & Lazarus (30) and Laffal (72) contain suggestions as to how this dynamic structure of the psychoses may be investigated by selected methods specially attuned to the pathologic process.

Factor analytic studies.—Another trend this year in experimental psychopathology has been the increasing use of factor analytic techniques. For example, Eysenck's (31, 32) work points to a productive application of objective laboratory methods to the problems of differential diagnosis, with only a minimal attempt to define or specify the psychological properties of psychosis. However, in Eysenck's discussions, as in those of Crown (26) and of Pullen & Stagner (107), the performance of patients on assigned tasks is not correlated with the dynamics of their psychoses and evidence supporting the hypothesis of differential specificity is given a great deal of attention while contradictory evidence is given too little consideration. This is particularly true of Pullen & Stagner's study in which eight of nine tests are explicitly designed to measure rigidity and the ninth to measure intelligence. After the correlation matrix was rotated, a rigidity factor and an intelligence factor were extracted without allowance for the fact that four of the tests which before rotation were supposed to measure rigidity were later interpreted to tap intelligence. While it is true that the rigidity tests had loadings similar to the Wechsler-Bellevue comprehension, arithmetic, and similarities tests, it is not clear as to why flicker-fusion overlap is taken as a measure of intelligence. Even were such a relationship to be based on Halstead's (50) thesis of biological capacity, the correlations between biological and psychological intelligence would still remain unclear, and the extent to which these factors generalize beyond the specific tests employed would remain undetermined.

Projective.—Ritter & Eron (117) attempted to set up statistical criteria to differentiate normal from other populations by the use of the Thematic Apperception Test. The authors found that when formal and content variations were combined in a single score the nonnormal populations were clearly differentiated from the normal on the basis of deviant responses, although certain normal responses occurred in both groups. Mussen & Krauss (93) employed the Szondi test on a group of students who had been diagnosed neurotic in a university neuropsychiatric clinic, as contrasted with a control group who had never felt the need for psychiatric help; despite Susan Deri's claims they found the test of little diagnostic or prognostic value. McKinnon's (80) concluding sentences are applicable in this context.

> Knowledge is the result of playing with what we know, that is, with our facts. A knowledgeable person in science is not, as we are often wont to think, merely one who has an accumulation of facts, but rather one who has the capacity to have sport with what he knows, giving creative rein to his fancy in changing his world of phenomenal appearance into a world of scientific constructs (p. 145).

Trends and Omissions

Two additional lines of thinking and experimentation have been developed on the thesis that the functions which most consistently differentiate psychotic individuals from nonpsychotics are primarily intellective or cognitive ones. These have been (*a*) our rapidly expanding knowledge of neurophysiology, particularly the work reported this year by Penfield (100), Jasper (60), and Magoun (81) and (*b*) a renewed interest in neuropsychologic correlations. Kubie (71), for instance, attempts to integrate psychoanalytic constructs with neurophysiological processes, but admits that such formulations remain essentially vague as to the relationship of motivation, memory, and symbolism to neural organizations. Malmo *et al.* (83) also apply Hebbian principles of neuropsychologic synthesis to the therapy of a case of hysterical deafness. While it is true that this kind of theorizing has not as yet led to definitive formulations, the concepts of cell assemblies, dynamic system families, neural feedback, resonancies, etc., may eventually be correlated meaningfully with determining tendencies, sets, expectancies, and other terms relevant to the molar dynamics of behavior.

Psychologic Factors in Diagnosis and Therapy

Diagnosis.—Comprehensive reviews on personality questionnaires by Ellis (29), on methodology by Berg (11), and on prognosis by Windle (155) highlight the difficulties and the disheartening results obtained from the use of standard clinical tools in attempts to sharpen differential diagnostic criteria. This year's literature, in general, confirms White's (148) observation that psychologists are losing interest in the re-examination of the classical nosological categories. For instance, the studies of Geist (46), Wittenborn &

Weiss (158), and Cohen (21) indicate that although various factors may be rotated out of correlation tables of ratings or test scores, they have relatively little relationship to the commonly accepted criteria for classifying a particular patient in one or another of the currently accepted categories. True, Guertin (49), in an analysis of symptom ratings, extracted three factors labeled paranoia, hebephrenia, and withdrawal; however, Wittenborn & Bailey (156) and Wittenborn & Weiss (158), using essentially the same techniques, did not distinguish these factors and were unable to differentiate involution psychosis or manic depressive manics from other psychiatric groups. Mehlman (89) and Forer *et al.* (36), with special regard to the Rorschach, likewise present data which further justify general dissatisfaction as to meaningfulness of current psychiatric diagnosis. In many cases behavior changes may be observed to vanish in the protocols of the tests, either because: (*a*) the underlying structure of various psychoses is roughly the same and is so reflected in the diagnostic instruments or, (*b*) these instruments are not sufficiently sensitive to discriminate different processes. The latter is true in the studies of Winder (154)and Rausch (110) in which they were able to distinguish between paranoid and nonparanoid patients. Similarly, Theisen (142) employed five pathological Rorschach patterns supposed to discriminate normal subjects statistically from schizophrenic patients, yet found that 51.6 per cent of schizophrenic patients showed no pathological signs. In view of such large lacunae in the diagnostic sieve, the relationship of psychotic processes to Rorschach patterns remains questionable.

Another study this year substantiates Siipola's (132) observations that subjects respond primarily to the interaction of characteristics within the stimulus objects rather than being affected by isolated factors; Sanders & Pacht (122) point out that the interaction among variables (i.e., color sequence interactions) rather than the variables taken singly produces significant results in distinguishing between normal and schizophrenic patients.

Evaluation.—A survey of the year's work on evaluation and treatment indicates: (*a*) that our standard psychological tests do not show improvement in psychological structure after therapy despite clinically favorable changes; (*b*) that in the majority of instances the criteria used to assay therapeutic progress have not been remarkably successful in differentiating patient groups or in predicting behavior; and (*c*) that there is increasing need of restudying past criteria by methods of cross validation and validity generalization. Appeals in the latter regard are forcefully made by Windle (155), and by Auld & Eron (6) who failed to confirm clinical predictions derived from the formula developed by Kotov & Meadow (69).

The testing programs conducted in psychiatric institutions on the comparative effects of various therapies present essentially the same picture of indeterminacy. Jones & Peters (63) conclude that tests which are more sensitive to overt behavior detect alterations after therapy which are indicative of improvement, whereas isolated Rorschach variables show no significant changes in basic personality processes. Because of a growing dissatisfaction with standard psychologic tests for the evaluation of psychotherapy, there seems to be an increasing use of behavior rating scales for this purpose. Wittenborn and his co-workers (157), Guertin (49), and Rackow *et al.* (108) exemplify this trend, but Kubie (70), in his discussion of the values and uses of rating scales points out quite forcefully that the external behavior of the patient may tell us relatively little about his underlying personality structure, a position illustrative of Adolph Meyer's definition of psychoanalytic theory as "the cult of the something else." Nevertheless in the present state of our knowledge it appears that information provided by relatively objective rating scales must continue to be given proper heuristic weight in much of our clinical research.

Prognosis.—Holzberg & Belmont (55) found that out of 45 predicted common factors in the Rorschach and the Wechsler-Bellevue, only four predictions were supported at a statistically significant level and two merely approached significance. Similarly, Filmer-Bennett (35) and Rogers & Hammond (118) were unable to find definite prognostic signs in their Rorschach results. In contrast, Stotsky (137) reports reliable findings with both the Wechsler-Bellevue and the Rorschach. Freeman (40) tested the Malamud-Sands Rating Scale as a prognostic indicator of the effects of lobotomy and concluded that those patients likely to benefit from other forms of treatment were also favorable candidates for the lobotomy operation. Similar conclusions were drawn by Feldman (33) in his use of the profiles from the Minnesota Multiphasic Personality Inventory for the prognosis and evaluation of shock therapies, again indicating the possibility of utilizing such findings as a more reasonable basis for developing a treatment oriented nosology than the descriptive diagnostic categories now employed. However, in his review of the field, Windle (155) emphasizes the necessity for careful cross validation of such prognostic signs before accepting the findings of any particular study and suggests the organization of a general psychological research exchange which would facilitate coordination in this area of research.

Social Evaluations

Etiology.—The year produced few detailed investigations of the social psychology of the psychosis in relation to their treatment. Mark (84) studied the attitudes of the mothers of male schizophrenic patients and Redlich *et al.* (111) conducted a demographic study in this field, but no specific conclusions were derived as to the characteristics or the functions of social groups in relation to individual conduct.

Social therapy.—Caudill *et al.* (19) report the experiences of a participant observer on a ward of neurotic patients undergoing treatment and stress the importance of group therapeutic orientation. Rioch & Stanton (115) also discuss various factors in *milieu* therapy and support Sewall, Gillin & LeBar (128) in their appeal for an analysis of the impact of the hospital on the patient. It has been a widely held belief that institutionalization has a deleterious effect on the ability of many patients to make adequate adjustments outside the hospital, yet few attempts have been made to understand the specific intramural factors that produce these effects. Recent reports by

Galioni, Adams & Tallman (45), Sines, Lucero & Kamman (133), and Miller & Clancy (91) on improvements in hospital attitudes and regimen confirm their favorable effects on the behavior of many patients, but again such correlations remain impressionistic. It is in the relatively controlled microcosm of the hospital that such reciprocal relationships between the individual and his social environment can be studied in psychological depth, configuration, and detail; the knowledge so derived may perhaps then be applied to urgent problems in extramural human affairs.

LITERATURE CITED

1. Abramson, H. A., *J. Am. Med. Assoc.*, **150,** 569–74 (1952)
2. Alexander, F., and Ross, H., *Dynamic Psychiatry* (University of Chicago Press, Chicago, Ill., 578 pp., 1952); Abstract in *J. Am. Med. Assoc.*, **149,** 1170 (1952)
3. *Am. J. Psychiat.*, **110** (1953)
4. Arthur, H., *Am. J. Orthopsychiat.*, **22,** 484–98 (1952)
5. Ascher, E., *Am. J. Psychiat.*, **108,** 901–8 (1952)
6. Auld, F., Jr., and Eron, L. D., *J. Consulting Psychol.*, **17,** 104–9 (1953)
7. Bailey, C. J., and Miller, N. E., *J. Comp. Physiol. Psychol.*, **45,** 205–8 (1952)
8. Beach, F. A., *Psychosomat. Med.*, **14,** 261–75 (1952)
9. Bender, L., *Child Psychiatric Techniques* (Charles C Thomas, Publisher, Springfield, Ill., 335 pp., 1952); Abstract in *J. Am. Med. Assoc.*, **149,** 1258 (1952)
11. Berg, I. A., *J. Clin. Psychol.*, **8,** 46–50 (1952)
12. Bettelheim, B., *Am. J. Orthopsychiat.*, **22,** 76–88 (1952)
13. Bowman, K. M., and Rose, M., *Am. J. Psychiat.*, **109,** 177–82 (1952)
14. Braceland, F. J. (Personal communication)
15. Brewster, H. H., *Psychosomat. Med.*, **14,** 154 (1952)
16. Brill, N. Q., and Beebe, G. W., *U. S. Armed Forces Med. J.*, **3,** 15–33 (1952)
17. Brody, S., *Psychosomat. Med.*, **14,** 94–99 (1952)
18. Cameron, D. E., *Can. Med. Assoc. J.*, **66,** 1–6 (1952)
19. Caudill, W., Redlich, F. C., Gilmore, H. R., and Brody, E. B., *Am. J. Orthopsychiat.*, **22,** 314–34 (1952)
20. Chapman, A. H., *U. S. Armed Forces Med. J.*, **3,** 805–9 (1952)
21. Cohen, J., *J. Consulting Psychol.*, **16,** 272–77 (1952)
23. Cohen, M. E., Badal, D. W., Kilpatrick, A., Reed, E. W., White, P. D., *Am. J. Human Genetics*, **3,** 126–58 (1951)
24. Coleman, J. V., Holmes, E. H., Lord, J. P., Tulchin, S. H., Garrett, A., Anderson, H. H., Wickman, K. M., and Krug, O., *Am. J. Orthopsychiat.*, **22,** 1–51 (1952)
25. Cowen, E. L., Wiener, M., and Hess, J., *J. Consulting Psychol.*, **17,** 100–3 (1953)
26. Crown, S., *J. Consulting Psychol.*, **17,** 92–99 (1953)
27. Daston, P. G., King, G. F., and Armitage, S. G., *J. Consulting Psychol.*, **17,** 50–53 (1953)
28. Drayer, C. S., *Am. J. Psychiat.*, **109,** 259–61 (1952)
29. Ellis, A., *J. Consulting Psychol.*, **17,** 45–49 (1953)
30. Eriksen, C. W., and Lazarus, R. S., *J. Abnormal Social Psychol.*, **47,** 302–8 (1952)
31. Eysenck, H. J., *J. Personality*, **20,** 345–84 (1952)
32. Eysenck, H. J., *The Scientific Study of Personality* (George Routledge & Kegan Paul, Ltd., London, England, 320 pp., 1952)
33. Feldman, M. J., *J. Consulting Psychol.*, **16,** 376–82 (1952)
35. Filmer-Bennett, G., *J. Abnormal Social Psychol.*, **47,** 502–6 (1952)

36. Forer, B. R., Farberow, N. L., Meyer, M. M., and Tolman, R. S., *J. Projective Techniques*, **16**, 346–51 (1952)
37. Fowler, E. P., Jr., and Zeckel, A., *J. Am. Med. Assoc.*, **148**, 1265–68 (1952)
39. Freeman, T., *British J. Med. Psychol.*, **25**, 148–55 (1952)
40. Freeman, W., *Am. J. Psychiat.*, **109**, 595–602 (1953)
41. Friedman, A., *J. Child Psychiat.*, [3]**2**, 266–69 (1952)
42. Frosch, J., Ed., *Annual Survey of Psychoanalysis*, **1** (International Universities Press, Inc., New York, N. Y., 556 pp., 1950)
44. Futterman, S., and Pumpian-Mindlin, E., *Am. J. Psychiat.*, **108**, 401–8 (1951)
45. Galioni, E. F., Adams, F. H., and Tallman, F. F., *Am. J. Psychiat.*, **109**, 576–83 (1953)
46. Geist, H., *J. Clin. Psychol.*, **8**, 184–88 (1952)
48. Grant, J. D., *U. S. Armed Forces Med. J.*, **3**, 631–34 (1952)
49. Guertin, W. H., *J. Consulting Psychol.*, **16**, 371–75 (1952)
50. Halstead, W. C., *Brain and Intelligence* (University of Chicago Press, Chicago, Ill., 206 pp., 1947)
51. Hebb, D. O., *Organization of Behavior* (John Wiley & Sons, Inc., New York, N. Y., 335 pp., 1949)
52. Hemphill, R. E., Hall, K. R. L., and Crookes, T. G., *J. Mental Sci.*, **98**, 433–40 (1952); Abstract in *Dig. Neurol. Psychiat.*, **20**, 406 (1952)
53. Hill, H. E., Kornetsky, C. H., Flanary, H. G., and Wikler, A., *Arch. Neurol. Psychiat.*, **67**, 612–19 (1952)
54. Hollender, M. H., *Psychosomat. Med.*, **14**, 306–8 (1952)
55. Holzberg, J. D., and Belmont, L., *J. Consulting Psychol.*, **16**, 23–29 (1952)
56. Hulse, W. C., *J. Am. Med. Assoc.*, **150**, 846–49 (1952)
57. Huston, P. E., and Senf, R., *Am. J. Psychiat.*, **109**, 131–38 (1952)
58. Jackman, A. J., and Schorr, C. A., *J. Clin. Exptl. Psychopath.*, **13**, 17–30 (1952)
59. Jackson, K., Winkley, R., Faust, O., and Cermack, E., *J. Am. Med. Assoc.*, **149**, 1536–39 (1952)
60. Jasper, H., *Arch. Neurol. Psychiat.*, **67**, 145–54 (1952)
61. Johnson, A. M., and Szurek, S. A., *Psychoanal. Quart.*, **21**, 323–43 (1952)
63. Jones, F. D., and Peters, H. N., *J. Abnormal Social Psychol.*, **47**, 345–53 (1952)
64. Joseph, H., Thieman, A., and Hamilton, E., *Am. J. Orthopsychiat.*, **22**, 557–69 (1952)
65. Karnosh, L. J., and Quinn, T. W., *Cleveland Clin. Quart.*, **19**, 57–61 (1952)
69. Kotkov, B., and Meadow, A., *J. Consulting Psychol.*, **17**, 16–20 (1953)
70. Kubie, L. S., *Proceedings of the Second Research Conference on Psychosurgery* (Public Health Service Publication, No. 156, Govt. Print. Office, Washington, D. C., 116 pp., 1952)
71. Kubie, L. S., *Psychoanal. Quart.*, **22**, 21–68 (1953)
72. Laffal, J., *J. Abnormal Social Psychol.*, **47**, 454–62 (1952)
74. Liber, B., *N. Y. State J. Med.*, **52**, 1019–22 (1952)
75. Lidz, T., Carter, J. D., Lewis, B. I., and Surratt, C., *Psychosomat. Med.*, **14**, 368–77 (1952)
77. Luton, F. H., *J. Am. Med. Assoc.*, **150**, 529–31 (1952)
78. McGinnies, E., and Adornetto, J., *J. Abnormal Social Psychol.*, **47**, 833–37 (1952)
79. Mackay, R. P., Lewis, N. D. C., and Bailey, P., Eds., *Year Book of Neurology and Psychiatry* (Year Book Publishers, Inc., Chicago, Ill., 603 pp., 1952)
80. McKinnon, D. W., *Am. Psychologist*, **8**, 138–46 (1953)
81. Magoun, H. W., *Arch. Neurol. Psychiat.*, **67**, 145–54 (1952)

82. Mahl, G. F., *Psychosomat. Med.*, **14,** 182–210 (1952)
83. Malmo, R., Davis, J. F., and Barza, S., *J. Personality,* **21,** 189–204 (1952)
84. Mark, J. C., *J. Abnormal Social Psychol.*, **48,** 185–89 (1953)
85. Masserman, J. H., *Diseases of Nervous System,* **13,** 233–40 (1952)
86. Masserman, J. H., *J. Mt. Sinai Hosp., N. Y.*, **19,** 639–52 (1953)
87. Masserman, J. H., and Pechtel, C., *Ann. N. Y. Acad. Sci.*, **56,** 253–65 (1953)
88. Masserman, J. H., and Pechtel, C., Report to the Mental Hygiene Division of U. S. Public Health Service (1952)
89. Mehlman, B., *J. Abnormal Social Psychol.*, **47,** 577–78 (1952)
90. Menninger, K. A., *A Manual for Psychiatric Case Study* (Grune & Stratton, Inc., New York, N. Y., 355 pp., 1952)
91. Miller, D. H., and Clancy, J., *Psychiatry,* **15,** 435–43 (1952)
92. Miller, M. M., *Arch. Neurol. Psychiat.*, **67,** 620–24 (1952)
93. Mussen, P. H., and Krauss, S., *J. Abnormal Social Psychol.*, **47,** 399–405(1952)
94. Nardini, J. E., *Am. J. Psychiat.*, **109,** 241–48 (1952)
95. Noble, D., Roudebush, M. E., and Price, D., *Am. J. Psychiat.*, **108,** 495–99 (1952)
96. Paley, A., *Bull. Menninger Clin.*, **16,** 14–19 (1952)
97. Pascal, G. R., and Swensen, C., *J. Personality,* **21,** 240–49 (1952)
98. Paul, L., *Psychosomat. Med.*, **14,** 378–82 (1952)
99. Pearlman, J., *Bull. Menninger Clin.*, **16,** 92–97 (1952)
100. Penfield, W., *Arch. Neurol. Psychiat.*, **67,** 178–98 (1952)
101. Persky, H., Gamm, S. R., and Grinker, R. R., *Psychosomat. Med.*, **14,** 34–40 (1952)
102. Peterson, D. E., and Chambers, R. E., *Am. J. Psychiat.*, **109,** 249–54 (1952)
103. Postman, L., Bronson, W. C., and Gropper, G. L., *J. Abnormal Social Psychol.*, **48,** 215–24 (1953)
104. Potter, M. G., *U. S. Armed Forces Med. J.*, **2,** 1821–28 (1951)
106. Prick, J. J. G., and Calon, P., *Folia Psychiat., Neurol., Neurochir., Neerl.*, **55,** 129–36 (1952); Abstract in *Dig. Neurol. Psychiat.*, **20,** 349 (1952)
107. Pullen, M. S., and Stagner, R., *J. Consulting Psychol.*, **17,** 79–86 (1953)
108. Rackow, L. L., Napoli, P. J., Klebanoff, S. G., and Shillinger, A. A., *Am. J. Psychiat.*, **109,** 561–66 (1953)
109. Raines, G. N. *et al., Diagnostic and Statistical Manual of Mental Disorders* (Prepared by the Committee on Nomenclature and Statistics of the American Psychiatric Association, American Psychiatric Association Mental Hospital Service, Washington, D. C., 1952)
110. Rausch, H. L., *J. Personality,* **21,** 176–87 (1952)
111. Redlich, F. C., Hollingshead, A. B., Roberts, B. H., Robinson, H. A., Freedman, L. Z., and Myers, J. K., *Am. J. Psychiat.*, **109,** 729–34 (1953)
112. Reid, J. R., and Finesinger, J. E., *Am. J. Psychiat.*, **108,** 726–34 (1952)
113. Renneker, R., and Cutler, M., *J. Am. Med. Assoc.*, **148,** 833–38 (1952)
115. Rioch, D. M., and Stanton, A. H., *Psychiatry,* **16,** 65–72 (1953)
116. Ripley, H. S., and Wolf, S., *Am. J. Psychiat.*, **108,** 409–16 (1951)
117. Ritter, A. M., and Eron, L. D., *J. Abnormal Social Psychol.*, **47,** 147–57 (1952)
118. Rogers, L. S., and Hammond, K. R., *J. Counsulting Psychol.*, **17,** 8–15 (1953)
119. Roseman, M., *J. Personality,* **21,** 48–58 (1952)
120. Rosen, H., *Am. J. Psychiat.*, **109,** 120–27 (1952)
121. Sager, C. J., *Mental Hygiene,* **36,** 210–19 (1952)
122. Sanders, R., and Pacht, A. R., *J. Consulting Psychol.*, **16,** 440–44 (1952)
123. Sandford, N., *Brit. J. Med. Psychol.*, **25,** 2–15 (1952)

124. Scheidlinger, S., *Am. J. Orthopsychiat.*, **22,** 394–403 (1952)
125. Schneck, J. M., *J. Nervous Mental Disease*, **116,** 48–58 (1952)
126. Schwartz, L. A., and Inwood, E. R., *U. S. Armed Forces Med. J.*, **3,** 991–1002 (1952)
127. Seitz, P. F. D., and Shipley, R. E., *J. Invest. Dermatol.*, **19,** 49 (1952); Abstract in *J. Am. Med. Assoc.*, **150,** 1148 (1952)
128. Sewall, L. G., Gillin, J., and LeBar, F. M., *The Hospital from the Standpoint of the Patient* (Presented at meeting American Psychiatric Association, May, 1953)
129. Shakow, D., *The Nature of Deterioration in Schizophrenic Conditions* (Nervous and Mental Disease Monographs, No. 70, Nervous and Mental Disease Publishing Co., New York, N. Y., 88 pp., 1946)
132. Siipola, E., *J. Personality*, **19,** 358–82 (1950)
133. Sines, J. O., Lucero, R. J., and Kamman, G. R., *J. Clin. Psychol.*, **8,** 189–93 (1952)
134. Sontag, L. W., Crandall, V., and Lacey, J. I., *Am. J. Orthopsychiat.*, **22,** 534–41 (1952)
135. Spiegel, E. A., Ed., *Progress in Neurology and Psychiatry*, **7** (Grune & Stratton, Inc., New York, N. Y., 604 pp., 1952)
136. Spitz, R. A., *Psychoanal. Study of the Child*, **6,** 255–75 (1951)
137. Stotsky, B. A., *J. Abnormal Social Psychol.*, **47,** 489–96 (1952)
138. Sturup, G. K., *Brit. J. Med. Psychol.*, **25,** 31–38 (1952)
139. Symposium on Psychologic Aspects of Medicine, *Med. Clin. N. Amer.*, **36,** 445–592 (1952)
141. Taylor, J. A., and Spence, K. W., *J. Exptl. Psychol.*, **44,** 61–64 (1952)
142. Theisen, W. J., *J. Consulting Psychol.*, **16,** 365–70 (1952)
144. Tissenbaum, M. J., Harter, H. M., and Friedman, A. P., *J. Am. Med. Assoc.*, **147,** 1519–21 (1951)
145. *Twenty-seventh Annual Conference of the Milbank Memorial Fund: The Biology of Mental Health and Disease* (Paul B. Hoeber, Inc., New York, N. Y., 654 pp., 1952)
146. Weber, L. G., *J. Abnormal Social Psychol.*, **47,** 713–21 (1952)
147. Weiss, E., *Psychosomat. Med.*, **14,** 150 (1952)
148. White, R. W., *Ann. Rev. Psychol.*, **4,** 273–94 (1953)
149. Whitehorn, J. C., *J. Am. Med. Assoc.*, **148,** 329–34 (1952)
150. Wilcoxon, H. C., *J. Exptl. Psychol.*, **44,** 324–33 (1952)
151. Wilkinson, W. E., Sutherland, G. F., and Betts, W. C., *N. Carolina Med. J.*, **13,** 11–15 (1952)
153. Wilson, D. C., *Virginia Med. Monthly*, **79,** 264–68 (1952)
154. Winder, C. L., *J. Abnormal Social Psychol.*, **47,** 86–100 (1952)
155. Windle, C., *Psychol. Bull.*, **49,** 451–82 (1952)
156. Wittenborn, J. R., and Bailey, C., *J. Consulting Psychol.*, **16,** 13–17 (1952)
157. Wittenborn, J. R., Herz, M. I., Kurtz, J. H., Mandel, W., and Tatz, S., *J. Consulting Psychol.*, **16,** 107–9 (1952)
158. Wittenborn, J. R., and Weiss, M., *J. Consulting Psychol.*, **16,** 193–98 (1952)
159. Wolfe, E. L., *U. S. Armed Forces Med. J.*, **3,** 1195–1203 (1952)
160. Wolff, E., and Bayer, L. M., *Am. J. Orthopsychiat.*, **22,** 510–21 (1952)
161. Wolpe, J., *Brit. J. Psychol.*, **63,** 243–67 (1952)
162. Wulff, M., *Psychoanal. Study of the Child*, **6,** 169–79 (1951)

THEORY AND TECHNIQUES OF ASSESSMENT[1,2]

By E. Lowell Kelly

Department of Psychology, University of Michigan, Ann Arbor, Michigan

Many readers will be surprised to discover that this volume of the *Annual Review* contains no chapter on psychodiagnostics, and that this topic, together with the diagnostic aspects of counseling and the methodological aspects of personnel selection, have all been treated in a single chapter. The writer accepted the challenge of treating these formerly separate topics in a single chapter because of a conviction that although the essential problems confronting these several applied fields are the same, each has suffered in its development by the lack of acquaintance of workers in one with the orientation and methods of the others.

Whether the applied psychologist functions in the clinical, counseling, or industrial personnel field, he is faced with the necessity of evaluating individual subjects (patients, clients, or applicants) and characterizing them (by categories, types, test scores, profiles, or verbal personality formulations) for the purpose of doing something, saying something, or implying differential prediction of the future behavior of the subjects in another domain (adjustment, performance, etc.). In general, it would seem that the explicit recognition of this total assessment process has been greater among personnel psychologists than among clinicians, many of whom delimit their diagnostic function to making a "personality study" for the purpose of describing the personality dynamics of the patient or "arriving at a better understanding" of him. Presumably, however, the psychologist (or someone else who reads his report) utilizes the personality evaluation to make explicit or implicit predictions regarding the patient; in other words, the assessment is used in a manner which makes a difference in the disposition of the case or the treatment of the patient. Diagnosis that is not also prognostic would hardly seem defensible.

While personnel psychologists seem to have been somewhat more systematic in carrying assessment research through to its logical conclusion by testing their predictions against life criteria, they seem to have been far less imaginative and creative in the construction of new types of tests and test items which might add measurably to the accuracy of their predictions. Clinicians and personality psychologists on the other hand, while more

[1] This summary is based primarily on references published between June 1952 and May 1953, with an occasional reference to earlier background studies. Because of the scope of the topic, the reviewer has been able to refer to less than a third of the articles and books which appeared during the year. Inevitably, some readers (and many authors!) are likely to feel that essential references have been omitted.

[2] The following abbreviations were used in this review: MMPI (Minnesota Multiphasic Personality Inventory); TAT (Thematic Apperception Test).

creative with respect to novel hunches for test construction, seem to have been remarkably negligent in the utilization of rigorous procedures to separate good hunches from bad.

In spite of the broad array of content encompassed in this review, it may serve to encourage varied groups of applied psychologists to look at their old problems with new perspectives and perhaps to read a few references which they otherwise might have overlooked.

Since most published papers relating to assessment are concerned with relatively specific problems of evaluation or prediction encountered by their authors in day-to-day applied duties, it is difficult to discern the major theoretical and methodological issues. Work in this field is in no sense systematic or clearly delineable with respect to either theories or methods. And, although all assessment psychologists are in general agreement that prediction of a selected sample of future behavior (the criterion) must be based on selected samples of behavior, this is about as far as the agreement goes. On other issues: what theory?, what variables?, what techniques?, how to combine the data?, etc., there are wide differences of opinion and practice.

General Contributions

Without doubt, one of the most valuable general publications in the field of assessment is Buros' (18) *Yearbook of Mental Measurement*, listing 793 tests and containing 596 original test reviews. The objectives of the test review section remain the same as those announced for the third *Yearbook* published in 1940. One of these eight objectives is "To impel authors and publishers to place fewer but better tests on the market and to provide test users with detailed and accurate information on the construction, validation, uses, and limitations of their tests at the time they are first placed on the market." While it is impossible to evaluate the degree to which the successive *Yearbooks* fulfill this or its other worthy objectives, this reviewer believes they serve a series of most useful functions and hopes that Buros will find it possible to continue this heroic undertaking. He would further hope, however, that before too long, the editor might find his task made easier by a marked reduction in the number of different tests which need to be included. Perhaps it is asking too much to suggest that the author and publisher of a test declare it obsolete, but the idea does not seem without merit, especially since the profession seems loathe to establish any procedure for "certifying" the quality of tests and other assessment techniques. Surely, there must be some way to get rid of old tests as well as to encourage higher standards in the development of new ones.

Perhaps, the job of cleaning out the test attic will be speeded up by the important work of the American Psychological Association Committee on Test Standards. In its "Technical Recommendations for Psychological Tests and Diagnostic Techniques" (3) this Committee attempts to develop standards, not for tests, but for test manuals. These proposed standards are grouped in three levels: "Essential," "Very Desirable," and "Desirable."

It is the writer's impression that, even if judged by the minimal standards recommended by this Committee, relatively few of the most widely used tests would be judged ready for publication and use.

Of especial relevance to assessment are the Committee's distinctions among four kinds of test validity: predictive, status, content, and congruent. "Predictive validity" is defined as correlation of test and subsequent criterion measures, "status validity" as correlation of test and concurrent external criteria. "Content validity" refers to the degree to which the test samples the universe of content specified, as in an achievement test. Finally, "congruent validity" is defined as demonstration, by any one of a variety of procedures, that the test actually measures the psychological variable it is alleged to measure. The familiar example is that of showing a substantial correlation with other measures of accepted validity, e.g., validating a new group test of intelligence against Binet I. Q.'s.

Much more difficult is the task of demonstrating the validity of a test designed to measure a hypothetical construct. Here, the task is that of demonstrating that scores on the test correctly predict behavior differentials deduced from the same theory that led to the construct and to the test; i.e., "the validation process is much the same as that involved in evaluating a theory itself." This type of validation is well exemplified by the program of research on the Blacky Pictures, originally published by Blum as a research tool rather than a diagnostic technique. In their recent paper, Blum & Hunt (15) review a dozen studies relating performance on the Blacky test to a wide variety of behavioral criteria selected on the basis of deductions from psychoanalytic theory. All findings seem to point to the probable validity of the scores for at least certain of the "psychosexual dimensions." Further, the findings indicate that these are evaluated with sufficient reliability to discriminate between groups of subjects. As yet, little is known about the reliability of these measures for individual subjects or their usefulness as a tool in the assessment of individuals for the prediction of their future performance.

In assessment, psychologists are necessarily concerned with predictive validity of a technique for the specific criterion. If a technique has been shown to have status validity for group differentiation relevant to the criterion, or if there is good evidence of its having congruent validity for a relevant variable, this makes the technique promising as a predictor. The proof, however, lies in putting it to an actual test in the assessment situation and correlating it with the relevant criterion.

The possible hazard of using a technique in assessment by extrapolating too far solely on the basis of data regarding congruent validity is illustrated in a paper by Ellis (31). For an individual subject, using only the Blacky protocol (administered after 200 hours of analytic treatment), clinical psychologists attempted to make a number of inferences about the personality and adjustment of the patient. The judges showed reasonably high agreement among themselves but not with the criterion judgments of the therapist and patient. Apart from any limitation of this particular study, it seems clear that congruent validity is no guarantee of predictive validity in the assessment of individuals.

Reliance on congruent validity alone as the basis for the selection of assessment techniques appears hazardous in another respect: validity is usually regarded as demonstrated when it can be shown that scores or ratings differentiate two known groups at the .01 level of significance. Now if the groups are large enough, or if they are extreme enough with respect to the criterion dimension, one can achieve a P of .01 and still account for precious little variance in the criterion. The assessment psychologist is obligated to evaluate techniques on the basis of the amount of variance in the criterion predictable from a given predictor. Thus, it is entirely possible that a test which has been shown to measure an attribute or variable essential for a given prediction, may prove to be useless in actual assessment because the test measures so little of the variable or attribute. Even if the test scores are sufficiently saturated with the variable to yield significant validity coefficients against an external criterion, the assessment psychologist is still obliged to ask whether another test will yield even higher validity or, if no higher, if it is more efficient in terms of cost, professional time, and convenience to the subjects.

The Empirical versus Theoretical Continuum

In general, it appears that the most valid assessment procedures developed thus far by psychologists are those in which the investigator has (*a*) selected a criterion and (*b*) searched widely and diligently for behavior samples (tests) which elicit differential responses correlated with the criterion measure. Scoring keys thus derived are cross-validated on a new sample and the test is ready for use. This empirical approach has been shown to work in a variety of assessment situations. It seems likely that such empirically derived instruments will be necessary for a long time, that is, until we know far more about personality and its evaluation.

The limitations of the extreme empirical approach are well recognized and serious. It leads to techniques with an unknown but probably limited degree of generality. The validity of the scoring key or regression weights can be expected to decrease or even to disappear if used with subjects differing in certain respects from those on whom the weights were developed or or if it were used to predict a related but different criterion. Its usefulness must therefore be empirically tested anew in each situation, and even in the same situation with changes over time. Worse still such empirically derived instruments are not likely to make systematic contributions to personality theory. They do not permit ready identification of the variables or dimensions of personality relevant to effective performance on the criterion and hence do not, except in a very general way, add to the psychologist's ability to come up with fruitful hypotheses for use in the next assessment situation.

At the other end of this continuum, we find the theory or technique oriented assessment psychologist, who because of his particular orientation, is convinced that one or more personality variables are salient in determining the behavior of persons in a wide variety of situations. Any specific assessment problem is, therefore, seen largely as that of evaluating these assumed "key" personality variables in each subject and then predicting, on an a priori basis, each subject's performance in the criterion situation. Such predictions may or may not be subjected to empirical test, but even when they are, this investigator is likely to be satisfied with a demonstration that the key variable or variables is significantly related to the criterion. Having proved to his satisfaction the correctness of his theoretical deduction, he feels free to use both his theory and his technique in a variety of assessment situations. It is rare for the investigator to show the slightest concern as to whether his favorite assessment variable accounts for more than the tiniest fraction of the variance in the criterion, and he is likely to be blissfully unaware of the above noted hazards of generalizing on the basis of a demonstrated correlation between a predictor and a specific criterion.

In between the empirical approach and that of emphasizing particular variables, or favorite techniques, are the systematic research programs of Cattell, Eysenck, and Thurstone directed toward the identification and measurement of the "primary" variables of personality. In spite of differences in the details of their work, all of these investigators are convinced that further progress in the evaluation of personality and the prediction of behavior demands, first, an orderly taxonomy of the personality domain and, second, the development of objective measures of the variables which emerge. All are sampling and measuring a large number of variables and all are using factor analysis as a means of testing the degree of overlap or independence of the variables which they are measuring. Cattell & Wenig (22) even go so far as to invade the domain of projective tests with the factor analytic approach. Eysenck, in his book *The Scientific Study of Personality* (33) unabashedly argues for not only the desirability but the absolute necessity of developing a firm taxonomy of personality as a basis for further progress in psychology. In contrast to the more widely accepted organismic orientation among most clinical psychologists, Eysenck takes an outspokenly atomistic, elementaristic point of view and is well along on an elaborate program of research directed at the classification, identification, and objective measurement of personality types and traits.

In this reviewer's opinion, Eysenck's book was easily the most important publication in the entire field of psychology during the past year. It presents important experimental findings on a large number of controversial issues in personality theory and psychopathology; furthermore, the findings point to conclusions considerably at variance with current teaching: e.g., "psychoticism" and "neuroticism" are independent dimensions of personality; both are continuous variables in normals as well as pathological subjects; neuroticism, as objectively measured, is apparently as much a genetic factor as general intelligence! Whether the reader agrees or disagrees with the interpretations, he simply cannot afford to overlook Eysenck's results.

That personality variables identified by the factor analytic process may have predictive validity for a wide range of criteria is strongly suggested by Barron's paper (5) on the Complexity-Simplicity dimension of personality. This factor independently identified by two investigators, using different tests, appears to correlate with a great many socially relevant behaviors.

Gough's work during the last five years, leading to the development of the California Psychological Inventory (51) represents a nice blend of the theoretical and empirical approach to assessment. Although guided by the goal of identifying and measuring personality variables of general predictive value, Gough has also developed a number of empirically derived scales for the inventory designed to predict a variety of criteria; e.g., social participation, delinquency, and academic achievement. It is of interest to note that different scales are necessary for the prediction of academic achievement in high school, in college, and in graduate schools. This suggests either that different motivational variables are operative or that they interact in different ways to influence academic achievement at the three educational levels.

The Role of the Psychologist in Assessment

In perhaps no other respect do psychologists differ so completely as in their answer to the question of the appropriate role of the psychologist in assessment. In the absence of objective tests of personality, psychologists have been forced to rely heavily on the human observer to discriminate essential personality variables and "to rate" subjects on these variables. Furthermore in the development of projective methods, the human interpreter came to be regarded as essential for the proper evaluation, integration, and interpretation of the behavior sampled by these techniques.

Even before the days of psychological tests and projective techniques, the practical problems of assessment were for the most part met by the selection or diagnostic interview in which a human being plays the role of the test, scoring key, and regression equation all rolled into one. The authors of *Assessment of Men* (90) state baldly that the interview is probably the best and only indispensable method of assessment. Rodger (91) goes as far as to say "the interview is the standard means whereby people are judged for many purposes, and it is likely to remain so, maybe till the end of time." In an interesting paper entitled "The Worthwhileness of the Interview," Rodger admits the generally low reliabilities and validities of interview assessment found in most studies, but takes the curious position that none of the studies proves its uselessness. He defends the interview on the basis of its "acceptability" and calls on psychologists to improve rather than abandon the technique. Crissy (26) also emphasizes the crucial need for research on the selection interview. His paper includes a good discussion of the inherent difficulties in such research and methods of meeting them.

Rodger's defense of the interview seems to have been brought about largely by the findings of the Michigan project (71) in which the interview did not contribute essentially to assessment. He appropriately notes a number of features of the research design which could have contributed to low validities found for the interview. In the meantime, Holt & Luborsky (67) have published a second interim report on the Menninger Assessment Program which relied most heavily on judgments based on the interviews and a battery of individually administered psychological tests. In this project, each applicant was interviewed independently by three psychiatrists, each of whom made a global prediction regarding the candidate's probable success in psychiatric training. Note that in this study the interviews were conducted by staff psychiatrists, presumably experts in the art of interviewing and maximally familiar with the expectations and demands of the criterion situation. Even so, the validities of the judgments based on these interviews are extremely low: for 14 interviewers who rated from 9 to 98 applicants, the median validity is only .08

In spite of accumulating evidence of this sort, the interview seems to have no serious competition as the most popular assessment technique. Swenson & Lindgren (111), in a survey of Minnesota industries, found it to rank first among personnel selection procedures. Crissy (26) also notes that it continues to be the most widely used personnel selection method in private industry. Stalnaker & Eindhoven (107), in a survey of medical school admission requirements, reports that applicants are required to report for a selection interview in 53 of 80 medical schools.

Although the interview is the primary diagnostic technique employed by psychiatrists, there are very few published studies bearing on its predictive validity. With respect to reliability, the evidence from older studies suggests inter-interviewer agreement is likely to be considerably better than chance but still relatively low. Since in most instances no external criteria are available, no estimate of predictive validity is possible, and "correctness" is assumed on the basis of consensus in interviewer judgments.

Two newer studies provide slight evidence on this point. In a study of the relationship among several measures of anxiety, Gleser & Ulett (49) report that the ratings of psychiatrists of "anxiety proneness" correlate .55 with scores on the Saslow Screening Inventory and .54 with the ratings of clinical psychologists based on a battery of individual tests. Even here, however, it was of interest to note that the objective measure correlates as high with each set of ratings as did the ratings of the psychiatrists and psychologists with each other. Furthermore, since the objective scores on the Saslow Inventory correlate higher with the average of the two ratings than with either set of ratings, it must be concluded that the Inventory is a better measure of whatever the judges were rating than either set of judges.

The other study involving a check of psychiatrist-interview judgments against outside criteria is not so encouraging. Eysenck (33) reports an unpublished doctoral dissertation by Heron which involved an assessment of factory workers and an analysis of the relationship between personality variables, productivity, and work adjustment. In this study, the psychiatrist's rating of "mental health" was found to be essentially uncorrelated with any of the other variables. (As a matter of fact, its low correlation with "neuroticism," objectively measured, was in the wrong direction!) Eysenck attributes these unexpected findings to the fact that the psychiatrist was forced to make his evaluations under unfamiliar conditions, e.g., the subjects were asked to come in for the interview and the psychiatrist did not have access to any records of the subject's work history.

The role of the psychologist in the assessment process is even more important for the proponents of "organismic assessment," who assume that "the trained psychologist or psychiatrist, with a fund of additional facts at his disposal is, today, capable of improving to a significant degree the accuracy of mechanical predictions derived from test scores alone" (90, p. 52). Although the blunt statement of this position is rarely encountered in print, it appears to be an implicit belief on the part of most users of diagnostic and selection interviews, projective techniques, situation tests, and other procedures which depend on the human interpreter or integrator of data.

The curious state of affairs wherein the most widely (and confidently) used techniques are those for which there is little or no evidence of predictive validity is indeed a phenomenon appropriate for study by social psychologists. This reviewer can only assume that in the absence of evidence of their predictive validity, such techniques must serve an important function other than assessment. Is it that they serve primarily to reduce threats of anxiety for persons confronted with the necessity of making significant decisions in the lives of individual clients or patients? Lacking dependable validated techniques for making the predictions essential to wise decisions, it should not be surprising if persons responsible for professional decisions were to gravitate to the use of techniques which yield a relatively large amount of information concerning the subject, regardless of how irrelevant most of the information may be. Add to extensity of information provided by the technique a theoretical orientation sufficiently flexible to permit using the information in a manner which seems "to explain" any subject, and we have what would seem to be the necessary ingredients for an anxiety-reducing prescription! Whether this analysis is correct or not, it cannot be denied that in most practical assessment situations, the choice of techniques seems to be largely a function of user confidence rather than demonstrated validity.

The organismic hypothesis and the essentiality of the human being in the assessment process is also discussed at considerable length by Eysenck (33) in a chapter entitled "The Organization of Personality." Eysenck reviews the evidence from three levels: total assessment; an intermediate level, as in the case of Rorschach interpretation along statistical or intuitive lines; and a more fundamental level, as in perceptual organization. All of the evidence serves to cast serious doubt on the correctness of the organismic position.

In any event, the introduction of the human interpreter or integrator in the assessment process greatly complicates the problems of validation, since individual differences in the human being may contribute to the variance of the predictions which emerge. Since, in such situations one cannot properly speak of the validity of a technique but only of a "technique-user combination" it would follow that for any given assessment situation, there should be a prior determination of the person-technique-criterion validity of each staff member!

Perhaps, as the result of accumulating evidence concerning the low predictive validity of judgments based on projective techniques, most recent studies have shown a trend toward the objectification of scoring and the utilization of categories of responses as variables. This trend has been viewed with alarm by Hanfmann (59), who while admitting there is no good reason why projective techniques should not be used objectively, takes the position that attempts to improve projective techniques by making them more objective " . . . may be expected to fail precisely to the extent that they succeed." She believes that the essence of projective psychology lies in " . . . what the psychologist does with the data obtained and in the nature and goal of treatment he accords them." She goes ahead to plead for the use of projective data via the technique of "symbolic interpretation" as a means of ferreting out "personal meaning" of the material for the case under study and for arriving at new insights. While she does not insist that this approach is necessarily superior to others, she believes it is an approach worth developing in its own right and argues for "further study of the interpretative process."

With this plea, the present reviewer is in complete accord. In fact, as he and Fiske have argued elsewhere:

> It is entirely possible that an extensive investigation would reveal some gifted persons who by procedures not presently communicable, can make clinical predictions superior to those possible by statistical psychometric procedures. If this should be the case, it is essential that efforts be made to identify the methods employed by such persons so that these methods may be communicated to others in training. If their methods cannot be identified or communicated, it would still be worthwhile to identify the essential characteristics of such persons so that others similarly gifted might be selected to function in a similar manner (71, p. 202).

However, in the absence of supporting evidence concerning the contribution of "understanding" to predictive validity, this reviewer cannot concur with the position taken by Rotter in the Volume 4 of the *Annual Review of Psychology* (94) condoning the choice of assessment techniques on the basis of "best fit—own theoretical orientation and purpose," to be used as "a personal instrument," etc. If the interpretative approach, and the feeling of "understanding" engendered by the use of certain techniques is of value, there must be some way of demonstrating it other than by "testimonials." If its value cannot be demonstrated, psychologists might well utilize at least a part of the time currently expended on techniques of doubtful validity in developing more valid tools for the tasks at hand. All too frequently, the feeling of "understanding" in the user of a technique is regarded as adequate "validation," i.e., the technique is said "to work." Worse still, new generations of students are taught to arrive at similar "understandings" of individual cases with no validity other than consensual judgment, which unfortunately, can be as invalid as the judgment of an individual. If, "explanation" is a doubtful criterion for use in personality research as MacKinnon suggests in "Fact and Fancy in Personality Research" (82), it is even more doubtful as the proper criterion of validity in a single case!

While this reviewer doubts that the approach suggested by Hanfmann will lead to the development of human beings capable of handling the complex problems of best weighting data for the prediction of criteria, he is quite convinced that the interpretative approach is most promising for the development of hypotheses leading to better objective procedures. The apparent "understanding" of a single case can lead to many creative hypotheses, each susceptible of empirical test. Since persons most gifted in developing intuitive hypotheses are frequently not inclined to feel it necessary to subject them to rigorous verification, psychologists seeking to develop new and better objective tests might well look to the clinical literature for such worthwhile leads. Thurstone in a recent publication goes so far as to state:

> Projective procedures are the nearest approach to personality tests. A projective test is essentially an ambiguous presentation to which the subject can respond in a variety of ways. In so doing he may reveal his personal idiosyncrasies. The best form of projective test is one which is quite unstructured for the subject but fairly well structured for the examiner. In this manner a projective test can be objectively scored; but the interpretation of the scores is often as unstructured as the test is for the subject, and then the test is useless for scientific inquiry (112, p. 1).

In summary, the role of the human being in the assessment process continues to be a much argued question. For some, he is the *sine qua non* in the assessment process. For others, he is the necessary architect, designer, and engineer, but to the degree that he enters into the assessment process itself, he is merely an added source of error variance!

General Reviews Relevant to Assessment

Although of varying relevance, a number of review articles published during the year help to provide a perspective of recent trends and developments in assessment methodology.

Schofield (100) in his third annual review of research in clinical psychology classifies 143 papers into 20 research areas and notes changes over a three year period. For 1951, fully 90 per cent of all articles reviewed concern one or another aspect of clinical diagnosis and assessment as used in this chapter. In Schofield's opinion, the most significant contribution of the year was the series of related papers by Wittenborn and his associates describing the development of an objective, quantitative system for multiple psychiatric diagnosis, a procedure which results in a profile of scores on seven factors or clusters of symptoms.

The most extensive review of the year was that done by Windle (120) on "psychological tests in psychopathological prognosis." Windle analyzed 90 research studies, organizing the findings on the basis of the particular test employed. In a master table covering seven pages of fine print, he has abstracted each investigation indicating: the author; the number and type of patients involved; the duration of illness; the follow-up time; the type of therapy, if any; the prognosis made for each of the prognostic indices and the level of significance of the finding. Where the original author did not report statistical significance, but did provide the necessary data, Windle calculated it. The over-all picture is one which should serve to shake any existing complacency regarding the predictive validities of our most widely used diagnostic tests. Even more alarming: "Many of the studies failed to demonstrate empirical justification for the conclusions drawn. Further, comparison among studies revealed little agreement among findings." Windle emphasizes the need for better research studies in this field and notes that most of the published investigations fail to contribute significantly because: (*a*) they fail to specify the conditions of the experiment, e.g., description of the patient population, conditions of therapy and criteria of outcome; (*b*) they fail to deal with homogeneous populations and conditions; (*c*) they fail to report their results in terms amenable to statistical evaluation; and (*d*) the reported findings are only rarely subjected to cross-validation. Unfortunately, most of the new studies appearing during the past year have likewise been defective in one or more of these aspects. Perhaps the most frequent error is the over-optimistic estimates of P values growing out of misconceptions and misapplications of the laws of probability. In the absence of statistical sophistication and with the motivation to "prove" that a particular test score or index is valid, many investigators appear all too anxious to rush into print with "promising findings."

Ellis (32) undertook a summary of all research using personality inventories published between January 1946 and December 1951. He presents a tabular analysis based on 499 studies with respect to the discriminations tested. Although this analysis shows inventory scores to have discriminated significantly in over half of the studies, Ellis is generally critical of their validity and suggests that where inventories are most effectively used they tend to become as time consuming as alternative psychodiagnostic procedures, such as interview and projective techniques, which to Ellis, "are more clinically incisive and valuable." Evidence for this latter opinion is not presented!

Ghiselli & Barthol (47) provide a more limited review of the validity of personality inventories in the selection of employees as reflected in 113 studies since 1919. They report that inventories have been found useful in a variety of jobs but that there are enough negative results to suggest caution in their use. In general, the validities reported were higher for sales clerks and salesmen and lower for supervisors and service workers.

Levine & Tupes (78) summarize postwar research in pilot selection and classification. The pilot selection tests developed during World War II have shown surprisingly stable validity over a period of eight years under a variety of conditions, their validity being particularly good for the criterion of flying deficiency against which these scores were originally validated.

Criterion Problems

In general, assessment psychologists are becoming increasingly aware of the complexity of the criterion problem. Traditionally, they were likely to select a criterion on the basis of its availability, its simplicity, or simply to take for granted that the most commonly used measure would serve as an acceptable criterion. If efforts at predicting the criterion were not successful, it was generally supposed that the fault lay in the predictor variables used. Gradually, we seem to be discovering that the behavior constituting performance in the domain to which we wish to predict is fully as complex, probably as multidimensional and as difficult to measure as the personality variables used as predictors. A variety of papers reflected this trend during the previous year.

Diagnostic categories as criteria.—Following his earlier publication outlining the method of criterion analysis, Eysenck (34) argues for the utilization of socially relevant criterion measures (e.g., psychiatric diagnoses) as transitional criteria for the identification of psychological variables which can, in turn, be used to sort people into more meaningful diagnostic categories and with greater accuracy than is now possible. Lorr (79) presents a logical analysis of the essentials of diagnosis, emphasizing the multidimensional nature of most psychiatric conditions and the desirability of describing patients on dimensions which are relatively homogeneous. Du Mas (30) in a stimulating paper entitled "On the Mathematical Representation of a Syndrome" suggests a procedure for selecting and ordering the components of a diagnostic profile. That even the older diagnostic categories may have some predictive validity is suggested in a paper by Hunt, Wittson & Hunt (70) who found that naval personnel labelled with a definite psychiatric diagnosis were more likely to receive neuropsychiatric discharges than those with less specific diagnoses.

Wittenborn & Weiss (121) using the quantified multiple diagnostic procedure report wide differences among patients diagnosed with manic depressive psychosis, manic state, and argue that the conventional diagnosis obscures important differences among them. Guertin (56) on the basis of a factor analytic study of behavioral symptoms identifies six factors in a group of patients even though are all classified as schizophrenic. In an inverted factor analytic study of a sample of the same group of patients Guertin (57) identifies three types of schizophrenic patients corresponding essentially to the present typology. The paranoid and hebephrenic types appeared to be the most frequent mixture. He failed to find any evidence whatsover of a general factor of schizophrenia. Turning to another diagnostic category Lorr & Jenkins (80) report a factor analytic study of the symptoms of maladjustment in delinquent children and conclude that there are at least five relatively independent factors in the global diagnoses of juvenile delinquency.

Other criterion studies.—Related studies from many other fields emphasize the multidimensional nature of most criteria. Ryans & Wandt (97) report that five factors are necessary to describe the behavior of teachers in elementary school; in a related study, Ryans (96) found six factors are needed to describe the behavior of secondary school teachers. Rush (95) identified at least four factors in sales success and concludes that the attempt to predict the global criterion may obscure important relationships between the predictor and the true criterion. Severin (103) notes that in the industrial field performance during the period of training correlates only about .20 with later job performance and hence the two cannot be considered as equivalent criteria. Brown & Ghiselli (17) also note that tests which predict training criteria may have little or no predictive power for the criterion of job proficiency or vice versa. Heron (65) finds that even among unskilled factory workers it is necessary to differentiate at least two dimensions of job success: average productivity and the supervisor's rating of job adjustment. Similarly, Fleishman (38) identifies two dimensions of supervisory behavior, each of which can be measured with respectable reliabilities and yet correlate −.02. Only if the criterion represents a relatively limited domain of behavior does it seem likely that a single criterion measure is adequate for assessment study: Gaier (45) reports a single common factor adequate to explain variance in the performance of medical school freshmen in five courses. Enlargement of the domain of criterion behavior seems, however, to lead almost immediately to more dimensions. Thus, Newman, French & Bobbitt (89) in two independent analyses of successive classes at the Coast Guard Academy find three independent clusters of cadet performance: (*a*) adaptability to academy life and practice, (*b*) athletic proficiency and attitudes, and (*c*) academic grades.

New Studies of Assessment

Only two reports describe new applied programs of assessment. Harrison & Jackson (61) describe a program for the placement of young engineers in a large organization. On the basis of a battery of objective and projective tests a personality description is prepared for each employee. The authors report that "... ninety-one per cent of the supervisors of these men report that the evaluation was correct." Similarly Higham (66) describes the use of tailored situation tests and staff judgments in a personnel selection program of a British industry. He regrets being unable to report any validity but says that the sponsor seems to be satisfied!

A systematic series of investigations dealing with the one variety of global assessment, Leaderless Group Discussion (LGD), is being conducted by Bass and his associates at the University of Louisiana. At least six additional studies growing out of this program have appeared during the last year.

The first study, by Bass & Coates (7), reports on the use of the LGD technique in forecasting Officer Potential. Subjects were third year ROTC cadets, the criteria were two sets of ratings by tactical officers. Reported validities were approximately .40 for the Army cadets and .46 for the Air Force cadets. Since the subjects studied were already selected for ROTC training, the authors suggest that the validity of the technique in screening applicants might be even higher.

Another study (122) deals with the validity of leaderless group discussions amongst strangers. Trained judges were found to agree .92 and to predict the criterion (sociometric choice for leaders by fraternity members) with an *r* of .40. Bass & Wurster (10) direct their attention to the effect of the nature of the problem on LGD performance. In still another paper, Bass, Klubeck & Wurster (8) find that the validity varies from discussion to discussion even though the interjudge agreement remains stable. Validity was also found to vary with the participant's outside leader status, the more stratified status the better being the discrimination. In a related study, Bass & Wurster (11) reported a correlation of .88 between participant rank in an industrial concern and his leader behavior in a supposedly leaderless situation. This leads to the conclusion that LGD rating are not valid where participants are of known different rank and prestige.

In spite of the demonstrated predictive validity of LGD scores, two questions appear relevant. First, do such scores, obtained in this rather eleborate procedure, predict the criteria of leadership any better than more economically obtained predictors? In one of the studies noted above, the ACE test correlated .28 with the criterion and in another a correlation of .54 was reported between paper-and-pencil predictors and supervisory success.

A related question concerns the identification of the personality variables contributing to the rated leadership. In an earlier study Bass (6) reported the amazing correlation of .93 between the ratings of judges and the actual number of words spoken by subjects in the LGD situation! In a more recent paper, Bass and four coauthors (9) report correlations of .37 and .22 with Guilford-Zimmerman Ascendancy and Sociality Scores, and a significantly larger number of Rorschach responses for subjects judged as good leaders. While it is of theoretical interest to determine the personality variables in the subjects which lead judges to rate them high or low on "leadership," one may well ask, why not use measures of these variables to predict the criterion directly? Only if it can be demonstrated that the LGD ratings of trained observers predict leadership criteria better than more economical measures of personality variables would it seem defensible to use the LGD procedure in practical assessment situations.

Also in an effort to identify the major personality variables assessed in situation tests, Sakoda (98) subjected the correlational data published in *Assessment of Men* to a modified cluster analysis. He reports that O.S.S. (Office of Strategic Services) ratings were a function of at least two varieties of situations in which the candidates were observed: verbal and active. In another cluster analysis of ratings on the ten traits, he finds three clusters: abilities, interests and motivation, and social adjustment. On the basis of these findings, Sakoda argues that a personality trait must be defined in terms of context and kind of situation in which behavior occurs. It should be noted that this analysis deals with traits as rated, and like all factor studies of ratings could reflect, at least in part, perceptual clusters in the minds of raters as well as actual clusters in the behavior of subjects being rated.

In spite of often reported high interjudge agreement in the evaluating of subjects by interview or other techniques, it is rare to find such reports accompanied by information pointing to the basis for the agreement. McKeachie (86) in a controlled experiment found that the presence of lipstick significantly affected certain personality ratings assigned six female subjects on the basis of a ten-minute interview. Inquiry revealed that the raters were totally unaware of this cue. Grossack (55) reports that first impressions are influenced both by identifiable cues and by expectations. Interjudge agreement can thus result, in part, from common expectations among judges. Fensterheim & Tresselt (35) demonstrate a significant influence of the value system of the judges on judgments based on photographs. Gage (44) reports that the prediction of responses of subjects on the Kuder Preference Record are more accurate when made on the basis of stereotype (expectations?) than when made after observing subjects in a series of brief situation tests.

This finding suggests the possibility that at least part of the often reported agreement between supposedly independent judgments may result from the fact that judges use a common "stereotype" as the basis of their evaluations. That this is more than a possibility was shown by Malcom (83) in an unpublished doctoral dissertation. Using data from the Michigan assessment study, and a technique of profile correlation, Malcom computed the congruence between sets of ratings assigned each subject by assessment staff members on the basis of different techniques. He found that much of the "apparent validity" of the rated profiles based on specific techniques was a function of a common stereotype of "the prospective clinical psychologist." In fact, for certain of the ratings, a "modal profile" turned out to be more predictive of the criterion profile than were the unique evaluations of individual subjects!

The danger that judgments or ratings may be contaminated or reflect spurious cues is dramatically shown by Hemphill & Sechrest (64) in a study of the relation of different criteria of aircrew effectiveness in combat over Korea. One of the criteria was the actual bombing error objectively measured from aerial photographs. In spite of the fact that the reliability of this objective criterion was zero, it was found to correlate .80 with the ratings of superiors on "objective achievement." Further analysis showed that this correlation was generated by the fact that the raters each had access to the same official bombing records, and, consequently, based their ratings primarily on shared but unreliable information. This resulted in spuriously high interjudge agreement and also spuriously high correlations of the judgments and the objective but completely unreliable criterion.

A more direct analysis of the basis of clinical judgment is reported by Forer & Tolman (39) who asked 30 clinical psychologists to judge the value of each of 100 items in a sentence-completion test. In general, the judges assigned higher values to those items which appeared to elicit reactions toward specified situations and which seemed to throw light on the causes of emotional states. They also report that confidence of ratings was associated more with extreme than with moderate judgments. Davenport (28) studied the "semantic behavior" of six clinical psychologists in the evaluation of six TAT[2] records from a heterogeneous group of subjects. Each judge was asked to decide whether or not each of 207 typical interpretive statements applied to each TAT record. To provide an index of the ambiguity of the statements, each statement was rated by 26 other clinical psychologists. She found (*a*) relatively little agreement among judges in the differential use of the statements for the six TAT records and (*b*) that the judges tended to apply statements rated as universal to almost any patient while avoiding the use of more specific statements. Analysis of the statements rated as the most ambiguous showed them to be more heavily loaded with psychoanalytic terminology. Davenport also found that her subjects rarely made statements about positive traits or assets of personality even though some of the TAT records were obtained from normal subjects.

Klieger & Mosel (74), in a study of performance ratings in a training division of the army, found no difference in the reliability of the ratings of judges indicating greater as compared with those indicating less opportunity to observe the specific trait rated. In general, ratings by superiors showed higher reliability than ratings by peers, regardless of the degree of familiarity claimed. The authors suggest that the higher interjudge agreement among superiors may be a function of greater communality of perceptual habits in the observation and categorizing of the particular variables rated in this situation. Conceivably peer judges might show higher agreement in rating other variables, e.g., those not related to behavior in the military situation.

Studies of Predictive Validity by Type of Criterion

Relatively few published papers provide evidence on the predictive validity of techniques for specific criteria. In this section, we shall review those noted, grouped by the type of criterion predicted.

The course and outcome in psychotherapy.—One of the most important and frequent assessment problems confronting the clinical psychologist in mental hygiene clinics is that of evaluating patients for critical decisions regarding psychotherapy. Several studies dealing with this problem appeared during the past year. All investigators relied almost exclusively on a single technique, the individual Rorschach. Some of the studies were concerned with predicting continuation-termination of therapy, others used improvement in therapy as a criterion.

In 1951 Rogers, Knauss & Hammond (93) published a study showing only chance differences in 99 Rorschach "signs" for mental hygiene patients staying in therapy for less than five as compared with more than five interviews; they also found no relationship between clinical judgments based on Rorschach protocols and termination in therapy. Kotkov & Meadow (75), using nine interviews as the criterion of continuation in therapy, analyzed the Rorschach records of 98 patients in group psychotherapy and calculated discriminant function weights (to eight decimal places and six significant figures!) for three out of an unspecified number of Rorschach scores. Application of these weights and a cutting score to a new group of patients in individual therapy resulted in the correct prediction for 69 per cent for 52 cases ($P=.01$). However, for this group of patients one of the three Rorschach variables, D%, not only failed to discriminate but the direction of the difference was reversed. P values for the other two variables, R and FC-CF, were .01 and .02. Parenthetically, it is of interest that these authors criticize the use of the "sign method" as violating the Gestalt quality of classical Rorschach interpretations but defend the use of the discriminant function method and theorize about the meaning of the variables weighted in their formula.

Auld & Eron (4) applied the Kotkov & Meadow formula to 33 patients in another clinic and used the same criterion for continuation in therapy, nine or more interviews. They found the formula predicted correctly for only 52 per cent of their cases, this in spite of the fact that the tetrachoric correlation between R and the criterion was .55. In this study, FC-CF (the only other Rorschach variable which had held up in Kotkov & Meadow's cross-validation attempt) showed a difference ($P<.10$) in the wrong direction. Furthermore, for 23 of the 33 patients to whom the W-B had been given, the correlation between verbal I.Q. and the criterion was .71. Auld & Eron conclude by emphasizing the need for cross-validation and validity-generalization studies of proposed methods of diagnosis and formulae for predicting behavior.

Rogers & Hammond (92) in another study evaluate the accuracy with which outcome in psychotherapy is predictable from the Rorschach. The criterion groups were 59 patients judged as improved and 50 patients judged as unimproved at the termination of therapy. As in their earlier study these investigators first used clinical judgments of the total Rorschach record. Categorized judgments (successful-unsuccessful) were made by three experienced clinical psychologists under four conditions: (*a*) a snap judgment (in two or three minutes); (*b*) a studied judgment using as much time as desired; (*c*) the same as (*b*) but with knowledge of the name of the therapist; and (*d*) from knowledge of the therapist only. Although both the intrajudge and interjudge agreement were generally good, none of these global judgments showed other than chance relationships with the criterion.

Next, the Rorschach scoring weights previously reported by Harris & Christianson (60) were applied. No significant discrimination was found between the scores for the two groups of patients. Rogers & Hammond then analyzed 99 Rorschach scores or indices in relation to the criterion. All of the resulting differences were chance only. Similarly negative findings were found for certain a priori combinations of variables.

Still undaunted, Rogers & Hammond (92) derived a set of empirical "rules" from the data from this group of patients and tested their validity on a cross-validation group. They report that: "the rule most useful permitted prediction in about one third of the cases examined, and showed correct predictions at the 1 per cent level of confidence." This reviewer cannot but wonder how even their best rule would work for the patients studied by Auld & Eron.

Prognosis, i.e., outcome of treatment of hospitalized neuropsychiatric patients was used as the criterion in an investigation reported by Filmer-Bennett (36). Using 12 matched pairs of improved and unimproved patients, he found significant differences (at the .20 level) for only 9 of 60 Rorschach signs. (Twelve of the 60 would have been expected by chance.) Even though none of these nine signs was regarded as warranting using it alone, "certain constellations of the nine appeared promising." However, after testing these patterns with a new sample of improved and unimproved patients, the author ruefully concludes: "There are no prognostic signs common to the Rorschach records of both psychotics and nonpsychotics which have the predictive accuracy claimed for the Rorschach signs reported in earlier studies."

In one study, the predictive validity of several Rorschach variables and of certain other test scores shows up in a much more favorable light. Stotsky (108), using two samples of matched groups of remitting and nonremitting schizophrenic hospitalized patients, made a series of predictions regarding their differential psychological test performance. Practically all of his predictions were confirmed with respect to the direction of the differences of scores for the two groups, several of them at a respectable level of significance in both samples. In general, the test records of the remitting groups reflected impairment in intellectual and emotional function, tending to resemble more those of neurotics than hospitalized schizophrenics. In spite of these significant differences in the test variables, some of which appear large enough to permit useful prediction of remission in schizophrenics, it should be noted that the nonremitting group had a history of more previous shock therapy. Also of interest is Stotsky's finding that although certain Rorschach variables showed significant differences for these two groups of patients, the total Rorschach protocols could not be sorted better than chance by six Veterans Administration trainees.

Sales performance.—Bills & Taylor (13) report that over achievement in a sales school, i.e., greater than that predicted from an intelligence test, is significantly related to three different criteria of later sales success. Wallace & Twichell (115) show that the early (first few months) performance in life insurance selling is such an accurate predictor of later success that they urge its use for the advantage of both the company and the salesmen.

Spencer & Worthington (106) describe in part an elaborate procedure for projectively evaluating the Worthington Personal History form and report a validity of .34 against tenure and .31 against amount of sales for a group of house to house salesmen.

The highest validities of the year are those reported by Tobolski & Kerr (113) who report that the Empathy Test scores of 23 auto salesmen correlated .71 with rankings by the sales managers and .44 with an objective index of sales success (cars sold divided by attempts). Interesting is the fact that scores on this same test were found by Van Zelst (114) to show similarly high validities for several criteria of performance of labor union officials.

Achievement in college and professional schools.—Nearly a score of papers, of which that by Melville & Frederiksen (87) is typical, were concerned with the prediction of success in academic or professional school programs. In general, high-school standing continues to be the best single predictor of college grades, followed closely by a score on some test of scholastic aptitude. Several of the studies show that for the prediction of performance in professional schools, some measure of interests (motivation?) will improve the multiple R obtained.

Turning to the Menninger project, in which the criterion is over-all competence in psychiatry, we have already noted the extremely low validities found for the selection interview. Although it will be some time before the full report is available, Holt & Luborsky (67) also report additional samples of the predictive validities being obtained for other techniques. Judgments based on the TAT, which had earlier been reported as yielding very promising validities, are now reported as −.03, .00, −.02, and .10 depending on the judge and the criterion. For the Rorschach alone, the comparable values are .26, .22, .02, and .05. That the criterion contains predictable variance is indicated by predictive validities of .30 and .50 for two judges using all available data (Credentials, W-B, a Word Association test, Rorschach, TAT, Self-Interpretation, Picture Reaction Test, and Interview). Although this project relied very little on objective tests, it is of interest to note that validities of −.29 and +.24 were found for two Strong Vocational Interest Scores, Production Manager and Lawyer.

Performance in social work training is the criterion used by Frankle in a research program for which as yet but preliminary reports are available. Frankle has been particularly interested in predicting the field work performance of social work students as distinguished from academic grades. In a symposium at the 1951 American Psychological Association meetings, he had reported that this criterion was predictable with very respectable validities in two independent samples, by two very different predictor variables.

The first was scores on the Michigan Speed of Reading Test, which showed correlations of approximately .50, even though this particular criterion was not predictable by intelligence tests. The second promising predictor was a set of scores derived from the Minnesota T-S-E Inventory. Although none of these scores yielded by this inventory showed useful validities, a "perseveration score" (based on the number of times the subject gives the same answer to successive pairs of items) yielded validities of −.63 and −.44 for the two samples.

Frankle's ingenuity in locating still other predictors of this same criterion is shown in a further report (40) dealing with objective indices derived from the Harrower Group Rorschach. Whereas H and Hd scores looked promising in one small sample, these did not hold up in cross-validation samples. Analyses of M+ scores showed more promise in all groups, but still yielded only low validity. However, another objective score (the M+ latency index) derived by weighting M+ responses by the position in the sequence of responses to each card, looks still more promising. In fact an empirically derived "pattern" utilizing this index as the key variable yields validities of .42 to .72 for different groups and different criteria. That the human movement Rorschach variable, objectively scored and empirically validated, may have considerable general validity is suggested by the fact that M+% was reported by Kelly & Fiske (71) to correlate significantly with most of their criterion measures for clinical psychologists even though none of the global predictions based on the Rorschach was significant.

Teacher performance.—Gough & Pemberton (52) found no significant relationships between grades in practice teaching and conventional scores derived from the MMPI[2] or group Rorschach; but empirically derived sign approaches to the MMPI yielded a *P* value of .05 in cross-validation. Callis (19) reports that scores on the Minnesota Teacher Attitude Inventory correlate .49 with pupils' evaluation of the teacher using a 47 item inventory. Two judges evaluated the same teachers and although their ratings correlated only .33, their combined rating was predicted by the Inventory scores with an r of .40. When the ratings by principals were used as the criterion, the validity of the inventory scores was only .19.

Other criteria.—Martin (85) reports an r of .37 between the score on a simple number checking test (same-different) and the accuracy with which 300 checks were listed on an adding machine after 10 to 12 hours of practice; the reliability of the criteria being .71. Seashore (101) reports significant validities for the prediction of clerical performance in banks but calls attention to relevant criterion problems encountered in validational studies in this field. For International Business Machine operators, Gadel & Kriedt (43) report fair predictions of performance by aptitude tests. Job satisfaction of the same subjects was not predicted by any of the Kuder scores, but the authors report the development of a special International Business Machine Interest Test which held up well on cross-validation.

The quality of student drawings was found by Crannell (25) to correlate

.59 with scores in the Meier Seashore Art Appreciation Test when the criterion was the pooled judgment of many fellow students. When the judgment of three artists was used as a criterion, the validity falls to .37 for the same subjects. Reliability of the two criteria were .90 and .80 respectively.

Gough (51) reports the development of a scale for predicting Social Participation and validities of .35 and .55 using as a criterion the number of activities in four schools participated in by high school students.

Hathaway & Monachesi (62) report on the follow up of a large scale study of 4,000 ninth grade children administered the MMPI in 1947–48. During the next four years, nearly one sixth of the group had one or more encounters with the police. This group included nearly three times as many boys as girls. Both sex groups showed significantly high elevations on the F, Pd, and Ma Scales of the MMPI. The delinquent girls also showed high Hy, Pa and Sc scores. Gough & Peterson (53) describe the development and validation of a promising inventory designed to assess predisposition to crime and delinquency. Clark (23) reports additional validation data based on his AWOL Recividist Scales for a small group of MMPI items.

Driscoll (29) was concerned, not with the assessment of delinquency, but with predicting the institutional adjustment of prison inmates. Prisoners who adjusted were, in the judgment of officials and guards, significantly lower on the D, F, and Pa Scales of the MMPI. A modified TAT failed to differentiate the good and poor adjustment groups.

Test Oriented Studies

A large proportion of the published studies relating to assessment procedures continue to be oriented around single tests rather than focused on (*a*) the prediction of a specific criterion or (*b*) the identification and measurement of a particular variable. Instead of selecting or devising tools and techniques most appropriate and effective to the task, all too many authors seem to be motivated by an attitude "here is our instrument. Let's see how many different variables we can infer from the behavior sampled by it or how many group differences we can find with it."

Whatever the reasons, the majority of the published papers continue to be most readily classifiable by tests or techniques. Even using such a classification, it is not possible to undertake a meaningful summary of these papers in a brief review. In fact, the output is so staggering as to make one wonder if even specialists with the technique are able to read it. As an example the *Fourth Mental Measurements Yearbook* lists 618 references to the Rorschach alone as appearing between 1947 and 1951 inclusive! During the same period of time, 1947–51, 197 additional references were noted for the TAT, and for the more recently introduced Szondi 67 references had already been noted by the end of 1951.

Several new texts in clinical psychology were published during the year; all include discussions of the more popular tests used in diagnosis. The most comprehensive treatment of this group of techniques will be found in Weider's *Contributions toward Medical Psychology* (116). In Volume II of this work, devoted entirely to psychodiagnostic methods, some 30 specialists describe the techniques with which they are most closely identified.

Rorschach.—Although the writer does not claim to have digested all of the more than 100 recent Rorschach references, they appear to reflect a trend toward a somewhat more critical evaluation of this technique than characterized studies of previous years. In only a few of the studies did the author rely on "clinical interpretation" as the main source of data. As usual, several papers were concerned with Rorschach signs as related to diagnostic categories. Although most authors are able to report a few "significant" differences, most studies report a very large amount of overlapping of groups known to be widely different. Furthermore, there seems to be relatively little consistency of the findings of different investigators. Friedman (41) for example, compared the Rorschachs of hospitalized schizophrenics and normals, and although he found statistically significant differences for eight variables, these were so generally small as to lead him to this final conclusion:

> It would seem, then, that consideration should be given to the redefinition of the customary Rorschach scores or the construction of new ones. In order to be most fruitful new variables should reflect vectors of a systematic and comprehensive theory of personality rather than isolated traits or independently considered aspects of psychological functioning.

Nearly a score of the authors contributing to the Rorschach literature during the past year were concerned only with factors affecting the Rorschach performance treated as an end in itself. Thus, Siipola & Taylor (105) report that "pressured instructions" result in more "symptomatic" responses; Gibby (48) reports that the examiner as well as the cards influence the the obtained protocol, especially that part of it obtained in the inquiry, and Klatskin (73) found that the testing situation (hospital versus factory) affects the Rorschach record. Maradie (84) employing a series of randomized sequential card orders found that position in the sequence is positively correlated with number of responses but that some cards elicited more responses than others regardless of position. Allen *et al.* (1) on the other hand, reports no relation between sequence of presentation and responses to the cards. Two or three additional papers this year report no relationship between color and responses.

Fiske & Baughman (37) in a detailed analysis of the relationships between Rorschach scoring categories and the total number of responses, found many significant relationships, several of them nonlinear. In their opinion, the computation of per cents by dividing by R is only a partial solution to the problem; they would prefer to see the development of new and better measures of the promising Rorschach variables.

Just what Rorschach variables are most promising and what they really are would still seem a moot question, especially in view of an exploratory study reported by Lotsof (81), who factor analyzed the intercorrelations among 10 variables: a test of verbal intelligence, three measures of verbal fluency derived from recordings of oral descriptions, and seven Rorschach variables believed to be relatively unaffected by verbal fluency. Although based on relatively few cases, four fairly clear-cut factors emerged. The loadings of the Rorschach variables strongly suggests the possible need for a revision of scoring categories and conventional interpretations of the Rorschach determinants.

In spite of these and other studies which raise certain doubts regarding the validity of conventional Rorschach interpretations, the year also saw the publication of several new texts. These include a third volume by Beck (12) and from the Gesell Institute of Child Development a book entitled *Child Rorschach Responses* (2). The subtitle here is "Developmental Trends from Two to Ten Years." This is essentially a book of age norms based on 50 children, 25 of each sex representing half year levels from 2 to 6 and year levels from 7 to 10. A subsequent publication is promised to cover years 10 to 16.

While the present reviewer does not pretend to the kind of expertness needed to evaluate these texts, he does feel qualified to at least question the impact of the last mentioned one. It can be predicted with reasonable confidence that this "book of norms" will lead to marked increase in the use of the Rorschach with children. How unfortunate, then, it would seem that the authors chose to base their "norms" on subjects anything but representative of the population with respect to intelligence and social status. Actually over three-fourths of the children fall in the professional and managerial group and a like proportion are in "above the average categories" in intelligence. In view of the known relationships between intelligence and R and between R and many other scoring categories, such "norms" seem likely to be most misleading. Of equal concern is the authors' completely uncritical acceptance of the conventional interpretations of determinants even when applied to the records of children.

Szondi.—During the past year, the Szondi seems to have replaced the TAT as the second most frequently studied projective device. Most of the Szondi articles deal with specific hypotheses regarding the stimulus value of the cards; only a few are in the nature of validational studies. The simplicity with which this test can be administered, the objectivity of the scores, and conflicting theories of its proponents will probably lead to many more papers. For anyone planning research with this instrument, the excellent Szondi review and critical evaluation by Borstelmann & Klopfer (16) is a must. This article contains not only reviews of previous work on the Szondi test but includes a thoroughly sophisticated discussion of the theoretical and methodological issues of personality testing and a plea for rigor in research on the validation of projective devices. The authors regard the evidence thus far available as not supporting the theories of either Szondi or Deri and suggest the need for systematic research which will permit, first, the reclassification of the cards in terms of their empirically determined stimulus values, and second, the validation of differential patterns of responses to the cards. In other words, pictures of human faces would seem to offer considerable promise as alternatives to verbal symbols as items for a "personality inventory" but validation of the resulting scores would follow by relating test performance to external criteria. These authors conclude their review as follows: "Any clinical instrument is not a shibboleth to be defended or refuted, but a provocative tool which requires careful investigation as to the nature of its contribution to the understanding of human behavior."

Publication of such articles, together with other evidence of increasing methodological sophistication on the part of persons doing research with projective tests should result in markedly improving the quality of future research in this domain.

Drawing techniques.—On the basis of the number of papers seen, a close competitor of the Szondi are the various techniques utilizing drawings of one sort or another. Among these, the most popular seems to be the Draw-a-Person technique, and some of the investigators use highly objective procedures for testing hypotheses. For example, Weider & Noller (117) find that 61 per cent of younger as compared with 48 per cent of older children use the upper-left quandrant of the paper. Does this mean that adults who do so are more regressed?

The next most popular drawing test seems to be the House-Tree-Person. An example of the ridiculous inferences which may result from a priori interpretation of drawings without norms is contained in a publication by Hammer (58) who asked three clinicians to evaluate the over-all adjustment of large samples of white and Negro children using only the H-T-P drawings. Although the reported interjudge reliabilities are very high, the median rating assigned Negro children was "severe neurotic" or "borderline psychotic" at all grade levels. White children fared somewhat better but still the median rating for the junior high school age groups was "neurotic."

TAT.—Relatively few new TAT papers appeared during the year. One showed that TAT stories told can be matched with greater than chance accuracy even by untrained judges. Two studies (54, 118) showed that modification of the TAT pictures by making the central figure more similar to the subject do not elicit greater productivity. Fry published a new scoring blank and manual (42). Shipley & Veroff (104) report the development of a measure of Need for Affiliation, and Clark (24) reports an attempt to use the TAT to measure Sexual Motivation.

Bender-Gestalt.—Turning to the Bender-Gestalt references, one reports a significant difference (but still large overlap) between schizophrenics and normals in Pascal-Suttell scores, another no relationship between recall of B-G figures and Shipley Hartford Scores, another analyzes the 41 Billingslea variables in B-G into six correlated clusters. Suttell & Pascal (110) report the use of the B-G in a study of regression in schizophrenia.

They conclude that regression as measured "is not peculiar to the schizophrenic."

Other techniques.—Studies of individual intelligence tests are still numerous. A number of papers agree that the Wechsler Intelligence Scale for Children is a pretty good intelligence test. Although we seem to be getting out of the period when the Wechsler-Bellevue is being used to evaluate almost everything but intelligence, there are still a few papers on scatter and a few authors still looking for "signs" of reading difficulty, delinquency, and deterioration, etc. Hunt & French (69) summarize their developmental work on the CVS scale and offer it not only as a good short test of intelligence but as a coarse diagnostic screen. Bluett (14) reports normative data for a battery of tests found useful in the rehabilitation of handicapped adults.

Using the Rosenzweig Picture Frustration technique, Holzberg & Hahn (68) compared adolescent psychopaths and normals, finding no differences in hostility and guilt. Another study fails to confirm previously reported findings of differences in stutterers and nonstutterers. In another paper, 5 out of 18 variables were found to differentiate anxiety neurotics and normals at the .05 level of significance.

As contrasted with the single technique approach reflected in so many papers, Lehmann & Dorken (77) report the use of a battery of projective tests. Although composed of four short tests, all of which can be scored relatively objectively, this battery shows promising discrimination among diagnostic categories.

As usual, several papers proposed new projective techniques, which to their creators, at least, "appear promising." To this reviewer, Kinget's "Drawing Completion Test" (72) seemed the most promising, perhaps because the author presented considerable data based on the technique.

Among the paper-and-pencil inventories, the MMPI was the most frequently studied instrument, followed closely by the Strong Vocational Interest Blank. Both instruments continue to show promise of utility for certain assessment situations, but in some instances the predictive validity is so low as to suggest the desirability of searching for other predictors instead of relying entirely on a favorite one. Typical papers are those by Williams (119) reporting the development of a "Caudality Scale" for the MMPI and that by Kriedt, Stone & Paterson (76) on the Vocational Interests of Industrial Relations Personnel. Both Navran (88) and Healy & Borg (63) report no validity of interest scores for the prediction of success in nurses' training.

Methodological Contributions

The failure of self-report inventories to show predictive validities in some selection situations has led to a number of efforts to identify and correct for "faking" on the part of the subject. A paper by Schlesser (99) suggests a number of possible solutions to the problem. Another approach lies in the development and use of more "subtle" items as suggested by Seeman (102) and as followed by Gough (50) who in the development of a new M-F scale, eliminated items for which judges could recognize the characteristic M or F response.

Still another approach to the problem of "faking" on self-report inventories is the development of "objective tests" measuring the same variables as traditionally approached by the Yes-No type of item. The development of such tests calls for ingenuity, but that it is possible is shown by the success of Cattell & Horowitz (21) in the construction of a series of short objective tests of "altruism" most of which turn out to be highly saturated with two or three personality factors previously identified through ratings and inventories.

Much of the reluctance of many psychologists to use objective measures of personality and statistical combination of such measures appears to stem from a conviction that the most accurate representation of an individual's personality and the most accurate prediction of his future behavior requires the use of mathematical models other than the "additive" one embodied in the widely used multiple regression technique. That an objective and statistical approach need not be limited to this or other specific models is reflected in the increasing use of procedures for quantifying the congruence of profiles, summarized by Cronbach & Gleser (27), and in the development of promising techniques of configural analysis of both profiles and item responses as suggested by Sullivan & Welsh (109) and by Gaier & Lee (46). A still more dramatic demonstration of the possibility of objectifying and statistically analyzing variables which the clinician regards as relevant is the P-technique factor analysis of the day-to-day variation in motives in a single subject reported by Cattell & Cross (20).

Conclusion

In this review of the theory and techniques of assessment the writer has attempted to report the present state of affairs as objectively as his obvious biases would permit. In doing so, it has been necessary to admit an almost complete absence of relevant theory and a discouragingly large number of studies yielding negative results. In spite of extensive efforts in the field, as reflected in an almost fabulous number of publications, an unfortunately large proportion of the researches reported do not seem to make any real contribution to theory or to practice. Furthermore, all evidence points to the fact that much of current practice involves the use of tests and techniques for which there is almost no evidence of predictive validity for the relevant criterion.

In spite of this dismal over-all picture, the reviewer is not discouraged regarding the future possibilities of assessment. Already, there is evidence that it is possible to predict a number of very different socially relevant criteria with a sufficient degree of accuracy to be useful. While the proportion of variance in the criterion accounted for may still not be large, there is reason to believe that psychologists have the necessary creativity, ingenuity, and skills to develop still better measures of both predictor and criterion variables. Even more important, assessment psychologists are peculiarly equipped with the methods and skills to carry out both the necessary evaluation of present procedures and crucial tests of new procedures suggested by advances in personality and measurement theory. To the extent that they utilize this unique competence, we may expect continued progress in the prediction of socially significant criteria. And to the degree that the prediction of real life behavior constitutes the acid test of the validity of hypothetical constructs, research in assessment may serve a "reality testing" function for theoretical developments in psychology.

LITERATURE CITED

1. Allen, R. M., Stiff, M. P., and Rosenzweig, M., *J. Clin. Psychol.*, **9,** 81–82 (1953)
2. Ames, L. B., Learned, J., Metraux, R. W., and Walker, R. N., *Child Rorschach Responses* (Paul B. Hoeber, Inc., New York, N. Y., 310 pp., 1952)
3. American Psychological Association Committee on Test Standards, *Am. Psychologist*, **7,** 461–75 (1952)
4. Auld, F., Jr., and Eron, L. D., *J. Consulting Psychol.*, **17,** 104–9 (1953)
5. Barron, F., *J. Abnormal Social Psychol.*, **48,** 163–72 (1953)
6. Bass, B. M., *J. Appl. Psychol.*, **33,** 527–33 (1949)
7. Bass, B. M., and Coates, C. H., *J. Abnormal Social Psychol.*, **47,** 321–25 (1952)
8. Bass, B. M., Klubeck, S., and Wurster, C. R., *J. Appl. Psychol.*, **37,** 26–30 (1953)
9. Bass, B. M., McGehee, C. R., Hawkins, W. C., Young, P. C., and Gebel, A. S., *J. Abnormal Social Psychol.*, **48,** 120–28 (1953)
10. Bass, B. M., and Wurster, C. R., *J. Appl. Psychol.*, **37,** 96–99 (1953)
11. Bass, B. M., and Wurster, C. R., *J. Appl. Psychol.*, **37,** 100–4 (1953)
12. Beck, S. J., *Rorschach's Test. III. Advances in Interpretation* (Grune & Stratton, Inc., New York, N. Y., 301 pp., 1952)
13. Bills, M. A., and Taylor J. G., *J. Appl. Psychol.*, **37,** 21–23 (1943)
14. Bluett, C. G., *J. Clin. Psychol.*, **8,** 237–44 (1952)
15. Blum, G. S., and Hunt, H. F., *Psychol. Bull.* **49,** 238–50 (1952)
16. Borstelmann, L. J., and Klopfer, W. G., *Psychol. Bull.*, **50,** 112–32 (1953)
17. Brown, C. W., and Ghiselli, E. E., *J. Appl. Psychol.*, **36,** 370–72 (1952),
18. Buros, O. K., *The Fourth Mental Measurements Yearbook* (Gryphon Press, Highland Park, N. J., 1163 pp., 1953)
19. Callis, R., *J. Appl. Psychol.*, **37,** 82–85 (1953)
20. Cattell, R. B., and Cross, K. P., *J. Personality*, **21,** 250–71 (1952)
21. Cattell, R. B., and Horowitz, J. Z., *J. Personality*, **21,** 103–17 (1952)
22. Cattell, R. B., and Wenig, P. W., *J. Abnormal Social Psychol.*, **47,** 797–809 (1952)
23. Clark, J. H., *J. Clin. Psychol.*, **9,** 62–64 (1953)
24. Clark, R. A., *J. Exptl. Psychol.*, **44,** 391–99 (1952)
25. Crannell, C. W., *J. Psychol.*, **35,** 131–42 (1953)
26. Crissy, W. J. E., *Personnel Psychol.*, **5,** 73–86 (1952)
27. Cronbach, L. J., and Gleser, G. C., *Similarity between Persons and Related Problems of Profile Analysis* (Bureau of Research and Service, College of Education, Univ. of Illinois, Urbana, Ill., 53 pp., 1952)

28. Davenport, B. F., *J. Consulting Psychol.*, **16**, 171–75 (1952)
29. Driscoll, P. J., *J. Abnormal Social Psychol.*, **47**, 593–96 (1952)
30. Du Mas, F. M., *J. Clin. Psychol.*, **8**, 347–54 (1952)
31. Ellis, A., *J. Clin. Psychol.*, **9**, 167–71 (1953)
32. Ellis., A., *J. Consulting Psychol.*, **17**, 45–49 (1953)
33. Eysenck, H. J., *The Scientific Study of Personality* (The Macmillan Co., New York, N. Y., 320 pp., 1952)
34. Eysenck, H. J., *Am. Psychologist*, **8**, 105–14 (1953)
35. Fensterheim, H., and Tresselt, M. E., *J. Abnormal Social Psychol.*, **48**, 93–99 (1953)
36. Filmer-Bennett, G., *J. Abnormal Social Psychol.*, **47**, 502–6 (1952)
37. Fiske, D. W., and Baughman, E. E., *J. Abnormal Social Psychol.*, **48**, 25–32 (1953)
38. Fleishman, E. A., *J. Appl. Psychol.*, **37**, 1–6 (1953)
39. Forer, B. R., and Tolman, R. S., *J. Consulting Psychol.*, **16**, 347–52 (1952)
40. Frankle, A. H., *Am. Psychologist*, **7**, 289 (1952)
41. Friedman, H. *J. Projective Techniques*, **16**, 352–60 (1952)
42. Fry, F. D., *J. Psychol.*, **35**, 181–96 (1953)
43. Gadel, M. S., and Kriedt, P. H., *Personnel Psychol.*, **5**, 207–12 (1952)
44. Gage, N. L., *Educ. Psychol. Measurement*, **13**, 14–26 (1953)
45. Gaier, E. L., *J. Appl. Psychol.*, **36**, 316–22 (1952)
46. Gaier, E. L., and Lee, M. C., *Psychol. Bull.*, **50**, 140–48 (1953)
47. Ghiselli, E. E., and Barthol, R. P., *J. Appl. Psychol.*, **37**, 18–20 (1953)
48. Gibby, R. G., *J. Consulting Psychol.*, **16**, 449–55 (1952)
49. Gleser, G., and Ulett, G., *J. Clin. Psychol.*, **8**, 279–82 (1952)
50. Gough, H. G., *Educ. Psychol. Measurement*, **12**, 427–39 (1952)
51. Gough, H. G., *The California Psychological Inventory* (University of California Press, Berkeley, Calif., 1951)
52. Gough, H. G., and Pemberton, W. H., *J. Appl. Psychol.*, **36**, 307–9 (1952)
53. Gough, H. G., and Peterson, D. R., *J. Consulting Psychol.*, **16**, 207–12 (1952)
54. Greenbaum, M., Qualtere, T., Carruth, B., and Cruickshank, W., *J. Clin. Psychol.*, **9**, 40–43 (1953)
55. Grossack, M., *J. Psychol.*, **35**, 245–52 (1953)
56. Guertin, W. H., *J. Consulting Psychol.*, **16**, 308–12 (1952)
57. Guertin, W. H., *J. Consulting Psychol.*, **16**, 371–75 (1952)
58. Hammer, E. F., *J. Clin. Psychol.*, **9**, 7–10 (1953)
59. Hanfmann, E., *J. Personality*, **21**, 1–12 (1952)
60. Harris, R. E., and Christianson, C., *J. Psychol.*, **15**, 49–74 (1943)
61. Harrison, R., and Jackson, T. A., *J. Appl. Psychol.*, **36**, 373–76 (1952)
62. Hathaway, S. R., and Monachesi, E. D., *Am. Sociol., Rev.*, **17**, 704–9 (1952)
63. Healy, I., and Borg, W. R., *Educ. Psychol. Measurement*, **12**, 767–75 (1952)
64. Hemphill, J. K., and Sechrest, L. B., *J. Appl. Psychol.*, **36**, 323–27 (1952)
65. Heron, A., *J. Appl. Psychol.*, **36**, 385–87 (1952)
66. Higham, M. H., *Occupational Psychol. (London)*, **26**, 169–75 (1952)
67. Holt, R. R., and Luborsky, L., *Bull. Menninger Clin.*, **16**, 125–35 (1952)
68. Holzberg, J. D., and Hahn, F., *Am. J. Orthopsychiat.*, **22**, 776–97 (1952)
69. Hunt, W. A., and French, E. G., *J. Consulting Psychol.*, **16**, 181–86 (1952)
70. Hunt, W. A., Wittson, C. L., and Hunt, E. B., *J. Clin. Psychol.*, **8**, 314–15 (1952)

71. Kelly, E. L., and Fiske, D. W., *The Prediction of Performance in Clinical Psychology* (The University of Michigan Press, Ann Arbor, Mich., 311 pp., 1951)
72. Kinget, G. M., *The Drawing Completion Test* (Grune & Stratton, Inc., New York, N. Y., 224 pp., 1952)
73. Klatskin, E. H., *J. Projective Technique,* **16,** 193–99 (1952)
74. Klieger, W. A., and Mosel, J. N., *Personnel Psychol.,* **6,** 57–64 (1953)
75. Kotkov, B., and Meadow, A., *J. Consulting Psychol.,* **17,** 16–20 (1953)
76. Kriedt, P. H., Stone, C. H., and Paterson, D. G., *J. Appl. Psychol.,* **36,** 174–79 (1952)
77. Lehmann, H., and Dorken, H., Jr., *Can. J. Psychol.,* **6,** 164–72 (1952)
78. Levine, A. S., and Tupes, E. C., *J. Appl. Psychol.,* **36,** 157–60 (1952)
79. Lorr, M., *J. Clin. Psychol.,* **9,** 143–44 (1953)
80. Lorr, M., and Jenkins, R. L., *J. Clin. Psychol.,* **9,** 16–19 (1953)
81. Lotsof, E. J., *J. Consulting Psychol.,* **17,** 21–24 (1953)
82. MacKinnon, D. W., *Am. Psychologist,* **8,** 138–46 (1953)
83. Malcom, E. V., *A Study of the Validity of Individual Personality Profiles Based on Each of Four Projective Techniques* (Doctoral dissertation, Univ. of Michigan, Ann Arbor, Mich., 1951)
84. Maradie, L. J., *J. Consulting Psychol.,* **17,** 32–35 (1953)
85. Martin, H. G., *Educ. Psychol. Measurement,* **12,** 699–700 (1952)
86. McKeachie, W. J., *J. Social Psychol.,* **36,** 241–44 (1952)
87. Melville, S. D., and Frederiksen, N., *J. Appl. Psychol.,* **36,** 169–73 (1953)
88. Navran, L., *J. Appl. Psychol.,* **37,** 31–32 (1953)
89. Newman, S. H., French, J. W., and Bobbitt, J. M., *Educ. Psychol. Measurement,* **12,** 394–407 (1952)
90. Office of Strategic Services Staff, *Assessment of Men* (Rinehart & Co., Inc., New York, N. Y., 541 pp., 1948)
91. Rodger, A., *Occupational Psychol.,* **26,** 101–8 (1952)
92. Rogers, L. S., and Hammond, K. R., *J. Consulting Psychol.,* **17,** 8–15 (1953)
93. Rogers, L. S., Knauss, J., and Hammond, K. R., *J. Consulting Psychol.,* **15,** 368–71 (1951)
94. Rotter, J. B., *Ann. Rev. Psychol.,* **4,** 295–316 (1953)
95. Rush, C. H., Jr., *Personnel Psychol.,* **6,** 9–24 (1953)
96. Ryans, D. G., *Educ. Psychol. Measurement,* **12,** 333–44 (1952)
97. Ryans, D. G., and Wandt, E., *Educ. Psychol. Measurement,* **12,** 574–86 (1952)
98. Sakoda, J. M., *J. Abnormal Social Psychol.,* **47,** 843–52 (1952)
99. Schlesser, G. E., *Educ. Psychol. Measurement,* **13,** 77–86 (1953)
100. Schofield, W., *J. Clin. Psychol.,* **8,** 255–61 (1952)
101. Seashore, H. G., *Personnel Psychol.,* **6,** 45–56 (1953)
102. Seeman, W., *J. Consulting Psychol.,* **16,** 278–83 (1952)
103. Severin, D., *Personnel Psychol.,* **5,** 93–104 (1952)
104. Shipley, T. E., Jr., and Veroff, J., *J. Exptl. Psychol.,* **43,** 349–56 (1952)
105. Siipola, E., and Taylor, V., *J. Personality,* **21,** 22–47 (1952)
106. Spencer, G. J., and Worthington, R., *Personnel Psychol.,* **5,** 125–44 (1952)
107. Stalnaker, J. N., and Eindhoven, J., in *Admission Requirements of American Medical Colleges,* **6** (Association of American Medical Colleges, Chicago, Ill., 106 pp., 1953)
108. Stotsky, B. A., *J. Abnormal Social Psychol.,* **47,** 489–96 (1952)

109. Sullivan, P. L., and Welsh, G. S., *J. Consulting Psychol.*, **16**, 383–88 (1952)
110. Suttell, B. J., and Pascal, G. R., *J. Abnormal Social Psychol.*, **47**, 635–57 (1952)
111. Swenson, W. M., and Lindgren, E., *Personnel Psychol.*, **5**, 19–24 (1952)
112. Thurstone, L. L., *Psychometric Lab. Univ. Chicago*, **78**, 1–5 (1952)
113. Tobolski, F. P., and Kerr, W. A., *J. Appl. Psychol.*, **36**, 310–11 (1952)
114. Van Zelst, R. H., *J. Appl. Psychol.*, **36**, 293–95 (1952)
115. Wallace, S. R., Jr., and Twichell, C. M., *Personnel Psychol.*, **5**, 347–58 (1952)
116. Weider, A., *Contributions toward Medical Psychology*, **II** (The Ronald Press Co., New York, N. Y., 426 pp., 1953)
117. Weider, A., and Noller, P. A., *J. Clin. Psychol.*, **9**, 20–23 (1953)
118. Weisskopf, E. A., and Dunlevy, G. P., Jr., *J. Abnormal Social Psychol.*, **47**, 441–45 (1952)
119. Williams, H. L., *J. Clin. Psychol.*, **8**, 293–97 (1952)
120. Windle, C., *Psychol. Bull.*, **49**, 451–82 (1952)
121. Wittenborn, J. R., and Weiss, W., *J. Consulting Psychol.*, **16**, 193–98 (1952)
122. Wurster, C. R., and Bass, B. M., *Educ. Psychol. Measurement*, **13**, 122–23 (1953)

PSYCHOTHERAPY[1]

By George Saslow

Departments of Medicine and Neuropsychiatry and Division of Psychosomatic Medicine, Washington University School of Medicine, Saint Louis, Missouri

Professor Wrenn (author of the chapter on Counseling) and I have made no attempt to delimit counseling and psychotherapy by means of a definition. We are inclined to consider such an attempt as little likely to succeed as the recent search for a definition of psychoanalysis [Committee on Evaluation of Psychoanalytic Therapy (1)]. We shall therefore leave psychotherapy "as an undefined technique which is applied to unspecified problems with nonpredictable outcome" [Lehner (2)]. This chapter will concern itself with the therapeutic process in medical settings, and with conceptual, clinical, and research activities in the field of therapy which seem highly relevant to such settings. The available materials for the period from May, 1952, to May, 1953 will be dealt with under the headings individual psychotherapy as process, individual psychotherapy in relation to outcome of therapy, multiple psychotherapy, group therapy, and general comments. Emphasis will be more upon critique than upon bibliography.

Individual Psychotherapy: As Process

The possibility of predicting which patients will continue in psychotherapy after the ninth interview has been studied by means of Rorschach scores [Auld & Eron (3)]. A proposed prediction formula, combining the total number of responses *R*, the percentage of these that are large usual details *D*%, and the number of form-color responses minus the number of color-form responses *FC—CF*, had been derived from 98 patients receiving outpatient group psychotherapy and subsequently applied successfully to another sample of 52 patients in individual therapy in the same clinic [Kotkov & Meadow (4)]. The developed formula was tried with a new sample of 33 psychiatric clinic patients in another city. It failed to predict which patients would continue individual psychotherapy and which would not. Auld & Eron therefore emphasize that, until cross validation and validity-generalization studies have been done, no confidence can be placed in the general applicability of any method of diagnosis or any formula for predicting behavior.

An improvement in the assessment of certain changes in individuals during psychotherapy is suggested by Butler (5). Procedures used so far by the Rogers group involve the construction of categories of recorded verbal behavior to be studied through time, counting the frequencies of behavior within the categories, and expressing these as percentages. Butler

[1] The survey of the literature to which this review pertains was completed in May, 1953.

points out that the categories set up generally neglect the context of behaviors outside them and that such neglect leads easily to unjustified inferences from the numerical data. He therefore proposes a "context coefficient" which does take account of the context of behaviors outside the categories being explored, and reduces to the narrower type of coefficient when noncategory responses are zero.

Raimy's method of studying self-references during psychotherapy has been extended by Bugental (6). One recorded case, the "Herbert Bryan" case in Rogers' 1942 book, was examined as an example of the new procedure. The thought units are divided into six self, not-self categories, called the Conceptual Matrix. The feeling tone of each unit is evaluated in terms of four categories (positive, negative, etc.). Interrater reliability was adequate. Consistency of the rank order of the categories in the Conceptual Matrix, from interview to interview, was high. The sample analyzed indicates the possibility of a fuller description of the patient's verbal participation in the therapeutic process in objective and quantified terms. The material is permanently available for the study of hypotheses, for making comparisons with other patients, examining the patient's achievement of defined goals of therapy, etc.

Various methodological approaches to the study of therapy as a process, with indications either that work is in progress or that unexpected difficulties have been encountered, are described in the recent book edited by Mowrer (7). Nearly all the material referred to in the book has already appeared in print, but the unusually high level of organization of it in various chapters is provocative and rewarding. Review of studies (since 1943) of the process of client centered therapy leads to the inference that they have been mainly studies in conceptualization; they have helped build ways of looking at therapy which have added to the theory-building process. They are not self-contained validity studies of therapy, but represent stages in the acquisition of knowledge which will need subsequently to be verified through independent measures of the phenomena examined [Seeman & Raskin (8)]. The considerable amount of work which has been done since 1947 with the discomfort-relief quotient (DRQ) is assessed by Dollard & Mowrer (9) and by Mowrer, Hunt & Kogan (10). The DRQ appears to be a reliable and valid indicator of other objective measures of personal change during therapy and of therapeutic success as estimated by psychotherapists. But it is not valid for social casework, the procedure from which it was derived, for reasons not now evident. Nor does it appear to be correlated with "tension" in schizophrenic subjects, again for reasons not evident. A description, historical outline, and critique of the procedures known as "Q technique" are given by Mowrer (11). Of major import is his demonstration that contemporary research in the field of personality is moving rapidly toward the development of a valid statistics of the individual case. Subdivisions of the developments in the general field are presented by Cronbach (12) in "Correlations between persons as a research tool," Luborsky (13) in "Intraindividual repetitive measurements (P technique) in understanding psychotherapeutic change," and McQuitty (14) in "A statistical method for studying personality integration." These four chapters in Mowrer's book, which do not permit easy summary, suggest that methods of study of individuals in clinical situations may soon be more clearly related to traditional research methods that use a statistics of groups. New ways of looking upon verbal behavior in psychotherapy are discussed by Mowrer (15). He considers them to have possibilities in the study of the process. Among them are the relative frequency of different parts of speech (pp. 503–21, 526–30); percentage of references to others and to self (pp. 522–24); content analysis through time to show the rise and fall of expressed concern with various problem areas (pp. 524–25); changes in the meanings of key words during therapy (pp. 530–36); study of consistency and contradiction during therapy (pp. 536–44), etc. All of the procedures have interesting aspects, and none has been supported by adequate systematic study. The beginnings of such study are described in a chapter dealing with tension, discomfort-relief quotient, and palmar sweat changes during psychotherapy, with special reference to resistance [Mowrer *et al.* (16)]. Transcribed interview recordings of 20 subjects are being used (the study is as yet unpublished). "Tension" was reported by each subject on a five-point scale, just before and after each interview; "happiness," similarly on a seven-point scale. Persons who completed therapy (n, 15) were distinguishably and appropriately different with regard to these simple measures from the five who did not. In 10 cases, subjective ratings and objective perspiration measurements were available; these showed good congruence, and thus both methods seem to have high face validity. Striking discrepancies occurred, which proved illuminating on detailed examination of the interview material: in one such case, the palmar perspiration measure appeared congruent with the interview material and the self-ratings were not. In the five recorded cases, the correlation between discomfort-relief quotient and palmar perspiration was .54; the changes were thus in the expected direction. In a chapter canvassing the possible inclusion of physiological changes during therapy as a necessary part of study of the process, attention is called to the so-far relatively unexploited use of skeletal muscle action potentials [O'Kelly (17)].

An experimental study of two definably different psychotherapeutic techniques has been published by Grossman (18). Two groups of 10 males each were matched for interest in obtaining therapy, temperament test scores, verbal and reasoning ability, etc. Each subject had three 60-min. interviews, the last being recorded. The therapist's statements were classified by himself and another judge; the therapist rated each subject's insight and progress on a five-point scale after the third interview, a day or two later, and four weeks later. Two hypotheses were examined: (*a*) subject's insight is greater following therapist responses that recognize explicitly expressed feelings or attitudes; (*b*) subject's insight is greater following therapist responses that recognize feelings or attitudes inferred from subject's verbal or motor behavior ("interpretations"). For some unaccountable reason, the desired matching was not fully achieved in the subjects' interview behavior: seven of the 10 in one group did not behave as if they had a definite problem. Despite this unforeseen difficulty, the data warranted accepting hypothesis (*b*) and rejecting (*a*). It seemed clear that the independent variable (therapist behavior) could be manipulated in a predetermined manner, that objective criteria could be used, and that several dependent variables could be held constant. Similar observations, apparently originally part of a doctoral dissertation, have been published by Dittman (19). Several judges evaluated 965 recorded verbal responses of one subject in 30 successive interviews with one therapist. Therapeutic movement (as defined in terms of progressive self-exploration) was found to be associated with (*a*) high level of participation by the therapist (in the sense of completeness of understanding of what the subject is communicating), (*b*) either response to feeling or to behavior of subject with therapist, or to both, provided the response occurs in the context of consistent response to both feeling and interpersonal behavior, and (*c*) therapist responses which were "slightly deeper" than pure reflection.

In a study bearing upon the above topic, the nature of psychotherapeutic interpretation was examined by Porter (20). He utilized transcribed client-centered interview material. He found that the interpretations by therapists of patients' verbal and gestural productions could be grouped into five classes. He suggested that characteristic patterns in the use of favored classes would be found in therapists of different but known training frames of reference, but that so long as an interpretation relates accurately to the attitudinal state being expressed by the patient, therapy will take place. He thought it possible that each class of interpretation influences differently the speed and the pathways of conceptual and affective reorganization.

The three papers just described provide a framework for the remark of Rogers (21) that he has "reluctantly come to concede the possibility that the process, directions, and end points of therapy may differ in different therapeutic orientations." Butler (22), in a detailed consideration of the interaction of client and therapist, compared client-centered therapy with classical psychoanalytic therapy from the point of view that therapists of these two orientations may well set in motion quite different therapeutic processes. He focussed his comparison upon the hypothesis that "in two-way personal-social interaction, each individual concerned displays anticipatory behavior which in turn elicits anticipatory behavior on the part of the other, the anticipatory behavior of the other in each case confirming the prior learnings of the individual about himself." These prior learnings have been learned early and slowly and are quite fixed. Resistance and transference are, in terms of Butler's hypothesis, joint functions of the social learning of the client and of the stimuli presented by the therapist to the client. When, at a particular point in psychoanalytic therapy, systematic interpretation is undertaken, the patient perceives the stimuli produced by the therapist as resembling those connected with his maladjustment, in that interpretation is similar to parental behavior. Since the therapist believes the transference and resistance behavior to originate in the patient alone, he presents certain stimuli to him rather than others, and then the typical psychoanalytic phenomenon transpires: an interpersonal struggle which is the transference relationship. The sequence of behavior in client-centered therapy appears quite different: incipient transference and resistance reactions often appear early, but die out presumably because the therapist's behavior continues to be directed toward understanding the frame of reference of the client as expressed verbally and nonverbally. Butler believes the particular behavior of client-centered therapists serves to deny and extinguish anticipations of the client with regard to the therapist. Butler's considerations make clear why each type of therapist is likely to be convinced of the inevitable course of therapy done his way, for the course of therapy is largely determined by patient responses evoked by the therapist. He remarks also that it is at present by no means certain that the same learnings must occur to produce a satisfactory therapeutic outcome: only the end product may be decisive for success. Grossman's and Dittman's results must be interpreted in the light of this remark.

The clear definition of therapeutic orientations, as shown above, has obviously been productive of new knowledge about therapy as a process. But it seems to be quite difficult, at the level of practice, to keep the therapeutic orientations firm and easily separable. Thus client-centered therapists, like other therapists, are faced with involuntary clients [Beier (23)]. A willingness to deal with such clients implies expansion of the views of client-centered therapy. Beier includes children, delinquents, prisoners, employees, and persons referred by courts among involuntary clients, and gives a few brief examples of three pretherapeutic procedures designed to assist such clients to become motivated clients. It should be noted that Beier's definition of an involuntary client, as one who engages in maladaptive behavior and who has some wish to free himself from such behavior but who does not seek the assistance of a therapist, is easily extended to encompass the common problem of a patient in a medical setting whose behavior is in one way or another relevant to his illness. Often such a patient has a strong wish to free himself from disabling medical symptoms, which are associated with maladaptive behavior, but he does not recognize the association, does not necessarily wish to alter the behavior, and does not seek a therapist for alteration of his behavior. Yet experience shows over and over that his wish to free himself from medical symptoms, combined with medical study (which excludes or gives proper place to alternative explanations) and pretherapeutic procedures which include but go beyond those described by Beier, are often successful in leading to long-term alterations of behavior through psychotherapy. Thus a determined refusal to expand the client-centered orientation probably implies refusal to benefit a great many clients by attributing in advance the alleged low probability of success entirely to the client. Observations like those of Beier have also been made by Moustakas & Makowsky (24). They found a strictly nondirective approach to fail with a number of parents who came for help for their children. Slight changes from orthodoxy were effective in increasing their clients' motivation (hence one should again point out the relevance of Butler's hypothesis that the resistance of clients may be produced by the therapist's technique).

Starting with a different type of client, the college student, Perry & Estes (25) also reject the strictly nondirective approach. They present a carefully reasoned argument for abandoning the notion that directiveness and nondirectiveness are processes in a unidimensional continuum, in favor of the concept that they belong to different realms. They are regarded as complex processes with many possibilities of conflict and of coordination. It is postulated that "any counselor-participation which is assimilated by the client to a set in which he perceives himself as ultimately responsible for initiative and evaluation is properly describable as client-centered." Once the client has assumed this set, the counselor may put at his service (through activities conventionally excluded from the nondirective repertoire) the knowledge and skills of that part of the culture in which the counselor is a specialist.

The difficulty of holding to sharply drawn lines is brought home by occasional instances that refuse to stay inside them. Thus, the advisability of undertaking psychotherapy against the will of the patient is discussed by Odenwald (26). A single case is described in which a delinquent boy ordered to have psychotherapy while on probation became, after probation was over, a well-motivated patient. An extraordinary case is described by Ring (27). A 51 year old man, severely ill with paranoid schizophrenic psychosis, for 30 years, had been considered completely hopeless. After a bimedial leucotomy, he had nine months of carefully planned treatment, including psychotherapy up to two hours a day, five days a week. He received much planned emotional support from his relatives and various hospital personnel who were instructed to practice systematic nonresponse to his delusional behavior, and interested discussion of his lucid behavior. During therapy the patient's ideation, behavior disturbances, etc., resembled markedly those of the Schreber case discussed by Freud. He was discharged after nine months and remained well for two years, at which time Ring's report was written. Here leucotomy appears to have made the patient accessible to behavior therapy, which was highly flexible and not dependent upon either nondirectiveness or insight alone. Of interest also is a single case described by Sifneos (28). A young woman with anorexia nervosa, a disorder generally considered to be related significantly to early social learnings, had remained ill for seven years. Unsuccessful treatment had included psychoanalysis, electroshock, and insulin. Neurosurgical intervention, in the form of a unilateral lower quadrant right frontal leucotomy, was followed by much improvement.

Unusual instances such as the three cited not only raise questions of great general interest with regard to the dependence of new learning upon age, upon severance of thalamocortical pathways, etc., with regard to the extinguishing of old learnings in relation to severance of thalamocortical pathways, etc., but also challenge the framers of psychotherapeutic orientations to fit them in.

If we turn our attention to another therapeutic orientation, the psychoanalytic, from the point of view of therapy as process, we may begin with some conclusions of Cameron (29). In a discussion of the "activity of the therapist in integrative forms of nondirective psychotherapy," he portrays him as an active participant, contrary to much now believed and practiced. He considers free association (strictly defined in practice and expectations) a scientific tool congruent with nineteenth century scientific premises, but not with those of the twentieth century, and as having serious limits to its effectiveness. He describes the therapist as a social invention capable of many different kinds of actions and of a great number of actions, in addition to sitting, hearing, and interpreting. He mentions in outline four major categories of action a therapist may show: (*a*) resolving capacity, i.e., ability to identify patterns in the streaming events of psychotherapy, an ability of which we have little knowledge; (*b*) power, the ability to effect the reorganization of the patient's handicapping behavioral patterns, about the working of which we know little; (*c*) acting as an agent of change, by the way in which he facilitates and maintains communication with the patient and supplies models of more effective behavior patterns; and (*d*) functioning as a working model, with whom a patient can safely try out hitherto unsuccessful relationships. These observations of a nonpsychoanalyst may be compared with some comments upon individual psychoanalytic and group analytic therapy by a Freudian psychoanalyst [Foulkes (30)]. He emphasizes strongly how often individual psychoanalysis reveals only half the story about a patient, and often the less important half at that. He is impressed by how much that was not clear or suspected is learned by observing the patient in a group situation. He writes with conviction, mentions the opportunities for research that his groups provide, but presents no data. A Kleinian psychoanalyst points out that the psychoanalytic method has largely ceased to be a historical method involving a reconstruction of the patient's past and has largely become a method for investigating the influence of (characteristically unconscious) situations and relationships in inner reality upon contemporary experience and behavior [Fairbairn (31)]. The method may therefore now be described as ahistorical, not genetic. The patient, it is assumed, is therefore helped most by dealing with his "here and now" behavior in either a dyadic or a group setting. A Kleinian analyst interested in a strictly psychoanalytic approach to group therapy remarks that patients show greater changes by devoting one or two hours of treatment per week to such group therapy than to individual psychoanalytic sessions [Sutherland (32)]. In a symposium on group therapy, another psychoanalyst discusses various important difficulties of group therapy, the saving of time for the therapist rather than for the patient, and the fact that patients behave differently in individual and in group sessions [Klein (33)].

Thus a number of psychoanalysts have found it necessary to expand their therapeutic orientation, and appear to be approaching Cameron's emphasis upon the necessity, during therapy, for the patient to interact with one or more persons in a variety of ways, if the therapist is to understand enough about him, and the patient is to change significantly in a reasonable time.

Since apparently clearly defined therapeutic orientations are so difficult to sustain in their initial forms, the interesting question arises whether factors common to the various orientations exist which may be more relevant to the therapeutic process experienced by the patient than the philosophy or technique of the orientation. As is well known, the question has been studied ingeniously by Fiedler and his co-workers. Their work is summarized by Fiedler (34). The conclusions that the essential aspects of a therapeutic relationship are a more elemental component in therapy than methods or techniques and that good therapeutic relationships are primarily a function of expertness and are independent of school make one skeptical of the virtues claimed for new techniques, especially when unsupported by some kind of evidence beyond assertion. The conclusions also direct attention to the need for more explicit definition of "expertness," "good therapeutic relationship," etc.

When therapy has taken place, presumably the patient has learned something new during the good therapeutic relationship he has experienced, and what he has learned has generalized to interactions with other persons. Thus therapy may be considered to deal with the notion of behavior disorder as interpersonal incompetence, and to be a form of social learning [Shoben (35)]. Shoben presents a formulation of neurosis that stresses its social origins within the family and its social consequences as they affect later interpersonal behavior, drawing from laboratory studies of conditioning and instrumental learning the principles by which these experiences produce neurotic patterns of behavior. He is able to do this without postulating discontinuity between human data and those from other biological sources, and without the necessity of falling back upon such difficult-to-define concepts as id, ego, superego, and psychic energy. Utilization of the same sources and principles permits him to give a description of psychotherapy as a resocialization experience, within the framework of the two-factor learning theory, and (again) without the need of the difficult-to-define concepts above mentioned. An attempt to describe in more detail the events in a psychotherapeutic sequence as they may be pictured in terms of the principles utilized by Shoben and by Dollard & Miller (36) is given by Hofstaetter (37). His hypothetical model for the psychotherapeutic process leans chiefly upon avoidance and approach generalization-gradients involving tabooed acts, neutral acts, pertinent verbalizations, and neutral verbalizations, and appears to be congruent with the known psychotherapeutic orientations.

Mowrer (38) presents clearly the major emendations of Freud's conceptions of neurosis and psychotherapy with which he has been concerned for some years. He finds it congenial to utilize those difficult-to-define concepts which Shoben has demonstrated can well be dropped, cites telling general considerations in favor of his view that repression is directed against the superego rather than the id, but submits only small samples of the kind of evidence that could be crucial in deciding between his views of the direction of repression (and important related aspects of neurosis and psychotherapy) and Freud's. He indicates that a book with sufficient evidence on these matters is in preparation, and judgment will have to wait upon its appearance. There are significant differences between Shoben's and Mowrer's ways of looking upon neurosis and psychotherapy in the light of the same learning theory, for appreciation of which the references themselves must be studied.

Very few attempts have been made to design an experiment in which present knowledge of learning is utilized to fashion deliberately a technique of psychotherapy, in contrast to the effort which has gone into applying the conceptual framework of learning theory to psychotherapy as a process [Shoben (35), Mowrer (38)]. One such experiment is available in mimeographed form from the Veterans Administration Hospital at North Little Rock [Peters & Jenkins (39)]. In an earlier publication, the hypothesis was stated that the schizophrenic process is a replacement of adaptive behavior by stereotyped "frustration behavior"; that such a process sets in when an individual's frustration tolerance is passed; and that when the resulting maladaptive stereotyped behavior results in more frustration, the process is typically progressive [Jenkins (40)]. The hypothesis suggested a possible method of treatment consisting of the reestablishment of flexible adaptive behavior by a process of retraining, utilizing simple techniques developed in learning studies with animals. The hypothesis rests upon the experimental work of various students of learning and frustration, particularly Maier, who has also shown that the stereotyped behavior is reversible by a process of guidance to "correct solutions" of previously frustrating situations (41). The study by Peters & Jenkins is an effort to evaluate the effectiveness of such "guidance" in patients with chronic schizophrenic psychoses not showing a favorable response to other methods of treatment. A small number of patients, 12, was chosen for each experimental run. They were selected from one closed-ward building, met certain predetermined criteria, were matched with regard to a behavior rating scale and placed randomly into three groups: group I to receive the special learning treatment; II, to receive treatment identical with that of group I, except for the absence of the learning treatment; and III, to receive the routine treatment given all patients on their ward. Groups I and II received subshock insulin injections every morning, then attended occupational therapy, where in a few minutes group III joined them. Every week-day morning, groups I and II received intense occupational therapy, working with one or two nurses, two aides, two student nurses, and occasionally an occupational therapist. During the two-hour occupational therapy period, patients in pairs (one from each group) were taken to another room for breakfast; the order of eating breakfast early or late was rotated. The patients in group II, on reaching the breakfast room, received breakfast at once; group I patients went to the experimental room, where they spent 20 to 30 minutes at problem solving with fudge as a reward. The problem solving was done individually with one patient and a psychologist in the room. After his test run, the patient had breakfast and returned to occupational therapy. The group III patients were not known as such to the building personnel.

The experiment was continued for three months. In this experiment, insulin-induced hunger was used to motivate, on a biological level, learning by human beings. After 1½ months, the insulin was dropped for groups I and II; it no longer seemed necessary for motivation of their problem solving behavior.

Solution and learning of problems was the critical variable. It began with a simple obstruction problem: getting a piece of fudge covered by a transparent plastic tunnel 18 in.×2 in.×2½ in., with three 6 in. sticks that were available at one end of the tunnel. Once a patient had perfected a method of solving this problem (2 to 4 days), he went on to a more difficult one, and so on. Modified stylus mazes, circular pencil mazes, multiple choice boxes, reasoning problems and proverbs were used. Fudge was used as a reward for all these types of problems. The last type of problem was an interpersonal relation or social type of problem, chiefly simple psychodrama to stated themes.

The patient thus moved from simple to complex problems, from motor to ideational problems, from individual to social problems, and from problems in which there was a direct reward (his movements automatically got him the fudge) to those in which the reward was indirect (fudge handed him by the psychologist for correct solutions to circular maze and to reasoning problems, no fudge as reward in the psychodrama situation, but praise from the group leader for the least of efforts).

No patient completed all of the problems without some help. This guidance was given in a planned, consistent manner, even to the psychologist's moving a stylus correctly through the maze pathways while the patient was required to hold the end of the stylus. The procedure for each patient was planned carefully from day to day.

Four different kinds of measurements were used to evaluate the effectiveness of treatment, three were made during the six months after the experimental period. The measurements were objective ward incidents (transfer to a better ward, home on trial visit, destroying property, etc.), the behavior rating scale, occupational therapy ratings, and number of days worked in "special occupational therapy."

At the time of the mimeographing of the material here summarized, three sets of 12 patients each had been observed for six months after completion of the experimental period. The hypotheses investigated would lead to the expectation of evidence of greater improvement in group I than in II or III and in group II than in III. The observed group differences for groups I and II were favorable to group I for all four measurements, and the three possible differences for groups I and III were favorable to group I. The results obtained with the objective ward incidents are statistically reliable between group I and the other two groups, and suffice for a rejection of the null hypothesis that there are no real differences between the groups. The results as to differences between groups II and III were inconclusive. Thus the results indicate that guided problem solving, motivated by hunger, is an effective method of improving the social adjustment of chronic schizophrenics. The effects of the treatment seem great enough to be measurable in small samples. The procedure appears to warrant much further study.

I shall conclude this section of the review with notice of various unrelated contributions. Some important points are made about the importance of cultural understanding to psychotherapy in a description of three child guidance cases [Chess *et al.* (42)]. These came to a clinic which dealt with patients from varied national and ethnic backgrounds. The material is of anecdotal type. It indicates that diagnosis, prognosis, understanding of what is happening in therapy, and of the therapist's proper behavior may all be seriously in error if there is insufficient awareness of cultural differences between therapist and patient. Though so slight in substance, this paper is one of the very few existing applications of the cultural approach to personality in clinical psychiatry. A broad consideration of various social factors in therapy, with some illustrative survey and case material concerning therapists and patients, is to be found in Ruesch's contribution to a meeting of the Association for Research in Nervous and Mental Disease (43). A number of the points made are generally neglected, yet are of considerable importance to the more effective practice of psychotherapy in situations of significant differences between therapist and patient as to social class, cultural background, status, etc. Seven dramatic examples (anecdotal) of the hypnotherapeutic unmasking, intensification, and recognition of an emotion are given by Rosen (44). One of the therapeutic techniques made possible by the hypnotic interpersonal relationship is the encouragement to show some real feeling. Under such circumstances, a number of patients who blot out conscious awareness of emotions may experience intensely sex desire, rage, fear, etc. These emotional responses and their contexts of situation and symptoms may be worked with therapeutically. The seven patients so treated have been followed for 1 to 2½ years. The considerable dangers of such a technique (self-deception of the therapist, suicide of the patient) are pointed out. Practical necessity in an inpatient child psychiatric setting led to the awareness that separate therapists need not be assigned to the several members of a child's family [Szurek (45)]. One therapist could be effective in individual therapy with several adults. As this was realized, it seemed also to become clear that the previous procedure, customary and taken for granted as standard, implied that several therapists, each working with one member of a child's family, could work effectively with each other. This, it was now realized, could not be assumed to be so, but depended upon practice and experience of the several therapists in collaborating in just this way. Thus a therapist's experience in psychotherapy of individuals does not necessarily become, by transfer, an acceptable level of skill in interpersonal dealings with other therapist-colleagues: such skill needs to be learned. The material is anecdotal. A book is available in which specialized techniques in psychotherapy are described [Bychowski & Despert (46)]. The material is impressionistic, with no evidential support other than summarized clinical experience. The techniques range from narcotherapy to the use of the telepathy hypothesis. A new book on the roots of psychotherapy, has been published by Whitaker & Malone (47). They describe therapy in terms labelled "experiential," as essentially intrapsychic, nongenetic, ahistorical, atemporal, therapist-activated, and dealing mainly with id processes until the patient's fantasy needs are fulfilled. The patient's growth processes having been thus catalyzed, preferably as intensively and quickly as possible, therapy is terminated. There are many provocative observations and ideas in the book, and many unconventional ways of looking at therapy. Therapy is viewed as a symbolic fantasy relationship, and the therapist may use aggression, physical contact, or going to sleep, as techniques. The "brief depth therapy" is insufficiently explicitly described, and no systematic data are shown that deal with the process or its results.

Individual Psychotherapy: As Outcome

Because of the unsatisfactoriness of our criteria for the outcome of psychotherapy, the present state of this subject is one of extreme confusion. We have to deal, on the one hand, with the enthusiastic conviction of psychotherapists and of many of their patients that the time, effort, and money expended have been associated with long-lasting fruitful changes in the life pattern of the patient; and, on the other hand, with the contradictory or disillusioning results of the efforts to study outcome in a systematic manner. Eysenck (48) has for some time pointed out that his survey of the available reports of improvement of neurotic patients after and without psychotherapy fails to support the hypothesis that "psychotherapy facilitates recovery from nervous disorder." The criteria of improvement used in the studied reports are discharge from a hospital, employment, and the like. In an unpublished study (by other investigators) of 100 patients with neurotic and psychotic types of behavior disorder, who did not have any planned psychotherapy, and who were re-evaluated from 1½ to 6 years later, it was found that criteria such as job stability, marital stability, geographic mobility, and amount of health care did not discriminate the minority of the patients who showed significant improvement in adjustive techniques and symptoms from the majority who did not show such improvement [Peters & Saslow (49)]. Observations of this kind, if confirmed, would make necessary the search for rather different classes of criteria of outcome, such, for example, as those suggested by Seeman & Raskin (50): degree to which irrelevant cues are disregarded or are distracting, speed with which hypotheses are rejected when the evidence for them becomes negative, number of different hypotheses which are formed, etc.

A careful study in which clear-cut criteria of the outcome of therapy were defined and, in addition, would be generally considered highly relevant to the kinds of changes looked for when therapy had been successful, is reported by Teuber & Powers (51). This was a social experiment, in which for the eight years 1937 to 1945, 325 underprivileged boys in the Cambridge-Somerville (Massachusetts) area had guidance, counseling, and therapy, in the hope of preventing delinquency. Provision was made for the following: existence of an untreated control group, with 325 members matched individually, at the outset, with the members of the treatment group; systematic attempts at an objective description of the therapeutic relationships; and quantitative measurement of the effects of therapy. Matching variables included age, intelligence quotient, school grade, delinquency rating, ethnic background, etc. Ten counselors whose treatment activities were not of one therapeutic orientation, but ranged from a big-brother relationship to psychiatric case work therapeutic interviews, participated originally. With the passage of time, a psychoanalytically trained supervisor was added to the staff. All treatment consisted of individual, face-to-face contacts. After eight years, treatment had lasted for two to eight years in individual cases, with a median duration of four years two months.

From 1937 to 1948, the total number of court appearances was 264, as a result of offenses committed by 96 boys in the treated group, and 218, committed by 92 boys in the control group. From 1938 to 1946, 49 boys in the treated group appeared one time before The Crime Prevention Bureau, and 65 boys two or three times; corresponding figures are 49 and 52 boys in the control group. Unless further trends change the present picture (and they might), the direct comparison between the two groups fails to sustain the major hypothesis that treatment would reduce the incidence of adjudged delinquency.

The counselors believed that the treatment program had substantially benefited about two-thirds of the treated boys; more than half the boys volunteered (after the treatment period was over) that they had been helped. Careful examination of the records of the treatment process (not verbatim records but daily logs) showed that a counselor-boy relationship which was poor was characterized by mutual misinterpretation persistently from the beginning [thus being illustrative of the considerations of client-therapist interaction put forward by Butler (22)]. It also appeared that certain counselors developed such relationships more frequently than others [thus illustrating the conclusions reached later by Fiedler (34)].

Before the evaluative results were known, all but two members of the treatment staff predicted significant success with the treated group. Hence an evaluation in the style characteristic of the vast majority of articles on outcome of therapy ever published, based on the therapist's own story and lacking objective indices of observed behavior, would certainly have resulted in another report of very successful therapy. To some of the counselors, the ideas of control group and of objective indices, etc., were meaningless; they felt the relationships established were valuable in themselves, even with the negative results of the delinquency prevention program. Others believed that all the necessary rules for conducting therapy were known and that research was superfluous. When informed of the final results, the psychoanalytic members of the treatment staff who had this idea asserted that the results would have been positive had there been consistent application of psychoanalytic principles, while the Rogerian counselors with this idea made identical assertions about systematic use of nondirective methods. The authors state dryly that one thing is clear from the data: the burden of proof is on anyone who claims specific results for a given form of therapy.

Appel *et al.* (52) discuss published reports of long term psychotherapy (over three months) by different methods. Their Table I, on p. 25, shows the results of treatment of 4131 psychoneurotic patients in 12 carefully made sets of observations available from Britain, Germany, and the United States, by psychoanalytic therapy, face-to-face psychoanalytically-oriented therapy, reassurance, re-education, hypnosis, distributive analysis, etc. The data accumulated from follow-up periods of from 1 to 20 years. The criteria of improvement of different observers are hardly comparable. Methods of obtaining follow-up information vary tremendously. Therapy processes are impossible to define, from the published data, in most reports. Nearly all the studies survey patients treated from 1910 to 1939.

Factors such as those above mentioned and various others make the validity of comparison between different methods of treatment very doubtful. Improvement seems to take place in about 67 per cent of psychoneurotic patients who have psychotherapy (range 55 to 76 for 11 studies, 87 for the twelfth).

Their Table II, on p. 25, shows the results of treatment of 1651 schizophrenic patients in seven centers before the introduction of insulin, electroshock, and brain surgery. Improvement was reported in 39 per cent (range, 25 to 50). More recent reports from groups especially interested in intensive psychotherapy with schizophrenic patients show improvement in 41 per cent of 139 patients (Chestnut Lodge 1944 to 1949) and in 60 per cent of 37 patients (J. Rosen).

The authors point out that, if the available figures mean anything, they may mean that psychotherapy has no effect whatever on patients, or that (if the natural history of the behavior disorders were known) nonspecific and common elements of the different types of therapy would be found to outweigh grossly in effectiveness their dissimilarities. On the grounds that it is contrary to experience, the authors reject the first possibility and accept the second.

That the common elements in different types of psychotherapy are of major relevance to the changes which take place in patients is a hypothesis congruent with the observations of Fiedler and with the impressions of various able psychotherapists; also, it is attractive and plausible in its own right. It has been clearly demonstrated, however, in far simpler situations, that reasoning of this kind does not necessarily answer questions of causal relationship in any specific manner [Klüver (53)]. He cites a number of observations from different fields which are examples of an "equivalence of stimuli"; in that heterogeneous stimuli, such as diverse chemical substances, disease processes, or sensory stimuli, often produce the same series of effects in an organism. If one attempts to account for such an equivalence of stimuli by specifying the set of properties or the common factor involved in producing the same effect, one may find no lack of general theories, or vague hypotheses purporting to account for particular forms of equivalence, or (as in the case of chemical agents) abandon all hope of explaining the results on a chemical basis, or that it is possible only to specify such common factors as are not relevant to the effects to be explained, or that the common factors must be located in the processes of the affected organism.

A few observations of the outcome of psychotherapy are available in the field of the psychosomatic or "stress" disorders. Stine & Ivy (54) made a preliminary report dealing with the effect of psychoanalysis on the course of peptic ulcer. Although they circularized the entire membership (368) of the American Psychoanalytic Association for help in the study, their material to 1951 is described as completely inadequate to shed light on the question, "How does psychoanalysis alter the course of peptic ulcer?" It was found possible to collect 17 cases, of which 7 proved suitable for a follow-up study. Two were unimproved, and five were improved. The paper discusses the difficulties which beset the authors, who propose to continue the study. A point of interest is that 80 per cent of the 253 psychoanalysts who replied to inquiries by the authors had not psychoanalyzed a single case of ulcer. A preliminary report of an appraisal of the results of treatment of various stress disorders is given by Berle *et al.* (55). The results of treatment of 739 patients in a clinic emphasizing psychotherapy, with follow-up of one to two years after discharge, are summarized. The physicians had been trained chiefly in internal medicine and were supervised by a senior psychiatrist. Therapeutic techniques varied from highly directive to nondirective, from suppressive to vigorously exploratory activity. Free association, dream analysis, correlation of health state with events and attitudes, and encouragement to free expression of feelings were used. Each patient was appraised by his own physician and (by review of the latter's appraisal) by the authors in terms of 852 items descriptive of him. Some of the disorders of the treated patients were irritable colon, asthma, peptic ulcer syndrome, essential hypertension, urticaria, vasomotor rhinitis, ulcerative colitis, and diabetes. A third of the patients failed to show improvement, two-fifths improved symptomatically, and a quarter showed improvement considered to be basic in that it appeared to include a reorientation or maturation of the personality. Since such data cannot answer the question whether the results achieved might have occurred spontaneously, other studies were planned in which matched treated and control groups would be compared. Thus 34 patients with ulcerative colitis treated in the special (psychosomatic) clinic were carefully matched with 34 other patients with ulcerative colitis treated in various other clinics of the New York Hospital (where the main emphasis of therapy had been placed on diet, medication, and antibiotic agents). For each patient treated in the special clinic, another was sought who matched him in age, sex, duration and severity of illness as judged by x-ray and other criteria, etc. Comparison showed consistent advantages in the group receiving psychotherapy, with regard to deaths (psychotherapy group 9 per cent and matched group, 18 per cent), operations (3 per cent versus 29 per cent), worse (0 versus 6 per cent), same (23 versus 21 per cent), improved (39 versus 18 per cent), symptom free (26 versus 15 per cent). The samples are small, but the differences are thought to be significant. Subsequent material dealing with other stress disorders in which the same matching procedure was followed has been made available by Grace (56). For 23 untreated patients with peptic ulcer matched with 23 ulcer patients who had psychotherapy, the outcome was better in the group having psychotherapy (number of operations, number worse, same, improved). For 27 patients with asthma matched with 27 with asthma who had psychotherapy, the outcome was better in the patients having psychotherapy (number worse, same, improved). Similar data are being collected for publication by Grace on all the stress disorders studied in the psychosomatic clinic of the New York Hospital.

Zubin (57) copes with the problem of delineating a design for the evaluation of various types of therapy. Basic criteria for such an evaluation are met by less than a dozen published long-term follow-up studies. In these studies, nearly all the immediate outcomes indicate a definite advantage for the specific treatment (whether psychotherapy, psychoanalysis, or other) but no advantage for the long-run comparison. At present, no one is able to explain such observations.

Hunt (58) argues that the question of the outcome of psychotherapy cannot be neglected, as a matter of professional responsibility, and cannot be solved by studies limited to changes in the patient during the process. Nor, if change in the patient is in fact associated with psychotherapy can we omit to ask if the relationship is causal, which question requires determination of the frequency with which the same kinds of change occur without psychotherapy. He proposes a large-scale design, complex in execution, that would provide three kinds of data: (*a*) about the initial state of the patient (*b*) about the patient and therapist during the psychotherapeutic process, and (*c*) about changes in the patient's subjective state, behavior, and effects on others.

MULTIPLE THERAPY

Interest in the therapy of one patient with several therapists has been shown in several quarters. The material published is anecdotal, but, from a number of points of view, illuminating. Dreikurs *et al.* (59), in a second paper on the subject, describe briefly four patients who had simultaneous multiple therapy. The authors believe the process to have certain obvious advantages for the patient: (*a*) he can be more detached, (*b*) he can interact with two persons, (*c*) he can see a therapist make mistakes, (*d*) he can see an example of a sustained working relationship (between the two therapists) despite disagreements, (*e*) he can observe one therapist act out patient's role in difficult situations and learn more quickly his own cues and responses in that role, and (*f*) his dependency problems are more easily dealt with. Multiple therapy with juvenile delinquents is described by Buck & Grygier (60). Anecdotal material is presented about seven boys and two girls. The patient worked with a male and a female therapist, simultaneously, successively, or alternately, or with one therapist while the other therapist worked with mother. Home visits were made by either one of the therapists. The authors consider the advantages of these procedures to be: (*a*) the therapists have more insight into the patient, (*b*) the therapists have more awareness of the patient's total situation, material and human, (*c*) there is direct dealing with the total sphere of the patient's disturbed relationships, and (*d*) there is better handling of transference behavior in all the cases. So impressive has the procedure of multiple therapists seemed to the staff at Chestnut Lodge, that it appears to have become a recognized part of the treatment program [Dryud & Rioch (61)]. They use the term multiple therapy to mean treatment by interview of one patient by more than one therapist at the same time. They describe therapy of seven patients, each of whom had been having intensive individual psychotherapy. All but one continued with individual therapy, after multiple therapy was stopped. In six, there were less than seven multiple therapy interviews. Thus multiple therapy was used as a type of brief therapeutic intervention within the framework of long-term individual therapy. The material presented makes the following remarks pertinent: (*a*) the goals, methods, and results seem as varied as in individual therapy, (*b*) the procedure seems to have much possibility for dramatic resolution of an impasse in long-term intensive individual therapy, and (*c*) it apparently has this possibility because new observers see quickly and easily so much that psychoanalyzed therapists do not see about the patient's and especially about their own behavior. In addition, the individual and the multiple therapists seem subsequently to be better able to deal with each other as colleagues, are less competitive, less defensive, etc. The improvements in the therapist's perceptions and behavior occur in so little time that we must consider the multiple therapy situation one of high learning potentiality, yet it simply amounts to observation of and participation in a labelled overt interpersonal situation a few times. The perceptual distortions, rationalizations, ineffective behaviors, etc. of the individual psychoanalyzed therapist in an impasse with his patient constitute observations confirmatory of those published from Chestnut Lodge previously by Stanton & Schwartz (62): i.e., adequate ability to see oneself objectively as a therapist and to perceive one's patients and colleagues objectively is evident after personal psychoanalysis and formal psychoanalytic institute training with a frequency which leaves much to be desired. Yet objective appraisals of the necessary kinds are relatively easily made if others can observe the therapist in action, and, moreover, can easily be communicated to said therapist, who, still more surprisingly (in view of his and our preconceptions) quickly puts them to good use in the form of new responses to old cues involving his patients and his professional colleagues. As might be expected, Dryud & Rioch found therapists initially reluctant to face the multiple therapy situations, though later appreciating their usefulness. The implications of these observations for the training of therapists and for therapy are not discussed in the paper. Yet the difficulties in perceiving, evaluating, and utilizing a patient's and a colleague's verbal, nonverbal, and social behavior are by no means limited to the therapists at Chestnut Lodge, who are trained in the manner advocated by H. S. Sullivan. Very similar difficulties are indicated among therapists observed at Yale, where the training is closer to Freudian psychoanalytic procedure [Caudill *et al.* (63)], and just as little therapeutic use appears to be made of the interpersonal relations among their patients and between themselves and their colleagues by therapists observed at Washington University [Henry (64)]. The therapists at Washington University are trained by a wide variety of methods (none like that of Sullivan): some follow the Freudian procedure, some follow that of the Chicago Psychoanalytic Institute, some are eclectic in their practice. The implications of observations of such similar difficulties of therapists in centers utilizing training procedures thought to be so dissimilar are, therefore, well worth a glance. Perhaps all present methods of training psychiatrists as therapists, long and expensive though they are, omit learning in social situations to such a degree as to fall far short of achieving certain definable results with even fair frequency. It is conceivable that therapeutic effectiveness could be learned more quickly by systematic application of the observations made by Dryud & Rioch. And if therapists could increase in effectiveness by learning so much more quickly than we now think they can learn, why not patients? Thus the observations of the multiple therapists suggest important new ways of looking at therapy, the chief feature of which is that we accept considerably lower expectations of the ability of a patient to generalize individual interview learnings to other interpersonal situations without practice in those situations.

Group Therapy

Since Sanford's 1953 survey (65) of the ideas about psychoanalytic group therapy held by psychoanalysts in Britain who are followers of M. Klein, was published, no research material by members of this group seems to have appeared.

A book summarizing a project in group psychotherapy which started in 1946 has been published by Powdermaker & Frank (66). The project was undertaken within the United States Veterans Administration under the auspices of the Washington School of Psychiatry. It began in 1946 with a seminar group which discussed informally the available material on the psychology of group behavior and on research methods in the field; next there was therapy of an ambulant (chiefly neurotic) patient group (July, 1947 to December, 1948) and of a hospitalized chronic schizophrenic group (July, 1947 to May, 1949); and finally, came the analysis and publication of what was done and learned. The type of therapy used may be described as psychoanalytic in orientation, and much more like that of Foulkes (30) than of Sutherland (32). Most or all of the 24 psychiatrists had had, or were having, psychoanalytic therapy and analytic institute training. Five clinical psychologists and two psychiatric social workers were members of the project staff. All group therapy sessions were conducted by psychiatrists (including psychiatric residents), and observers (social worker or clinical psychologist) were present at nearly all sessions. Various methods of studying the process of therapy, e.g., using verbatim transcripts, categorizing and rating defined items in the group sessions, utilizing all or a representative sample of the available material, were looked into and discarded. The investigators found it necessary to limit themselves to the study of the problems of therapy which were of most immediate concern to the doctors and on which they had the most material. They tried to isolate the specific problems so defined, and to devise methods for valid study of them. They came to rely primarily upon data obtained by trained observers, working closely with the psychotherapists, and analyzed qualitatively.

The basic data consisted of the following: running accounts by observers of the activity in the group; a selection of what seemed to be therapeutically significant; summaries of meetings prepared by observer and therapist; situation analyses of events which appeared to have negative or positive therapeutic significance; therapist's judgment about a patient; psychologist's test data; and social worker's interview with patient, focussed on patient's interpersonal relations.

The patients studied in the clinic consisted of 124 white male veterans (9 psychotic.) Of the patients studied in the hospital, 88 were on an experimental ward and 86 on a control ward. Very few of the therapists had any prior experience with group therapy, and a number who worked with schizophrenic groups had practically no experience with individual therapy of schizophrenics. All therapists were volunteers. Most of the patients had both group and individual therapy sessions.

The difficulties of the project, such as inexperienced mobile personnel, administrative problems in the hospital project, thwarted desire to deal with the many variables of the group therapeutic process that could be explicitly defined and yet appeared mutually dependent, and unsolved methodological problems of criteria of outcome of therapy, were staggering. Despite them, much was learned for subsequent studies on a smaller scale. The careful presentation of the operation of the project and of a number of situation analyses will be found very rewarding. Only a few points will be mentioned here.

Careful study of the completeness and accuracy of the observer's running account of a session showed by no means such a great inferiority to mechanical verbatim recording as might be suspected (Appendix B, pp. 531–48). The psychiatrist's evaluation of individual patients, upon which much depended for evaluation of outcome of therapy, seemed to the reader as unsatisfactory here as elsewhere (Appendix C, pp. 549–52). The psychologist's use of the Rorschach test in the project (Appendix E, pp. 565–79) is subject to the most serious criticism since it was used in a global fashion that implied, without evidence to prove it, confirmation in a patient's social and group behavior of his overall Rorschach test performance and of specific aspects of that performance. Such use of the Rorschach ignores the great many published studies which show failure of specific determinants, patterns of Rorschach signs, or global Rorschach interpretations to predict any specific or general behavior of a subject [see for example, Auld & Eron (3); Roe (67)]. Roe found it impossible to guess from the Rorschachs of eminent American scientists either their high sustained achievement level or how they differed from hospitalized patients. Group therapy was more taxing and complicated than individual therapy, the doctors thought; and even those with considerable experience in individual therapy showed little quick generalization to the group therapy situation, or even quick learning in it. The idea that personal psychoanalysis frees a therapist to behave or to learn more easily in interpersonal situations is weakened (*a*) by one doctor's awareness that he fantasied his observer (who was being psychoanalyzed by the doctor's own analyst) reporting to his analyst what the doctor did poorly (p. 328), and (*b*) by another's feeling threatened at the prospect of closeness between two members of the group, and especially anxious in the presence of social conversation (p. 325, 326). There are suggestions in brief hints like these to make one wonder: (*a*) if transference relationships are ever worked through; or, (*b*) if worked through, facilitate easier interpersonal relations; or, (*c*) if working through them means a new permanent irrational tie to one's analytic therapist; or, (*d*) if having worked through them, one now needs to spend an equal amount of time learning how to deal with closeness, social conversation, or group therapy situations. Some remarkable observations are presented that have to do with intense rivalry situations set up between schizophrenic patients in a group in relation to a definable kind and intensity of doctor-patient relationship in that group (pp. 392–434). Under certain conditions, two such patients and the doctor appear to have undergone a symbolic fantasy experience of very high intensity, certainly for the patients and probably for the doctor, with subsequent sudden strikingly favorable behavioral alterations in one of the rivalrous patients: the whole procedure reading like an illustration of the thesis of catalyzed growth through satiation of intense infantile needs in the book by Whitaker & Malone (47). A unique description is that of therapy with a group of 87 chronic schizophrenic patients, most of whom also attended the small therapy groups (pp. 466–92); the large group functioned for 1½ years and had advantages of its own.

As to outcome, in the clinic group, improvement occurred in 61 per cent of those who had individual and group therapy and in 52 per cent of those who had only group therapy (pp. 38–65). A weakness in such an evaluation was the fact that chief weight was given to the doctor's judgment; even though this was influenced by social worker and psychologist information, one should recall the study of Teuber & Powers (51) which showed how little relation the intense conviction of interested parties in therapy may have to explicitly defined outcome. In the hospitalized group, analysis of many categories of comparison with the control ward group showed critical ratios significant at the 1 or 5 per cent level in only a few instances (pp. 344–58). In general, the data indicate that the experimental patients tended more often to react overtly in stressful situations than the controls, and that the group therapy had a stimulating effect upon outwardly purposeful activities and verbal relationships with others.

Some provocative illustrations scattered throughout the book (66) show that in group therapy the presence of a new doctor may elicit transference reactions, new life history material, etc., which had not appeared before; or may enable patients for the first time to express certain attitudes toward the former doctor or feelings thought unacceptable to him. It will be recalled that Foulkes (30) is impressed by how much is learned in a group situation that was not clear or not suspected in individual therapy sessions. Taken together, these observations suggest that psychotherapy might be more effective if the patient's therapy included either (*a*) interacting in a representative sample of his life situations or (*b*) being encouraged to give adequate descriptions of such a sample of his interactions, trying out new ones, evaluating them with the therapist, again trying, etc.

The second idea is undoubtedly used more or less systematically by many therapists who are not of a single therapeutic orientation. The first idea leads, by a natural extension, to the plan of making the patient's entire life situation therapeutic for a limited period. This has been attempted by Jones, and described in his book *The Therapeutic Community* (68). The plan of the Industrial Neurosis Unit (a hospital) grew out of two earlier experiences with therapy in groups, the first dealing with 100 patients who had neurocirculatory asthenia, and the second with 1200 exprisoners of war (who represented the most maladjusted 1 per cent of the 100,000 British repatriates from the European theatre of war). Therapy in the Industrial Neurosis Unit covers the whole working day of the patient and includes all his contacts with other persons. Intensive individual treatment is discouraged, few patients had uncovering psychotherapy, and none had psychoanalytic therapy. The patient-sample was drawn from desocialized patients with severe character disorders (chronic unemployed neurotics) consisting of drug addicts, prostitutes, prison offenders, schizoid personalities, sexual perverts, aggressive psychopaths, etc. One-third of 104 patients traced in follow-up visits were failures, 22 per cent made a "fair adjustment," and 44 per cent held good records (health, work experience, family life) for six months after a duration of three to four months of treatment. All treatment was free through the Ministry of Health of the United Kingdom, and many of the patients have war pensions. Over 85 per cent of the patients admitted had a history of psychiatric treatment.

It appears to have been demonstrated that it is possible to change social attitudes in relatively severely desocialized patients, if they are treated in a group by a staff which develops clear concepts of each member's role and which becomes a therapeutic community. The community workshops simulate normal factory conditions where the patients can practice mastering their tensions associated with work roles, while in the hospital. The level of common staff responsibility and of free communication necessary for an entire staff to function actively in therapy is of course very high, and cannot be achieved without major alterations taking place in doctor-doctor, doctor-nurse, and all-other-staff relationships. It is doubtful that the results achieved by Jones could have been achieved by conventional psychiatric hospitalization and individual psychotherapy (many of his patients are regarded by psychotherapists as incapable of socialization). It is of interest also that criteria of general adjustment such as job holding may be discriminating among patients of the kind treated by Jones.

General Comments

The experimental studies of the psychotherapeutic process appear to be leading to an enriched general and comparative psychology. The most satisfactory studies of the outcome of therapy, if we define this as modification of patients' behavior through the planned behavior of professional persons, appear to be those of the New York Hospital group on stress disorders (55, 56) and of the Belmont Industrial Neurosis Unit (68). Both studies suffer from the short duration of follow-up and from other admitted deficiencies, and neither utilizes the most intensive types of psychotherapy now known.

In 1950, at the Hixon Symposium on psychoanalysis as science, Hilgard (69) remarked that

> anyone who tries to give an honest appraisal of psychoanalysis as a science must be ready to admit that the bulk of the articles in its journals cannot be defended as research publications at all. Having said this, I am prepared to reassert that there is much to be learned from these writings. The task of making a science of the observations and relationships may, however, fall to others than the psychoanalysts themselves.

My reading of the published material on psychotherapy this year leads me to conclude that Hilgard's remark is as appropriate in 1953 as it was in 1950. It also leads me to conclude that it applies not only to psychoanalysts, but rather generally to medical psychotherapists as a class. The most promising and the soundest work in the field is being done by psychologists, in the sense of work that will ultimately be part of a general, comparative psychology.

The quantity and quality of the scientific work of psychiatrists is related to progressive loss of curiosity with professional age, in a report to be published by the Committee on Psychopathology from the Group for Advancement of Psychiatry (70). Related to the postulated decline in research motivation with age are thought to be at least four obvious factors: lack of personnel, lack of free time, lack of funds, and lack of training in research. The last factor, even when investigation is done, perhaps explains the large proportion of single case reports and simple counting procedures. It is also notable that the psychiatrist's constant therapeutic activity orients him towards research on therapy exclusively, often of a retricted character, when he does research.

The possibility that the psychoanalysts, who gave the impetus to the enormous enrichment of psychological understanding of the last decades, will save the general situation is made to seem rather remote by the picture of psychoanalytic research presented by Glover (71). His address before the International Psycho-Analytical Congress on research methods in psychoanalysis is based on his own long clinical experience and his observations as Director of Research of the London Institute of Psycho-Analysis for 16 years. He believes there has been an increasing tendency by psychoanalysts not to apply to their data such scientific controls as are available. He describes vividly how hearsay evidence becomes attested conclusion (given an analyst with seniority, enthusiasm or plain dogmatism); how a student whose professional career depends on overcoming "resistance" to the satisfaction of his training analyst can hardly be expected to defend his own scientific integrity against his analyst's theories and practice, so that inherent in the training situation is a tendency to perpetuate error; how, no matter how ideal their own analysis, individual analysts tend to show at meetings and elsewhere their own conflicts and "favorite pathological mechanisms"; how these three factors lead to the stereotyped proceedings of the Psycho-Analytical Association; and how peculiarly susceptible to fashion, "canalized no doubt through a hierarchy of transferences and countertransferences" are psychoanalytic groups. He has the impression that present-day psychoanalytic teaching preserves many of the disadvantages of mid-Victorian pedagogy and few of its advantages, and that the deficiencies of such authoritarian spoon-feeding are not remedied, as is often thought, by the candidate's training analysis. He believes it is time these issues were faced, and that a first task of psychoanalysts is to settle down to the arduous task of defining terms, verifying criteria, and developing reliable statistics. His portrayal of the association between lack of scientific productivity and the psychoanalytic training procedure is that of a self-reinforcing system with tremendous internal resistance to change.

If we relate Glover's appraisal to the observations of Powdermaker &

Frank, already mentioned, and to those of the multiple therapists, it is difficult to avoid the question, "could some other method of training psychotherapists and psychiatric research workers be found?" And if the most thoroughly psychoanalyzed persons, the psychoanalysts themselves, appear to have undergone so little change in their "pathological mechanisms," is it not time for careful study of the outcome of psychoanalytic therapy of patients?

So far as I know, the only published material on the training of psychotherapists which presents an explicit alternative to the difficulties of which Glover gives so clear a picture is a paper by Cameron (72) describing a program of postgraduate instruction in psychotherapy in operation at McGill University for five years. The program there makes no special point of personal psychoanalytic therapy or of psychoanalytic institute training, but does make a point of providing for the low generalization of the complex skills and understandings needed by psychotherapists, through a wide variety of types of study and experience over a four-year period.

LITERATURE CITED

1. Report of Committee on Evaluation of Psychoanalytic Therapy, *Bull. Am. Psychoanal. Assoc.*, **6**, 17–19 (1950)
2. Lehner, G. F. J., *Am. Psychologist*, **7**, 547 (1952)
3. Auld, F., Jr., and Eron, L. D., *J. Consulting Psychol.*, **17**, 104–9 (1953)
4. Kotkov, B., and Meadow, A., *J. Consulting Psychol.*, **17**, 16–20 (1953)
5. Butler, J. M., *J. Clin. Psychol.*, **8**, 199–202 (1952)
6. Bugental, J. F. T., *J. Consulting Psychol.*, **16**, 435–39 (1952)
7. Mowrer, O. H. *et al.*, *Psychotherapy Theory and Research*, Chap. 9–19 (The Ronald Press Co., New York, N. Y., 700 pp., 1953)
8. Seeman, J., and Raskin, N. J., in *Psychotherapy Theory and Research*, 205–19 (Mowrer, O. H., Ed., The Ronald Press Co., New York, N. Y., 700 pp., 1953)
9. Dollard, J., and Mowrer, O. H., in *Psychotherapy Theory and Research*, 235–56 (Mowrer, O. H., Ed., The Ronald Press Co., New York, N. Y., 700 pp., 1953)
10. Mowrer, O. H., Hunt, J. McV., and Kogan, L. S., in *Psychotherapy Theory and Research*, 257–95 (Mowrer, O. H., Ed., The Ronald Press Co. New York, N. Y., 700 pp., 1953)
11. Mowrer, O. H., in *Psychotherapy Theory and Research*, 316–75 (Mowrer, O. H., Ed., TheRonald Press Co., New York, N. Y., 700 pp., 1953)
12. Cronbach, L. J., in *Psychotherapy Theory and Research*, 376–88 (Mowrer, O. H., Ed., The Ronald Press Co., New York, N. Y., 700 pp., 1953)
13. Luborsky, L., in *Psychotherapy Theory and Research*, 389–413 (Mowrer, O. H., Ed., The Ronald Press Co., New York, N. Y., 700 pp., 1953)
14. McQuitty, L. L., in *Psychotherapy Theory and Research*, 414–62 (Mowrer, O. H., Ed., The Ronald Press Co., New York, N. Y., 700 pp., 1953)
15. Mowrer, O. H., in *Psychotherapy Theory and Research*, 463–545 (Mowrer, O. H., Ed., The Ronald Press Co., New York, N. Y., 700 pp., 1953)
16. Mowrer, O. H., Light, B. H., Luria, Z., and Zeleny, M. P., in *Psychotherapy*

Theory and Research, 546–640 (Mowrer, O. H., Ed., The Ronald Press Co., New York, N. Y., 700 pp., 1953)
17. O'Kelly, L. I., in *Psychotherapy Theory and Research*, 641–56 (Mowrer, O. H., Ed., The Ronald Press Co., New York, N. Y., 700 pp., 1953)
18. Grossman, D., *J. Consulting Psychol.*, **16**, 325–31 (1952)
19. Dittman, A. T., *J. Abnormal Social Psychol.*, **47**, 236–44 (1952)
20. Porter, E. H., Jr., *J. Consulting Psychol.*, **16**, 343–46 (1952)
21. Rogers, C. R., in *Psychotherapy Theory and Research*, 44–68 (Mowrer, O. H., Ed., The Ronald Press Co., New York, N. Y., 700 pp., 1953)
22. Butler, J. M., *J. Abnormal Social Psychol.*, **47**, 366–78 (1952)
23. Beier, E. G., *J. Consulting Psychol.*, **16**, 332–37 (1952)
24. Moustakas, C. E., and Makowsky, G., *J. Consulting Psychol.*, **16**, 338–42 (1952)
25. Perry, W. G., Jr., and Estes, S. G., in *Psychotherapy Theory and Research*, 95–119 (Mowrer, O. H., Ed., The Ronald Press Co., New York, N. Y., 700 pp., 1953)
26. Odenwald, R. P., *Am. J. Psychiat.*, **108**, 856 (1952)
27. Ring, F. O., *Psychiat. Quart.*, **26**, 372–86 (1952)
28. Sifneos, P. E., *Am. J. Psychiat.*, **109**, 356–60 (1952)
29. Cameron, D. E., *Am. J. Psychiat.*, **109**, 183–87 (1952)
30. Foulkes, S. H., *Brit. J. Med. Psychol.*, **26**, 30–35 (1953)
31. Fairbairn, W. R. D., *Brit. J. Med. Psychol.*, **25**, 122–27 (1952)
32. Sutherland, J. D., *Psychiatry*, **15**, 111–17 (1952)
33. Klein, S., *Brit. J. Med. Psychol.*, **25**, 223–28 (1952)
34. Fiedler, F. E., in *Psychotherapy Theory and Research*, 296–315 (Mowrer, O. H., Ed., The Ronald Press Co., New York, N. Y., 700 pp., 1953)
35. Shoben, E. J., Jr., in *Psychotherapy Theory and Research*, 120–39 (Mowrer, O. H., Ed., The Ronald Press Co., New York, N. Y., 700 pp., 1953)
36. Dollard, J. and Miller, N. E., *Personality and Psychotherapy* (McGraw-Hill Book Co., Inc., New York, N. Y., 488 pp., 1950)
37. Hofstaetter, P. R., *J. Psychol.*, **34**, 191–96 (1952)
38. Mowrer, O. H., in *Psychotherapy Theory and Research*, 69–94, 322, 532 (Mowrer, O. H., Ed., The Ronald Press, Co., New York, N. Y., 700 pp., 1953)
39. Peters, H. N., and Jenkins, R. L., "Improvement of chronic schizophrenic patients with guided problem solving motivated by hunger" (Unpublished data obtainable from Dr. Peters)
40. Jenkins, R. L., *Arch. Neurol. and Psychiat.*, **64**, 243–62 (1950)
41. Maier, N. R. F., *Frustration: The study of behavior without a goal* (McGraw-Hill Book Co., Inc., New York, N. Y., 264 pp., 1949)
42. Chess, S., Clark, K. B., and Thomas, A., *Psychiat. Quart.*, **27**, 102–14 (1953)
43. Ruesch, J., in *Psychiatric Treatment, Proc. Assoc. Research Nervous and Mental Disease*, **36**, 59–93 (1953)
44. Rosen, H., *Am. J. Psychiat.*, **109**, 120–27 (1952)
45. Szurek, S. A., *Am. J. Psychiat.*, **109**, 296–302 (1952)
46. Bychowski, G., and Despert, J. L., Eds., *Specialized Techniques in Psychotherapy* (Basic Books, Inc., New York, N. Y., 371 pp., 1952)
47. Whitaker, C. A., and Malone, T. P., *The Roots of Psychotherapy* (The Blakiston Co., New York, N. Y., 237 pp., 1953)
48. Eysenck, H. J., *J. Consulting Psychol.*, **16**, 319–24 (1952)
49. Saslow, G., and Peters, A. DeH. (Submitted for publication)

50. Seeman, J., and Raskin, N. J., in *Psychotherapy Theory and Research*, 227–34 (Mowrer, O. H., Ed., The Ronald Press Co., New York, N. Y., 700 pp., 1953)
51. Teuber, H. L., and Powers, E., in *Psychiatric Treatment, Proc. Assoc. Research Nervous and Mental Disease*, **36,** 138–47 (1953)
52. Appel, K. E., Lhamon, W. T., Myers, J. M., and Harvey, W. A., in *Psychiatric Treatment, Research Publs. Assoc. Research Nervous and Mental Disease*, **31,** 21–34 (1953)
53. Klüver, H., in *Cerebral Mechanisms in Behavior* (*The Hixon Symposium*), 166–71 (John Wiley & Sons, Inc., New York, N. Y., 311 pp., 1951)
54. Stine, L. A., and Ivy, A. C., *Gastroenterology*, **21,** 185–211 (1952)
55. Berle, B. B., Pinsky, R. H., Wolf, S., and Wolff, H. G., in *Psychiatric Treatment, Proc. Assoc. Research Nervous and Mental Disease*, **36,** 167–77 (1953)
56. Grace, W. J. (Personal communication)
57. Zubin, J., in *Psychiatric Treatment, Proc. Assoc. Research Nervous and Mental Disease*, **36,** 10–15 (1953)
58. Hunt, J. McV., *J. Consulting Psychol.*, **16,** 237–46 (1952)
59. Dreikurs, R., Mosak, H. H., and Shulman, B. H., *Psychiat. Quart.*, **26,** 590–96 (1952)
60. Buck, A. E., and Grygier, T., *Am. J. Psychother.*, **6,** 711–24 (1952)
61. Dryud, J. E., and Rioch, M. J., *Psychiatry*, **16,** 21–26 (1953)
62. Stanton, A. H., and Schwartz, M. S., *Psychiatry*, **12,** 339–54 (1949)
63. Caudill, W., Redlich, F. C., Gilmore, H. R., and Brody, E. B., *Am. J. Orthopsychiat.*, **22,** 314–34 (1952)
64. Henry, J., "Study of the social structure of an in-patient psychiatric ward" (Unpublished data)
65. Sanford, N., *Ann. Rev. Psychol.*, **4,** 317–42 (1953)
66. Powdermaker, F. B., and Frank, J. D., *Group Psychotherapy* (Harvard University Press, Cambridge, Mass., 615 pp., 1953)
67. Roe, A., *Psychol. Monographs*, **67**(2), 1–55 (1953)
68. Jones, M., *The Therapeutic Community* (Basic Books, Inc., New York, N. Y., 186 pp., 1953)
69. Hilgard, E. R., in *Psychoanalysis as Science*, 3–45 (Pumpian-Mindlin, E., Ed., Stanford University Press, Stanford, California, 1952)
70. Huoton, P. E., Chairman, *Collaborative Research in Psychopathology* (Report of the Committee on Psychopathology, Group for Advancement of Psychiatry, being prepared for publication)
71. Glover, E., *Intern. J. Psycho-Anal.*, **33,** 403–9 (1952)
72. Cameron, D. E., *J. Assoc. Am. Med. Coll.*, **25,** 338–44 (1950)

COUNSELING METHODS[1,2,3]

By C. Gilbert Wrenn
University of Minnesota, Minneapolis, Minnesota

This chapter is slightly different in content and emphasis from the corresponding chapters in earlier volumes. Action taken by the Editorial Committee simplified the title of the chapter and provided for the inclusion of studies in psychological measurement only as these related directly to counseling. A further restriction has been made in order to minimize the confusing overlap of the terms "counseling" and "psychotherapy." With the cooperation of Professor Saslow, author of the chapter on Psychotherapy, it was decided to make no attempt to distinguish between counseling and psychotherapy but, in the main, to include in this chapter only studies that have a nonmedical setting. Studies in medical settings, whether using the term psychotherapy or the term counseling, are covered in the chapter on Psychotherapy. This decision will not please every reader but the confusion in terminology required some such definitive action as this. Rogers (57) reports a study of members of the American Psychological Association who, in the APA *Directory*, express an interest in the "practice of psychotherapy." Forty-four phrases indicating this interest were isolated, 16 of which involved some use of the rubric "counseling." Incidentally, Rogers finds an increase in mention of this combined function in the *Directory* from 1948 to 1951 of almost 5 per cent (from 23.5 per cent to 28.3 per cent). The proportion rises to 35 per cent for psychologists born at the quarter-century mark as compared with 21 per cent for those born at the beginning of this century.

The Development of Counseling as a Profession

Counseling, as a field within psychology, is making progress toward status as a profession. Much of this chapter is devoted to studies of instruments, procedures, and methodology in research, in some of which lie the claim to being a science. The practice of counseling is the other side of the coin.

The attention of psychologists in general has been drawn to the field of counseling by two events of the past year. The first of these is the designation of "Counseling Psychologist" as a new position in Veterans Administration mental hospitals and in Veterans Administration guidance centers (two separate programs). The second event was the publication in June, 1952, of

[1] The survey of the literature to which this review pertains was completed on May 1, 1953.

[2] The following abbreviations are used in this chapter: APA (American Psychological Association); MMPI (Minnesota Multiphasic Personality Inventory); OL (Occupational Level).

[3] Assistance in the review of literature for this chapter was given by Edward H. Seldon, Court Psychologist, Minneapolis, Minnesota.

two reports of the then Division of Counseling and Guidance, one on recommended standards for the doctoral training of counseling psychologists (12) and one on recommended standards and procedures in the practicum aspects of this training (77). It would seem to the writer that these two reports, officially adopted as the statements of Division 17 of the APA[2], will inevitably exert a strong influence in the development of this field. This may suggest a personal bias for he was president of Division 17 at the time and became personally involved in this culmination of committee work that had extended over several years. Even now, however, these reports are providing the basic structure for the evaluation of doctoral training programs by the American Psychological Association that was requested by the Veterans Administration. In this connection Long's review (40) of Veterans Administration Guidance Centers points out that the 29 million dollars that has been spent in counseling some one and one-half million veterans represents only two-tenths of 1 per cent of the total cost of veterans' educational benefits. He points up both the restrictions of this vast program of counseling and the gains made. A small amount of research on counseling outcomes is cited.

The selection and professional education of counselors is outlined by Wrenn (88) together with a description of a small research project in selection. He stresses the problems involved in balancing content (science) and procedure (practice) in graduate training programs. Cottle (16) reviews the existing research on the characteristics and the selection of counselors as the first in a series of studies to be reported on this topic. A seven-year study of psychotherapists at the Menninger Clinic by Luborsky (41) has some significance for counselors; in this he reports on a comparison of the top and bottom 13 per cent in rated competence as psychotherapists. The high group, in contrast to the low group, were more apt to be: sensitive to others, independent in thinking and judgment, subdued in warmth, quiet rather than expressive, able to express themselves appropriately, younger, married, and conventionally adjusted. No levels of confidence for the significance of these differences is reported.

Inservice development after attaining the doctorate is described by Samler (61) as more important than preservice professional training. Some attractive procedures in this field are suggested. Failor & Williams (23) describe the coordinated program of four universities and colleges in Colorado for taking graduate training to the counselors in the schools of the state. This is one of the better examples of what is done in over one-half of the states to develop school counselor competence.

Another phase of professional development is the attention given to ethical standards and practices. A code of 104 statements of ethical practice for counseling is drawn by Gluck *et al.* (27) from existing codes in medicine, law, psychology, and social work. An adaptation of the APA code is made for counselors by Wrenn (89) who analyzes ethical responsibilities under the headings of responsibility to the client, to the employing institution and society, and to the profession.

Systematic Formulations and Theory

Several basic statements on counseling theory have appeared during the past year. One of these is a formulation of the counseling process that is based upon learning theory. Perry & Estes (53) believe that the learning process in counseling involves both selective, or self-learning, and directed learning. The nondirection and direction in learning are not a continuum but occupy two distinct realms; not polar opposites, but part of a complex that requires coordination.

With this learning theory as foundation, Perry & Estes propose that the process of counseling with most college students is one of ego-building, not release of infantile conflicts. There are two stages in Perry & Estes' "integrational counseling": (*a*) the permissive or nondirective, which is used until the client accepts the responsibility for initiative and evaluation of his own problems (until he achieves "the heuristic set"), and (*b*) the collaborative phase, in which the counselor is accepted as an aid in the process of counseling. This latter phase requires the use of skill in helping the student to see the problem as external both to himself and to the counselor, as upon a screen in front of both of them. The authors provide a few data from interview analyses intended to indicate that the interview proceeds from nondirective to collaborative in accordance with their theory.

Another basic theoretical proposal is made by Butler (14) who considers the behavior of the psychotherapist in terms of the following hypothesis: "In two-way personal-social interaction each individual concerned displays anticipatory behavior which in turn elicits anticipatory behavior on the part of the other, the anticipatory behavior of the other in each case confirming the prior learnings of the individual about himself." He develops an extensive learning theory, involving considerable reliance upon transfer and social learning, and with this proceeds to indicate how the therapist's behavior becomes the stimulus for the learning of the client. The article is particularly illuminating with regard to the resistance phenomenon.

A theory of vocational development proposed by Super (78) takes issue with Ginsberg's occupational choice theory, particularly his failure to define clearly the nature of the compromise process which is at the heart of the choice made. Super constructs a ten-point theory of vocational development stressing the dynamics of the long process of choice and adjustment, and the interplay of interests, aptitudes, self-concept, and work satisfactions. A monograph by Small (71), referred to later, suggests that the compromise process "is a function of the adequacy or strength of the ego." He limits the vocational counseling process (a limitation which would not be acceptable to Super) by saying, "Vocational counseling, emphasizing as it does realistic factors, is best able to benefit the realistically oriented individual. Strengthening such weak (non-realistically oriented) egos is the problem of the therapist rather than the counselor." The reviewer is reminded of the distinction made several years ago by Butler between the adjustment and the distributive (planning) phases of counseling.

Another attempt to reduce complexity to orderliness was that of Black (10) who analyzed the features of counselor-client relationship that are common to all therapies. He summarizes five common factors and suggests that we be cautious in attributing successful counseling to any particular method or procedure when the nature of the relationship between counselor and client may be the potent factor in the situation. Hahn (32) also attempts to find common elements in different approaches to counseling. He believes that there is a trend toward considering therapy as a phase of counseling, quoting Bordin to the effect that counselors work primarily with the normal range of personal adjustment, and Pepinsky's statement that counselors work with "minor, functional maladjustments." It is apparent that counseling is far from being integrated, however, and that any man's statement may be one which he wishes he might modify at a later stage in his or the profession's development.

Two expositions of client-centered therapy are made by Rogers, one (58) in Mowrer's recent book (48a) and one in the *Scientific American* (59). In the first of these Rogers restates some of his convictions regarding the self-concept and the positive and constructive nature of basic personality factors. He opens this chapter by limiting his discussion to client-centered therapy "since I have reluctantly come to concede the possibility that the process, directions, and end points of therapy may differ in different therapeutic orientations" and closes it in the hope that "gradually some of the speculations and opinions and clinical hunches of this paper may be put to operational and definitive test." No one can quarrel with a theory that states its boundaries and asks that it be tested. It is interesting to note the research studies Rogers selects to use in his second paper, which is for "nonpsychological" consumption: those by Snyder, Sheerer, Haimowitz, and Thetford. Rogers concludes that the research thus far has contributed more to increased knowledge of the dynamics of the personality than to improvement of therapeutic procedures.

Four papers contribute to self-concept theory. Two of these by Roberts (56) and Bills (9) use the Index of Adjustment and Values to test the relationship between emotionality and the discrepancy between self-concept and ideal self-concept. The results support the assumption of a definite relationship which is persistent over a period of time. The other two papers support each other in showing a relationship between degree of self acceptance and measures of emotional adjustment. One, by Taylor & Combs (79), used a list of questions which are probably true of all children yet which are damaging to the self-concept to admit. Using sixth grade children who had been divided into those who were well and those poorly adjusted, they found that the well adjusted group were able to accept significantly more of the damaging statements. The other, by Calvin & Holtzman (15), used college fraternity members to whom was given the MMPI[2] and a "self-other" rating form using seven traits. One finding was that those who deprecated self (in comparison with others) tended to be more poorly adjusted generally.

A constructive attempt to integrate counseling operationally was made by Maclean (42) who drew upon learning concepts of differentiation and integration for his argument. Stating that differentiation (specialization, many approaches) has been paramount in counseling thus far, he pled for advancement to the state of integration and listed some effective steps to be taken in that direction.

Research and Evaluation Methodology

The eleven chapters on research procedures in *Psychotherapy Theory and Research*, by Mowrer and his associates (48a), defy analysis within the limited scope of a chapter such as this. Perhaps outstanding for counselors is the chapter by Seeman & Raskin (64) on research in client-centered therapy. They summarize between 40 and 50 published studies in this field under the headings of "Internal Dimensions of Therapy Research," (research on elements of the counseling process) and "Studies in Outcomes of Therapy." These are rich pages, to be read carefully,

Without listing each chapter, the other features of the research section of the book involve a lively 90 pages by Mowrer on the constellation of Q Techniques and by Luborsky on the P Technique. Another group of three chapters deal with the tension factor in therapy and with tension as an evaluation criterion. Eighty pages, again by Mowrer, analyze the verbal factor in therapy, including the semantic researches by Grummon, Osgood, and Winthrop. Fiedler's chapter on the function and measurement of the therapist's feelings toward the client, and McQuitty's chapter on configural analysis are other examples of the research value of this volume. The volume should add much to the resources of anyone contemplating research in counseling.

An ambitious coordinated effort to analyze research methods in counseling is reported by a team from the Division of Counseling Psychologists consisting of Dressel (19), Shoben (68), and Pepinsky (50). The first paper outlines the problems of criteria, design, subtle versus obvious aspects of the process of counseling, contamination, and financing. Dressel believes that outcomes must be established before process can be studied and that these outcomes should be sought regardless of any value judgments regarding them. Shoben takes issue with this, believing that the results of counseling per se are not sufficient, that they must be tested against the client's psychological health in the client's "extraclinical world." The client's psychological health is of necessity related to the values (acceptance) of his community, so that evaluation is in terms of not only the client's extraclinical behavior but also of "the way that behavior is evaluated by himself and others." After summarizing five common theories of counseling research, Pepinsky makes a case for the development of design upon a clear statement of the psychological rationale (bias, assumptions) that is involved. He outlines five basic steps essential in any counseling research: (*a*) research objective (theory based upon interaction of observations and conceptualizations), (*b*) testable hypotheses, (*c*) unambiguous design for testing hypotheses, (*d*) explicit and detailed planning before executing any part of the project, and (*e*) discussion, in which restraint is used in the drawing of conclusions. Dressel advocates use of statistical control through covariance methods of analysis in preference to control groups while his team mate, Shoben, issues a strong warning against use of criteria residing wholly within the interview.

Eleven basic conditions that must be satisfied before successful therapy can be claimed, which might well become the criteria for any study purporting to evaluate counseling, are given by Thorne (80). To be noted in particular is the need for demonstrating that (*a*) the process is not self-limiting or in a self-curative phase and (*b*) the effects are more than the results of a simple treatment of behavior symptoms. Watson in this same issue of the *Journal of Clinical Psychology* (84) bares five shortcomings of all published research on the effectiveness of psychotherapy.

In a carefully safeguarded study of the amount of verbal participation in a group as a criterion that might be useful in counseling evaluation, Pepinsky *et al.* (51) used performance on a Rorschach and sociometric ratings as the dependent variables. With 184 variables, six multiple *R*'s were found to be significant. These provide the basis for three hypotheses: (*a*) the talkative, socially sensitive individual tends to receive a larger proportion of favorable role choices in a group, ($R = .87$), (*b*) the frequently chosen, intellectually striving individual will tend to talk relatively often in the group, ($R = .82$), (*c*) the more mature individual who tends to perceive the unusual will tend to be more accepting of others in the group, ($R = .70$). Pepinsky and two associates also developed a Group Participation Scale for use as a criterion in evaluating counseling (52). This sociometric device, when administered in five fraternities, resulted in a distribution that was spread over almost the entire scale (from 2 to 8 out of a possible 1 to 9) and that had only slight negative skewness. More careful studies of criteria such as these by Pepinsky are urgent needs in the counseling field.

The tricky factor of client motivation, as a variable in counseling research, is well illustrated in a study by Gutherie & O'Neill (30) and a report by Rothney & Mooren (60). In the first study a perhaps too-simple design was used in evaluating the outcomes of a program of dormitory counseling on study habits. Because no differences in grades were found after 10 weeks between counseled and noncounseled groups the author proposes that the missing factor is that no distinction was made between students who wanted counseling and those who did not. All in the experimental group received counseling whether they wanted it or not. Rothney & Mooren report on the nature of a 95 per cent response to a mail follow-up of counseling. Analysis shows that those who had been interviewed most and who had requested further interviews responded first of all. This is the type of motivation-factor which should be accounted for in all follow-up evaluations. The authors list other characteristics of those responding early, but no report on tests of significance accompanied these statements.

Although a number of studies reviewed (and not reported) showed great naivete, the reviewer is encouraged by some of the major studies in theory and in research methodology that are reported in this chapter. Careful theory will encourage research attacks: cautious and sophisticated research designs will demand basic theory for testing. The advance on the two fronts simultaneously seems essential. I am speaking here of such basic theory statements as those by Butler, Perry & Estes, and Super, and of the research proposals by the authors of Mowrer's chapters and by the Division of Counseling Psychologists' team.

Psychological Measurement in Counseling

Interest measurement.—The most significant study in interest measurement during the past year was that by Strong & Tucker (76). This was more than a study of medical interests; it was written to be helpful to those who are considering medicine as a career and to counselors who must answer such questions as these: "Do I have the interests of a medical man?" "If so do I have the interests of a specialist or of a generalist, and if the former, what kind of specialist?" With funds for a three-year study from the Office of the Surgeon General, four medical specialists' scales (Surgeon, Pathologist, Internist, and Psychiatrist) and a revision of the Physician Scale of the Strong blank were produced.

One feature of the research was the development of a "medical-men-in-general" group so that the interest patterns of the medical specialists could be compared with the interests of both "men-in-general" and "medical-men-in-general." The four specialty blanks differentiated the specialists from physicians-in-general with an average r of .79. They differentiated equally well among each other. Of special interest to psychologists is the consistent tendency in factor analysis and in other comparisons, for the psychiatrists to be most unique in their interests, of the four medical specialties, and furthest from the interests of physicians in general. In fact, in one factor analysis, psychiatrists had a slightly smaller loading of "medical interests" than did psychologists! On a loading called "interest in people" the psychiatrist was highest of all the medical groups and closer to psychologists and personnel men than to the other medical men. This study, both for its deliberate interest to be helpful to counselors and for its clear exposition of some significant research approaches, is a valuable "find" in the literature of the year.

Melville & Frederiksen (44) studied the relationship between interest patterns on the Strong blank and the first-year academic achievement of engineering freshmen and found several significant correlations between grades and the Strong scales. Layton (39), in a more elaborate prediction of academic success in veterinary medicine, found that scores on the Veterinarian scale of the Strong blank provided one of the significant predictors. Do these studies suggest that as universities select more carefully in terms of intellectual ability (provide a more intellectually homogeneous group) measures of interests as motivation indices become increasingly important in predictions? [See also the studies by Schofield (63) and Morgan (48), reported under Prediction.]

Three doctoral studies under the direction of Super were reported in a four-author monograph as a coordinated attempt to test the validity of the assumption that the Occupational Level (OL) score of the Strong test is a measure of motivation or drive (2). Barnett's study of several hundred vagrants yielded slight but inconclusive evidence that OL[2] score measured drive or ambition. Another study by Stewart compared OL score with social background and plans. The score was found to be related to immediate but not to long range plans, and to have but little consistent relationship to social background. Handelsman used high school students' statement of aspirations, two aspiration tests, and teachers' rating of student aspiration. Only the latter showed any relationship to OL score and that was not of any magnitude. Super concludes, "the evidence now available warrants interpreting the Occupational Level scale as a measure of status of interests. The evidence does not warrant interpreting the OL score as a measure of drive."

Among a number of other studies concerned with interest measurements, Dressel & Matteson (20) studied the relationship between interests and experience of college students. The analysis showed that: (*a*) in general the expressed interest was conditioned by the amount of experience; (*b*) there was a greater variability of expressed interest than of experience (not surprising perhaps for young men); (*c*) that interest was greater than experience in the science and music areas, but that the reverse was true in the clerical and persuasive areas. This is a suggestive study but one cannot help but agree with the authors that a forced-choice blank is not the most effective method of recording vocational experience.

Steinberg (72) used the Kuder Preference Record to study differences between two groups of disabled veterans classified as "neurotic" and "nonneurotic" (the latter, probably not a pure nonneurotic). He concluded that "A Kuder profile characterized by low interest in Mechanical and Scientific areas and a relatively high interest in the Literary and Musical areas, in the absence of other evidence to support the validity of these interests, may indicate maladjustment."

Strong (74) analyzes several bases for the differences found between the interests of several Negro occupational groups and corresponding groups of white men that were reported in Hartshorne's 1948 study. He agrees that there is a real difference between the two samples in that Negroes seem to like more items than whites but believes that a Negro men-in-general group must be developed before any substantial answers can be found.

Personality measures.—If the reviewer were to accept at face value the gloomy review of personality inventories given by Ellis (22), there would be no need to write further in this section. Ellis reviewed "all researches on personality inventories" published from 1946 through 1951 and concludes that there is little good in any of them, because they are not measuring independent traits, they do not agree with each other or with projective measures, they are easily faked, they usually do not give significant group discriminations. Ellis has greater faith in "interviewing and the use of projective techniques that seem to be more clinically incisive and valuable."

Another and somewhat more helpful review of research is that by Cottle (17) which condenses the findings of 215 research studies using the MMPI that have appeared up to 1951; it also lists 38 such studies that were published in 1951. There is an excellent discussion of interpretation, including Welsh's two ratios, and a good description of the meaning of each scale with "normal" populations. A 1952 study by Blanton & Landsman (11) bears on the criticisms of Ellis since these two authors used the Group Rorschach and the MMPI on the same population which was retested after three months. They conclude that these two tests have different functions as far as college populations are concerned and that neither can be considered an effective substitute for the other. Another MMPI study, by Gough & Pemberton (29), developed a list of 15 clinical signs for interpreting the results of this test in a prediction setting wherein single scale analysis had proved futile. The signs were not too effective in a cross-validation check but "the results highlight the error involved in concluding that the MMPI does not work because single scale analysis fails."

Four other studies provide results on four different tests that are used in counseling. Shaw *et al.* (67) used the Minnesota Teacher Attitudes Inventory to measure changes in attitudes toward students and others produced by a two-weeks workshop. Drucker & Remmers (21) used the SRA Youth Inventory to test differences between students judged "good" and "poor" in school adjustment and found differences at the 1 per cent level between these groups in every area of the Inventory but two. Merrill & Heathers (45) provided another study of Wechsler-Bellevue subtests and found scatter to be such a common phenomenon among university students that any use of it in personality diagnosis seems highly inadvisable. Brogden (13) factor-analyzed the Allport-Vernon Study of Values and found that only four of the original scales were identified in this analysis: Aesthetic, Theoretical, Social, and Religious. The original Political and Economic scales become one secondary factor. (This latter point was also an outcome of Lurie's 1937 study but in that study the Aesthetic scale disappeared.)

Three attempts to provide new measures of academic efficiency or study habits belong only in part under the heading of "personality measures." Gough (28) developed a 38-item "achievement scale involving such personality factors as self-confidence, purpose, and acceptance of others, as well as items on study habits," that gave an r of .44 with high school grades on a cross validation population of 234 seniors. A scale of attitudes toward college was developed by Woodman (87) which revealed marked differences in attitudes between "over" and "under" achievers. When the attitude items were weighted and the blanks scored, the two distributions ("over" and "under" achievers) were independent for 68 per cent of cases, but with scores used or prediction purposes he secured an r of only .30 between scores and first semester grades. Michael & Reeder (46) developed a 47-item inventory of study habits, which produced an r of .55 against high school scholastic average, and, combined with the American Council on Education Psychological Examination, a multiple R of .83. These relatively high correlations dropped to an r of .31 and an R of .79 for high school girls, and to .32 and .56 respectively for college freshmen. No cross validation was reported. Here, as also suggested by some of the studies in interest measurement, are reported efforts to tease out attitude, motivation, and other nonintellectual factors that will contribute to the mystery of "Why do some students who are intellectually able achieve scholastically and others fail to do so?"

Aptitude tests.—Studies of the General Aptitude Test Battery are rereported by Storrs (73) and by Jex & Sorensen (33) in which retest reliability of six of the tests ranged only from .70 to .88 but in which test G correlated highly (.80) with the Verbal scale of the Wechsler-Bellevue test in one study. In another study, however, test G correlated no higher with first quarter college grades than did test Q for women and test V for men. Follow-up reports on the Differential Aptitude Test are given by Bennett *et al.* (5) and by Wesman (86), but the data are reported in such general terms that exactness of interpretation is difficult. In general, college curricula chosen or jobs held seem to reflect part scores on the battery, but no tests of significance of the differences between scores are reported. Wesman points out that the validity in terms of part-score correlation with course grades is specific to each situation, i.e., no general validity conclusions can or should be drawn because of variation in the criterion (course content and grading standard).

Prediction studies.[4]—Studies of scholastic prediction in the three professional schools of law, veterinary medicine, and medicine at the University of Minnesota are reported respectively by Berdie & Layton (7), Layton (39), and Schofield (63). Seven variables in Berdie and Layton's study of law students produced a multiple R of .75 with freshman grades. These were the conventional intellectual variables, with prelegal grades the best single predictor. Only one out of 46 students predicted to have grades of 80 or more failed to achieve them, while only 8 out of 43 predicted to have failing grades of 60 or less succeeded in passing. The prediction of success was better than prediction of failure, an unusual accomplishment. In the veterinary medicine study, Layton used only 3 variables out of 20 to produced an R of .60 with first quarter grades. As mentioned earlier one of these was the Veterinarian scale of the Strong Interest Blank.

The part of the medical school study reported by Schofield in the current article deals only with the relationship of MMPI scores to junior year medical school grades. Students in the upper quarter as compared with students in the lower quarter of grades have significantly lower mean scores on

[4] The title of this section is somewhat misleading for many of the studies grouped under test categories are primarily prediction studies.

scales 3 (hysteroid), 4 (psychopathic deviate), and 8 (schizoid). This finding was checked in various ways but held constant, which led Schofield to suggest that students who show both a restricted intellectual promise and marked elevations on these three scales will be likely to prove poor academic risks.

A comparison study of high achieving and low achieving liberal arts students of high ability again stresses nonintellectual differences. Morgan (48) found that the high group in comparison with the low group had: (*a*) more Strong scores in Group V and fewer in Groups VIII and IX; (*b*) fewer MMPI elevations on Scale 4 (*Pd*) (this checks with Schofield's finding), higher scores on special MMPI scales for Dominance, Social Responsibility, and Intellectual Efficiency; and (*c*) higher in the "achievement motivation" scoring of the Thematic Apperception Test (TAT). On the other end of the scale Wiegand (85) studied a group of 81 lower ability college entrants who had been placed in a special curriculum for the first year. All were presumably equally motivated to make high enough grades for transfer to a regular curriculum but the 41 who did so were different in several respects from those who had not made the required scholastic average. More of the "successes" (1 per cent level of confidence) had definite vocational choices, vocational choices that coincided with the "most desired" occupation, and choices that were related to the college major chosen. Here we have one of the few studies that gives some hope to those who believe that the fact of vocational choice influences scholastic success.

Lack of pressure from family as a favorable factor is attested to by Kirk (35). Puzzled by students who do well on objective tests of scholastic aptitude but poorly on classroom tests, she postulates that academic failure of this type probably provides unconscious satisfaction for hostilities directed toward some member of the family who demands success. She quotes a psychologist in the University of California Student Health Service: "On the basis of 1500 records collected here, the kinds of MMPI records most frequently associated with poor academic achievement are (*a*) Psychoneurosis with compulsive and depressive features, (*b*) Hysterical personalities." This latter point checks with Schofield's study.

Biographical factors enter the picture in studies reported by Myers (49) and Berdie (6). The former tested biographical items selected from one freshman class in a women's college as those that were related to achievement in a cross validation study using the succeeding freshman class. Items that differentiated between high and low achievement, at 1 and 5 per cent levels, were (in the direction of high achievement): Jewish family, from larger towns, with foreign born parents, youngest in family, low participation in high school activities but high in offices held. Berdie engaged in a follow-up of a large population of high school graduates one year after graduation to determine the outcome of plans stated during their senior year in high school. Students who were from homes high on the educational-vocational ladder were most likely to carry out their plans. The factor of economic determinism reared its ugly head again in the figures showing that 90 per cent of the high ability children whose parents were in top-level occupations were able to attend college. The contrasting figure was 55 per cent for equally able students whose fathers were factory laborers. In general, factors favorable to plans for college were these: (*a*) high economic and cultural level of home, (*b*) parents had attended college, (*c*) being a woman, (*d*) living in an urban area. There seems to be support here for the Warner-Havighurst-Davis school of thought.

One study, of general usefulness, is that by Abelson (1) who used high school grades and scholastic aptitude tests to predict college grades for 3500 students in seven coeducational institutions. He was able to state with some assurance that the greater predictability of women's grades (often found in such studies, illustrated in this chapter by Wesman's study) is not the result of predictor differences but is caused by the greater homogeneity of the criterion of women's grades in college.

Procedures in Counseling

A sorting of the published material of the year that contribute to one's knowledge of specific procedures in counseling aside from measurement and prediction, has resulted in the following grouping: (*a*) research studies involving a specific procedure or concept, (*b*) systematic but theoretical discussions of a procedure, (*c*) some representative textbooks.

In the first group the study by Richardson & Borow (55) examines the proposition that preparing students for the possible outcomes of counseling results in more effective counseling outcomes. Nineteen out of 25 criterion measures used to determine the effectiveness of the interview favored the experimental (prepared) group; six, significantly so. It seems clear that the prepared group got more from their interviews than the nonprepared group.

There is encouragement in the outcomes of a program of counseling by Serene (65) in which he was able to motivate high school eleventh-grade underachievers to better academic performance. He counseled 124 underachievers over the year regarding the realities of their past and potential accomplishment with the result that correlation between aptitude and achievement increased from .56 to .76; the number of pupils in the line of expectancy increased from 93 to 147 (out of 301 in class). No similar gains were found in the tenth and twelfth grades which served as controls. This study makes some contribution to self-concept theory.

Somewhat more specific procedural elements are studies by Toman (81) and Berg (8). Toman had clients dictate their life histories after which the record was played back and each client analyzed the pauses he had made in the dictation. Such analysis was used as an introduction to therapy. Berg analyzed types of words used in a completed and recorded interview series to find that certain types of words (empathetic, negative) tended to increase as therapy progressed while other verbal correlates decreased (ego words and expletive sounds). Another attempt to isolate correlates of therapy progress was the study by Dittmann (18) who found that a high level of counselor participation and counselor response to feeling or interpersonal behavior were characteristic of the later stages of successful counseling. In the field of marriage counseling Mitchell reports a study (47) indicating that some of the factors in the initial interview have a closer identification than others with the "whole case" factors. This suggests that they are more predictive and should be given more attention in the initial interview.

In the group of theoretical discussions of counseling procedures Porter (54) defines five classes of interpretations made by the counselor. He develops these as outgrowths of two broad types of counselor activities, interpreting the meaning of the client's productions and expressing to the client the meaning that will best help him. A different type of process analysis is made by Beier (3) who defines three approaches that may be used with the involuntary client, the one "in whom resistance toward giving up symptoms and substitute gratifications is greater than his desire for help."

Brief discussions of specific procedures are found in studies on the use of reassurance by Laing (38), the individualizing of test interpretation by Kirk (36), reduction of anxiety in the testing situation by Sinick (70), and handling therapeutic overambition by Beigler (4).

It is obviously impossible to characterize a textbook fairly in a single sentence and yet such is almost necessitated by the limits of this chapter. Soundly written, with stress on the dynamics of interviewing and with much practice and illustrative material, is the text for counselors and social workers by Fenlason (24). Another text is a thorough and clear analysis of the use of tests and many other procedures in studying students by Froehlich & Darley (25). Another text in a somewhat more general view and with a modified nondirective emphasis is that by Shostrom & Brammer (69) while the volume, *Counseling College Students During the Defense Period* (83), is specific in both purpose and the counseling procedures proposed. Hiltner's follow-up (31) of his earlier book in pastoral counseling is a casebook containing several chapters that will be suggestive to counselors in general; the chapters entitled "Action," "Externals," "Charm," and "Hostility" in counseling are penetrating and of general psychological usefulness.

Vocational Choice and Occupational Information

A monograph by Small (71) supplies some comments on Ginsberg's theory of vocational choice which has caused considerable discussion since the appearance of his monograph in 1951. Small gathered data on fantasy and reality factors in the vocational choices of 144 boys aged 15 to 19 which do not support Ginsberg's assumption of a linear relationship between age and realism. There may be a change from fantasy to realism or from realism to fantasy at each age level. The better adjusted boys were more realistic in their "first choice" than the more poorly adjusted boys, but were less realistic in their "second choice." Small proposes that choice involves the interplay of fantasy and reality, with reality perception being given full weight in the first choices of the better adjusted boys but fantasy given some satisfaction in the second choices. Kirk (37) reports the changes in vocational choice of 3100 veterans after the "brief counseling contacts" of a Veterans Administration Guidance Center to be in the direction of current vocational trends, i.e., the change in choices seem to reflect realism.

Strong (75) reports a significant finding from one of his numerous analyses of earlier and follow-up data. Choices made in the college sophomore year show a reliability of .80 with choices made in the freshman year, with measured interest reliabilities of from .88 to .91 for the same period. When choice and interest pattern were compared, however, it was found that the closer the relation between the two measured interest patterns the closer the relationship between the choices made in the two years. Samson & Stefflre (62) studied the relationship between parental occupation and the vocational choice of 1136 high school seniors in Los Angeles who had been exposed to 10 months of vocational counseling on a city wide basis. Use of chi-square indicated a clear relationship between parent's occupation and child's choice which they term a "significant secondary factor." The primary tendency is still to choose a vocation at a higher prestige level than that of the parent. (Incidentally, Strong's one-year follow-up showed no change in average prestige level of vocation chosen. This remained high, being 90 on the Stubbins' scale of 1 to 99.)

Another approach to a study of choice was made by Traphagen (82) who compared scores from the Strong Interest Blank for 30 veterans who had indicated a vocational choice of "high school teacher" at the beginning of counseling but had changed their choice during counseling, with 30 who still maintained their precounseling choice of high school teacher. A primary pattern in Group V with A or B ratings on the Teacher scales discriminated in favor of those who retained their vocational choice of teacher. Primary patterns in Groups IX, X, and XI discriminated in favor of those who changed from their choice of teacher.

The appearance of the second edition of Shartle's basic book on occupational information (66) will be welcomed by many. The revision contains several additions and changes such as the 1950 census classification data, the material of the revised Dictionary of Occupational Titles, and the North-Hatt Scale of Prestige Ratings. Kaplan (34) cites the availability of the P-B series of United States Census bulletins which give the numbers in each major occupational group by each county and each urban area in any state. The P-C series gives a more detailed occupational breakdown for states and cities. A special "national sample" report of all occupations is also available.

Psychologists will be interested in at least one phase of Mahoney's "expert-opinion" analysis (43) of the elements of occupational information that should be included in the professional education of school counselors. The area of greatest agreement between state supervisors, city directors, and university professors on the items that should be included was that of "vocational adjustment." This area, having the largest number of items of any of the nine categories of the study (34), contains such topics as "personal characteristics that contribute to job holding and job security," "relationship of intelligence levels to vocational selection and vocational adjustment," and "patterns of ability generally considered necessary for success in college." Germain *et al.* (26) presented their second report on the forms used by government and military agencies for categorizing physical characteristics used in job placement. The terminology of the physical capacity form and the physical demand (job) form should be common to both but is not. Only one U. S. agency, the United States Employment Service, shows any substantial correlation.

Conclusions

The past year has seen the beginning acceptance of "counseling psychologist" as the professional title at the Ph.D. level in this field without abandonment of the term "counselor." There has also developed an improved understanding of what is involved in professional training, in the research needed on the nonintellectual qualities presumed essential for practitioners, and in the application of a code of ethics to counseling. Professionally, this field of psychology is a little more nearly mature than it was a year ago. Knowledgewise and researchwise we have greatly benefited by a dozen studies of major significance. A prediction is made by this writer that some of the past year's writing on counseling and vocational choice theory, on research and evaluation methodology, on the Strong Interest Blank and on the MMPI will influence thinking and research on counseling for several years to come.

It is common to have reviewers of research shake their heads and cluck their tongues sadly over the scarcity of "good" research. On the contrary, this reviewer is encouraged regarding the quality of much that he has read. Although there are still goodly amounts of shoddy research and ill proved claims there is enough also of that of which we can be proud to encourage us regarding future developments in this area.

LITERATURE CITED

1. Abelson, R. P., "Sex Differences in Predictability of College Grades," *Educ. Psychol. Measurement*, **12**, 638–44 (1952)
2. Barnett, G. J., Handelsman, I., Stewart, L. H., and Super, D. E., "The Occupational Level Scale as a Measure of Drive," *Psychol. Monographs*, **66**(10), 1–37 (1952)
3. Beier, E. G., "Client-Centered Therapy and the Involuntary Client," *J. Consulting Psychol.*, **16**, 332–37 (1952)
4. Beigler, J. S., "Therapeutic Ambition—Handicap for Counselors," *J. Rehabilitation*, **18**, 9–11, 15 (1952)
5. Bennett, G., Seashore, H. G., and Wesman, A. G., "Aptitude Testing: Does it 'Prove Out' in Counseling Practice?" *Occupations*, **30**, 584–93 (1952)
6. Berdie, R. F., "Why Don't They Go To College?" *Personnel Guidance J.*, **31**, 352–56 (1953)
7. Berdie, R. F., and Layton, W. L., "Predicting Success in Law School," *J. Appl. Psychol.*, **36**, 257–60 (1952)
8. Berg, I. A., "Verbal Correlates as Measures of the Effectiveness of Clinical Counseling," *Am. Psychologist*, **7**, 382 (1952)
9. Bills, R. E., "A Validation of Changes in Scores on the Index of Adjustment and Values as Measures of Changes in Emotionality," *J. Consulting Psychol.*, **17**, 135–38 (1953)
10. Black, J. D., "Common Factors of the Patient-Therapist Relationship in Diverse Psychotherapies," *J. Clin. Psychol.*, **8**, 302–6 (1952)
11. Blanton, R., and Landsman, T., "The Retest Reliability of the Group Rorschach and Some Relationships to the MMPI," *J. Consulting Psychol.*, **16**, 265–67 (1952)
12. Bordin, E. S. *et al.*, "Recommended Standards for Training Counseling Psychologists at the Doctorate Level," *Am. Psychologist*, **7**, 175–81 (1952)
13. Brogden, H. E., "The Primary Personal Values Measured by the Allport-Vernon Test, A Study of Values," *Psychol. Monographs*, **66**(16), 1–31 (1952)
14. Butler, J. M., "The Interaction of Client and Therapist," *J. Abnormal Social Psychol.*, **47**, Suppl., 366–78 (1952)
15. Calvin, A. D., and Holtzman, W. H., "Adjustment and the Discrepancy Between Self-Concept and Inferred Self," *J. Consulting Psychol.*, **17**, 39–44 (1953)
16. Cottle, W. C., "Personal Characteristics of Counselors: I," *Personnel Guidance J.*, **31**, 445–50 (1953)
17. Cottle, W. C., *The MMPI: A Review* (University of Kansas Publications, School of Education, Lawrence, Kansas, 82 pp., 1953)
18. Dittmann, A. T., "The Interpersonal Process in Psychotherapy: Development of a Research Method," *J. Abnormal Social Psychol.*, **47**, 236–44 (1952)
19. Dressel, P. L., "Some Approaches to Evaluation," *Personnel Guidance J.*, **31**, 284–87 (1953)
20. Dressel, P. L., and Matteson, R. W., "The Relationship Between Experience and Interest as Measured by the Kuder Preference Record," *Educ. Psychol. Measurement*, **12**, 109–16 (1952)
21. Drucker, A. J. and Remmers, H. H., "A Validation of the SRA Youth Inventory," *J. Appl. Psychol.*, **36**, 186–87 (1952)

22. Ellis, A., "Recent Research With Personality Questionnaires," *J. Consulting Psychol.*, **17**, 45–49 (1953)
23. Failor, C. W., and Williams, H. E., "Carrying Guidance Training Out to Colorado Schools," *Personnel Guidance. J.*, **31**, 380–83 (1953)
24. Fenlason, A. F., *Essentials in Interviewing* (Harper & Brothers, New York, N. Y., 352 pp., 1952)
25. Froehlich, C. P., and Darley, J. G., *Studying Students* (Science Research Associates, Chicago, Ill, 411 pp., 1952)
26. Germain, G. L., Browne, C. G., Bellows, R. M., "Measuring Men and Jobs: Criteria for Physical Analysis Forms," *Personnel Guidance J.*, **31**, 245–49 (1953)
27. Gluck, S. *et al.*, "A Proposed Code of Ethics for Counselors," *Occupations*, **30**, 484–90 (1952)
28. Gough, H. G., "What Determines the Academic Achievements of High School Students," *J. Educ. Research*, **46**, 321–31 (1953)
29. Gough, H. G., and Pemberton, W. H., "Personality Characteristics Related to Success in Practice Teaching," *J. Appl. Psychol.*, **36**, 307–9 (1952)
30. Guthrie, G. M., and O'Neill, H. W., "The Effects of Dormitory Counseling on Academic Achievement," *Personnel Guidance J.* **31**, 307–9 (1953)
31. Hiltner, S., *The Counselor in Counseling* (Abingdon-Cokesbury Press, New York, 188 pp., 1953)
32. Hahn, M. E., "Conceptual Trends in Counseling," *Personnel Guidance J.*, **31**, 231–35 (1953)
33. Jex, F. B., and Sorensen, A. G., "G.A.T.B. Scores as Predictors of College Grades," *Personnel Guidance J.*, **31**, 295–97 (1953)
34. Kaplan, D. L., "Occupational Information from the 1950 Census," *Personnel Guidance J.*, **31**, 368–70 (1953)
35. Kirk, B. A., "Test Versus Academic Performance in Malfunctioning Students," *J. Consulting Psychol.*, **16**, 213–16 (1952)
36. Kirk, B. A., "Individualizing of Test Interpretation," *Occupations*, **30**, 500–5 (1952)
37. Kirk, B. A., "How Counseling Affects Vocational Goals," *Educ. Psychol. Measurement*, **12**, 692–98 (1952)
38. Laing, L. D., "The Use of Reassurance in Therapy," *Smith Coll. Studies Social Work*, **22**, 75–90 (1952)
39. Layton, W. L., "Predicting Success of Students in Veterinary Medicine," *J. Appl. Psychol.*, **36**, 312–15 (1952)
40. Long, L., "The V. A. Guidance Program: An Evaluation," *Personnel Guidance J.*, **31**, 104–7 (1952)
41. Luborsky, L., "The Personality of the Psychotherapist," *Menninger Quart.*, **6**, 1–6 (1952)
42. Maclean, M. S., "Counseling and the Tower of Babel," *Personnel Guidance J.*, **31**, 357–62 (1953)
43. Mahoney, H. J., *Occupational Information for Counselors* (World Book Co., Yonkers, N. Y., 70 pp., 1952)
44. Melville, S. D., and Frederiksen, N., "Achievement of Freshmen Engineering Students and the Strong Vocational Interest Blank," *J. Appl. Psychol.*, **36**, 169–73 (1952)

45. Merrill, R. M., and Heathers, L. B., "Deviations of the Wechsler-Bellevue Subtest Scores from Vocabulary Level in University Counseling Center Clients," *J. Consulting Psychol.*, **16**, 469–72 (1952)
46. Michael, W. B., and Reeder, D. E., "The Development and Validation of a Preliminary Form of a Study-Habits Inventory," *Educ. Psychol. Measurement*, **12**, 236–47 (1952)
47. Mitchell, H. E., "The Interrelation of Factors Associated with the Initial Interview to Factors Related to the Marriage Counseling Process as a Whole," *Am. Psychologist*, **7**, 381–82 (1952)
48. Morgan, H. H., "A Psychometric Comparison of Achieving and Nonachieving College Students of High Ability," *J. Consulting Psychol.*, **16**, 292–98 (1952)
48a. Mowrer, O. H. *et al.*, *Psychotherapy Theory and Research* (The Ronald Press Co., New York, N. Y., 700 pp., 1953)
49. Myers, R. C., "Biographical Factors and Academic Achievement: An Experimental Investigation," *Educ. Psychol. Measurement*, **12**, 415–26 (1952)
50. Pepinsky, H. B., "Some Proposals for Research," *Personnel Guidance J.*, **31**, 291–94 (1953)
51. Pepinsky, H. B., Clyde, R. J., Olesen, B. A., and Van Atta, E. L., "The Criterion in Counseling: I. Individual Personality and Behavior in a Social Group," *Educ. Psychol. Measurement*, **12**, 178–93 (1952)
52. Pepinsky, H. B., Siegal, L., and Van Atta, E., "The Criterion in Counseling: A Group Participation Scale," *J. Abnormal Social Psychol.*, **57**, 415–19 (1952)
53. Perry, W. G., Jr., and Estes, S. G., "The Collaboration of Client and Counselor," in *Psychotherapy Theory and Research*, 95–119 (Mowrer, O. H., Ed., The Ronald Press Co., New York, N. Y., 700 pp., 1953)
54. Porter, E. H., Jr., "On the Nature of Psychotherapeutic Interpretation," *J. Consulting Psychol.*, **16**, 343–46 (1952)
55. Richardson, H., and Borow, H., "Evaluation of a Technique of Group Orientation for Vocational Counseling," *Educ. Psychol. Measurement*, **12**, 587–97 (1952)
56. Roberts, G. E., "A Study of the Validity of the Index of Adjustment and Values," *J. Consulting Psychol.*, **16**, 302–4 (1952)
57. Rogers, C. R., "Interest in the Practice of Psychotherapy," *Am. Psychologist*, **8**, 48–50 (1953)
58. Rogers, C., "Some Directions and End Points in Therapy," in *Psychotherapy Theory and Research* 44–68 (Mowrer, O. H., Ed., The Ronald Press Co., New York, 700 pp., 1953)
59. Rogers, C. R., "Client-Centered Psychotherapy," *Sci. American*, **187**, 66–68 (1952)
60. Rothney, J. M., and Mooren, R. L., "Sampling Problems in Follow-up Research," *Occupations*, **30**, 573–78 (1952)
61. Samler, J., "Professional Training: End Goal or Kick-off Point?" *Personnel Guidance J.*, **31**, 15–19 (1952)
62. Samson, R., and Stefflre, B., "Like Father . . . Like Son?" *Personnel Guidance J.*, **31**, 35–39 (1952)
63. Schofield, W., "A Study of Medical Students with the MMPI: III, Personality and Academic Success," *J. Applied Psychol.*, **37**, 47–52 (1953)
64. Seeman, J., and Raskin, N. J., "Research Perspectives in Client-Centered

Therapy," in *Psychotherapy Theory and Research* 205–34 (Mowrer, O. H., Ed., Ronald Press, New York, N. Y., 700 pp., 1953)

65. Serene, M. F., "An Experiment in Motivational Counseling," *Personnel Guidance J.*, **31,** 319–24 (1953)
66. Shartle, C. L., *Occupational Information*, 2nd ed. (Prentice-Hall, Inc., New York, N. Y., 448 pp., 1952)
67. Shaw, J. *et al.*, "Changes Occurring in Teacher-Pupil Attitudes during a Two-Week Guidance Workshop," *J. Appl. Psychol.*, **36,** 304–6, (1952)
68. Shoben, E. J., Jr., "Some Problems in Establishing Criteria of Effectiveness," *Personnel Guidance J.*, **31,** 287–91 (1953)
69. Shostrom, E. L., and Brammer, L. M., *Dynamics of the Counseling Process* (McGraw-Hill Book Co., New York, N. Y., 213 pp., 1952)
70. Sinick, D., "Anxiety in the Testing Situation," *Personnel Guidance J.*, **31,** 384–86 (1953)
71. Small, L., "Personality Determinants of Vocational Choice," *Psychol. Monographs*, **67**(1), 1–21 (1953)
72. Steinberg, A., "The Relation of Vocational Preference to Emotional Adjustment," *Educ. Psychol. Measurement,* **12,** 96–104 (1952)
73. Storrs, S., "Evaluative Data on the G.A.T.B.," *Personnel Guidance J.*, **31,** 87–90 (1952)
74. Strong, E. K., Jr., "Interests of Negroes and Whites," *J. Social. Psychol,* **35,** 139–50 (1952)
75. Strong, E. K., Jr., "Amount of Change in Occupational Choice of College Freshmen," *Educ. Psychol. Measurement,* **12,** 677–90 (1952)
76. Strong, E. K., Jr., and Tucker, A. C., "The Use of Vocational Interest Scales in Planning a Medical Career," *Psychol. Monographs,* **66,** 1–37 (1952)
77. Super, D. E., "The Practicum Training of Counseling Psychologists," *Am. Psychologist,* **7,** 182–88 (1952)
78. Super, D. E., "A Theory of Vocational Development," *Am. Psychologist,* **8,** 185–90 (1953)
79. Taylor, C., and Combs, A., "Self-Acceptance and Adjustment," *J. Consulting Psychol.*, **16,** 89–91 (1952)
80. Thorne, F. C., "Rules of Evidence in the Evaluation of the Effects of Psychotherapy," *J. Clin. Psychol.*, **8,** 38–41 (1952)
81. Toman, W., "Pause Analysis as a Short Interviewing Technique," *J. Consulting Psychol.*, **17,** 1–7 (1953)
82. Traphagen, A. I., "Interest Patterns and Retention and Rejection of Vocational Choice," *J. Appl. Psychol.*, **36,** 182–85 (1952)
83. United States Office of Education, *Counseling College Students During the Defense Period* (Superintendent of Documents, Government Printing Office, Washington, D. C., 25 pp., 1952)
84. Watson, R. I., "Research Design and Methodology in Evaluating the Results of Psychotherapy," *J. Clin. Psychol.*, **8,** 29–33 (1952)
85. Weigand, G., "Goal Aspiration and Academic Success," *Personnel Guidance J.*, **31,** 458–61 (1953)
86. Wesman, A. G., "The Differential Aptitude Tests," *Personnel Guidance J.*, **31,** 167–70 (1952)
87. Woodman, E. M., "Description of a Guidance Instrument Designed to Measure

Attitudes Related to Academic Success in College," *Educ. Psychol. Measurement,* **12,** 275–84 (1952)

88. Wrenn, C. G., "The Selection and Education of Student Personnel Workers," *Personnel Guidance J.,* **31,** 9–14 (1952)

89. Wrenn, C. G., "The Ethics of Counseling," *Educ. Psychol. Measurement,* **12,** 161–77 (1952)

EDUCATIONAL PSYCHOLOGY

By James Maxwell
Moray House, Edinburgh, Scotland

Introduction

The topics discussed in this review are derived from those publications, containing material of interest to educational psychologists, which have appeared during the period March, 1952 to March, 1953. It was not always possible to obtain in Britain the most recent issues of periodicals published in the United States in time for inclusion in this review; and it is probable that some contributions have been overlooked. The purpose of the review, however, is more to examine and evaluate the current trends in educational psychology than to comment critically on individual articles, so the omission of some of the published material may not significantly disturb the general picture.

No clear-cut definition of the term "Educational Psychology" has been attempted; the scope of the review has been empirically determined by the selection of such material as would interest those directly or indirectly concerned with the process of education, within the limitations that the topics should be discussed from a psychological point of view, and that they should to some degree be an original contribution to the field of knowledge.

Research and practice.—The relationship between research and educational practice is discussed in several articles. Brownell (1) points out the value of pure as well as applied research, indicating that the results of research on rats may in the end have as much influence on education as research on children. He also thinks it is not a bad thing that researchers are not able to insist on their findings being applied immediately; a time lag is necessary for proper understanding and evaluation of research findings; and the results of research are influencing educational practice, though not as speedily as the research worker may wish. Also among the optimists are Gray & Iverson (2), who, in a discussion of the teacher's attitude to criticisms, argue that the standards of attainment are at present at least as high as in the past, and that modern teaching methods are founded on the research results of a considerable number of years. It is worthy of note that both Gray and Brownell are in the fortunate position of having been concerned with research in the elementary school subjects for a long enough time to see the results of their work appearing in school practice. It is also noteworthy that both use Reading as the example which best supports their thesis. Others are not so sanguine. Leonard (3) stresses the change in emphasis in education from skills to citizenship, and calls for further research in the nature and climate of the group, in the acquisition of moral values, and in children's development. He accepts by implication the thesis of Gray and Brownell on the school subjects, but disregards their plea for time and patience. Leonard's plea for research in group relationships has been responded to in the period of this review, in quantity if not in quality, and some of the articles reviewed do give added force to the argument for a time lag for adequate evaluation of their results. Buswell (4) emphasises the difference between "Frontier" research and "Follow-up" research. Frontier research is exploratory, empirical, and less rigorous. "Follow-up" research is rigorous, carefully designed, and aimed at elucidating the theoretical implications of the frontier research. The distinction is a good one for the evaluation of research. Much of the research reviewed here is frontier research; it is exploratory, and often inconclusive and unconvincing, but to apply rigorous standards would be misleading, and for the findings to be put into practice might be disastrous. The follow-up research is less interesting, possibly, but it is on that type of research that changes in educational practice are made.

There does appear, however, to be a gap between the researcher and the teacher which could be closed. Gray & Iverson, in the article quoted, advocate some national establishment to co-ordinate research. Mackenzie (5) deplores the lack of co-ordination between studies in curriculum subjects and the work in schools, and suggests more team work in research with the participation of teachers. Corey (6) makes the same plea for greater participation in research by serving teachers, and suggests methods by which teachers' observation and records could meet the more exacting requirements of the research worker.

None of this is new, but it is good that these issues should be kept alive. It is heartening to find that experienced research workers are satisfied that research work in educational psychology is affecting school practice, though perhaps slowly. But both Buswell's stages must be passed through before the findings are tested in the ultimate trying ground, the classroom. Closer liaison between teachers and research workers seems needed, but the fault is not wholly with the teacher. Many articles contributed by teachers have been excluded from this review because they were anecdotal, hortatory, and too specific; many research articles cited are open to the charge of being rather remote from classroom realities and frequently concerned with tests rather than children. Too often the educational purpose appears to be the acquisition of a higher degree rather than the extension of knowledge of children and education. In the end, however, time will prove to be a better evaluator than any reviewer.

School Subjects

Reading.—Reading still holds first place among the school subjects investigated, though there has of recent years been a shift of emphasis from the elementary to the later stages of reading instruction. The complaint of Hill (7) that too little attention is given to research in higher education in the United States is not borne out in the field of reading. Half the articles cited below deal with higher education.

Elementary school reading.—It appears as if the subject of elementary reading had been virtually exhausted. The frontier research in reading skills was done many years ago, follow-up experiments have been extensive, and the outcome of all this investigation is presented in two very comprehensive text books on reading by Anderson & Dearborn (8) and by Tinker (9). The title of Anderson & Dearborn's book, *The Psychology of Teaching Reading*, is a good indication of the treatment. Reading is treated initially as a function of the child's growth, but this approach is not systematically pursued through the book. Considerable attention is given to the perceptual aspects of learning to read, and it is here that the authors draw most upon the very large volume of research available. An excellent critical examination of methods of teaching reading is followed by a short discussion of evaluation. Though pedagogically useful, this book merits mention here as an example of the way in which a large and scattered body of research work can be brought together to enlighten and instruct the practising teacher. The title of Tinker's book, *Teaching Elementary Reading*, is also an indication of its approach. The stress is on teaching methods, and more attention is paid to training than to maturation. A large portion of the book is devoted to reading readiness and Grade I methods. Preparatory activities and training programmes are fully described, though little evidence is quoted in the text as to their effectiveness. The bibliography, though, is extensive. The book is apparently addressed to the serving teacher and suffers from the defects of most digests. It tries to be too comprehensive, forgetting sometimes that the field is governed more by the knowledge available than by the needs of the classroom. The result is a tendency to dogmatism and over-simplification, without adequate distinction being made between principles well-founded on research and those less well-founded. Though a bit diffuse, the treatment aims at covering the ground that the school teacher is concerned with, which it succeeds in doing comprehensively, if at times uncritically.

The remaining studies are mainly concerned with the tidying up of the odd corners of the field of reading skills. Triggs (10) shows that word recognition, defined in terms of ability to match the printed and spoken word and to divide words into their syllables, does not appear to show improvement after Grade IV. It is probable that the essential skills have been mastered before that stage. Bond (11) and Smith (12) both raise doubts about the efficacy of present group methods of teaching reading. Both desire more individual instruction, which they maintain raises the standard of reading attainment, though neither explains how the teacher is to cope with largish classes. Haugh (13) investigates the effectiveness of radio listening as a supplement to reading. For 539 Grade XI pupils,[1] it was found that after seven weeks, a greater gain in information was made by the readers than by the

[1] We adopt the British usage of describing one still in attendance at school as a pupil, reserving the term "student" for one attending a college, university, or other institution for further education.

listeners. The same applied to changes in attitude. Studies by Freeburne & Fleischer (14) and Hall (15) investigate the effects of background music on reading efficiency. Hall, with 278 Grade VIII and IX pupils, finds music helps reading. Freeburne & Fleischer, with 208 students, find no significant differences. Both studies overlook the probable incentive inherent in the experimental situation; and it does not appear likely that musical accompaniment would be an aid to long-term serious reading. McKillop (16) tackles a more fundamental aspect of reading, the interaction between the reader's emotional attitudes and the material read. She gave 512 pupils in Grade XI attitude tests of the Negro versus white variety and found that the pupils' responses on matters of factual detail in their reading were not affected by attitude, but there were significant differences in their interpretation and evaluation. This study, conducted on sound lines, would indicate a need for teaching pupils to read accurately and without bias. Though no indication of the differences in reading efficiency in relation to attitudes is given, it is possible that poor readers are more susceptible to emotional bias and to read into the passage what is not there. But it does seem that reading skill alone does not make a good reader. Burton (17) attempts to determine the nature of literary appreciation with Grade XII pupils. He finds it related to verbal intelligence, social background, and silent reading skill, but all correlations are rather low. There is the usual difficulty of the criterion; and though the results are unconvincing, appreciation has been a neglected aspect of reading studies.

College reading.—The remainder of the studies deal with the reading difficulties of college students. Such students appear to be a growing problem to American psychologists, and, during the period under review, are the major concern of those working in the field of reading. Krisa (18) found that his 20 adults showed no reversals in reading, but continued to show them with artificial symbols. He concludes that reversals in reading are mastered by training and practice, and not by maturation as is often stated. The number of cases is too small and the experimental conditions too artificial for this conclusion to be wholly accepted. Manolakes (19) trained an experimental group of adults, using a tachistoscope. This training had no effect on their reading eye movements. It remains to be found whether this applies to children, as there are many advocates of perceptual training as preparation for learning to read. Witty, Stolartz & Cooper (20) gave 42 students, all low scorers on the Co-operative English Text, a nine week intensive training which raised their reading percentile rank from 48 to 76. The permanence of the improvement is not stated. Barbe (21), in a similar twelve week course, obtained a 64 per cent improvement in rate of reading, which dropped to 49 per cent six months later. Mouly (22) similarly found improvement, but points out that the personality of the students electing remedial reading may be a factor in the results. Johnson (23), with small groups of students, found improvement in reading both from training in techniques and from group therapy. In all such studies, it must be remembered, the validity of the findings depends on the validity of the measuring instruments, and it is all too easy to balance one set of test results against another and claim improvement in reading as the result. Timely warnings are given by Carillo & Sheldon (24) who point out that flexibility of reading rate is more important than mere speed, which is so often taken as the criterion of reading efficiency. The appropriate measure should be the relationship of speed to difficulty. Barbe & Grilk (25) show that reading rate and intelligence correlate only $r=.12$, whereas if other reading abilities are considered as well, the correlation rises to $r=.72$. Finally Dahlberg, Rosewell & Chall (26) stress that reading efficiency is not merely a matter of skills; disabilities are often associated with psychological disorder, which must be taken into account in any scheme of remedial training.

The reviewer remembers a well-known American psychologist asking an equally well-known Scottish psychologist what was done in Britain with students with reading disabilities. The answer was that we do not let them into college. The absence of any British contributions to the literature reviewed is an indication of the way in which educational research is influenced by educational needs. From the safety of the other side of the Atlantic the reviewer may perhaps offer a few critical comments. The presence of college students who cannot read effectively would seem to call for greater attention to the school reading programme, particularly in diagnosis of difficulties in the upper grades. There is little sign of such interest. Another doubt concerns the efficiency of intensive courses at a late stage in reading progress. There are too many studies which take reading tests as their own criterion; more confidence would arise from proof that such courses resulted in improvement in college work, which Mouly uses, and in a longer term follow-up of the benefits gained. Such researches would be more difficult than those cited, but more valuable.[2]

Other school subjects.— The other school subjects are poorly represented. In art, there are one or two studies of interest. Whipple (27) assessed the features of book illustration most interesting to Grade VI pupils. The favoured features were a definite centre of interest, action, colour, and size. Readers with many pictures were preferred to those with few. Two very neat investi-

[2] The reviewer received too late for inclusion in the text a report of the Annual Conference on Reading, edited by Gray (107). It is impossible to summarize such a comprehensive survey, consisting as it does of some 50 papers on various aspects of the topic. The opening paper confirms the view that the field of study of reading as such is virtually exhausted, but points out that a new field is now being explored, the relationship of reading skills to other areas of the school curriculum. It is to the latter topic that the volume is devoted, and the discussion is thorough. Throughout, the requirements of the high school are kept in mind, and in this respect, as in others, the volume goes some way towards meeting the reviewer's criticisms about neglect of certain aspects of the study of reading. The contributors ask questions rather than attempt to answer them, and it is likely that further research in reading will arise from the questions they ask.

gations by Rudisill (28) and French (29) discuss pupils' development in appreciation. Rudisill, using a variety of coloured and uncoloured pictures, finds that realism rather than colour appeals to children from kindergarten to Grade VI. The conclusion is that adults over-emphasise the attraction of colour for children. French finds that young children are quite consistent in their judgements of pictures. They prefer clear outline and isolated objects, similar to their own productions. Adults and pupils of Grade V upwards prefer impressionistic pictures, with true perspective. There is a fairly clear maturational change both in drawings and appreciation, and the findings are well worth study by teachers endeavouring to train children in art. The remaining studies are slight. Elkisch (30), in a subjective analysis of Grade V and VI boys' drawings, concludes that they think of themselves as machines. Knopp & Richards (31) find girls' drawings more complex than boys', and younger children's more constricted. The main interest in these investigations is in appreciation, and studies like those of French and Rudisill are contributions to the understanding of children's development which could profitably be carried further.

An over-elaborate factor analysis of a spelling test of 100 words by Knoell & Harris (32) does not leave us much wiser. Wiliard (33) finds 19 high school pupils given formal spelling instruction were 18 per cent better than a control group, which is fair enough. Dressel, Schmidt & Kincaid (34) reveal a state of affairs among college students which requires attention. Excluding English, the hours per year spent in writing varied from 131 to 4. It was found also that frequency of essay writing in subjects other than English gave rise to no improvement over a year.

The work on arithmetic is disappointingly small. As a skill, arithmetic is as essential as reading, and yet hardly a single article is found dealing with the learning and teaching of arithmetic. Crawford & Zylstra (35) show that the level of accuracy with which high school pupils can estimate quantities is low, and that ability to estimate size, volume, etc., is independent of IQ and mathematical ability. The other contributions deal with the writing of numbers. Perry (36) points out the superiority of arabic over roman numerals, and Wright (37) in an extensive discussion, examines the sources of confusions in numbering and the current practices in teaching. From these he derives the optimal system of numbers, including the small zero and round-topped three. The book is voluminous but readable, though the validity of the proposed system is not fully established. Halloran (38) shows that for a four-year period, Esperanto is a useful introduction to the study of French for poorer pupils, but is of no benefit to the abler ones. The four-year span of the experiment gives confidence in his findings.

Measuring progress.—The theoretical implications of measurement of educational progress have produced some thoughtful papers. English (39) discusses the concept of learning and maintains that there is no need for a systematic theory; learning is a technological term, and is established by an empirical measurement of improvement. Without necessarily adopting this extreme empirical attitude, Durost & Prescott (40) stress the need for careful consideration of what is involved in measuring improvement. Units in both measurements should be comparable and equally variable at all levels, and there should be equal opportunity for improvement for all subjects, differences in curriculum, length of school year and so on, being taken into account. There is rather a counsel of perfection, but more attention to these requirements would produce more valid results. Tilton (41) also discusses the question of a general learning ability, basing his findings on the intercorrelations of school subjects after a 20-month interval through Grades IV and V. He very properly emphasises that measures of improvement must be reliable as well as the tests used, and tentatively concludes that there is a general learning ability. This is an initial approach to a topic which calls for further research in two dimensions, the constancy of growth of the general learning ability and the maturational development of specific abilities. The theoretical implications are important, but the technique of investigation will require careful consideration.

The year's work in the school subjects has, with a few exceptions, been disappointing. Interest in this field seems to be stagnating. This is explicable in reading, where a large mass of research has still to be digested, but the drift of interest in the United States to evaluation and social relationships and in Britain to measurement and selection, does not wholly excuse the paucity of contributions to the scientific psychological study of the basic school subjects. The lack of interest in arithmetic is especially disturbing.

Social Aspects

Under this heading are such topics as interpersonal relations, home background and interests, and attitudes to social questions. These topics are becoming of increasing interest to educational psychologists and reflect a shift of attention from the teaching of skills to the teaching of citizenship and how to live. Greater attention has always been paid in the United States to personal and group relations than in Britain, as the problems of American society are more manifest and urgent. The feature of the present period is an outburst of sociometry.

This is still frontier research and much is exploratory and descriptive. Techniques are yet to be established, and the findings are far from conclusive, even at times appearing rather pointless. But implicit in it all is a felt need for adjusting the individual to a social group. The "isolate" is by implication requiring rescue, the "star" is approved. What will come out of it when sound working techniques have been established is not yet clear, but the positive purposes to which these techniques will be applied require watching. The pupil of independent mind and character may fare badly.

Sociometric studies.—Wrightstone *et al.* (41) use sociometric techniques to assess and improve school staff relationships. The claim is made, despite inadequate statistical support, that service on committees increases the acceptability of isolate teachers. Kuhlen & Collister (42) find the social acceptability of Grade VI and IX pupils who leave school is lower than that of those who remain. The social acceptance is here clearly specific to the situation, and cause and effect are not distinguishable. Holmes (43) shows that abler students have a better attitude towards the worth of others. Again a normative implication is present. Ausubel, Schiff & Gasser (44) investigate pupils' awareness of their own and others' sociometric status. Using four methods of assessment, mainly five point ratings, they find ability to assess status increases with age. Their ratings are not shown to be very reliable, and their conclusions are more sweeping than their evidence warrants. The Alexanders (45) ask whether socially acceptable children are best adjusted. Joe, who was most frequently chosen by a group of nine-year-olds, was clinically examined to see if he was well adjusted. He was not. Bretsch (46) separates 696 fourteen-year-olds into well, medium, and poorly accepted groups. There is a significant difference between the groups in respect of social skills and activities in favour of the well accepted, but there is no check upon the validity of the social skills ratings, and the differences are very small. The two Graces (47) find no relationship between verbal behaviour and the opinion of the rest of the group about how an individual would actually behave. The criterion is rather artificial; the article is full of jargon. Goodnow & Taguiri (48) use sociometry (choice of roommate) to find that boys tend to choose mates of their own religious denomination. They expect also to be chosen on the same principle. Hallworth (49) gives what is essentially a descriptive account of the personal relationships in a grammar school of pupils aged 11 to 16. Under the ambitious title of *Studies in the Social Psychology of Adolescence* (50) and under the editorship of C. M. Fleming are published four studies of social relationships in school. Richardson (50) groups a class of girls according to their sociometric choices, and claims improvement in English and social relationships in comparison with a control class. There is too much description and the evidence is essentially subjective. Forrester (50), in an inconclusive study of attitudes of adolescents to their own development uses questionnaire methods, but without check on their validity. The adolescents are concerned mainly with adventure and with growing up, but these findings may be as much a function of the questionnaire as the pupils. Shukla (50), also using unvalidated questionnaires, finds friends have common interests. Higginbotham (50) records discussions by Grammar School and Approved School girls, but little else. Taylor (51) used sociometric techniques in an attack on a more vital problem, the desirability of promotion by age in elementary schools. Over 1000 children in 38 classes were studied, and it was found that there was no relation between age and acceptability, this not justifying age promotion. A slightly lower constancy of social acceptance was found in progressive as opposed to traditional classes, which was taken to mean that teacher's efforts at social adjustment were not wholly ineffective. This is a more competent research than most quoted in this section; but what they all add up to is not clear. Though strict standards should not be applied to exploratory research, yet some regard must be had for scientific logic and relevance to educational problems. Though the chalk legends on school walls that AB loves CD have not yet attained the status of educational research, some of the contributions cited above, especially the British, are only about one stage beyond this.

There are attempts, however, to bring order into the field. Moreno (52) objects to the extensive use of sociometric techniques without relation to the theory behind them. There is inadequate analysis of the group situation, ignoring of the observer-actor relationship and gross oversimplification of experimental design. Clark & McGuire (53, 54) jointly attempt to derive working indices from sociometric data. Assuming that a sociometric valuation gives information about the valuer as well as the person valued, a "sociograph" can be made showing social clusters and cleavages. Similarly they find two indices of peer status. The analysis is thorough and it may prove that the indices are practicable measures like the well-established IQ, but there does remain the doubt that social relationships are less constant than IQ is assumed to be and the data not susceptible to a single measure. Still, until something like these indices can be used, it is unlikely that anything of permanent value will emerge from the current sociometric studies. Wityrol & Thompson (55) compare the stability of two sociometric measures, Partial Rank Order and Paired Comparison, on Grade VI pupils over five weeks. Paired Comparison is both more rigorous and reliable, and the two methods agree with a median correlation of $r=.7$. This is the kind of investigation that should have been done before sociometric techniques were applied as freely as they have been. Whether sociometric techniques will prove a fruitful instrument of research remains to be seen, but much progress is unlikely till there are more investigations of the kind of the last two cited.

Attitude studies.—The attitude studies produced during the period under review are in continuation of those of the past few years and present no unusual features, though they add to the fund of information. Estvan (56) makes a comprehensive study of the attitudes of eleven-year-old children to poverty. Distinctions between social class are shown in awareness of the effects and incidence of poverty, the lower class children having a more sympathetic, immediate, personal awareness. Children of high intelligence have greater recognition of poverty as a social as well as personal affair. Boys tend to look at poverty from an objective and father's point of view, the girls more at the family and home aspect. The feature of this study is the care taken in experimental design, which lends confidence to somewhat subjective methods of interpretation. This research has a direct bearing on the teaching of social studies in school. Himmelweit, Halsey & Oppenheim (57) investigate differences between grammar school (IQ, 115 plus) and modern school boys in their attitudes to social class. Sixty per cent of the boys did not understand what social class meant, and the remainder defined it in several frames of reference, e.g., work, income, politics, etc. They did, however, agree with the sociologists in ranking occupations, though working-class boys overranked manual professions. The most significant finding was that most boys expected their occupations to be higher than their fathers'. This study would suggest that the attitude of most boys to the social structure is not far removed from that of the community in general. Prothero & Miles (58) take a representative group of adults, and find that their attitudes to race and religion are very similar to those of college students. Young, Mayans & Corman (59) find that 83 per cent of their Grade XI pupils have the same political views as their parents and the same complex of attitudes associated with these politics. All these studies raise the question of what effects school education has on the social attitudes of pupils. It appears, very little.

Children's interests.—There are also a few studies of the effects of children's interests outside school. Malter (60) analyses children's comics, finding only about 5 per cent of the space is used for printed matter, and that humour and crime between them account for half the contents. Crime is not so predominant as it is alleged to be. McKellar & Harris (61) find British children aged 8 to 14 years uniformly prefer radio to cinema programmes and prefer humorous variety and adventure serials. They find the children not uncritical of crime and adventure features, and like Malter, they conclude that the effects of such stories can easily be exaggerated. Another commonly held belief is deflated by Smith (62). In an experiment using control and experimental groups, it was found that instruction by films led to gains by the more intelligent pupils, there being no evidence of gain by the less intelligent. Though the methods used were rather cumbersome, the conclusion appears sound enough.

Guidance and Selection

Educational psychologists in both Britain and the United States are faced with what is fundamentally the same problem, though the settings are different. The problem is to reconcile individual differences in ability and circumstances with an egalitarian educational policy. In the United States, where the students' choice is freer than in Britain, students are liable to elect courses for which they are not suited and become academic misfits. In Britain the pupils are allocated to different types of secondary education and again misfits occur. In Britain the psychologists have to talk themselves out of misfitting; in the United States the psychologist has to talk the student out of it. In both countries there is constant need of valid and reliable assessment of an individual's suitability for various courses of study.

Prediction of academic success.—Most of these studies are American and are concerned with college students. A review of the practice in many colleges is given by Cosand (63). Intelligence tests plus language-skill tests give prediction up to $r = .8$, though no single test appears to give more than $r = .5$; and high school marks appear to be better predictors than any single test. A comprehensive table of results from various sources is given. Bolton (64) reports that, of a battery of intelligence and scholastic tests, the best predictor was the American Council of Education Psychological Examination

(A.C.E.), but that its prediction of college progress was considerably higher for the first than for the second year. This well-conducted study confirms previous findings. Similar results are given by Frederiksen & Schrader (65), who report that high school marks are slightly better than A.C.E. test scores. Doppelt & Wesman (66) investigate the use of Differential Aptitude Tests rather than general intelligence tests as predictors of academic progress in school, and find that these tests give a correlation of $r = .7$ with the Iowa Tests of Educational Development one year later. This study has the weakness of many such, balancing one set of test results against another, but the authors are aware of the weakness of their criterion. Sutherland (67) compares the predictive value of different types of arithmetic tests given to twelve-year-olds with their school marks two to three years later. Problem arithmetic is found to be the best predictor, but not so good as an intelligence test. Differences in time allowance for the tests made little difference.

Validity of intelligence tests.—In all these studies, the conventional intelligence test still appears the best predictor. In Britain, the use of intelligence tests for selection of pupils for secondary education has recently been criticised. In England particularly, the accuracy of selection is important, as the many pupils' chances of obtaining an academic secondary education largely depend on their performance on such tests. Vernon (68), giving the question of coaching and practice effects on IQ an airing, reports gains of about 14 points in IQ from coaching and lesser gains from practice, but the investigation appears to have been done in circumstances giving the maximum effects, and the conversion of scores to IQ is suspect. Wiseman (68) reports an extensive experiment in which a control group gained about four points IQ, a coached group six points, and a practice group, eleven points. This reverses Vernon's results, and Wiseman's groups were both larger and more representative. Watts, Pidgeon & Yates (69) find that practice gives slightly greater gains than coaching, and their results agree fairly closely with Wiseman's. The upshot appears to be that IQ on verbal group tests is raised by about seven points by practice and coaching, but that the greatest effect occurs after the first practice or coaching period; and if a practice test is given shortly before the test proper, substantial justice would be done. Emmett (70), justifying intelligence tests for selection, claims that less than 2 per cent of the children are affected by coaching, but admits that about 9 per cent of the grammar school entrants are affected. He also ignores the resulting lack of confidence in the larger proportion of the scores from which the suspect cases are drawn. He also reports a correlation of $r = .84$ between selection tests and school certificate examinations as evidence of the efficiency of the tests. But the criterion is not how well pupils perform in the grammar school; it is whether the tests have selected the best pupils for the grammar school. More relevant validation is given by a report on Edinburgh pupils (71). The Leaving Certificate successes are compared with test results of six years earlier, and it is clearly shown that the chances of any pupil, not selected for full secondary education, gaining this Certificate are extremely small. This workmanlike study, together with those of Wiseman and the National Foundation (69) are sound contributions to this very important educational problem in Britain. These studies are unlikely to lead to any radical changes in practice, but it is all to the good that current procedures should be examined, exaggerated claims exposed, and sound practices confirmed.

The use of the IQ in educational practice has been under examination from other aspects. Estes (72) finds significant differences between the average intelligence of upper and lower economic groups in Grade II, but no corresponding difference in Grade V. It is not clear, however, whether this is attributable to the levelling effect of common education, or the retardation of less able pupils. With three-year-old children, Sacks (73) reported an increase in Binet IQ when favourable social relations were established with the children. Boger (74) found training with jigsaw and other geometric puzzles increased average IQ, and Pitts (75) showed the importance of reading skill in the intelligence test scores of negro girls. The larger question of intelligence tests and cultural environment is discussed by Stenquist (76) and Biesheuvel (77). The former doubts the value of a "culture free" IQ, which would lose the cultural heritage of the schools and advocates the use of specific aptitude tests instead of a general composite IQ. The latter reaches the same conclusion through difficulties in standardising tests on a bilingual population, who are to be educated in a common school system. It does not seem likely, though, that intelligence tests will fall into disuse, as aptitude tests are specific to a given field of behaviour, whereas in education the aptitudes required are so many and various that the overall IQ is likely to remain the most practicable and efficient instrument. Periodic reminders of the limitations of IQ are not amiss, and the comments of both writers are pertinent.

School success, however, does not depend on ability only; social differences also operate. Halsey & Gardner (78) find greater differences in social class between grammar and modern school children in England than can be accounted for by differential selection by intelligence. Even within the grammar schools, the children from the middle classes have better prospects of success than children of the same measured intelligence from the working classes. Campbell (79) examined the home conditions of pupils who had been selected by test for different levels of secondary education and were found to be misplaced. Those who failed to make progress were found to have poorer home background than those who were progressing better than expected. His conclusions are cautious and sound. These two studies throw further light on the factors influencing school progress, and it appears that the influence of cultural and social differences in measured intelligence is not disadvantageous in educational selection, but in fact is underestimated in intelligence test scores. The study of social differences in education is developing slowly, probably because of the egalitarian basis of educational policy, but the principle that educational progress is not a function of intellectual ability only requires both emphasis and further study. It is possible to be as scientific about social differences as about cognitive differences, but it is less popular.

Teachers

The characteristics of the teacher, no less than those of the pupils, have an important bearing on education. Educational psychologists have always paid more attention to the learner than to the teacher; and it is gratifying that the teacher as a person, as distinct from an applier of methods, is attracting some attention. The problems of the assessment of the teacher's influence on the pupils, the teacher's attitudes and technical competence, and in the selection of fit persons as teachers are very considerable, and have not yet received the intensive study they deserve. Most of those engaged in training teachers are aware of the subjective and arbitrary nature of their judgements, and any critique founded on sound psychological investigation is very welcome.

Teaching competence.—The main difficulty lies in the criteria of teaching competence. Orleans *et al.* (80) point out that the ultimate criterion is change in the pupil, but this must be considered in relation to at least three essential variables, the kind of teacher, the kind of pupil, and the kind of educational aim. Assessment is not a simple matter, and basic thinking on the subject is much needed. In their study of teacher competence, Grim & Hoyt (81) show awareness of the complex criterion by approaching the assessment through both the teacher and the pupil. They obtain both the pupils' and the principals' points of view on certain topics and propose to compare the results with the rating value given to the teacher. Validation is awaited, but the approach is promising. Ryans (82) endeavours to unravel the complexities of the criterion by a factor analysis of a classroom observation scale, but the five factors obtained do not add much to the understanding of the problem. The identification of factors is rather naive.

Teachers' attitudes.—A more thorough investigation into the various components of successful teaching is needed before the training, selection, and assessment of teachers can be placed on a scientifically validated basis. The question of teachers' attitudes has, however, attracted a few investigators. Ringness (83) examines the reasons students give for choosing teaching as a career; these reasons can be subsumed under 13 headings. A comparison of two methods of assessing these reasons, however, failed to reach sufficient agreement to confirm their reliability. The investigation is inconclusive, but seems worth repeating with larger numbers and a careful follow-up. Evans (84, 85) also reports negative conclusions in a study of the relationship of favourable attitude to teaching to intelligence and socioeconomic status. With students in training as teachers, no correspondence was found between attitude and teaching marks, or between teaching marks and intelligence, though a small negative correlation was found between attitude and intelligence. Possibly this last is a reflection on training college courses, but the main conclusion seems to be that a favourable attitude to teaching is in itself an independent component. As college teaching marks cannot be taken as a measure of teaching competence, the connection between attitudes and successful teaching remains unknown. Shaw *et al.* (86) and Cook & Hoyt (87) investigate the Minnesota Teacher Attitude Inventory. Shaw finds an improvement in attitude of teachers after a two-week refresher course, but this is hardly validation. Cook & Hoyt find that attitudes appear to be independent of length of teaching experience, but that there are variations according to type of school, size of school system, and subjects taught. If this Inventory is to be related to teaching competence, it appears as if several validations will be needed, and the complexity may be sufficient to render the instrument impracticable. Bach (88), using both a comprehensive and thorough battery of predictors and criteria, finds reasonable agreement within the predictor variables and within the criterion variables, but virtually no correlation between them. Practice teaching, done here under unfavourable conditions admittedly, is in particular a poor predictor. Shaw (86) taking the rather weak criterion of supervisors' assessments during students' teaching practice, claims the judgement of a single interviewer to give the most reliable and valid prediction. But in view of Bach's findings, the application of this to teacher selection is more than doubtful.

The feature of all these studies in teacher assessment is their negative conclusions. No positive pointer has emerged, and such studies must cause serious misgivings in the minds of those who train and select teachers. The investigations quoted are by no means superficial or incompetent, yet no foundation for teacher assessment and selection has even begun to be laid. This field of educational psychology is one which is crying out for systematic and concerted investigation. The pupil is only one part of the educational situation, the teacher is another, and vital one too.

Problem Children

Under this head are included studies of children who present special educational problems as a result of exceptionally high or low intelligence, sensory defects, behaviour disorders, or differences in race or language. Such children have for long been a standing concern of educational psychologists, and this year's contributions are in line with those of the past; no new ground is broken, but understanding of these complex topics is increased.

Intelligence.—The education of the mentally defective child was one of the earliest studies of educational psychologists, and a fairly satisfactory level of practice now seems to have been attained. The papers cited below are contributions on a broad basis to the assessment of mental defect. Porteus & Corbett (89) examine the various statutory definitions of feeblemindedness in the United States and find for children that educational, psychometric and psychiatric criteria are confused. They stress the need for a clear legal definition which could be uniformly applied, which would certainly help educators in knowing what the special needs of these children were. It appears that a child may at present be certified in one state but not in another. Fraser Roberts & Mellone (90) find that the variance of IQ in the Terman-Merrill revision of the Binet test is not independent of age, as it should be; therefore extremely high or low IQ's are not comparable from age to age. A table of corrections to give uniformity of variance is provided, and some of the corrections are large. A child aged six, with tested IQ of 70, has three points deducted, a child aged eleven with the same tested IQ has six points added. The importance of this for the diagnosis of mental defect among children is obvious.

The education of the highly intelligent pupil is no longer being as neglected as it used to be. Wilson (91) finds that the artistic, musical, scientific, and mechanical abilities of gifted pupils are above average, but that there is a wide range of variation and that special abilities are not highly correlated with IQ. This raises the question of the kind of total education suited to those children, and the question of what abilities are being measured when the children are designated gifted. Blackmer (92) and Thomas (93) discuss the gifted student and the transition from school to college. Blackmer advocates linking certain colleges and schools to avoid retardation, and Thomas finds that such students present no difficulties in the academic or social sides of college, despite their youth and not infrequent poor home background.

Sensory defect.—The pupil with sensory defect remains a problem, and it is perhaps proper that the child with probably the greatest disability, the deaf child, should receive mention. Smith (94) finds deaf children of average intelligence in nonverbal tests, but very retarded on verbal tests, which is not unexpected. Albright (95) finds almost three-quarters of deaf children and adolescents are below average on the California Mental Health Analysis. These findings depend entirely on the validity of this Analysis, which is very doubtful. Neither of these studies of deafness can be called a major contribution. Barger (96) discusses the reading difficulties of congenitally aphasic children, most of them being boys. A mirror reading technique is found to be effective, but the important point in the article is the suggestion that many reading difficulties may be a result of mild undiagnosed aphasia.

Delinquency.—This is another field in which interest seems to be waning. The problem remains, but it is possible that attention has shifted to clinical treatment of individual cases, a topic which is not included in this review. The average intelligence of delinquent girls on the Wechsler-Bellevue Intelligence Scale is compared with that of nondelinquent girls by Diller (97). The finding is the usual one, but the delinquents are found relatively better in performance than in verbal test items. England (98), making a distinction between delinquent and problem children, finds the latter most distinctive in their use of colour in drawings, this being very slapdash and careless. The criterion seems to be subjective, and it is doubtful if the results have any practical application. Another aspect is discussed by Crane (99). Over three-quarters of a group of student teachers report having been members of gangs, and the boys' activities were more antisocial than the girls'. These activities did not necessarily denote prospective delinquency, as the students had grown up into well-behaved adults, by Australian standards at least. Crane suggests that much minor delinquency may be only a necessary phase in the process of social development and is temporary. This sounds reasonable, but it does raise problems in the field of prevention of delinquency in its educational aspects.

Race and language.—Differences in race and language from the norm of the community will always be an educational problem. It is perennial in the United States, at least so long as a democratic concept of education co-exists with what attitude studies show to be a fairly prevalent resistance to certain racial groups. The question is, of course, much more than an educational one, but psychological examination can at least help to establish facts and indicate certain lines of amelioration. Lee (100) demonstrates how the process of acculturation raises difficulties for Chinese children. Their acceptance of American standards leads to a cleavage from the parents, and the disgrace of appearance in court seems to intensify the cleavage. Boyd (101) finds that in a mixed school for Negroes and whites, the level aimed at by Negroes is the higher; this is another aspect of the influence on education of the felt inferiority of certain groups. Billingualism is linked to race differences, but it appears from a study by Fishman (102) that where racial absorption has occurred, bilingualism is of minor importance. In a Yiddish school, Fishman found no difference between the play and leisure activities of unilingual and bilingual children. A study by Anastasi & D'Angelo (103) suggests that linguistic and intellectual differences between whites and Negroes may be cultural in origin. No significant racial difference was found for preschool children in either language tests or Goodenough's Draw-A-Man. The groups were carefully selected, and the procedure carefully planned, but the author's impression was that the white children were more mature linguistically. A further study by Anastasi & Cordova (104) of bilingual Negro children found that it made little difference whether a nonverbal test was administered in English or in Spanish. The group was below average, but this is not necessarily the result of bilingualism as such. Johnson (105) concludes that neither verbal nor nonverbal intelligence tests are valid for bilingual children. This does not agree with Darcy's (106) summing up of research findings. Most studies seem to show a more marked inferiority of bilingual subjects in verbal tests. The question must be left open, but as long as intelligence tests play a part in the educational system, the problem remains one of practical importance, and full information is vital. It may be, as some contend, intelligence tests are unsuitable instruments for the purpose, or it may also be that the tests are in fact reflecting cultural differences associated with bilingualism. The studies quoted above are suggestive, but not final.

The whole problem of racial and cultural differences is one which psychological research will in itself not solve. It is, nevertheless, desirable that educational psychologists should continue to be aware of the psychological aspects of this question and continue to add to the common fund of educational knowledge, for along whatever lines a solution is reached, the educator will be playing a vital part. The studies cited tackle competently specific aspects of the larger problem, and though none is in itself conclusive, a steady stream of such studies cannot but be beneficial. Time and knowledge are good solvents of prejudice.

Conclusion

Though the scope of this review has necessarily been limited by considerations of space and the fact that a number of topics of interest to educational psychologists are reviewed elsewhere in this volume, certain trends of interest are evident. There are some perennial major currents of interest, e.g., the learning of elementary school subjects like reading or the measurement of abilities; there are other lesser and more fluctuating currents determined by changes in educational needs and policies, such as reading of college students or coaching in intelligence tests; and there are certain more ephemeral currents, such as the prevailing indiscriminate use of sociometric techniques in researches for which these techniques are not always fitted. The individual contributions are, as is to be expected, a mixed bag. Most of those in the well established fields of investigation are of sound workmanship, but in more recently opened fields there is more trivial and poorly designed work than is really necessary. Research, the reviewer believes, should have reference to some general educational issue, either practical or theoretical. Rather too many investigations begin and end in themselves, and the need for a clear and relevant criterion for any tests, procedures, or groups investigated cannot be overstressed. The point is well illustrated in the selection of teachers, where the investigators show themselves particularly aware of the need for a well founded criterion before further investigation is possible.

Perhaps as significant as the centres of interest are the centres of neglect. Reading attracts considerable attention, Arithmetic is virtually neglected. Reading of college students is the subject of several articles, reading of high school pupils inspires hardly any. The interpersonal preferences and popularities of pupils and students are extensively described, their relationship to the personal development and qualities of the individual is almost passed over. Much attention is paid to the effects of practice and coaching on selection tests for pupils, much less to the social and economic factors which appear to play a considerable part in their school progress. It would be Utopian to demand that all articles conform to rigorous standards of research design and execution, and that all topics receive their due attention; but, in the period under review, it is felt that more could have been done to achieve this standard and this balance. It is to be hoped that future reviewers in this field may find evidence which will enable them to disagree with this verdict.

LITERATURE CITED

1. Brownell, W. A., *Calif. J. Educ. Research*, **3**, 51–60 (1952)
2. Gray, W. S., and Iverson, W. J., *Elem. School J.*, **53**, 1–44 (1952)
3. Leonard, J. P., *Calif. J. Educ. Research*, **4**, 3–9 (1953)
4. Buswell, G. T., *Calif. J. Educ. Research*, **3**, 195–203 (1952)
5. Mackenzie, G. N., *Teach. Coll. Record*, **53**, 423–28 (1952)
6. Corey, S. M., *J. Educ. Psychol.*, **43**, 331–38 (1952)
7. Hill, G. E., *School and Soc.*, **76**(1959), 1–3 (1952)
8. Anderson, I. H., and Dearborn, W. F., *The Psychology of Teaching Reading* (The Ronald Press Co., New York, N. Y., 382 pp., 1952)
9. Tinker, M. A., *Teaching Elementary Reading* (Appleton-Century-Crofts, New York, N. Y., 351 pp., 1952)
10. Triggs, F. O., *Educ. Psychol. Measurement*, **12**, 345–49 (1952)
11. Bond, G. W., *Childhood Educ.*, **29**, 134–38 (1952)
12. Smith, N. B., *Natl. Educ. Assoc. J.*, **41**, 280–83 (1952)
13. Haugh, O. M., *J. Educ. Research*, **45**, 489–98 (1952)
14. Freeburne, C. M., and Fleischer, M. S., *J. Educ. Psychol.*, **43**, 101–9 (1952)
15. Hall, J. C., *J. Educ. Research*, **45**, 451–58 (1952)
16. McKillop, A. S., *Teachers' College Studies in Education* (Columbia University Press, New York, N. Y., 102 pp., 1952)
17. Burton, D. L., *J. Educ. Psychol.*, **43**, 436–39 (1952)
18. Krisa, M., *J. Educ. Psychol.*, **43**, 408–22 (1952)
19. Manolakes, G., *J. Appl. Psychol.*, **36**, 410–12 (1952)
20. Witty, P., Stolartz, T., and Cooper, W., *School and Soc.*, **76**(1982), 376 ff. (1952)
21. Barbe, W. B., *J. Educ. Psychol.*, **43**, 229–37 (1952)
22. Mouly, G. J., *J. Educ. Psychol.*, **43**, 459–66 (1952)
23. Johnson, G. B., *J. Educ. Research*, **46**, 192–205 (1952)
24. Carillo, L. W., and Sheldon, W. D., *J. Educ. Psychol.*, **43**, 299–305 (1952)
25. Barbe, W., and Grilk, W., *School and Soc.*, **75**(1941), 134–36 (1952)
26. Dahlberg, C. C., Rosewell, F., and Chall, J., *Elem. School. J.*, **53**, 211–17 (1952)
27. Whipple, G., *Elem. School J.*, **53**, 262–69 (1953)
28. Rudisill, M., *Elem. School J.*, **52**, 441–51 (1952)
29. French, J. E., *Elem. School J.*, **53**, 90–95 (1952)
30. Elkisch, P., *Am. J. Orthopsychiat.*, **22**, 379–85 (1952)
31. Knopp, I. J., and Richards, T. W., *J. Genetic Psychol.*, **81**, 99–112 (1952)
32. Knoell, D. M., and Harris, C. W., *J. Educ. Research*, **46**, 95–111 (1952)
33. Willard, C. B., *Calif. J. Educ. Research*, **4**, 14–18 (1953)
34. Dressel, P., Schmidt, J., and Kincaid, G., *J. Educ. Research*, **46**, 285–93 (1952)
35. Crawford, B. M., and Zylstra, E. W., *J. Educ. Research*, **46**, 241–48 (1952)
36. Perry, D. K., *J. Appl. Psychol.*, **36**, 346–47 (1952)
37. Wright, G. G. N., *The Writing of Arabic Numerals* (University of London Press, for Scottish Council for Research in Education, London, England, 424 pp., 1952)
38. Halloran, J. H., *Brit. J. Educ. Psychol.*, **22**, 200–4 (1952)
39. English, H. B., *J. Educ. Psychol.*, **43**, 321–30 (1952)
40. Durost, W. N., and Prescott, G. A., *Educ. Psychol. Measurement*, **12**, 741–55 (1952)
41. Wrightstone, J. W., Beaumont, F. S., Forlano, G., and Gastwirth, P., *J. Exptl. Educ.*, **20**, 301–4 (1952)

42. Kuhlen, R. G., and Collister, E. G., *Educ. Psychol. Measurement*, **12**, 632–37 (1952)
43. Holmes, D. C., *Educ. Research Bull.*, **31**, 63–66 (1952)
44. Ausubel, D. P., Schiff, H. M., and Gasser, E. B., *Child Development*, **23**, 111–28 (1952)
45. Alexander, T., and Alexander, M., *Child Development*, **23**, 207 ff. (1952)
46. Bretsch, H. S., *J. Educ. Psychol.*, **43**, 449–58 (1952)
47. Grace, G. L., and Grace, H. A., *J. Educ. Research*, **46**, 123–31 (1952)
48. Goodnow, R. E., and Taguiri, R., *J. Abnormal Psychol.*, **42**, 316–20 (1952)
49. Hallworth, H. J., *Sociometry*, **16**, 39–70 (1953)
50. Richardson, J. E., Forrester, J. F., Shukla, J. K., and Higginbotham, P. J., in *Studies in the Social Psychology of Adolescence* (Fleming, C. M., Ed., George Routledge & Kegan Paul, Ltd., London, England, 266 pp., 1952)
51. Taylor, E. A., *J. Educ. Psychol.*, **43**, 257–72 (1951)
52. Moreno, J. L., *Sociometry*, **15**, 146–63 (1952)
53. Clark, R. A., and McGuire, C., *Child Development*, **23**, 129–40 (1952)
54. McGuire, C., and Clark, R. A., *Child Development*, **23**, 141–54 (1952)
55. Wityrol, S. L., and Thompson, G. G., *J. Educ. Psychol.*, **44**, 20–30 (1953)
56. Estvan, F. J., *Genetic Psychol. Monographs*, **46**, 3–60 (1952)
57. Himmelweit, H. T., Halsey, A. H., and Oppenheim, A. N., *Brit. J. Sociol.*, **3**, 148–72 (1952)
58. Prothero, E. T., and Miles, O. K., *J. Social Psychol.*, **36**, 53–58 (1952)
59. Young, N., Mayans, F., and Corman, B. R., *Teach. Coll. Record*, **54**, 340–44 (1953)
60. Malter, M. S., *Elem. School. J.*, **52**, 505–10 (1952)
61. McKellar, P., and Harris, R., *Brit. J. Educ. Psychol.*, **22**, 101–23 (1952)
62. Smith, H. A., *J. Educ. Research*, **46**, 249–61 (1952)
63. Cosand, J. P., *Calif. J. Secondary Educ.*, **28**, 12–21 (1953)
64. Bolton, E. B., *Peabody J. Educ.*, **29**, 345–60 (1952)
65. Frederiksen, N., and Schrader, W. B., *J. Appl. Psychol.*, **36**, 261–65 (1952)
66. Doppelt, J. E., and Wesman, A. G., *J. Educ. Psychol.*, **43**, 210–17 (1952)
67. Sutherland, J., *Brit. J. Psychol., Statist. Sect.*, **5**, 189–96 (1952)
68. Vernon, P. E., *et al.*, *London Times Educ. Suppl.* (January 2–March 14, 1952)
69. Watts, A. F., Pidgeon, D. A., and Yates, A., *Secondary Schools Examinations* (Natl. Foundation Educ. Research, No. 6, London, England, 77 pp., 1953)
70. Emmett, W. G., *The Use of Intelligence Tests in the 11 Transfer Examination* (University of London Press, London, England, 8 pp., 1952)
71. Edinburgh City Education Dept., *The Edinburgh 1946 Group; Scottish Leaving Certificate Results* (Mimeographed, 8 pp., 1953)
72. Estes, B. W., *J. Consulting Psychol.*, **17**, 58–62 (1953)
73. Sacks, E. L., *J. Abnormal Psychol.*, **47**, 316–20 (1952)
74. Boger, J. H., *J. Educ. Research*, **46**, 43–52 (1952)
75. Pitts, R. J., *J. Educ. Psychol.*, **43**, 486–91 (1952)
76. Stenquist, J. L., *Teach. Coll. Record*, **54**, 185–90 (1953)
77. Biesheuvel, S., *S. African J. Sci.*, **49**, 120–38 (1952)
78. Halsey, A. H., and Gardner, L., *Brit. J. Sociol.*, **4**, 60–75 (1953)
79. Campbell, W. J., *Brit. J. Educ. Psychol.*, **22**, 89–100 (1952)
80. Orleans, J. S., Clarke, D., Ostreicher, L., and Standlee, L., *J. Educ. Research*, **56**, 641–48 (1952)

81. Grim, P. R., and Hoyt, C. J., *Educ. Research Bull.*, **31,** 89–91 (1952)
82. Ryans, D. C., *Educ. Psychol. Measurement,* 12, 333–44 (1952)
83. Ringness, T. A., *J. Expt. Educ.*, **21,** 1–55 (1952)
84. Evans, K. M., *Brit. J. Educ. Psychol.*, **22,** 63–69 (1952)
85. Evans, K. M., *Brit. J. Educ. Psychol.*, **23,** 58–63 (1953)
86. Shaw, J., Klausmeier, H. S., Luker, A. H., and Reid, H. T., *J. Appl. Psychol.*, **36,** 304–6 (1952)
87. Cook, W. W., and Hoyt, C. J., *Educ. Psychol. Measurement,* **12,** 562–73 (1952)
88. Bach, J. O., *J. Exptl. Educ.*, **21,** 57–80 (1952)
89. Porteus, J. D., and Corbett, G. R., *J. Psychol.*, **35,** 81–105 (1953)
90. Fraser Roberts, J. A., and Mellone, M. A., *Brit. J. Psychol., Statist. Sect.*, **5,** 65–79 (1952)
91. Wilson, F. T., *J. Genetic Psychol.*, **82,** 59–68 (1953)
92. Blackmer, A. R., *Coll. Board Rev.*, **18,** 301–4 (1952)
93. Thomas, R. B., *Coll. Board Rev.*, **18,** 305–8 (1952)
94. Smith, D. I., *Brit. J. Educ. Psychol.*, **22,** 71–72 (1952)
95. Albright, M. A., *Exceptional Children,* **19,** 107–13 (1952)
96. Barger, W. C., *Am. J. Orthopsychiat.*, **23,** 158–70 (1953)
97. Diller, L., *J. Genetic Psychol.*, **81,** 167–83 (1952)
98. England, A. O., *J. Child Psychiat.*, **2,** 343–49 (1952)
99. Crane, A. R., *J. Genetic Psychol.*, **81,** 113–23 (1952)
100. Lee, R. H., *J. Social Psychol.*, **36,** 15–34 (1952)
101. Boyd, G. F., *J. Social Psychol.*, **36,** 191–96 (1952)
102. Fishman, J. A., *J. Social Psychol.*, **36,** 155–65 (1952)
103. Anastasi, A., and D'Angelo, R. Y., *J. Genetic Psychol.*, **81,** 147–65 (1952)
104. Anastasi, A., and Cordova, F. A., *J. Educ. Psychol.*, **44,** 1–19 (1953)
105. Johnson, G. B., Jr., *J. Genetic Psychol.*, **82,** 3–19 (1953)
106. Darcy, N. T., *J. Genetic Psychol.*, **82,** 21–57 (1953)
107. Gray, W. S., Ed., *Improving Reading in All Curriculum Areas* (Suppl. Educ. Monographs, No. 76, University of Chicago Press, Chicago, Ill., 262 pp., 1952.)

STATISTICAL THEORY AND RESEARCH DESIGN[1]

By Hubert E. Brogden

Personnel Research Branch, AGO, Department of the Army, Washington, D. C.

No very definite or novel trends seemed noticeable in the literature on statistical methods and research designs during the period covered by this review. Increasing specialization seemed pretty generally evident. Although few publications have appeared on the topic, increased activity in applications of statistical problems to high speed computers suggests that such devices will soon have marked influence in this field. Foreseeable effects include the tabling of functions hitherto regarded as unmanageable, and the use of more exact but computationally difficult methods, such as principal component solutions in factor analysis.

An overview of the literature having general interest to psychologists led this author to the conclusion that some of the more significant advances were achieved in the areas of test theory and personnel classification methods. As a consequence, these areas were accorded special emphasis. It is possible, of course, that the writer's area of specialization may have been responsible for such emphasis.

Test Theory

Lord (39) sets about determining the effect of item difficulty distributions on certain relations between test scores and a perfect measure of their underlying common ability. He investigates this for the case where multiple choice responses are involved and guessing is permitted, making use of Carroll's (14a) adjustment for guessing. A convincing argument is presented showing that the test scores necessarily have curvilinear relation to underlying ability. He infers that relations between test scores and ability should be expressed in curvilinear form. Lord then shows that if a group of individuals all have the same common underlying ability the intercorrelations of the items are zero. As a consequence, the curvilinear correlation of true score on the normally distributed underlying ability is always plus one; true score being defined as the score on an infinitely long test. The curvilinear correlation of test score on the underlying ability is shown to be equal to the square root of the test reliability. Hence, conclusions derived with regard to reliability can be readily applied in the case of the curvilinear correlation of test score on ability. From here he proceeds to the derivation of equations and presentation of numerical results. He concludes that "maximum test reliability and the maximum curvilinear correlation of test score on criterion, for a test composed of equivalent items, is obtained when the item difficulty

[1] The survey of the literature pertaining to this review was completed in May, 1953.

is somewhat easier than halfway between chance level and 1.00," and that "reliability and curvilinear correlation of test score on criterion decrease as the variability of the item difficulties increase."

With respect to the conclusion that curvilinear correlation of test score on underlying ability decreases as the dispersion of the item difficulties increase, Lord himself points out that he might not have reached this conclusion had he investigated the curvilinear correlation of criterion on test score in lieu of the curvilinear correlation of test score on criterion. In "A Theory of Test Scores" (which will be reviewed shortly) Lord indicates that $\sigma_{s \cdot c}$ is likely to be smallest when $\sigma_{c \cdot s}$ is largest. The subscript s is the test score and the subscript c the underlying ability. It seems, then, very likely that the effect of item dispersion on the curvilinear correlation of underlying ability on test score is not necessarily the same as the effect of item dispersion on the curvilinear correlation of test score on ability. While the findings regarding curvilinear correlation of test score on underlying ability is important to a general theory of test scores, the major interest must center in findings bearing upon the curvilinear correlation of underlying ability on test score. The central problem is in reducing errors of the test when related to underlying ability not in errors of underlying ability in predicting test score.

Cronbach & Warrington (18) attack the problem of item difficulty distribution in relation to test efficiency by use of a technique which is in part the same as one also suggested by Lord (40). The technique will be discussed separately since it appears to be a definite contribution to test theory.

Bivariate surfaces relating scores on various hypothetical tests to true ability were prepared by the technique mentioned above. The efficiency of the test for a wide range of cutting points (on the test) was then evaluated by computing biserial correlations between the test score and true ability, true ability being defined as a perfect normally distributed measure of the factor common to the test items. The test types investigated included those with free response items and, by application of Carroll's development on guessing, tests consisting of multiple choice items in which guessing is permitted.

Cronbach & Warrington conclude, in general, that tests with all items at .5 difficulty have optimal validity for a wide range of cutting scores. The range of advantage over tests having spread of item difficulties increases as the saturation of the items in the common underlying ability becomes less. The author of this review might note here that the data they present do not seem to warrant their emphasis on the superiority of the test with peaked distribution of item difficulties. With one exception, all of the patterns of item difficulty distribution they investigated gave very close to the same r_{bis} at most cutting points in dealing with sets of items having saturations in the common underlying ability typical of most tests. It seemed clear to this reviewer that the major conclusion could well have been that, within wide ranges, item difficulty distribution makes little difference in the efficiency of a test. The exception noted was a test made up of items 60 per cent of which would normally be regarded as extreme (per cent passing below 20 or above 80).

Cronbach & Warrington also consider the optimal item difficulties for tests when the selection ratio is known in advance. Their results indicate that, contrary to general belief, maximum validity of a test having constant item difficulty is at a selection ratio such that the per cent selected is higher than the average difficulty level of the items as measured by the per cent passing the item.

In one of the most definitive papers so far published in the area of test theory, Lord (40) develops formulae relating the characteristics of test items to various characteristics of the test score. The formulae developed include those yielding the bivariate surface of test score and ability, the product moment correlation between test score and ability, the frequency distribution of test scores, the frequency distribution of true score (the score on an infinitely long test), the bivariate frequency surface of two tests measuring the same ability, the regression of test score on ability, the standard error of measurement at a given ability level, and the curvilinear correlation of test score on ability.

In general, these formulae depend upon assumptions that the items of the test are dichotomous and that all items are measures of the same underlying ability. Normal distribution of ability is assumed for certain of the developments but is unnecessary in some instances. Lord restricts consideration to items in which guessing is not a factor.

Expressions for the regression of ability on test score, and for the standard error of estimate of ability around test score proved too complex to permit a practical solution. However, the formula permitting the preparation of the bivariate frequency surface of test score and ability allow computation of both of these expressions for any given hypothetical test. The development involved here will be discussed in greater detail later.

Findings expected from theory were compared with those obtained from empirical data. In general, agreement appeared to be surprisingly high. The theoretical developments appear to offer a sound basis for predicting various characteristics of test scores from knowledge of the item parameters.

From examination of the formulae, Lord concludes: (*a*) the regression of true score on ability is necessarily curvilinear (although with low item intercorrelations this curvilinearity has a negligible effect); (*b*) the standard error of measurement on a given test is ordinarily least for examinees at an ability level at which the test is least discriminating; (*c*) errors of measurement for typical test scores have binomial rather than normal distributions (while such errors are not correlated with ability they vary in magnitude with variation in ability and the skewness of their distribution also varies with ability); (*d*) maximum discrimination at a given ability level is provided by a test, all items of which are passed by 50 per cent of examinees at that ability level; (*e*) unless the item intercorrelations are high, a test consisting of items of 50 per cent difficulty will be more discriminating for practically all examinees than will a test having a spread of item difficulties; (*f*) the shape of the test score frequency distribution does not necessarily reflect the shape of the frequency distribution of ability.

The technique discussed by Lord and used by Cronbach & Warrington appears to have special importance since it can be applied in attacking various as yet unsolved problems pertaining to the efficiency of a test score as a function of the component items or of the test score distribution. This technique permits preparation of the full scatter plot showing the relationship between a hypothetical test score and the ability common to the test items.

Basically the technique derives from the point that, within a group of individuals having the same underlying ability, the item intercorrelations will be zero. Knowing this, it readily follows that the mean, standard deviation, and, in fact, the full frequency distribution of the scores of a set of individuals having the same underlying ability can be obtained for a hypothetical test by means of a binomial expansion. Since the distribution can be obtained for each array, an entire scatter plot showing the relation between test score and underlying ability can be prepared. Scatter plots so constructed depend upon the assumption that all items have the same difficulty and the same saturation in their common underlying ability. However, for a set of individuals having the same underlying ability the frequency distributions obtained for two sets of items, each having different difficulty levels, are statistically independent and may be readily combined by multiplying into each other. Thus, an array of a scatter plot can be obtained for tests having various difficulty levels and, as a consequence, the entire scatter plot can be constructed for such a test.

Possible applications of the technique have not been exhausted by the work of Cronbach & Warrington. A number of writers have expended considerable effort in developing theories of item difficulty distribution in relation to the discriminative power of a test, with attention directed toward factors such as the shape of the frequency curve. Many such investigations seemed highly speculative. It appears that the basic problem could have been more adequately handled by use of the technique we have just considered.

A tie-in of work on test theory with various developments in scaling should prove instructive. Lord started his development with consideration of an item's characteristic curve, a construct very similar to those often used in scaling work. The basic objectives of scaling and of test construction seem to have much in common. Yet a major conclusion of Lord, and of Cronbach & Warrington, was that tests with peaked distributions of item difficulties are probably best. Such a conclusion seems in opposition to the very notion of scaling.

A final comment on the foregoing developments seems in order. Lord's work seems important in laying the groundwork for a generally acceptable theory of test scores. It should have a number of practical applications to test construction, particularly when it is desired to specify in advance a test-score frequency distribution, to set up tentative norms, or to estimate in advance the proportion of cases in an area of a bivariate surface. It is unlikely, however, that direct application will result in validity higher than that obtained by following current practices.

Lord (41) applies the method of maximum likelihood to problems associated with the estimation of underlying ability from the responses to the items. His development offers verification of certain conclusions reached by different reasoning in his earlier monograph (40). A new development which seems important allows estimation of confidence intervals for test scores within which the examinee's true ability may be expected to lie.

Correlation, Regression, and Selection

The shrinkage formula proposed by Wherry has been commonly used by psychologists to obtain an unbiased estimate of a multiple correlation coefficient. More recently, with widespread discussion of the principle of cross-validation, most psychologists dealing with such prediction problems feel that experience with empirical data suggests that Wherry's formula considerably overestimates the shrunken multiple. Regardless of the adequacy of empirical evidence on this point, two papers, neither of which have been published, show rather convincingly the source of the difficulty.

Nicholson (46), and Lord (42) both point out that Wherry's (or various equivalent) formula gives the expected universe value of the multiple correlation. Although the value of R obtained in the sample used in computing the weights is biased upward, this bias is not the only possible source of shrinkage. The universe value of the multiple is usually relevant only if the universe values of the weights are known. In practice, only estimates of these weights are available. Thus, further shrinkage must be expected when a regression equation is applied to a second sample as a function of the sampling error in the regression weights.

While Wherry's formula is correct, if the universe value of the multiple is desired, another formula is needed to estimate the efficiency of a regression equation when it is applied to a second sample from the same universe. Nicholson and Lord both give an expression for the mean squared error of estimate when a regression equation is applied to a second sample. The formula, from Lord, is

$$E_1E_2S^2 = \frac{N+k+1}{N-k-1} S^2_{y.(x)}$$

where $E_1E_2S^2$ is the expected value of the mean squared error of estimate of y when a regression equation developed in one sample is applied to a second sample, N is the number of cases in the sample used to determine the regression equation, k is the number of independent variables, and $S^2_{y\cdot(x)}$ is the mean squared error of estimate in the sample in which the regression equation is developed, (x) being the independent variables in vector notation.

Neither of the two authors gave the above formula in this exact form.

The formula can be obtained in both instances by simple manipulations. A discussion of the differences in their presentation would be unnecessarily time consuming.

The formula given above cannot be simply translated to give an estimate of the cross-validity, the correlation between the predicted and actual values of y. The reasons for this are discussed by Nicholson and are of sufficient interest to justify added comment. It has been known for some time [see, for example, Schultz (51a)] that if a regression equation for estimating y is derived in one sample and applied in a second sample, all values of y are not estimated with the same precision. Precision is greater at the mean value and less for both high and low values of y. Consider the bivariate surface formed by plotting, in the second sample, the estimates of y derived from the first sample regression equation against the actual y values. The estimates of y would ordinarily be expected to equal the means of the arrays of y (in a scatter plot based on the sample in which the regression equation was derived). In the bivariate surface in the second sample, the estimates of y no longer equal the means of the arrays of y values. The estimates are biased and consistently overestimate for high positive values of y and underestimate for values of y below the mean. This bias is of interest if we wish to estimate the absolute value of y. The above formula gives the expected error of estimate which includes the error involved in this bias. If we are interested in predicting only the relative values of y, as we imply in computing a cross-validity, greater accuracy can be obtained.

Nicholson, in considering aspects of the problem just discussed, decides that interest should center in the prediction of the absolute rather than the relative values of y. Hence, a formula giving the expected cross-validity derived from a regression equation is not provided. This reviewer feels certain that such a formula can be obtained by further derivation. Space does not permit detailed discussion of this additional problem.

A further development by Nicholson is pertinent to many present day discussions of cross-validation problems. Suppose a regression equation is developed in sample one. Suppose, further, that the independent variables are known in sample two, but the values of the dependent variable is unknown. Nicholson asks whether the estimates of the regression equation of sample one can be improved upon, with or without use of the additional information given in sample two. He demonstrates that the estimates provided by the regression equation of sample one are best in the maximum likelihood sense.

Flanagan (24) discusses short methods for calculating correlation coefficients that have been widely used for item analysis purposes. He investigates tetrachoric correlations, biserial correlations, the well-known upper and lower 27 per cent estimates of product moment correlations, and several variants of this latter procedure. The variants of the upper and lower 27 per cent estimates are obtained by double, or in some cases, triple tallies of a specified proportion of cases with extreme scores in the criterion. The process is analogous to digiting on IBM tabulators in computing cross-products. While the method used for the upper and lower 27 per cent estimate creates a three-category variable (values of 1, 0, and −1), the variants of this procedure approach biserial correlations in that, in effect, a five or seven category variable is created. The computing labor involved with the several variants of the upper and lower 27 per cent seems generally less than that required in computing a tetrachoric correlation since the data for a substantial middle group need not be manipulated at all. By any of the short methods employed only two values (which might be regarded as weighted percentages) need be computed. These are used to enter tables previously prepared by Flanagan. Computing times are given which indicate that the short methods involve about ⅕ the time required for biserial coefficients.

To investigate the effectiveness of these various short-cut methods, three populations of 10,000 cases was established in which the product moment correlations were known to be .00, .45, and .90. One hundred samples of 100 cases each were drawn from each of the three populations. The coefficients were then computed by the methods enumerated above. The mean values and empirical estimates of the standard errors of each of the coefficients were determined in this way and compared with each other and with the standard error of the coefficient, when it could be computed by formula.

The data support Flanagan's contention that various of the short-cut methods give standard errors considerably less than tetrachoric r and very little greater than those of r_{bis}. The findings seem in close agreement with those anticipated by Flanagan through consideration of the variance within categories in relation to total variance of the categorized variable. An added finding of considerable interest is the close agreement between the standard error of the biserial coefficient shown by the empirical findings and the standard error given by formula. The adequacy of the formula has, of course, often been questioned. Flanagan's findings suggest that this formula might well be used with reasonable confidence in its accuracy. It must be admitted, however, that a larger number of samples would have to be used to allow a definite conclusion on this point.

This reviewer agrees with Flanagan's conclusion that it would seem generally desirable to use the shorter methods and, if necessary, plan to obtain additional cases to offset the slightly higher standard errors associated with such short methods.

Suppose, in solving a set of normal equations, the full inverse of a matrix is computed. This is often done so that the standard errors of the regression coefficients can be computed. West (54) develops computing methods for resolving the normal equations after deleting, adding, or replacing a variable. The computing methods employ direct operations on the inverse matrix itself.

Hamilton (31) suggests an iterative procedure for computing the inverse of a matrix. He reports that considerable time can be saved over that required by conventional methods.

Doppelt & Bennett (20) investigated empirically the cost of hiring and training employees and showed graphically how the use of tests will reduce the cost per satisfactory employee. They found generally decreasing costs with increase in the cutting score used with the test. With very high scores, however, the curve reversed and increases became evident. Such increases were anticipated in an earlier theoretical analysis by the author of this review (9b). They are explained by the high cost of testing per employee hired when, say, only one out of 25 or 50 is selected.

Arbous & Sichel (5) also discuss this problem. They point out that the high cost of hiring an employee, when a small proportion of those tested are hired, can be offset by use of short prescreening devices. Mathematical formulae, charts, and graphs are developed to establish the effectiveness of such prescreening devices.

Several writers discuss various aspects of the problem of reliability. Dudek (21) believes that the term reliability has come to be used too loosely and suggests that the type of coefficient be kept in mind when reliability is discussed. He points out that inexact usage may lead to incorrect inferences. For example, increasing the length of a test will generally yield greater reliability as measured by internal consistency coefficients. Such increased reliability is not necessarily obtained, however, when test-retest coefficients are involved. Lawshe & Nagle (37), using five sets of empirical data, investigated the practical effect of weighting individual ratings according to the reliability of the rater before combining them into a composite. They conclude that the decision to eliminate a low-reliability rater from the rater pool, or to apply differential weights to different ratings, has little practical effect even when there are wide differences in the reliabilities of the raters. Examination of their empirical findings gives strong support to their conclusions. It was noted that the improvements obtained were, in any event, very small. Often elimination of a low-reliability rater resulted in a lower reliability for the composite of the ratings. Psychologists attempting to improve the reliability of any composite of criterion variables by weighting according to reliability might well take note of their findings. Angoff (4) considers the problem of determining the reliability of a speeded test. With speeded tests it is well known that the usual internal consistency estimates are invalid. Angoff proposes a way of determining reliability which will save some time over that needed to construct an alternate form. In effect, he proposes that a short equivalent of a longer form be used for this purpose. Formulae are given for estimating reliability of the speeded test with this arrangement.

Schmid (51) describes the steps in the use of sequential analysis in the selection of discriminating test items. Anastasi (2) tried an empirical study of sequential analysis as used in item selection. She started with use of extreme cases and added, in successive steps, the cases closer to the mean. She concludes that sequential methods are useful in item selection since the results obtained correspond to those that would have been obtained if all cases had been used. It seems likely that her findings could be explained on other bases.

In an article reviewed elsewhere in this chapter, Flanagan (24) gives both theoretical and empirical evidence supporting the idea that short methods of estimating the product moment item validity involving extreme groups are almost as effective as biserial estimates of the product moment validity. His findings may explain Anastasi's results. Kuang (36) reports another empirical study of three methods of item selection. He employs Davis's indices, biserial correlation, and probit analysis methods, as means of improving the reliability of tests. He finds no significant differences in the reliability of the scores for sets of items resulting from the use of the three different methods.

Webb & Jones (53) take note of the controversy between those using the "Poisson fit" technique and those using correlational techniques in the study of accident proneness. They report uses of the two techniques which give very similar results. A method of their own, labelled the binomial correlation method, is found to give identical results with a "Poisson fit" technique developed by Newbold (45a) and Cobb (14b). Burke (11) shows mathematically that the two methods are identical in their end effect.

This reviewer was struck with the similarity of the basic ideas behind the accident proneness methods to those used in computing reliability coefficients of aptitude tests. The Newbold-Cobb technique involves, essentially, a comparison of the obtained variance of the distribution of the number of accidents with that to be expected from chance alone. A similar comparison is basic to the Kuder-Richardson reliability formulae, where the variance of a total score is related to the variance expected if the items have zero intercorrelations. Correlational methods used in the study of accident proneness have obvious similarity to split-half or odd-even reliability coefficients.

Fisher (23) gives a readable, although somewhat condensed, discussion of some general logics related to the idea of sequential tests. Some points he makes regarding the logic of selection, as used by eugenicists to improve animal stocks, are pertinent in the present context. Fisher argues that if attention is directed to only one dependent variable, the resulting improvement in that variable may be offset by losses in another dependent variable. The applicability of his points to the logic of criterion construction in personnel selection problems is fairly apparent.

Geary (26) discusses Berkson's (7a) distinction between controlled and uncontrolled measurements of the independent variable. With error of measurement in the independent variable, use of uncontrolled measurements will give biased estimates of the slope of the regression line. In controlled observation of the independent variable, no bias will result even though error of measurement is present in the independent variable. Controlled measurement might be likened to measurements obtained through manipulation or experimentation, while uncontrolled measurement is concerned with observational data not involving manipulation.

Berkson's conclusions were limited to the case in which the true relationship is linear. Geary considers the implication of this distinction for the nonlinear case and develops a theory of estimation and sampling distribution.

Gaier & Lee (25) review a variety of approaches to nonadditive or configural methods of scoring or combining variables and reach rather enthusiastic conclusions concerning their probable value. It should be noted that most such approaches when used for prediction can be duplicated or approximated by regression techniques involving higher order curvilinearity. In view of findings reported in Air Force research during World War II that simple culvilinearities noted on samples of 1,000 or more failed to reappear in subsequent samples, it seems likely that the promise of configural methods will be most evident if analysis is confined to a single sample and cross-validation is not attempted. More evidence of the value of such methods with adequate cross-validation is certainly needed before wide-spread use can be justified.

Personnel Classification

Several authors have discussed solutions to the personnel classification problem. The classification problem as approached by these authors may be stated in the following manner. Suppose a matrix of n columns and N rows whose elements, C_{ij}, are measures of the productivities of N individuals in each of n jobs. If individuals are assigned to jobs according to specified quotas, a sum S can be defined, the elements of which are drawn one from each row and so that the total number from each column agrees with the number specified by the quota for this job. This sum may be regarded as the total productivity of assigned individuals. The objective is to maximize S. Two cases should be distinguished. If the total of the quotas equals N, complete classification is involved. A second case occurs when the total of the quotas is less than N and a portion of the group is to be rejected.

Lord (43) reformulates and gives a more rigorous proof of a solution presented earlier by Brogden (9a). His solution is also stated in more general form since Brogden's development applies to the case in which a portion of individuals are rejected entirely. Lord shows that if cases are represented spatially, the boundary between the regions for any pair of jobs must be defined by some constant value of the difference between the scores on the two jobs. There would be $\frac{1}{2}n(n-1)$ such boundaries and, consequently, $\frac{1}{2}n(n-1)$ constants applying to an equal number of possible difference scores. Each boundary is an $(n-1)$ space. Since all $\frac{1}{2}n(n-1)$ boundaries pass through the same straight line, it is possible to make a translation so that they will all pass through the origin. It can be shown to follow then that the equations for the $\frac{1}{2}n(n-1)$ boundaries can be written with n constants, one for each estimate of productivity, replacing the $\frac{1}{2}n(n-1)$ constants. For example, the constant k_{12} required to define the boundary between jobs one and two would be replaced by the difference between v_1 and v_2, where k_{12} is an instance of the $\frac{1}{2}n(n-1)$ constants while v_1 and v_2 are instances of the n constants.

Lord also provides a solution for the case involving a rejection group which is effectively the same as that given by Brogden.

The integrals from which, in theory, the n constants could be determined for any set of quotas are written out, but Lord decides that the expressions thus obtained are too cumbersome to be of practical use.

Votaw (52) applies the simplex method used in solving the Hitchcock-Koopman transportation problem to the personnel classification problem. It will be convenient to take some liberties with Votaw's statement of the optimal solution to allow a more direct comparison with that of Lord or Rao (49).

In effect, Votaw indicates that an optimal solution is obtained if the proper number of individuals is placed in each job and if for any individual i

$$C_{ik} + v_k + u_i \geqq C_{ij} + v_j + u_i$$

where k is the job to which the individual is assigned and j is any of the remaining jobs. The v's in the above equation were defined earlier while the u's are constants applying to individuals. The reader will notice that u_i is repeated on both sides of the equation and is, consequently, unnecessary for definition of the optimal solution. The u's are necessary, however, in solving sets of equations used in the simplex method.

To solve the problem encountered when a portion of the population are to be rejected, a dummy job is set up with the productivity estimates of all individuals in this job being zero. It can be seen that individuals placed in this dummy job have zero contribution to S. Since their contribution to S would be zero if they were rejected, the use of a dummy job in this way gives results equivalent to those obtained with a more direct approach. This rather clever device permits use of the simplex method in the same way as it is used when no cases are to be rejected. Votaw also considers a number of additional special problems and shows how adaptations of the simplex method can be used to solve them. For example, the method can be used to minimize the cost of training.

In general, the methods proposed by Votaw have been rigorously developed and include solutions to a number of related or subsidiary problems. An iterative procedure for accomplishing the actual allocations of men to jobs is given as an integral part of the mathematical development. Provisions are made to avoid degenerate problems. The principal difficulty seems to be in the labor required to accomplish the solution. Since the solution becomes lengthy if the number of individuals or jobs is large, Votaw prefers to group them in classes. It is possibly an open question whether the use of a small number of classes will materially affect the efficiency of the final allocation of men to jobs.

Rao (49) proves a lemma which, in effect, provides a solution to the classification problem. He first gives the proof for a solution needed when it is desired to classify so as to maximize the product rather than the sum of the scores of classified individuals. While his proof is compact and may be of interest for that reason, it will not be discussed in detail at this point since the end solution is essentially the same as Lord's.

Rao's lemma may be stated as follows. If there exist quantities, $v_i, \cdots, v_n$ such that each element, C_{ik}, of the Q_k elements chosen from the k'th column, satisfies the relationship

$$C_{ik} + v_k \geqq C_{ij} + v_j$$

and if similar relationships held for elements similarly chosen from any other column using the same set $v_i, \cdots, v_n$, then for this choice of $Q_1, \cdots, Q_n$ elements the sum S is a maximum. $Q_1, \cdots, Q_n$ are the quotas for the n jobs. The remaining symbols were defined earlier by this reviewer.

Some general comments on the several solutions to the classification problem so far considered should be helpful. First, it should be noted that the end solutions achieved are all effectively the same. While it might appear that Votaw's u_i's introduce a real difference, we have already indicated that the u_i's are pertinent to the iterative procedure and have no bearing upon the final solution. In fact, any set of u_i's may be added to various individual's scores without affecting the final outcome, except where a reject group is involved.

One basic difference in the approach of Votaw and that of Lord and Brogden should be made explicit. The simplex method of Votaw starts with any allocation of men to jobs that satisfies the specified quotas. He then solves a set of equations and interchanges men between two jobs in a way that will give maximum improvement in over-all productivity. Each of the successive steps in reaching the solution improves the sum total productivity. By contrast, the iterative method proposed earlier by Brodgen yields a maximum allocation sum at each stage. An approximate fit to quotas is taken as a starting point with each successive step aimed at an improved approximation to the quotas. The latter type of iterative solution seems in general much faster and more adaptable to use with large N's. The iterations are based on subjective considerations, however, while Votaw's procedure boasts objective mathematical bases for each iteration. The advantages of the latter may be important if it is desired to use modern high speed computers.

Applications of the classification theory can, in some instances, be quite simple and straightforward although the bases for such application were not made explicit in any of the papers just discussed. Suppose a set of v_j's have been determined for specified quotas using a large sample. If the samples were sufficiently large, operating use of the findings in a second large sample could be as follows. First, v_1 is added to all of the productivity scores for job 1, v_2 to all of the productivity scores for job 2, etc., for all jobs. Classification could then be accomplished by assigning each individual to the job in which he received his highest score. Thus, if the v_j's could be determined beforehand, in some way, application is extremely simple. The basis for such application is readily seen by relating the steps involved to the equations or solutions previously given.

Two as yet unpublished papers on the classification problem which have come to this reviewer's attention will be briefly discusseed. Paul Dwyer gives a clear and readable account of theory and practice relating to classification problems. He develops new proofs and proposes a method of "optimal regions" which permits a more rapid solution for the v_j's. Paul Horst proves, for the two-job case, that if estimates of productivity are used as the C_{ij}'s, these estimates are "best" if determined by the conventional least squares procedures.

To conclude, there seems little question but that the nature of optimal solution to the personnel classification problem is well established. Various iterative procedures for arriving at this solution are known, and improvements on these will probably be forthcoming. It is possibly unnecessary to add that a host of related problems still remain to be solved.

Factor Analysis

Burt (13) reviews at length the literature on significance tests related to factor analysis. He concludes that no really satisfactory solutions are available. The more rigorous tests are too elaborate and are still not fully rigorous, while the more practical tests are based on seemingly untenable assumptions.

The main theoretical difficulties arise from (*a*) the fact that the errors of the observed intercorrelations are themselves correlated, and (*b*) multivariate analysis is not equipped to deal with the assumptions of specific factors. The only apparent exception to Burt's general conclusion relates to the principal component factor solution where exact tests are available, permitting one to decide when to accept factors as established. He concludes that no very rigorous solutions are available when centroid or group centroid procedures are used in factoring.

In treating the problem of when to stop factoring, Burt again feels that none of the solutions so far proposed are very useful. He states his own preferences in the matter which involve extraction of several centroid factors beyond the point where the loadings "appear" to be significant.

Guttman (29) discusses two theorems that had been presented in an earlier paper of his, and considers their relation to group factoring methods and to the factoring of score (as opposed to correlation) matrices. He also considers the "inverted" factor methods in relation to the factoring of score matrices.

His first theorem is contained in the matrix equation

$$G_1 = G - GX'(XGX')^{-1}XG$$

where G_1 is the residual matrix, G is the correlation matrix to be factored and X is a matrix of weights of the order s by n, s being the number of factors to be extracted and n the number of variables. The matrix X may take various forms according to the methods of factoring actually used. In its simplest form the weight matrix could consist of 0's and 1's and could represent the experimenter's identification of variables used to define the group centroids for the s factors to be extracted. Proper definition of X can, in theory, eliminate the need for rotation.

His second theorem is contained in the matrix equation

$$S_1 = S - SY'(XSY')^{-1}XS$$

where S_1 is the residual score matrix, S the original score matrix and Y a matrix of weights of the order s by n, s being the number of factors to be extracted and n the number of cases. X is defined as in his first theorem. This theorem implies that factors can be extracted directly from the test scores. Guttman discusses this problem in detail and relates his discussion to other proposals to accomplish this end result. The point is made that the choice of Y in no way affects "the common factor space of tests as studied by X." Similarly, the choice of X in no way affects the results from a given Y.

It seems clear that Guttman's earlier article contains some definite contributions that have often been overlooked in subsequent discussions of similar problems. It also seems clear that the matrix equations given, plus the accompanying more detailed discussion, are not equivalent to a fully developed method for factoring a matrix of intercorrelations.

A point of Guttman's on the general logic of experimental designs in factor analysis will bear emphasis. Guttman suggests that hypotheses concerning factor structure can be explicitly stated in the weight matrix X and the analysis then used as a check on the initial hypothesis. By conducting analyses in this fashion, the possibility of capitalizing on chance error can be avoided. His point seems cogent in view of the meager amount of information available on sampling errors of factor loadings together with the extensive bias and shrinkage found in prediction studies involving cross-validation designs. It must be realized, on the other hand, that statement of hypotheses with sufficient precision to make Guttman's approach a fruitful one is, possibly, easier said than done.

Carroll (14) proposes that a new matrix τ be formed which contains the squares of the entries in the "simple structure" matrix V, and that the major requirements of simple structure will be satisfied by minimizing the non-diagonal entries of $\tau'\tau$.

Carroll's formulation provides a unique solution. However, he indicates that the solution provided is an approximation to simple structure, and that the computations are too involved for most applications. Adaptation to high speed computers may allow widespread application. The solution is an approximation since the presence of complex tests makes the primary axes more highly correlated than would be the case if they were located by graphic rotations.

When tests and people are located in the same factor space, a test having the same direction cosines may be called the test-equivalent of that person. Sandler (50) suggests that such test equivalents of persons will aid in rotating and interpreting factors. He provides the necessary equations for identifying them.

Adcock (1) discusses Thurstone's multiple group method of factoring and suggests that improvement would obtain if an alternative method were available for rotating the oblique group centroids to orthogonality. Such an alternate method should keep the resulting orthogonal reference axes as close as possible to the positions suggested by all the clusters and thus reduce the labor of rotation. A precise solution attributed to Ledyard Tucker is given together with an approximate solution which reduces the computations involved.

It is of interest to note that principal component solutions are being obtained on high speed computers in less than an hour's time. Wrigley & Neuhaus (55) report on the use of such computing methods. D. J. Wheeler, R. T. Gregory, and R. F. Klippinger are credited with developing the programs on the ORDVAC electronic computer. The program can, presumably, be made available to others.

Analysis of Variance and Related Designs

The statistical literature on analysis of variance is extensive and specialized. Developments with regard to both design and methods of analysis have far outstripped the practices of those who use them in psychology. It seemed wise, as a consequence, to avoid attempting full coverage of new developments and seek papers that emphasize the problems of design and analysis pertinent to current usage in this area.

Kogan (35) gives a clear and well-organized discussion of the use of variance designs in psychological research. While not all of the points he makes are new, many will bear repetition. Instances are cited in which the investigator fails to use methods of analysis which are appropriate to the design which he sets up. For example, equality of means and standard deviation may have been forced, but this feature of the design was not taken into account in the analysis of results.

Kogan criticizes the use of t tests in order to check on the significance of the difference between various pairs of means. He points out that such t tests are not independent, and cites Cochran & Cox (15b) who show that apparent significance will be found with much greater frequency than would be indicated by the chosen level of significance. It seems that the problems involved in the use of a series of t tests recur frequently in various types of statistical applications.

Kogan stresses, as others have done before, the practical advantages of "confounding" in the planning of experiments. Repeated findings of insignificant interactions should be more often utilized by investigators as the basis for a confounded design. The basic idea is to improve precision of selected comparisons while neglecting others which prior investigations have shown to be unimportant. He points out that experiments involving repetitive measures of criterion variable for one or more groups of subjects characterize many psychological researches but do not appear in other research areas for which analysis of variance designs have been developed. He regards methods in current use by psychologists as somewhat questionable, pointing out that, in general, successive measures takes on the same subjects should not be regarded as either randomly distributed or independent. There seems to be need for further theoretical work on the topic of repeated measurements, preferably with the aid of mathematical statisticians.

Kogan notes the undesirability of designs which allow all subjects to undergo several different experimental treatments in the same order. Such a design is increased in sensitivity by the separation of individual variations in regression on time from the estimate of error, but this does not overcome the confounding of differences in "set" means with possible temporal effects of fatigue, adaptation, etc. Such confounding of the main experimental factor should be avoided by randomizing the sequence of experimental conditions among the subjects.

Kogan notes that most psychologists dealing with higher order multiple classification or factorial designs proceed from the bottom up in setting up F ratios from an analysis of variance table. That is to say, successive interactions are tested starting with the higher order ones and, if all are found to be insignificant, a denominator for the F ratio is used which consists of the pooled interactions and residual terms. This procedure is criticized as having no sound basis. He refers to Cochran (15a) for a discussion of the problems involved and a solution that will often be applicable. In some further discussion of individual tests of significance in connection with analysis of variance, Kogan suggests that procedures presented by Tukey (51b) are the most simple and practical. Tukey's procedure involves use of a "gap" test, a "straggler" test, and a new F test to subgroups among the treatment means after a significant F has been found for a set of treatment means. Kogan points out that psychologists have given consideration to the Neyman-Pearson Type I errors and have generally omitted consideration of the possibility of Type II errors. While most investigators appreciate that failure to reject the null hypothesis does not prove the null hypothesis, there is a strong tendency to draw conclusions in a fashion that suggests that the null hypothesis is proven. He suggests that the power function of the analysis of variance test could be useful for estimating the sample sizes needed to reduce the probability of a Type II error to some specified level. Consideration of the power concept in relation to current psychological research leads to the conclusion that many experiments are carried out with a design such that there is too high a probability that findings of practical significance will fail to show statistical significance.

Archer (6) describes greco-latin designs adapted for use in learning studies. Since, in learning studies, the subject rarely learns the same content under all conditions, but the content must be presented in the same order for all subjects, a simple latin square is inappropriate. Order of presentation would be confounded with a practice effect to be described. To avoid such confounding, order of, say, a list of words can be presented according to a "latin" square independent of the latin square for conditions, or in other words, a greco-latin square can be used.

Practice effects of the usual sort can be handled by designs previously developed. The design proposed by Archer deals with practice effects that generalize from the learning of, say, one list of words to the learning of a second series of words. With such practice effects the several conditions of learning under investigation would not be experimentally independent. Two basic designs plus a variant of one of these designs are described. The chief limitation noted is the loss of the possibility of evaluating higher order interactions.

Apart from Archer's paper there is a considerable body of literature appearing in the *Annals of Mathematical Statistics*, *Biometrika*, and other similar journals which set forth designs, or sets of designs, for a considerable variety of problems. There is no attempt at thorough coverage of such papers. A brief discussion of certain of the more pertinent papers is given below.

Patterson (47) is concerned with construction of the type of experimental designs in which treatments are applied to the experimental material in a number of successive periods, each experimental unit receiving a different treatment in each period. Elements of balance required for simple statistical treatment are set out.

When partially balanced incomplete block designs were first developed, there was concentrated attention on designs involving two or three accuracies in the treatment comparisons. Nair (45) deals with designs involving four accuracies, and the necessary formulae are worked out in detail. Illustrations are given.

An experimental design in which there is no randomization by the experimenter, except possibly in naming the treatments, is called systematic. Cox (17) reviews recent work on systematic designs for use when the residual variation is (*a*) auto-correlated, and (*b*) formed from a trend plus random error. Cox points out that systematic designs have been considered questionable following criticisms by R. A. Fisher. He adds that randomized designs (as opposed to systematic designs) always give unbiased estimates of error and that this is a completely convincing argument for randomizing in all cases except those in which we have special reason to expect a systematic design to be either more accurate or more convenient.

Kempthorne (34) discusses a class of designs using blocks of two plots. Bose & Connor (8) consider the combinatorial properties of group divisible, incomplete block designs. Connor (16) discusses some relations among the blocks of symmetrical group divisible designs, while Bose & Shimamoto (9) give a long detailed discussion of partially balanced incomplete block designs involving two associate classes.

Tests of Significance

Cochran (15) presents a readable account of the history of χ^2 test with discussion of a number of the more important papers involved. His subsequent discussion of the practical use of the test will be of interest to psychologists. It is customary to recommend in applications of χ^2 that the smallest expected number in any class should not fall below 5 or 10 cases.

Cochran points out that, while use of small frequencies is undesirable, the exact choice of numbers was originally arbitrary, and that subsequent investigations have been too few or too narrow in scope to allow definite conclusions. He offers recommendations, however, for a number of separate cases. His recommendations are based on the viewpoint that disturbances in P at the .05 level may be permitted to range from .04 to .06, while those at the .01 level may be permitted to range from .007 to .015.

In testing for goodness of fit for bell-shaped curves such as the normal distribution, problems arise because expectations at the tails are quite small. However, little disturbance in χ^2 at the 5 per cent level occurs even with a single expectation as low as ½, or 2 expectations as low as 1. This conclusion holds at the 1 per cent level if the number of degrees of freedom in χ^2 ex-exceeds 6. Since important discrepancies will most likely occur at the tails in applying the test to bell-shaped curves, Cochran suggests using cells with as small expectations as possible without introducing disturbance.

If all expectancies involved in a χ^2 test are small, expectancies as low as 2 may be used without appreciable loss of accuracy. For 2×2 tables Cochran indicates that Fisher's exact test should be used if $N<20$, or if N is between 20 and 40 and there are expectations below 5. If continuous data are involved large expectations should be avoided. Expectations should be kept down to 12 per cell for $N=200$, 20 per cell for $N=400$, and 30 per cell for $N=1{,}000$.

A number of alternate and supplementary tests are discussed. A suplementary test of some interest deals with the case when systematic departure from theoretical distributions seem evident. The number of runs (consecutive departures from the theoretical distribution in the same direction) is the basis for this test. The distribution of the number of runs has been shown to be independent of χ^2 and may, consequently, be used in addition to this test.

Brožek & Tiede (10) consider the problem often faced after completion of an item analysis. If 5 per cent of the items are significant at the 5 per cent level, the statistical significance of the 5 per cent with high critical ratios is obviously suspect. If, in general, N significance tests have been performed and n show significance at some given level, how do we know whether the n occurrences could be attributable to chance? The probability of n significant results at the .05 level in N tests can be obtained by expanding the binomial $(.05+.95)^N$ and summing an appropriate number of terms. The computations involved are prohibitive if N is large. However, with a large N the authors indicate that the binomial distribution can be approximated by the normal distribution with the mean equalling NP and the S.D. equalling $\sqrt{NPQ}$. The P's for the set of items are assumed to be statistically independent of each other.

One difficulty with their solution derives from the fact that the sampling errors in a set of item coefficients are themselves correlated (to approximately the same degree as the items are correlated). Consequently, the assumption of independence of the probabilities may not always be appropriate in applications to item analysis problems.

Baker (7) takes various writers to task for failing to distinguish between joint and compound probability, when probabilities are combined from two samples in item selection. Compound probability is proper although, since compound probability is a monotonic function of joint probability, the same items will be selected in the end. An abac is presented for easy computation of compound probability.

Gordon, Loveland & Cureton (28) contribute to the solution of the same problem. They present extensions of tables for χ^2 for two degrees of freedom. Such tables can be used to combine the probabilities of rejecting the null hypothesis, when the latter is determined in two separate samples.

Moses (44) considers the problem of testing for significance when experimental manipulation is believed likely to produce both high and low scores without, possibly, having effect on the mean. He proposes that the significance of the difference between an experimental and control group can be shown by a test which he develops. After all subjects, experimentals, and controls are ranked in order a statistic s_h^* is to be computed. The least number of consecutive ranks necessary to include all the members of the experimental group except for the h least and the h greatest of them is s_h^*. Significant values of s_h^* are tables for a few situations, and a formula is available for direct computation.

Paulson (48) investigates problems arising in the identification of the best treatment or control category when a number of experimental (treatment) categories are compared with a control. Specifically he seeks to devise a statistical test so that if none of the categories is superior to the control the probability that it will be selected will be $\geqq 1-\alpha$. Paulson also asks the size of the sample needed so that, if one of the categories is really superior to all others by a given amount, the probability will be $\geqq 1-\beta$ that this experimental category will be selected as best.

Solutions, both exact and approximative, are developed both for the case when (a) the observations are normally distributed, and (b) the observations have a binomial distribution. Even the approximative solution leads to fairly involved equations and requires, seemingly, considerable computation. The problem may sometimes be important enough, however, to warrant added effort needed to apply Paulson's solution.

Suppose in a group of N individuals, each chooses d possible associates. Individuals not chosen are isolates and, if N and d are fixed, the number of isolates has often been regarded as an important characteristic of the social group. If it is desired to say whether the number is large or small the chance distribution of this number must be known. The expected number of isolates was previously given as

$$\text{mean} = N[(N - d - 1)/(N - 1)]^{N-1}.$$

Katz (32) determines an exact expression for the distribution of a number of isolates and then proceeds to find an approximation that will reduce the computations. The variance of the distribution is

$$\text{variance} = N\left(1-\frac{d}{N-1}\right)^{N-1}\left[1+(N-1-d)\left(1-\frac{d}{N-2}\right)^{N-2}-N\left(1-\frac{d}{N-1}\right)^{N-1}\right].$$

The nature of the distribution obtained may be judged roughly from the statement that a modified Poisson distribution gives a good fit.

Burke (12) makes the very cogent point that arguments concerning the nature of scales are irrelevant to statistical treatments, either descriptive or inferential. In using statistical tests we merely wish to be in a position to say that we do or do not have confidence that, with repetitions, essentially the same results will be obtained. Stated otherwise, if we are willing to assume a universe of biased or otherwise inadequate measurements, then samples from this universe will behave according to the same statistical principles that govern the behavior of samples drawn from universes of unbiased or more adequate measures.

Truncated Distributions

Suppose records are available giving the number of accidents per person for those having accidents but the number of persons having no accidents is unknown. David & Johnson (19) discuss various problems of estimation involved in such a situation and give a solution. Tables are given to aid in certain of the computations. Halperin (30) develops solutions to a number of similar truncation problems involving different frequency distributions.

Scaling

Edwards & Thurstone (22) describe a modification of the method of equal-appearing intervals together with an internal consistency check. The basic data are sortings by a number of judges of a number of stimuli into an arbitrary set of scale categories. The frequencies for each of the stimuli are expressed as proportions and used, assuming normal distribution of judgments, to estimate the location of the boundaries of the scale categories in relation to each of the stimuli. By subtraction several estimates of the widths of the boundary of each category (except the two extreme categories) are obtained. The average is taken to estimate the width of each boundary. A new scale is thus obtained and the stimuli are placed on the scale according to median value of distribution of judgments pertaining to each stimulus.

Using the scale values of the stimuli and the widths of the categories, theoretical frequency distributions (expressed as proportions) can be determined for each stimulus and compared with observed frequencies. Such a comparison was made for a particular set of data with a resulting average discrepancy of .025. This average discrepancy compares favorably with similar values reported in the literature when internal consistency checks were applied via the method of paired comparisons. Paired comparisons were obtained on the same set of empirical data. The correlation between the values obtained by the two procedures was nearly perfect. The evidence presented indicates rather conclusively that the two methods yield equivalent results.

Katz (33) criticizes status indexes in current use and proposes a new index that takes into account the status of the persons providing the basic data.

Gibson (27) shows the existence of a least squares solution for case IV of the law of comparative judgment. Because of the heavy computations involved, he does not propose that his solution be used in paractice.

General

Few textbooks on statistical methods of general value to psychologists were published during the period of this review. Lacey's *Statistical Methods in Experimentation* (38) seems too limited in coverage to be suitable. Anderson & Bancroft's *Statistical Theory in Research* (3), and Rao's *Advanced Statistical Methods in Biometric Research* (49) would be found somewhat heavy. Rao's book, however, should prove useful to many psychologists. His verbal statements of statistical problems and use of examples are especially helpful. A number of applications to psychological problems were noted.

LITERATURE CITED

1. Adcock, C. J., "A Note on Cluster-Directed Analysis," *Psychometrika*, **17**, 249–54 (1952)
2. Anastasi, A., "An Empirical Study of the Applicability of Sequential Analysis to Item Selection," *Educ. Psychol. Measurement*, **13**, 3–13 (1953)
3. Anderson, R. L., and Bancroft, T. A., *Statistical Theory in Research* (McGraw-Hill Book Co., Inc., New York, N. Y., 399 pp., 1952)
4. Angoff, W. H., "Test Reliability and Effective Test Length," *Psychometrika*, **18**, 1–14 (1953)
5. Arbous, H. G., and Sichel, H. S., "On the Economies of a Pre-Screening Technique for Aptitude Test Batteries," *Psychometrika*, **17**, 331–46 (1952)
6. Archer, E. J., "Some Greco-Latin Analysis of Variance Designs for Learning Studies," *Psychol. Bull.*, **49**, 521–37 (1952)
7. Baker, P. C., "Combining Tests of Significance in Cross-Validation," *Educ. Psychol. Measurement*, **12**, 301–6 (1952)

7a. Berkson, J., "Are There Two Regressions?" *J. Am. Statist. Assoc.*, **45**, 164–80 (1950)

8. Bose, R. C., and Connor, W. S., "Combinatorial Properties of Group Divisible Incomplete Block Designs," *Ann. Math. Statistics*, **23**, 367–83 (1952)
9. Bose, R. C., and Shimamoto, T., "Classification and Analysis of Partially Balanced Incomplete Block Designs with Two Associate Classes," *J. Am. Stat. Assoc.*, **47**, 151–84 (1952)

9a. Brogden, H. E., "An Approach to the Problem of Differential Prediction," *Psychometrika*, **11**, 139–54 (1946)

9b. Brogden, H. E., "When Testing Pays Off," *Personnel Psychol.*, **2,** 170–83 (1949)
10. Brožek, J., and Tiede, K., "Reliable and Questionable Significance in a Series of Statistical Tests," *Psychol. Bull.*, **49,** 339–41 (1952)
11. Burke, C. J., "Notes Concerning the Webb-Jones Article," *Psychol. Bull.*, **50,** 133–36 (1953)
12. Burke, C. J., "Additive Scales and Statistics," *Psychol. Rev.*, **60,** 73–75 (1953)
13. Burt, C., "Tests of Significance in Factor Analysis," *Brit. J. Psychol.*, (*Stat. Sect.*), **5,** 109–33 (1952)
14. Carroll, J. B., "An Analytical Solution for Approximating Simple Structure in Factor Analysis," *Psychometrika*, **18,** 23–28 (1953)
14a. Carroll, J. B., "The Effect of Difficulty and Chance Success on Correlations between Items or between Tests," *Psychometrika*, **11,** 1–19 (1945)
14b. Cobb, P. W., "The Limit of Usefulness of Accident Rate as a Measure of Accident Proneness," *J. Appl. Psychol.*, **24,** 154–59 (1940)
15. Cochran, W. G., "The χ^2 Test of Goodness of Fit," *Ann. Math. Statistics*, **23,** 315–45 (1952)
15a. Cochran, W. G., "Testing a Linear Relation Among Variables," *Biometrics*, **7,** 17–32 (1951)
15b. Cochran, W. G., and Cox, G. M., *Experimental Designs* (John Wiley & Sons, Inc., New York, N. Y., 454 pp., 1950)
16. Conner, W. S., "Some Relations Among the Blocks of Symmetrical Group Divisible Designs," *Ann. Math. Statistics*, **23,** 602–9 (1952)
17. Cox, D. R., "Some Recent Work on Systematic Experimental Designs," *J. Roy. Stat. Soc.*, **114,** 211–19 (1952)
18. Cronbach, L. J., and Warrington, W. G., "Efficiency of Multiple-Choice Tests as a Function of Spread of Item Difficulties," *Psychometrika*, **17,** 127–47 (1952)
19. David, F. N., and Johnson, N. L., "The Truncated Poisson," *Biometrics*, **8,** 275–85 (1952)
20. Doppelt, J. E., and Bennett, G. K., "Reducing the Cost of Training Satisfactory Workers," *Personnel Psychol.*, **6,** 1–8 (1953)
21. Dudek, F. J., "Concerning 'Reliability' of Tests," *Educ. Psychol. Measurement*, **12,** 293–99 (1952)
22. Edwards, A. L., and Thurstone, L. L., "An Internal Consistency Check for the Method of Successive Intervals and the Method of Graded Dichotomies," *Psychometrika*, **17,** 169–80 (1952)
23. Fisher, R. A., "Sequential Experimentation," *Biometrics*, **8,** 183–87 (1952)
24. Flanagan, J. C., "The Effectiveness of Short Methods for Calculating Correlation Coefficients," *Psychol. Bull.*, **49,** 342–48 (1952)
25. Gaier, E. L., and Lee, M. C., "Pattern Analysis: The Configural Approach to Predictive Measurement," *Psychol. Bull.*, **50,** 140–48 (1953)
26. Geary, R. C., "Non-Linear Functional Relationship Between Two Variables When One Variable is Controlled," *J. Am. Stat. Assoc.*, **48,** 94–103 (1953)
27. Gibson, W. A., "A Least-Squares Solution for Case IV of the Law of Comparative Judgment," *Psychometrika*, **18,** 15–21 (1953)
28. Gordon, M. H., Loveland, E. H., and Cureton, E. E., "An Extended Table of Chi-Square for Two Degrees of Freedom, For Use in Combining Probabilities from Independent Samples," *Psychometrika*, **17,** 311–16 (1952)
29. Guttman, L., "Multiple Group Methods for Common-Factor Analysis: Their Basis, Computation, and Interpretation," *Psychometrika*, **17,** 209–22 (1952)

30. Halperin, M., "Maximum Likelihood Estimation in Truncated Samples," *Ann. Math. Statistics*, **23**, 226–38 (1952)
31. Hamilton, M., "An Iterative Method for Computing Inverse Matrices," *Brit. J. Psychol.* (*Stat. Sect.*), **5**, 181–88 (1952)
32. Katz, L., "The Distribution of the Number of Isolates in a Social Group," *Ann. Math. Statistics*, **23**, 271–76 (1952)
33. Katz, L., "A New Status Index Derived from Sociometric Analysis," *Psychometrika*, **18**, 39–43 (1953)
34. Kempthorne, O., "A Class of Experimental Designs Using Blocks of Two Plots," *Ann. Math. Statistics*, **24**, 76–84 (1953)
35. Kogan, L. S., "Variance Designs in Psychological Research," *Psychol. Bull.*, **50**, 1–40 (1953)
36. Kuang, H. P., "A Critical Evaluation of the Relative Efficiency of Three Techniques of Item Analysis," *Educ. Psychol. Measurement*, **12**, 248–66 (1952)
37. Lawshe, C. H., and Nagle, B. F., "A Note on the Combination of Ratings on the Basis of Reliability," *Psychol. Bull.*, **49**, 270–73 (1952)
38. Lacey, O. L., *Statistical Methods in Experimentation: An Introduction* (The Macmillan Co., New York, N. Y., 249 pp., 1952)
39. Lord, F. M., "An Investigation of the Relation of the Reliability of Multiple-Choice Tests to the Distribution of Item Difficulties," *Psychometrika*, **17**, 181–94 (1952)
40. Lord, F. M., "A Theory of Test Scores," *Psychometric Monograph*, No. 7 (1952)
41. Lord, F. M., "An Application of Confidence Intervals and of Maximum Likelihood to the Estimation of an Examinee's Ability," *Psychometrika*, **18**, 57–76 (1953)
42. Lord, F. M., "Efficiency of Prediction When a Progression Equation from One Sample is Used in a New Sample," *Research Bull. 50-40*, Educational Testing Service (1950)
43. Lord, F. M., "Notes on a Problem of Multiple Classification," *Psychometrika*, **17**, 297–304 (1952)
44. Moses, L. E., "A Two-Sample Test," *Psychometrika*, **17**, 239–48 (1952)
45. Nair, K. R., "Analysis of Partially Balanced Incomplete Block Designs Illustrated on the Simple Square and Rectangular Lattices," *Biometrika*, **8**, 122–55 (1952)
45a. Newbold, E. M., "Practical Applications of the Statistics of Repeated Events, Particularly of Industrial Accidents," *J. Roy. Stat. Soc.*, **90**, 487 (1927)
46. Nicholson, G. W., *The Application of a Regression Equation to a New Sample* (Doctoral thesis, Univ. of N. Carolina, 1948)
47. Patterson, H. D., "The Construction of Balanced Designs for Experiments Involving Sequences of Treatments," *Biometrika*, **39**, 32–48 (1952)
48. Paulson, E., "On the Comparison of Several Experimental Categories with a Control," *Ann. Math. Statistics*, **23**, 239–46 (1952)
49. Rao, C. R., *Advanced Statistical Methods in Biometric Research* (John Wiley & Sons, Inc., New York, N. Y., 390 pp., 1952)
50. Sandler, J., "A Technique for Facilitating the Rotation of Factor Axes, Based on an Equivalence between Persons and Tests," *Psychometrika*, **17**, 223–29 (1952)
51. Schmid, J., "Sequential Analysis of Test Items," *J. Exptl. Educ.*, **20**, 261–64 (1952)

51a. Schultz, H., "Standard Error of a Forecast from a Curve," *J. Am. Stat. Assoc.*, **25,** 139–85 (1930)
51b. Tukey, J. W., "Comparing Individual Means in the Analysis of Variance," *Biometrics*, **5,** 99–114 (1949)
52. Votaw, D. F., "Methods of Solving some Personnel-Classification Problems," *Psychometrika*, **17,** 255–66 (1952)
53. Webb, W. B., and Jones, E. R., "Some Relations Between Two Statistical Approaches to Accident Proneness," *Psychol. Bull.*, **50,** 133–36 (1953)
54. West, V. I., "Replacing Variables in Correlation Problems," *J. Am. Stat. Assoc.*, **47,** 185–90 (1952)
55. Wrigley, C., and Neuhaus, J. O., "A Refactorization of the Burt-Pearson Matrix with the ORDVAC Electronic Computer," *Brit. J. Psychol.* (*Stat. Sect.*), **5,** 105–8 (1952)

COMMUNICATION[1]

By George A. Miller

Massachusetts Institute of Technology, Cambridge, Massachusetts

Communication presents many aspects worthy of scientific scrutiny, but only a few have been selected for this review. The necessary selection was achieved by rigid adherence to a single rule: Only those studies were covered that interested the reviewer. Anyone who resents the omission of his work should know that personal appeal, not merit, was the reviewer's yardstick.

The review begins with two linguists, Jakobson and Harris, who have recently published summaries of different theoretical positions. For a broader view of the many activities in linguistics that are related to psychology, the reader is referred to the report of a recent conference of anthropologists and linguists (19).

Roman Jakobson

Both psychologists and linguists are apt to be impressed by *Preliminaries to Speech Analysis* (13), but for different reasons. Psychologists will be impressed by the forceful exposition of the distinctive features and the way these crucial dimensions of speech are related at the acoustic, physiological, and psychological levels of analysis. Linguists have heard most of that story before, however, and they are more interested in technical points, such as how /p/[2], /t/, and /k/ should be handled in a system of binary oppositions, or whether "minimum redundancy" is a satisfactory criterion for a unique phonemic solution of a given language.

Jakobson, who is probably the outstanding linguistic theorist alive today, has devoted much of his theorizing to the distinctive feature. The linguist's "distinctive feature" is almost (but not quite) synonomous with the psychologist's "discriminative stimulus." The spoken utterances in any language differ among themselves in many ways, but reinforcement is contingent upon just a few of those differences. Those aspects of the stimulus which must be discriminated in order to understand a language are the distinctive features, and all other features are nondistinctive. For example, the utterances "pill" and "bill" are heard as different by people who speak English, so these people must discriminate voiceless /p/ from voiced /b/, or tense /p/ from lax /b/. Unless they respond with respect to the significant dimensions of the stimulus, they will not be able to communicate. A listener who ignores the dimensions of voicing and tenseness, but discriminates on the basis of pitch, will not prosper in an English-speaking community.

[1] The survey of the literature pertaining to this review was completed in May, 1953.

[2] Phonemic symbols are indicated by placing them inside slanted lines.

The idea of distinctive features has been familiar to linguists for several years. What Jakobson has done is to shift the emphasis, i.e., to make distinctive features, rather than phonemes, the ultimate entities of linguistic analysis. This shift in emphasis has some interesting consequences. One of them is to show that when a linguist defines a phoneme, he is reducing to a minimum the number of phonetic dimensions that must be used to describe the language. This problem is formally similar to a factor analysis problem. Another consequence of shifting from phonemes to features is that the relation to psychological theories of discrimination learning becomes more obvious and direct.

The changed emphasis also leads at once to the observation that most features, and perhaps all, are discriminated dichotomously. Jakobson has exploited the dichotomous nature of the features in his phonemic notation by writing "+" if the phoneme has one value of a feature and "−" if it has the other value. Cybernetics fans, already at home with binary logic, binary relays, binary neurons, binary digits to measure information, etc., are intrigued by Jakobson's binary notation for phonemes. The binary notation aligns speech firmly on the side of the digital computer as opposed to the analogue computer, as discrete rather than continuous. This discrete description contrasts with the kind of continuous description in acoustic terms that one expects to get from, say, the Bell Telephone Laboratories (4, 5, 15, 29, 30).

The difference between a linguist's and an engineer's approach to the sounds of speech is interesting. The engineer possesses powerful analytic methods that enable him to distinguish quite precisely among the sounds of speech, or among any other sounds whatsoever. He can describe exactly the differences among "ah" and "oo" and a clarinet tone and a frying egg. His trouble is that he can describe too accurately. Many of the differences he measures are irrelevant. He must learn to ignore many of the descriptive data that his analyzing machines are able to report. Therefore, he sees the problem as one of abstraction, as a matter of ignoring things until some essential property emerges as the invariant. The linguist, on the other hand, has cruder instruments, his ears and his memory. He can distinguish perceptually among sounds, and he can remember the contexts in which similar sounds occur. Therefore, he sees the problem as one of patterning, as a matter of discovering the structure that relates the elements.

The engineer's description is absolute, in terms of distance, mass, and time. The linguist's description is relative, in terms of perceptual dimensions and contextual constraints. The linguist knows that the same physical pattern can be perceived as phoneme A in one context and as phoneme B in another context.

A clear experimental demonstration of the relativity of perceptual judgments of speech is now available in the work of Liberman, Delattre & Cooper (17). They put the same acoustic patterns in front of all the different vowel sounds. By this systematic procedure they were able to discover, for example, a consonant-like sound that listeners called "p" in front of "oo" or "ee," but called "k" in front of "ah." The same stimulus is phoneme "p" in one context and phoneme "k" in another context. The engineer, by concentrating on how physically different sounds can be judged as identical, has tended to overlook the disturbing fact that physically identical sounds can be judged as different. The linguist is better prepared to let the particular stimulus be judged in terms of its position in a larger linguistic Gestalt. Pike (31) has recently described the concept of linguistic relativity in some detail. This relativity will make the construction of speech-recognizing machines a difficult engineering task (4, 15). However, Licklider (18) has offered some interesting suggestions as to how a nervous system might make use of known engineering techniques—filtering and correlating—to achieve the results it does.

In the *Preliminaries to Speech Analysis* Jakobson, Fant, and Halle have undertaken a tentative catalog of all the distinctive features. These include grave versus acute, compact versus diffuse, strident versus mellow, nasal versus oral, tense versus lax, sharp versus plain, flat versus plain, voiced versus unvoiced, checked versus unchecked, interrupted versus continuant, vocalic versus nonvocalic, and consonantal versus nonconsonantal. For each feature the reader is told what acoustic properties of the stimulus are involved, how those properties are produced by the vocal apparatus, how the feature is perceived, and in what languages the feature is known. At many points in the survey the evidence is fragmentary. Probably the details will be revised. But the broad outline into which these details must fit is clearly prescribed.

An important consequence of the emphasis on features rather than phonemes is that it encourages the linguist to accept the psychological nature of many linguistic problems. A willingness to use psychological techniques distinguishes Jakobson from Harris. The difference is worthy of elaboration.

Zellig S. Harris

In his *Methods in Structural Linguistics* (9) Harris describes a rather different kind of analysis that emphasizes "distributional techniques." The "distribution" of a particular linguistic element is the set of all contexts which will become utterances in the language when that element is substituted into them. In order to give the flavor of the difference between Harris and Jakobson, a fictitious example is useful.

An exotic language has three kinds of phonetic segments (physiological coordinations or acoustic spectra) that are designated A, B, and C. People who speak this language have been heard to say only BA, AC, and AA. Examination of these utterances (the "corpus") leads to the discovery that B and C never occur in exactly the same context. They have "complementary distributions": B occurs only before A and C occurs only after A. When this situation arises, it is unnecessary (or "redundant") to retain a distinction between the segments so distributed. It is possible to call both B and C by the same name, say D, so that the three utterances become DA, AD, and AA, respectively. The two segments B and C, although phonetically distinguishable, have now been classed together as variant forms ("allophones") of the same phoneme, C. (If A and B or A and C are combined, however, confusions will result because their distributions are not complementary.) Notice that the principle of complementary distribution makes no reference to meaning or to any nonlinguistic evidence. In fact, nothing is said even about the sound of the three segments.

Harris advocates the use of distributional methods to discover the basic units, or phonemes, of any language. (Similar techniques are also advocated for isolating morphemes, but that half of *Methods in Structural Linguistics* will not be considered here.) The method can squeeze out much of the redundancy of a phonetic transcription without reference to phonetics or semantics. It has the disadvantage that the solution is not unique and that a subsidiary principle of "phonetic similarity" is usually required to rescue the solution from minor absurdities. And the method takes for granted the prior existence of an accurate phonetic transcript, a document that could not exist without the prior segmentation of the utterances into discrete temporal units.

For comparison, consider Jakobson's approach. First, construct sets of utterances that are identical except for minimal segments: BA and AA are identical except for their initial segments. The existence of these sets of utterances is proof that the language contains an initial opposition between B and A and a final opposition between C and A. The fact that BA and AA produce different behaviors from these people indicates that B and A must be distinguishable (and similarly for C and A). Second, examine the phonetic nature of the oppositions. If any of the phonetic features are common to B and C but not to A, so that a single feature can distinguish both B from A and C from A, then B and C can be equated in a single phoneme, D.

Thus Jakobson and Harris reach the same result, but by quite different routes. Jakobson stresses the importance of the initial segmentation (which probably requires a knowledge of the meanings of the language) and the phonetic features of the utterances, while taking distribution for granted. Harris emphasizes distributional analysis, and takes the initial segmentation and the phonetic similarities more or less for granted.

In his attempt to purify his methodology, Harris would like to eliminate the intuitive, psychological concept of meaning from linguistics. The meaning can give useful hints that help the analyst reach a solution more rapidly, but for complete rigor the same solution should be attained by considering the distributions in very large contexts. On the other hand, Jakobson might proceed without knowing the meanings, but he has little desire to try. Whether or not a linguist can work without meanings, his job is certainly simpler if he knows them. In any event, the kind of meanings that the linguist needs can be defined with considerable objectivity in terms of behavioral discriminations. No appeals need be made to subjective intangibles in order to use meaning in a linguistic analysis. However, the spirit of Harris' work is strong in many American linguists, and the *Methods* summarizes a self-consciously scientific approach to language.

Harris' position that context can, in sufficient quantity, substitute for meaning has some interesting repercussions if it is generalized beyond the realm of linguistic description. It is a general observation that events taken out of context are ambiguous, and that their true meaning is usually not clear until related facts are known. Does this imply (shades of E. B. Titchener!) that the context is the meaning? The relation of context to meaning is a slippery but interesting one that arises repeatedly in studies of communication. Some recent work by Kaplan throws a little light on the relation.

Abraham Kaplan

When a philosopher does psychological experiments in linguistics to solve an engineering problem, the interdisciplinary character of modern communications research is boldly revealed. As a logician and philosopher, Kaplan is familiar with the ambiguities of natural languages. An incentive for studying linguistic ambiguity was provided by the problem of engineering a computer that could translate mechanically from one language to another. The methods Kaplan adopted were purely psychological (14).

A list of words was presented in isolation and in contexts selected from sentences in which the words had occurred. The contexts were:

P1 one word preceding,
F1 one word following,
B1 one word preceding and one following,
P2 two words preceding,
F2 two words following,
B2 two words preceding and two following, and
S the complete sentence.

Judges were asked to indicate which one of several alternative definitions was correct.

With no context there were on the average about 5.5 senses that the words might have. Context reduced this number. For example, accurate judges were able to reduce the number of senses as follows: to 59 per cent for P1; 51 for F1; 46 for B1; 48 for P2; 52 for F2; 36 for B2; and to 26 for S. P1 was least effective. B1 was more effective than P2 or F2. B2 was almost as effective as S.

A short verbal setting can reduce the ambiguity of a word on the average from 5.5 possible senses to about 1.5 or 2.0 senses. Most of this reduction is contributed by context not more than two words away. Kaplan's result seems to mean that there is a high probability that a B2 context will include some substantive word (one of semantic rather than mere syntactic function) that will give a clue as to which sense is appropriate. That is to say, the context probably acts quite specifically and not by gradual accretion of meaning as words are added to the context.

The engineering significance of these results is that a translating machine needs to remember only five words of text at a time. The status of mechanical translation schemes has recently been reviewed by Bar-Hillel (2) and will not be pursued here.

CLAUDE E. SHANNON

The question of context appears in a different light in the work of Shannon. He considers the problem of a communications engineer who wants to send as much information as possible over a communication channel that has a finite capacity. If the context of an item tells something about that item, then the context effectively repeats the information in the item. This repetition of the same information by the symbol and its context is redundant and inefficient. In order to use a channel efficiently, an engineer would like to remove this redundancy so that every symbol could carry the maximum amount of information.

Shannon's measure of redundancy is, therefore, a measure of covariance between the verbal elements and their contexts, a measure of how predictable the future of a message is when only its past is known. It is intuitively apparent that the more history that is given, the more predictable the future can be. That is to say, if you can predict the next letter with a given level of accuracy when you know n-1 preceding letters, then on the average you will not predict less accurately if you know n preceding letters. In order to obtain additional accuracy from the additional unit of context, however, it is necessary to know the statistical properties of the message source. In order to calculate how much redundancy (or predictability) is introduced by a context of n-1 preceding letters, you must know the probabilities for all possible sequences of length n. As n increases, the number of possible sequences goes up rapidly and the feasibility of actually measuring all the necessary probabilities goes down at the same rate. Thus it seems as though the theory of information requires a calculation that is impractical, if not impossible.

Shannon's most recent contribution to this problem, however, has been a short-cut method for estimating upper and lower bounds on the amount of redundancy (35). Like Kaplan, Shannon resorted to a psychological experiment. He avoided the statistical labor that is required in theory by using a simple guessing game. His assumption is that people who know a language will guess approximately in accordance with those otherwise unknown probabilities. We will consider one of the bounds that Shannon developed.

Shannon's argument can be presented as follows. Imagine identical twins who have exactly the same guessing habits about language. The first twin sends a message to the second, say, "There is no reverse on a motorcycle." Now, because their guessing habits are the same, the transmitting twin knows that the first guess his receiving brother will make for the first letter is "t." Instead of sending "t," therefore, he can send "1," meaning "Your first guess is right." If the receiving twin is wrong on the first 6 guesses, the transmitter just sends "7," meaning "Your seventh guess is right," etc. By recoding the original message into guessing numbers, the twins arrive at a new sequence of symbols:

T H E R E — I S — N O — R E V E R S E — O N — A — M O T O R C Y C L E

becomes

1 1 1 5 1 1 2 1 1 2 1 1 15 1 17 1 1 1 2 1 3 2 1 2 2 7 1 1 1 1 4 1 1 1 1

For the twins, the two sequences of symbols contain exactly the same information (one can be recoded into the other, and vice versa), so they must contain exactly the same amount of information. Note, however, that successive symbols in the sequence of digits are effectively independent; the fact that it took 6 guesses to get this letter does not say anything about how many guesses will be needed for the next letter. The sequence of digits, therefore, has no contextual constraints, the context repeats none of the information given by the individual digits. It is an easy matter to calculate how much information per symbol there is in the digit sequence because no knowledge of probabilities for long sequences is required. So Shannon computes the amount of information per symbol in the nonredundant digit sequence and assumes that this is equal to the amount of information per symbol in the redundant sequence of letters. The difference between this estimate of information actually encoded and the theoretical calculation of how much could be encoded with no redundancy provides Shannon's measure. It is usually convenient to transform into percentages.

The experiment ran as follows: A sequence of n-1 letters ($n=1, 2, \cdots,$ 100) was selected at random from English prose writing and presented to a judge. The judge read the n-1 letters and then guessed at the n-th letter. If he was wrong, he guessed again. He continued to guess until he got the right letter. After this procedure had been repeated for several contexts of length n-1, Shannon had a frequency distribution for the number of times the first guess was right, the number of times the second guess was right, the third guess, the fourth, etc. From those frequencies he estimated $q_i^{(n)}$, the probability that guess i is correct when a context of n-1 preceding letters is known. Shannon used only the 26 letters of the alphabet and the space, so i runs from 1 to 27. The amount of information per letter in the original message is, therefore,

$$H_n = -\sum_{i=1}^{27} q_i^{(n)} \log_2 q_i^{(n)}$$

The theoretical maximum information per symbol that could be obtained with a 27-letter alphabet is $\log_2 27$. The difference between this maximum and the estimate, H_n, measures the amount of redundancy involved in a context of n-1 letters. [Pollack (32) has used this technique in a study of the memory span].

Translated into percentages, the function Shannon obtained was

n:	1	2	3	4	5	6	10	15	100
Per cent Redundancy:	0	15	25	35	33	45	48	48	68

Thus 15 per cent of the information conveyed by a letter is also contained in the letter immediately preceding it; 25 per cent is contained in the two preceding letters; 68 per cent is contained in the 99 preceding letters. A similar but somewhat flatter curve was later estimated by Newman & Gerstman (24), by a different method.

Here again it is found that contextual effects decline rather rapidly with distance from the target item. If one remains in the realm of verbal context, the redundancy is somewhere between 50 and 80 per cent and most of this is contributed by context within a span of about 10 letters. It is also possible, however, to supply the nonlinguistic, or situational, context of the communication. Frick & Sumby (6) used Shannon's technique to estimate the redundancy in spoken messages sent from an airport control tower to an approaching airplane. With only the verbal context, these messages were 80 per cent redundant. With situational context added, the redundancy was 96 per cent. The tower was sending only four per cent as much information as it could have sent with an efficient language.

In comparing these results with Kaplan's, however, it is necessary to remember that Shannon is interested in how much the context determines what the message can be, whereas Kaplan wants to know how much the context determines what the message can mean. Confusion between the amount of information, in Shannon's sense, and the meaning of the information, in Kaplan's sense, has led to a certain amount of nonsense in the cybernetic literature. Carnap & Bar-Hillel have recently endeavored to clarify the difference.

Rudolph Carnap

Shannon's measure of the amount of information in a message is the negative logarithm of the probability that the message will occur. The less probable the message, the more information it contains. Of the two sentences, "This is a pencil," and, "This is a writing implement," the first is more probable to occur in normal, conversational English. Therefore, according to Shannon, the first message must contain less information than the second. If we examine the meanings of these two sentences, however, Shannon's measure seems wrong. "This is a pencil" implies that it is a writing implement, but "This is a writing implement" does not say whether it is a pencil, pen, typewriter, etc. Semantically, therefore, the first message contains more information than the second.

Obviously, there are two different senses of "amount of information" involved in this example. The engineer's sense, which ignores meanings and concentrates on the probabilities of the different messages that the channel will need to transmit, has been beautifully developed by Shannon and his colleagues. The application of this engineering measure to psychology has been reviewed by Miller (23). The second sense, which concentrates on the meanings of the messages, has received far less attention. It is the second sense of "amount of information" that Carnap and Bar-Hillel have tried to develop in their *Outline of a Theory of Semantic Information* (3).

If sentence X logically implies sentence Y, then the information carried by X includes the information carried by Y, and possibly more. This is the necessary condition that Carnap and Bar-Hillel impose upon the concept of semantic information. The detailed development of the idea is beyond the scope of this review, but some of the obvious consequences can be stated here. If X implies Y and also Y implies X, then X and Y contain equal amounts of information. A tautology (e.g., "Today is either Tuesday or it is not Tuesday") is logically implied by every sentence and so contains no information. A logically false sentence (e.g., "Today is both Tuesday and not Tuesday") logically implies all other sentences and so contains the maximum amount of information—semantic information is not necessarily truthful information. The amount of information in the conjunction of two sentences is equal to or less than the amount of information in the first plus the amount of information in the second (equality holding only if two sentences are logically disjunct).

The theory of semantic information is a ramification of the theory of inductive probability developed by Carnap. Psychologists interested in the application of information theory to psychology owe themselves a careful perusal of this work. If nothing more, it should clarify some of the limitations of Shannon's theory.

An interesting question for a semantic theory of information is whether there is a semantic equivalent to the engineer's concept of noise. For example, if a sentence can have two meanings and if one meaning is intended by the talker and the other is received by the listener, then there is a kind of noise in the communication even though the physical signals were transmitted perfectly. Carnap and Bar-Hillel wish to call this "semantic noise." Kaplan's work, for example, might be characterized as a study of the extent to which context reduces semantic noise. In many situations, however, it is difficult or impossible to decide whether the receiver's misunderstanding is due to a semantic misevaluation or to a random error in perception or response. The question of human errors in communication systems is currently receiving close study by psychologists.

WILLIAM J. MCGILL

Communication engineers usually have two human beings in their idealized systems, a source and a destination for messages. Between them is the equipment that provides the channel. The psychologist's idealized system exactly reverses the positions. The psychologist has equipments that generate stimuli and record responses. Between them is a single human being who provides the channel. The first clear statement of this inversion was supplied by Garner & Hake (7).

The measure of transmitted information becomes, in the psychological application of Shannon's theory, a measure of the covariance of stimuli and responses. The channel capacity defined by the engineer becomes the subject's discriminative capacity. The subject's behavior upon stimulation is recorded and analyzed without reference to what the stimuli mean. This engineering approach to the discriminative processes (and even to memory) offers considerable promise and is being pursued vigorously by experimental psychologists (1, 6, 7, 8, 10, 11, 12, 14a, 14b, 16, 22, 23, 24, 32, 33, 34).

McGill (22) has recently contributed an important extension to the Shannon-Garner-Hake development. He has shown that the measure of transmitted information closely resembles analysis of variance. The total information in the subject's responses can be analyzed into the sum of several components, one for each stimulus variable used, plus an error (or noise) term. In this way an experimenter can show which of the stimulus variables influenced the responses. With McGill's model each stimulus dimension can be regarded as a separate (but not necessarily independent) input to the subject. For example, it should be possible to tease out Jakobson's distinctive features by applying McGill's analysis to speech-perception data.

According to the Shannon-Wiener definition,

$$H(x) = -\sum p_n \log p_n,$$

is the measure in bits of the amount of information per event drawn from the discrete population described by the probabilities p_n. Only one random variable, x, is involved. When two random variables, x and y, are observed. it is possible to define $T(x,y)$, a two-dimensional quantity, in addition to $H(x)$ and $H(y)$. If x is the input to a communication system and y is the output, then $T(x,y)$ is a measure of the transmitted information, i.e., of the covariance of output with input. By definition,

$$T(x,y) = H(x) + H(y) - H(x,y)$$

where $H(x,y)$ is computed from p_{nk}, the probabilities for the joint occurrence of a given input value with a given output.

The one- and two-dimensional quantities, $H(x)$ and $T(x,y)$, are well known as a result of Shannon's work. McGill has simply continued the argument for more than two random variables. For example, x and y are two different stimulus inputs and z is the organism's response. Then $H(x)$, $H(y)$, and $H(z)$ are the amounts of information in the two stimuli and the response. $T(x,y)$ is the covariance of the two stimuli, $T(x,z)$ is the transmission of information about x, and $T(y,z)$ is transmission about y. Now it is possible to define a three dimensional quantity,

$$A(xyz) = -H(x) - H(y) - H(z) + H(x, y) + H(x,z) + H(y,z) - H(x,y,z),$$

so that all the various quantities of information are combined in a single expression. McGill points out that $A(xyz)$ is closely related to the three-way interaction term in analysis of variance.

By some algebraic rearrangement it can be shown that

$$H(z) = H_{xy}(z) + T(x,z) + T(y,z) + A(xyz),$$

where $H_{xy}(z) = H(x,y,z) - H(x,y)$. In this equation $H(z)$, the output or response information, is analyzed into several components: (*a*) $H_{xy}(z)$ is "noise," the response information that cannot be attributed to either input x or input y; (*b*) $T(x,z)$ is the response information attributable to input x; (*c*) $T(y,z)$ is response information attributable to y; and (*d*) $A(xyz)$ is that part of the response information that can be attributed to x by virtue of the fact that y is also known (or conversely, to y because x is known). This partitioning of response information into components parallels quite closely the analysis of variance into an error term, two main effects, and an interaction term. It would seem that information theory effectively corresponds to a nonparametric analysis of variance.

Although most of McGill's results were foreshadowed in the one and two dimensional cases, there is one rather unexpected result. All quantities of information with one or two discrete random variables must be nonnegative. However, the three-variable term, $A(xyz)$, can be negative. In other words, a knowledge of input y may decrease the amount of information that z has about x—communication from x to z would actually be better if no data about y were collected at all! This interesting feature of informational analysis is not found in analysis of variance, since variances are always nonnegative. The A-term is not a measure of information in the sense that H-terms and T-terms are. The A-term measures the gain (or loss) in transmission that results from considering the several stimuli together instead of one at a time.

A communications engineer has ways of measuring the noise that interferes with his transmissions. A psychologist who tries to apply communication ideas, however, has no such independent estimates of the psychological noise. All he can say is that some fraction of the response output is signal (is attributable directly to the known stimulus inputs). The remainder is, presumably, random noise. What McGill does is to break the noise term into parts that can be attributed to different sources. If he knows where some of the psychological noise comes from, his chances for getting rid of it are considerably improved.

In psychological applications it is perhaps a limitation of the engineering theory that semantic relations are ignored. The distinction that Carnap and Bar-Hillel propose between "semantic noise" and "random noise" is intuitively appealing, but the Shannon-Garner-Hake-McGill theory contains no rules for distinguishing these two kinds of noise. After McGill has taken out all the noise that he can correlate with various stimuli, the residual error that the person introduced remains untouched. It may be either semantic or random.

Possibly the Carnap theory and semantic noise can be applied to certain psychological problems in a manner analogous to the way Shannon's theory and random noise are used to study discriminative problems. In fact, Hovland's "communication analysis" of concept formation (12) suggests one direction this application might take.

Charles E. Osgood

It seems that everyone who studies communication becomes involved in problems of meaning and the more involved he becomes, the slower he gets ahead. The psychologist who unravels the meaning of meaning will break the worst bottleneck in communications research. It is conceivable that Osgood may do just that.

Osgood (28) has proposed a "mediation hypothesis" based on some early Hullian ideas in order to explain how it is that something which is not the object becomes a sign of the object. A sign, he argues, evokes a mediating reaction that is a fractional part of the total behavior elicited by the object. Furthermore, the mediating reaction produces self-stimulation which in turn becomes conditioned in varying strengths to different instrumental responses or response sequences. This mediating reaction is what Osgood refers to as the meaning of the sign. [A more recent elaboration adds grammatical functions to this purely semantic mechanism (see 19, p. 51).] A sign can elicit more than one mediating reaction; it will tend to elicit other mediating reactions in proportion to their similarity to the original reaction, and it will inhibit others in proportion to the directness of their antagonism to the original reaction.

Whether or not this translation of "meanings" into "mediating reactions" really converts the horse fly into a flying horse need not be decided in this review. In the reviewer's opinion, however, the more significant half of Osgood's contribution is his technique for measuring meanings, a technique that grew out of work on synesthesia by way of attitude measurement. Over this circuitous path, Osgood arrived at a kind of multidimensional psychophysical method that may be applicable to a wide variety of complicated psychological problems.

The "semantic differential" is a combination of association and scaling methods. A judge is asked to indicate the position of a concept (e.g., "pacifist") along an experiential continuum defined by a pair of polar terms (e.g., "kind-cruel"). This indication can be made in terms of a seven-point rating scale or by measurement of the judgment time required. The judgment is repeated by a group of judges for all combinations of several different concepts and polar continua.

The polar continua can be regarded as the coordinates of a "semantic space." Each concept is assigned experimentally a value along each coordinate, and so can be specified as a point in the semantic space. Points that are near together in the space should be semantically similar, for they evoke nearly the same judgments on all the polar continua. The distances in this space are a little tricky, however, for the coordinates are probably not all at right angles (that is to say, are not independent). Factor analytic techniques can be used to isolate a limited number of general coordinates of the semantic space that will have the maximum differentiating power. Factors discovered so far include an evaluative factor (good-bad), a strength factor (strong-weak), an activity factor (active-passive), and several specific factors.

It is no great trick to criticize this technique of measurement, but the fact remains that it is the most promising approach yet proposed. Semantic conditioning, associative interference, word associations, tachistoscopic recognition times, and the like are even more limited in scope than the semantic differential. For example, Noble's (25, 26, 27) recent work, in the tradition of Glaze, Hull, Krueger, Witmer, etc., is not concerned with the measurement of meaning, but with the more limited problem of measuring meaningfulness. That is to say, when Noble reports that "maelstrom" and "tumbril" evoked the same number of associations per minute from his subjects, he argues that "maelstrom" and "tumbril" have the same meaningfulness. He would not claim that they have the same meanings. For two meanings to be the same, the associations should not only be equal in number, but identical in content. Osgood proposes to measure the meanings themselves, which is a more ambitious and potentially more useful project.

Benoit Mandelbrot

A relation between frequency and rank order, often called "Zipf's Law," has turned up over and over in statistical studies of language. Zipf formulated the law as follows:

$$p_n = Pn^{-B}$$

when n is the rank of a word when all words are ordered by decreasing frequency of use, p_n is the probability that the word at rank n will be used and P and B are constants. Although this relation appears with regularity in linguistic data, no one has claimed more than a vague appreciation of its cause or significance. No one, that is, until Mandelbrot (20).

Mandelbrot's argument is complicated and even an over-simplified version requires several steps for its development. The first step is to find the assignment of probabilities p_n to the different words that will make the average cost of transmitting a word as small as possible, subject to the side condition that the average amount of information per word is a constant. There is some cost associated with communication. Let j_n represent the cost of transmitting the n-th word. Then $\sum p_n j_n$ is the average cost per word. Assume that the cost of each word is given, but the frequencies of use can be varied at will by the transmitter. What frequencies will minimize his average cost? Obviously, he should always send the cheapest word. This answer, while cheap, has the disadvantage that an unchanging message conveys no information to the receiver. It is necessary to impose the auxiliary condition that the amount of information, measured by $-\sum p_n \log p_n$, must be a constant.

Any mathematician (and many nonmathematicians) can solve this problem with a trick devised by Lagrange. He introduces some dummy constants, called "Lagrange multipliers," and comes out with the result that

$$p_n = Pe^{-Aj_n},$$

where P and A are constants introduced in order to obtain the solutions for p_n.

The answer to the first problem, therefore, is that the p_n should be selected so that the cheapest words are used most and the most expensive words are used least. The greater the cost j_n, the smaller must be the probability p_n. This answer seems intuitively correct and coincides with the common linguistic observation that frequent words are usually short (presumably cheap) and rare words are usually long (presumably expensive). The answer is not completely satisfying, however, because it does not contain a clear idea of what the cost might be or how the costs of different words could be measured. The second problem, therefore, is to examine the costs j_n.

Mandelbrot considers this situation: The language has many more "words" than "letters," so each word must be represented by a sequence of letters. Furthermore, the communication system that Mandelbrot wants to study can remember only one word at a time and must transmit a sequence of letters for the present word before it can begin to encode the next word. Furthermore, no letter can be transmitted without cost. Some letters may be cheaper to send than others, but none are free.

Under these conditions, the cost of a word is given as the sum of the costs of each of the letters in the sequence of letters used to represent that word. Words, however, are delimited by spaces (or pauses) that indicate where the word ends. To the cost of each word, therefore, it is necessary to add the cost of the space that is used to separate it from the next word. Although it may seem trivial, the introduction of the space between words is the crux of Mandelbrot's contribution and the main feature that leads him to results different from Shannon's. In Shannon's problem, the entire message is remembered and then coded in the most efficient form for transmission. In Mandelbrot's problem, the message is remembered only one word at a time, so that every time the space occurs the transmitter makes the most efficient coding he can of that word and then begins anew on the next word. Obviously, a transmitter of the kind Shannon studied will be more efficient, but one of the kind that Mandelbrot is studying will be more practical.

Mandelbrot has shown that, for any assignment of costs to the individual letters, the relation between the cost of the word j_n and its rank n is given (at least to a first approximation) by

$$j_n = \log_M n.$$

For example, suppose all letters are equally expensive, so that the cost of the word is given by its length (plus one for the space at the end), and suppose there are M different letters available in the alphabet. Then there are M different, one-letter words which are the cheapest. Next cheapest are the M^2 different, two-letter words, then the M^3 three-letter words, etc. Therefore, when all words are ranked from cheapest to most expensive, the rank n increases exponentially as the cost (or length) j_n increases linearly. The fact that the same kind of relation holds approximately when the different letters have different costs is less obvious but no less true.

The result of the second step in Mandelbrot's argument, therefore, is that the cost of a word will be given approximately by the logarithm of its rank order with respect to increasing cost. This result is true under very general conditions and is not a unique outcome of some particular assignment of costs to letters. It reflects the two facts: that, in general, if the cost of a word is the sum of the costs of its letters, then the more letters it has the more it is apt to cost, and that it is not possible to construct as many short, cheap words as there are long, expensive words. If these two facts are accepted, then the logarithmic relation of cost to rank order is a direct consequence.

The third step in the argument is to substitute the logarithmic solution for j_n into the earlier equation relating word probabilities to word costs:

$$p_n = Pe^{-Aj_n} = PM^{-Bj_n} = Pn^{-B}$$

And there, *mirabile dictu*, is Zipf's law. In fact, Mandelbrot is able to improve upon Zipf's law. If the relation of word cost to rank order is solved more precisely, the second-order approximation gives

$$j_n = j_o + \log_M (n + m).$$

When this result is substituted into the first equation for p_n,

$$p_n = P(n + m)^{-B},$$

where m is another constant. It is clear that m will have the greatest influence when the rank n is small—it makes the curve somewhat flatter for the commonest words. This modification of the law enables Mandelbrot to describe the empirical results much more accurately.

What does Mandelbrot's result mean? He says that if one wants to communicate efficiently word-by-word, then one must obey Zipf's law. There is a strong temptation to reverse the implication and to argue that because we obey Zipf's law we must therefore be communicating word-by-word with maximal efficiency. The work on the effects of context seems to indicate that a speaker's encoding process involves a longer memory span than Mandelbrot postulates for his word-by-word encoder. And the calculations of the actual redundancy in natural languages indicate that they are far less efficient than they could be under the constraints Mandelbrot imposes. The question of redundancy is a technical one, however, and the interested reader can best pursue it in Mandelbrot's monograph.

One interesting suggestion that comes out of this work is a reinterpretation of Hick's data for multiple choice reaction times. W. E. Hick (10) reported that

$$t_r = 0.27 \log_e (n + 1)$$

described the relation of disjunctive reaction times to the number n of alternative responses where n ranged from 1 to 10 fingers. For simple reaction times, $n = 1$, Hick was led to argue that the brain makes a binary choice between the presence and the absence of a signal at any instant. With this assumption he was then able to say that reaction times are directly proportional to the amount of information needed to make the correct response. Mandelbrot was struck by the similarity of Hick's function to the cost function, stated above, when $j_0=0$ and $m=1$. That is to say, Mandelbrot thinks that the reaction time is a measure of the cost of making the discrimination. This thought implies that the disjunctive reaction time can also be used in verbal perception experiments as a measure of the cost of a word. Since rare words are theoretically more costly than common words, rare words should take longer to read, as indeed they do. There is no reason why Mandelbrot's logarithmic cost function and the reasoning behind it should not be generalized to a variety of reaction time and latency experiments.

Mandelbrot's thesis takes him into game theory, mathematical statistics, thermodynamics, psychology, linguistics, and communication theory. His general frame of reference comes from the theory of games; transmitter and receiver form a coalition against nature in order to minimize the information lost during the communication. In these general terms, the cost of a message is the amount of information lost in transmitting it.

Jacob Marschak

A tie between communication and economic theory has been effected in a different way by Marschak (21). Whereas Mandelbrot proposes to consider information as the currency in a game between men and nature, Marschak considers information as a commodity that can be bought and sold in the market place.

Marschak's concern is to generate an economic theory for teams. Here we will consider only a small fragment of this ambitious program, the question of how much a person or a team should be willing to pay for information. The direction of Marschak's thought can be indicated by some examples.

A dollar is bet on the toss of a coin. The probability of the coin falling heads is known to be p. If the result of the toss is not known, then the best bet is heads if p is greater than 0.5, or tails if p is less than 0.5. That is to say, over a long series of trials a smart gambler can expect to win $p-q$ dollars per bet if $p>0.5$, or $q-p$ dollars per bet if $p<0.5$. This fact can be expressed by writing that his expected value $U_0=|p-q|$. Now this question can be asked: How much should the gambler be willing to pay for information about the outcome of a toss prior to placing his bet? If he knows the outcome in advance, he can win on every toss, so the expected value now becomes $U_1=1$. The difference between his expected values with the information and without it, U_1-U_0, is the amount that the gambler should be willing to pay for the information. In this example, the value of an inquiry is $w=1-|p-q|$.

Note that the value of inquiry is similar, but not identical to the amount of information (in Shannon's sense) that the inquiry produces. In this example, the amount of information is given by $-p \log p-q \log q$. Both the amount and the value are maximal when p is 0.5 and minimal when p is 0 or 1. Therefore, Marschak agrees with Mandelbrot in spirit if not in detail. Both theorists treat cost and amount, dollars and bits, as closely related measures of information.

Marschak's notion generalizes readily to the value of inexact information. Imagine that, in the preceding example, the gambler had the opportunity of buying information that he knew was correct only 90 per cent of the time. If he buys this information and uses it, his expected value is $U_1=0.8$ dollars per bet (in 10 bets, he expects to win 9 and lose 1). Therefore, the value of inquiry becomes $U_1-U_0=0.8-|p-q|$. When p, the probability of heads, is less than 0.1 or more than 0.9, the gambler will lose money if he buys the inexact information. Under these conditions he will decide not to buy. In a sense, Marschak offers the gambler his choice of two games, both with the same opportunities for profit. In one game he gambles on his knowledge of p. In the other game, he pays a price to get a safer bet. In the general case, the gambler may be permitted to buy information of any degree of precision that he chooses.

The value of inquiry can also be defined for multidimensional situations where the event is characterized by several aspects. For example, if future weather is one dimension and future prices another, a farmer might want to buy information about either or both of these aspects before he decides what to plant. If the several aspects of such a complex situation are not independent, then there is not so much advantage in knowing both over knowing only one. In this way the value measure generalizes to dependent probabilities as well.

A simple example may suggest how these ideas are related to the problem of team organization. Imagine that two partners run a shoe factory. Partner A is an expert on leather prices, partner B on shoe prices. A can commit the firm to buy leather, and B can commit the firm to sell shoes. Now suppose that A and B try to run their firm without talking to each other about leather prices or shoe prices. Then the only way they can operate is for A to buy leather only if the cost is below average and for B to sell shoes only when the price is above average. By failing to communicate, the firm will miss the chances it has to make a profit when leather is expensive but shoes are more so, or when shoes are cheap but leather is cheaper. The profit that the firm can expect if the partners operate independently is U_0 and the larger profit they can expect with two-way communication is U_1. Here, as before, $w=U_1-U_0$ is the value of communication to the firm, the amount that they should be willing to spend for telephones, conferences, etc. Cases of considerable interest arise if we consider the possibilities of one-way communication, the effects of correlation between the two price variables, and the consequences of greater variability in one price than the other.

Marschak's development of the value of inquiry is in itself a useful contribution to communication theory, and the possibilities it suggests for optimizing team organizations look quite promising. However, all the stock criticisms raised by psychologists against normative economic theory can also be raised against the type of work represented by Marschak's paper. Perhaps social psychologists will be more grateful for a normative approach to groups than their experimental colleagues have been for a normative approach to choice and motivation. A purely descriptive science of group behavior is certainly a tedious alternative.

Conclusions

Perhaps the reader of this review has been struck by a persistent and recurring theme in nearly all the recent work reported here. This theme has to do with the question of context. In linguistics there is a real division of opinion about how far context can be used to replace meaning in linguistic analysis. Kaplan wanted to relate context and ambiguity. Shannon wanted to relate context and redundancy. McGill resolved psychological noise into components by a careful examination of contextual stimuli in the experimental situation. Mandelbrot examined the effect of limiting the amount of context used during encoding to one word at a time. After years of neglect, verbal context has now become a very popular problem.

A second theme that runs through most of the recent work is an old favorite. The treatment of meaning is an important aspect of the work by Jakobson, Harris, Kaplan, Carnap, and Osgood.

Finally, a third trend in this work is reflected in the many attempts to optimize something. Kaplan wants to minimize ambiguity, Shannon wants to minimize redundancy, McGill wants to maximize transmission, Mandelbrot wants to optimize the encoding procedure, Marschak wants to find the best rules for communication within teams. This normative approach is attributable in part to engineering, in part to economists, and it makes many psychologists uncomfortable.

LITERATURE CITED

1. Aborn, M., and Rubenstein, H., *J. Exptl. Psychol.*, **44,** 260–66 (1952)
2. Bar-Hillel, Y., *Am. Doc.*, **2,** 229–37 (1951)
3. Carnap, R., and Bar-Hillel, Y., *An Outline of a Theory of Semantic Information* (Technical Report No. 247, Research Laboratory of Electronics, Massachusetts Institute of Technology, Cambridge, Mass., 48 pp., 1952)
4. Davis, K. H., Biddulph, R., and Balashek, S., *J. Acous. Soc. Amer.*, **24,** 637–42 (1952)
5. Fletcher, H., *Speech and Hearing in Communication* (D. Van Nostrand Co., New York, N. Y., 461 pp., 1953)
6. Frick, F. C., and Sumby, W. H., *J. Acous. Soc. Amer.*, **24,** 595–96 (1952)
7. Garner, W. R., and Hake, H. W., *Psychol. Rev.*, **58,** 446–59 (1951)
8. Hake, H. W., and Hyman, R., *J. Exptl. Psychol.*, **45,** 64–74 (1953)
9. Harris, Z. S., *Methods in Structural Linguistics* (University of Chicago Press, Chicago, Ill., 384 pp., 1951)
10. Hick, W. E., *Quart. J. Exptl. Psychol.*, **4,** 11–26 (1952)
11. Hick, W. E., *Trans. Soc. Instrument Technol.*, **4,** 67–77 (1952)
12. Hovland, C. I., *Psychol. Rev.*, **59,** 461–72 (1952)
13. Jakobson, R., Fant, C. G. M., and Halle, M., *Preliminaries to Speech Analysis* (Technical Report No. 13, Acoustics Laboratory, Massachusetts Institute of Technology, Cambridge, Mass., 53 pp., 1952)
14. Kaplan, A., *An Experimental Study of Ambiguity and Context* (P-187, Rand Corp., Santa Monica, Calif., 18 pp., 1950)
14a. Klemmer, E. T., *The Rate of Handling Information* (HFORL Memo Report No. 34, Bolling Air Force Base, Washington, D. C., 11 pp., 1953)
14b. Klemmer, E. T., and Frick, F. C., *J. Exptl. Psychol.*, **45,** 15–19 (1953)
15. Kock, W. E., *J. Acous. Soc. Amer.*, **24,** 625–28 (1952)
16. Krulee, G. K., and Sinclair, E. J., *Some Behavioral Implications of Information Theory* (Report 4119, Naval Research Laboratory, Washington, D. C., 11 pp., 1953)
17. Liberman, A. M., Delattre, P., and Cooper, F. S., *Am. J. Psychol.*, **65,** 497–516 (1952)
18. Licklider, J. C. R., *J. Acous. Soc. Amer.*, **24,** 590–94 (1952)
19. Levi-Strauss, C., Jakobson, R., Voegelin, C. F., and Sebeok, T. A., *Results of the Conference of Anthropologists and Linguists* (Indiana University Publications in Anthropology and Linguistics, Memoir 8, Bloomington, Ind., 67 pp., 1953)
20. Mandelbrot, B., *Contribution a la Theorie Mathematique des Jeux de Communication* (Institute of Statistics, University of Paris, Paris, France, 124 pp., 1953)
21. Marschak, J., *Basic Problems in the Economic Theory of Teams* (Cowles Commission Discussion Paper, Economics No. 2051, University of Chicago, Chicago, Ill., 53 pp., 1952)
22. McGill, W. J., *Multivariate Transmission of Information and Its Relation to Analysis of Variance* (HFORL Report No. 32, Human Factors Operations Research Laboratories, Air Research and Development Command, United States Air Force, 19 pp., 1953)
23. Miller, G. A., *Am. Psychologist*, **8,** 3–11 (1953)
24. Newman, E. B., and Gerstman, L. J., *J. Exptl. Psychol.*, **44,** 114–25 (1952)
25. Noble, C. E., *J. Exptl. Psychol.*, **43,** 437–46 (1952)
26. Noble, C. E., *Psychol. Rev.*, **59,** 421–30 (1952)

27. Noble, C. E., *Psychol. Rev.*, **60,** 89–98 (1953)
28. Osgood, C. E., *Psychol. Bull.*, **49,** 197–237 (1952)
29. Peterson, G. E., and Barney, H. L., *J. Acous. Soc. Amer.*, **24,** 175–84 (1952)
30. Peterson, G. E., *J. Acous. Soc. Amer.*, **24,** 629–37 (1952)
31. Pike, K. L., *J. Acous. Soc. Amer.*, **24,** 618–25 (1952)
32. Pollack, I., *The Assimilation of Sequentially Encoded Information* (HRRL Memo Report No. 25, Human Resources Research Laboratory, Washington, D. C., 71 pp., 1952)
33. Pollack, I., *J. Acous. Soc. Amer.*, **24,** 745–49 (1952)
34. Senders, V. L., and Sowards, A., *Am. J. Psychol.*, **65,** 358–74 (1952)
35. Shannon, C. E., *Bell System Tech. J.*, **30,** 50–64 (1951)

AUTHOR INDEX

C

G

T

SUBJECT INDEX

D

P

R